EUROPEAN NATIONS

GREAT BRITAIN

A REFERENCE GUIDE
FROM THE RENAISSANCE TO THE PRESENT

Richard S. Tompson

Frank J. Coppa, General Editor

Facts On File, Inc.

Great Britain: A Reference Guide from the Renaissance to the Present

Facts On File, Inc.
132 West 31st Street
New York NY 10001

Library of Congress Cataloging-in-Publication Data
Tompson, Richard S.
  Great Britain : a reference guide from the Renaissance to the present /
  by Richard S. Tompson.
    p. cm. — (European nations series)
  Includes bibliographical references (p.) and index.
    ISBN 0-8160-4474-0
  1. Great Britain—History—Bibliography. I. Title. II. Series.
  Z2016.T66 2003
  [DA30]   941′.003—dc212002192540

Facts On File books are available at special discounts when purchased in bulk quantities for businesses, associations, institutions, or sales promotions. Please call our Special Sales Department in New York at (212) 967-8800 or (800) 322-8755.

You can find Facts On File on the World Wide Web at http://www.factsonfile.com

Text design by David Strelecky
Cover design by Semadar Megged
Maps by Dale Williams © Facts On File

Printed in the United States of America

VB FOF 10 9 8 7 6 5 4 3 2 1

This book is printed on acid-free paper.

CONTENTS

FOREWORD

This series was inspired by the need of high school and college students to have a concise and readily available history series focusing on the evolution of the major European powers and other influential European states in the modern age—from the Renaissance to the present. Written in accessible language, the projected volumes include all of the major European countries: France, Germany, Great Britain, Italy, and Russia, as well as other states such as Spain, Portugal, Austria, and Hungary that have made important intellectual, political, cultural, and religious contributions to Europe and the world. The format has been designed to facilitate usage and includes a short introduction by the author of each volume, a specialist in its history, providing an overview of the importance of the particular country in the modern period. This is followed by a narrative history of each nation from the time of the Renaissance to the present. The core of the volume consists of an A–Z dictionary of people, events, and places, providing coverage of intellectual, political, diplomatic, cultural, social, religious, and economic developments. Next, a chronology details key events in each nation's development over the past several centuries. Finally, the end matter includes a selected bibliography of readily available works, maps, and an index to the material within the volume.

—Frank J. Coppa, General Editor
St. John's University

INTRODUCTION

Great Britain is the largest offshore island in the North Sea. Geography helps to explain its history, its internal structure, and its relation to the world outside. Britain was for centuries the destination or target of continental migrations and invasions—Roman, Saxon, Christian, and Scandinavian. From about A.D. 1100 there was a period of five centuries of struggles with French, Spanish, and papal powers on the continent. By A.D. 1600 there were clear signs of political, religious, and economic independence in Britain. These were accompanied by a reversal of the flow of power and influence, and a British empire took shape in the 17th century, with outposts in the Americas, Asia, and Africa. That great international enterprise grew in size and strength until the 20th century, and then it rapidly shrank. As the empire contracted, the British entered a new stage of relations with Europe, joining that continent's new community structure in 1972 and fitfully enlisting in the new institutions of Europe from then on.

While engaging in these long phases of international relations, the countries and peoples within Britain were constantly evolving and defining themselves. It was over four centuries after the end of Roman occupation before centralized kingdoms emerged in England and Scotland (A.D. 850–900). Wales, on the other hand, was ruled by tribal leaders, as was Ireland; both were subjected to English intervention and eventual domination. Scotland, on the other hand, was able to survive a period of "wars of independence" in the early 1300s. While England built a wealthy and centralized kingdom by 1400, it took 300 years more to assert English power firmly over its near neighbors.

By the end of the 20th century there were two major measurements of the importance of British history: first, in the evidence of the many British "exports" that spread across the globe; and second, in the complex and contradictory position of Britain in the world. The major exports were represented by emigrants, the English language and literature, and institutions of government. Beginning in the age of the American rebellion, there was rapid population growth in Britain. The increase continued through the 19th century, and by 1900 the number of people who had emigrated was greater than the entire population of Britain in 1801. These emigrants and exiles carried British influence in their luggage and in their lives. They used a language which became a universal medium before the end of the 20th century. With that language came a literary heritage of immense power, with Chaucer, Shakespeare, Milton, and Dickens. The British migration paralleled the construction of empire. And in that enterprise political and legal institutions, shaped primarily in England, were exported to the colonies. Even in places where the colonists later rejected the authority of the crown, their parliaments and statutes and their form of courts and common law typically survived as the essential fabric of government.

But the British Empire did decline and almost disappear. In its finale, this once mighty institution was transformed. Perhaps the experience of defeat in America in 1781 gave Britain a sense that imperial losses could be profitable. For from that situation, the once-dependent colonies became a stalwart and powerful ally by the 20th century. Indeed, there developed what some called a "special relationship"—a cultural and political alliance of unusual closeness. Also, in the course of the century after the American revolt, the more mature, white-dominated British colonies evolved into "dominions" of the crown, with virtual independence in domestic affairs. African and Asian peoples did not receive the same treatment. Nevertheless, those colonial peoples were encouraged by the grants of autonomy made to Canada, Australia, and New Zealand. When Britain and the United States proclaimed as their war aims "self-determination of nations" (1918) and "four freedoms" (1914), the road to liberation seemed to be open.

The British formal title is "The United Kingdom of Great Britain and Northern Ireland." This name was created in 1922 with the foundation of the Irish Free State, itself a dominion government. That event ended a period of over seven centuries of English rule of Ireland. Ironically, in the years since 1922 the leaders in Northern Ireland have fought to *maintain* union with Britain. But elsewhere, the trend was all in the opposite direction. The vestiges of empire are visible today in the Commonwealth of Nations. Originally made up of the dominions, the Commonwealth met at first in colonial conference and formed imperial committees during World War I. After the war the dominions insisted on looser ties, which were ratified by statute in 1931. By 1957 the adjective "British" was dropped from the name of the Commonwealth, and it became an international organization for trade and other relations.

As Britain forged new relations with its commonwealth nations in the aftermath of World War II, there also had to be new ties to Europe. The destruction of Germany in 1945 brought terrible misery to much of the continent, and the ambition of one of her conquerors—the Soviet Union—was to take advantage of that weakness. Western Europe was fortified by aid from the United States (the Marshall Plan, the International Monetary Fund, and the World Bank) and a new joint military force in the North Atlantic Treaty Organization (NATO). By 1957, in the Treaty of Rome, a new idea of European cooperation was adopted. But Britain declined full participation at first, out of a concern for her historic trade partners in the empire and commonwealth. This position was reversed in 1972 when Britain joined the Common Market. Still, Britain remains deeply divided as to her relation with Europe.

Great Britain has always included a group of linked national histories. For many years these were overshadowed by English rule and English history. In the last century the histories of Ireland, Scotland, and Wales have gained greater prominence. Meanwhile the United Kingdom has had vital and changing relations with Europe and the world, especially the United States. Thus in Britain we can see an array of shifting national and imperial identities. Britain's history is our key to understanding the roots of the culture and institutions which have had such enormous influence around the world.

—Richard S. Tompson

HISTORY OF
GREAT BRITAIN

EARLY BRITAIN

Britain is both a geographical entity and a political idea. The space has been searched, excavated, and mapped with great thoroughness. Archaeology can now explain much about the earliest habitation and the evolving cultures of prehistory and the early years of the historical era. The political past is far harder to describe, because of the rarity of written evidence and other clues.

The record on the ground tells us of inhabitants who built remarkable stone monuments and equally remarkable stone dwellings. These prehistoric people are known to have been present from the end of the ice ages; they began a succession of cultures that probably spanned 10,000 years. The later cultures began to use bronze and to practice agriculture (starting around 4000 B.C.). With the Iron Age (from 700 B.C.), Britain was soon inhabited by incoming peoples loosely referred to as Celts, who originated in central and eastern Europe. These tribes had warrior-kings whose hill-forts were centers of tribal government. An agrarian people, they used iron swords and worshiped nature gods that were described by Roman observers. Substantial physical evidence of their existence can be found in all parts of Britain.

ORIGINS OF BRITAIN

The idea of Britain as a political entity is an abstraction beyond the imagination of the tribal king. It is clear that no central rule was in place either before or after the Roman occupation. The many small, pre-Roman tribal kingdoms formed shifting alliances, and some of them survived as subjects of Roman rule. The first Roman contact came with the invasion by Julius Caesar in 55–54 B.C. The occupation by the Roman legions lasted from A.D. 43 to 406. In the empire's wake, a long turbulent period of upheaval followed, with many invasions and many realignments, again featuring tribal units that sometimes merged into larger allied groups. The one common element for Britain, Ireland, and all of Europe was the spread of Christianity. This conversion began in the later days of the empire, and it was maintained in Ireland but snuffed out by Germanic invaders of Britain (A.D. 400–600). There was no central political authority for nearly 500 years after the end of Roman occupation. The meager political record consists of a few chronicles and rare commentary, plus some later king lists that named the predecessors of medieval rulers, far into the distant and mythical past.

The Roman conquest was most advanced in the area roughly corresponding to modern England. Much of Wales and Scotland was controlled from garrisons but not completely subdued by the invaders. The northern frontier was marked by Hadrian's Wall, which ran 73 miles across the narrow isthmus between the Tyne and the Solway Firth. On the western frontier, Roman garrisons in Wales and Cornwall marked limits of imperial rule. Beyond these boundaries the native Celts maintained their tribal rule and culture. Their cousins inside the Roman-occupied territory became known as "Britons"—that is, Celts whose culture had merged with the Romans. From the end of the fourth century, the imperial structure began to break down, and it was lost in the early years of the fifth century. It was then that new invasions of Angles, Saxons, and other continental peoples began. They overran much of the former Roman zone but failed to penetrate some frontier areas. Numerous Anglo-Saxon tribal kingdoms took shape in the sixth and seventh centuries. In that period they were converted to Christianity by twin missions: in the north by the Irish Celtic church (Iona in Scotland and Lindisfarne in northern England) and in the south by the Roman church, via Canterbury. The first contemporary history by the monk Bede in Northumbria was called the *Ecclesiastical History of the English People* (A.D. 731). In Bede's day a set of seven kingdoms (called the "heptarchy") ruled most of Anglo-Saxon England. They were probably the result of mergers of many smaller tribal groups. In the early eighth century, Wessex, Mercia, Northumbria, Kent, Essex, Sussex, and East Anglia were the most powerful kingdoms. Kingdoms rose and fell, and the most powerful ruler was sometimes known by the name "Bretwalda," literally a "wide-ruler" or an over-king. But still there was no unified Britain.

The Anglo-Saxon kingdoms became the target of Viking raids and invasions between A.D. 793 and 870. The result was the defeat of all of them except Wessex, which, led by Alfred the Great, began the process of reconquering the land that would become "England." Alfred could only begin the process, and it took nearly a century before a form of unified rule evolved under later Saxon kings. One of the main obstacles was the large settlement of Vikings across central and northern England, known as the "Danelaw." Edgar, king of Wessex and Northumbria, held an imperial coronation at Bath in 973, and later in the year, on the river Dee at Chester, he was rowed in a boat by eight sub-kings, including the rulers of Scotland, Strathclyde and Gwynedd. The ceremonial acknowledgment of Edgar's lordship may have been temporary, but it was early evidence of English unification. That unity was tentative and short-lived, for by the end of the century there were more Scandinavian invasions, leading to Cnut of Denmark's conquest and rule of a united England. The period of Danish rule lasted from 1016 to 1042, followed by restoration of the Anglo-Saxon king Edward (the Confessor, ruled 1043–66).

NORMANS AND ANGEVINS

After Edward's death and the very brief rule of King Harold, there were two powerful invasions in 1066: the Norwegians in the north and the Normans in the south. Although Harold defeated the king of Norway, the Norman invasion succeeded. William the Conqueror (1066–87) wiped out most of the Anglo-Saxon nobility and introduced a new aristocracy. The conquest linked feudal lordship to strong existing royal institutions, so the Normans were able to create a powerful and centralized English (or Anglo-Norman) kingdom. But the first half-century of Norman rule also produced a cross-channel empire with divided objectives. The English unit was strong and centralized, and it was fortified *against* its Welsh and Scottish neighbors. There was hereafter no ready way to assimilate all of Britain; the English would dominate them for nine centuries, but assimilation and a unified culture and society lay a long way ahead.

Scotland had an even cloudier early history, with little documentation before the 12th century. The prehistoric people called "Picts" were contemporary with the Romans, and they were joined in the sixth and seventh centuries by Irish invaders (called "scotti"—whence the name Scotland). Also, parts of Scotland were inhabited by Britons (Strathclyde) and by incoming Angles (Lothian) and Vikings. The mission of the Irish (Celtic) church greatly assisted unification around 850. Scottish kings followed the custom of *tanistry,* or inheritance by near male relatives. This provided ample opportunity for royal bloodshed. King Malcolm (1005–34) killed a number of tanists, and his grandson Duncan succeeded him, only to be murdered by Macbeth (1040). He in turn was slain by Malcolm III (1058), the king who faced the new Anglo-Norman regime in England. He successfully resisted the Norman advance in the 1060s, although the next two centuries saw considerable movement of Anglo-Normans into the south of Scotland.

Wales was made up of a collection of small tribal groups. Here Britons (Celts) spoke one form of Celtic language and had much in common with kin in Cornwall and Brittany, with whom they shared cultures and engaged in trade. Wales itself was hilly, remote, and poor. It was isolated by the Norman conquest when William I created frontier earldoms (Chester, Shrewsbury and Hereford), which were granted extensive powers and made responsible for defense of the border. This arrangement assured both subordination and separation for Wales.

Monmouth was on the southern Anglo-Welsh border, an area that was the home of a churchman named Geoffrey. In 1136 Geoffrey wrote the most compelling story about Britain in all of the middle ages, *The History of the Kings of Britain* (Historia Regum Britanniae). He lived and taught for much of his life in Oxford (before there was a university there), and he was a singular champion of the Britons. A mixture of myth, romance, and history, his book was one of the most popular works in the Middle Ages, with nearly 200 copies of the manuscript still in existence. Geoffrey claimed that he translated the story from an old book written in Welsh (which has never been found). He told of Brutus, a descendant of Aeneas of Troy, who came to Britain around 1200 B.C. From him a line of kings was traced down to the last British ruler, Cadwallader, who was defeated by the Saxons in the seventh century. One of the high points in Geoffrey's narrative was the story of Arthur, king of the Britons and heroic leader of the ancestors of the Welsh, whose return to power was prophesied by the seer Merlin. The real significance of Arthur's story did not lie in British political history, however. This mythic figure, of prophetic birth and prodigious valor, was a cultural stereotype for the age of chivalry. He was thus adopted by continental writers and went on to a long literary life over the next five or six centuries. But as a British political figure, Arthur represented a ruler who could legitimize native aspirations in the void that was British political history. The real world of the 12th century saw very different tendencies.

Just as Geoffrey of Monmouth died, the throne of England was reclaimed by Henry of Anjou in 1154. The grandson of Henry I and great-grandson of William the Conqueror assumed the throne that had been bequeathed to his mother and contested by another prince. When Henry II restored his family's rule, he also brought back the cross-channel empire and the French orientation of William the Conqueror. This again made British interests secondary to continental ones, a condition that would endure until the 15th century. Henry had earlier married Eleanor of Aquitaine and thus enlarged the royal domain. But she and the four sons she bore him caused endless political turmoil.

England in the 1150s was a source of wealth, and its tax revenues probably were its most appealing feature to continental rulers. This wealth might be directly exploited through the exactions of feudal overlords, but from the 12th century the process of exploiting that wealth became entangled with critical legal developments: the birth and growth of a common law dispensed by royal judges; the tradition of petitioning the Crown, which issued charters of liberties; and the summoning of councils to approve taxes and other measures, which eventually produced the institution of parliament.

The king's authority was supported by the church, but he was subject to church authority. In the 12th century there was a major clash between the authority of the pope and that of the Holy Roman Emperor, a dispute that echoed through all royal courts. The issue was whether the pope or the secular rulers controlled the appointment of bishops—a source of continuing tension in the Middle Ages. There were many other points of friction between clerical and lay leaders. Henry II had a dispute with his archbishop of Canterbury, Thomas Becket, which ended in a particularly grisly episode. Four of the king's knights murdered Becket, and while the king denied giving the order, he did public penance for the crime. In the wake of this event, Henry made his famous expedition to Ireland (1171), mainly to discipline his vassal, the earl of Clare, who seemed to be assuming too much power there. But Henry also carried a papal bull vesting him with the power of lordship in Ireland.

Henry's son Richard I (1189–99), known as the Lion Heart, succeeded to the throne of England, but he spent five years on crusade (and in captivity) and five more in wars on the continent. His youngest brother John succeeded him (1199–1216). Due to the loss of Normandy in 1204, John spent more time in England, but his harsh rule brought resistance and, in turn, the issue of charters to the church, to the city of London, and eventually to his barons in 1215. A large proportion of that document, the "Great Charter" (Magna Carta) was reissued some years later under John's son Henry III.

Henry III managed his inherited territories with indifferent success. He faced a strong French king, Philip II, and he encountered resistance in Wales, Scotland,

and Ireland. In all his dealings, Henry was less warlike than his ancestors, but this did not make his subjects less rebellious. During Henry's reign there were periodic meetings of barons and clergy, sometimes augmented by the attendance of commoners (knights and burgesses). These were the earliest examples of the institution of Parliament. When a serious revolt occurred in 1265, a so-called model Parliament was summoned. This unusually representative body was dismissed by the king's son, Prince Edward, who became a much more strong-willed ruler than his father. Edward I (1272–1307) wanted tighter control of his domin-

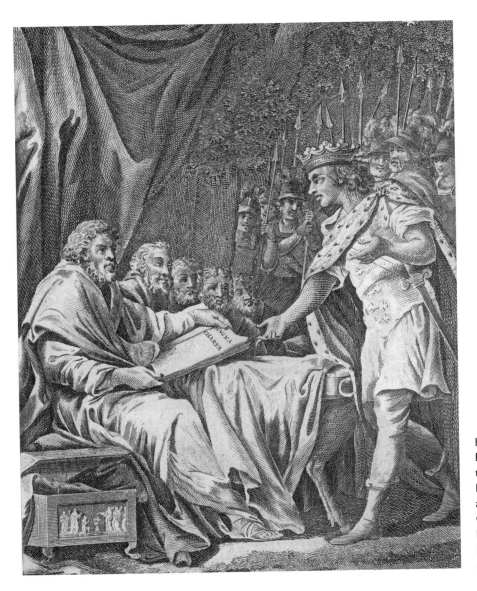

King John of England submits to the Barons at Runnymede and agrees to sign the Great Charter of British Liberties, the Magna Carta, 1215. *(Hulton/Archive)*

ions and began with a campaign to improve the government of Gascony. Wales was soon brought to heel, and a statute was enacted to annex its government (1284). Edward also enacted a series of major statutes to increase his power over the feudal nobility, and when the Scottish line of succession ran out, he intervened to assure a pliable ruler in 1290. But Edward met his match in Scotland: a prolonged series of campaigns added to the demands for revenues already inflated by castle-building in Wales and costly ventures in France. Victory eluded Edward, as William Wallace led a popular campaign against the English (1297), and Robert Bruce energized a revived claim to the throne (1306).

Bruce's efforts were capped by a victory at Bannockburn in 1314, and in 1320 the Scottish clergy produced a declaration of independence (Arbroath). These events occurred during the troubled reign of Edward II (1307–27), one of the least martial of English rulers. His ineffective government and his personal character were fuel to hostile nobles, who led an unsuccessful palace revolt in 1310. The contrast between Edward II and his son could hardly have been greater. Edward III (1327–77) was placed on the throne after his father was deposed and murdered by his mother and her lover. Soon Edward III took power in his own right, and about 1340 he launched the English campaigns that began the Hundred Years' War with France. This conflict had roots in a failed French succession, but it had more to do with trade and dynastic power. During the 14th century it was no accident that the focus on France was accompanied by a serious loss in English authority in Ireland, fitful intrusions in affairs of Scotland, and growth of rebellious sentiments in Wales.

FOURTEENTH-CENTURY CRISES

The convergence of a number of crises in the second half of the 14th century marks the period as one of unusual significance. As the English continued to fight in France, the awesome toll of the "Black Death"—the bubonic plague, which struck in 1348—was not only terrifying in itself, but it led to a host of major social changes. The deadly disease would kill somewhere between 10 and 50 percent of the population in communities small and large. Modern attempts to assess the toll are hindered by lack of population data in the Middle Ages, at which time there was limited interest in statistical information. Estimates of the general population before the plague range from 4 million to 6 million; for the end of the century, between 2.5 million and 3 million. There is no way to calculate the precise impact, but there are many chilling accounts from specific communities, monastic houses, and towns or neighborhoods. There is no question that the mortality rate was severe. Moreover, the plague was not a single event: it returned in 1361, 1369, 1375, 1390, and 1405. Recurrence made it even more frightening and reinforced major impacts: a shrinking work force, declining land values, and falling production. There were desperate acts to offset these effects; for example, the Statute of Labourers was enacted to freeze wage levels (1351). The plague unleashed powerful forces of social and economic change, forces which no government, certainly none in the Middle Ages, would be able to control.

The consolation of religious faith was never more essential than in the plague years, and yet the church was subject to unprecedented stresses at the same time. Due to the warfare between England and France, there were extraordinary pressures on the Catholic Church. One manifestation of this was a debate over the powers of the papacy to appoint clergy for positions in the English Church during the 1350s. The roots of this resistance went back to the period when the popes moved to Avignon, a papal enclave in southern France (1305–78). Parliament passed laws banning papal appointments and restricting appeals to the Roman curia. This tension appeared again when a schism split the church in 1378.

In this era of war and unrest, there was significant theological controversy. The central figure was John Wycliffe, an Oxford teacher and diplomat. Wycliffe (ca. 1329–84) was one of the foremost critics of church government and papal power. An early advocate of translation of the scriptures into English, he eventually disputed central doctrines of the church (e.g., "transubstantiation," the belief that the bread and wine of the eucharist become the body and blood of Christ in the course of the sacrament). Wycliffe was condemned by the church but, protected by the university and by his patron, John of Gaunt, he was able to live out his life in peace. However, his followers, known as Lollards, persisted in some of these views and were to suffer later on.

While Wycliffe was on trial in the 1370s, the government faced its own problems in France. Needing new resources, Parliament adopted "poll" taxes in 1377, 1379, and 1380. The last of these triggered the Peasants' Revolt of 1381. A large body of rebels marched on London from Essex and Kent. Their leaders included a renegade priest named John Ball, who called for the removal of all bishops and archbishops. They entered the city, destroyed a number of buildings, and killed the king's chancellor and treasurer. But the rebels were outnumbered by government supporters. When the 14-year-old King Richard II (1377–99) rode out to meet them at Smithfield, the rebel leader Wat Tyler presented a list of demands. However, during a scuffle Tyler was killed by the lord mayor of London. Soon all the rebels dispersed, and the unrest in a number of counties was followed by arrests and harsh punishments. Yet it may not be just a coincidence that the next generation saw the ending of villein status (unfree tenants who were bound to a lord's estate). And there could never be quite the same social order after events such as these, especially as there were severe strains at the upper end of society.

The reign of Richard II witnessed a breakdown of relations between the crown and the nobility, and the stresses magnified commonplace feuds into constitutional clashes. Of course, these were not without precedent: barons had opposed King John (1215), they had resisted Henry III (1258 and 1265), and they tried to impose restraints on the royal power of Edward II (1310). The reign of Edward III had a long spell of amity thanks both to his victories and to his support of chivalric ideals (e.g., the Order of the Garter). But the king's later years saw this harmony evaporate. Defeats in France and distrust of Edward's advisers brought about the so-called Good Parliament in 1376. The Commons brought charges of court corruption and military incompetence, and the process of impeachment (against two of the king's ministers) was used for the first time.

When Richard II took the throne the next year (1377) there was some relaxation. But the tensions revived after the Peasants' Revolt. Richard made this worse by his choice of advisers and his reckless tactics against those who opposed him. Upon coming of age, he encountered more opposition. In 1386 Parliament impeached his chancellor, Michael de la Pole. In 1387 his advisers were charged with treason by a faction known as the "Lords Appellant." In 1388 the "Merciless Parliament" executed some of the king's supporters. Richard reasserted his power in 1389, arresting some opponents and exiling others. The king also confiscated some estates, including those of Henry Bolingbroke, the heir of John of Gaunt, duke of Lancaster. Richard unwisely made expeditions to Ireland during this tense period, and on the second of these, in 1399, Bolingbroke led a small invading force, which defeated and captured the king. This coup removed Richard and inaugurated the Lancastrian dynasty under Henry IV (1399–1413). The events of 1399 did not restore stability. Indeed, the years after 1350 saw multiple crises in government, religion, and society—a pattern that would continue for much of the 15th century.

THE END OF
THE MIDDLE AGES

1399–1509

The condition of the English monarchy in the 15th century was chaotic: five depositions, a devastating defeat in France, and a generation of civil warfare. Until recently, historians allowed this chaos to represent the entire period and the general character of the century, which was then rescued by the appearance of the Tudors and a "new monarchy" in 1485. Now it seems evident that this picture was one that served the interests of contemporary and later authors, exaggerating the misery before and the recovery after 1485. The central point is that the government system was not defective: weak kings and ambitious nobles robbed it of the essential bonds it needed to function.

A second major correction recognizes that the rest of British history was not dependent upon or represented by the crisis in government. There were in fact multiple developments—in religious, intellectual, social, and economic life—which together were creating a different Britain from that of the medieval period. England, with its weak crown and its strategic vulnerability, commanded little respect in Wales, Scotland, and Ireland. But England's wealth and its central position, sometimes challenged, would be the basis of British unification in the 16th century.

WAR AND LORDSHIP

It is helpful to relate the events of this century to the evolving ideas of lordship, the crux of politics. Already in the 14th century the classic feudal ties were replaced by "bastard feudalism," or contracts of service on cash terms. The 15th century saw this process extended, and the evolution of private armies, or "liveries" in the pay of a wealthy nobleman, became a regular feature. There was not as yet a national army, for as yet there were only fledgling ideas of nationality. The "nations" of this century were unsettled. Were the English a nation or a group of regions? Were the Welsh, Scots, and Irish coherent national groups? Were the French the same as the Burgundians, Bretons, and Gascons? It was still easier to find one's identity with a lord, whether a king or aristocrat. Further, it should be remembered that in the 15th century the kings and great men could gather forces of several thousand under their banner, and this number would be considered quite substantial. The armies that would invade France under Henry V (1413–22) were 5,000–6,000 strong; the armies fighting in Wales under Henry IV (1399–1413) were almost as large on some occasions. The forces in battle during the Wars of the Roses (1455–1485) were usually small, and the 10,000 of both sides at Towton (1461) far exceeded all the other battles. Thus any rebel group, with skill and luck, might pose a serious threat.

In summer 1399 Henry Bolingbroke invaded England with a tiny force of 300 men. He had come to reclaim his Lancaster inheritance, which King Richard II had taken from him. The king hastily returned from his campaign in Ireland but was captured by Bolingbroke, whose allies included the Percys of Northumberland. By August Bolingbroke had claimed the crown as Henry IV, by descent from Edward III through his third son, John of Gaunt. His claim was fortified by the fact that Richard had no heirs, but Henry's coup spawned a whole series of rebellions: a plot to kill him by Richard's supporters, leading to the former king's murder; a revolt in Wales led by Owen Glendower; a revolt by the Percys in 1403; and a related challenge from the archbishop of York, who was executed in 1405.

The Welsh rebellion was not a simple reaction to Richard's deposition, although Henry might be forgiven for seeing the hand of his rival's followers in it. The revolt was an attack on English colonial power by native Welsh rebels. Glendower attacked English castles and town settlements; he made alliances with Northumberland and with the Scots and the French; and he eluded capture by the king's forces, even though they invaded Wales several times. But Glendower's plan for an independent Wales was crushed. Henry was able to dispose of most of the threats to his rule, and when he died he left four sons to succeed him. There was only one competing claim to the throne, and the earl of March chose not to advance it, though it would later be adopted by Richard of York in the 1450s.

Henry V succeeded his father in 1413. His hold on power was quite secure, threatened only by two inept revolts in 1415. Sir John Oldcastle, a Lollard and a military servant of the king, was convicted of heresy, and he and his supporters were crushed. The earl of Cambridge tried to exploit the March claim to the throne, but the earl of March exposed him, and he was executed with his fellow plotters. But Henry V was intent on plans for French conquest by this time. He prepared an army of 10,000, made an alliance with Burgundy, and set sail in August 1415. After a long siege at Harfleur, Henry marched across country and engaged a much larger French force at Agincourt, winning a stunning victory. He followed this in the next few years with further victories in Normandy, and by the Treaty of Troyes (1420) he became regent of France and heir to the throne, taking the princess Catherine as his bride. But Henry died just before the French king in 1422, leaving a nine-month-old heir, Henry VI. The boy would be crowned both in France and in England, but he would also preside over the final expulsion of the English from France.

Henry VI did not rule in his own right until 1437. In the interim his uncles— John, duke of Bedford, and Humphrey, duke of Gloucester—and his great-uncle, Cardinal Henry Beaufort, vied for authority. At the same time there was

King Henry V
(Hulton/Archive)

growing resistance in France, led by Joan of Arc and by resurgent factions. The coronation of Charles VII, the death of the duke of Bedford, and the loss of the alliance with Burgundy made it essential to make peace. Henry married the princess Margaret of Anjou as a conciliatory gesture in 1445, but French resistance continued, sweeping the English out of Normandy in 1450 and Gascony in 1453. The great continental adventure was over, with only the colony at Calais remaining in English control.

The failure in France tended to mask early success at home. The English succession was untroubled by revolt, as the royal council imposed its control firmly. The house of Lancaster seemed to have brought a new stability to English politics, but in a short time the royal uncles and other leaders fell out over the events in France and the constitutional vacuum in England. Henry had his first coronation in London in 1429. He was then taken to France, but the planned coronation there was delayed and then had to be conducted quickly so that he could return to safety in England (1432). There was now a joint royal council for the two kingdoms, but this did little to reduce the conflicts between the senior advisers. Even when Bedford died in 1435, there was no cessation of friction. Henry VI began to assume power in his own right in 1437, sharing authority with the royal council. The timing was not in his favor: heavy expenses had been demanded from parliaments since 1415 and before, and the tide of victory in France was being reversed. The cost and trouble of a French crown was now clear to see. And in the next few years his subjects would see that Henry VI was not a king like his father.

Even a skillful ruler would have struggled with the conditions facing the young king. But he was inexperienced, extravagant, and lacking in good judgment. His courtiers assumed more and more control of the royal council, and in so doing they aroused increasing hostility. One of the king's leading advisers, the duke of Suffolk, was murdered in 1450. In the same year there was a serious popular revolt known as "Cade's Rebellion." Even more serious, at the time when the French inflicted the defeat in Gascony in 1453, Henry suffered a mental collapse, and Richard of York asserted himself as regent. He carried on the claim to succession of the earl of March, which had been bypassed in 1399. Although Queen Margaret presented Henry with a son in 1453, there was conflict over the succession, and the fighting which soon began would later be dubbed the Wars of the Roses after the symbols of the Houses of York (white rose) and Lancaster (red rose). After several battles, Richard claimed the throne in 1460, but he died soon after in a battle at Wakefield. His son assumed the title, supported by the earl of Warwick ("the kingmaker"), and as Edward IV defeated the army of Queen Margaret and Henry VI at Towton in March 1461, affirming his title as king.

NEW MONARCHS

Edward's reign can be divided into a troubled first half and a much more successful second. At first he was confronted with the forces of King Henry (captured in 1465) and Queen Margaret (in exile in Scotland). He also could not rally all the nobility to his side; indeed, by 1469 he had alienated his most powerful backer, the earl of Warwick. Thus in 1470 there was a coup: Warwick forced Edward out and restored Henry VI. This lasted but a short time. In March 1471 Edward returned and defeated Warwick (Battle of Barnet) and Margaret (Battle of Tewkesbury). Her son Edward was killed in the battle, and Henry VI died in the Tower of London, probably murdered. The major phase of the Wars of the Roses had ended with a decisive Yorkist victory. Edward IV had secured his throne, and his rule for the next 12 years proved successful. He placed his brothers—George, duke of Clarence, and Richard, duke of Gloucester—alongside a set of loyal noblemen, in charge of the several regions of the kingdom. Edward resumed the English royal quest for a French title, but his allies deserted him during his expedition in 1475, and the king settled for a ransom and trade and marriage settlements from the king of France. At home Edward's policies included financial reforms, support for merchants, and significant reduction in the level of taxation. But this reign was also troubled by noble factions: the king's brother George, duke of Clarence, was involved in treacherous acts, and the king had him attainted by Parliament and executed in 1478. The treachery of his other brother would dominate affairs after Edward's death in 1483.

The king's son would have become Edward V, but his accession was prevented by his uncle Richard, duke of Gloucester. The 12-year-old prince was declared illegitimate, and Richard assumed the throne as Richard III. The prince and his younger brother were never seen again, apparently murdered in the Tower on their uncle's orders. Richard had ruthlessly silenced most of the leaders of the court who opposed him, and his acts reopened the gates of dynastic warfare. His short reign was preoccupied with numerous efforts to buttress his claim to the throne. But there was a rival in exile, who soon would challenge him.

Henry Tudor was the son of Edmund Tudor and Margaret Beaufort, descended from the ubiquitous John of Gaunt. As earl of Richmond, he was a minor Lancastrian supporter who went into exile after Tewkesbury. Henry received enough support from France to mount an expedition in 1485. He landed in Pembroke and marched through Wales and western England, rallying support. Richard's army marched to meet them, and they fought at Bosworth in Leicestershire. The king's army was larger than Henry's, but it was not as loyal. When Richard was killed, his forces dissolved. Henry marched to London and claimed the throne as Henry VII.

The new dynasty, a partial restoration of the Lancaster line, was deliberately joined to that of York by Henry's marriage to Elizabeth (daughter of Edward IV). But the chaos of factional warfare was not quickly nor easily ended. Henry's own claim was tenuous; his wife's legitimacy had been denied; there were rumors that the young princes were still alive; and of course no one expected a sudden end to the bitter and bloody disputes, deceptions, and treachery of the last generation. Indeed, the first half of Henry's reign was consumed by the fallout from this atmosphere. There was a Yorkist rebellion in the name of Edward, earl of Warwick (son of the late duke of Clarence and nephew of Edward IV). Led by an imposter named Lambert Simnel, posing as the earl, this group was defeated at the Battle of Stoke in 1487. Another imposter named Perkin Warbeck posed as Richard, duke of York. The king beat his forces in 1497, and Warbeck was later executed along with the real earl of Warwick in 1499. It is perhaps significant that Henry had the apparently easy task of crushing fraudulent enemies, but the main point was that the Crown was not yet secure.

The reign of Henry VII was for a long time regarded as a "new monarchy." The new king's effectiveness, against the background of previous instability, goes far to explain this impression. But Henry only made better use of existing royal powers. What was new was the reduced size of the English nobility and the exhaustion after 30 years of aristocratic factional fighting. The king restored order and discipline, was attentive to royal finance, exploited diplomatic opportunities to improve trade and secure his own position, and generally brought an efficient and determined approach to royal government. The outcome was strict monitoring of aristocratic factions and stronger royal justice, with a consequent decline in rebellion. Henry achieved this by use of a strong royal council, with enhanced judicial powers in its meetings in the court of Star Chamber. He exploited regular assets like feudal dues, crown lands, and forfeitures, plus occasional heavy levels of parliamentary taxation. But Henry husbanded these resources, and with a pacific foreign policy and steady support of trade, he accumulated an unheard-of surplus in the royal treasury in the course of his reign.

Little has been said here of Parliament. It once was thought that the early Lancastrian parliaments had begun a precocious democratic development, claiming to control purse strings and public debate. But it appears that the crisis conditions surrounding so many meetings, the need to raise ample revenues for French campaigns, and the recurrent use of parliamentary councils to ratify royal power and title lent an appearance of power to these councils that was misleading. Henry Tudor convened Parliament frequently in the first half of his reign, but as his power solidified and his finances stabilized, he only had to summon Parliament twice in the second half.

Finally, Henry performed the most essential of royal duties by providing legitimate heirs: his sons Arthur (1486) and Henry (1491) and daughters Margaret (1489) and Mary (1496). Arthur was wed to Catherine of Aragon in 1501 but died six months later. She would later marry the younger son, Henry, in 1509. Margaret was married to James IV of Scotland, a union that eventually united the two crowns in 1603. The Tudor dynasty brought an end to the debilitating series of conflicts that had plagued England and Britain during the 15th century. How had the rest of society fared in this same period?

SOCIAL AND ECONOMIC CHANGES

English religious life at the end of the Middle Ages is hard to see clearly because of the glare of the 16th century's reformation. The Church of the 15th century was deeply involved with papal appointments, judgments, and finance. It also included large orders of monks and friars—in Britain, some 900 religious houses in all. To the later Protestant, these were potential sources of corruption and abuse, but to contemporaries they were quite normal. From the archbishops and bishops and other senior clerics, many of whom held important positions in royal government, to the parish priests—rectors, vicars, curates—churchmen were a competent and comprehensive administrative corps. They attended to the souls of their flock, but they also managed estates, collected tithes, and conducted courts at all levels. The 40,000–50,000 clergy in the British Isles were for the most part dutiful and conscientious. But recent relations between Rome and the national churches had injected a dangerous division. After the "captivity" of the papacy in Avignon (1308–78) there was a schism for the next 40 years, during which there were two and sometimes three rival popes. Such a crisis opened the door to criticism, already manifest in such measures as the statutes passed in England to prevent papal appointments and to limit its legal jurisdiction (Statute of Provisors [1351] and Statute of Praemunire [1392]). Out of this situation there came mounting anticlerical criticism and rising reform ideas. When movements for reform began, attention was always drawn to the most vulnerable individuals and practices. The Lollards in the early years of the 15th century were numerous enough to provoke major reaction; statutes and orders to root them out had had some effect by the second decade. But another reaction, just as important in the overall picture, was the growth of individual expressions of faith. There was considerable interest in devotional literature and lay piety in the 15th century—for example, the writing of Richard Rolle, a Yorkshire hermit, and Margery Kempe, wife of a burgess of Lynn; or the devotional work of Lady Margaret Beaufort, mother of Henry VII. Much of the writing was in the vernacular, and lay involvement in the church was greatly encouraged.

The 15th-century economy experienced some changes that would have created problems even without the extraordinary burdens of warfare, foreign and civil. A declining population meant contraction in agriculture; a shrinking money supply and falling prices were common features; and trade disruptions and harvest failures were compounding problems, especially in the middle of the century. The most significant developments included a shift to pastoral farming and the transfer from export of wool to manufacture and trade in woolen cloth. The phenomenon of failed villages, difficult to trace but evident in many comments and complaints, reflected the combined effects of population decline, falling wool exports, and conversion of farmland to pasture. Part of the picture had to be the improved ability of peasants and workers to move from one place to another: a fairly high demand for labor gave the worker unprecedented mobility.

Towns and trade showed important signs of growth in the 15th century. London grew more rapidly than other towns, consequently increasing its share of trade and economic activity. There and in other urban centers, the life of the community was controlled by the powerful guilds, which provided the mayors and aldermen and other leaders. Many of the most successful among them bought estates and entered the gentry. Cities like York, Bristol and Norwich were also thriving by the end of the century. The towns that suffered most had been dependent on the trade in raw wool. Their trade had been burdened by high duties during the war years of the 14th and 15th centuries, which added costs to the continental manufacturers, a de facto tariff behind which English cloth manufacturing was able to develop. This was aided by the availability of water power for mills as well as other natural advantages. Several regions of England (the Cotswolds, Yorkshire, and East Anglia) produced special products which became highly competitive. As the trade expanded, London's share grew, and merchants there became more involved in the growth of English shipping. Where much of English trade had been carried in Florentine and Venetian vessels, the second half of the 15th century saw English shipping ventures into the Mediterranean and the Atlantic, the precursors of 16th- and 17th-century mercantile growth.

Society saw several very important changes. The laws of supply and demand favored the peasantry and brought reciprocal shifts in standards of living; landlords lost ground while tenants and workers improved. The decline of villeinage had begun in the previous century, and it was completed in the 15th. This was marked by the increase in copyhold tenure; that is, the granting of a copy of the manor court roll to a tenant, which amounted to a permanent lease. This much more favorable tenancy was a direct consequence of the relative advantage tenants possessed due to population decline (the Black Death). That condition began to be reversed by the end of the century.

There were some steps toward defining the class that became known as the "gentry." The higher nobility, the peerage, had been defined more fully in the 14th century. They were the elite of the landowning class; the lesser but still wealthy landowners were consigned to the ranks of knights, esquires, and gentlemen. These were indeterminate groups whose ranks were swelled by increasing fortunes and new purchases of landed estates. In the 1440s those with incomes of £40 or more were enjoined to take a knighthood, though many did not. That status was required for one to be elected as a knight of the shire to attend Parliament (1445). There were no such clear delineations pertaining to the esquire and the gentleman. The terms placed their bearers in the wide zone between nobility and yeomanry, or small farmers. These were the more affluent local men, who were expected to serve in Parliament or as justices of the peace or as grand jurors—in other words, the governing class.

The 15th century also saw significant intellectual development and, apparently, increasing literacy. Sir Thomas More made the implausible claim that by 1500 half of the English population was literate. Assuming that he was correct in seeing significant improvement, some credit must be given to the popular devotional literature of the time and to the growing number of schools and colleges founded in the second half of the century. Moreover, the appearance of the printing press by 1476 aided the circulation of reading material. The century had a significant rise in the number of laymen who held official posts, many of which were formerly occupied by churchmen. There was also the oft-noted but elevated category of the intellectual elite, many of them exposed to and influenced by the humanist scholarship of both Italian and northern European origin. The number who traveled to these regions, returning to teach and write, was increasing. At another level, the study of law was being expanded in the Inns of Court, the schools for English lawyers. While it was too soon to speak of an English "renaissance," the 15th century was providing some essential foundations.

England's political troubles might have enabled her neighbors to resist her control. But there was intermittent exercise of that control, and there was no concerted effort to destroy the foundations of English power, with the exception of the Glendower revolt in the early years of the century. That exception to the rule also indicated the difficulty of resistance. While the revolt was of great duration (1400–15), its accomplishment was negligible. When the English captured James I of Scotland, an ally of France, and held him for ransom (1406–24), that seemed to show the weakness of the northern kingdom, but there was never a genuine threat to the Scottish monarchy. Perhaps only the increasing autonomy of Irish and Anglo-Irish leaders was cause for real concern. Yet England experienced no apparent fundamental weakening in relation to her immediate neighbors, and a restoration of English royal authority began to counteract the chaos of the 15th century. Sir John Fortescue, a constitutional lawyer of the time, had recommended a government less dependent upon public finance and less subject to the interests of powerful aristocrats; Edward IV and Henry VII began to achieve this. By the 16th century the power of the English monarchy had been stabilized. In the testing crises of the new century, a more centralized British state would be formed.

Britain Reformed

1509–1603

The Tudors presided over a century in which Britain was reformed in almost every aspect. The most dramatic change was in the church, but there was also a revolution in government (both in the English monarchy and in the British state), and wide-ranging social and intellectual change. Henry Tudor was perhaps an unlikely progenitor of such sweeping alterations. He himself was not a reformer, but rather a skillful manager of existing institutions. As seen in the last chapter, his reign as Henry VII (1485–1509) was notable for the restoration of stable royal administration. He prepared the ground for his son by accumulating a surplus in the treasury, affirming the Crown's authority over the aristocracy and Parliament, strengthening royal courts of law, and avoiding costly military adventures. Finally, he assured the succession of his younger son Henry and arranged for the renewal of an alliance by marriage with Spain.

THE TUDOR DYNASTY

Henry VIII (1509–47) had much grander visions of his role than were ever entertained by his father. He thought that his realm should share the stage of European power with France and Spain and that the royal succession justified all manner of expedients, including a succession of royal wives and a reform of the church. Henry's reign began smoothly enough, as he carried out his father's wish and married Catherine of Aragon in 1509. She and Henry had five children, but only Princess Mary survived infancy. In search of a male heir, Henry decided to divorce Catherine, a process that took six years (1527–33) and led to England's break with the Roman Catholic Church. As head of the new Church of England, Henry married Anne Boleyn, who gave birth to Princess Elizabeth in 1533. Anne was found guilty of treason and executed. She was replaced by Jane Seymour, who gave birth to Prince Edward but died afterward (1537). Henry later married and divorced Anne of Cleves (1540); married Catherine Howard, who was executed for adultery (1540–42); and finally married Catherine Parr in 1543, who survived him.

Henry's ambition in international affairs was as ill-conceived as his marital conduct. Dreaming of victory in France, he invaded in 1512, captured Tournai, and married his sister Mary to Louis XII. But the cost of the war (which also led to the defeat of the French allies, the Scots, at Flodden in 1513) was its most serious result. In 1518 Henry and Cardinal Wolsey devised the Peace of London, leading to a temporary balance of power in Europe. But when a Spanish Habsburg became Holy Roman Emperor (Charles V in 1519), that illusion evaporated. Henry engaged in another diplomatic fantasy in 1520, meeting the French king Francis I at the Field of the Cloth of Gold, near Calais. This was a summit meeting, arranged with inordinate display and again designed to promote Henry's international importance, but it mainly resulted in a drain on the

Portrait of Henry VIII
(Hulton/Archive)

treasury. Further campaigns against France and Scotland marked the last 20 years of his reign, all to no effect.

Henry's personality was morbid, suspicious, and brutal. Wives, officials, clergymen, and suspected enemies were in mortal danger. The king had less to fear from court intrigues, rebels, or foreign agents than they had to fear from him. In his will, Henry directed that his son and successor Edward VI (1547–1553) have a council and no one adviser as a regent or protector. Edward Seymour, uncle to Edward and duke of Somerset, nevertheless assumed a protectorate. The duke pursued the fulfillment of the Treaty of Greenwich (1543), which was supposed to arrange the marriage of Edward to his cousin Mary of Scotland, daughter of James V. This policy was thwarted by French diplomacy, and Seymour was overthrown in 1549 by John Dudley, duke of Northumberland, who was protector for the rest of Edward's reign. As the king's protectors and his royal council were strong supporters of Protestant reform, the Church of England moved much further away from Roman Catholicism during these years. Edward himself never took power in his own right, as he became ill and died at the age of 15. Before his death, Northumberland persuaded the king to designate Lady Jane Grey (the duke's daughter-in-law) as his successor. But those loyal to Princess Mary defeated this coup attempt.

Mary I (1553–58) was a devout Roman Catholic, spurned by the court and sometimes in mortal danger as she grew up. Her goal was to restore the old church, and she tried to advance that cause by undoing the legislation and policy of the previous two reigns. Her most ambitious move, however, was to marry King Philip of Spain, thus creating a dynastic union that would endow any heir with the strongest ties to the papacy and the traditional church. But the marriage was not successful; Philip lost interest in his bride, and while Mary was sure she was carrying his child, she was in fact dying of stomach cancer. Her death came in the midst of the efforts to undo the reformation, and it gave the throne to her Protestant half-sister, Elizabeth.

Elizabeth I (1558–1603), the daughter of Anne Boleyn, had lived in an unstable situation for much of her early life. Declared illegitimate by her father in 1537, and suspected by her half-sister of being a plotter, she had learned to conduct herself in a circumspect fashion. Her own religion inclined toward the traditional features of Catholic worship, but she adopted the royal supremacy and limited aspects of the reformed religion. Elizabeth chose what some called a "via media," or middle way, between Catholic and Protestant. She did have herself styled as "supreme governor" of the church, and she allowed much of the reformers' agenda to be followed. But in this and other areas of policy—especially questions about her designs for a husband—Elizabeth was careful to conceal her true opinions. This was very helpful in staving off excommunication until 1570. Even after that, the catholic powers held back from a full assault, until in 1586 Philip of Spain decided to launch his *armada católica* against England. This decision was followed by the queen's anguished choice to execute her cousin Mary, queen of Scots, for plotting against her. Elizabeth's admirals succeeded in beating the Spanish Armada in 1588, and some later fleets were turned back by weather and other problems. Thus England was spared an invasion, while her privateers and explorers harassed Spanish treasure fleets and made early forays into American exploration and colonization. Elizabeth harbored none of her father's illusions about English power, but her reign saw the development of English maritime strength. Elizabeth never married, never had a child, and at the end she named her cousin Mary's child, James VI of Scotland, as her successor. With this the Tudor dynasty ended, and the Stuart dynasty began.

The Tudors, particularly Henry VIII and Elizabeth I, guided the realm toward significantly new destinations. Their calculated plans were not all successful, but the end result for Britain was a striking set of new institutions and ideas, the most important being the formation of the Church of England.

THE CHURCH REFORMED

The Church of England was the product of what is called the English Reformation. That series of events was essentially the conversion of the church from a branch of the Western Christian Church to a department of the English state. Its immediate cause was Henry VIII's struggle to annul his marriage to Catherine of Aragon. However, that struggle occurred within a context of popular discontent with the church, humanist scholarship and debate, and continental Protestant reform movements. Therefore, the "Henrician" reformation, as it is sometimes called, was tied to many different, and sometimes unrelated developments, and its explanation must try to describe each of them.

There was widespread discontent within the English Christian community in the early 16th century. Whether it was sufficient to support a broad Protestant movement may be doubted, but there was a good deal of anticlerical feeling: a perception that there was an excessive number of clergy and that they absorbed large amounts of resources (tithes, rents, and fines) was accompanied by stories of inefficiency (clergy holding multiple benefices and not residing in them) and tales of injustice at the hands of church courts. A second problem was the formality and impersonal nature of religious worship, symbolized by the reading of the Latin mass to uncomprehending worshippers. More personalized worship by individuals, whether reading scripture or private meditation, was only available to the wealthier educated class. With Erasmus's *Handbook of a Christian Knight* (1503), or his satire *In Praise of Folly* (1514), the English reader found devotional guidance and subversive entertainment; but again, that audience was severely limited in size.

The "king's great matter" (his divorce from Catherine of Aragon) gave the ignition to reform, although it was not expected to have that effect. Indeed, in 1521 Henry VIII wrote a pamphlet attacking Martin Luther's heretical views, called *The Defense of the Seven Sacraments*. The pope bestowed the title "defender of the faith" (*fidei defensor*) on the king, a title which ironically is still used on British coinage. Henry conceived of himself as something of a theologian, and when he decided to discard his wife Catherine in 1527, he marshaled several biblical arguments and urged Cardinal Wolsey to convince the pope that the annulment was correct. Such a concession was indeed common for royalty and aristocrats, but in this case the pope had to invalidate his predecessor's dispensation allowing Henry to marry his brother's widow. The matter was complicated by the fact that Catherine's nephew, the Holy Roman Emperor, happened to have an army in control of Rome at the time. All of Wolsey's efforts to win a trial and verdict in the king's favor failed, and he died soon after being removed from office.

A member of Wolsey's staff, Thomas Cromwell, soon became Henry's chief advisor in church matters. He conducted a clever campaign to coerce the clergy into submitting to the king, prior to issuing directives and introducing legislation that gave the king supreme authority over the church in England. There was a series of legislative acts that denied revenues to Rome, terminated Roman legal authority, and finally declared the king to be the "supreme head" of the church. This involvement of Parliament as the vehicle for the king's directives gave that body the appearance of greatly increased power. But for the time being, Henry was the principal beneficiary, and he used the oaths recognizing his supremacy as a tool to beat down his adversaries, such as his lord chancellor, Sir Thomas More; his bishops, including John Fisher; and other members of the church, such as the Carthusian monks of London—all of whom were executed by the king in 1535. The supreme head of the church could not tolerate the divided loyalty of the monks and friars, who were by definition under direct Roman authority. Hence, in 1535 Cromwell made a survey, the *valor ecclesiasticus,* which assessed the value of monastic properties and the management of their assets. This was used as a pretext for dissolving the houses, first the smallest and then the rest (1536–38). A reaction to the dissolution took place in the Pilgrimage of Grace (1536), a popular demonstration against the destruction of monastic houses. Henry promised leniency to the pilgrimage's leaders, but they were arrested and executed.

While the pretext for dissolution was to discipline errant monks, the purpose was to seize their wealth. Most of it was soon spent on the king's wars or granted to members of the landowning class. Some was used to found schools, almshouses, and hospitals. The spoliation of the monasteries was a crude exercise in public looting, worthy of a rabid reform, but the king's policy was still not of that type. He reluctantly authorized the English Bible in parish churches in 1539, a few years after his agents had hunted down William Tyndale, who was responsible for the first English translation of the New Testament. His archbishop of Canterbury, Thomas Cranmer, worked on a Book of Common Prayer, but it was not produced until after the king's death. Meanwhile, numerous articles of religion were adopted, with later alterations in the 1530s and 1540s. The upshot of the Henrician reformation was the total reorganization of the Church of England under the authority of its "supreme head," without coherent attention to change in doctrine.

This new Church of England was not the only reformed church in the British Isles, for of course the church in Wales, Scotland, or Ireland could hardly be insulated. Each of the other three areas had a unique experience. Since Wales was part of the English province of Canterbury, it was subject to all of the reforms instituted in England. There were pockets of resistance, just as there were in England, and Cromwell decided that the annexation of Wales was

Sir Thomas More
(Library of Congress)

required in order to better secure the settlement there. Ireland was directed to adopt the English changes, but only the Pale, that part of Ireland under English control, was likely to be affected. Moreover, the majority of the Irish church remained Catholic and was likely to provide a strong base for papal reaction. The reformed church was definitely in a minority position, even though it wielded the apparent powers of the state. In Scotland, the church was under the Scots crown and influenced by the French alliance. Thus it was resistant to reforms, but when the French retired and Scottish leaders took control in 1560, the country experienced a popular and Protestant reform. These differences reflect the varied pattern of government in the British Isles, a pattern which itself was being reformed in the 16th century, both in the English center and in the British periphery.

THE ENGLISH MONARCHY REFORMED

About 50 years ago a thesis was advanced that during the 16th century there was a "revolution in government"—a shift from medieval to modern—in church, Parliament, and administration in England. There has been much debate and many amendments to the thesis, but the basic argument seems sound. The royal government of Henry VIII became something very different from its predecessors, and the modern elements, though buffeted over the next 150 years, remained visible and vital.

At the center of this revolution, Thomas Cromwell took old offices, combined them and their revenues, and applied new and more efficient accounting and management methods. He also reformed the king's privy (private) council, forming a smaller and more efficient body to effectively manage the newly empowered Parliament, which alone could produce (at the king's behest) the new statutes, so vital to the functioning of the reformed government. When Cromwell was deposed in 1540, a clerk to the council was appointed, and a regular register of council acts was begun.

These changes were not so surprising when it is seen that the problems of the 15th century had to do with the ability of powerful aristocrats to overawe the royal councils and intimidate royal officials. At first, under Henry VII, the council was an important new judicial forum. Sitting as the Court of Star Chamber, or the Court of Requests, the king's councillors heard cases against powerful subjects or, in the second case, on behalf of poor persons, and administered justice outside the rules of the common law courts. Beside the obvious tension this created in the judicial sphere, these prerogative courts were a notable addition to royal authority.

Thus, some change was already under way when the storm of the Reformation blew through the English government. Several major governmental changes can be tied directly to the church's reform. First, the powerful churchmen—the extreme example being Cardinal Wolsey as the lord chancellor—would never again dominate the highest level of civil government. Second, the former wealth of the church, a basis for its role in public affairs, was put directly under the control of the Crown and, in the case of the dissolution, converted to civil uses. That process was managed by new secular courts, the Court of Augmentations (1536) and a Court of First Fruits and Tenths (1540), coupled to a Court of Wards (1540) for feudal revenues and a Court of General Surveyors (1542). These bodies were an attempt to bypass the ancient Court of Exchequer, to give the Crown more direct control over revenues. A third change, which did not last, was the creation of a secular manager of church affairs. "The King's Vicegerent for Spirituals" was Cromwell's title, and in this capacity he ordered the important survey of monastic properties that preceded the dissolution. The importance of the title is that it is more evidence of the radical experimentation then being undertaken, particularly in connection with church reform.

The further argument for revolution hinges on the work of Cromwell, and of some of his successors, in creating the post of secretary of state. The king's chief officer had been the lord chancellor, who was the keeper of the great seal; head of the chancery or writing office, and as such the nominal supervisor of royal correspondence; and the head of the Court of Chancery, the court of equity jurisdiction. In the 1530s Cromwell held the office of king's secretary, and under him an attempt was made to supplant the clerical functions of the chancellor. The emergence of a new office that managed the king's business in more efficient manner was undeniably important. This post would be used by a later Tudor servant, William Cecil, Lord Salisbury, to establish the post of secretary of state, a major position in modern government.

Cromwell's work also influenced the unique English system of local government, which depended on the unpaid services of the justices of the peace in each county. He sent circular letters to the justices of the peace (JPs) in the king's name, handwritten by his clerks. These directives, coupled to the reports he received from the JPs and justices on circuit, created a network of government with two novel features: it took precedence over the church hierarchy, and it took power away from the many local feudal jurisdictions that had arisen during the Middle Ages.

There are other ways in which royal government, especially that of Henry VIII, was reformed in the mid-16th century. The king's martial endeavors have been noted, and their expense seems foolish next to a pragmatic view of England's power in Europe. However, in two ways they added to monarchic reformation: Henry's ambition prompted him to push for early development of an English royal navy, and the expense of this, plus his other ventures, applied enormous pressure to royal finances. However wasteful, that pressure forced innovation in organization and finance, and these processes continued into the later 16th century. Finally, there was the king's relationship with Parliament. Historically that body was an enlarged council summoned by kings, mainly for the approval of revenue measures. Certainly that role continued, but with the Parliament that met during the Reformation, there was an important development. The preamble to the Act in Restraint of Appeals (drafted by Cromwell) stated:

> This realm of England is an empire and so hath been accepted in the world, governed by one supreme head and king having the dignity and royal estate of the imperial crown of the same . . ., he being also institute and furnished by the goodness and sufferance of Almighty God with plenary, whole, and entire power, preeminence, authority, prerogative and jurisdiction . . .

This act, like all others, was passed at the instigation of the Crown, and with its approval. And yet the action was more than the proverbial rubber stamp. Kings had never included Parliament in the definition of their fundamental power; hereafter they mutually endorsed a stream of statutory definitions and ratifications. Parliament was a very useful tool for the Crown, although a tool that would someday become a check on royal power. The strength of the "imperial crown" was also being employed in other ways in the 16th century, as it extended its power throughout Britain.

REFORMING THE BRITISH STATE

The "empire" cited in Henry's Act in Restraint of Appeals referred to the myth of an ancient British kingdom, when in fact the Crown was creating a much more modern British state in the middle of the 16th century. The driving force was the church's reformation, which was allied with traditional motives of security and dominion.

The map of the British Isles in 1500 showed an England hedged about with buffer zones: the Scottish borders; the Welsh marches; and, outside Britain, the Irish Pale, the Channel Islands, and Calais. Within England, in fact, there were semiautonomous zones in Chester, Lancaster, and Durham—palatine counties whose feudal authority showed that there was as yet no fully dominant central power in England. These special jurisdictions were similar to the delegated royal authority of the marcher lordships in Wales, wardens of the marches on the Scottish border, and a lord deputy in Ireland. One of the major accomplishments of Tudor rule was the centralization of power at the expense of these jurisdictions.

Edward I had formally annexed the principality of Wales, and most of the country was held by marcher lords, perhaps as many as 130 of them in the early 16th century. During Henry VIII's reign it was decided to end those lordships and bring all of Wales into the system of shires, with members of Parliament and with the institutions of local government and laws as they were in England. This process was completed by statutes in 1536 and 1543. The stated reason was to end disorder and bring good government to Wales. But the real aim was to secure the country against a backlash directed at the Reformation and the dissolution. Wales was already within the English church province of Canterbury, so no new action was required on that front. But the possibility of papal counterattack was taken seriously.

Irish government, or that of the small area around Dublin known as the Pale, was in the hands of a lord deputy, an Anglo-Irish nobleman ruling in the king's name. Under Henry VIII this system was replaced by English deputies, and the king himself assumed the title king of Ireland in 1541. No such simple step would solve the myriad problems of Irish rule, but this was part of a larger effort to import the reformed church and to extend English-style government institutions to the Irish. These measures had limited success, and only the creation of plantations (with English and Scottish settlers) and the military defeat of Irish clan leaders would eventually give English authority effective control, which was achieved by the end of the Elizabeth I's reign.

With Scotland the English king faced a poor but formidable adversary. The Tudors managed to complete the Scots' military defeat, which Edward I had sought. But even though the English destroyed Scottish armies at Flodden (1513) and Solway Moss (1542), and both cases resulted in the death of the Scottish king (James IV and James V, respectively), the Scots remained independent. Part of the reason for this was their alliance with France; the other part was their bitter hatred of the English. This was given renewed life when Henry VIII invaded in the 1540s, attempting to force the dynastic union set out by the Treaty of Greenwich. But Edward VI never married Mary, who briefly became the bride of the king of France. It was Elizabeth who smoothed the road to union by negotiating the withdrawal of the French and English armies from Scotland in 1560. England and Scotland would ultimately be joined through the royal marriage of English princess Margaret to Scottish king James IV, arranged by Henry VII in 1503. The unifier would be their great-grandson, the son of Mary, queen of Scots. When his mother abdicated he became James VI of Scotland (1567), and at Elizabeth's death he became James I of England (1603).

In the week Elizabeth died, the Irish who had fought against her in Hugh O'Neill's rebellion in Ulster surrendered to the English deputy. This brought the English conquest of Ireland to a conclusion. England now commanded all of the British Isles, although the new king of "Great Britain" would find that many liabilities came with these assets.

THE ELIZABETHAN AGE

Queen Elizabeth I (1558–1603) had the longest reign of any Tudor and oversaw the Church of England's settlement, victory over the Spanish Armada, and less dramatic but equally important economic and social changes during the 16th century. The Elizabethan Age, as it was known, also witnessed the flowering of intellectual life known as the English Renaissance.

The church's settlement was the climax of the English reformation after the turmoil of Henry VIII's break with Rome and the succeeding swings under Edward and Mary. The Marian bishops would not serve under Elizabeth, and the exiles who began returning from Geneva and elsewhere were determined to build a sound Protestant church. The queen's dexterity and determination produced a moderate settlement, one in which she took the title "supreme governor" of the church. In 1559 a prayer book was adopted, much like that of 1552. An Act of Uniformity of 1559 put the enforcement powers of the civil government behind the new church. But its detailed doctrine was still to be decided. In a convocation in 1563 this was hammered out in the 39 Articles of Faith, which had just enough ambiguity at critical points that most of the diverse Protestant flock could support them. Elizabeth's *via media* resulted in powerful challenges from both Protestant and Catholic adversaries. From the Protestants came continuing agitation over clergy vestments, forms of prayer, and the allowance for individual interpretation. The last of these led Elizabeth to sack Archbishop Edmund Grindal in 1583 and to promote John Whitgift, who became a symbol of Puritan persecution in the queen's later years. On the Catholic side, Elizabeth had to deal with a rebellion of nobles in the north in 1569, her own excommunication in 1570, and a series of plots against her life, ending with the trial and execution of her cousin Mary, queen of Scots, in 1587.

The most serious threat to Elizabeth, and to her Protestant subjects, was the Spanish Armada in 1588. Philip of Spain had had hopes of taking Elizabeth as his wife after her sister Mary died. But as this prospect faded, it seemed that the Catholic Mary of Scotland might become queen, especially when, in 1562, Elizabeth was stricken with smallpox; however, she managed to recover. There were a number of plots aimed at bringing about Mary's succession. By 1570 Elizabeth had been excommunicated, and as a heretic she became a legitimate target. Yet it was not until 1585 that Philip declared war on England and set in motion his plan of conquest. He prepared a giant fleet to sail into the English

Engraving of
Queen Elizabeth I
(Library of Congress)

Channel and rendezvous with an army under his lieutenant, the duke of Parma, governor of the Netherlands. The armada would shield the army's channel crossing. If that trained force of 30,000 had landed, there is little doubt that it could have overthrown the Elizabethan regime. But the English escaped this fate for several reasons. First, an expedition in 1587 had attacked the port of Cádiz and destroyed some of the Spanish fleet's stores and equipment. Second, when the armada arrived in the channel in 1588, English long-range guns and tactics proved effective against the closed mass of Spanish ships. Third, when the armada anchored at Calais, the English launched fire-ships into the fleet at night, causing havoc. The next day the disorganized Spanish were beaten in the Battle of Gravelines and forced to retreat by sailing around the north of the British Isles. There were several later attempts to mount a similar attack, but none got as far as this, and the victory became a celebrated moment in English naval history. Equally important, though, was the cost of this venture combined with the other expeditions and campaigns of Elizabeth's reign. Some estimates put the cost of the war against Spain at £250,000 per year. On top of that, the queen ordered expeditions to France and Holland to aid Protestants and campaigns in Ireland to suppress the Gaelic rebels there. She sold off vast amounts of Crown lands, spent the income from privateers, borrowed heavily, and left a debt of £400,000 at her death. In short, the kingdom's finances suffered, and the expedients used to deal with the problem (grants, sales of offices, new taxation) caused escalating discontent and government weakness.

Government finance faltered in the context of a rapidly changing economy. The population had begun to grow again, and it doubled by the end of the 16th century. At the same time there was astronomical inflation—a 500 percent increase over the course of the century. Real wages fell about 50 percent, and that translated into severe pressure on jobs and a rapid increase in vagrancy. Landowners were under pressure to increase production and profits, forcing many to enclose their land, among other things to convert from crops to pasture, in hopes of greater profits.

Elizabethan society proved resilient throughout this period of rapid religious, economic, and political change. The essential hierarchy of social ranks did not change. The aristocracy consisted of peers, knights, esquires, and gentlemen, amounting to about 5 percent of the population. The vast majority of the elite were the gentlemen, or "gentry," an amorphous, ill-defined group covering a wide range of wealth and position that provided the bulk of the magistrates and clergy. Below the aristocracy were the "middling sort" of people: merchants, farmers, and craftsmen who made up probably 20 percent of the population. They directed most of the business of society, managed estates, carried on trade, and produced the necessary tools for daily work. The poorer sort, including farm workers, laborers, and the poor, made up the remaining 75 percent.

This society, or at least its upper ranks, experienced a further kind of reform over the course of the 16th century, one which often bears the label "renaissance." The advent of humanist scholarship combined with Tudor patronage and display were the engines of a major reform of education, the arts, and literature. The church's reformation was a counterpoint that involved displacement of the arts, the libraries, and the trappings of the old faith into a more public arena. In the later decades of the century, the Elizabethan period saw a revival of patronage, royal and aristocratic, which supported the flourishing construction of country houses and the literary work of Sir Philip Sidney, Edmund Spenser, and the great William Shakespeare, among others. The century had also seen a notable increase in schools, from the humanist John Colet's foundation at Westminster (1509) to the more humble town grammar schools, especially numerous after the dissolution of the monasteries caused the loss of many schools. Religion remained the centerpiece of the newer schools. The catechism might be altered, but its method and purpose lost no importance. Elementary schooling probably expanded its audience, but the numbers were small; advanced schooling in Latin—and, less often, Greek grammar—was for an elite destined for the university and, primarily, for the church. As with schools, so the universities went from church to secular control, though with no less emphasis on their divine vocation. Indeed, humanists thought the universities were not fit to train a true gentleman, but as the best established scholarly bodies they became the training schools of the new gentry as well as the vocational schools of the church.

The Tudor era brought a compound of reforms. Settling the Church of England was the central change, and the sometimes brutal impact on society, education, and culture sent shock waves through all of Britain. These waves coincided with secular alterations in the functioning of the English monarchy and in the government of the regions. The new state and society reached a peak of cultural development in Elizabeth's reign, but her government was weakened by financial erosion while society was still bitterly divided by religious conflict. That combination became the fuel for a century of revolution.

BRITISH REVOLUTIONS

1603–1707

The 17th century was largely a period of civil war and revolution, marked by the execution of Charles I (1649) and the forced exile of James II (1688). These events were the blunt instruments that formed a constitutional monarchy, a change that was amplified by radical religious, social, and economic forces. The upshot was the transformation of Britain by the most comprehensive revolution Europe had seen.

ORIGINS OF THE CIVIL WAR, 1603–1642

In 1603, when James VI of Scotland traveled south to take the English throne as James I, there was general relief and rejoicing. After all, a Protestant king would assure the safety of the religious settlement. In addition, a king who was dedicated to peace would bring an end to European wars, which in turn would lead to reduced government spending. Yet all of these expectations were crushed, and the next king found himself at war with his own subjects within four decades. Clues to the causes of that war can be found in examining the reign of James I (1603–25) and the reign and character of Charles I (1625–49).

James was born in the early days of the Scottish Reformation, and his tutors included staunch Presbyterians, so many of the English Puritans expected a royal ally. They were soon disappointed, for when James convened the Hampton Court Conference to discuss the settlement of the church in 1604, he made it clear that he wanted no part of advanced Protestantism. In fact he valued the role of the bishops, and he did his utmost to restore them in Presbyterian Scotland. James wanted an episcopal church only slightly more reformed than that of Elizabeth. The king was also fiercely opposed by the more extreme Roman Catholics, a group of whom plotted to blow up the houses of Parliament at the opening session in 1605. The so-called Gunpowder Plot was exposed, and the deliverance of the king and his councillors was praised, while the plotters were tortured and executed. Although they were outside the mainstream, they signaled the depth of difficulty in solving religious disputes. This was ominous, for James was conciliatory, albeit strict in the enforcement of the church settlement.

James had ambitious plans for the union of his two monarchies. But their different forms of protestantism, their different institutions (parliaments, courts of law, local governments), and their different social and economic conditions did not aid his plans. James immediately proposed that his parliaments undertake the business of unification, but at once many objections arose. The king unilaterally declared his title to be "king of Great Britain," and he designed a new royal flag and minted new coins. Yet with two discordant and frustrated parliaments, there was no progress on the wider project of union. Subjects on both sides of the border did not lose their ingrained hostility overnight, but as a matter of law, a suit known as Calvin's Case found that all persons born in Scotland after James's accession in 1603 were on an equal footing with English subjects.

In the area of foreign policy, James tried to be a moderating influence in European religious affairs, hoping to bring about a reconciliation between Rome and her Protestant enemies. Likewise, he wanted to pursue a pacific foreign policy with European states, in line with his general desire for Catholic-Protestant reconciliation. He was able to make peace with Spain in 1604, ending 20 years of warfare. He also negotiated the marriage of his daughter Elizabeth to Frederick V, the Protestant elector Palatine. He wanted a dynastic marriage for his son Charles with Spain, thinking that these ties would support his role as a mediator. In 1609 James helped to arrange a treaty between Spain and the Netherlands. Although peace with Spain frightened Protestants who remembered the Armada, it also pacified English Catholics and profited English merchants who gained some protection from Spanish imperial power. The whole policy was shattered by the outbreak of the Thirty Years' War (1618–48), which had been, ironically, exacerbated by Frederick's acceptance of the crown of Bohemia in 1619. After Frederick's defeat the following year by imperial forces, James was seen as supporting both sides in a war that became especially brutal. His Protestant subjects were outraged by continued overtures to Spain, in particular the sudden trip that Prince Charles and the duke of Buckingham made in 1623 to try to woo the Spanish princess. The escalating conflict in Europe also forced James to seek more financial support from his subjects. But royal finances were in serious jeopardy already.

There was a tradition that the king was supposed to pay for his government out of ordinary revenues. Profits from land, customs, and routine fees had long since ceased to be adequate due to inflation and the sale of Crown lands, to which Elizabeth had frequentiy resorted. James inherited Elizabeth's heavy debts, and he himself was a profligate spender. The king resorted to a range of expedients to increase his revenue: raising customs duties (impositions), collecting money from ancient feudal obligations (purveyance—the supply of food at fixed prices; wardships—the guardianship of minor heirs), and even the sale of titles. Older peerages were not sufficient, and in 1611 James created the new rank of baronet, which initially sold for over £1,000. But all of these tactics were not enough; even in peacetime, the king needed more revenue. This meant frequent demands for funds from Parliament, where there was opportunity to question royal policies. James encountered this kind of opposition in 1604,

King James I
(Library of Congress)

1610, 1614, and 1621. On these occasions the fundamental issue was being defined: the Crown demanded the means to conduct government, and Parliament insisted that grievances be addressed before supply. James had to struggle mightily during his reign, but his long experience and his political skills preserved a basic harmony. This was not to be the case for his son.

Charles I was a very different ruler: fastidious where his father was uncouth; rigid in his faith, where his father wanted moderation; youthfully dogmatic regarding his power, where his father was stubborn but also learned and studious. Charles was primarily responsible for the estrangement that brought on civil war. This occurred through a string of poor decisions and attempts to assert his power.

Charles pursued belligerent policies toward France and Spain, but in 1626 Parliament refused to fund his military operations. The king nevertheless continued to collect taxes, and he resorted to a forced loan. There was widespread resistance, and some 70 gentlemen were arrested for their refusal to pay the money demanded from them. Five were tried and convicted in 1627, raising the central questions of whether the king could levy taxes without Parliament's consent, and whether the Crown had the power to arrest without a specific charge. The following year Parliament passed a "Petition of Right," which held that the king should have Parliament's approval for taxation, that subjects should not be arrested arbitrarily, and that billeting of troops and martial law should not be used (as they had been in the recent situation). Charles gave his approval but claimed that the petition merely affirmed traditional rights and that it placed no new limits on his prerogative. If he truly believed this, he was ill-advised. In 1629 Charles ordered Parliament to dissolve. In the heated atmosphere, several members of the Commons held the Speaker in his chair so that he could not dismiss them, while they read a set of resolutions on the rights of Parliament. The king's next move was to decide to govern without Parliament.

It was entirely lawful for the king to summon or not summon a Parliament. The typical occasion for a parliamentary session was when the Crown needed revenues. Those occasions had become routine by the 1630s, but Charles decided to try executive government. He might have succeeded, as long as there was peace and as long as his financial expedients worked. One particular expedient was called ship money. In the past, coastal towns had been expected to raise funds to operate a ship during a maritime emergency. In 1635 this obligation was extended to all towns regardless of emergency. For a while the income from ship money assessments was substantial, but it fell off after the tax was challenged in court and only narrowly approved in 1638.

The period of personal rule was brought to an end by disputes over the Scottish kirk (church). Charles had continued his father's efforts to bring the kirk into line with the episcopal church in England. But with less sympathy and understanding, his archbishop, William Laud, ordered the adoption of new church canons (1636) and the introduction of a new prayer book (1637). These touched off a broad campaign of Scottish resistance, the signing of a national covenant against the innovations, and the meeting of a general assembly that abolished the office of bishop. A Scottish army entered England in 1639, but there was no fighting. A treaty made in 1639 was merely a cease-fire, and in 1640 a Scottish army again crossed the border and occupied Newcastle and much of northern England. Charles had summoned Parliament in April, but dissolved this "Short" Parliament in the midst of debate over the rights of subjects. Now he had to summon another, and the "Long" Parliament was about to remake the English constitution.

The leaders of Parliament were determined to achieve their demands, and Charles was forced to accept serious inroads on his power. He surrendered his principal minister, Thomas Wentworth, earl of Strafford, who was tried and executed; the prerogative courts (Star Chamber and High Commission) were abolished; and acts were passed requiring a meeting of Parliament at least every three years, while the current Parliament was not to be dissolved without its consent. When a rebellion broke out in Ireland in October 1641, even more radical demands were made. Now the issue was whether or not an army would be provided to meet the rebels—an army that might also be used to discipline the king's English enemies. At this point a split developed in Parliament between those loyal to the king and those determined to oppose him. In January 1642 Charles entered the Commons to arrest five of its radical leaders, but they had been warned and had hidden in London. The contest then became one of securing forces for war. The king withdrew from London, and in August 1642 he declared war on the insurgents.

CIVIL WAR AND REVOLUTION, 1642–1659

The Civil War began with monarchists on both sides, but the fury unleashed across the British Isles produced a revolution that killed the king and brought a decade of turmoil. In England a military dictatorship deepened religious divisions, seized property, and never developed a majority of support. In Scotland and Ireland the period brought English invasion and occupation and a temporary unification, but in the end there was alienation between the areas.

The division of forces for the king and for Parliament cut across county and community lines, but generally the north and west of England stood for Charles and the south and east for Parliament, London in particular. In Wales, Scotland, and Ireland there were no clear regional lines, and there were more complex divisions among Presbyterians and Catholics, Irish settlers and natives, Scottish highlanders and lowlanders. The campaigns went on for four years. No decisive battles came until Marston Moor in 1644 and Naseby in 1645, and those victories for Parliament were due in part to the arrival of allied Scottish forces. There was a plan to bring Irish troops to the king's aid, but that did not come to pass. The war brought very heavy taxation, confiscation of property, the destruction of many communities, and severe loss of life. The Scottish alliance required the planning for a new English Presbyterian church. Parliament reformed its army on a "new model" in 1645, removing aristocratic leaders and promoting the most skilled soldiers, including one named Oliver Cromwell. The new force was more professional and also more imbued with religious radicalism. This army became a political vehicle once it had defeated the king; for at that point Parliament decided to disband the army without meeting payroll arrears, offering service in Ireland as an alternative. The army demanded payment, and some of its units marched on London in 1647. Meanwhile King Charles, who had surrendered to the Scots in 1646, was taken prisoner by units of the army.

Within the regiments of the new model army, there were agents of the troops known as agitators. Many of them were influenced by the religious doctrines of the anti-episcopal and anti-Catholic Independents, who wanted self-governing congregations. The army also included members of the radical Levellers, a group led by John Lilburne, who advocated the end of aristocracy and a wide range of democratic reforms against the tyranny of kings, parliaments, and armies. Army leaders such as Cromwell were determined to suppress such radical ideas, while at the same time they set out to protect themselves from control by Parliament or king.

During his captivity Charles formed an alliance with royalists in England and Scotland, and a brief second civil war in 1648 saw the final defeat of his forces.

Now the army was even more determined to secure its position. Parliament was purged of the members who opposed the army, reducing it by half. This "Rump" Parliament joined with the army council to set up a high court of justice to try the king. In January 1649 Charles was tried, convicted of treason, and executed.

The revolution eliminated the Crown, and it was followed by the abolition of the House of Lords and the termination of the episcopal church. Names had to be altered: e.g., the court of "king's bench" became the "upper bench." Far more important, however, was the continued role of the army. In 1649 and 1650 English armies under Oliver Cromwell invaded Ireland and then Scotland. In the first case, there were brutal punishments awaiting the Catholic subjects of Ireland (Drogheda, Wexford, 1649). In the latter, Cromwell decisively defeated Scottish armies (Dunbar, Stirling, and Worcester, 1650–51).

In his capacity as the head of the army council, Cromwell established a commonwealth run by the Rump Parliament and the army leadership. Disputes between them led Cromwell to dismiss the Rump in 1653, and a nominated Parliament, a body of 150 Independent ministers, was installed in 1653. It too drew Cromwell's wrath and was dissolved before the end of the year, upon which a new protectorate was established. Cromwell designated himself as Lord Protector. Several different parliaments (including Scottish and Irish members) sat during this period, and for a time (1654–56) England was ruled by a military regime in which major generals ruled over English districts. None of these expedients was popular, all of them were provisional, and when Cromwell died in 1658, his son Richard was unable to wield power effectively. There was a period of great political instability, and order was restored only when General George Monck, Cromwell's commander in Scotland, brought his army to London in 1660. The mission of this army was to pave the way for the restoration of the monarchy, in the person of Charles II.

RESTORATION AND REVOLUTION, 1660–1688

Charles II had been proclaimed king by the Scots and the Irish after his father's death. He had a large following in England as well, where there were unsuccessful rebellions of royalists in the 1650s. When Monck arrived in London with his army, the remnant of the Long Parliament met long enough to call an election for a "Convention" Parliament. Meanwhile Charles presented the Declaration of Breda, in which he promised a general pardon; a settlement of confiscated estates (by Parliament); payment of arrears to the army; and "liberty to tender consciences," i.e., a vague form of religious toleration. The Convention Parliament invited the king to return, and he reached London in May 1660. This initial Parliament passed an act of indemnity, granted Charles a fixed income (in lieu of feudal dues), and passed acts regarding confiscated lands. The restoration affirmed the acts of the late king prior to 1642, thus accepting the elimination of the prerogative courts and several other measures.

This very promising beginning was soon disturbed by the resurrection of key issues from the 1620s and 1630s: religious uniformity, foreign affairs, and questions of royal authority once again threatened to disrupt the political scene. The first Parliament elected under Charles II sat from 1661 to 1678. This body was dominated by staunch royalists and was thus labeled the "Cavalier" Parliament, after the nickname for royalists in the Civil War. Such a parliament was not inclined to be moderate, as can be seen in the religious settlement. Charles II had hoped to include Presbyterians in the new church, but the new bishops and members of the Cavalier Parliament would not hear of it. Their policy was embodied in what was called the "Clarendon Code" named after the king's chancellor, Edward Hyde, earl of Clarendon, who in fact did not endorse some of its provisions. The code included a Corporation Act (1661), which applied religious tests to members of local corporations; and an act of

Oliver Cromwell; reproduction of a painting by Robert Walker
(Library of Congress)

uniformity (1662), which enjoined the use of a new prayer book. The latter act prompted the king to issue a Declaration of Indulgence in 1662, which dispensed with the law's operation. Thus religion had very quickly raised a serious constitutional issue. Later parts of the code included a conventicle act (1664), which governed the religious meetings of dissenters; and a Five Mile Act (1665), which restricted the movements of dissenting preachers. The latter acts were in response to outbreaks of unrest, and clearly religious tensions were still strong. They could also still be fanned by fears of foreign powers.

In foreign affairs Charles was both pragmatic and deceitful. His pragmatism was evident in his policy of trade war with the Dutch, designed to strengthen the British merchant navy. This policy, first used during Cromwell's war in 1652, was revived by the reissue of navigation laws. War broke out in 1665, but the English fleet was both underfunded and embarrassed by a Dutch raid on the fleet anchorage in the Thames in 1667. This was followed by the Treaty of Dover with Louis XIV in 1670. A third Dutch war in 1672–74 was less for commercial than for diplomatic purposes, but its major effects came in related areas. First, in order to finance the fleet, the king stopped payment to creditors in 1672. This "Stop of the Exchequer" was a radical step which helped to assure that government finance would be separated from the personal finances of the king. The second and more telling matter was that the Treaty of Dover had secret clauses in which Charles promised to declare his conversion to Catholicism as part of a plan to bring about a Catholic restoration in England. For this the French promised him a subsidy along with the prospect of dividing the spoils of the Dutch empire. But the king's policy brought little imperial profit and great domestic hostility.

In 1672 Charles issued another Declaration of Indulgence, allowing private Catholic worship and easing laws against dissenters. The Dutch war did not provide an English victory, and in 1673 Parliament demanded the declaration's removal. It went on to pass a Test Act, which required all officers and officeholders to take Anglican communion publicly and to take an oath denying transubstantiation. Charles was forced to assent to this in order to obtain parliamentary funding. Even more important, this act forced his brother James to resign as lord high admiral, thus publicly acknowledging his religion. That in turn created a controversy over the royal succession. Charles had no legitimate heirs, but he did have an illegitimate son, the duke of Monmouth, who was a Protestant. His brother James had converted after the death of his first wife, Anne Hyde (who gave him two daughters, Mary and Anne, both raised as Protestants). When she died in 1672, James remarried, taking as his wife the Catholic princess Mary of Modena. Would the throne pass to a Roman Catholic? If so, what would be the fate of the Church of England and of Scotland?

These questions drove the events of the next few years in a continuing drama called the "exclusion crisis." A dramatic climax was reached in 1678 with reports of an alleged plot to murder Charles and place his brother James on the throne. This "Popish plot" was the product of the frenzied imaginations of Titus Oates and Israel Tonge—both Anglican clergymen and both rabid haters of the Roman church. Oates had made a deposition to a London magistrate, and when that man was found murdered, the sensational stories acquired credibility. The House of Commons heard testimony from Oates, resulting in numerous trials and 24 executions. Anti-Catholicism exploded, a new Test Act was passed (1678), Catholic peers were sequestered, and the king's chief minister was impeached. Charles was forced to dissolve his longstanding Parliament in the midst of this hysteria. The issue of excluding James from the succession was presented in bills before the Commons in successive parliaments. During the crisis a political group called the Whigs were prominent advocates for James's exclusion; a rival group of Tories staunchly supported the succession, with their doctrine of nonresistance claiming that it was illegal to deny the lawful heir to the throne. Three parliaments could not settle the issue, and Charles decided in 1681 not to summon any more. He had returned to the point of his father's fateful decision in 1629. But in this case, the king was able to govern for four more years, and the atmosphere cooled for several reasons: Oates was proven to have lied; a plot hatched by radicals had led to the execution of several Whig leaders, William, Lord Russell and Algernon Sidney among them; and the panic had brought harsh memories of the 1640s.

James II came to the throne after his brother died in 1685. He was welcomed by a new and pliant Parliament that provided him with ample revenues and with supplements when it was learned that there were rebellions in England and Scotland. Charles II's son, the duke of Monmouth, led a rebel force in western England, and the earl of Argyll another group in Scotland. Both were easily defeated, and Monmouth was executed in London, while 300 of his followers were executed in the rebel areas and hundreds of others were sentenced to transportation to the West Indies. The major outcome of all this was to strengthen support for James.

Yet in spite of his early popularity, James managed to lose most of his support over the next three years as he took actions that revived all the fears of absolutism, amid a growing certainty that he planned to restore the Catholic religion. Since there was only a minority of some 2 percent who were Catholic, most Anglicans preferred to accept an anointed legitimate ruler in 1685. But that opinion quickly began to change as James exercised his power. He wanted to repeal the Test Acts; appointed Roman Catholics as army officers; opened seminaries in London; sent emissaries to Rome; and began remodeling local corporations, university colleges, and the county commissions of the peace. His zealous conduct turned widespread support into frightened opposition in short order.

BRITAIN AND THE GLORIOUS REVOLUTION, 1688–1707

A crisis in 1688 precipitated the fall of James II. The previous year he had issued yet another Declaration of Indulgence, and in May 1688 his council ordered the clergy to read it from their pulpits. Seven bishops who petitioned the king to delay his order were arrested and sent to the Tower of London. Their trial for sedition resulted in an acquittal on June 29, which set off rejoicing in London. Meanwhile, on June 10, however, the queen had given birth to a male heir, and it was apparent that a legitimate successor would guarantee the continued advance of the Catholic restoration. With that in mind, on June 30 a group of seven leading Whigs and Tories sent a message to William of Orange, asking him to come to England to protect their church and preserve their liberties. As the main Protestant prince and foe of French king Louis XIV, William had for some time been communicating with English allies and planning such a move. Knowing that King James was in league with France, he had every reason to launch a preemptive assault.

William's invasion force sailed into the channel and landed in Southwest England on November 5, 1688. James failed to see soon enough that Dutch preparations were directed against him and not France. By the fall he was hard pressed to mount a defense, and he hastily reversed many of his orders, canceling an upcoming Parliament (for which many Catholics would have been seated), restoring Anglican bishops, closing his Commission for Ecclesiastical Causes, and revoking the new borough charters he had created. Meanwhile William issued a declaration of his intent to come as a guardian of liberties, to see that a free Parliament was chosen, and to guarantee the protection of the established church. His fleet of 500 vessels brought an army of 20,000, mainly veterans of continental wars. James would have had a fair chance of defeating the invasion, had he acted with resolve. He failed to do so, and he fled London, only to be captured by Kentish fishermen. A second escape was facilitated by his guards, as William had no desire for a confrontation. By December William was in London proposing that he and his wife Mary (James II's eldest daughter by Anne Hyde) be declared joint sovereigns. The English eventually accepted this settlement, and they presented the king and queen with a declaration of rights as their part of the bargain. This document itemized James's errors and set out agreed principles: the Crown's power to suspend or dispense with laws was denied; the king's prerogative in judicial matters was also overturned; the standing army in peacetime was banned; Parliament alone was to raise revenue; and free elections, the right to bear arms, and judicial protections were all included. In addition, the declaration set out the line of succession and prohibited a Catholic from taking the throne. The plain consequence of these measures was a constitutional monarchy.

With regard to Scotland, William had to accept the Claim of Right, which was actually more radical than the English declaration. It provided that no Catholic could be king, that royal prerogative could not overrule law, that parliaments should meet frequently and not be subject to the Lords of the Articles, that only Parliament could raise revenues, and that the office of bishop was to be abolished. While William did not immediately accept all of the terms, the Presbyterian structure of the church did become the established model by 1690, and all the remaining terms were eventually accepted.

In Ireland, the Glorious Revolution, as William and Mary's accession was called, was countered by widespread Catholic resistance. Consequently, James came from France to lead a rebel Catholic government in its fight against an invading Anglo-Dutch force under William. After some early victories, James was defeated at the Battle of the Boyne in 1690. His forces had also failed to conquer the besieged Protestants in Londonderry, and that victory became a symbol for Protestant loyalists for centuries to come. The war in Ireland was only concluded in 1691 with a surrender at Limerick. French troops were allowed to depart, and fair terms were promised to the defeated Catholics. But over the next few years, these terms were not honored, and a rigid Protestant regime was established. Strict penal laws were enforced, reducing Catholics to subordinate status.

But there was much more to the outcome of William's invasion. Foremost was the fact that he had achieved a diplomatic revolution. Instead of England, Scotland and Ireland being allied with France, he had shifted those realms to the Protestant cause, with access to all their resources for his destined struggle with Louis XIV. The Nine Years' War (1689–97) and the War of the Spanish Succession (1702–13) incurred enormous expenditures, and there was a successful effort to preserve Dutch independence and to strengthen English maritime power. The heavy burden of this effort assured that the king met Parliament annually, and its finances were guaranteed by the establishment of the national debt and the foundation of a Bank of England (and a Bank of Scotland) in 1694–95.

The Nine Years' War was between France and a Protestant alliance over the division of the faltering Spanish power in Europe and abroad. A series of bloody and inconclusive battles on the Dutch frontier as well as a number of naval engagements brought no clear conclusion. The peace of Ryswick in 1697 saw France returning its conquests and recognizing William as king of Britain, while a set of partition treaties were drawn up in a futile effort to divide the former Spanish territories. This process broke down in 1701 when Louis XIV recognized James "III" (James II's son with Mary of Modena) as the lawful king of Britain. King William had begun war preparations, but he died suddenly in a riding accident in 1702, to be succeeded by his sister-in-law Anne (1702–14). Nevertheless, the English and allied armies led by John Churchill, later duke of Marlborough, defeated the French and their allies in a stunning series of battles in Europe, while English sailors won a number of naval engagements. The Treaty of Utrecht in 1713 recognized an overwhelming British victory in the War of the Spanish Succession.

A dominant political feature of William's reign was the emergence of political parties in government. The Whigs and Tories of the exclusion crisis became accepted groupings of politicians, though they were not the only ones or the most important at all times. Whigs tended to represent aggressive foreign policy, mercantile interests, and more liberal religious views. Tories by and large were the party of landowners who opposed heavy government taxation and spending and supported the established church. The labels were far from precise, but the point was that the king found ministers to run his government from groups who could manage Parliament along defined lines of policy. The king still chose the ministers, but they now had a new identity and strength in a party. These were still far from modern organized parties, but they were also no longer the individual royal servants of the early 17th century.

The royal succession dominated the politics of the end of the 17th century. William III had no heirs; his sister-in-law Anne lost her only son, William, in

1700; and the son of James II born in 1688 assumed his father's claim to the throne in 1701. The Jacobites (from *Jacobus* for "James") saw a possibility of regaining power. But in 1701 the English Parliament passed an Act of Settlement that provided that the succession should pass to the descendants of James I's daughter Elizabeth, who had married Frederick V of Bohemia. The successor would be the electress Sophia of Hanover, or her children, who also happened to be Protestants. One other aspect of this law was that it silently presumed to provide for the Scottish succession as well.

The Scots had not accepted the Glorious Revolution without a fight. There was a strong but small Jacobite element that won the Battle of Killiecrankie in July 1689, but the forces of the Crown soon overcame them. The divisions in Scottish society, roughly Highland and Lowland, Gaelic and English-speaking, provided some guide to the state of politics. Support for William and for any English ruler always had limits. The Scots cherished their separate government institutions—church, courts, and parliament. They also saw the Scottish Crown as a separate entity. Thus in 1703–05 Scottish patriots pushed for laws giving the Scottish Parliament an independent voice in deciding the royal succession. This action was spurred by a long list of Scottish grievances over English intervention: control of Scottish affairs from London, complaints about English navigation laws, and the failure of a Scottish colonial company due to English interference.

Challenged by the Scottish Parliament, the English government began to work toward a plan of parliamentary union, and in 1706 Queen Anne appointed commissioners to negotiate the terms. In 1707, after a treaty was signed, acts were passed in both legislatures, and the union of the two parliaments was completed. In 1707 the first Parliament of the United Kingdom of Great Britain convened. Scotland was represented by 45 members of Parliament (MPs) in the Commons and 16 elected peers in the House of Lords. In all other respects it was still the English parliament. The act of union also preserved the Church of Scotland and Scottish courts and laws, and it promised to link the two economies through a complex formula for integration. The act was also meant to assure Scotland's security from Jacobite rebellion, though the future would show that no law could achieve that.

In 1707 the monarch, Parliament, the Churches of England and Scotland, and communities throughout the British Isles still bore traces of the previous century's revolutions. At the same time, because of the economic changes of the later 17th century, they were about to build a new society in the 18th.

A NEW SOCIETY

1707–1850

The Stuart dynasty was supplanted by the House of Hanover when Queen Anne died in 1714. Over the next half-century Britain became the strongest military power in Europe, built a global empire, and refined the constitutional monarchy inherited from 1689. The government was dominated by an entrenched Whig oligarchy until 1757, owing in part to the threat of a Jacobite restoration, which was identified with Tory supporters. This threat was defeated on two major occasions, in 1715 and 1745, and then subsided. The main concern then became the status of the American colonies, whose rebellion in 1776–81 threw off British rule. This coincided with a period of political instability in England, ending when the French Revolution of 1789 brought major European war (1793–1801, 1803–15). A victorious coalition led by Britain defeated Napoleon Bonaparte, but the postwar years, while peaceful, were a time of tremendous social stress and political tension, all of which helped to induce a remarkable series of reforms from 1820 to 1850.

The new society that emerged in this period enabled the middle classes to gain in numbers and affluence by 1800, and over the next half-century that momentum carried the poor toward a social recognition hitherto unknown. In 1850 British society still had old familiar outlines, but its structure was coming to resemble that of today. There was also a new appreciation of social class and social justice. For over a century Britons had absorbed the fruits of a new consumer culture fed by a global empire, and this broad wave of development was destined to remake society.

In the 17th century the old society had featured a tiny elite ruling in a patriarchal order with a focus on the land and a dominant religion, and with the lower orders settled in seemingly permanent subservience. This order of things was now and then marred by famine, plagues, and pestilence. More significantly, in the middle of the century an apocalyptic revolution had overturned the old structure. The attempt to restore the old order after 1660 could not succeed, as many new elements—and some old frictions—were present.

What was distinctive and valuable in the changes that occurred was the flexible stability that the older British society, and its newer forms, retained throughout the period. Numerous observers commented on the differences between most of Britain and her continental neighbors: mobility among classes, commercial opportunities, and broad access to law were paramount. This flexible stability enabled Britain to move through the changes that this chapter will trace, without the trauma of revolution. And when pressure for political reform grew in the 19th century, the memories of two revolutions—the bad in 1649 and the good in 1689—also promoted moderation. One of the most pervasive factors associated with the changing climate of the latter half of the 17th century was a broad stream of intellectual development that reconfigured the natural world and in so doing challenged elementary ideas of society.

THE ENLIGHTENMENT

The term "enlightenment" has had an odd history. It was first a self-conscious description of contemporaries who saw themselves escaping the "darkness" of the world of medieval thought, dominated by religion and religious controversy, heedless of man's mental capacity, and dogmatic in its treatment of new ideas. They found their escape route by way of empirical study and logical deduction. Historians looking for the roots of the French Revolution of 1789 found a brilliant corps of writers (the *philosophes*) in 18th-century France (Montesquieu, Diderot, Voltaire) who seemed to be the inspiration for later events. They were joined by an amazing band of intellectuals in 18th-century Scotland (Hume, Hutcheson, Kames, Smith) whose work received recognition as the "Scottish Enlightenment." But there had also been nearly a century of philosophic thought in England (Bacon, Boyle, Newton, Locke) that formed part of the basis for the Age of Enlightenment, as it was called. Whether or not these thinkers should be credited with triggering Europe's enlightenment, their contributions to Britain's social and political history must be considered.

The notable thinkers and early scientists in 17th-century Britain rebuilt the understanding of the cosmos, the natural world, and the human function within it. Francis Bacon was the most influential early figure, noted for his works on inductive method. William Harvey was a physician who described the circulatory system of the human body, Roger Boyle experimented with gases and their properties, and Sir Isaac Newton developed a theory of gravity to explain the operation of the universe. After the Restoration (1660), the Royal Society was incorporated to foster the work of such men. Their significance was to open a new avenue for human intelligence, outside the bounds of traditional, theological explanation. At the time of the Glorious Revolution (1688), the greatest thinker of his age, John Locke, recast the understanding of government, evaluated the role of the church, and speculated on the nature of human psychology in his books *Treatises on Government* (1689) and *Essays Concerning Human Understanding* (1690).

This same period saw passage of a Toleration Act (1689), which allowed (and regulated) the practice of Protestant dissent. It was not generous (Catholics and Quakers were excluded) and it was intended more to fortify the Anglican establishment than to honor the beliefs of others. Nevertheless, the next generation became an important time for the growth of dissent (Presbyterians, Baptists,

John Locke
(Hulton/Archive)

Congregationalists), as well as a time of emerging public expression of deism, that is, the belief in a god whose existence was proven by nature, not revealed truth. This was confined to a very small segment, and orthodox churchmen regarded with it horror. Nevertheless, it was another sign of the Enlightenment's influence, which would continue to stimulate religious diversity and debate.

In a more pragmatic way, the end of the century saw the flourishing of political and social economics. A powerful dose of empiricism was added to the operation of government: systematic calculation in finance and the development of banking and exchange facilities were important advances. They were, of course, subject to manipulation, as in the infamous South Sea Bubble scheme, which caused widespread ruin when it collapsed in 1720. But on balance the new type of finance was the key to Britain's commercial growth in that era. In the wider society there was an effort to count the population. The economist Sir William Petty pioneered in this, beginning in mid-century Ireland. In 1688 the statistician Gregory King calculated the size of the various levels of English society, using hearth tax returns as a basis for computation. Only slowly did society accept the idea of precise statistics: the Ordnance Survey mapped the country from 1791, and the decennial census began in 1801.

Another form of the Enlightenment can be seen with the expiration of the Licensing Act (1695), when toleration for all manner of publications began to increase. Newspapers, journals, and other printed works multiplied, and clubs and associations for the sharing of information and ideas grew rapidly. While both of these were primarily urban phenomena, they made singular contributions to a new view of knowledge and information. And in one dimension, this was decidedly not just an urban matter.

AGRICULTURAL REVOLUTION

This term is now out of favor. Earlier historians, inspired by the revolutionary change in industry later in the 18th century, saw a comparable set of changes in agriculture at the beginning of the century. Now the consensus of historians is that although there were indeed very important improvements, they were spread out over a very long time, were not adopted for all cultivation, and are very difficult to measure accurately. Given those qualifications, it is undeniable that England (and other parts of Britain) ended famine by the middle of the 18th century, feeding a population that grew very rapidly for the next century even as large numbers of the farming population migrated into the growing new industrial towns.

Some of the change was due to technical experimentation: new patterns of crop rotation, some borrowed from Dutch farming; the use of fertilizers, such as marl (a clay soil rich in lime); and mechanical inventions, like Jethro Tull's seed drill. Food supply was made more manageable with the growth of better inland transportation, e.g., the turnpikes that began to expand in 1730, then canals, and, much later, railroads.

One factor long held to be critical was the movement to enclose open fields. These fields had been cultivated for centuries on a system of strips held by different tenants who did the major work in common and shared the product. Also, woodland and common pasture under this older system were part of the design. Such common lands had no discernible legal title, and in order to reallocate them it was necessary to obtain an act of Parliament to create a title and dispose of it. Thus, private enclosure acts became a common event. Their numbers grew quickly in the later 18th century, and they may have increased the pace of change, because those landlords seeking enclosure were usually the ones intent on using newer methods as a means to increase output.

The most important ingredient in agricultural growth was reminiscent of some features of the Enlightenment: empirical study, sharing of information, and stimulation of "improvement." Progressive landlords used this term to describe themselves. One of the more famous, Thomas Coke of Norfolk, organized meetings at his estate, conducted experiments in crop rotation and live-stock breeding, and gave incentives to his tenants to adopt the changes. In the farmer's notoriously conservative environment, he and others promoted a wide range of improvement. Of course, the forces of an expanding market provided a traditional incentive that all farmers understood.

Growth in the British population was a striking feature of the later 18th century. There had actually been a leveling or decline in population in the late 17th century. Then, after four or five decades of slow growth, a large increase began around the 1780s. Historians and demographers who have studied the process intently have not found a dramatic explanation for the rise. Several factors produced a drop in death rates (especially among young children) and an accompanying increase in the birth rate. There was no single trigger, but some of the causes included better diet and better medical care (including inoculation against smallpox) and the disappearance of plague (the last outbreak was in 1665; cholera would revive the horror in the 1830s). Probably most important was an increase in fertility rates, i.e., earlier and more numerous marriages. This change could be caused by higher earnings and changes in living patterns: whereas farm workers might have lived in a single enlarged household, urban and industrial workers might more often have had separate dwellings or apartments. Whatever the explanation, the consequence was that population in England and Wales nearly tripled in the century after 1750. In the same period Scotland's rose by 130 percent and Ireland's population, up to 1846, increased by 450 percent.

To the extent that there was an agricultural revolution, those who profited most from it were an agrarian ruling class of peers and gentry who owned most land and leased it to tenant farmers. Parliament's business was very much tied to the land in 1700, and that business was done by members of this class. The land was taxed—an innovation to pay for William III's wars—and other burdens of government fell on the landowner, who was responsible for local government (the commission of the peace; the militia; and county offices such as sheriff, service on grand juries, etc.) However, the landowning class was about to meet its greatest social and political challenge, as the small corps of professional people and merchants of the 17th century was transformed into a much enlarged middle class—great colonial merchants known as nabobs, bankers and brokers, factory owners and industrialists—who created a new capitalist layer in the social hierarchy.

TRADE AND INDUSTRY

Those people once called the "middling sort" were a small group in the old society, one that enjoyed better incomes than the laboring poor as well as some social standing. This was particularly true for the more notable professionals and traders. By the middle of the 19th century their numbers would explode, along with their aggregate wealth. The reasons for this growth were the creation or mobilization of capital; the expansion of trade, especially over-seas; growth of industrial production; and the creation of a consumer society.

Some economic historians speak of a "financial revolution" at the end of the 17th century. This is more than an attempt to echo the better-known industrial revolution. Vast amounts of money were raised to fight William III's wars, much of it raised by loans through the Bank of England, with the government pay-ing 8 percent annual interest. In London and the provinces, banking grew steadily. Stock exchanges facilitated the link between shareholders and entrepreneurs and employed armies of agents and solicitors. Landowners and merchants continued to invest in government bonds but also lent increasing sums to underwrite shipping, road building, and canals. This capitalization was essential to the coming age of industry.

No less essential to economic growth was the expansion of England's (and later Scotland's and Ireland's) trade. From the latter days of the 17th century, the contest for imperial trade went more and more in Britain's favor, while the conditions of internal trade in the British Isles offered a cooperative marketing structure. The two components reinforced each other. The wars of the period 1756–1815 secured Britain's place as the leading international trader. The cost of war was high, but the gains for commerce outweighed the losses. Imports and exports increased by 500–600 percent, most notably in imports of raw materials and exports of manufactured goods. Particularly important in these areas were colonial markets, including the West Indies, India, and the onetime American colonies. The share of national income from overseas trade doubled in the 18th century.

Internal trade grew as well. The previously noted transport improvements in roads and canals, plus improvements in river navigation, helped the movement of goods. By the 1830s there were 22,000 miles of turnpikes and 4,000 miles of canals in use. These connections helped the growth of towns in England and Scotland. Most towns had been small, with only a few over 5,000. The 18th cen-tury saw a doubling in the share of population living in such larger towns. Lon-don remained an outsized exception, growing still more in this period, but alongside it grew major trading centers and new manufacturing towns. In the 1851 census there were 63 towns with more than 20,000 inhabitants, whereas in 1801 there had only been 15. By mid-century the urban population was about 50 percent of the total; it had about half of that in 1700.

Another factor in Britain's favor was that the island constituted the largest free-trade area in Europe: most continental states had tariff barriers and border limits to trade. It may be that this feature was one of the stimulants to a radi-cal new theory of economics. The idea of free trade was promoted by the Scot-tish philosopher Adam Smith, notably in his *Inquiry into the Causes of the Wealth of Nations* (1776). His thinking was that the effect of regulation must be to limit trade; and while some circumstances (war, famine, and natural disasters) might require government intervention, the general unregulated dealings of mer-chants and customers ought to produce the most benefit to all. This statement of what came to be called classical economics marked the opening of a new phase in British economic thinking. It was only slowly incorporated into government policy through extended debates in many areas. But by 1850 the corn laws, navigation laws, and other restrictions had been repealed, and Britain had begun a new era of "free trade." Some accounts suggest this was the core of an age of *laissez faire,* or noninterference by government. Though that became a slogan for many and a social philosophy for others, the performance of British governments presented a mixed picture of regulation and distance.

The most studied feature of British society in the 18th century was the rise of industry—the "industrial revolution." Historians are now retreating from this usage, but its essential point has validity. There was a massive shift in employment, production, and creation of wealth, from older agricultural sectors to that of industry. This process took more than a half-century (approximately from 1780 to 1830), but it was an undeniably major change. The earlier 18th century witnessed a scattered number of innovations: in coal production (1720s), iron manufacture (1730), and textiles (1760–80). After the 1780s, improvements in steam engineering (James Watt) and the manufacture of iron (Henry Cort and John Wilkinson) and textiles (Richard Arkwright) launched a new wave of growth. By the 1830s a large portion of the industrial workforce worked in factories, their location concentrated in some of the new towns.

The classic image of the factories as "dark satanic mills" is overstated, but it conveys one contemporary reaction, and it suggests the likelihood of a social response sympathizing with the new worker's hard lot. But just as much sympathy should go to the obsolescent handloom weavers of the 1800–30 period, and the dynamic of workers' complaints was enhanced by

English textile factory, 1877 *(Hulton/Archive)*

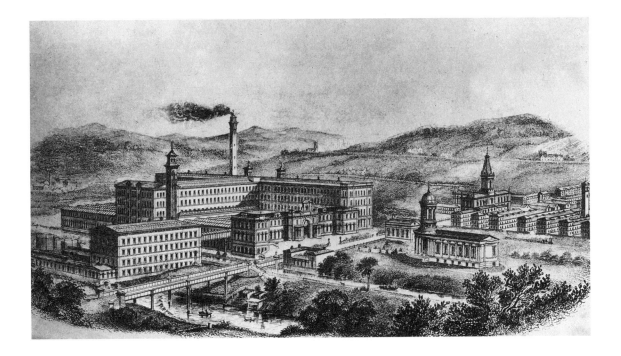

their collective presence in the new workplace. What this meant in terms of ammunition for reforms will be examined in the next section. What the output of factories meant for society as a whole was to provide one more impetus to a consumer revolution.

Leaving aside the question of pace, it is acknowledged by recent historians that this period witnessed a radical change in spending and consumption. There was a sufficient increase in income levels in the 18th century to provide the means for many members of society to obtain goods that were simply not available to many before 1700. Household furnishings, clothing, and luxury items were all in conspicuously greater supply in the course of the period, and Britain had, by comparison, far more of all of these than other countries in Europe. In addition, along with the rise in quantity came a new environment of acquisition: mass production, promotion, and competition became basic features of the consumer society. Moreover, the inequalities that were bound to occur, plus the awakened demand accompanying these changes, must have played a part in responses to those truly revolutionary events—in 1776 and 1789—which marked the later years of the period.

REVOLUTION AND SOCIAL CHANGE

Political revolutions in the later 18th century had important effects on British society and government. Basically, the upheavals in America and France put British institutions under the microscope and added significant pressure to existing ideas for reform. The consequence was a series of changes that helped to transform society by 1850. By then society was aware of and responding to the first coherent demands of its "working class."

To understand the events of this period, an outline of its politics is necessary. The War of the Spanish Succession (1702–13) ended with the Treaty of Utrecht, which confirmed Britain's imperial gains in 1713. At home the main issue was the royal succession. Pursuant to the 1701 Act of Settlement, when Queen Anne died in 1714, George I (eldest son of the electress Sophia of Hanover) succeeded her. After taking the throne in 1714, he insisted on Whig ministers, believing that all Tories were supporters of the Jacobite cause. That movement brought on a Jacobite rebellion in 1715, which was crushed by royal troops, and the last in 1745, with the defeat of Bonnie Prince Charlie at Culloden in 1746. Whigs were able to capitalize on the threat to prove their loyalty. In 1721 Robert Walpole became the king's first minister, and he continued in that post when George II came to the throne in 1727. Walpole's main achievement was a long period of peace, reducing the demands of the land tax while showing skill in managing the government's finances. But part of that skill was in the use of patronage, for which he was both feared and admired. After the outbreak of war with France in the 1740s, he was removed from office, and the king turned to Walpole's lieutenant, Henry Pelham. By the later 1750s, the Seven Years' War brought William Pitt to the post of first minister. He was forced to resign in 1761 just after George III came to the throne. That king began his long reign (1760–1820) by relying on his former tutor Lord Bute as chief minister. This odd choice opened a period of instability, and there was a quick succession of ministers until Lord North assumed control in 1770. His government would last until 1782, though North often tried to resign during the American Revolution.

The war in America was precipitated by Britain's efforts to make the colonies pay for their defense, first with the Stamp Tax (1765) and then with tariffs on colonial trade. Resistance to this policy finally generated a colonial rebellion, which British troops attempted to suppress, but George Washington led a successful campaign to defeat the forces of the Crown. After victory (1781) and a peace treaty (1783), the 13 colonies became independent. This crisis naturally caused serious repercussions: Britain's colonial policies were severely criticized, and the Colonial Office was temporarily abolished. But there was still keen interest in colonial development, particularly in the Pacific, the Caribbean, and Africa. In domestic affairs, the loss of American colonies brought on a period of angry debates over government failure; election reform, finances, and colonial policy were all disputed.

During the crisis in 1783, the king removed his ministers and selected William Pitt (the young son of the former chief minister) as leader of the government. Pitt won an election in 1784 and went on to serve the Crown for the rest of the century. He put forward a mix of progressive policy (reducing sinecures, carefully managing finances) and conservative philosophy (crackdowns on sedition, vigorous monitoring of critics of the Crown). Pitt was in office when the French Revolution broke out. He and others did not sense its danger at first, and indeed, he thought there was no likelihood of war; but France, having disposed of her king, declared war on Britain in 1793. Pitt had to gather a coalition of European states (the first of four), which he subsidized with British money while using the British fleet to control the seas.

Pitt was forced to resign in 1801, after the king rejected his plan for an act of union with Ireland. Pitt wanted to include Roman Catholics in the settlement, but the king refused. The plan of union was a reaction to the Irish rebellion in 1798, which was supported by a small amount of French assistance. That created a fear of future assault on England and the chance of being surrounded. Union also addressed the fear of the minority Anglo-Irish population toward the Catholic majority.

War continued in 1802 with a new opponent in Napoleon Bonaparte, the feared revolutionary general and, later, emperor. His plan for an invasion of England was made impossible by Admiral Nelson's victory at Trafalgar (1805). But Napoleon still conquered most of Europe, faltering only when he tried to conquer Russia (1812). His final defeat by Wellington at Waterloo (1815) marked the ascendancy of Britain in European and world politics. A period of 40 years of peace for Britain followed, though there were several serious bouts of revolution on the continent.

At home in Britain there was great distress in 1815. Heavy taxation, agricultural depression, loss of foreign trade, and massive military commitments all made of life more difficult. After the war there were riots and demonstrations, both being met with government force (Spa Fields, 1816; Peterloo, 1819). Later, limited economic improvement was paralleled by an increase in the number and intensity of supporters of a wide range of political, social, and economic reforms. A cluster of debates and decisions put the finishing touches on the new society by 1850.

Since the later 18th century there had been mounting criticism of the system of parliamentary representation. In the rural areas there were fairly large electorates, as the vote was granted to owners or occupiers of land worth 40 shillings per annum—a level set in the fifteenth century. In the boroughs (old townships with the right to send a member to Parliament), some electorates might be very large, but many had become small or even nonexistent. The latter "rotten" boroughs were under the control of landowners who could decide the member who would sit in the House of Commons. As early as the 1780s there had been a movement among county gentry to transfer some of these seats to the counties, thus obtaining more representative membership. This movement was swept aside in the 1790s, but criticism of the old order mounted. In 1830 a new ministry undertook reform, though it took two years, plus much debate and pressure, before the important reform was enacted. In 1832 the vote was given to all those who held property worth £10 per annum, and a number of the rotten boroughs lost their seats, which were transferred to new towns that had had no members. Bills were passed for England and Wales, Scotland, and Ireland. The greatest increase in voters was in Scotland, the smallest in Ireland.

In none of these cases, however, was there an effort to go beyond the principle of representation for property owners. This clearly left out the vast majority of the population. In 1836 the London Workingmen's Association was organized to press for universal manhood suffrage. This was the root of the Chartist movement, so called for its main document, "The People's Charter," which called for votes for all males and the conversion of Parliament into a genuine democratic assembly. This document was presented to Parliament on several occasions in petition form, but it was rejected every time. These failures discredited the moderate reformers, and more radical approaches were proposed. Though the movement ended in 1848, almost all of the charter's points were made law by 1910.

Social reforms were also put forward, again with roots in the 18th century. Many of these were the result of agitation by "evangelical" reformers—those who wanted, in keeping with holy scripture, to remedy what were seen as immoral policies. The first major target of the movement was the slave trade, and a 20-year agitation resulted in an act abolishing that trade in 1807. The next target was slavery itself, which was abolished in the British Empire in 1833. There were also dedicated secular reformers, most notably the followers of Jeremy Bentham, known as utilitarians. Their aim was to introduce reforms for the "greatest good for the greatest number." Among other things, utilitarians supported reform of prisons, criminal law, and the poor law. The latter was the system of parish support for the able and disabled poor. This had been instituted on a national basis in the Elizabethan era, but it had become extremely costly during years of economic stress at the turn of the century. Thus many, especially ratepayers, were anxious to introduce a new system. A controversial act in 1834 tried to do just that, but it had mixed results. Meanwhile a serious crisis in public health arose in 1832 with the outbreak of cholera, which took 31,000 lives. There was serious debate on the means of preventing such epidemics, and after many hearings and discussions, the first general public health laws were enacted.

In another closely related category, the conduct of economic life came into the purview of legislators in several ways. Worker efforts to organize and protect their livelihood were challenged by Combination Acts (1799, 1800). Any combination, or union, in restraint of trade (by employers or workers) was illegal in common law, but Parliament chose to invoke special enforcement provisions against workers. After two decades of campaigning, these acts were repealed in 1824, allowing an increase in legal organization by workers. There were also significant reforms in the workplace. Conditions for factory workers were a matter of serious complaint, and as early as 1802 there was some legislation. The title of the first act was a sign of the times: the Health and Morals of Apprentices Act was aimed at protecting young workers from poor conditions in contemporary factories. There were more real dangers—from long hours of work, from dangerous machinery, and from unscrupulous employers. A roster of reforms came forward, especially after 1830. Another area of economic reform was the campaign to abolish the "corn laws," which were protective tariffs on various grains. The laws were enacted during the French wars to encourage cultivation of marginal land and were kept after the wars at the request of landowners. They were not beneficial to consumers, especially poor workers. In 1839 a group of progressive manufacturers organized the Anti-Corn Law League. This was a new type of pressure group, with well-funded and well-orchestrated campaigns, touring speakers, publications, and an intense lobbying effort in Parliament. The league targeted Robert Peel, the conservative leader, as the laws' chief supporter, but ironically it was he who, in the Irish Famine crisis of 1846, pushed through the repeal. This was followed soon after by repeal of the navigation laws—and the beginning of the era of free trade in Britain.

In 1851 the census revealed that Britain had become 50 percent urban. It also took measurements of religious observance for the first (and only) time. The results of that tabulation were very disturbing. Less than half the population was attending church at some time on Sunday. Tallies of the several different congregations revealed that dissenters outnumbered Anglicans; and Catholics, whose worship had been lately recognized as lawful, showed significant attendance. The society glimpsed in that census was vastly different from the early 18th century. It boasted a broad and wealthy middle class and a literate and demanding working class. Those two would no longer accept the old regime; indeed the reforms of the last generation pointed to further change ahead. And this society, growing rapidly and sending its products across the globe along with missionaries and merchants, was fast becoming the leading imperial power. That fact would shape the new society of the late 19th century.

THE BRITISH EMPIRE

1850–1914

The building of the British Empire spanned several centuries and resulted in the world's most extensive concentration of military and economic power. It was also unplanned empire, evolving from the efforts of semiautonomous traders, religious refugees, soldiers, and administrators, with no early central direction. This complex creation was rooted in territorial growth, international politics, and domestic political change many years prior to 1850.

The beginnings of the empire were not auspicious. In the 16th century the dominant empires were Spain and Portugal. English ships and sailors conducted raids, and only late in the century were there plans and attempts to make colonial settlements. As the senior empires began to decline in the 17th century, opportunities for English settlement grew in North America, the West Indies, West Africa, and the Far East. Although the Dutch Wars of that century had not gone in England's favor, the alliance of 1689 neutralized another major imperial adversary. The victories over France at the beginning of the 18th century signaled a dominant theme of that period, and the ultimate winner was Britain.

The one major setback in America was in fact offset. Strong trade ties with the new United States were rebuilt after 1783, while colonial expansion continued in Canada, Australia, and India. Indeed, the period from 1815 to 1850, once regarded as a time of "anticolonialism," saw the continued growth of imperial power. That came from conquests (Ceylon, 1802; the Cape Colony, 1806; British Guiana, 1814; Malta, 1814; Nepal, 1816; Burma, 1824–52; the Straits Settlements [Penang, Malacca, and Singapore], 1826; the Falkland Islands, 1841; Hong Kong, 1842); from extensions of former holdings (Sierra Leone, 1807; Van Dieman's Land, 1825; Western Australia, 1826; New Zealand, 1840; Zanzibar, 1841; British Columbia, 1849); and from treaty arrangements (Argentina, 1825). The free traders and government critics such as Adam Smith and Jeremy Bentham did indeed regard formal colonies as expensive and unprofitable. Nevertheless, the momentum of expanding free trade assured that the imperial network would grow, if in a bewildering variety of connections (direct rule, trading company government, alliance with native rulers, self-governing colonies, and trade treaties).

This growth was fostered by a set of favorable conditions. First, there was no major European war for a century (1815–1914). Only the Crimean War

(1854–56) broke this long peace, and that was an isolated struggle between an Anglo-French alliance and Russia over the future of the declining Ottoman Turk-ish Empire; it had very little effect outside the Black Sea region and eastern Europe. A second factor was the absence of competition: Spain and Portugal had receded, the French had been restrained, and other potential competitors were either too weak (the United States, Russia, Prussia) or were themselves in decline (Turkey, China). Third was what contemporary British observers thought mat-tered most: the ingenuity and drive of British imperialists. Their ships, finances, factories, and, most of all, free trade policies did give them an extraordinary advantage. With the world's most powerful economy, it would have been diffi-cult not to enjoy several generations of unrivaled imperial success.

The economic good news was an important antidote to domestic political dif-ficulty. After 1815 the monarchy had fallen in public esteem, domestic politi-cal violence had escalated, and there were serious social problems. George III had suffered a loss of mental capacity, and a regency was declared in 1810. His son Prince George had married Princess Caroline (1795), but he had also had a long-term affair (and a secret marriage in 1785) with Maria Fitzherbert, a Roman Catholic. When he was crowned as George IV in 1820, his estranged wife returned, demanding her conjugal rights and recognition as queen. This led to a divorce trial, accompanied by riots on Caroline's behalf—in all, a most unseemly affair. George had no heirs, and his brother William succeeded him as William IV (1830–37). A former naval officer, he had held the post of lord high admiral, but his private life was awkward. He had 10 illegitimate children by his longtime mistress, but his marriage to a German princess had produced only two daughters who died in infancy. Thus, at his death the crown passed to the daughter of another brother, the duke of Kent, who had died in 1836. The 17-year-old Princess Victoria became queen in 1837. This diminutive and homely woman restored the image and the stature of the crown as a symbol of sovereignty. But it was not within her power to reactivate royal power in full form. Parliament now governed the country subject to very limited royal authority. The sovereign was the formal head of the empire, and very real power and considerable executive influence were wielded in her name. But the men and measures lacked coherent organization.

There was a certain ambivalence about the government's role in the man-agement of the imperial enterprise. At one level this was consistent with the general attitude of relaxing trade regulation and removing barriers to commerce. Colonial affairs were nominally under the secretary of state for the colonies—a post that had been abolished in frustration in 1782 but restored in 1812. The clerks of that office were not expected to engage in grand strategy, but that did not prevent others from doing so. The following are just a few examples of the ad hoc process of developing colonial policy in the early 19th century.

Most administrators in India in the 18th and early 19th centuries had rec-ognized the value of native culture. But by the 1830s, reformers led by Thomas Macaulay argued for India's "reformation." They envisioned the transfer of English law and institutions to the subcontinent. By the 1850s, British viceroys in India were trying to introduce systems of land, taxation, and education on an English model. This was not just cultural imperialism: its basis was also the belief that such a reformed society would be more open to the goods produced by British manufacturers.

On the other side of the globe, in British North America, there had been a rebellion in 1838. A commission was created to investigate the circumstances, and in 1839, under John Lambton, Lord Durham, this body proposed that Britain should pursue a policy of "responsible government"—that is, granting limited autonomy to the several provinces. In 1848 Nova Scotia and the Province of Canada were given this status, as were Prince Edward Island in 1851, Newfoundland in 1854, and New Brunswick in 1855.

In the 1830s in Australia, the colonial statesman Edward Wakefield championed what he called "systematic colonization," a deliberate policy to regulate entry of immigrants. He wanted to balance the ratio of male and female settlers and otherwise stimulate and control the population and land use of new areas. As a pioneer in Australia and a leader of the New Zealand Company, he was a major figure in the early settlement of those colonies.

These examples indicate some of the sources—all of them outside the official colonial establishment—of policy development in the colonies. While many British colonial officials seemed uninterested in planning the Colonies' future, there were plenty of substitutes willing to do the job. The nature of Britain's industrial and commercial strength assured that there would be those who would step in to try to manage the direction of its development. In that regard one of the most interesting entrepreneurs was Prince Albert, Queen Victoria's husband and chief planner of an event that symbolized the new age: the Great Exhibition of 1851.

WORKSHOP OF THE WORLD

Prince Albert was the major force behind "The Great Exhibition of the Industrial Works of All Nations," an event loaded with symbolism and packed with material evidence of progress. There actually was a long continental tradition of exhibitions, but this was the first and greatest of its kind for Britain. The giant trade show attracted exhibits from many countries, but it was meant primarily to showcase British manufactures and scientific progress. There were over 100,000 exhibits housed in a giant "Crystal Palace," which covered 26 acres in Hyde Park in the center of London. More than 200 designs for the structure had been submitted, and there was some controversy over the selection of the winning entry: Joseph Paxton, the head gardener for the duke of Devonshire, was known for the great conservatory he had designed on the duke's estate. Built of iron frames and glass panels, the Crystal Palace was to be more than 1,800 feet long and was itself a symbol of the modern mechanical skills of the nation. One announced object of the event was to engage interest in the working class. In the end, some 6 million people visited the exhibition, many of them coming by way of railroad excursions, with fares ranging from one shilling to three guineas (63 shillings). The prince's plan was a great success, as it reflected the awesome power of Britain's industry, trade, and capital in the mid-19th century.

Britain was the sole true industrial power in 1851. Two-fifths of the work-force was engaged in industry, a figure well beyond that of other countries. There was continued growth (in real terms) up to 1914, though rates varied widely. By the end of the period, Britain was still the industrial leader, but her lead had dwindled to a very slim margin. Economic historians argue over whether there was a "Great Depression" in the British economy in the last quarter of the 19th century. All that is certain is that some sectors of the industrial economy performed more poorly than others. Textiles had been a leading sector, but they faltered at the end of the century. Other areas, such as mining and metal manufacture were stronger, but all of them faced growing international competition after 1870. In 1851 the country was absorbing the effects of the first railway boom—trackage had just passed the 6,000-mile mark. That would continue to grow, nearing 19,000 miles in 1900. That industry saw its income grow in the same period from £12.7 million to £101 million. While the basic industrial sectors showed signs of healthy growth, one danger sign at the end of the century was Britain's slow development in more modern areas of industry such as chemicals and electricity.

British trade dominance was a second key area. Between 1840 and 1860, British trade doubled in value. This growth rate was not an aberration: the country carried about a fourth of the world's goods in the 1860s, and Britain's dominance of trade in manufactured goods continued into the 1890s. The basic pattern of British trade showed exports being led by manufactured goods (85 percent), while imports were led by raw materials (over 60 percent) and food-stuffs (over 30 percent).

As for markets, Britain's trade with Europe remained strong (40 percent in the 1870s, and growing), and while trade with the western hemisphere declined, that in the East and Africa grew. By the 1890s about 28 percent of world trade

The Crystal Palace during the Great Exhibition, London, 1851–1852 *(Library of Congress)*

was with the empire. Yet in the 1890s Britain had more trade with Belgium than with all of Africa. The value of colonial markets was not just seen in current terms: to have them under control was to deny them to competitors, and their nurture was expected to produce results over the longer term.

In terms of value, Britain's imports began to outgrow exports; in fact, by the 1890s imports were 50 percent higher, but the difference was masked by the earnings from "invisible exports"—the profits from investment and shipping and banking. However, in the years before 1914, all trade figures improved: imports and exports increased, trade was more often in balance, and foreign investment began to rise rapidly. Trade with the colonies increased to about 35 percent of the total, and investment levels there rose to 42 percent.

The expanding role of British capital was impressive. Foreign investment grew five times between the 1850s and the 1890s. In the years 1900–14, total foreign investment went from £45 million to £200 million. Besides investment, British companies dominated international trade in brokerage, insurance, and banking. The profits from these "invisible exports" were becoming essential to keep trade in balance. This sector became ever more important as the "workshop of the world" found itself in competition with others by 1914.

A look at different areas of industry shows how the British were still successful but encountering a new era of competition as the 20th century began. In cotton textiles, employment reached a peak (646,000) in 1911. But British industry had not adopted many recent technical improvements, because continuing strong demand for her products gave little incentive to do so. Coal output had doubled between 1870 and 1900; the peak year was 1913, by which time one-third of production was destined for export. But output per man was declining, and many old seams were wearing out. British steelmakers produced more than all of Europe combined in 1879, but by the mid-1890s, even though Britain's production was still increasing, she had been surpassed by the United States and Germany. At the turn of the century, shipbuilding was in a period of rapid change in design and engineering. Strong markets for ships were increasing demand, creating a risk of excess capacity.

Meanwhile, in some newer industrial areas, Britain was not dominant. Germany became a leader in the chemical industry, particularly in dyestuffs, solvents, and pharmaceuticals. Use of the new power source of electricity was another area where Britain lagged. Early systems of electric lighting and telephones were run by U.S. companies in Britain. In motor vehicles, France did pioneering work in internal combustion engines, Germany's Daimler was building vehicles by 1885, and Britain had some obstacles, like the infamous "red flag" law. Railroads wanted to stem competition from steam carriages, so a law required any powered vehicle to have someone walk in front of it with a red flag. This was repealed at the beginning of the 20th century, and by 1914 Britain had some 265,000 vehicles, produced by nearly 200 small manufacturers in the automobile business. Clearly the competitive situation was entirely different from the early days of the Industrial Age.

The "workshop of the world" held its own until 1914, but its rivals were growing and multiplying. Britain had built a system in which it had to sell a large surplus production, and it had to import massive quantities of raw materials and food to keep its factories working. Its colonial markets became an ever more important part of that system. But since Britain had flooded the colonies and other parts of the world with a prodigious export of people, that did not seem to be a problem.

DIASPORA

In the century before 1914, some 22.6 million people left the British Isles for other parts of the world. Why they left, how they traveled, where they landed, and what they took in their baggage are all important clues to the meaning of this phenomenon for Britain, for the empire, and for the world. Emigration did not follow a simple pattern. The numbers rose in the 1830s, jumped sharply in the late '40s and early '50s due to famine in Ireland, declined in the late '50s, and rose sharply again after 1870. Peak years came between 1907 and 1912. Overseas migration was mainly triggered by poverty, by the promise of a better life, and by the prospect of employment, either in the colonial service or in the varied missions of churchmen, explorers, and adventurers.

The movement of poor emigrants was an organized effort from early in the process. For many years the authorities had transported convicts, first to North America or the West Indies, later to Australia and Van Dieman's Land, and even later to Tasmania, an island off Australia, used for a convict settlement in the early 19th century. Scottish clearances in the early 19th century were planned efforts to depopulate parts of that country for sheep farming, which resulted in many thousands of people emigrating to Canada. Numerous societies fostered emigration (the British and Colonial Emigration Society, the Colonial Emigration Society); many of them were local or specialized (the British Women's Emigration Association, the Salvation Army Emigration Department). Paupers were an attractive cargo, especially to the ratepayer and parish overseer. By 1840 the government had set up the Colonial Land and Emigration Commission, which sent out over 330,000 emigrants over the next 30 years. That same body was also involved in large movements of workers from India and China to other parts of the empire where laborers were needed. On another level, the social worker Thomas Barnardo organized the emigration of orphans, many to Canada, beginning in 1882. His workers were able to help over 100,000 in this process.

Another dimension was colonial recruiting. In the 1850s Australia had the Highlands and Islands Emigration Society working to attract new settlers. Other colonies published notices, including offers of cheap land and other inducements. It is important to note that emigration from anywhere but a major seaport also involved some inland movement in the British Isles—for example, the Irish departing via Liverpool or the numbers of British emigrants leaving via London.

Traveling overseas was long and difficult, and it was expensive, even for the passengers in steerage. A passenger was required to pay a fare (if not subsidized) and usually to provide his or her own food—no mean task for journeys which might take anywhere from five to 10 weeks. The early stages of the trade treated them as so much cargo. Numerous examples of accidents and widespread fraud led to Parliament's adoption of the Passenger Acts, which were designed to protect the unwary traveler. The Colonial Land and Emigration Commission was instrumental in preparing some of the more effective legislation, and by about 1870 the colonies themselves began to regulate immigration.

Travelers were divided by destination. In the 19th century about 25 percent of British and Irish emigrants headed for the United States. The proportion among the Irish was substantial. It is estimated that prior to 1921, some 7 million migrated from Ireland to the United States. Other favored destinations for settlers or business-minded emigrants were Canada and Australia. Missionaries headed for Africa, soldiers and civil servants for India. There were also important internal flows within the British Isles and between India, China, etc., and expanding frontier sites in Africa and North America.

The "baggage" of immigrants involved much more than their often meager possessions. Figuratively, their belongings included British "civilization"—religion, values and ideals, and institutions. One popular theory in the 19th century was championed by Sir Charles Dilke, whose *Greater Britain: A Record of Travel in English-Speaking Countries in 1866 and 1867* (1868) argued that the emigrant and colonist carried an imprint of British civilization, and their settlements, including the United States, were therefore extensions of British society and culture. This of course was not obvious to Irish emigrants, who, it may be assumed, were not happy to be perceived as repositories of anything British. Indeed, many of their communities and customs and cultural features rejected British influence in any form. It does remain a fact, however, that the governments, laws, courts, and jury systems they took with them were copies of the English or British originals. The language they spoke was the same; their worship was the same; and their literature, music, and other entertainment belonged to their original communities.

The great diaspora of British and Irish folk in the 19th century did many things: it rescued some from lives of poverty, peopled large areas, confirmed ties between Britain and the colonies, and brought a mobile workforce to places where it was needed. Lastly, in contrast to the thesis of "Greater Britain," it may have stimulated the desire for colonial independence.

PAX BRITANNICA

Britain enjoyed unchallenged imperial power for most of the 19th century. The British navy was by far the world's strongest; in 1815 there were over 200 battleships and 800 other vessels. In 1817 Foreign Secretary Lord Castlereagh set forth the policy of maintaining a fleet that matched the power of the world's next two largest navies. This "two-power" standard would be official policy until sometime after it was no longer feasible (ca. 1910). Britain's army, on the other hand, was small by European standards, though a large (mainly native) army was deployed in India.

Beside its obvious importance in the colonies, political leaders knew that imperial power was a major factor in domestic and foreign affairs. All British political leaders were imperialists, though their perspectives varied. In 1850 political parties were in a state of flux. After the repeal of the corn laws in 1846, Robert Peel had been deposed as Tory leader and there was a fluid period of party realignment, which only clarified in the later 1860s with the emergence of new Liberal and Conservative Parties.

In this intermediate period, the country was prospering as never before, displaying its wealth in the Great Exhibition, but struggling to address problems of maldistribution of that wealth. The first item on the Liberal agenda, however, was free trade and laissez faire. William Gladstone's budgets, from 1853 onward, fulfilled these pledges by reducing expenditures. In so doing, the task of redressing social ills was made harder. Cities and slums could only grow. The population, which was 50 percent urban in 1851, saw that share increase to 80 percent by 1901. Original industrial cities such as Manchester and Birmingham sprouted satellite towns. The railroads that facilitated movement of people and goods added their share to the grime and vapor. Workers were bound to be attracted to unions, and a minority to the more extreme protests of socialism, in spite of the fact that living standards for many were increasing in the second half of the century. Workers' wages were falling, but not as fast as prices. This might satisfy the economist, but the worker was bound to feel threatened whenever his or her employer cut wages. This contributed to rapid growth of unions, which by the end of the century included many unskilled workers. Studies by Booth and Rowntree in the last years of the century found levels of poverty as high as 30 percent, while the other 70 percent were in many cases doing very well. Trade union growth continued into the next century, helping along the formation of the Labour Party, a new organization committed to advancing of workers' interests.

Many more of those workers had gained the right to vote by the end of the 19th century. While the People's Charter had been rejected in 1848, the debate on its proposals went on. In 1872 the secret ballot was granted, and in 1867 and 1884 the franchise was widened to include 70 percent of men. The great Liberal of the 1850s and '60s, Lord Palmerston, had opposed reform—but mainly because Tories were unable to win elections in those years. This explains why reform came in a bill proposed by Tory leader Benjamin Disraeli in 1867. The urban worker was enfranchised, and while he did not show his appreciation in the first election after the act (1868), the Tories did win in 1874, and they became the dominant party after 1881. They had begun to strengthen their party's organization by forming a union of local conservative groups in 1867 and a central office for the party in 1870. The Liberals' loss in 1874 inspired Radical leader Joseph Chamberlain to bring in stronger party organization in Birmingham. A National Liberal Federation was set up in 1877, but the real shaper of Liberal fortunes was William Ewart Gladstone. He introduced a new style of campaigning, making speaking tours and using an electoral platform to focus voters' attention. In the elections of 1876 and 1880, many of the issues Gladstone addressed were imperial ones. However, his government in the 1880s was a series of imperial failures, for example, in southern Africa and the Sudan.

The Liberals, having lost their dominance, became a more progressive party in the 1890s, reaching out toward a wider working-class electorate. Their positions on home rule, social reform, and higher taxes on the wealthy were oddly linked to a segment of the party which had favored imperial growth. A portion of that group of Liberal imperialists helped the Conservatives under Lord Salisbury and Arthur Balfour stay in power for most of the period 1885–1902. With Joseph Chamberlain at the Colonial Office during that time, they championed strong imperial policies. Other Liberals who remained in the party (Lord Rosebery, Lord Haldane, Sir Edward Grey, Herbert Asquith) were also strong advocates of empire who fought with the more advanced social reformers in the party during the Boer War (1899–1902).

The British position in foreign affairs naturally was linked to the empire. Because of growing global strength, British leaders were content to withdraw from continental involvements. They preferred to act on the principle of the balance of power. Britain reserved the right to intervene in European affairs to redress a perceived imbalance—for example, negotiating Belgian neutrality in 1839 and intervening in the Crimea in 1854. In fact, by the end of the 19th century, Lord Salisbury had coined the phrase "splendid isolation" to describe British aloofness from diplomatic commitments. Other states could easily interpret this as proof of typical British arrogance or deviousness.

In the mid-century, a dominant policy theme was Cobdenite liberalism; peace and trade were seen as interdependent. Thus, in 1860 the Cobden-Chevalier treaty between Britain and France agreed to reduce tariffs and promote peaceful relations. Yet by the 1870s there was talk of a "new imperialism"—a more aggressive, conscious effort to advance the size and strength of the empire. This was clearly popular with the new working-class voters. Disraeli had been an early beneficiary of this policy, and as prime minister he gained popularity by unilateral acts to extend influence, for example, by buying shares in the Suez Canal (1875) and by creating the title "Empress of India" for Queen Victoria (1876).

After Disraeli died in 1881, Lord Salisbury succeeded him as Tory leader. About the same time, the "scramble for Africa" began, with many European countries trying to carve out some holdings there, both as a matter of prestige and for (elusive) economic benefit. A similar process soon began in Asia, particularly aimed at China. Also in the 1880s, there was the beginning of a feeling of insecurity about British naval power. First there was a stir when the French began building new ships. Then, in the later 1890s, Germany passed a naval law directing the expansion of the high seas fleet, a move clearly aimed at challenging British supremacy. Britain responded by building the new type of battleship known as Dreadnoughts (1906) and adding to that class of very expensive vessel over the next few years. By this time the cost of competing in this manner had escalated, and it became a major political issue.

Meanwhile the diplomatic picture had changed. After Britain's struggles in the Boer War, there was a general shift in European attitudes. German support for the Boers and general hostility to Britain's exertion of power in South Africa were both cause for concern. The policy of isolation was also being challenged on other imperial fronts: Russia's presence in the Far East was a reason why Britain broke its ban on alliances in 1902 and signed an agreement with Japan. A showdown in Africa with France led to a diplomatic truce known as the Entente Cordiale in 1904. Further efforts to resolve tension in and around Afghanistan, plus the mounting tensions in Europe, brought an entente with Russia in 1907. Thus imperial tensions, on top of a dawning sense of relative weakness, contributed directly to a fundamental modification of British foreign policy. In these same years, Britain began to realize that her conduct in colonial affairs faced new and difficult challenges for which she would have to fashion new responses.

CHALLENGE AND RESPONSE

The empire's colonial subjects expressed their hostility to British control in escalating fashion in the later 19th century, first in isolated outbreaks and later moving toward systematic colonial nationalism. The British government's responses were signs of hardening British attitudes toward empire and of more belligerent moods between imperial powers. Time seemed to be running out on the Pax Britannica.

By the mid-19th century it was apparent that white-majority dominions (Canada, Australia, New Zealand) were destined to gain more autonomy. But in colonies with nonwhite majorities, or in cases of conflict with nonwhite populations, British policy reflected the belief that these were "lesser breeds without the law." A series of episodes in the third quarter of the century clearly demonstrated this.

The most serious insurrection occurred in India when native troops at a station near Delhi mutinied in 1857. They had been issued Enfield rifle cartridges which rumor said were treated with pork and beef fat—contriving at once to offend both the Hindu and Muslim soldier. A regiment had been severely disciplined for refusing to touch the cartridges, and shortly several bodies of troops mutinied, murdered their officers, and marched on Delhi. There they were joined by other disaffected troops. The mutiny spread, often resulting in the deaths of wives and children of British soldiers. There was too small and dispersed a garrison to strike back at once, but as reinforcements arrived over the summer, the British retaliated. They recaptured Delhi in September, other cities in the fall, and completed the reconquest in 1858. The British had ample support from other native troops—Sikhs, Gurkhas and Pathans—and most of the insurgency was concentrated in the north-central provinces. The violence and retribution were brutal on all sides. After the mutiny was suppressed, the East India Company lost its role in Indian government, and a separate cabinet level post of Secretary of State for India was created. The government recognized that the mutiny was the result of the British policy of attempting to convert the population to western customs, thus threatening to destroy native culture. While that policy was discontinued, British influence continued to be exerted through railroad construction, road building, irrigation, sanitation, and impartial administration of justice.

The remains of the Chutter Munzil Palace, Lucknow, destroyed by Indian mutineers in an uprising against British rule *(Hulton/Archive)*

In the West Indies a different sort of crisis brewed as the result of a different sort of British intervention. Having imported slaves to build a bustling sugar plantation economy, the slave status had been abolished in 1833. This transformed the economy, as planters now had to deal with free laborers. In Jamaica many of those workers had left plantations and taken plots of land, which were later seized from them, causing riots. A rebellion there in 1865 was brutally repressed, and the local assembly surrendered its powers to the Crown. Governor Edward Eyre was the focus of bitter controversy in Britain. He had proclaimed martial law and ordered the execution of 354 black insurgents. Angry liberals formed a committee to seek his prosecution, while others organized in his defense. He was prosecuted but found not guilty.

In South Africa the British had been mainly interested in the Cape and the port facilities there. There was little interest in the ongoing frontier conflicts between white farmers (mostly Dutch, or Afrikaner) and their black tribal adversaries. With the discovery of gold and diamonds in the 1860s, the situation changed. The British annexed the Afrikaner state of Transvaal in 1877, galvanizing a nationalist movement there. Actually the most dangerous enemy of the Transvaal was the Zulu kingdom of Cetewayo. His army was poised to attack, but the British commissioner delivered an ultimatum and then attacked. A British force was soundly beaten in January 1879 at Isandhlwana, with 800 killed. That day another British unit defeated the Zulus at Rorke's Drift, and some months later, the Zulu army was destroyed at Ulundi. There was ample criticism over the handling of these conflicts, in addition to one unforeseen consequence. The British victory over the Zulus in 1879 only increased Boer nationalism. A rebellion was followed in 1881 by renewed Boer independence, and the Transvaal became rich in 1886 with the discovery of diamonds in the Witwatersrand.

In Afghanistan an uprising in Kabul led to the murder of Sir Louis Cavagnari, the British resident. Frederick, Lord Roberts occupied Kabul in August 1880 from where he led a force of 10,000 men on a forced march over the mountains to relieve the garrison at Kandahar, a journey of 320 miles in 23 days. The British installed a new native ruler under an arrangement that gave Britain control over the foreign affairs of Afghanistan.

In Egypt the British had been anxious about the Suez, especially since the opening of the canal there in 1869. The French had been involved in its construction, and the Khedive, the deputy of the Ottoman Turks, was the political authority for the region. He was deeply in debt, and in 1875 Disraeli authorized the purchase of 44 percent of the shares in the canal company. With this foot in the door, Britain joined with France in sorting out Egyptian finances and demanding a number of fiscal reforms. Those measures were an incentive to rebel nationalists, and the British and French decided to establish a protectorate. This only increased native hostility, and after France withdrew, Britain bombarded Alexandria and sent in troops.

One effect of British action in Egypt was to cause instability in the large area to the south, the Sudan. There a revolt was begun by a fanatical Muslim leader, the Mahdi. General Charles Gordon was sent to evacuate an Egyptian force in Khartoum, but he tried instead to hold the city, and he was killed in 1885. A decade later the British dispatched General Herbert Kitchener to retake the city, and he defeated the rebel forces and reestablished British authority (1898).

In the meantime, affairs at the other end of the continent were becoming critical. The Cape Colony under Cecil Rhodes was fomenting unrest with the Boer republics, Transvaal and the Orange Free State. The pretext was the denial of civil rights to foreigners (*uitlanders*) in the gold and diamond mines. The real cause probably had more to do with a plan to take over these lucrative assets. Rhodes already had built up the DeBeers Mining Corporation to a position of monopoly power, and he had equally ambitious political aims. In 1895, a Rhodes agent named Colonel Jameson led a raid across the border of Transvaal, but he was repelled. A period of protracted negotiation followed, ending in 1899 with an ultimatum from the Transvaal president Paul Kruger. War began in October that year. Initially the Boers had numerical superiority and better weapons; in addition, they were defending their own territory. As a result, they won early victories and besieged British forces in several towns. By 1900, with reinforcements and a change in command, the British turned the tide. But the Boers then resorted to guerilla warfare and prolonged the fighting for another 18 months. In that time, British leaders employed "concentration" camps for women and children, while they systematically destroyed Boer farms and crops. More than 20,000 died in the camps, about twice as many as the total losses in battle; Britain lost 5,800, the Boers 4,000. The war was a shock to all, even to imperialists: it cost over £220 million, brought humiliating defeats, and displayed serious military weaknesses. Furthermore, the camps and the campaigns aroused bitter controversy at home and created a more critical attitude toward empire.

Something similar came from Britain's actions in China, an old established power but one which was terribly weak by modern standards. Along with other European states, the British had carved out port zones where they exercised a limited sovereignty and supervised a lucrative trade. The key commodity that Britain imported was opium from India. Wars were fought over this trade in the 1840–60 period, and later the European intrusions escalated, creating numerous grievances. These boiled over in 1899 with the organization of the "Righteous and Harmonious Fists"—known to the Europeans as the Boxers. Though the Boxers had troubled relations with the Chinese empress, they joined in a raid on the Peking legations in 1900. An international army was sent to relieve the legations, and the episode provoked even more foreign intervention.

The European powers realized that their normal response to incidents such as this was likely to bring down the dynasty, which could lead to China's total collapse, causing untold conflict. Therefore they drew back from full use of their power, in fear of the consequences. In fact the world situation had progressed to the point where the unchecked use of imperial power was ever more likely to result in serious collisions. The Pax Britannica had clearly ended.

WORLD POWER

1899–1945

Great Britain confronted mounting international competition in the last decades of the 19th century. Her competitors became strong enough and ambitious enough to challenge the Pax Britannica in the 20th century. Of course there were multiple causes for the horrific wars unleashed over this period, and antagonism toward Britain was probably not the major one. Militarism, nationalism, and totalitarianism were more potent elements. Britain had a share in these, but none would say she had a monopoly. Before, during, and after the hostilities, domestic politics moved rapidly into the age of democracy, bringing added energy for social reform and compounding the pressures on the economy.

BRITISH ISOLATION, 1899–1914

Britain's imperial power had engendered a strong sense of superiority, especially in the governing class. Paradoxically, the empire had also evoked growing unease in the old aristocratic order at home and abroad. Political and social reformers were becoming more strident. Irish Home Rule, parliamentary reform, social welfare, and votes for women were key sources of agitation in the early 20th century. In Ireland the efforts to reverse the act of union of 1801 were revived in the 1870s, and in 1886 Prime Minister Gladstone proposed "Home Rule" for Ireland in the House of Commons. He was badly beaten, and the defection of a large number of Liberals shifted power for the rest of the century. The home rule measure would return (1892, 1912) but it would only be realized in a divided Ireland after a civil war (1922).

Meanwhile, other political issues stoked hostility. The naval race with Germany required heavy spending on ship construction, and that threatened to scuttle plans for social welfare programs. In 1909 the Liberals proposed higher taxes on the wealthy to pay for old-age pensions and other social insurance. The House of Lords, dominated by Tories, rejected the budget. Such a vote was against parliamentary convention, and indeed the lords had not rejected a budget since the 17th century. There followed a long and bitter debate on limiting the powers of the upper house, which was accomplished by the Parliament Act of 1911. The lords could not veto a budget measure, and further, they could only negate an ordinary bill in two successive sessions. On its third passage, the same bill would become law, with or without their assent. The act also altered the length of a parliament from seven to five years. This reform of the traditional constitution was paralleled by rising voices of workers and women: the former agitated for more power for unions, while a workers' party (Labour) was organized and began to gain seats in Parliament (1903–18). The women, for their part, escalated the campaign for women's suffrage with protest demonstrations from 1908 on. They initially failed to gain any concession, but in 1918 the vote was given to women over the age of 30. The same act gave the vote to all men over 21, clearly as a consequence of the sacrifice made in World War I (1914–18).

How Britain came to be involved in "The Great War" was, of course, a consequence of international affairs. During the 19th century the country had enjoyed economic supremacy and an unusually long period of peace. A major corollary of Britain's peace and prosperity had been what Lord Salisbury called "splendid isolation." Without alliances, Britain was free to act independently in foreign affairs. This luxury, if that is what it was, could not survive in the new century. The Boer War had embarrassed Britain, and it had given Germany the chance to pose as a protector of the Boer Republics. A faltering Turkish empire in the Balkans and an expansive Russian one in the Far East were both serious threats to peace. Thus, in 1902 Britain broke out of isolation with an Anglo-Japanese alliance. This enlisted Japan as a counterweight to Russia, and it allowed Britain to concentrate its naval strength in the Atlantic and the Mediterranean. That arrangement proved successful when Japan beat Russia in the Russian-Japanese war of 1905. Before that Britain had come to terms with France, signing an entente (not an alliance) in 1904 to sooth tensions over contested colonial claims. In 1907 a similar agreement was signed with Russia (dealing with Persia, Tibet, and Afghanistan). But these agreements had another dimension. France and Russia were allies, having signed a Dual Alliance in 1893. They were ranged against the Triple Alliance of Germany, Austria, and Italy (1882). That framework had been the result of growing national rivalries on the continent since about 1870. Britain had purposely remained aloof, and even with her ententes she was still hoping not to become a full military ally. That hope proved to be futile in 1914.

The most explosive area in Europe was in the Balkans. There were strong national independence movements throughout the region (Rumania and Serbia, 1878; Armenia, 1890s; Bulgaria, 1908). All were seeking to escape the Ottoman Empire's control, while internally that government was losing power to the Young Turk movement. The neighboring Austro-Hungarian and Russian Empires fostered some of these efforts and looked for chances to expand their territory and influence. Several earlier crises in this area were resolved by international conferences (the Congress of Berlin, 1878; the Mediterranean Agreement of 1887; the Treaty of London, 1913, ending the first Balkan War, followed quickly by the Second Balkan War, 1913). The area remained a major confluence of national ambitions with a very long history of hostilities.

In 1914 Archduke Franz Ferdinand of Austria was assassinated in Sarajevo by an agent of the Serbian terrorist Black Hand Society (June 28). Austria issued an ultimatum demanding a Serbian crackdown on nationalists, surrender of those involved, and apologies (July 23). Britain proposed an international conference to adjudicate, but Austria and Germany rejected this (July 26). Austria declared war on Serbia (July 28), Russia ordered mobilization (July 30), and Germany declared war on Russia (August 1) and France (August 3). The German invasion of France required movement of German forces through neutral Belgium, and on the ground that this violation of international law had to be resisted, Britain declared war on Germany (August 4). In fact, Britain had become more closely allied with France in the preceding years, making agreements for shared naval responsibility. But whether she would join the war, and in what capacity, were questions answered only at the last minute.

ARMAGEDDON, 1914–1918

In 1914 the Liberal prime minister Herbert Asquith led the nation into war. Britain was not well prepared, except at sea, where the only major encounter with the German fleet was the indecisive Battle of Jutland in 1916. The German invasion of Belgium required the dispatch of the British Expeditionary Force to the continent. The allied armies stalled the German advance, and soon a line of battle stretched from the coast of Belgium across northern France to the border of Switzerland. Trenches were dug along that line, with barbed wire and fortifications placed on both sides. Millions fought on the western front for four years, taking massive casualties. The greatest impact, both physically and psychologically, came from the devastating and unprecedented losses in individual battles or campaigns—for example, the 1916 Battle of Verdun, which saw the French lose 550,000 and the Germans 450,000. In summer that year, the British lost 60,000 in the first day of the Battle of the Somme and 400,000 overall. This kind of destruction was inflicted with long-range artillery, machine guns, mines, and poison gas. The war also saw the first tanks and aircraft used in battle—and, more importantly, the submarine. On the eastern front, battles raged across central and eastern Europe, the Germans and Austrians taking large amounts of territory and forcing the new revolutionary government of Russia to accept a humiliating treaty (Brest Litovsk) in early 1918. This effort had exhausted all of the old prewar empires, and the regimes of the Habsburgs, Turks, and Bulgarians had collapsed by 1918.

Meanwhile, there were efforts to develop some flanking strategy to relieve the horror of the western front. The most dramatic of these was the Gallipoli campaign fostered by Winston Churchill, then a prominent Liberal. The plan was for British and French fleets to force their way through the straits of the Dardanelles, take Constantinople, and open a route of communication to Russia through the Black Sea. In March 1915 a naval assault very nearly succeeded, but the commander withdrew after losing several ships to mines and bombardment. The Turkish forces were bolstered by some assistance from their German ally, and they were able to repel an allied amphibious assault on the rugged Gallipoli peninsula, near the straits. This campaign proved to be a disaster, and allied forces withdrew in late 1915 after taking heavy casualties. By then Churchill had resigned as head of the admiralty and taken an infantry post in France.

The other leading young Liberal of the prewar era, David Lloyd George, was chancellor of the exchequer when war broke out. In 1915, in the "shell scandal," it was said that British troops were running out of ammunition—an inexcusable failure which, true or not, would have wide political repercussions. Conservative politicians threatened to oppose the government, and Asquith

British troops prepare for the charge over the top at the Battle of the Somme. *(Hulton/Archive)*

bought their temporary cooperation with a coalition. Lloyd George was sent to head a new Ministry of Munitions, and ammunition factories were placed under direct government control. With the wide powers he had been granted, Lloyd George was very successful in expanding production. In 1916, as discontent with Asquith's leadership mounted, Lloyd George joined the Conservatives in forcing him out and taking over as prime minister. This was an important improvement in wartime government, but a disaster for the future of the Liberal Party, which never recovered from the split in its ranks. In 1917 and 1918, Lloyd George brought energetic leadership, but he could not hold back the tide of losses and discouragement.

Part of the disarray came from within the British Isles. In Easter week of April 1916 there was an uprising in Dublin. A band of rebels seized the general post office and several other buildings and proclaimed an Irish republic. Within a week they had been routed by the British army, their leaders rounded up and summarily executed. The Easter Rising was the end result of pent-up frustrations over the past generation: Irish home rule had been promised, but it was shelved in 1914 because of the war. For two years prior to that, the threat of home rule had galvanized Ulster Protestants to swear to defend the union, and there was a serious prospect of civil war when a home rule act passed in 1914. The suspension of that law only proved to ardent Irish nationalists that the British government intended to continue to rule Ireland. Ironically, the small rebel band of the Easter Rising, who had become martyrs to their cause, was incorrectly labeled as the "Sinn Féin" by the British government. In fact that name applied to a moderate nationalist party, which benefited from British policy and in 1918 was successful in parliamentary elections for the first time. Sinn Féin took nearly three-fourths of the Irish seats, but the party (having become considerably more radical) chose not to send its MPs to Westminster but stayed in Dublin and formed a provisional government in January 1919.

A long list of national movements sprang up during the war. As the three old empires crumbled in the East, many people saw the opportunity for political self-expression. As the war dragged on, it was imperative that Britain enlist the support of these movements. Britain had not made its goals clear, other than defense of Belgian neutrality, France, Russia, and its own possessions. This was especially important since the United States, which was a vital potential ally, had remained neutral. Britain was helped in this regard by Germany's decision to resume unrestricted submarine warfare in February 1917. America formally entered the war in April, and though U.S. troops did not arrive until much later, shipments of grain from the United States and Canada were critical. Britain lost about 30 percent of her merchant fleet in 1917, and Lloyd George had to coerce the admiralty to accept the use of convoys to reduce the losses of merchant ships. However, the German tactic did not succeed.

There were many who called for a negotiated end to hostilities, including most of the Americans. What would a British negotiating position be? Why was Britain fighting? On January 5, 1918, Lloyd George issued Britain's first statement of war aims, claiming that Britain was not waging war against the German people, only Germany's authoritarian government, and that Britain wanted to see a free Poland, plus recognition of national identities in Austria-Hungary and in parts of the Middle East. There were vague references to a "League of Nations" in Lloyd George's speech. His remarks were aimed mainly at British voters, but he was also directing his statement to the American audience. On January 8, 1918, in a speech to Congress, President Woodrow Wilson announced his famous Fourteen Points, which outlined a more expansive agenda: no secret treaties; freedom of the seas; free trade; reduced armaments; settlement of colonial and national ambitions on a fair basis; evacuation of territory seized in the war; and adjustment of frontiers, plus an international body to protect integrity of all states.

In spring 1918 the allied armies held off a last German offensive, and by summer U.S. forces had joined an allied assault that forced the German army back. With serious political instability in Berlin, and fearing for the collapse of his army, General Ludendorff advised the government to sue for peace. An armistice was declared on November 11, 1918.

In all, the great powers had mobilized about 56 million men, and the total casualties amounted to approximately 7.7 million dead and more than 28 million wounded. From Britain's standpoint, another major global aspect was the participation of British Empire forces, and later of the United States. Britain began the war with its small regular army. A highly successful volunteer campaign drew a million men by Christmas 1914. But as the war dragged on, casualties mounted, along with criticism of Britain's war leaders. Conscription was implemented in 1916. Compared to the U.K. total of 5.7 million, India, Canada, Australia, New Zealand, and South Africa provided 2.77 million soldiers and another 1.3 million auxiliary workers.

Several major developments altered British politics during the war. Generally these were emergency acts intended only to enhance the war effort and to be dismantled in peacetime. But the effects were sometimes long-lasting. In the first days of the war, ministers assumed dictatorial powers with the Defence of the Realm Act. This allowed the government to seize property and to control individuals in the name of prosecuting the war. The basic act had to be spelled out in detailed Defence of the Realm Regulations. These were in most cases rescinded at war's end, but the process of legislative command followed by regulatory elaboration, a practice used slightly before the war, was employed much more extensively thereafter.

The executive was reorganized: a "war cabinet" of five members was formed, which oversaw all major decisions. Traditional cabinets, with 20 or more members, each operating more or less independently, were simply not considered capable of running a war. Consultation with the larger cabinet continued, but there ceased to be regular interaction with Parliament. In order to maintain more careful records and to keep track of complex issues, a cabinet secretariat (staff and clerks) was established in 1916. That body continued after the war and has become a permanent part of what is now regarded as a more "presidential" executive.

A cardinal feature of the war at home was the eventual involvement of the whole population in the war effort. After the success of the Ministry of Munitions, the government control model was applied to whole sectors of the economy: coal mines, railways, and shipping were put under emergency state control. An agreement was made with unions to suspend strikes in exchange for a guarantee of collective bargaining (1915), and while this was violated in a number of instances, the step was a notable one.

More important to British subjects was the degree to which individual lives had been subject to control, such as conscription after 1916. Meanwhile, daily life marked by rationing and regulation was also greatly altered by radical new developments. There were measures for housing and public health during the war, and there was a huge expansion in employment for women in nursing and related work and in replacement positions in industry. Within a month after the war's end, the Representation of the People Act of 1918 seemed to acknowledge the huge contribution from all sectors of society. The road was open to universal suffrage.

BETWEEN THE WARS, 1919–1939

Although the victory in 1918 brought euphoria for a time, it did not bring peace for very long. The reasons why may be found in the settlement of 1919, the nature of politics in the 1920s and '30s, the faltering world economy in the '30s, and finally in the rise of totalitarian states in the period.

The Paris Peace Conference convened in January 1919 amid signs of hope and scenes of devastation. Added to the destruction and economic dislocation, there were massive numbers of refugees and the horror of an influenza pandemic that crossed the continent in 1918–19. Called the Spanish flu because of its ferocity in that country, the illness killed far more than the war, perhaps as many as 25–30 million.

In the peace conference, the Council of Four (Britain, France, the United States, and Italy) had the greatest influence, and a plenary body of the 27 states represented ratified their decisions. In that larger body were representatives of Canada, Australia, New Zealand, and South Africa. Separate treaties were drafted for each of the defeated powers (Germany, Austria, Hungary, Turkey, and Bulgaria), who were not invited to participate. Russia, which had become the Union of Soviet Socialist Republics (USSR), was also not present. Each of the treaties laid down terms for peace, including concessions of territory, arms limitations, and reparations. Each treaty also had embodied in it the covenant of the League of Nations: a new international body in which member states promised to provide protection for each other, submit disputes to binding arbitration, and pursue general disarmament as well as solutions to a range of social problems. When the drafting was complete, delegations of the defeated powers were told to sign; there was no negotiation. Germany accepted the Treaty of Versailles in June, having complained that it was not in line with the conditions of the armistice. The German government was forced to accept the famous "war guilt" clause (article 231), admitting responsibility for the war. In turn, this was the pretext for levying heavy reparations and drastically limiting German arms and military strength. The other four treaties were signed over the next 12 months.

Britain's delegation at Paris, led by Lloyd George, followed a policy between the vengeful French, led by Georges Clemenceau, and the idealistic Americans, led by Woodrow Wilson. Lloyd George had stayed at the head of his wartime coalition government, which won a decisive victory in the general election of 1918. This was derisively called the "coupon" election, for those Liberal candidates who backed the prime minister were given a letter of endorsement, which Herbert Asquith dubbed the "coupon" in a sarcastic reference to wartime rationing—a reminder that the government was perpetuating wartime alignments as well as capitalizing on the glory of victory. Lloyd George's followers swept all others, taking 478 seats, while Asquith's Liberals won a mere 28. The fledgling Labour party took 63 seats and proceeded to adopt its formal party constitution.

Party politics was not as stable as the 1918 results seemed to suggest. A number of scandals and postwar problems shook the government, and the Conservatives belatedly withdrew their support from Lloyd George in 1922. A series of elections came over the next three years, and they showed a rise in Labour's vote and a fall in the total for Liberals. There was a minority Labour government in power briefly in 1924, before the Conservatives returned to office in 1924–29. Several key events highlighted this period.

When the provisional government was set up in Dublin in 1919, the British countered by sending troops to Ireland, and the unionists in the North refused to recognize the rebels. A period of raids and atrocities was finally ended by a truce in 1921. Meanwhile, the British Parliament had passed a Government of Ireland Act in 1920, enabling the formation of two legislatures; one had already been convened in Belfast. Late in 1921 an agreement was reached for the formation of an Irish Free State, a dominion with a governor general and with its own parliament responsible for domestic affairs. The more radical members of Sinn Féin, led by Eamon de Valera, a hero of 1916 and former president of the provisional regime, held out for independence and began an assault on the Free State government that continued for two years. De Valera would eventually return to regular political activity and head the government, leading the Free State on an independent political path, beginning with a new, self-proclaimed constitution in 1937.

The most serious domestic problem facing the British government in the 1920s was the reestablishment of a peacetime economy. This seemed to be well under way in 1919–20, because there was a brief period of growth caused by the postwar need to restore stocks of goods. In 1921 this momentum stopped, business faltered, and unemployment rose to high levels that only began to recede in the late 1930s. One of the most troubled industries was coal mining. Government had taken over the industry and had provided subsidies to mine owners during the war. When it tried to terminate the arrangements, the owners planned to cut wages, the miners opposed the cuts, and there was a stalemate. Several government commissions studied the industry and recommended reforms, none of which were adopted. In 1926 the owners prepared to cut wages as the subsidy ran out, and the miners' union, together with its allied unions, declared a general strike in May. Its object was to bring the economy to a halt and force the government to intervene on its behalf. But the government instead used troops, police, and mobilized civilians to drive trams and fill in for other strikers. Winston Churchill, who was then the chancellor of the exchequer, published a government newspaper (*The British Gazette*) and directed other antistrike operations. After 12 days the strike ended, but the miners stayed out until the fall, when they were forced to return to work on the owners' terms. The next year the government passed a trades disputes act, which prohibited general strikes and sympathy strikes.

The overall picture for the economy and for employment did not improve in the late 1920s. After the first majority Labour government took office in 1929 (Labour was in the minority in 1924), there was even worse news. A financial crisis meant choosing between cutting spending or increasing taxes; according to economic orthodoxy, the budget had to be balanced. A dispute within the cabinet ended with the resignation of the prime minister, Ramsay MacDonald, in 1931. However, he immediately resumed office at the head of a coalition government, in effect turning his back on his party in order to retain power. For this he was expelled from the Labour Party, the only sitting prime minister in British history to suffer this fate. The "National" government proceeded to end free trade by adopting a policy of preferential tariffs at the Ottawa Imperial Conference in 1932. But neither this nor any other economic measures were able to soften the impact of the depression. Unemployment doubled the already high levels of the 1920s, and it did not begin to recede until 1936. Pockets of destitution were tragic: some shipyard and factory towns had upwards of 70 percent unemployment. Strikingly, real wages increased throughout the years 1920–38 (by about 20 percent), but this was small consolation to those out of work.

Similar economic conditions prevailed in other countries, and in some of them the political consequences were alarming. By the 1930s there was an alignment of autocratic states—"totalitarian" in that they claimed popular political majorities that they used as a pretext to assume broad dictatorial powers. In postwar Italy, Benito Mussolini headed a Fascist movement that took power in 1922. In Germany, Nazi Party leader Adolf Hitler took power in 1933. In Spain, Francisco Franco led a victorious National Front in that country's civil war in 1936–39. These ominous events formed the background for a major foreign crisis in the 1930s.

Britain in the 1920s had reduced its military strength, partly in keeping with the aims of the League of Nations and partly for reasons of economy. The government adopted a general policy known as the "Ten-Year Rule"—namely, that no war was expected for at least 10 years. Consequently, army and navy budgets were cut, the country agreed with others at the Washington Naval Conference (1921–22) that there would be limits on warship construction, and the process of general disarmament negotiations was given support in the years 1926–32. Besides this trend, there was an effort to fulfill the League's goal of using arbitration to settle international disputes. That target was in sight in 1924, when the organization debated but failed to approve the Geneva Protocol, which called for binding arbitration for international disputes. Meanwhile, many states lost faith in the League's ability to protect them, and a wave of international agreements were made to assure security. Britain did not enter into any of these, not out of nostalgia for "splendid isolation," but because she did not want to be bound to any military alliance.

From about 1935, diplomatic and military concerns and threats began to change this picture, producing the British response of "appeasement,"—that is, a policy of meeting some demands so that there were fewer chances of open warfare. The main source of pressure came from the German desire to right the wrongs of Versailles. Why should Germany be the only power to be disarmed? Why should German territory still be demilitarized? Why should Germany not annex territory inhabited by Germans? These were views which Hitler manipulated to bring himself to power, and they served equally well to embarrass and unbalance his western diplomatic adversaries.

In 1935 the British government made a naval agreement with Germany, allowing an increase in German ships, limited to one-third of the tonnage of British vessels. But this came only months after Germany had unilaterally repudiated the arms limits of the Versailles treaty and had announced the formation of the Luftwaffe. There was little security gained for Britain, though there also was little chance that German naval construction would have been controlled otherwise. In 1936 Hitler announced that he was going to send German troops into the demilitarized Rhineland. Britain and France had no response to this additional treaty violation. Germany, meanwhile, introduced conscription and entered into military alliances with Italy and Japan (1936). By 1938, Nazi sympathizers in Austria and Czechoslovakia actively supported German expansion. In March a planned plebiscite on unification to be held in Austria was preempted by an unopposed German invasion and annexation.

In the next few months, German troop movements on the Czech border caused alarm, the Czech army mobilized, and talks were held on the subject of autonomy for the Sudeten Germans. But Hitler demanded the annexation of the Czech border, and in September British prime minister Neville Chamberlain and French premier Edouard Daladier flew to Munich to meet Hitler and Mussolini. There an agreement was signed to allow the annexation, and Hitler gave Chamberlain a signed statement that he had no further territorial ambitions. This proved worthless in March 1939, when Hitler annexed the rest of the Czech state. With appeasement a failure, Britain made an alliance with Poland, which seemed to be the next target on Hitler's list. But in August 1939 Stalin trumped this with an agreement to divide Poland with Hitler. This "nonaggression" pact sealed Poland's fate, and the subsequent German and Russian invasions signaled the beginning of World War II in Europe in September 1939.

Actually, the war may be said to have begun two years earlier, when Japan, with no formal declaration of war, attacked Chinese forces in 1937, seizing Beijing (Peking), Shanghai, and Nanjing (Nanking). Indeed, the Japanese had seized Manchuria as far back as 1931–32, capitalizing on the deteriorating state of internal affairs in China. But soon the Japanese government began a more ambitious campaign of expansion in the western Pacific, highlighted by the attacks on Pearl Harbor and the Philippines in December 1941.

The British governments of the 1930s have been criticized for their foolish policy of appeasing the dictators. They had no formal allies, but they did begin to increase military spending in 1936. The "Ten-Year Rule" no longer applied, but the nation's economy could not begin to catch up in the few remaining years of peace. It seemed likely that any policy that could stall the aggression of Germany was a worthwhile expedient. Unfortunately, Germany was not operating in a vacuum: Italy, Japan, and the USSR were eager partners in the race to expand and build military machines in the 1930s. Among the most outspoken opponents of appeasement was Winston Churchill, the former head of the admiralty and political maverick, somewhat of an outcast in his own (adopted) Conservative party in the 1930s. When the war began, he was summoned back to the admiralty in September 1939.

HOLOCAUST, 1939–1945

World War II saw far higher levels of destruction than the First World War. There was also greater loss of human life, far more of it in the civilian populations and much of it due to deliberate policies, including genocide. The later war was truly a global event, with very few places in the world untouched. This magnitude accounts for the more sweeping impact of the war on Britain and its empire by 1945.

Britain did not see major fighting for eight months after the invasion of Poland. This period was called "the phony war" by some, but it would end soon enough. In fact, preparations were begun as soon as war was declared; a "war book" had been created after the experience of 1914, and many wartime regulations were implemented swiftly. But there was little contact with the enemy. After Germany invaded Denmark and Norway on April 9, 1940, a British naval assault at Narvik (April 13) briefly took that port; and an Anglo-French force landed in the south (April 20) but was driven out in two weeks. Norway fell in early June.

By then the main German invasion was launched (May 10) on the Netherlands, Belgium, and France. Having lost the confidence of the House of Commons, Chamberlain was forced to resign, and Winston Churchill was appointed prime minister on the same day. He inherited a grim military situation: German mechanized units were conquering Belgium and overwhelming the French. Large armies were trapped near Dunkirk, and only by an incredible effort were 335,000 British and French troops rescued from the beaches (June 4). France signed an armistice on June 22, and Britain faced Germany alone.

The swiftness of France's defeat caught everyone by surprise, including Hitler. He had no immediate plan for an invasion of Britain, and in any event he was only now in possession of airfields to use for preliminary attacks. A campaign against Royal Air Force (RAF) installations began in August, but before there was time to seriously disable British air power, the targets were shifted to London and other major cities in September. This "Blitz" lasted through the winter and killed some 43,000 civilians, but its military effectiveness was dubious, in that civilian morale was if anything stronger afterward. That experience, contrary to the apostles of air power, was to be repeated many times throughout the war.

The other major aspect of German attack was at sea, where U-boats threatened to cut Britain's lifelines in the Battle of the Atlantic. The United States, still neutral, provided weapons and ammunition as early as June 1940; in September a deal was made to send 50 destroyers from the First World War in exchange for leases to British bases in Newfoundland, Bermuda, and the Caribbean; and sharing of American arms production was arranged in November. Further aid was authorized by the Lend-Lease Act of March 1941, and large food shipments helped Britain stave off the worst effects of the submarine war. Britain had begun the war with 21 million tons of shipping in 1939. By summer 1941 shipping losses were estimated to be over 7 million tons. (It would get worse: over 800,000 tons would be lost in a single month, twice, in 1942). By that time the United States had launched a major shipbuilding program, and its navy was gradually patrolling farther into the Atlantic to protect convoys bound for Britain. In August, U.S. president Franklin D. Roosevelt and Prime Minister Churchill met on a warship in Placentia Bay, Newfoundland, where they signed the Atlantic Charter, a lofty statement of peace aims. The occasion was an odd one, given that America was still a "nonbelligerent," but the meeting presented an opportunity for the military staffs of both countries to begin to work together.

Before the top-level meeting, one of the first critical turning points of the war came on June 22, 1941, when Hitler launched an invasion of his erstwhile ally, the Soviet Union. This major miscalculation immediately created an ally for Britain, though Churchill found that dealing with Stalin was a special challenge. In any case, Britain no longer fought alone. In December the Japanese surprise attack on Pearl Harbor instantly brought the United States into the war. Several days later, Hitler declared war on the United States. Churchill and Roosevelt agreed that the first priority was victory in Europe, but that was not an easy proposition. Much to the dismay of Stalin, who wanted early attacks on mainland Europe, the Anglo-American allies began a campaign of defeating the German and Italian forces in North Africa, after which they invaded Sicily and Italy. These long and bloody campaigns took over two years, and the invasion of occupied France only came in June 1944. Within a year, the Western forces and the advancing Russians met in Germany, completing Hitler's defeat (May 1945).

In the Pacific, the Japanese had conquered vast island and mainland territories by 1942. At the same time as Pearl Harbor, Japan attacked the Philippines and British stations in Hong Kong and Malaya. Britain lost Singapore and was forced out of Burma in 1942. That same year the United States began a series of naval battles and island invasions (Coral Sea, May; Guadalcanal, August; Solomon Islands, November). Advancing across the Pacific, the American were able to begin attacks on Japan and on the home fleet by the end of 1944. The most devastating blow came with the dropping of atomic bombs on Hiroshima and Nagasaki in August 1945. These fierce assaults brought a Japanese surrender and the country's occupation by U.S. forces.

When Churchill took power in 1940, he assembled a small war cabinet and appointed himself as minister of defense. This naturally put him at loggerheads with military commanders, and his active interference (including some notably dangerous schemes) forced intense debate, but most of the time Churchill acceded to the professional judgment of his chiefs. The British generals were fortunate to have access to German communications via the secret decoding of the Enigma machine, known as the "Ultra Secret." It had been Britain's good luck to get possession of a German encoding machine in Poland in 1939, and a special secret office was set up in Bletchley Park, where cryptographers worked out the machine's operation. Intercepted messages were then deciphered and turned over to Churchill and the highest-ranking officers of his staff; the information was later shared with the United States. Allied commanders often enjoyed an advantage over their adversaries because of this intelligence asset.

Churchill's deputy prime minister was Clement Attlee, the head of the Labour Party. That group had recovered from its self-destruction in the early 1930s and was now the second-ranking party. However, there had been no general elections since 1935, and thus it was seen as urgent to return to peacetime politics as soon as Germany was defeated in May 1945. The election was held in July, with a delay in counting so as to include the votes of servicemen. The stunned public—and their prime minister—learned that Labour had won with 393 seats. Churchill resigned and was replaced at the postwar Potsdam conference by Attlee, the new prime minister. The upset could be attributed to Churchill's campaign, which compared Attlee and his socialist policies to the Nazi regime. There had also been a long interval since the last election, and the equally long memories of the depression era were associated by many with the Tories (or at least with the incumbent government).

Even as Churchill was being hailed as a victorious war leader, it was hard for him to avoid the negative impressions that the war had left on so many. While there were many more in uniform in this war (from 2 million in 1940 up to 5 million in 1945), there were fewer who died (360,000). Civilian populations had carried a tremendous burden, most of all in central Europe and Asia, where policies and programs had brutalized whole populations (Jews, Chinese, Koreans, and others). By those standards, British suffering was minor, though there was unprecedented loss of life and limb from enemy bombs, and 30,000 merchant seamen lost their lives. There were heavy losses of homes and material goods, topped by strict rationing, shortages, and scrap drives. Through it all, patriotism was not diminished, even on the Left, but there were rising expectations. The government multiplied its spending by a factor of six between 1939 and 1945, defying all conventional wisdom. Of course, it did so in large part by borrowing and raising taxes. The income tax was raised to a standard rate of 50 percent, and a purchase tax was introduced along with a compulsory deduction from employees' wages and salaries. Early in the war Churchill appointed William Beveridge to head a committee to review Britain's social services. Some 600,000 copies of his report were in circulation in December 1942. It elicited a powerful response: comprehensive social services were now seen as a practical goal—though not by Churchill's government, which did not accept the report.

In foreign affairs, Britain had become a member of the Big Three; the United States, the Soviet Union, and the United Kingdom. While it might seem a mark of status (and by 1945, many thought it was an exaggerated position), in the longer view this was a demotion. Britain had stood supreme 50 years earlier; and even in the 1930s, with her empire at its greatest size in population and territory, she had cause to feel superior. The events of 1940–41 had destroyed those illusions. For the duration of the war, it was expedient for the United States and the USSR to keep this valuable, but junior, ally in their company. Once victory was achieved, all that would change. But the first diplomatic task after the Japanese surrender was to make arrangements for postwar government.

This postwar planning had a long pedigree. It began in the waters off Newfoundland in 1941, when Churchill and Roosevelt signed the Atlantic Charter. It started to take more practical shape in 1943 with the organizing of refugee and relief assistance in a conference of 44 nations (United Nations Relief and Rehabilitation Administration). In July 1944 the Bretton Woods conference (United Nations Monetary and Financial Conference) created the International Monetary Fund and a bank for reconstruction and development to stabilize currencies and exchange rates. In October 1944 the Dumbarton Oaks conference prepared a proposal for the United Nations, and its first meeting was held in San Francisco in April 1945; the 50 nations there adopted the organization's charter in September. Meanwhile the great powers meeting at Potsdam in July and August had begun to arrange the terms of surrender and occupation of Germany.

Victory in the Second World War came at the cost of losing an empire and relegating Britain to the second rank of world powers. Hints of her former greatness were still visible, in her position as a great power in the United Nations, in her possession of atomic secrets, and in her "special relationship" with the United States. But these only thinly disguised a seriously weakened state. The war had consumed 28 percent of Britain's national wealth and left her with a debt of £3 billion and a deficit in the balance of payments of £1 billion in 1945. The United States was her major creditor—a very *special* relationship—but lend-lease was terminated abruptly in 1945, and further loans would be needed. The debts in 1945 were all the more serious because so much property had been lost and so many foreign investments had been sacrificed in the war. These losses were the bleak background to the celebrations in 1945. Soon the business of postwar reconstruction was under way, and with it an ambitious new program of social reform amid a gloomy scene of economic distress, bread rationing, coal shortages, and currency crises.

DECLINE AND DEVOLUTION SINCE 1945

Most of the commentary on Britain in the second half of the 20th century has concentrated on its decline—imperial, industrial, and economic. The many meanings given to that word add up to a negative consensus that is not fully deserved. It seems that decline is a motif, a conventional framework rather like some of its predecessors, such as "progress" or "change." The idea of decline can be given more coherence by coupling it with a less common term: devolution. This has a specific political meaning from which a more general one can be derived. After the American Revolution, British colonies found authority devolved upon them (Canada, 1867; Australia, 1901; New Zealand, 1907; South Africa, 1910; Southern Rhodesia, 1923). The nations of the British Isles also sought more devolved political authority—Ireland by force (1922), Scotland and Wales by referenda (1979 and 1997). The idea and process of devolution were reactions to English power and influence, a domination whose credibility was lost in the modern era. The remote dominions had a strong claim to some kind of independence. Nearer home, the strength of devolution was greatest in the Irish nation because of its eight centuries of colonization. Conversely, in Wales and Scotland, devolution gained support from the wider process of decolonization which emerged after 1918 and accelerated after 1945.

It is possible to see dominion growth, decolonization, and U.K. devolution as symptoms of decline, particularly from the standpoint of the old imperialism. But it is not an objective fact. Ruling the world's largest empire did not win the wars of the 20th century for Britain. That depended on the alliance with a wealthy former colony and, later, a rival communist empire, plus the limitations of an encircled German state. Britain's world-power status was in jeopardy long before 1939, and the heavy cost of her victories contributed to further weakening after 1945. It is therefore important to draw a distinction between decline and devolution and between the absolute weakening of any measures of power and their relative effects in Britain as compared to other states or regions.

DOMESTIC POLITICS

The mood of Britain in 1945 was a mixture of elation with final victory and exhaustion from deprivation, continued shortages, and rationing, which was to continue for years to come. The election of that year brought the Labour party its first landslide victory, and that was followed by what some called the "revolution" of 1945: the inauguration of the "welfare state." One of the most powerful arguments against Labour's plans was that the country could not afford the luxury of welfare programs because of its battered economy. To the governing party the goal of social reform was too important to set aside, and its radical policies were implemented over the next few years. Some contemporaries called it socialism, but it was far short of the expropriation and governmental control that true socialist states demanded. British politics from 1945 to the end of the century was in fact a vigorous two-party democracy contained within the traditional constitutional monarchy, one that generated a large bureaucratic structure alongside an increasingly "presidential" executive.

British democracy is based on an open electorate operating within a strictly regulated campaign system (short campaigns, spending limits on candidates, and party political broadcasts paid for by the public). When voters went to the polls in 1945, all men and women aged 21 or older were entitled to vote. This was the third election (after 1929 and 1935) in which women participated, and in the postwar years there would be further fine-tuning to make the system more democratic. An act of 1948 ended plural voting (one vote in a place of business or a university, another in a place of residence). In 1969 the voting age was lowered from 21 to 18.

The major political parties, Conservative and Labour, are joined by many smaller parties: Liberal Democrats, Scottish Nationalists, Plaid Cymru (Welsh Nationalists), Greens, Communists, National Front, and others. General elections are required at no more than five-year intervals. From 1945 to 2001 there were 16 elections, with only three occasions where they were at very short intervals (1950–51, 1964–66, and two elections in 1974); the average time between elections was 3.5 years. Two long Conservative "reigns" (1951–64 and 1979–97) were offset by shorter and more contentious periods of Labour government. The Liberal Party won from six to 12 seats as a rule until 1981 when it formed an alliance with right-wing Labourites; and this Social Democratic Party took 23 seats in 1983 (on 26 percent of the vote). By 1990 this alliance had collapsed, and the Liberal Democrats, descendants of the old Liberals, won 20 seats in 1992 and 46 in 1997. The minor parties are at a great disadvantage because their total voting strength does not translate into an equivalent number of seats. The "first past the post" system, where the leading candidate, regardless of percentage of the vote, wins the seat, gives a disproportionate weight to parties that can contest all 650 seats. Liberal Democrats have thus been inclined to support systems of "proportional representation," which allocates seats according to voting strength, as in the system used in the Republic of Ireland.

Clement Attlee's government held power from 1945 to 1950, and it narrowly won reelection, but its slim majority forced Attlee to hold another election in 1951. The Conservatives won, and although they received 230,000 fewer votes, they took 321 seats to 295 for Labour. Winston Churchill returned to office, but due to his advanced age he retired in 1955. Anthony Eden, the longtime foreign secretary, took over and won the 1955 election with an increased margin. He resigned after the Suez crisis in 1956, allowing Harold Macmillan to take the helm. Macmillan won the next election in 1959 with an expanded majority. After his retirement, the Conservatives replaced him with Sir Alec Douglas-Home, who lost the 1964 election to Labour by the slim margin of 317 to 304. This meant a short-lived Parliament, and the next election in 1966 gave Labour a solid margin of 90 seats. Harold Wilson called an election in 1970, but he was surprised by a Conservative victory. That party, now led by Edward Heath, lost the first election of 1974 by only 0.8 percent of the popular vote; a second election in October gave Labour a margin of 42 seats. However, serious economic problems and recalcitrant union behavior turned the voters to the Tories. Margaret Thatcher, Britain's first female prime minister, won a margin of 70 seats in 1979. She won reelection with an even greater majority in the wake of the Falklands War in 1983. Labour's extreme left-wing manifesto in that election reduced its share of the popular vote to 27 percent. A solid victory in 1987 gave Thatcher the longest tenure of any 20th-century leader. However, in 1990 she was forced to resign as a result of party friction, mainly over her poll tax proposals. In 1992 her successor, John Major, won a surprising 65-seat majority. In 1997 he was beaten by Labour's new leader, Tony Blair, in the century's most resounding victory. Labour took 419 seats and an overall majority of 179, based on only 43 percent of the popular vote. The only evidence of decline in all of this was a somewhat lower voter turnout (71 percent in 1997, as opposed to 84 percent in 1950).

Meanwhile, the British monarchy seemed to decline in public esteem in the late 20th century. At the 1952 coronation of Elizabeth II (Queen Victoria's great-great granddaughter), there was a period of ecstatic praise for the young queen and the durability and poise of the institution. Writers even promoted a "new Elizabethan age"—an echo of the greatness of the nation under the 16th-century queen. Publicity was first an asset, but it soon turned against the monarchy. Elizabeth's coronation was televised, as was Prince Charles's investiture as prince of Wales, and the queen agreed to make the family more open to public view. In the film *Royal Family* in 1969, Elizabeth was shown with her husband Prince Philip and their four children as a model family. The

Margaret Hilda Thatcher *(Hulton Archive)*

children's weddings were also public spectacles—and thanks to the tabloid press, so were the marital problems that followed. The divorces of three of the queen's children, including that of the heir to the throne and his popular bride, Princess Diana, brought unwanted exposure and criticism. In 1993, after a fire had ravaged parts of Windsor Castle, raising the prospect of costly public expense for repairs, the queen agreed to pay taxes on part of the royal income, and she opened part of Buckingham Palace to tourists to raise added funds. The overall effect of these events is difficult to gauge. There had been harsher criticisms of the monarch in the 19th century, but now—thanks to the press—the institution came under even closer scrutiny. With measures to limit the power of the House of Lords and questions about the continued state sanction of the Church of England, a trend may have already begun to reduce the role of the sovereign, although its outcome is far from clear.

The scope and control of civil government grew markedly in the late 20th century. Its most visible additions were in nationalized industry: the British Broadcasting Corporation (BBC) was formed in 1926, London Transport in 1933, and British Airways in 1939. The Bank of England was nationalized in 1946, as were the coal mines. Railways were nationalized in 1947, along with roads, docks, and inland waterways; to these were added electricity in 1947, gas in 1948, and iron and steel in 1949—in all, about 20 percent of the nation's economy. The form of control in most cases was an autonomous public corporation, nominally not a government body, whose shares were usually available to former private owners, often on generous terms. This form of state intervention was popular at first, though by the 1980s it had lost that support, and by 1995 it was all but extinguished.

On another front, government control was boosted somewhat by wartime mobilization and more so by postwar expectations. It became accepted doctrine that the planned use and integration of resources and technology would produce more effective results for the economy. Whole ministries were devoted to this concept (Town and Country Planning, 1943; the Economic Planning Council, 1947; the National Economic Development Council, 1962; the Department of Economic Affairs, 1966). In fact, the story of economic planning agencies is one of drift and erratic movement, the consequence of severe economic pressures on the balance of international payments and disagreement over the aims of progressive planners. This has always been set against the traditional budget watchdogs, known to Labour leaders as the "mandarins" of the Treasury: the civil servants.

The most flourishing part of government in the second half of the 20th century was undoubtedly the bureaucracy. Its size and importance grew, not merely with the creation and growth of the welfare state, but in response to the increased intervention of modern government. The civil service began to grow in the 19th century, and it grew even more in the 20th. The Second World War produced a major increase, from 387,000 in 1939 to 704,000 in 1945. At the top of this large body of government workers is an elite of perhaps 700 administrators, their highest levels being the permanent secretaries of government departments. One effect of such a service is to maintain continuity, not always a positive feature. In 1973 Sir William Armstrong, one of the country's top civil servants, said that the business of the civil service was "the orderly management of decline." The numbers of civil servants kept growing until it reached some 730,000 employees in 1979. Mrs. Thatcher cut that number down to about 560,000 by 1990, mainly by privatizing a number of government departments. The highest levels are dominated by graduates of Oxford and Cambridge, and critics see them as having little of the scientific, technical, and legal skills required in modern government. In 1988 a new program of reform began to reorganize the service. New agencies were made accountable for the delivery of services; these were separated from their respective policy-making departments and given targets of productivity and efficiency.

Since the time of World War I, the power of the prime minister has increased. His or her power in the cabinet, in control over Parliament, and through a host of traditional forms of influence and patronage make the office one that approaches the power of a president, but without the restraints of the separation of powers in the U.S. government system. Indeed, the office is sometimes referred to as an elective dictatorship. The prime minister chooses and dismisses cabinet ministers who manage the main departments of state. They meet as a group, follow an agenda set forth by the prime minister, and defend their decisions in Parliament and before the public. Any serious dissent will usually lead to resignation. The cabinet members represent various factions in the governing party and thus are not easily expelled, for they will still have seats in the House of Commons. The powers of the prime minister in the Commons have not changed drastically. He or she still has the classic powers of setting the agenda, leading the party in debate, and calling general elections. The party whip keeps tight control over the MPs' voting attendance and behavior. However, debates in the Commons and Lords are less and less meaningful, as decisions are made in the cabinet or among smaller groups of advisers. The prime minister has access to broadcasting and television, which sometimes is used to shape opinion and bypass Parliament. When it was decided to televise debates in the House of Commons, it was considered a further boost to the party in power. One of the popular features for viewers is "Question Time" on Tuesdays and Thursdays, when the prime minister answers questions from the opposition; in the format used, he always speaks last.

As party leader, the prime minister presides at annual conferences, heads the party in campaigns, and can support or oppose individual candidacies. Outside the party, the leader's patronage includes approval of posts in the Church of England, appointments to the judiciary (via the lord chancellor), and a large number of more formal appointments throughout the country. Thus the term "elective dictatorship" may not be too far off the mark.

SOCIAL CHANGE

However one assesses the state of British politics, the motif of decline does not apply to social conditions, at least not in absolute terms. The historic experiment of the welfare state began a period of social and economic improvement for many, augmented by a policy of full employment. There was general improvement in the living conditions of most of the population. These changes were accompanied by significant reforms in education, and while the class structure of British society was not shaken, there were many radical cultural changes by the end of the century.

The welfare state was a conscious effort to raise the level of material standards for the bulk of the British population. Partly a reaction to the 1930s, partly a recognition of wartime deprivation, and partly a fulfillment of the doctrines of the Labour Party, the program of national insurance set a subsistence level of household income that would be assured for all. State retirement pensions were expanded to cover more people. The National Health Service was established, against powerful lobbying by doctors. It provided free medical treatment and reorganized the varied types of hospitals into a rational, regionally managed system. The government also implemented its full employment policy. From 1948 to 1970 the level of unemployment was usually below 2 percent, and average wages nearly tripled, rising much faster than prices.

In these conditions, diet, health, and housing all showed signs of improvement. The revolution in domestic appliances brought stoves, refrigerators, and televisions to many homes. Those homes were increasingly owned rather than rented: in 1914 only 10 percent owned their houses; in 1939 that had risen to 35 percent and in 1981 to 59 percent. Private car ownership went up tenfold between 1945 and 1985. But in these years, the nation's economy was only growing about 2.5 percent annually, whereas other countries' rates were well above 4 percent. Thus the puzzle: was the country declining while individuals were advancing?

One of the most basic measures of a society's health is in its population. Population decline had been the intermittent aspect of the years 1901–45 in Britain. After 1945 the fertility rate increased, at first as a postwar phenomenon, but over the next few decades it was the simple result of more marriages at earlier ages. The birth rate among women of childbearing age rose from 6 percent before the war to 9 percent in the 1960s. The general population of Britain increased from 48.9 million in 1951 to 53.9 million in 1971 and 56.2 million in 1991. One more population source, even more visible, was immigration from former colonies: West Indian, Asian, and African. From Commonwealth countries, the numbers rose from 597,000 in 1961 to 2,635,000 in 1991. This incoming wave was a source of anxiety for the formerly all-white society. There were immigration restrictions enacted in the 1960s, but there were also race relations acts designed to prevent discrimination. Racial mixing was an explosive subject but, given Britain's imperial past, certainly not a novel one, and only from the most racist viewpoint was it a measure of decline.

"Secondary education for all" was the slogan of the Butler Education Act (1944). All students were to be placed in either grammar, technical, or "secondary modern" schools, and a state-funded education was guaranteed. The school-leaving age was raised to 15; but the "eleven plus" exam meant that working-class children still faced long odds on admission to grammar schools, and then entry to higher education. Consequently, the traditional class system persisted. In the 1960s the Labour government introduced the "comprehensive" school, combining grammar and secondary modern. The comprehensive schools came to educate over 90 percent of secondary students in the state system. There was, of course, still a private sector, commonly referred to as the independent schools. This group contained the ancient "public" schools and those fee-paying schools that had grown from the late 19th century to cater to a more select group of students. Today some 2,250 schools in this category teach about 7 percent of the children of secondary school age.

The other major development in education has been the great expansion in higher education since 1945. In 1900 there were already 10 universities that stood beside—and well below—Oxford and Cambridge; these were attended by about 20,000 students. In the 1960s expansion began, and by 1980 there were 47 universities in Britain. Along with them were about 30 polytechnics—originally technical colleges, but most of them expanding toward a full university curriculum. There were also 125 teachers colleges. In all there were about 600,000 full-time students and 350,000 part-time students. In addition, the Open University, a novel experiment of the 1960s, was aimed at working adults who wished to earn degree credits. It offered televised courses and tutorials, and by the 1990s it was teaching 9 percent of students in higher education. Efforts were made in the 1980s and 1990s to increase higher-education enrollment, and the proportion of secondary students going on to higher education rose from about one in eight (1980) to one in five (1991).

Many expected education reform to be a critical solvent of the "class society," the highly stratified and exclusive social regime of earlier centuries. But the extensive reforms did not erase the function of private education. Much was said about the corrosive effects of the war on class, such as the large numbers of working-class children evacuated from London, or the large numbers of servicemen and women who enjoyed interclass relationships during the war. But social class was not dissolved by war, and the distribution of wealth did not change, even if distribution of income did to a degree. In fact, the 1980s saw some reversal of redistribution: lower tax rates in that decade tended to increase the disparity of incomes. The most striking social changes of the late 20th century were in the form of challenges to the old order, frequently seen as a cultural revolution. Music, literature, and the arts reflected conscious rejection of old standards, and rebellious artists created one of the most successful export industries in postwar Britain (the Beatles, the Rolling Stones, Monty Python). At the same time, the increase in drug use, the public flaunting of old moral standards and sexual permissiveness were unsettling to the older generation. Aside from these changes, there were important social landmarks in other areas: abolition of capital punishment (1965), divorce by mutual consent (1969), and the selection of a woman as leader of the Conservative party (1975).

THE EMPIRE AND EUROPE

Britain was caught in an apparent trap between "keeping" the empire and the Commonwealth or joining European integration. This stalled eventual entry

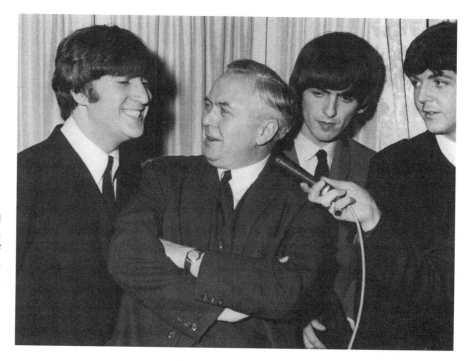

Labour leader Harold Wilson, center, speaks to John Lennon of the pop group The Beatles. To his left are members of the band George Harrison and Paul McCartney.
(Hulton/Archive)

into the European Community. The pull of the empire was a force beyond reason. Imperial decline got a lot of its input from the victory in 1945, and on paper the empire was larger than ever. But this assessment was based on a wobbly structure that included occupied but uncontrolled areas of the Middle East; large and failing imperial regimes such as India; and very large and autonomous dominions such as Canada and Australia, as well as smaller dominions like South Africa. Only willful blindness could allow these supposed colonial areas to support great power notions. Yet such ideas lingered, either because they fit a perceived (Tory) image of greatness or because they gave some hope for postwar power and authority.

The empire was also part of the strategic yearning of the 1950s and early '60s: a Britain dependent on American handouts was either too proud or too stubborn to accept the implications of such penury and demotion, so her governments cultivated their strategic assets. When the United States declined to share atomic secrets (fearing British spies), Britain went ahead with a costly independent program to develop atomic weapons. On similar lines, British governments, both Labour and Conservative, tried to maintain a military power well beyond their means, and they kept a National Service program of conscription in place until 1960. But great power status was impossible to maintain for long. As the cold war began, the shrinking imperial economy, plus the shifting world trade structure and the British currency's place in it, conspired to undermine Britain's power.

In 1945 Britain entered a world dominated by two superpowers, the United States and the Soviet Union. Despite the country's precarious financial condition, Labour leaders maintained an army of nearly a million men and pushed ahead with weapons development, trying to maintain an independent voice in world affairs. Ironically, this effort succeeded only in making Britain an adjunct to U.S. power while it deprived the British economy of resources that might have speeded recovery. This effort was concluded in the early 1960s, when it was recognized as futile. Meanwhile, Britain had been embarrassed and exposed as a second-rank power by the Suez Crisis of 1956.

Britain had previously agreed to withdraw its troops from Egypt. When President Gamal Abdel Nasser nationalized the Suez Canal in July 1956, Prime Minister Anthony Eden, seeing signs of communist expansion, wanted to take military action to prevent loss of British influence. Rather than mounting a direct assault, a secret plan was made whereby Israel would attack Egypt, while Britain and France would intervene in the guise of peacemakers, thereby gaining access to the canal. When British troops landed in November, there was a major rift with the United States, and Britain was forced to withdraw, her troops replaced by a U.N. contingent. This vividly demonstrated the loss of British power and marked the last such venture into a strategically vital part of the world.

The imperial economy remained critical to Britain well into the postwar era. Nearly half of British exports went to the empire in 1950. At the same time, her inflated defense spending and her heroic efforts to maintain sterling, the Commonwealth's monetary standard, were incredibly heavy burdens. By 1950 Britain had been forced to leave India (1947), Ceylon and Burma (1948), and Palestine (1949). There was simply no affordable way to maintain colonial governments in so many places. Some liberated colonies chose to remain in the Commonwealth and thus retained important trading connections with Britain. Elsewhere there were colonial wars, for instance in Malaya and Kenya. There were also growing numbers of nationalist movements in other colonies, all seeking to escape from British rule. Yet it is surprising how quickly, and peacefully, the rest of the empire dissolved. In the short period of 1957–67 most of the remaining colonies were given up. In the simplest terms, the only alternative was to imagine a British government with the will and the resources to govern, say, Nigeria, a country with four times the area of the United Kingdom and a roughly equal population. The better option clearly was some form of devolution of power. But these were not the only realities. There was also an increasingly attractive prospect of closer relations with Europe.

In 1945 Britain was not interested in European cooperation. A French offer of economic partnership in 1949 was spurned, as was an invitation to join the European Coal and Steel Community in 1950. Britain did participate in Marshall Plan aid and in the formation of the North Atlantic Treaty Organization (NATO, 1949), because in both cases those moves served their interests. But when the move to unify Europe and create a common market really gathered steam, Britain was chilly to the prospect. The Treaty of Rome of 1957 inaugurated the Common Market without British participation. The new organization enjoyed the advantages of reduced tariffs and restrictions and led to increasing trade and accelerating economic growth.

Britain in the 1960s was falling behind; consequently, in 1963 the first attempt was made to join Europe. Harold Macmillan found his Conservative party divided on the idea, as was the Labour party. This effort was blocked by French president Charles de Gaulle because of his annoyance at Britain's close strategic partnership with the United States. A similar scenario played out in 1967, as de Gaulle once again prevented Britain's entry into the Common Market. With the 1970 election of Edward Heath, a vigorous supporter of European union, coupled with the 1969 resignation of de Gaulle, a third British application went ahead and was accepted. The Treaty of Brussels of 1972 authorized British entry. However, there was considerable debate over the entry terms, and after some renegotiation a referendum on membership passed in 1975. British entry had finally been settled.

Today the British government and people remain sharply divided over most European policies—for example, deciding not to adopt the new European currency (the euro) and showing great aversion to further steps toward European political unification. This tendency was accentuated by Margaret Thatcher's policies in the 1980s. Yet by the time she was first elected in 1979, the basic illusion of Britain as a "great power" had been fully exposed. She might show scorn for foreigners, denouncing the European Community at every turn and even launching a colonial war to recapture the Falkland Islands from Argentina (1982). But even that venture proved expensive for Britain, and it did little for the nation's status as a world power.

REVIVING NATIONS

Although Britain lost her status as a great power, so had most others who aspired to that rank in 1939. But none of them made the efforts Britain did to regain that status. After 1945 only the Soviet Union and the United States had real pretensions to the rank of world power; and by 1989 the Soviet Union had forfeited its claim. There was no single state approaching the United States' capacity. There was no doubt that in the league of world powers, Britain's rank had fallen sharply. But that was not the only measure being used. In terms of income, productivity, trade and other indices, Britain was being compared with the countries of Europe, and found wanting. The simple fact was that after the war many states enjoyed a significant revival. Even Germany and Japan became economic powerhouses within a generation of their defeat, and other countries that the British felt were inferior showed signs of beating Britain in some statistical areas. By the 1970s there was talk of a British "disease" of low productivity and economic weakness. This was the most galling view of British decline. A frequent comparison used to demonstrate the decline is in the "league table" of European states. For instance, the numbers for 1991 in per capita gross national product (GDP) ranked Britain eighth on the list, behind Italy and just ahead of Spain.

Since the 1960s, most of the measurements of British economic performance have been poor relative to other countries, despite many signs of prosperity in

British society. There have been innumerable explanations, none of which has seemed satisfactory. On large measures, Britain's place has fallen. For example, between 1950 and 1983 British growth rates of 2–3 percent per annum were lower than in the United States (3.3 percent), Western Europe (4.5 percent), and Japan (7.9 percent). British manufacturing accounted for 25 percent of the world total in 1880; it was about 4 percent in 1980. In trade of manufactured goods, the numbers fell from 40 percent to 9 percent. These changes were due to the emergence of powerful industrial giants and to a leap in the numbers of competitors. Those elements overpowered the once-dominant British economy, because its population and resources were no match for the others.

The decline in once-great British industries made a powerful impression on most people. The coal industry fell on hard times in the 1920s, and with competition from oil and, later, natural gas, lagging British mines were forced to close. Desperate government efforts to ban imports and increase usage in the 1960s were futile. The national economy was given a lift by the discovery of oil in the North Sea during the 1970s, but this was another blow to the old energy industry, which was also adversely affected by the advent of nuclear power. Its declining years were marked by a violent struggle between the miners' union and the Thatcher government in the 1980s. The government won.

In cotton textiles the decline was also evident in the 1920s. By 1958 there was actually a net import surplus in cotton goods. Iron and steel were overwhelmed by large competitors. The nationalizations of 1950 and 1967 did not help, and Britain was reduced to a small share of world production in specialized sectors. Shipbuilding was also in decline, as Japan emerged as the greatest competitor. Yards had to close, and shipbuilders went bankrupt. British car makers were profitable until the 1960s. Then a series of mergers failed to stem falling sales and profits.

While industry stagnated and faltered, services and finance seemed to thrive. This was not cause for cheer to many, as it was inconceivable that Britian could be an economic success without producing material goods. But economists were divided. For one thing, only about 43 percent of the workforce were in manufacturing, mining, and construction in the middle of the 19th century. The number did not change before 1970. But by 1975 it was 30 percent, and, in 1995 it fell to 20 percent. Yet no one can tell exactly what this structural change will mean.

Students of this subject have offered a variety of explanations for Britain's economic decline. One theory is that elite British culture did not accept the industrial lifestyle; another is that the British entrepreneur lacked sufficient enterprise; another said that organized labor thwarted efficient production; yet another found fault with interfering government policies; and yet another saw the dominant financial community to blame. Of course, none of these features was unique to Britain, and most kinds of general explanation have proven to be unsatisfactory.

When looking at the relative economic weakness of the United Kingdom, one should also consider the impacts of the parallel forms of devolution the country experienced between 1950 and the end of the century: the decolonization of the 1960s, the devolved power tied to entering the European Economic Community, and devolved power within the British Isles. Each of these changes, singly and together, contributed to British decline.

There were economic burdens accompanying the devolution of power to colonies and dominions. In the period of disconnection, 1947–70, Britain bore heavy overhead costs. Maintaining sterling as a major currency was a liability, clearly displayed in the continuing balance of payments crises (1945–70). While Winston Churchill made rousing speeches in 1947 at the head of a "United Europe Movement," there was never a solid British commitment to Europe, as was evident from the constant internal feuding over each step of policy. What would the economic effect of early and full participation have been? Would Britain's economic performance have been better? No one knows, but it is fair to assume that joining Europe would have allowed Britain to participate in the rapid growth continental countries enjoyed in the 1960s and 1970s.

Devolution within the British Isles has taken many different forms, and it is a continuing story. The earliest episode involved the search for Irish Home Rule (1870–1922). This produced a dominion government that was converted to a republic (1937–49). At the same time, the separate dominion in Northern Ireland remained part of the United Kingdom. In Ulster, civil war and unrest plagued the province (1969–98) as the IRA tried to force British withdrawal. Instead, in 1972 the dominion legislature was closed, and Britain used the army to exert control for over two decades. Much more benign events in Scotland and Wales fostered the slow growth of nationalist parties from the 1880s. They made some slight headway in Parliament after 1945, and by 1969 there was enough concern to create a Royal Commission on the Constitution. This body looked at governance in the different parts of the United Kingdom and acknowledged that there might be grounds for reform. But there was no consensus as to the shape of reform, and the commission produced multiple suggestions. Meanwhile, political leaders had created a secretary of state for Wales (1964), on the lines of the office created for Scotland in 1885. There was growing interest in preserving the native languages, literature, and history of the Scots and the Welsh. In 1979 there were votes to form national assemblies, but both failed, the one in Wales by a wide margin. All the same, interest was revived in the 1980s, partly due to Margaret Thatcher's policies. As her Conservative party had fewer and fewer votes from these areas, her policies reflected a disdain for them, particularly in the plan for a poll tax, to be implemented first in Scotland in 1989. Consequently, the proposals for a parliament for Scotland and an assembly for Wales were both approved in 1997. Through all of this discussion, there have been suggestions that English regions should receive some devolution, but the trend has been toward greater centralization of English government, and the English regions did not develop the kind of political voice used by the nationalist parties.

How much did the connections and conflicts between England, Scotland, Wales, Northern Ireland, and the Irish Republic "cost" in terms of economic development? Some of the areas affected include the tariff battles with the Irish Republic from the 1930s, army occupation of Ulster (1969–98), disputes over

BALKAN ST. 12

regional development (for instance, North Sea oil), and issues of taxation (poll tax) and other policies (for instance, the disputes between central and local government over health and education). All were negative factors in the U.K. balance sheet. Since 1997 improved relations with the Irish Republic helped to achieve a cease-fire in Northern Ireland while a fragile peace process got under way. The new Welsh Assembly and Scottish Parliament (the latter with some taxing powers) may or may not prove to enhance the local (and national) economies. But the struggle, real and rhetorical, has definitely had costs, economic as well as political and psychological.

A Belfast woman looks out of her door to see two British soldiers in the street (1970). *(Hulton/Archive)*

CONCLUSION

Britain in the 21st century is a mature democracy with a longstanding monarchy and no written constitution. That is, its government has evolved from roots in absolutism and aristocracy, with no experience of revolutionary upheaval since the 17th century. Thus, the story of political reform has had the unlikely outcome of "elected dictatorship." There are still strong feelings for proportional representation, a quasi-bill of rights has been approved in the Human Rights Act (1998), and there were moves toward abolition and/or replacement of the House of Lords. What each or all of these may do to the essential nature of British government remains to be seen.

The modern British economy grew from poorly capitalized industry, surpassed all competitors, and built a solid financial empire. In the 21st century Britain's industry deserted its erstwhile essentials and turned toward a "post-industrial" model, running on the fuel of "invisible exports" from the financial and commercial community. This trend has recently been augmented by information technology, and Britain has reluctantly joined the European community. The economic effects of these changes may well halt the decline of relative growth in Britain.

The hierarchy of British society became part of a welfare state in 1945. The whiff of socialism did not erode the aristocracy, but it may have made it irrelevant. And even Thatcher's harsh assault on state control in the 1980s did not erase national insurance and the health service. The culture of 21st-century Britain has seen major transformations. For example, the place of the churches in society has been undermined, the established church in particular. Art, literature, music, drama, and dance have been stimulated by the eruption of popular culture via old and new media. There has been a transformation of ideas and institutions beyond that of the traditional constitutional and social forms. Britain has entered the new millennium with less power in the world at large, but with an abiding confidence in the strength and stamina of her society and culture.

HISTORICAL
DICTIONARY
A–Z

A

Abbot, Charles See COLCHESTER, CHARLES ABBOT, FIRST BARON.

Abbot, George (1562–1633)
archbishop of Canterbury
Born in Guildford, Surrey, the son of a cloth-worker, Abbot attended Guildford grammar school and Balliol College, OXFORD UNIVERSITY, earning his M.A. in 1585. He studied theology and became a notable preacher. He rose to become a leading figure in the university and the church hierarchy. An advocate of the PURITANS, he was made a BISHOP in 1609 and ARCHBISHOP in 1611. He was employed in efforts to reestablish bishops in SCOTLAND, under the authority of James I (JAMES VI AND I), who had come to the English throne from that country. Abbot was at odds with the government of CHARLES I, and was briefly suspended (1627–28).

See also CHURCH OF SCOTLAND; REFORMATION.

abdication crisis (1936)
Edward, prince of Wales, succeeded his father, GEORGE V, on January 20, 1936, as king EDWARD VIII. He intended to marry Wallis Simpson, a divorced American socialite. The planned wedding encountered strong opposition from the church and from political leaders, and Edward was forced to abdicate in December 1936, taking the title of Duke of Windsor and marrying the woman he loved.

Aberdeen, George Hamilton-Gordon, fourth earl of (1784–1860)
prime minister, 1852–55
Lord Aberdeen was educated at Harrow school and St. John's, CAMBRIDGE UNIVERSITY. A Scottish representative peer (1806–14), he served in several diplomatic assignments. He was a supporter of Robert PEEL and was foreign secretary 1828–30 and again 1841–46. After Peel resigned in 1846, Aberdeen became the leader of the Peelite faction of the CONSERVATIVE PARTY. His period of leadership coincided with the CRIMEAN WAR (1854–56), for which his government was charged with serious mismanagement, and he resigned after a vote of censure. He also was the founder of the Athenian Society and president of the Society of Antiquaries (1812–46).

Aboukir Bay (1798)
The French fleet anchored off Alexandria after landing Napoleon's army for the conquest of EGYPT. Admiral Horatio NELSON had pursued the enemy across the Mediterranean and he attacked on August 1, 1798, achieving one of the most decisive victories in English naval history, in what became known as the Battle of the Nile.

act of Parliament
The highest legal authority in the United Kingdom; however, it may be amended or repealed

by a later act of PARLIAMENT. Making an act begins with drafting a bill, usually by the ministers of the Crown. Until the 20th century, individual members often introduced legislation, but that became far less common with the rapid growth of government business in the 19th century. The bill is introduced in either the HOUSE OF COMMONS or the HOUSE OF LORDS, and it must pass three readings in each house. During these stages, members may debate and offer amendments. When both houses have passed the final version of the bill, it must receive royal assent, after which it becomes law.

See also BUDGET; CABINET; PARLIAMENT; REFORM ACTS; SELECT COMMITTEE; UNION, ACTS OF.

Acton, John, first baron Acton (1834–1902)
essayist, historian

A renowned historian, Baron Acton was born in Italy and raised on the continent. His father was English, his mother German and Roman Catholic. His religion prevented his entry into OXFORD UNIVERSITY or CAMBRIDGE UNIVERSITY. He gained notoriety with essays supporting liberal Catholic views and opposing papal infallibility in the 1870s. He was a member of the HOUSE OF COMMONS before assuming his PEERAGE in 1869 and entering the HOUSE OF LORDS. He was made Regius Professor of History at Cambridge in 1895, and he planned the *Cambridge Modern History* (1899–1912). His lifetime project, "A History of Liberty," was never completed. He is best remembered for his remark, "Power tends to corrupt and absolute power corrupts absolutely."

Adam, Robert (1728–1792)
architect

Adam was the best-known of four architect brothers, sons of William Adam, an important architect in Scotland in the early 18th century. He attended Edinburgh University and then studied architecture in Italy. Adams's work was in the neoclassical style, taking inspiration from many Greek and Roman models. He built a number of famous country houses in England, and he was the designer of important public buildings in EDINBURGH, including Charlotte Square and Register House.

Addington, Henry, viscount Sidmouth (1757–1844)
prime minister, 1801–1804

Addington attended Winchester School, Brasenose College, OXFORD UNIVERSITY, and Lincoln's Inn. Elected to Parliament in 1783, he was made SPEAKER OF THE HOUSE (1789–1801). In 1801 he was selected by GEORGE III to succeed William PITT as PRIME MINISTER. He opposed Catholic emancipation, favored a peace policy and repeal of the INCOME TAX, but when the Peace of Amiens failed, Pitt was returned to office in 1804. Addington was raised to the PEERAGE in 1805, and he served in various posts in the governments of the next 25 years. Home secretary during the radical agitations of 1819 and 1820, he is remembered for the notorious SIX ACTS (1819), the government's response to the PETERLOO MASSACRE (1819).

Addison, Joseph (1672–1719)
essayist, politician

Educated at Charterhouse and Queen's College, OXFORD UNIVERSITY, Addison was a distinguished classical scholar. A member of PARLIAMENT (1708) and a WHIG supporter, he wrote essays for *The Tatler,* published by Richard STEELE (1709–11), and together they published *The Spectator* (1711–12). These popular essays were reprinted many times until the 19th century. Upon the accession of GEORGE I, he returned to office with the Whigs.

Aden

Port city at the entrance to the Red Sea (now part of Yemen). Controlled by the Turkish Empire, it became a British base and a coaling station in 1839. Administered from INDIA, it was an important outpost connecting GREAT BRITAIN and its eastern colonies. It was made a crown COLONY in 1937. British forces were withdrawn in 1967, after a period of civil turmoil.

admiralty

The term is used for the court of law, established in the 14th century and dealing with maritime acts and merchant disputes on the basis of the civil (Roman) LAW. This aroused the hostility of the common lawyers, and maritime jurisdiction was gradually taken over by the COMMON LAW courts. While this legal shift was underway, English officers of state in the 17th century fashioned an Admiralty Board, a government department that had control over the naval forces of the Crown. The board was made up of "lords of the admiralty," the First Lord being a member of the CABINET. The admiralty board was paralleled by a NAVY board, responsible for the administration and maintenance of the fleet. The two boards were merged in 1832.

See also COURTS OF LAW; MERCANTILISM.

Afghan Wars

When Russian forces appeared to threaten the British colony in INDIA in the 19th century, the area of Afghanistan became a buffer zone. The first major violence was a British invasion in 1838, when nearly 20,000 British troops died. A second war in 1878 was caused by diplomatic rivalry and it produced a pro-British ruler. In 1919 the Afghan leaders asserted independence, and although British forces again imposed control, Afghanistan's sovereignty was recognized in 1921.

Africa

GREAT BRITAIN's relations with Africa fell into four distinct stages. The earliest involved contact with various coastal communities through the trading companies created during the reign of Queen ELIZABETH I in the 16th century. This contact expanded when British merchants joined in the SLAVE TRADE (Royal Africa Company, 1676). The second stage of territorial expansion began in the early 19th century when Britain seized the Dutch colony at the Cape of Good Hope; elsewhere, explorers and missionaries began to search the interior of the continent. The most aggressive phase began in the last quarter of the 19th century, when other European states were also busy carving out imperial holdings. Britain's main steps were to take control of EGYPT (1882), THE SUDAN (1898), and east-central Africa; and, after the BOER WAR (1899–1902), forming the Union of SOUTH AFRICA (1910) and the diamond- and gold-driven colony of Southern RHODESIA (1923). By the middle of the 20th century, Britain entered the final stage, the reluctant liberation of its African colonies (their former names are given in brackets) after WORLD WAR II, including Egypt (1952); Sudan (1956); [Gold Coast] GHANA (1957); NIGERIA (1960); SOMALIA (1960); TANGANYIKA (1961); South Africa (1961); UGANDA (1962); KENYA (1963); [ZANZIBAR and TANGANYIKA] TANZANIA (1963); [NYASALAND] MALAWI (1964); [Northern Rhodesia] ZAMBIA (1964); Southern Rhodesia (1965); THE GAMBIA (1965); [BECHUANALAND] BOTSWANA (1966); [BASUTOLAND] LESOTHO (1966); and SWAZILAND (1968).

See also ANTISLAVERY MOVEMENT; FASHODA; IMPERIALISM; ORANGE FREE STATE; RHODES, CECIL; ZULU.

Agincourt, Battle of (1415)

HENRY V led an army of 10,000 men to France in August 1415. He laid siege to the town of Harfleur, but it held out for more than a month. The French army (numbering nearly 20,000) tried to prevent the English from moving toward Calais and forced a battle on October 25. By this time, the English army was much reduced, but it still included about 5,000 archers. The French cavalry charged, but the two flanks of the English were manned by the archers, whose deadly fire killed large numbers of French knights. The victory opened the way for the conquest of Normandy and led to Henry's victory over France. This was the high point of the HUNDRED YEARS' WAR for England.

agricultural revolution

A conventional expression for the rapid technological changes that brought increased productivity to English agriculture in the 18th and 19th centuries. The term was coined as a companion to the INDUSTRIAL REVOLUTION, though recent research suggests that the duration and direction of agricultural changes do not fit well with the metaphor of revolution. The most important fact was the undeniable increase in food production, which helped to support a rapid increase in British population after 1760. The major elements of change were: new root crops, which allowed soil regeneration without LAND lying fallow;

improved livestock breeding; improved transport (especially canals and turnpikes); advances in land drainage; and ENCLOSURE of common land, bringing more land into cultivation.

See also COKE, THOMAS, EARL OF LEICESTER; YOUNG, ARTHUR.

air raids

The earliest attacks on Britain by air came with the ZEPPELIN raids on LONDON in WORLD WAR I. The fear of air power and its ability to destroy major cities was a pronounced theme between the two world wars. Air-raid precautions for civilians were initiated in the 1930s, including distribution of gas masks, construction of shelters, and organization of medical personnel and facilities for emergency use. On the military side, the construction of fighter aircraft and the invention of

Sir Winston Churchill tours the blitz-damaged streets in the city of London. *(Hulton/Archive)*

RADAR detection began to offset the prevailing view that "the bomber will always get through." The sustained German raids of 1940–44, including the assault on ROYAL AIR FORCE facilities and the bombing of cities (especially the London BLITZ between August 1940 and March 1941), tested these preparations. In the later stages of the war, German V-1 and V-2 rockets added a more frightening dimension to air warfare, although casualties were much lower. The British and American forces, for their part, launched a heavy bombing campaign against Germany that took many civilian lives, destroyed German industrial capacity, and set off a continuing debate over its contribution to the final victory.

See also DOWDING, HUGH; HARRIS, ARTHUR TRAVERS.

Aitken, Max   See BEAVERBROOK, MAX AITKEN, LORD.

Alamein, Battle of El (1942)

The first major British victory over German ground forces in WORLD WAR II. General Bernard MONTGOMERY had about twice the number of troops plus air superiority, while his German adversary General Rommel was faced with overstretched supply lines and forced to retreat 1,500 miles into Tunisia. Together with the Soviet victory at Stalingrad and the allied landings in North Africa, there now was a turn in the tide of war.

Alanbrooke, Alan Francis Brooke, first viscount
(1883–1963)

chief of the Imperial General Staff

Son of an Irish baronet, Alanbrooke studied in France and at the Royal Military Academy, Woolwich. He served as an artillery officer in Ireland, in India, and on the western front in WORLD WAR I. Commander of the air defense forces before WORLD WAR II, he took the high command of home forces in 1940, and became chief of the Imperial General Staff in 1941. His strategic vision and careful planning were a valuable antidote to the ambitious ideas of his civilian superior, Winston CHURCHILL.

Albany, dukes of

The Stewart family in SCOTLAND, unlike its English royal cousins, usually had a large supply of male descendants, though they were not always of full age when they inherited the throne. This assured rivals, regents, and presumptive heirs in abundance. Robert Stewart (1339–1420) was the uncrowned ruler of Scotland, 1388–1420 (during the reigns of Robert II, Robert III, and JAMES I), during which time he took the title Duke of Albany in 1398. The second duke, Murdac Stewart, succeeded his father, but was executed by King JAMES II in 1425. The dukedom was created again for that king's younger son, Alexander Stewart (1458). He in turn was forced to flee to France, but his son, John Stewart, took the title and acted as guardian for the infant JAMES V (1515–24).

Albemarle, George Monck, first duke of

See MONCK, GEORGE, FIRST DUKE OF ALBEMARLE

Albert, Prince (1819–1861)

prince consort of Queen Victoria

Prince of the German state of Saxe-Coburg Gotha, Albert was shy and studious. Introduced to Princess VICTORIA in 1836, they were engaged in 1839 and married in 1840. Initially he was as unattracted to his new home as he was unpopular with its inhabitants. PARLIAMENT reduced his allowance, and he was not granted the title of Prince until 1857. Unable to assert himself in politics to the degree he felt he was entitled, Albert took on a series of nongovernmental public functions: chairman of the Fine Arts Royal Commission; chancellor of CAMBRIDGE UNIVERSITY; and most notably, the organizer, in 1851, of the GREAT EXHIBITION of the Industrial Works of all Nations. He died of typhoid fever at the age of 42, and Queen Victoria went into prolonged mourning.

She withdrew from active political life, which may have reduced the power of the Crown or, alternatively, allowed democratic trends to proceed without serious friction.

Alexander of Tunis, Harold Rupert Leofric George Alexander, first earl (1891–1969)
military commander

Educated at Harrow and at the Royal Military College, Sandhurst, Alexander served in WORLD WAR I and WORLD WAR II. In 1940, with the BRITISH EXPEDITIONARY FORCE in France, he took part in the DUNKIRK evacuation. He took command of British forces in the Middle East in August 1942. The next year he was commander of the ground forces in the invasion of Sicily. In December 1943 he was appointed supreme allied commander of the forces in the Mediterranean and as such was responsible for the campaigns in Italy (1943–45). He served as governor-general of Canada from 1946 to 1952.

Allen, William (1532–1594)
cardinal, founder of Douai College

Educated at OXFORD UNIVERSITY, and head of St. Mary's Hall there (1556), Allen went into exile (1561) when the CHURCH OF ENGLAND was restored to Protestant governance by Queen ELIZABETH I. He returned to ENGLAND but fled again in 1565. He founded the College at Douai in Flanders to provide university education for English Catholics and to train priests who might lead the English back into the Roman church. He was made cardinal in 1587.

See also REFORMATION.

Allenby, Edmund Henry Hynman Allenby, first viscount (1861–1936)
soldier, administrator

Educated at Haileybury and Sandhurst, Allenby served in African campaigns, including the BOER WAR. During WORLD WAR I he led the cavalry divi-

sion in France in 1914 and took command of the Third Army there in 1915. In 1917 he was assigned to command the army in PALESTINE, where he led a victorious campaign against Turkish forces. After the war he served as high commissioner in EGYPT.

almshouses

Buildings designed to house the aged and infirm, established and maintained by monastic orders and later by private benefactors. Discipline, clothing, and religious observances were often spelled out in the founder's bequest, and the almshouse was typically designed to serve a specific community.

Amboyna massacre (1623)

English settlers were tortured and executed by Dutch authorities on an island in the Moluccas in 1623. The incident was one of many collisions between the European colonizers, and as a result the EAST INDIA COMPANY withdrew from competition in the spice trade, and its activities were redirected to the Indian subcontinent. This episode remained a sore point through the DUTCH WARS of the later 17th century.

American colonies
SETTLEMENT

English, Scottish, Welsh, and Irish settlers, merchants, and proprietors came in growing numbers to the eastern shores of North America and the islands of the WEST INDIES in the 17th century. Immigrants included religious exiles, traders, indentured servants, and African slaves. Their communities were organized under various royal grants of power which authorized provincial governments. The grants were made to trading companies and to powerful individuals, and from time to time, new royal charters were issued over the first century of settlement. From the point of view of the Crown, these profitable outposts were to provide timber for ships and consumable commodities such as tobacco, rice, and sugar. The trade established was regulated by principles of MERCANTILISM, so as to maximize the commercial strength of the British nation. This colonial production justified the military and naval forces, the protective trade legislation (NAVIGATION ACTS), and the substantial bureaucracy (BOARD OF TRADE) of His Majesty's government.

EXPANSION

The mainland colonial population grew rapidly in the 18th century (from about 500,000 in 1715 to 2 million in 1770), causing the expansion of colonial settlements. This movement resulted in clashes with native peoples and with the subjects of other colonial powers, especially France, whose colonists had made inroads from their landing areas in the North (Quebec) and the South (Louisiana). Colonial wars were the corollaries of great power conflicts, mainly among GREAT BRITAIN, France, Holland, and Spain. Britain enjoyed an emerging naval superiority over the course of the 18th century, an edge that was enhanced by her early and rapid industrial development. Eighteenth-century American colonial society saw the growth of urban centers, complex social organization, and increasing autonomy in many areas. The colonial governments had achieved *de facto* independence by the middle of the century. But in the view of most Westminster politicians, the subordinate position of colonies had barely changed.

CRISES

Divergent views of the position of the colonies showed clearly in the STAMP ACT crisis (1765–66), when the LONDON government introduced a new form of taxation in the colonies to defray the cost of defense and administration after the heavy expense of the SEVEN YEARS' WAR (1756–63). The quick repeal of the Stamp Act in response to colonial resistance indicated metropolitan weakness, which was only underscored by the provocative wording of the DECLARATORY ACT (1766), which stated that PARLIAMENT had "full power

and authority" to make laws for the colonies. The Stamp Act generated the first significant colonial political organization, and in the next decade further clashes occurred. The British government and the colonies feuded over collection of revenue, quartering of troops, and the basic powers of colonial institutions. The atmosphere became more heated by mob violence, a campaign of nonimportation, and the British suspension of colonial government.

REBELLION

After the colonists assembled a Continental Congress in 1774, the British government increased its military forces and declared a state of rebellion in 1775. The British evacuated BOSTON in 1776, and the colonists declared their independence. Although Britain faced the challenge of fighting over a great distance in dispersed areas, there was support from loyalists, and there was no assurance that the colonies could organize effective forces or that the colonists would agree to give their soldiers adequate resources.

When the American armies defeated the British at Saratoga in 1777, the colonies gained the support of France. British armies began a successful campaign in the southern colonies in 1778, but the colonial army won a key victory at YORKTOWN in 1781 and forced Britain to surrender.

See also COLONY; INTOLERABLE ACTS.

Amritsar massacre (1919)

In INDIA in April 1919, a crowd of demonstrators in the holy city of Amritsar refused to disperse. Troops led by Brigadier General Reginald Dyer were called to support police after several days of rioting over new security laws. Dyer ordered his troops to fire on the unarmed crowd, and after the ensuing panic there were 379 dead and 1,200 wounded, including women and children. An official inquiry censured Dyer's conduct, and he was forced to resign. The incident became a symbol of British misrule and helped to spur the Indian national movement.

Anderson, Elizabeth Garrett
(1836–1917)
physician, feminist

Taking inspiration from the WOMEN'S MOVEMENT, Anderson became the first woman in ENGLAND to qualify in medicine. Licensed as an apothecary in 1865, she opened a dispensary for women and children in LONDON in 1866, which later became the Elizabeth Garrett Anderson Hospital, fully staffed by women doctors and nurses.

Anglican

A term referring to the CHURCH OF ENGLAND, used especially from the late 17th century. The expression denotes the faith of the members of the church, as it was formed from the time of the REFORMATION. It ranges from the most conservative or high church position, which reveres the historic connections to the Catholic Church, to the low church or evangelical position, which admires the radical Protestant reforms of the 16th and 17th centuries. Due to the colonial expansion that began in that era, there is a worldwide Anglican communion recognizing the leadership of the ARCHBISHOP of CANTERBURY.

Anglo-Dutch Wars   See DUTCH WARS.

Anglo-Irish Treaty (1921)

The denouement of British rule in IRELAND came after years of open hostilities at the end of the WORLD WAR I. There was a burst of violence during the EASTER REBELLION in April 1916. That was followed by temporary martial law and prolonged military occupation before the Irish nationalists won a major electoral victory in 1918 and chose to stay in DUBLIN to form a provisional government. This provoked violent clashes and the formation of the IRISH REPUBLICAN ARMY later in 1919. The war of 1919–21 was more a series of raids and reactions, without any formal campaigning. British forces included the infamous BLACK AND TANS, pitted against the Irish republicans' armed guerilla fighters. During the fighting,

and due to the unease about the safety of the Protestant population in ULSTER, the British government passed a Government of Ireland Act in 1920 which included the basic features of the aborted Home Rule Act of 1914, plus separate governing provisions for Ulster. Thus a dominion-style parliament was opened in BELFAST, the ceremony presided over by GEORGE V in 1921.

By July 1921 a truce had been arranged in the South, and negotiations began in September. A treaty concluded in December 1921 created the IRISH FREE STATE. In January 1922 the Irish republicans split over ratification, the pro-treaty group winning by only a narrow margin in the DÁIL ÉIREANN. The ardent republicans regarded this as a sellout, and they attacked their former allies, launching a period of renewed internal bloodshed (1922–24). In those same years, the structure of an Irish republic began to take shape, and Ireland's partition became a harsh reality.

See also COLLINS, MICHAEL; DE VALERA, EAMON; LLOYD GEORGE, DAVID; SINN FÉIN.

Anne (1665–1714)
queen of England, Scotland, and Ireland, 1702–07,
queen of Great Britain and Ireland 1707–14

Queen Anne was the second of two daughters of James, duke of York (JAMES VII AND II) and his first wife, Anne Hyde. Her schooling was Protestant, and she married Prince George of Denmark in 1683. James in the meantime had married a Catholic princess and made clear his own religious preference. When he succeeded to the throne in 1685, Anne was out of favor; when William of Orange (William III) invaded England in 1688, Anne gave her support to him, and to her sister MARY II as the new queen. The relationship with the new court soured, and Anne was again out of favor. She did succeed in bearing a son in 1689, but he died in 1700. With no heir, in spite of 17 pregnancies, Anne had to agree to an Act of SETTLEMENT in 1701, stating that only a Protestant could assume the throne and laying out the acceptable line of succession should she fail to have an heir. She succeeded William to the throne the following year. During her reign Anne had to deal with major problems, from the continuing warfare with France and the treaty of UTRECHT to the recurring threat of invasion from the JACOBITES to the union of ENGLAND and SCOTLAND. She was a wise and capable manager of the many political factions and interests that flourished in this early age of WHIG and TORY party politics.

Anne Boleyn   See BOLEYN, ANNE.

Anne of Cleves   (1515–1557)
queen of England, 1540
In a marriage arranged by Thomas CROMWELL, Anne of Cleves became the fourth wife of HENRY VIII in January 1540. The marriage was meant to cement a Protestant alliance, but Henry rejected the alliance and his new queen because he found them both unattractive and unnecessary. Cromwell's policy was discredited, and he was arrested and executed in June 1540. Anne received a pension and lived the rest of her life in ENGLAND.

Anson, George Anson, baron (1697–1762)
naval commander, administrator
Trained in the naval service from 1712, Anson served during the long years of peace after the Treaty of UTRECHT. His great opportunity came when he led an expedition to attack Spanish shipping in the Pacific in the early 1740s. His fleet was decimated, but he was able to capture a fabulous treasure and returned, after circumnavigating the globe, to receive rapid promotion and a PEERAGE. He played an important role in leading naval development before the SEVEN YEARS' WAR, as First Lord of the ADMIRALTY in 1751–56 and 1757–62.

Anti-Corn Law League
The CORN LAWS were protective tariffs on grain, which measures came under criticism by the new economists of the early 19th century. The laws had been passed to protect the landed interests from fluctuating prices for grain, and they restricted imports when prices fell. Such regulation encouraged the cultivation of marginal LAND during the NAPOLEONIC WARS, while it deprived consumers of the possibility of low prices. In 1838 a group of manufacturers, economists, and radicals began an organized campaign to repeal the corn laws. Led by Richard COBDEN and John BRIGHT, the League was a prototype for modern pressure groups. At the time, such concerted activity by persons "out of doors" was regarded as improper, if not faintly seditious. After years of organized meetings, publications, and petitions to PARLIAMENT, the corn laws were repealed in 1846. However, the repeal was the result of a decision by Prime Minister Robert PEEL, one of the League's great enemies, taken during the crisis of the IRISH FAMINE.

See also FREE TRADE; MERCANTILISM; RADICALISM.

antislavery movement
Opposition to the enslavement of Africans and to the SLAVE TRADE, which carried the human cargo to the Western Hemisphere, became a significant phenomenon in the second half of the 18th century. Led by evangelical Christians like Granville SHARP, Thomas CLARKSON, and William WILBERFORCE, committees were formed to oppose the slave trade, petitions were presented to PARLIAMENT, and numerous pamphlets were written and distributed. By 1807 this effort produced a vote to abolish the trade in the BRITISH EMPIRE. Then the movement turned to the abolition of slavery, and an Anti-Slavery Society was formed in the 1820s. The government that took office after the reform act of 1832 passed an act abolishing slavery in 1833.

See also SIERRA LEONE; SOMERSET CASE; WEST INDIES.

Appeal, Court of
A branch of the Supreme Court of Judicature created in 1873. At first it was only a civil court, but in 1966 the Court of CRIMINAL APPEAL was

merged with it, creating a body with two divisions. The civil division hears appeals from the HIGH COURT OF JUSTICE and the criminal division hears appeals from persons convicted in the CROWN COURT. The judges are the LORD CHANCELLOR (and any previous chancellors), the LORD CHIEF JUSTICE, the MASTER OF THE ROLLS, the president of the family division of the high court, and the lords justices of appeal. Appeals from the court of appeal may be heard by the HOUSE OF LORDS appellate committees.

appeasement

In the 1930s several countries, notably Germany, Italy, and Japan, were intent on changing the terms of the postwar settlements of the 1920s. Appeasement refers to a broad policy of accommodation of these regimes, a policy meant to defuse tension, but one that ultimately encouraged more aggressive behavior. British and French leaders were foremost in pursuing this policy, particularly evident in the years 1936–39. Adolf Hitler's Germany reoccupied the demilitarized zone west of the Rhine, and there was no attempt to stop him (nor was it clear how that might be done, as the zone was within German territory). Benito Mussolini's Fascist government in Italy launched an invasion of Ethiopia, and there was an Anglo-French agreement to ignore the aggression. In 1937 Japan invaded China, and again the Western states did not intercede militarily. In 1938 Hitler occupied Austria in an unopposed annexation (*Anschluss*). Then he proclaimed that Germans in the borderlands of Czechoslovakia (the Sudetenland) were entitled to join Germany. In September 1938 in a meeting in Munich, Neville CHAMBERLAIN, French premier Edouard Daladier, Mussolini, and Hitler met to resolve the issue. The Munich Agreement called for the transfer of the disputed territory to Germany, which meant the loss of major frontier installations and the neutralizing of a significant army. This agreement, adopted by the British and French, was followed six months later by the German annexation of the rest of the Czech state. Another six months later, Hitler and Stalin signed

a nonaggression pact, which appeasement preceded Hitler's invasion of Poland. This last, perhaps more than any other step, received the scorn of critics who blamed the outbreak of WORLD WAR II on the concessions made to the aggressor states.

apprenticeship

The period of contractual agreement between a master and an apprentice, in which the latter was trained in the skills of a trade, usually for a period of seven years, for a premium paid to the master. When completed, the new journeyman might be employed by others, or set up on his own as a master. This structure was fostered in the medieval and early modern periods by major GUILDS, or associations of craftsmen and skilled workers. It was subject to the governance of local guilds and to national regulation, such as the Statute of Artificers of 1563. Apprenticeship declined as the nature of work changed with the INDUSTRIAL REVOLUTION, and the nature of schooling was broadened and made mandatory in the 19th century.

Arch, Joseph (1826–1919)
agricultural labor leader

Born into a farmworkers' family, Arch was a lay preacher and the founder of the National Agricultural Labourers' Union in 1872. He led a strike of farmworkers in 1874, by which time his union numbered 80,000. The strike failed, but he continued to agitate, especially for votes for farmworkers. That goal (votes for all adult males) was achieved in 1884, and in 1885 he was elected to PARLIAMENT, the first farmworker to sit as a MEMBER OF PARLIAMENT. Defeated the next year, he won again in 1892 and served until 1902.

archbishop

Church official presiding over a province, i.e., a group of dioceses, each headed by a BISHOP. There are two provinces in the CHURCH OF ENGLAND: CANTERBURY and York. There was no archbishop for WALES (the jurisdiction falling to Canterbury). IRELAND had four archbishops in the 12th century, reduced to two in the 1830s. SCOTLAND had no archbishop until the end of the 15th century, when four were created. They lost their authority in the reformation of 1560, but it was intermittently restored until 1690, when a PRESBYTERIAN order was established. After the REFORMATION there were no Roman Catholic archbishops recognized by secular authority in the British Isles until the creation of the archbishop of Westminster in 1850.

archdeacon

The chief lieutenant of a BISHOP in his diocese, overseeing many of the duties of administration. Historically the archdeacon presided in the lowest and busiest of the church courts.

Argyle (Argyll), earls of See CAMPBELL FAMILY.

Arkwright, Sir Richard (1732–1792)
inventor, manufacturer

The son of a laborer in Preston, Arkwright was apprenticed to a barber and established his own business in Bolton, but he gave that up for a career as an inventor. Together with John KAY he invented the water frame, a spinning machine using rollers that was powered by horses or by water (patented 1769). His work encountered opposition from workers and from rival manufacturers. The former destroyed one of his mills, and the latter brought legal action to destroy his patent. He continued his work and is recognized as a pioneer in factory organization and in the foundation of the Lancashire cotton industry.

Armada, Spanish

In 1588 Philip II of Spain launched an unprecedented invasion of ENGLAND. His *armada católica* was partly aimed at the overthrow of the heretic

The Spanish Armada attacked by the English navy *(Hulton/Archive)*

queen ELIZABETH I; at the same time it would end the English threat to Spanish treasure fleets from America and reinforce Spanish influence in the Netherlands. Nearly 140 ships and 24,000 men of the Spanish fleet were supposed to rendezvous with an army of similar size in the Netherlands, move across the channel, and invade southern England. The English countered with a fleet of about 200, only 34 being warships of the royal NAVY. They could not prevent the progress of the enemy up the English channel and only annoyed them with their more effective long-range gunnery. When the Spanish fleet anchored at Calais, prior to the expected rendezvous, the English sent a number of fireships into their formation at night. The Spanish were forced to disperse, and the following day a long and costly sea battle left the armada in disarray. The remaining Spanish vessels sailed to the north and around the shores of the British Isles, losing many ships on the stormy journey down the coast of IRELAND. This extraordinary campaign failed because of weather and inadequate logistics, but that did not prevent the English (and others) from seeing providential signs and using the outcome to boost national spirit.

Arminian

Early in the reign of ELIZABETH I the English church showed considerable Calvinist influence, especially in the doctrine of predestination, that one was saved by God's will, regardless of human choice. An influential Dutch theologian, Jacobus Arminius, argued against this doctrine, and similar views became increasingly prominent in ENGLAND by the end of the 16th century. Though there was no formal connection, those members of the CHURCH OF ENGLAND who held these beliefs were labeled "arminians." By the accession of CHARLES I (1625), the so-called Arminian influence was very powerful in the church's hierarchy. In fact, the beliefs of Archbishop William LAUD and others were part of an older, authoritarian, Catholic tradition, which

was never extinguished and became one of the major issues in the rebellion of the 1640s.

armistice

As German forces fell back toward the frontier with France in October 1918, the German general Ludendorff advised Kaiser Wilhelm to sue for peace. The Kaiser abdicated and sought asylum in Holland, while a provisional German government negotiated the terms of armistice, formally ending WORLD WAR I at the 11th hour of the 11th day of the 11th month (November 1918).

army

From the earliest times there were twin sources of military manpower in ENGLAND: a militia based on a general obligation of service to the Crown (the Assize of Arms of 1181 is perhaps the earliest formal statement); plus an elite warrior group, an armed aristocracy with ancient roots. The modern royal army traces its origins to the time of the restoration of CHARLES II in 1660, when the king had a small permanent body of troops, containing officers and units and doctrines left over from the NEW MODEL ARMY of the later 1640s, which had defeated the king's father.

In the 18th century the British army was strictly limited in resources, in part because of civilian fear of a powerful standing army— another legacy of the CIVIL WAR. Thus the military record, and the military role in the society, were quite different from other European states. Typically the British fought wars with a powerful NAVY and a small army augmented by mercenaries from allied states who received British subsidies. This applied in varied ways to European and colonial wars. In fact, the largest British army in the 19th century was the one taken over from the EAST INDIA COMPANY in 1858.

Warfare in the 20th century transformed this pattern, as Britain resorted to conscripts in 1916 and 1939. The mass armed forces and the collateral mobilization of society and the economy were general in the two world wars, as was the urge to demobilize as rapidly as possible. But in both cases, international threats appeared to make a return to the old policy too risky. In the 1940s compulsory NATIONAL SERVICE was kept as a general source of military manpower and only dropped in 1960.

Arnold, Matthew (1822–1888)
poet, critic

Son of Thomas ARNOLD, the famous headmaster at Rugby School, Matthew Arnold was educated at Winchester and at OXFORD UNIVERSITY. Although a professor of poetry there (1857–67), he was better known as a social critic. An inspector of schools, he advocated secondary education reform, some of his inspiration coming from continental tours of schools. A religious liberal, he became a prominent critic of Victorian society in general. His major work was *Culture and Anarchy* (1869), in which he saw English society as materialistic and overly proud of its assumed superiority.

Arnold, Thomas (1795–1842)
schoolmaster

Educated at Winchester and OXFORD UNIVERSITY, Arnold was vicar of a parish in Middlesex before becoming headmaster at Rugby School in 1828. He was known for his special enthusiasm and sense of duty, both in sermons and in sports, which became a hallmark of Victorian schooling. His school was the model for the Tom Hughes novel *Tom Brown's Schooldays* (1857). He was the father of poet Matthew ARNOLD.

Ascham, Roger (1515–1568)
scholar, educator

Educated at CAMBRIDGE UNIVERSITY, Ascham became one of the leading authorities on classical languages. He was tutor to princess ELIZABETH I and EDWARD VI. He served in embassies in Germany and in Venice and was Latin secretary under Queen MARY I. His book *The Schoolmaster, or*

Plain and Perfect Way of Teaching Children the Latin Tongue (1570) was widely used for generations.

Ashanti

A West African native empire; in the later 18th century it expanded and came into contact with British coastal communities. Conflict broke out in 1824 with an Ashanti victory. After a settlement, there was strife again in 1863. British forces sent to Africa destroyed the Ashanti capital and claimed the territory as a Crown COLONY. Further resistance by the Ashanti during the competition for empire led to their total defeat by the British in 1901.

Aske, Robert (unknown–1537)
rebel leader

A Yorkshire gentleman and a LONDON lawyer (a fellow of Gray's Inn), Aske was a leader in the PILGRIMAGE OF GRACE, the protest ignited by the DISSOLUTION of the monasteries in 1536. A first outbreak in Lincolnshire was followed by another in Yorkshire. Aske negotiated with Thomas HOWARD, duke of Norfolk, and King HENRY VIII promised pardons and an audience in which he would address the grievances of the protesters. When another disturbance began in 1537, Aske was implicated, arrested on charges of treason, and executed at York.

Asquith, Herbert Henry, first earl of Oxford and Asquith (1852–1928)
prime minister, 1908–16

An orphan from a modest background, Asquith was educated at OXFORD UNIVERSITY, became a barrister, and in 1886 entered PARLIAMENT. A rising member of the LIBERAL PARTY, he fell out with the leadership over their opposition to the BOER WAR, but he regained respect by campaigning against tariff reform in 1903, and he became the heir apparent in 1905 when he was appointed CHANCELLOR OF THE EXCHEQUER. He became PRIME MINISTER in 1908 and presided over important domestic reforms: old-age pensions, increased taxation on the wealthy, reform of the HOUSE OF LORDS, and a pioneer program of NATIONAL INSURANCE. Asquith's government also resisted the efforts of the WOMEN'S MOVEMENT; had a troubled relationship with the labor movement and could not contain the emerging LABOUR PARTY; and found its parliamentary majority dependent on support of the Irish Nationalists, prompting the introduction of the third IRISH HOME RULE bill in 1912.

In foreign affairs, Asquith's time in office coincided with an escalating arms race with Germany, intensified nationalist rivalry in the Balkans, and the awkward ending of GREAT BRITAIN's diplomatic isolation. In the crisis of 1914, Britain was unsure of her role, but when WORLD WAR I began, and German troops marched into neutral Belgium, Asquith was able to rally his government to the side of France and Russia with only two CABINET members resigning. He led the British government for the first half of the war, but in late 1916, with mounting dissatisfaction over both the war and domestic politics, he was replaced as prime minister by his former colleague David LLOYD GEORGE, who had allied with the CONSERVATIVE PARTY to oust him. This bit of skulduggery so alienated Asquith that he led an angry section of the LIBERAL PARTY in opposition to the new government. He continued this opposition after the war, perhaps fatally dividing the party and making way for Labour to replace it as the second major party by 1924.

assize

Originally the term applied to any sitting of a court and to the pronouncements of some of those courts. From the 13th century it was connected to the regular circuits of royal judges through the English counties, where civil and criminal cases were heard. Criminal cases were presented by a GRAND JURY, and the matter was tried before a petty JURY. Some cases were transferred to judges sitting in Westminster while others were decided locally. The result was a

fairly efficient system of centralized but local justice. It was finally abolished in 1971.

See also COURTS OF LAW; NISI PRIUS.

association movement

In the 18th century, landowners and gentlemen concerned over perceived inefficiencies and corruption in elections and government formed county associations and petitioned PARLIAMENT for fiscal and electoral reform. Christopher WYVILL and the Yorkshire Association made the first such appeal in 1780, and a reform convention met in 1781. Some of the momentum for the movement came from discontent over the loss of the AMERICAN COLONIES, but the larger impulse for reform continued and assumed different forms in the 19th century, even though many of the same ideas remained strong.

See also ECONOMICAL REFORM; REFORM ACTS.

Astor, Nancy, Lady (1879–1964)
politician

Lady Astor was the American wife of Waldorf Astor, a Conservative MP who succeeded to a PEERAGE in 1919. She ran in the subsequent by-election for his constituency and became the first woman to sit in PARLIAMENT (1919–45). An outspoken campaigner for women's causes and for temperance, she was also a supporter of APPEASEMENT, though not a supporter of Hitler's Germany. The family estate at CLIVEDEN became a meeting place and symbol of the appeasers.

Atlantic, Battle of the (1940–1943)

As WORLD WAR II began, German submarines made British shipping highly vulnerable; their U-boats developed a "wolf pack" technique, where numbers of subs attacked convoys. Decoding of German orders helped to disrupt the attacks, but German successes mounted to a critical level in 1942. In 1943 massive new ship construction from America, plus improved tactics and weapons (longer-range aircraft, better detection, and more effective depth charges) enabled the allied forces to turn the tide in the Atlantic.

Atlantic Charter (1941)

The incipient alliance between GREAT BRITAIN and the United States took a step forward when President Franklin Roosevelt and Prime Minister Winston CHURCHILL held an unannounced meeting on warships off Newfoundland in August 1941. Since the United States was not yet at war, the idea of a top-level meeting with the leader of a belligerent state was a sensitive issue in America, where sentiment for remaining neutral was still strong. Although the senior military staff on both sides engaged in talks, the public product of the meeting was a "charter" of common political principles: opposition to aggression, freedom for people to organize their own governments, and freedom of expression.

atom bomb

During WORLD WAR II nuclear fission was applied to the manufacture of bombs of enormous power. Although German scientists had made some progress in this area, an American and British team was successful in an intense research effort, code-named the Manhattan Project. The atom bombs produced were dropped in two raids on Japan in August 1945, forcing that country to surrender. After the war, both countries developed peacetime uses for NUCLEAR ENERGY, and both were caught up in spy fervor, as the Soviet Union tried to obtain scientific information to aid its own program of weapon development. In October 1952 GREAT BRITAIN successfully detonated its first atom bomb.

See also CAMPAIGN FOR NUCLEAR DISARMAMENT.

attainder

Form of punishment by an ACT OF PARLIAMENT, in which the party convicted suffers loss of life, with property forfeited to the Crown, and heirs disinherited. Used extensively in the late 15th century, it was less common in the 17th century. JACOBITES were sometimes punished in this way, and attainder was last used was in the case of Lord Edward FITZGERALD in 1798. The procedure was abolished in 1870.

Atterbury, Francis (1663–1732)
Tory scholar, bishop

Educated at Westminster and at Christ Church, OXFORD UNIVERSITY, Atterbury was a leading member of the university and opposed the efforts of JAMES VII AND II to introduce Catholic fellows. But by the time he was bishop of Rochester (1713) he was driven to extreme JACOBITE positions by the tyranny of one-party WHIG rule. His enemies exposed his machinations in 1723, and for the so-called Atterbury plot he was exiled by PARLIAMENT's enactment of a bill of pains and penalties.

Attlee, Clement Richard Attlee, first earl (1883–1967)
prime minister, 1945–1951

Educated at OXFORD UNIVERSITY, Attlee prepared for the law but gave that up to work for the poor. After serving with distinction in WORLD WAR I, he became Labour mayor of Stepney in 1919, and entered PARLIAMENT in 1922. He became leader of the LABOUR PARTY in 1935, and when Winston CHURCHILL took office as PRIME MINISTER in 1940, Attlee joined his coalition cabinet. In 1942 he became deputy prime minister in charge of domestic affairs. At the end of WORLD WAR II, Attlee led his party in the election campaign against the war hero Churchill and won an overwhelming victory. Labour promised the electorate social reforms, which had tremendous appeal after the misery of the DEPRESSION and the war. The new government brought about major changes including NATIONAL INSURANCE, the NATIONAL HEALTH SERVICE and NATIONALIZATION of large sectors of the economy. Attlee led his party to a narrow victory in 1950, followed by a loss to Churchill in 1951. He resigned as party leader in 1955.

attorney

The representative of parties in lawsuits. In the medieval Court of COMMON PLEAS the staff of attorneys was barred from the INNS OF COURT, whose members became BARRISTERS. The office of attorney was ended in the reform of the courts in 1873. The title of Attorney General is given to the senior law officer of the Crown, a post with legal and political significance, assisted by the Solicitor General.

Attwood, Thomas (1783–1856)
economist, political reformer

An advocate of currency reform, especially the use of paper money, Attwood founded the Birmingham Political Union in 1830 as a vehicle for political reform. This body helped to spur the first major parliamentary reform in 1832. In the election of that year, Attwood was chosen as MEMBER OF PARLIAMENT for Birmingham. In 1839 he introduced the petition from the Chartists, which was rejected by the HOUSE OF COMMONS.

See also CHARTIST MOVEMENT; REFORM ACTS.

Aubrey, John (1626–1697)
biographer, antiquarian

A gentleman interested in antiquities, Aubrey was elected to the ROYAL SOCIETY in 1663. He studied the sites of Stonehenge and Avebury and helped to compile *The Antiquities of Oxford* in 1674. He also wrote a series of *Brief Lives*, published in the 19th century and in expanded form in 1949. These became the classic descriptions of many notable 17th-century figures.

Auchinleck, Sir Claude (1884–1981)
general

Commander in chief in the Middle East in 1941, Auchinleck engaged the German forces led by General Rommel and was nearly beaten in 1942. Winston CHURCHILL lacked confidence in his leadership, and though Auchinleck stopped Rommel at El Alamein, in August 1942 Churchill replaced him with generals Harold ALEXANDER and Bernard MONTGOMERY. Auchinleck later served as commander in chief of the army in INDIA.

Augmentations, Court of

With the DISSOLUTION of the monasteries, their revenues were taken over by this new government department in 1536, channeled into the royal financial system, and merged with the EXCHEQUER in 1554.

Austen, Jane (1775–1817)
novelist

The daughter of a country parson, Austen used portrayals of the lives of the gentry she knew firsthand to examine human nature. She composed and revised her first novel, *Sense and Sensibility,* in the 1790s, but it was not published until 1811. Other works similarly written and revised appeared over the next seven years: *Pride and Prejudice* (1813); *Mansfield Park* (1814); *Emma* (1816); and *Northanger Abbey* and *Persuasion* (1818), the latter two published posthumously. Her work received a mixed reception, but by the late 19th century she had attained the popularity her writing still enjoys.

Austin, Herbert (1866–1941)
automobile manufacturer

Austin attended Rotheram Grammar School and Brampton College and in 1884 went to Australia, where he worked in manufacturing. He returned to England in 1893 and produced a three-wheeled motor car, the "Wolseley," in 1895. He founded the Austin Motor Company in 1905, and in the first year of production the company produced 120 cars. The company aimed at a large general market, and by 1939 it was producing over 75,000 cars at the Longbridge site near Birmingham.

Australia

Occupying the smallest of the world's seven continents, modern Australia is composed of six federated states (New South Wales, Tasmania, Victoria, Queensland, Western Australia, South Australia). Populated for thousands of years by aboriginal peoples, the land was claimed for BRITAIN by Captain James COOK in 1770. The first British settlement was in 1788, when a fleet transporting convicts entered BOTANY BAY. This mode of settlement continued for about 80 years and totalled some 160,000 persons by the time it was abolished in 1867. Meanwhile, ordinary immigration gradually increased. At first the area's economy was not promising, but in the early 19th century the prospects were improved by the herding of sheep and export of wool. The exploration and development of the continent were propelled by the discovery of gold in 1851, which brought a significant increase in immigration.

The political institutions in the colonies soon developed democratic features. With male suffrage and secret ballot by the 1850s, and paid legislators as early as 1870, the institutions of the frontier society reflected its more open and enterprising economy. By the end of the century the colonies agreed (by referendum) to establish a federation, the Commonwealth of Australia (1901). That government remained a loyal part of the British Commonwealth as one of its new DOMINIONS. Political, diplomatic, and cultural ties with Britain remained strong through the great wars of the 20th century, but by the end of the century Australia was pursuing more independent policies.

Austrian Succession, War of (1740–1748)

When Frederick the Great of Prussia invaded Silesia in 1740, he violated the diplomatic guarantee of the Austrian throne occupied by Empress Maria Theresa. BRITAIN and Holland had pledged to support Austria; some in Britain, including King GEORGE II, were more worried about the power of France; and Britain was already fighting Spain in the War of JENKINS' EAR. With Austrian and Dutch allies, the British fought against France in the Low Countries. They provided financial aid to the Austrians fighting in Italy and in central Europe, but the greatest British victories came against French naval forces. The conflict ended with the Treaty of Aix-la-Chapelle in 1748. Prussia kept Silesia, and Austria retained imperial precedence for the Empress and her husband. Otherwise the eight years of conflict and the deaths of nearly half a million had been to little avail in terms of European politics. In British politics, the years of war saw the fall of Robert WALPOLE and other ministers, and the conflict coincided with the 1745 rebellion of the JACOBITES at home. It confirmed the general British foreign policy of supporting allies with subsidies while relying mainly on British maritime strength.

Avon, first earl of See EDEN, ANTHONY, FIRST EARL OF AVON.

B

Babington, Anthony (1561–1586)
conspirator

A Derbyshire gentleman from a Catholic family, Babington traveled in Europe and assisted missionaries to ENGLAND. A supporter of MARY, QUEEN OF SCOTS, he engaged in a plot to kill Queen ELIZABETH I. He was trapped by Sir Francis WALSINGHAM, Elizabeth's principal secretary, who used agents to infiltrate the conspirators and intercept correspondence. Babington was executed, and the plot's exposure convinced Elizabeth to bring Mary to trial.

backbencher

Term applied to a MEMBER OF PARLIAMENT who sits at the rear of the facing tiers of benches in the HOUSE OF COMMONS, the front rank of which is reserved for the leaders of the government and the opposition. Backbenchers are rank-and-file MPs who are not likely to achieve power themselves and are often critical of their own party leaders.

Engraving of Francis Bacon, Viscount St. Albans *(Library of Congress)*

Bacon, Francis, viscount St. Albans (1561–1626)
lawyer, philosopher

Son of Nicholas Bacon, lawyer and longtime royal servant, Francis Bacon studied at Trinity College, CAMBRIDGE UNIVERSITY, and subsequently at Gray's Inn. He pursued a political career in addition to his work in the law and his study and writing in philosophy. With the accession of JAMES I, he held a series of official posts: solicitor general in 1607, attorney general in 1613, and lord chancellor in 1618. His career in office was ruined by IMPEACHMENT on bribery charges in 1621. His published works include *Essays* (1597), *Advancement of Learning* (1605) and *Novum Organum* (1620). Bacon was a pioneer in scientific study in both practical and theoretical terms. The inductive method of careful observation of natural phenomena would remain a fundamental approach in scientific research. Some have speculated that Bacon was the author of William SHAKESPEARE's plays, a theory that appeared in the 19th century, based on the playwright's plebian background as well as the philosopher's acknowledged genius. This attribution still has its defenders, but most Shakespeare scholars do not share this view.

Baden-Powell of Gilwell, Robert Stephenson Smyth Baden-Powell, first baron (1857–1941)
founder of the Boy Scouts
A soldier since 1876, Baden-Powell specialized in reconnaissance. He developed training methods on duty in India and published *Aids to Scouting* in 1899. He fought in the BOER WAR and was instrumental in the victory at the siege of Mafeking. A hero to the British public, he went on to found the BOY SCOUTS in 1908 and the GIRL GUIDES in 1909.

Bagehot, Walter (1826–1877)
journalist
Educated at the University of London, Bagehot became the editor of *The Economist* in 1860. He is particularly noted for his book *The English Constitution,* published in 1867. Unlike other 19th-century writers on English institutions, his work analyzed the current operation of government, in its actual as opposed to theoretical powers and procedures.

bail
An arrested person may be released from custody on the condition he or she will appear for trial or further proceeding. This release on bail is granted at the discretion of a magistrate and upon an assurance given by persons known as sureties for the prisoner; or, more often, by a promise to provide monetary or other payment if the defendant does not appear.

bailiff
A medieval term for an official, often the agent for a lord, in a MANOR or BOROUGH. In Scotland a "bailie" was a senior councillor in a BURGH corporation. In modern terms, a bailiff is an agent of a COUNTY COURT.

balance of power
This expression refers to power relations between the states of Europe, particularly the idea that no one state or group of states should dominate the continent. It was often used by British statesmen to justify policies of assistance or intervention.

Baldwin of Bewdley, Stanley Baldwin, first earl (1867–1947)
prime minister, 1923–1924, 1924–1929, 1935–1937
Educated at CAMBRIDGE UNIVERSITY, Baldwin worked in the family ironworks. Upon his father's death, he stood for his seat in PARLIAMENT in 1908. He served with David LLOYD GEORGE in the coalition governments of WORLD WAR I, but Baldwin helped to topple Lloyd George in 1922. He became PRIME MINISTER in 1923, called an election the following year, and lost the CONSERVATIVE PARTY majority, thus allowing the formation of a (minority) LABOUR PARTY government, the first of its kind. He returned to office in 1924 after winning the next election with a majority of over 200 MPs in the HOUSE OF COMMONS. While historians have not considered him a leader of high intellect or powerful will, Baldwin successfully presided over a party with many rivalries and strong personalities.

Balfour, Arthur James, first earl (1848–1930)
prime minister, 1902–1905
Balfour entered PARLIAMENT in 1874 and served as head of the Local Government Board (1885), SECRETARY OF STATE for SCOTLAND (1886), and chief secretary for IRELAND (1887–91). The nickname "Bloody Balfour" came from his policy of suppressing of rural violence in Ireland, but he also applied a policy of social change, through sale of LAND to tenants and support for economic improvements.

Balfour's uncle, Lord SALISBURY, was PRIME MINISTER for most of the period 1885–1902 and seemed to be grooming his nephew for that position. Balfour was an intellectual and not a great orator or parliamentarian. When he took office in 1902, the BOER WAR was ending, and there was rising debate over TARIFF reform and over a cluster of social issues (rights of workers, women, and the Irish). At the 1906 election, his CONSERVATIVE PARTY was resoundingly defeated, and he was forced to resign as party leader in 1911 after an ineffective spell as leader of the opposition. However, he returned to office in 1915 as part of the wartime coalition government, served as foreign secretary (1916–19) and wrote the famous BALFOUR DECLARATION (1917), which outlined the British government's commitment to support a Jewish homeland in PALESTINE.

Balfour Declaration (1917)

In 1917, with British forces attempting to control the Middle East in the final stages of WORLD WAR I, and with pressure mounting to gain support from as wide a population as possible, the British government authorized the foreign secretary, Arthur BALFOUR, to announce GREAT BRITAIN'S endorsement of the concept of a national home in PALESTINE for the Jewish people. This was to be achieved without prejudice to the rights of the inhabitants of Palestine. The terms of the declaration were incorporated in the mandate of the LEAGUE OF NATIONS establishing British control of Palestine after the war.

Ball, John (d. 1381)
priest, rebel leader

A leader of the PEASANTS' REVOLT of 1381, Ball was an itinerant preacher who had been imprisoned in Kent. The rebels had opened the prisons on their way to LONDON to protest against a POLL TAX and other grievances. Ball joined them and preached to them. When the revolt collapsed, he was tried and executed.

Ballot Act (1872)

In 1872 the secret ballot was introduced for local and national elections. It had been one of the original demands of the Chartists (see CHARTIST MOVEMENT), but there was strong LIBERAL PARTY opposition to the measure, as it was deemed less honest than open voting. However, recent scandals in which farm tenants were punished for voting the "wrong way" in open elections, especially in a case in Wales, brought more pressure to pass the act. The act was most influential in Ireland, where voters became able to freely support nationalist candidates.

Baltimore, George Calvert, first baron (1580–1632)
founder of Maryland

A MEMBER OF PARLIAMENT and SECRETARY OF STATE, Lord Baltimore resigned upon announcing his conversion to Catholicism. In 1632 he received a grant of rights to land in the north of Virginia from CHARLES I. Maryland was named after the king's Catholic wife, Henrietta Maria. Baltimore wanted the colony to practice toleration in the hopes of encouraging Catholic immigration. He died before visiting his new land, and the colony's administration passed to his sons.

Bancroft, Richard (1544–1610)
archbishop of Canterbury

Promoted to BISHOP of LONDON in 1597 and ARCHBISHOP of CANTERBURY in 1604, Bancroft was a strong supporter of the hierarchical government of the CHURCH OF ENGLAND. He stoutly opposed the PRESBYTERIANS, and aided in the prosecution of some of their leaders. He helped the efforts of Archbishop WHITGIFT in restoring conformity, supported the publication of the canons of the church, and assisted JAMES VI AND I at the HAMPTON COURT CONFERENCE in the year he was made archbishop.

Bangladesh

A Muslim republic, Bangladesh was recognized as a member of the Commonwealth in 1972. It was formerly East Pakistan and, before 1947, part of Bengal province. It is the most populous

East Asian state, with over 71 million people in an area less than that of England and Wales. A succession of military dictatorships interrupted political development, and floods and famine cost an estimated 5 million lives in the first two decades of independence.

Bank of England

In 1694 PARLIAMENT established the Bank of England to aid in underwriting the costs of warfare with France. A joint-stock company, the bank bought government securities and was allowed to issue its notes as legal tender. It became the state's central financial institution over the next century, and its position was formalized by the Bank Charter Act of 1844. In 1946 the bank was taken into public ownership; it was privatized in 1998.

Baptists

One of the main groups of Protestant dissenters, the Baptists believed that only adults should be baptized, since only they could understand the ceremony. Their first group formed in 1612 in LONDON. Their numbers grew rapidly in the 19th century, even as the congregation divided between those favoring Calvinist ideals and those favoring the UNITARIANS.

Barbados

This easternmost Caribbean island was uninhabited until settled by the English in 1627. By 1660 the colonists had established sugar plantations worked by slave labor. It became a crown COLONY in 1662 and an independent member of the COMMONWEALTH in 1966. It is the most densely populated Caribbean island, with more than 250,000 people in an area of 166 square miles.

Barnardo, Thomas (1845–1905)
philanthropist
Active in the evangelist movement of the 1860s, Barnardo worked as a medical missionary and in 1867 founded the first of a number of homes for impoverished and neglected children. In the 1880s he began a program of sending children to CANADA. His work resulted in the rescue of nearly 60,000 children in his lifetime, and Dr. Barnardo's Homes continue to help homeless and deprived children today.

Barnet, Battle of (1471)

A critical battle in the Wars of the ROSES. King EDWARD IV had been expelled from the kingdom by his onetime supporter and "kingmaker," the earl of WARWICK. Edward returned, landing near Hull, and met Warwick's army north of London. At first the earl's forces had the advantage, but the tide turned against them and Warwick was killed. Edward followed this victory with an even greater one at TEWKESBURY and secured his hold on power.

baron

Title of nobility introduced by the Normans to describe the more important vassals of the king. A baron had a military rank and attended royal councils, which by the 13th century included PARLIAMENT. In the 14th century more senior titles were created, and the baron became the lowest rank in the developing PEERAGE. The rank of baron was employed when the practice of creating life peers was first used for judges in the 19th century, and for life peers generally after they were authorized by an act in 1958.

baronet

A special order created by JAMES VI AND I in 1611. The baronet was a hereditary knighthood, which title was purchased from the Crown. At first only an English dignity, the Irish baronet was created in 1619 and the Scottish in 1625. As commoners, baronets might sit in the HOUSE OF COMMONS.

Barrett, Elizabeth   See BROWNING, ROBERT.

barrister

A lawyer allowed to plead before the royal courts of COMMON LAW. This regulated status originated in the 16th century and was conferred after attendance at the INNS OF COURT. Selected members of this group were designated as King's (or Queen's) Counsel (KC or QC).

Basutoland

Mountainous territory in southern Africa inhabited by tribes that had fled the ZULU and then had troubled relations with the CAPE COLONY and the Boer (Dutch) settlers. The first attempt to seize their land was in 1856. After the discovery of diamonds, there were hostilities between the Basotho people and the Cape Colony. A British PROTECTORATE was formed in 1868 and then absorbed into the Cape Colony in 1871. Direct control was asserted over the area from 1884 until the independence of LESOTHO was proclaimed in 1966.

Battle of Britain   See BRITAIN, BATTLE OF.

Baxter, Richard   (1615–1691)
Puritan minister

A clergyman from a humble background, Baxter was ordained in 1638. He was opposed to extremes in religious controversy, both the ARMINIAN positions of Archbishop LAUD and the doctrinaire Calvinism of PRESBYTERIAN enemies of the royal court. He welcomed the restoration of CHARLES II, but in the SAVOY CONFERENCE of 1661, he was unable to fashion a compromise. He declined a bishopric and was expelled from the CHURCH OF ENGLAND under the act of UNIFORMITY of the same year. Imprisoned several times for unlicensed preaching, he supported the accession of WILLIAM III and MARY II in 1689.

Beardsley, Aubrey   (1872–1898)
illustrator

A leading member of the Aesthetic Movement, Beardsley's drawings in black and white had great detail and refinement, showing influences of French rococo and Japanese prints. He was the art editor of the *Yellow Book,* and he did the illustrations for Oscar WILDE's *Salome* (1893).

Beaton, David   (1494–1546)
archbishop of St. Andrews

Beaton had a bishopric in France and was made cardinal in 1538. The next year he succeeded his uncle as ARCHBISHOP at St. Andrews in SCOTLAND. He became chancellor in 1543 and was active in persecuting Protestants. He was responsible for the trial and execution of George WISHART, whose friends attacked and murdered Beaton in St. Andrews Castle.

Beatty, David, first earl   (1871–1936)
admiral

The youngest British admiral in over 100 years, Beatty was given command of the battlecruiser squadron in 1913 by Winston CHURCHILL. During WORLD WAR I his performance at the battles of Dogger Bank and JUTLAND was not brilliant, but his leadership was effective and helped to gain him command of the Grand Fleet in 1916. After the war he was made first sea lord (1919–27), in which capacity he supervised the reorganization of the fleet and the implementation of the disarmament agreement of the WASHINGTON CONFERENCE (1922).

Beaufort family

Descended from John of Gaunt (1340–99), duke of Lancaster and son of EDWARD III, the family held positions of the highest influence in English politics for over a century. John's eldest son and heir took the throne as HENRY IV (1367–1413). The youngest (legitimized) son of Gaunt, Thomas Beaufort (1377–1426) served his half brother and became chancellor to HENRY V. Another son, Henry Beaufort (1377–1447), was successively BISHOP of Lincoln and Winchester, and a cardinal of the church. In England he held the post of chancellor several times. Edmund

Beaufort (ca. 1406–55), a grandson of Gaunt, was duke of SOMERSET, held high office under HENRY VI, and was responsible for English losses at the end of the HUNDRED YEARS' WAR. His feud with Richard of YORK helped to precipitate the Wars of the ROSES, and Edmund was killed in the first Battle of ST. ALBANS (1455). Lady Margaret Beaufort (1443–1509) was a descendant of the Somerset line, married to Edmund TUDOR at the age of 12. Her only son became king as HENRY VII; she outlived him and was involved in the succession of her grandson HENRY VIII.

Beaverbrook, William Maxell Aitken, first baron (1879–1964)
newspaper publisher, politician

Born in CANADA, Lord Beaverbrook had a successful business career before immigrating to ENGLAND in 1910. There he entered politics as a Conservative MEMBER OF PARLIAMENT. He was soon working in the highest circles, and he had some part in the plot to remove Herbert ASQUITH and replace him with David LLOYD GEORGE as PRIME MINISTER in 1916. He purchased the *Daily Express,* one of the earliest mass-circulation newspapers, and built its daily circulation to about 2.25 million by 1936. He also purchased the *Evening Standard,* and he used both these papers to advance his own political views. In 1940 Winston CHURCHILL appointed Beaverbrook as minister of aircraft production; he is credited with a major role in accelerating output, critical to BRITAIN's victory in the air war with Germany. He served in other government posts and helped to negotiate the LEND-LEASE program with the United States.

Bechuanaland

A southern African territory, the site of the Kalahari Desert, Bechuanaland was made a British PROTECTORATE in 1885. Little was done to develop the area, and it served mainly as a source of labor for SOUTH AFRICA and other states. It became independent as BOTSWANA in 1966, and the discovery of diamonds in 1967 ushered in rapid economic growth, tripling per capita gross national product (1984–91).

Beckford, William (1709–1770)
merchant, politician

Born in JAMAICA, where his father was governor, Beckford was educated in ENGLAND and entered PARLIAMENT in 1747. He made a fortune as a merchant, and with an electoral base in LONDON, he was instrumental in rallying support behind William PITT the elder. Representing the commercial interest in 18th-century politics, Beckford was a critic of old political practices and an advocate of parliamentary reform. He supported John WILKES in his defiance of authority, and he served twice as lord mayor of London.

Bedlam

The slang reference to Bethlem Royal Hospital, the first insane asylum in ENGLAND. It was founded in the 13th century as part of the priory of St Mary Bethlehem, then converted into an asylum at the time of the REFORMATION. In the 17th and 18th centuries it was something of a tourist attraction, with visitors paying to view the inmates in their cells. The institution was moved to several different locations in London and finally to Beckenham in Kent in 1931.

Belfast

The principal city in NORTHERN IRELAND, Belfast's growth dates from the English conquest of ULSTER in the early 17th century and the subsequent commercial and later industrial development of the area. From a population of 8,500 in 1750, it grew to 20,000 a half-century later and to 350,000 by the end of the 19th century. Its primary economic activity was in linen manufacture, engineering, and shipbuilding. Incorporated as a city in 1888, Belfast became the capital of the new Northern Ireland dominion in 1920. The city had a long tradition of urban violence well before the outbreak of unrest in 1969, which lasted for the next three decades.

Belize

Formerly British Honduras, a British crown colony on the eastern coast of Central America. English settlers arrived from JAMAICA in the 1640s, and conflicts with Spanish colonial officials arose through the 18th century. After Guatemala and Mexico gained independence in 1821, the British laid claim to the area, renamed British Honduras in 1871. Because of Guatemalan claims to the territory, the British military presence remained until 1981.

Bell, Andrew (1753–1832)
educator
Educated at St. Andrew's University, Bell went to INDIA in 1787 where he was the superintendant of the Madras Male Orphan Asylum, run by the EAST INDIA COMPANY. There he developed a system of tutelage in which older boys were used as instructors for the younger ones. He described his system in a pamphlet in 1797, and it was adopted in a number of English schools, competing with a similar system devised by Joseph LANCASTER. In 1811 Bell was made the superintendant of the CHURCH OF ENGLAND's National Schools Society for Promoting the Education of the Poor.

Bengal

In 1633 the EAST INDIA COMPANY established a trading center in Bengal, the easternmost part of INDIA. The port city of CALCUTTA was at its center, and Fort William was the area's security outpost from 1696. In 1740 the ruling Nawab (prince) proclaimed independence from the Mogul empire. In 1756 an attack on Fort William was followed by the imprisonment of 146 British captives in a room that was no bigger than 18' by 15' (called the "black hole of Calcutta"). Only 23 persons survived this torture, which prompted the offensive led by Robert CLIVE at Plassey (1757), after which the government of Bengal and other provinces was vested in the East India Company. By the late 19th century the province had grown to twice the population of the UNITED KINGDOM. A plan to partition the province into Muslim and Hindu sections (1905) provoked sharp nationalist resistance and was dropped in 1912. However, after partition was imposed in 1947, and Bengal became East Pakistan, then BANGLADESH in 1972.

Bentham, Jeremy (1748–1832)
radical philosopher
Trained as a barrister, Bentham never practiced law. Instead, his career was devoted to a critique and reconstruction of English law on rational lines. In 1776 he published *A Fragment on Government,* an attack on the *Commentaries* of Sir William BLACKSTONE. His *Introduction to the Principles of Morals and Legislation* (1789) asserted that the aim of legislation should be "the greatest happiness of the greatest number." This theme of UTILITARIANISM was highly influential in contemporary and political thought. Bentham was the author of numerous projects of codified law. He developed a new model for prisons, and he was an advocate of parliamentary reform.

Berkeley, George (1685–1753)
philosopher, Bishop
Berkeley was born in IRELAND, studied at Kilkenny, and graduated from Trinity College, DUBLIN, where he became a fellow in 1707. He wrote *A Treatise Concerning the Principles of Human Knowledge* (1710), one of several works he published before moving to England in 1713. He was an associate of Alexander POPE, Jonathan SWIFT, Richard STEELE and Joseph ADDISON. He went to America (1728–32) to found a college for missionaries in BERMUDA. A charter had been granted, but no funds were provided. An influential philosopher in his day, he served as BISHOP of Cloyne (1734–52).

Berlin, Congress of (1878)
In June 1878 German chancellor Otto von Bismarck presided over a meeting of European

heads of state and Turkey. At the end of the Russo-Turkish War the Treaty of San Stefano had threatened a major change in the BALANCE OF POWER in the Balkans and the Near East. Essentially the conference (and secret negotiations beforehand) rewrote the settlement and propped up Turkish power in the region. The British were concerned with security for the SUEZ CANAL, and to that end they obtained a lease for the island of CYPRUS in exchange for support of Turkish interests.

Bermuda

A group of 150 small islands lying about 600 miles off the east coast of the United States. A dependency of GREAT BRITAIN, settled in 1609, it became a crown COLONY in 1684. Internal self-government was granted in 1968. An important naval base in the 19th century, today its economy depends on tourism and offshore business.

Besant, Annie (1847–1933)
radical reformer

After divorcing her husband, Besant joined forces with Charles BRADLAUGH and became vice president of the National Secular Society as well as coeditor of *The National Reformer.* Put on trial for publishing a tract on birth control in 1875, she lost custody of her daughter. She turned to SOCIALISM and organized strikes and demonstrations in the 1880s. She joined the Theosophical Society in 1889, emigrated to India, and became a supporter of Indian nationalism.

Bessemer, Sir Henry (1813–1898)
inventor

Bessemer was trained in his father's metal-working business. In the 1830s he invented a method of dating deeds and a type-composing machine. He experimented with combinations of cast iron and steel and in 1856 invented the steelmaking process that bears his name. Molten iron was injected with air to remove impurities, and when the technique was perfected, it allowed large-scale production of cheaper steel for railways, ships, and guns.

"Bess of Hardwick" (1518–1608)
(Shrewsbury, Elizabeth Talbot, countess of)
noblewoman

Known as "Bess of Hardwick," the daughter of John Hardwick of Derbyshire married four husbands, each wealthier than the last. With them she built or rebuilt great homes: Chatsworth, Worksop, and Hardwick Hall. But Bess gained the most notoriety from being custodian of MARY, QUEEN OF SCOTS (1569)—and accusing her husband George Talbot of adultery with the queen. Later Bess tried unsuccessfully to aid the claim of her daughter-in-law Arabella Stewart to be the successor to Queen ELIZABETH I.

Bevan, Aneurin (1897–1960)
politician

From a family of Welsh miners, Bevan worked in the pits and became an active labor organizer. After some time at the Central Labour College in London (1919–21) he became a MEMBER OF PARLIAMENT in 1929. He was a founder and later editor of *Tribune,* the voice of the left-wing socialists. As minister of health in the LABOUR PARTY government of 1945, he was the architect of the NATIONAL HEALTH SERVICE Act of 1946, which was the basis for the founding of the health service in 1948. He was a turbulent colleague, leader of the more radical element in the party, and unsuccessful contender for party leadership in 1958.

Beveridge of Tuggal, William Beveridge, first baron (1879–1963)
economist, social reformer

Baron Beveridge was a graduate of Balliol College, OXFORD UNIVERSITY, where he took a degree in civil law (1903). He went to work in LONDON at the social settlement Toynbee Hall, and he wrote articles for the *Morning Post.* An early advocate of social insurance plans, he helped to draft the Labour Exchanges Act (1909) and the national insurance Act (1911). He headed the London School of Economics from 1919 to 1937. In 1941 he was asked by the government of Winston CHURCHILL to prepare plans for postwar social services. The "Beveridge Report" of 1942 was not endorsed by the government, but it was a highly popular scheme that became the basis for postwar NATIONAL INSURANCE.

Bevin, Ernest (1881–1951)
unionist, politician

From very humble beginnings, Bevin began working at age 11, and by the turn of the century he was active in workers' organizations. He became a full-time officer of the Dockers' Union in 1911 and assistant general secretary in 1920. He helped to form the Transport and General Workers Union in 1922. By 1937 he had become the chairman of the TRADES UNION CONGRESS and one of the most influential members of the LABOUR PARTY. He served as minister of labor during WORLD WAR II (1940–45). He held the post of foreign secretary in the government of Clement ATTLEE. He also supported the Marshall Plan, NATO, and the building of a British ATOM BOMB. He used his stature to hold off those party members who strongly opposed these policies.

Bible

Although the books of the Old and New Testament were partially and occasionally translated in the Middle Ages, they were only available as a full text in Latin, and then only to a minority of the clergy. In the 14th century the first English versions were produced by the LOLLARDS. With the advent of printing in the 15th century, and with Greek translations of Erasmus (1516), a new era began. William TYNDALE made an English translation on the continent (1526), and for his trouble he was hunted down by agents of HENRY VIII. Within a decade, after the king's break from Rome, the translation by Miles COVERDALE

was authorized for use in English churches (1539). A later "Geneva" Bible was used by ELIZABETH I (1560). In 1604 JAMES VI AND I commissioned a group of churchmen who produced the King James Version (1611), a comprehensive revision which remained the authoritative text for many years. From the 19th century, translations of the Bible proliferated. In 1952 a Revised Standard Version was but one of a set of recent editions employing modern scholarship and some modern usage.

A Welsh New Testament was composed by William SALESBURY and Richard DAVIES in 1563–67. An Irish GAELIC New Testament was translated by Nicholas Walsh in 1573 (printed in 1602). A complete Bible in Welsh was prepared by William Morgan in 1588. In 1767 James Stuart produced a New Testament in Scots Gaelic, and a complete Irish Gaelic Bible was printed in 1810.

Bill of Rights

The constitutional product of the GLORIOUS REVOLUTION, the bill was a list of injunctions that had been presented in the DECLARATION OF RIGHTS to the new sovereigns, WILLIAM III and MARY II, and agreed to by them when they accepted the crown in February 1689. The bill was later enacted into law by PARLIAMENT, and it contained a list of traditional rights, a set of recent practices to be amended, and provision for a Protestant succession. This action created what came to be called the "balanced constitution"—the sharing of political power by the king, the lords, and the HOUSE OF COMMONS.

Unlike the Bill of Rights in the first 10 amendments to the U.S. Constitution, the document of 1689 did not contain a set of fundamental rights of individuals, but rather a set of rules for the functioning of the monarchical constitution. In the 1990s there was a movement for a British Bill of Rights on the American model, and in 2000 a Human Rights Act came into force. This act applied rights granted under the European Convention of Human Rights to British subjects.

Birkenhead, Frederick Edwin Smith, first earl of (1872–1930)
lord chancellor

An intellectual and a famous orator, Smith was a Conservative MEMBER OF PARLIAMENT and an outspoken supporter of ULSTER unionism who became attorney general in 1915. The following year he led the prosecution of Sir Roger CASEMENT for TREASON. He became LORD CHANCELLOR in 1919, at 47 one of the youngest ever. While in that office he played a part in the negotiation of the ANGLO-IRISH TREATY in 1921. He was also responsible for major changes in LAND law. He was later made SECRETARY OF STATE for INDIA (1924–28).

bishop

The bishop's office traces its ancestry to the early apostles, though in modern times its function is that of spiritual leader and clerical administrator of a diocese. These areas have been altered over time since the earliest bishops were chosen in Roman BRITAIN; and the authority of bishops has varied considerably over time among ENGLAND, WALES, SCOTLAND, and IRELAND. Often this variation was a byproduct of political power, often the corollary of the social and cultural role of the church.

See also CHURCH OF ENGLAND; CHURCH OF SCOTLAND.

Bishops' Wars (1639, 1640)

When CHARLES I imposed a new prayer book on SCOTLAND in 1637, there was widespread protest in the form of the SCOTTISH NATIONAL COVENANT (1638), a document subscribed to by thousands of Scots. This was a petition to restore the true kirk (church) on a PRESBYTERIAN rather than an Episcopal model. The GENERAL ASSEMBLY abolished the office of BISHOP, and the king assembled an army to send to Scotland, but it was ineffective and Charles had to accept a truce in 1639. The next year the Scots invaded ENGLAND and demanded an indemnity. The king's forces were weakened because he had disbanded PARLIAMENT in 1629. This conflict in fact forced the king to recall Parliament in 1640, which began the series of events leading to the CIVIL WAR (1642–48).

Black and Tans

A nickname for the auxiliary police sent to IRELAND during the crisis of 1920–21. They were noted for their lack of discipline and for reprisals and atrocities against their republican adversaries. These reinforcements for the ROYAL IRISH CONSTABULARY wore a khaki uniform with black caps, and thus were given the name of a pack of hunting dogs from County Limerick.

Black Death

In the summer of 1348 England was struck with the first appearance of a disastrous epidemic of the bubonic plague, commonly called the Black Death. This was part of a pandemic that spread from Asia across North Africa and Europe. By 1349 many parts of the British Isles had been affected. The occurrence of plague was not new, but apparently in this instance the disease was the more infectious pneumonic form, in addition to the typical variety carried by rats and fleas. There are no reliable statistics on the death toll, but the likelihood is that there were several million deaths in the British Isles. There is no doubt that this was the single most devastating demographic event of British history. Moreover, the plague was to return, in slightly less virulent form, several times in the later 14th century and over the next three centuries. The last episode was in 1665.

Blackstone, Sir William (1723–1780)
judge, jurist

Blackstone was a practicing barrister who held the first appointment as professor of English law at OXFORD UNIVERSITY. His lectures on that subject were published as *Commentaries on the Laws of England* (four volumes, 1765–69). This work

Tony Blair *(Paul O'Driscoll/Getty Images)*

was by far the most influential treatment of the COMMON LAW, for its own time and later. He also was a member of parliament and a justice in the courts of COMMON PLEAS and KING'S BENCH.

Blair, Anthony (1953–)
prime minister, 1997–
Born in EDINBURGH, Tony Blair's grandparents were English and Irish. He attended Fettes School and OXFORD UNIVERSITY, but only joined the LABOUR PARTY after leaving university. He was admitted to the bar from Lincoln's Inn in 1976. He was first elected to PARLIAMENT in 1983 for Sedgefield, a constituency in Durham in a

former mining area. He advocated a brand of progressive populism somewhat at odds with traditional Labour Party policies, and he pushed this direction on the party at large after becoming leader in 1994. In the general election of 1997 Labour won 418 seats, for a record majority of 177. This margin enabled them to put forward a stunning series of reforms, including assemblies for SCOTLAND and WALES and dismantling of the ancient HOUSE OF LORDS. Blair led his party to a second sweeping victory in June 2001, the first time that Labour won two consecutive parliamentary majorities.

Blake, Robert (1599–1657)
admiral
Blake served with the parliamentary army (1642–49) and was named admiral in 1649. During the CIVIL WAR he defeated the royalist naval forces and captured a treasure fleet returning from Brazil. He also scored several victories over the Dutch in the first Anglo-Dutch war (1652–54; see DUTCH WARS). Together with civilian administrators, he helped establish a permanent naval force in place of the old system of requisitioning private vessels.

Blake, William (1757–1827)
poet, artist
Trained in school and an apprenticeship to an engraver, Blake combined his art with a lifelong love of poetic expression and an evolving mystical philosophy. He studied at the ROYAL ACADEMY (1778) and was a partner in a printseller's shop. The death of his younger brother in 1787 marked a turn in his art. He developed a method of etching illustrations with text, which he called "illuminated printing." He was critical of 18th-century rationalism and industrialism. His earlier works included *Songs of Innocence* (1789) and *Songs of Experience* (1794). His visionary work began with *The Book of Thel* (1789–94). Ignored by most contemporaries, Blake's work attained a high stature among 20th-century critics.

Blenheim, Battle of (1704)

Victory of John Churchill, first duke of MARLBOROUGH, in the War of SPANISH SUCCESSION, in which the French and Bavarian forces threatening to capture Vienna were soundly defeated. The palace in Oxfordshire given to Marlborough in thanks for this victory is named after the site of the battle, and it was the birthplace of Winston CHURCHILL.

Bligh, William (1754–1817)
naval officer

Bligh served in the last voyage of Captain James COOK. In 1787 he commanded the voyage of the HMS *Bounty,* and when the crew mutinied, he was put in an open boat with 18 men. They drifted for 41 days and nearly 4,000 miles. Upon his return, he was court-martialled; cleared, he resumed his naval career. He later served as governor of New South Wales but was ousted by his subordinates in the so-called Rum Rebellion when he tried to force the end of the use of rum as currency (1808).

Blitz (1940–1941)

During WORLD WAR II, the first concentrated air assault on civilian population centers was launched by Germany in 1940. LONDON was the primary target, where over 40,000 lives were lost in the period between July 1940 and June 1941. Other cities targeted were Plymouth, Liverpool, Manchester, and Sheffield, as well as BELFAST, Glasgow, Hull, and Coventry. The term was derived from the German word *blitzkreig,* or lightning war, an expression coined to describe a concentrated and overwhelming assault.

Bloody Assizes (1685)

When James Scott, the duke of Monmouth, led the failed MONMOUTH'S REBELLION against the accession of JAMES VII AND II in 1685, the main disturbances were in the western counties. In September that year, Chief Justice George JEF-FREYS and his colleagues presided over the trials (ASSIZES) of 1,300 prisoners for treason. The mass convictions and sentencings were followed by several hundred executions, carried out in many towns in the region. The condemned were drawn and quartered, and parts of the corpses were put on display. Those not executed were transported to the West Indies. All of these procedures were within the law, but the scale of punishment was exceptional.

Bloody Sunday (1887, 1920, 1972)

1. November 13, 1887: In Trafalgar Square an illegal demonstration by socialists and radicals was suppressed by police and troops, with numerous injuries and two deaths.
2. November 21, 1920: In Dublin the IRISH REPUBLICAN ARMY murdered 14 British officers in their homes or hotels. In reprisal, BLACK AND TAN troops fired on a football crowd at Croke Park and killed 12 spectators.
3. January 30, 1972: A banned civil rights march in Londonderry ended in a confrontation in which 13 demonstrators were killed and 17 wounded by the British ARMY. This ended Catholic support for the British army presence in NORTHERN IRELAND, and it was soon followed by increased violence and the imposition of direct rule by the British government.

Bloomsbury Group

A group of writers, artists and intellectuals who used to meet in the area of central LONDON near the BRITISH MUSEUM. They rejected Victorian standards and were an important expression of more modern cultural and social views. The core of the group included Clive and Vanessa Bell and Leonard and Virginia WOOLF. Other members included E. M. FORSTER, John Maynard KEYNES, and Lytton STRACHEY.

Blount, Charles See MOUNTJOY, CHARLES BLOUNT, BARON.

blue book

The common name for parliamentary papers, printed in blue paper covers. Reports of parliamentary committees and ROYAL COMMISSIONS were important commentaries on current problems and remain as vital sources of data and contemporary opinions for social historians.

Blunt, Anthony (1907–1983)

art historian, spy

Educated at Trinity College, CAMBRIDGE UNIVERSITY, Blunt lectured on art at the Courtauld Institute, 1935–47, during which time he recruited agents for the Soviet Union. He worked in MI 5 during WORLD WAR II and passed information to the Russians. Afterward he became the surveyor of the king's pictures and the head of the Courtauld Institute. He received numerous British and French honors for his work. In 1964 he admitted privately that he had been a spy for 30 years, and he was given immunity for this confession. His admission was confirmed by the PRIME MINISTER in 1979, at which point he lost his knighthood.

Board of Trade

With colonial trade increasing in the late 17th century, the Board of Trade was established in 1696 to advise the PRIVY COUNCIL on trade matters. It was especially important in connection with the AMERICAN COLONIES. When they became independent, and the government was seeking measures of economical reform, the board was abolished in 1782. It was soon necessary to create a new committee to do the same sort of work, and over the course of the next two centuries, the new Board of Trade emerged as a key department of state. In 1970 it became the Department of Trade and Industry.

Bodley, Sir Thomas (1545–1613)

Sir Thomas Bodley was educated at Geneva, where his parents were in exile. He went on to study at Magdalen College, OXFORD UNIVERSITY, and later held several posts at the university. He went on diplomatic missions to Denmark and France, and he served as ambassador to the Netherlands (1589–96). He promoted the formation of the Bodleian Library, which opened in 1603 and for which he gave an endowment in 1611.

Boer War 1899–1902

The Boers (South African farmers of Dutch ancestry) were the first colonial settlers, and when GREAT BRITAIN seized the CAPE COLONY in 1806, a fundamental division occurred. The colonists migrated northward and founded two republics (the TRANSVAAL and ORANGE FREE STATE) independent of British rule. Discovery of gold in the Transvaal in 1886 made control of the area a more serious proposition. The possibility of a strong rival in the region put pressure on British leaders, some of whom advocated aggression. In 1899 fighting began, and the Boer army was initially very successful, advancing into enemy territory and placing several towns under siege. But with reinforcements the British turned the tide and defeated the Boers by 1902. In the later stages, the British evacuated the Boer civilian population and placed them in concentration camps, where the incidence of disease proved deadly. These policies caused deep divisions at home, not really offset by the formation of a Union of SOUTH AFRICA (1910) as a new self-governing DOMINION.

Boleyn, Anne (1507–1536)

queen of England, 1533–1536

Introduced to the English royal court in 1521, Anne Boleyn had many admirers, including HENRY VIII. Their affair probably began in 1526, when the king was seeking a divorce from CATHERINE OF ARAGON. By 1531 they were openly living together, and in January 1533 the king arranged a secret marriage. Anne was declared queen in May that year after the divorce from Catherine was proclaimed unilaterally by the

ARCHBISHOP of CANTERBURY, Thomas CRANMER. Her first child was the princess Elizabeth, born in December 1533. Her inability to bear Henry a son endangered her position, and in 1536 she was accused of adultery, divorced by Henry, and executed along with her accused lovers. Her daughter became Queen ELIZABETH I.

See also CROMWELL, THOMAS; REFORMATION; WOLSEY, THOMAS, CARDINAL.

Bolingbroke, Henry See HENRY IV.

Bolingbroke, Henry St. John, viscount (1678–1751)
politician

Viscount Bolingbroke entered PARLIAMENT in 1701 and held the posts of secretary at war (1704–08) and SECRETARY OF STATE (1710–14). He managed the negotiations for the Treaty of UTRECHT, but he was increasingly hostile to the chief minister, Robert HARLEY. Dismissed by GEORGE I, he was impeached and attainted. Fleeing to France, he briefly worked for the exiled JACOBITE court. After being pardoned in 1723, he returned to England and wrote many pamphlets and essays for the TORY party.

Bonnie Prince Charlie See STUART, CHARLES EDWARD.

Book of Common Prayer

In 1549 the first Book of Common Prayer was adopted for uniform worship in the CHURCH OF ENGLAND. A second version, published in 1552, showed more influence of continental reformers. Archbishop Thomas CRANMER is credited with the main authorship, and these books were the sole authorized form of prayer for the Church of England. Later modifications were made in 1559, 1662, 1928, and 1965. In 1980 an *Alternate Service Book* was issued to meet the desire for modernization of the liturgy.

Booth, Charles (1840–1916)
social reformer

Booth was a wealthy businessman who made the first scientific investigation of poverty. Doubting official statistics and the estimates of radical groups, he developed statistical techniques which he applied in his main work, *Life and Labour of the People in London* (1886–1903). This task filled 17 volumes, and it showed that over 30 percent were living in poverty, caused by low wages, high unemployment, and old age. His work provided ammunition for the early social reforms of old-age pensions and NATIONAL INSURANCE.

Booth, William (1829–1912)
Salvation Army founder

Booth grew up in Nottingham, where he entered the Methodist ministry. Finding that most middle-class churches failed to meet the needs of the people, he and his wife, Catherine, founded a mission in London's East End in 1865. They later organized the SALVATION ARMY, an authoritarian and disciplined form of mission, with Booth as its "general." He grew more convinced of the material obstacles to salvation, and his book *In Darkest England and the Way Out* (1890) gave a disturbing picture of poverty and a strong argument for social reform.

borough

Broadly speaking, a borough is a settlement with urban features and/or fortification. Its meaning has shifted, from the Anglo-Saxon *burh* (fortified place) to the Norman *burgus* (town) to the medieval *borough* (a community with certain privileges, often in a charter). Later boroughs were apt to have special courts, taxes, or trading rights; and, after the 13th century, the right to choose members of PARLIAMENT. The officials (mayor, aldermen, councillors, burgesses) operated under the terms of their charter, which was subject to royal revision or legal challenge, and later, in the 19th century, to statutory reform.

See also BURGH; MUNICIPAL CORPORATIONS; LONDON.

Boston

The state capital of Massachusets, named after the port city in Lincolnshire. In colonial times, Massachusetts Bay, as it was then called, was home to some of the colonies' most radical patriots, and it was the focal point of early resistance to British control. The Boston Massacre of 1770 was a clash between British troops and a crowd in which five people died, an event which aroused great indignation among American colonists. The Boston Tea Party in 1773 was a methodical protest against customs duties as "taxation without representation." Several hundred chests of tea were thrown into the harbor, provoking the government's passage of the INTOLERABLE ACTS (1774), which closed the port, altered the colonial government, and removed trials of soldiers from the Massachusetts Bay colonial courts.

See also AMERICAN COLONIES.

Boswell, James (1740–1795)
diarist

The son of a Scottish judge, Boswell was introduced to Samuel JOHNSON in 1763. Their friendship was recorded in detail in Boswell's journals. In 1773 they made a tour that was described in Boswell's *Journal of a Tour to the Hebrides* (1785). His *Life of Johnson* (1791) was a highly successful and pioneering biography. Boswell's journals were not published in full until the 20th century.

Bosworth, Battle of (1485)

Henry Tudor defeated RICHARD III, thus securing the throne and establishing the TUDOR dynasty. Coming from exile in France, Henry had landed with a small army in WALES and marched into ENGLAND. When the king's army came to meet him at BOSWORTH, some of its leaders defected, others refused to fight, and Richard himself was killed.

Botany Bay

A harbor on the east coast of AUSTRALIA, discovered by Captain COOK in 1770. It was supposed to be the site of the first penal colony in New South Wales, but when the first fleet landed there in 1778, it was decided to move the settlement north to what became Sydney harbor.

Botha, Louis (1862–1919)
prime minister of South Africa

Born in NATAL, Botha worked on a farm and campaigned against the ZULU in 1884. He raised volunteers to respond to the JAMESON RAID in 1895. In the BOER WAR he was the assistant general of the army of TRANSVAAL and won the battles of Colenso and Spion Kop. After the loss of Johannesburg and Pretoria, he led his troops in guerilla warfare for two years. At the end of the war, he supported reconciliation with Britain. He became the first prime minister of Transvaal (1907) and, after the union convention, the first prime minister of the Union of SOUTH AFRICA (1910–19). He supported GREAT BRITAIN during WORLD WAR I, but he faced a rebellion of pro-German Boers in 1914. He attended the Paris Peace Conference in 1919, and he died upon his return to Pretoria.

Bothwell, James Hepburn, fourth earl of (ca. 1535–1578)

A Protestant Scottish nobleman, but one opposed to the leaders of his group (the LORDS OF THE CONGREGATION), Earl Bothwell assisted MARY, QUEEN OF SCOTS, with the murder of her second husband, Henry Stewart, Lord DARNLEY, in 1567. He then divorced his wife and married Mary. Only a month later the couple was defeated in a confrontation with an aroused populace. She was made a captive in Lochleven Castle, but he fled the country. He was captured in Denmark and imprisoned there for the rest of his life.

Botswana

A landlocked country, the former PROTECTORATE of BECHUANALAND, and now an independent state, Botswana became a republic in 1966. Its neighbors are NAMIBIA to the west and north, Zimbabwe (formerly RHODESIA) to the north and east, and SOUTH AFRICA to the South. South Africa was the dominant force in the affairs of the protectorate and state until the end of apartheid.

Boulton, Matthew (1728–1809)
engineer

A manufacturer in Birmingham, Boulton built works at Soho, a large factory with 600 workers operating water-powered machines making iron, copper, and silver products such as chains and buttons. In 1775 he entered a partnership with James WATT and secured a share in the patent of the improved steam engine. The engines were not profitable for some time, but he continued to subsidize their development. After 1786 they were widely used in coal mining, mills, and coin presses.

Bow Street Runners

When Henry FIELDING was MAGISTRATE at the Bow Street POLICE office in LONDON, he established a number of CONSTABLES to investigate and pursue suspected criminals. This sort of work was previously done by "thief takers," who were independent entrepreneurs. After Fielding's experiment, the model was applied in other London police offices by legislation in 1792, but a metropolitan police organization was not created until 1829.

Boxer Rebellion (1900)

Increasing European influence in China prompted a revolt in 1900. When a secret society (the Harmonious Fists) attacked foreigners, an international military expedition was sent to Beijing (Peking), where unrest had led to the death of the German ambassador. The relief forces engaged in reprisals and looting, and the affair had a powerful influence on nationalist feeling in China.

Boycott, Charles (1832–1897)
estate manager

A retired army captain, Boycott came to IRELAND and served as land agent for Lord Erne in County Mayo. In 1880, with unrest growing over the LAND question, Charles PARNELL directed his followers to ostracize anyone who evicted tenants. Boycott was the first target of this campaign, and his crops had to be harvested by a special group of volunteers under military guard. In speeches and newspaper accounts, his name became synonymous with collective resistance.

Boyle, Robert (1627–1691)
natural philosopher

Son of Richard Boyle, the earl of Cork, Robert Boyle was educated at Eton and on the continent. He built a laboratory at OXFORD UNIVERSITY, and he joined other members of the early scientific community in forming the ROYAL SOCIETY. With Robert HOOKE, he developed an air pump and he formulated a new law of gas pressure and volume.

Boyne, Battle of the (1690)

After his expulsion in the GLORIOUS REVOLUTION (1688), JAMES VII AND II raised an army in France and landed in IRELAND in 1689, where support for him remained strong. WILLIAM III dispatched an army, and he himself came to Ireland in 1690. James had campaigned in the north, but he had failed to capture Derry. His army met that of William at the Boyne river, 30 miles north of DUBLIN, on July 12, 1690. The battle itself was inconclusive, but James returned to France and William took Dublin. Ever since, the victory has been commemorated by Protestants in ULSTER as marking their ascendancy over Catholic rule.

Boy Scouts

The youth organization founded by Robert BADEN-POWELL in 1907 was inspired in part by the Boys Brigade, founded in SCOTLAND by William Alexander Smith in 1883. The Brigade was a military-style religious organization. Baden-Powell's effort was to strengthen moral and physical attributes of youth; his *Scouting for*

Boys emphasized individual skills and resource-fulness in what he saw as a vital contribution to imperial service.

Bradlaugh, Charles (1833–1891)
radical

An outspoken radical, secularist, and atheist, Bradlaugh edited *The National Reformer* (1860–). Elected to PARLIAMENT in 1880, he was not allowed to take his seat because he would not take the oath. He campaigned for the right to make nonreligious affirmation in lieu of oaths, and was reelected three times before he was allowed to take his seat in 1886.

See also BESANT, ANNIE.

Brandon, Charles See SUFFOLK, CHARLES BRANDON, DUKE OF.

John Bright *(Library of Congress)*

Breda, Declaration of (1660)

While in exile in Holland, CHARLES II issued a declaration of his intentions upon returning to the throne after the fall of the COMMONWEALTH OF ENGLAND (April 1660). He offered general pardon and indemnity, pay for the army, and a vague form of toleration ("liberty to tender consciences"), leaving the resolution of most divisive issues to a "free parliament."

Bright, John (1811–1889)
politician, reformer

A Quaker manufacturer from Lancashire, Bright was a key figure in the anti-corn law league. Elected to parliament in 1843, he vigorously supported free trade, opposed the crimean war, and advocated reform of the government of india. He favored limited parliamentary reform and served in several of William gladstone's cabinets, but he broke with his leader over the issue of irish home rule in 1886.

Brighton, Laurence Kerr Olivier, baron Olivier of See OLIVIER, LAURENCE KERR, BARON OLIVIER OF BRIGHTON

Brindley, James (1716–1772)
canal builder

A self-taught engineer, in 1759–61 Brindley built the canal that connected the coal mines of the duke of Bridgwater with the town of Manchester. The great saving in shipping costs led to several other canal projects for Brindley, part of a boom in canal construction in the latter part of the 18th century. By 1830 there were 4,000 miles of canals in England, but they would soon be overtaken by the railway.

Britain

The Romans called the largest island *Britannia*, perhaps from the Greek name for the *Pretanic* islands. The use of the name by Julius Caesar may be a confusion with the *Britanni*, a name given to earlier Belgic invaders. The name *Briton* is usually applied to the CELTS living in the island to distinguish them from incoming Romans, Angles, Saxons, and others. The name GREAT BRITAIN, encompassing ENGLAND, WALES, and SCOTLAND, came into regular use from the time of the reign of JAMES VI AND I (1603–25).

Britain, Battle of (1940)

After the fall of France in June 1940, Hitler began preparing operations for an invasion of Britain. The first step was to achieve air superiority, and between July and September the Luftwaffe attacked ROYAL AIR FORCE (RAF) installations in southern England. Both sides suffered heavy losses, the Germans losing nearly twice the number of aircraft as the British. The campaign was close to success, but in September the air offensive was shifted to the BLITZ of LONDON, giving the RAF a much-needed respite. The German invasion plan was called off in October.

See also WORLD WAR II.

British Broadcasting Corporation (BBC)

The BBC was established in 1927 under a royal charter. Originally the British Broadcasting Company and subsequently Corporation, it was given a broadcasting monopoly funded by license fees. It began the first television service in 1936, but its monopoly status was ended in the 1950s with the introduction of commercial radio and television. The organization was a public-service body; hence at first it was strictly impartial, which limited its subject matter, perhaps critically, in the 1930s. During WORLD WAR II the BBC's reputation was enhanced by its effective and diversified coverage of foreign and home events, although of course it operated under the government's censorship.

British Empire and Commonwealth

The British Empire reached its greatest extent in the early 20th century, with about one-fifth of the world's land and over 400 million persons under its rule. From trading companies in the 16th and 17th centuries to colonial settlements from the 17th century to a vast collection of colonial markets and commodity sources in the 19th century, the empire had come to be the largest and wealthiest in world history.

EARLY GROWTH

ENGLAND's earliest overseas ventures gave no hint at future greatness. Both Spain and Portugal had made immense fortunes from imperial ventures in the Americas and the Far East before there was any sign of English activity. Indeed, the earliest efforts were directed at preying on the treasure fleets of those countries, and only later did English companies and captains seriously work on building garrisons and productive outposts.

MERCANTILE EMPIRE

The 17th-century commercial colonies in the Americas, the West Indies, East Indies, and Africa were designed to be sources of wealth for the home country—protected by the British NAVY, subjected to British commercial regulation, and producing a surplus income that would be the return on GREAT BRITAIN's investment. The reality did not often agree with the theory. First, the investment was usually larger than expected in terms of military and naval support, government infrastructure, and legislative time and effort. Second, the ventures into colonial commerce were all made with some kind of delegation of authority and promise of profit to the companies or individuals involved. Third, in the most serious cases, as with the AMERICAN COLONIES, the ungrateful settlers might decide that self-government was preferable to imperial rule. Indeed, by the early 19th century, a growing body of thought had rejected the canon of MERCANTILISM and accepted the doctrine of FREE TRADE.

FREE TRADE EMPIRE

It was said that the British Empire was made "in a fit of absence of mind." The comment pointed to the lack of any central policy or plan in empire-building. An erratic but escalating series of ventures in the 18th and 19th centuries brought an expanding number of colonial stations and settlements. The doctrine of free trade said that growth was maximized in inverse proportion to the regulation by government. Less restriction = more trade = more profit. This was further understood to mean less investment by government and more freedom for individual entrepreneurs and businesses, so that government expenditures declined for much of the 19th century. However, all of these rules were challenged in the years after 1870 when other states began to look for colonial markets and mandates.

TWENTIETH-CENTURY EMPIRE AND COMMONWEALTH

A combination of competition and reform undermined the Victorian empire. Competing industrial economies such as Germany, the United States, and Japan transformed the world economy, making British imperial investment less profitable. Indeed, considering commerce alone, the balance sheet for British colonies was probably in the red for much of the empire's history, and in the latter days the "invisible exports" (capital, investment income, insurance, and other services) were what kept the accounts reasonably sound. At the same time, political and social reform, at home and abroad, sharply undercut the ethos of British imperial authority. The most important reflection of this was the creation of DOMINIONS, or self-governing dependencies, with ties to Britain in matters other than domestic. Thus CANADA (1867), AUSTRALIA (1901), NEW ZEALAND (1907), SOUTH AFRICA (1910), the IRISH FREE STATE (1922), and Southern RHODESIA (1923) were recognized to have this status, and became members of the British Commonwealth.

IMPERIAL DECLINE

After WORLD WAR II, the remaining colonies all looked toward greater freedom, and many gained their independence with looser ties to the Commonwealth. INDIA and PAKISTAN divided the inheritance of British India. PALESTINE and EGYPT led the march to independence in the Near East. The colonies of AFRICA followed in the 1960s in rapid succession. This rather swift dismantling was naturally a subject of bitter debate and doubt in Britain itself. The British Commonwealth was rechristened the Commonwealth of Nations, and a secretariat was established in 1965 to manage relations within the group of former colonies. Even as this new formation was developing, however, Britain was being drawn into a closer relationship with the countries of the EUROPEAN COMMUNITY.

British Expeditionary Force

The small British ARMY sent to France in 1914 (four divisions) was important in delaying the German advance at Mons and at the Marne during WORLD WAR I. The same name was applied to the WORLD WAR II force sent to France and Belgium in 1939, eventually 10 divisions and a tank brigade. When the German assault came in May 1940, most of the force was evacuated from DUNKIRK.

British Honduras See BELIZE.

British Museum

The preeminent public research library and museum collection in Britain got underway with the British Museum Act of 1753. Its initial collections were the artifacts, books, and manuscripts from several private collections, augmented by many further additions, including the Royal Library (1756 and 1822). The new buildings in Bloomsbury were designed and constructed by 1857. They housed rapidly expanding departments of antiquities, not only from ancient Greece and Rome but from EGYPT, Asia, and prehistoric BRITAIN. Continued growth of the library meant that parts of the collection had to be dispersed. In 1973 the British Library was made a separate entity, and the books from the

British Museum and other locations were gathered in a new British Library in St. Pancras, which was opened in 1997.

Britten, (Edward) Benjamin (1913–1976)
composer, pianist

Born in Lowestoft, the son of a dentist, Britten became the most notable modern English composer. His work includes the operas *Peter Grimes* (1945) and *Death in Venice* (1973). He also wrote the *Spring Symphony* (1949) and *War Requiem* (1962). In all he composed 12 operas and 13 song cycles. He also was the founder of the Aldeburgh Festival in 1948.

Bronowski, Jacob (1908–1974)
scientist, writer

Born in Poland, Bronowski and his family moved to Germany in 1915 and to GREAT BRITAIN in 1920. He studied mathematics at CAMBRIDGE UNIVERSITY, but his main talent was in scientific writing and later in broadcasting. He wrote *Common Sense of Science* (1951); *Science and Human Values* (1958); and *William Blake and the Age of Revolution* (1965). He is best known for his 13-part television documentary, published in book form as *The Ascent of Man* (1973).

Brontë family

Charlotte (1816–55), Branwell (1817–48), Emily (1818–48), and Anne (1820–49) were the children of Reverend Patrick and Maria Brontë. The Anglo-Irish churchman took a parish in the Yorkshire village of Howarth, where his three daughters lived and wrote. They published poems and a series of novels under male pseudonyms (Cumer, Ellis, and Acton Bell): *Jane Eyre* (Charlotte) and *Wuthering Heights* (Emily) and *Agnes Grey* (Anne) in 1847. Emily and Anne died in the next two years. Their remaining novels were Anne's *The Tenant of Wildfell Hall* (1849) and Charlotte's

Shirley (1849) and *Villette* (1853). After a brief marriage, Charlotte died in 1855.

Brooke, Alan See ALANBROOKE, ALAN BROOKE, VISCOUNT.

Brougham and Vaux, Henry Peter Brougham, first baron (1778–1868)
lawyer, politician

Educated in EDINBURGH, Brougham was associated with liberal political figures there and helped to found the *Edinburgh Review.* Having qualified as an advocate in SCOTLAND, he was admitted to the English bar in 1808 and entered the HOUSE OF COMMONS in 1810. He was a supporter of popular education, the ANTISLAVERY MOVEMENT, and parliamentary reform. He accepted the post of legal adviser to the estranged queen CAROLINE OF BRUNSWICK at the time of the accession of GEORGE IV (1820), a step disapproved by many colleagues. When the WHIGS came into office in 1830 he was named LORD CHANCELLOR (1830–34) and was actively engaged in the passage of the REFORM ACTS of 1832. As a follower of Jeremy BENTHAM, he engaged in many efforts to reform and improve EDUCATION. He called for the inquiry into educational charities in 1819, which produced the Charity Commission; was one of the founders of the Society for the Diffusion of Useful Knowledge in 1825; and cofounded the University of London in 1828.

Brown, Lancelot (1715–1783)
landscape designer

Known as "Capability" Brown, because he always referred to the "capabilities" of a landed estate, Brown became one of the foremost designers of estate grounds in the 18th century. He preferred naturalistic settings to the formal designs of his predecessors. He designed 140 estates, including those at Croome Court, Longleat, Chatsworth, and Blenheim.

Browne, Robert (ca. 1550–1633)
Puritan separatist

A PURITAN preacher, Browne came from a wealthy family and attended CAMBRIDGE UNIVERSITY, where he was influenced by Thomas CARTWRIGHT. Increasingly alienated from all forms of church government, he established independent congregations. Arrested and released, he migrated to the Netherlands, where he continued to write and preach. Returning to ENGLAND, he was imprisoned, submitted to church authority, became a schoolmaster, and later was ordained (1591). He was rector of a parish in Northamptonshire for the rest of his life.

Browning, Robert (1812–1889)
poet

The self-educated son of a clerk, Browning spent some time at the University of London, traveled on the continent, and began to write for the stage. With little success there, he turned to publishing collections of poetry. He admired the work of Elizabeth Barrett (1806–61) and after corresponding and courting, they secretly married. Her *Sonnets from the Portuguese* (1850) and her verse novel *Aurora Leigh* (1856) were among her best-known works. His collections *Dramatic Lyrics* (1842) and *Dramatic Romances and Lyrics* (1845), as well as his *Men and Women* (1855) and *The Ring and the Book* (1868–69), made him extremely popular. He was buried in WESTMINSTER ABBEY.

Bruce, Thomas See ELGIN, THOMAS BRUCE, EARL OF.

Brunel, Isambard Kingdom (1806–1859)
engineer

One of the leading engineers of the Victorian age, Brunel designed the Great Western Railway (1835–41). He planned the ships *Great Western* (1838), *Great Britain* (1845), and *Great Eastern*, the largest steamship of its kind (1858). He also supervised construction of railways in Italy and engineering projects in Australia and India.

Bryce, James Bryce, first viscount (1838–1922)
intellectual, politician

Born in Belfast, Bryce revived the study of Roman law at OXFORD UNIVERSITY and traveled and wrote extensively about the Near East. Elected to PARLIAMENT in 1880, he served in the last cabinet of William GLADSTONE and chaired a ROYAL COMMISSION on education (1894–95). He was successful as the British ambassador to Washington (1907–13), having unusual insights, as evidenced by his book *The American Commonwealth* (1888). His last work was *Modern Democracies* (1921).

B.S.E.

Acronym for *bovine spongiform encephalopathy*, commonly known as "mad cow disease," first identified in 1985. The outbreak was initially confined to the UNITED KINGDOM, where it claimed 160,000 cattle in the first decade. Caused by feed contaminated by the rendered brains of infected sheep, B.S.E. attacks the nervous system of cattle. The disease can be transmitted from cows to their calves, but more disturbingly, it is now linked to the rare Creutzfeldt-Jacob disease in humans. During this crisis, exports of British beef were prohibited, and domestic consumption and prices fell, compelling the government to provide a subsidy for affected farmers.

Buchan, John, baron Tweedsmuir (1875–1940)
writer, statesman

The son of a Scottish minister, educated at Glasgow and OXFORD UNIVERSITY, Buchan was called to the bar in 1901 from the Middle Temple (see INNS OF COURT). He worked with the HIGH COMMISSION in SOUTH AFRICA (1901–03) on postwar reconstruction and served on the army staff during WORLD WAR I. A Conservative MEMBER OF PARLIAMENT from 1927 to 1935, he was governor general of CANADA, 1935–40. He published his first novel while at Oxford. In addition to nonfiction works, he wrote adventure stories, including *The Thirty-nine Steps* (1915), *Greenmantle* (1916), *Mr Standfast* (1918), and *John Macnab* (1925).

Buchanan, George (1506–1582)
Scottish humanist
Educated in Paris, Buchanan was influenced by the ideas of Erasmus. Returning to his homeland of SCOTLAND during the turbulent reign of MARY, QUEEN OF SCOTS (1561–67), he was connected with her court, but after her deposition he wrote a dialogue justifying resistance to tyranny, *De Jure Regni apud Scotos* (1579). He also compiled *Rerum Scoticarum Historia* (1582), and both works were dedicated to the young king JAMES VI AND I, who was his pupil.

Buckingham, George Villiers, duke of (1592–1628)
courtier
Favorite of JAMES VI AND I, Buckingham was appointed lord admiral. Involved in a failed plan to marry Prince Charles to the daughter of the Spanish king, he switched to an anti-Spanish policy, planning an abortive raid on Cadiz in 1625. He was kept as senior adviser by CHARLES I on the king's accession in 1625, and he was responsible for yet another failed expedition, this one to assist French Protestants in La Rochelle in 1627. PARLIAMENT tried to impeach him, and his wide unpopularity inspired an angry army officer to assassinate him in 1628.

Buckingham Palace
The official residence of the monarch in LONDON. Buckingham House was built in 1702–05 by John Sheffield, duke of Buckingham. It was purchased by GEORGE III in 1762 and altered and enlarged. In 1825–50 there were more extensive additions. Only in Queen VICTORIA's reign did the palace become the main royal residence. Some of the rooms have been opened to the public since 1993, in order to help pay for rebuilding of the sections of WINDSOR Castle destroyed by fire in 1992.

budget
The annual plan for government taxation and spending. The practice dates from the 18th century, and since the 19th century it has been the task of the CHANCELLOR OF THE EXCHEQUER to present the budget in PARLIAMENT each year, or more often in time of crisis. The budget message constitutes the government's most important overall statement of planning and policy.

Buller, Redvers (1839–1908)
soldier
Buller's early career included service in China and Africa. He became adjutant general and organized the Army Service Corps, which did much to consolidate procurement and transport. Decorated for bravery in the ZULU War (1878–79), he was given command at the start of the BOER WAR, but his orders to remain on the defensive were not obeyed, and several units were under siege by the time he arrived in SOUTH AFRICA. His early efforts were weak and ineffective, and he was replaced in command by Lord ROBERTS.

Bunker Hill, Battle of (1775)
With BOSTON surrounded by rebel troops, on June 17, 1775, a British force of 2,300 attacked rebel positions on Breed's Hill. The colonists held off two assaults before being overrun, and they lost less than half the number of men that the British did. This performance was an important boost to the morale of the rebels. The battle was mistakenly named for nearby Bunker Hill.

Bunyan, John (1628–1688)
Puritan writer
A BAPTIST preacher who had served in the rebel army in the CIVIL WAR, he was imprisoned for his refusal to comply with laws against DISSENTERS

after 1660. During his 12 years in jail he wrote numerous tracts. His most famous work was *Pilgrim's Progress* (1684), an extended story of his conversion and of the tribulations of dissenters.

Burdett, Sir Francis (1770–1844)
radical politician

A wealthy landowner and patrician reformer who opposed government restriction and advocated "ancient liberties," Burdett first entered PARLIAMENT in 1796, opposed war with France, and supported parliamentary reform. In 1810 he was imprisoned for breach of parliamentary privilege, and large crowds demonstrated for his release, causing a crisis in which troops had to be called out. He was imprisoned again in 1820 for his attacks on the government after the PETERLOO MASSACRE. He was MEMBER OF PARLIAMENT (MP) for Westminster, one of the most radical of constituencies, from 1807 to 1837, but his style of RADICALISM was that of the 18th century, not his own day. He later became a Conservative MP (1837–44).

burgess

The principal residents of a BOROUGH were summoned, usually in pairs, to attend the PARLIAMENTS of EDWARD I and later sovereigns. They, in addition to the KNIGHTS of the shire, represented the social classes below the aristocracy, and their presence was desired in order to endorse taxation and other royal policies. There is little evidence that they had any more significant role in the business of Parliament before the 17th century.

Burgess, Anthony (1917–1993)
fiction writer

One of the foremost contemporary writers, he served as an education officer in Malaya in the 1950s, during which time his first novel was published (*Time for a Tiger,* 1956, the first of his Malayan Trilogy; the others were *The Enemy in the Blanket* [1958] and *Beds in the East* [1959]).

Stricken with a brain tumor and given one year to live, he returned to England and wrote prodigiously, ultimately producing 29 novels and outliving most of his doctors. His best-known work was *A Clockwork Orange* (1962).

burgh

The Scots form of BOROUGH—towns with special privileges, either royal burghs or the more numerous burghs of barony or regality, established by feudal lords. Each was entitled to some self-government, and burghs were represented, from the 16th century, in the Convention of Royal Burghs. In addition, from the 14th century, one of the estates of the Scottish parliament had representatives from burghs, which provision was incorporated in the Scottish representation in the Union Parliament after 1707.

Burghley, William Cecil, first baron (1520–1598)
secretary of state

Queen ELIZABETH I's principal secretary (1558–72) and then lord high treasurer (1572–98), Cecil was a major figure in the settlement of the church after her accession. He helped the Protestants in SCOTLAND, but he had doubts about efforts to aid continental Protestants—the Huguenots in France (1567) and Calvinists in Holland (1585). He persuaded the queen to sign MARY, QUEEN OF SCOTS' death warrant (1587). A masterful administrator, he astutely managed the old TUDOR institutions, but he was not an innovator. He amassed a considerable fortune, which he used as a patron and as a builder of several great houses for his family.

Burgoyne, John (1722–1792)
general

During the American Revolution, Burgoyne commanded the British force that invaded New York from CANADA. He took Ticonderoga and Fort Edward, but was forced to surrender to the

Americans at Saratoga (1777). He returned to LONDON, defended his conduct, became an opposition MEMBER OF PARLIAMENT, and wrote plays, the most successful being *The Heiress* (1786).

Burke, Edmund (1729–1797)
politician, philosopher

An Irishman, Burke went to Trinity College in DUBLIN, briefly studied law in LONDON, and entered PARLIAMENT in 1766. He joined the Rockingham WHIGS and spoke in defense of the American colonists and in favor of ECONOMICAL REFORM. His *Thoughts on the Present Discontents* (1770) argued that the king was upsetting the constitutional balance by ignoring the place of political parties. He drafted a Civil List Act (1782), which proposed to have ministers' salaries unpaid until all other expenditures were met, but this failed to achieve the kind of fiscal reform he wanted. Burke was a proponent of religious toleration, and Catholic interests were among those for which he sought relief. His outspoken denunciation of the French revolution (*Reflections on the Revolution in France,* 1790) is seen as a manifesto for modern conservatism, though it may equally be read as a plea for the traditional liberty of the balanced constitution of 18th-century ENGLAND.

Burma

The EAST INDIA COMPANY had established trading centers by 1612. In 1824 the British saw the Burmese empire as a threat to trade, and a war in that year brought some annexation of territory, followed by more in 1852. Eventually another conflict saw Burma become a province of British INDIA in 1886. A separate administration was established in 1937, but Burma was overrun by the Japanese in 1942; British forces defeated them in 1944. After WORLD WAR II, an independent Burmese socialist republic was established in 1948, and the country left the Commonwealth. In 1988 the military government of Burma changed the name of the country to Myanmar.

Edmund Burke, ca. 1780 *(Hulton/Archive)*

Burnet, Gilbert (1643–1715)
bishop, historian

Educated at Aberdeen, Burnet became professor of divinity at Glasgow University, then moved to LONDON and attached himself to the opposition to the royal court. He wrote a *History of the Reformation* (1679), for which he received the thanks of PARLIAMENT. In exile in Holland, he was favored by WILLIAM III of Orange, whom he accompanied to ENGLAND at the GLORIOUS REVOLUTION in 1688. He was made BISHOP of Salisbury and wrote a *History of My Own Time,* which was not published until 1723–34.

Burns, John (1858–1943)
trade unionist

An engineer's apprentice and a figure in early socialist activity, Burns was a member of the SOCIAL DEMOCRATIC FEDERATION (1884), the Battersea Labour League, and the Metropolitan Radical Federation. He was prominent in unemployment demonstrations in 1886 and 1887 and the LONDON dock strike of 1889. Elected to PARLIAMENT in 1892, he broke with more extreme left wing groups and advocated alliance with the LIBERAL PARTY. In 1905 he became president of the BOARD OF TRADE, the first workingman to become a CABINET minister. He resigned in protest against the war in 1914.

Burns, Robert (1759–1796)
poet

Born into a farming family, Burns developed a love of literature and of his native culture. In 1786 he published *Poems Chiefly in the Scottish Dialect,* which brought him critical acclaim and demonstrated that the Scots language was a potent vehicle for polite literature. His next project came in contributions to James Johnson's *The Scots Musical Museum* (1789–1803), for which he produced over 100 vernacular songs and lyrics. Burns died at age 37 of rheumatic heart disease, but his birthday (January 25) continues to be celebrated by Scots around the world to the present day.

Burton, Sir Richard (1821–1890)
explorer, author

Burton joined the Indian army in 1842, absorbing as much knowledge as he could of culture and languages of the East and of Africa and America. From his extensive travels he produced a vast number of books, his best-known being the *Arabian Nights* (1885–88), the *Kama Sutra* (1883), and *The Perfumed Garden* (1886). His most notable travels were his pilgrimage to the forbidden city of Mecca (1853) and the expedition to the source of the Nile, which brought the discovery of Lake Tanganyika (1858).

Bushell's Case

When the Quakers William PENN and William Mead were tried for illegal preaching and acquit-

ted in 1670, the jurors in the case were fined and imprisoned. The jury foreman, Edward Bushell, obtained a writ of HABEAS CORPUS. When arguments were heard on the writ, Chief Justice Sir John Vaughan ruled that jurors were the sole judges of fact in a trial, and as such they could not be punished for their findings.

Bute, John Stuart, third earl of (1713–1792)
prime minister, 1762–1763

The tutor to GEORGE III was named as his PRIME MINISTER in 1762. His selection alienated the political leaders of the day, and indeed the young king had wanted to choose advisers who were not from their ranks. Bute's ability and influence were subject to so many scurrilous attacks that historians have some difficulty making a fair assessment of his career. One particular reaction was the publication by John WILKES called *The North Briton,* which triggered the important legal case over GENERAL WARRANTS.

Butler, James See ORMONDE, DUKES AND EARLS OF.

Butler, Josephine (1828–1906)
feminist, reformer

A determined social reformer, Butler led the campaign for the repeal of the Contagious Diseases Acts, which required the registration, licensing, and examination of prostitutes in garrison towns and ports. The acts were repealed by 1886. Butler was also active in campaigning for higher EDUCATION for women, in stopping the white slave traffic, and working with the National Vigilance Association of W. T. STEAD.

Butler of Saffron Walden, Richard Austen Butler, baron (1902–1982)
Conservative politician

A MEMBER OF PARLIAMENT from 1929, Butler joined Winston CHURCHILL's wartime CABINET. As minister of EDUCATION he was responsible for the 1944 Education Act, which introduced a three-tier secondary education system, designed to provide free education for all up to age 15. This plan also contained the "11-plus" examination, aimed at determining which level of the system was right for each child. A leader of the moderate wing of the CONSERVATIVE PARTY, Butler held most high posts in government, but he was passed over for the office of PRIME MINISTER in 1957 and 1963.

Butt, Isaac (1813–1879)
Irish lawyer, politician

A Protestant lawyer, Butt was defense counsel for the YOUNG IRELAND leaders in 1848. While once a conservative supporter of the BRITISH EMPIRE, he found himself leaning toward a nationalist position in Irish politics. He believed that IRELAND's economic woes would be offset by a measure of autonomy in an Irish parliament. He was the counsel for the FENIAN BROTHERHOOD bombers in 1868, thus polishing his nationalist credentials. In 1870 he helped in the formation of the Home Government Association, and in 1873 he assisted the HOME RULE League. By 1874 a corps of 58 MPs were supporting the cause, but more radical tactics like those of Charles Stewart PARNELL forced Butt into the background.

by-election

When a member of the HOUSE OF COMMONS dies, resigns, or becomes disqualified, a special election, called a by-election, is held to fill the vacancy. The contest is conducted in the constituency, with assistance from the national parties. The outcome of these elections is scrutinized carefully for any sign of trends which may affect national politics.

Byng, John (1704–1757)
admiral

A son of the naval hero George Byng (1664–1733), the victor over a Spanish fleet in 1718, John Byng was rear admiral by 1745. When the SEVEN YEARS' WAR began, he was sent to protect the garrison on the island of Minorca. Upon arrival he found that the French had already landed, so he retreated to GIBRALTAR, and the garrison had to surrender. There was an outcry at this performance, and Byng was court-martialled and executed. This was the opportunity for the French author Voltaire to comment that the English liked to execute an admiral from time to time *pour encourager les autres* ("to encourage the others").

Byron, George Gordon Noel Byron, sixth baron (1788–1824)
poet

Heir to a title and modest income, Lord Byron attended Harrow and CAMBRIDGE UNIVERSITY and then went on to a grand tour and a life of dissipation. He was nevertheless capable of hard work and zealous political involvement. In 1812 the publication of the first two cantos of *Childe Harold's Pilgrimage* brought him great acclaim and patronage. He published a series of verse romances and became a leading figure in ROMANTICISM. He left England in 1816, participated in the Italian nationalist movement, and in 1824 went to fight in the Greek war for independence. He died of a fever at Missolonghi.

C

cabinet

Royal government always required the active participation of advisers, councillors, or ministers. By the late 17th century the PRIVY COUNCIL, which had performed that function for TUDOR and STUART sovereigns, had become too large and unwieldy. CHARLES II began to consult a small inner group—as his ancestors had also undoubtedly done—which often met in the king's chamber, or cabinet. These meetings became more regular, and by the reign of GEORGE I the king attended less often, allowing one of his ministers, typically the first lord of the TREASURY, to chair the meetings. Thus began the development of the position of PRIME MINISTER.

The cabinet included the leading members (peers and commoners) of the party or parties controlling a majority of the seats in the HOUSE OF COMMONS. This convention emerged since that body had become the *de facto* controller of finance by the end of the 17th century. It was also at this time that the WHIG and TORY parties began to form, since partisan politics only became legitimate after the revolutions of that century. It took until the end of the 18th century for a clear idea of cabinet unity and party loyalty to evolve. By the 19th century, it had become an accepted convention that all members would support a cabinet decision once made ("collective responsibility").

In the 20th century cabinets became more highly structured. In 1916 a cabinet secretariat was established to maintain a record of the decisions and actions of the cabinet. It is remarkable that until such a late date there was no formal record of cabinet meetings. The debates and actions of cabinets were only recorded in the private papers of ministers, who took those with them when they left the government. But since 1916 the proceedings have become much more formal. Also, a system of cabinet committees has developed to cope with the increasing volume and complexity of government business. The prime minister can establish a committee to oversee policy and legislation in any area, and it will report to the full cabinet, thus streamlining the work of the central body. The sovereign still appoints all ministers, on the advice of the prime minister, although today that royal power is ceremonial.

Cabot, John (ca. 1450–1498)
explorer

A Genoese mariner who had sailed for Venice and Spain, Cabot came to Bristol in 1493 and mounted an expedition to cross the Atlantic with his son Sebastian Cabot (1474–1557). On their second attempt they reached NEWFOUNDLAND and NOVA SCOTIA. They mapped the waters of the Atlantic coast down to the Carolinas, but John died on his next voyage, while Sebastian went on to become cartographer to HENRY VIII and governor of the MERCHANT VENTURERS.

Cade's Rebellion (1450)

The defeats in France were accompanied by high taxes and rising public hostility to royal officials. The king's chief adviser, William de la POLE, duke of Suffolk, was being sent into exile in 1450, when he was murdered in a boat off Dover. The government inflicted reprisals on the people of Kent, and this produced a general uprising, wherein a large army of peasants and some gentry marched on London. Their leader was one Jack Cade, about whom little is known. After executing several courtiers, the rebels were forced to leave LONDON, and in spite of a royal pardon, Cade was hunted down and killed. The rebellion had no significant consequence, except that it was a prelude to battles within the aristocracy, known as the Wars of the ROSES.

Cairns, Hugh Cairns, first earl (1819–1885)
lord chancellor

A barrister and MP for BELFAST, Cairns was the first Irishman to be lord chancellor of ENGLAND. He was a legal reformer who worked closely with his counterpart in the LIBERAL PARTY, Lord SELBORNE. He headed a royal commission on the judicial system, which recommended sweeping changes in the judiciary, embodied in the JUDICATURE ACT of 1873. This created the modern structure of a HIGH COURT OF JUSTICE and a court of APPEAL. While it initially did away with the right of appeal to the HOUSE OF LORDS, that was restored by another act in 1876.

Calais

Port on the French coast of Flanders, opposite Dover. Captured by the English in 1347, it was held until 1558. A staging area for invasion and a port of entry for English wool exports, it was a colonial outpost which required heavy expenditure and a garrison of troops. The defenses were allowed to decline, and the French recaptured it in 1558.

Calcutta

English trading post established in 1690 in BENGAL, which began to rival the port of Madras. Fortified after English victories under Robert CLIVE, it became the administrative center for the EAST INDIA COMPANY. In 1834 it became the capital of British INDIA, until it was replaced by NEW DELHI in 1912.

Callaghan, James (1912–   )
prime minister, 1976–1979

James Callaghan grew up in relative poverty and left school at 16, taking a job as a tax officer. He joined his local union and rose to the position of assistant general secretary of the Inland Revenue Staff Federation in 1936. Callaghan was first elected to PARLIAMENT as a candidate for the LABOUR PARTY in Cardiff in 1945. An effective debater, he soon rose in the ranks of the party. When Labour formed a government in 1964, Callaghan was made CHANCELLOR OF THE EXCHEQUER, in which post he had to struggle with a series of financial crises that led to the devaluation of the pound sterling in 1967. Callaghan moved to the HOME OFFICE, where in 1969 he was responsible for sending troops into NORTHERN IRELAND to try to quell the violence there. In a later Labour government, Callaghan served as foreign secretary, and he was involved with continuing negotiations on the terms of Britain's entry into the EUROPEAN ECONOMIC COMMUNITY. When HAROLD WILSON resigned as PRIME MINISTER and party leader in 1976, Callaghan was chosen by the party to replace him. Due to high inflation and government deficits, Callaghan faced a period of serious economic discontent. The government was forced to seek financial aid from the International Monetary Fund, and Callaghan tried to bring in a policy of wage restraint. He was opposed by union leaders and confronted with a series of strikes. Because of that, his government lost a VOTE OF CONFIDENCE (by one vote) and then lost the ensuing general election of 1979 to MARGARET THATCHER and the Conservatives.

Calvert, George See BALTIMORE, GEORGE CALVERT, FIRST BARON.

Cambridge University

In the Middle Ages schools were conducted by the clergy in monasteries and cathedrals. More advanced learning came in communities of scholars under some form of patronage; these "colleges" became more numerous from the 12th century (Bologna, Paris, Oxford). Cambridge University dates its origin to around 1209, when a group of scholars left OXFORD UNIVERSITY after a local dispute and migrated to Cambridge. The first chancellor was recorded in 1225. The first college foundation was that of Peterhouse in 1284. The university provides the general governing structure and manages properties, libraries, laboratories, and awards degrees. The colleges are autonomous endowed institutions that house teachers, researchers, and students.

There were 11 college foundations before the REFORMATION, five more in the 16th century, and none thereafter until six were founded in the 19th century and six more in the 20th century. The major reform in the nature and structure of university education came in the middle of the 19th century, when general examinations were introduced. University lecturers were added in

King's College Chapel in Cambridge *(Hulton/Archive)*

1868, and soon after, courses were opened to women, religious tests were abolished, and modern scientific laboratories were added to the school. The main changes in the 20th century have been public provision of tuition and more open access to education based on merit. These have diluted the once aristocratic tone of all higher EDUCATION along with the rapid expansion of UNIVERSITIES after 1960.

Camden, William (1551–1623)
historian

Camden taught at Westminster School (1575–97) and helped to establish the Society of Antiquaries (1585). He traveled widely across ENGLAND and collected information for his *Britannia,* a survey of the counties of England, published in Latin (1586) and later in English (1600). He also wrote a contemporary history, *Annals of Queen Elizabeth* (1615), employing state papers to which he was given access by his patron, William CECIL, Lord Burghley.

Cameron, Richard (1648–1680)
Scottish religious leader

A schoolteacher in Fife, he later became a PRESBYTERIAN field preacher. He was not present when a group of COVENANTERS were beaten at the Battle of Bothwell Bridge in 1679, but in 1680 he issued a declaration denouncing CHARLES II and declaring him deposed. Royal troops hunted him down and killed him. This action hardened the resistance of covenanters, some now called "Cameronians." They rejected attempts at compromise in 1689, and they refused to join the restored Presbyterian CHURCH OF SCOTLAND.

Campaign for Nuclear Disarmament (CND)

The CND was formed in 1958 by a group of intellectuals who advocated unilateral nuclear disarmament, including Bertrand RUSSELL and J. B. PRIESTLEY. Annual marches were held from the Aldermaston nuclear base in Berkshire to Trafalgar Square in London, drawing as many as 100,000 people. In 1960 the LABOUR PARTY endorsed unilateral disarmament, but reversed this view the next year. A test-ban treaty in 1963 reduced the size of the CND, but it revived during the 1980s when the NORTH ATLANTIC TREATY ORGANIZATION announced plans to place cruise missiles at British bases. As many as 400,000 attended its Hyde Park rally in 1982, but after further arms treaties were signed, the group's membership declined again.

Campbell family

A major name in Scots history, the Campbells were leaders in Argyll from the early period of the revival of the MONARCHY in the 14th century. As allies of the Crown in the 15th century, the Campbell earls increased their power in the Southwest and the Isles, and with time there were important branches established throughout SCOTLAND. Members of the Campbell clan were adversaries of the STUART clan, but by the end of the century they had become Crown agents, as at the GLENCOE MASSACRE (1692). They were among the supporters of the UNION (1707), and they were allies of the Crown against the JACOBITES in the 1740s.

Campion, Edmund (1540–1581)
Jesuit martyr

The son of a bookseller in LONDON, Campion attended OXFORD UNIVERSITY, and after converting to Catholicism he made his way to Douai (1571) and thence to Rome, where he joined the JESUIT order in 1573. In 1580 he was sent on a mission to ENGLAND, news of which alarmed the government of Queen ELIZABETH I. He was apprehended in Berkshire, taken to London, and tortured on the rack. He refused to recant or to confess to the fabricated charges of treason against him. He was executed in December 1581.

Canada

There had been early English contact with the northern parts of the Americas, in the voyages of John CABOT and his son Sebastian (1497–1508) and the developing fur trade through the Hudson's Bay Company (1670). However, there was extensive French exploration and settlement in the areas to the south around Quebec and in the interior, extending along the valley of the St. Lawrence River into the lakes and the headwaters of the Mississippi River. The rivalry between colonial powers naturally produced conflict, but British influence only became preeminent after the victory of General James WOLFE at Quebec in 1759. In the previous generation the area of Acadia was ceded by treaty (1713) and repopulated and renamed NOVA SCOTIA. But this sort of draconian policy was not feasible for the rest of Canada, and there began a long-term effort at assimilation of the French and English colonial populations, which is still incomplete today.

When the AMERICAN COLONIES rebelled against British rule, many loyalists migrated to Canada. The refugees from the thirteen colonies joined the multicultural population, which, in the early 19th century, began to experience heavier migrations, especially from SCOTLAND. Canada was a source of minerals, timber, and wheat, but it was an uneasy colony, and GREAT BRITAIN tried several formulas for government in the 19th century. The British North America Act of 1867 seemed to offer a sound solution: a federation of provinces combined with a federal government and a colonial governor-general produced the first of the empire's DOMINIONS. New provinces were quickly added: the Northwest Territories and Manitoba in 1870, British Columbia in 1871, and Prince Edward Island in 1873. Somewhat later the Arctic Islands (1880), the Yukon (1898), Alberta and Saskatchewan (1905), and NEWFOUNDLAND (1949) entered the federation.

A secession movement among French Canadians gained momentum with their electoral victory in Quebec in 1976, but they failed to win a referendum on secession in 1980. A second referendum was narrowly defeated in 1995. Meanwhile the discussion of a possible breakup brought added interest to the long-running debate on the nature of the constitution. The Canadian constitution was, like that of Britain, subject to the legislative authority of the PARLIAMENT in Westminster. In 1982, after conferring with provincial governments, the Canadian parliament passed a Constitution Act which contained a Canadian Charter of Rights and Freedoms, a section on the rights of the aboriginal peoples of Canada, and a procedure for amending the constitution—by federal approval plus that of two-thirds of the provinces, without any reference to Britain. This act was not opposed by the British government, and it signaled Canada's formal independence.

In the latter part of the 20th century, the Canadian economy became a much more pressing issue. There was stress resulting from the antagonism between resource-rich western provinces and the historically more populous and powerful eastern ones. There was an attempt, in the North American Free Trade Agreement (1987), to generate more trade, but the economy seemed unable to break out of the grip of high unemployment and low public revenues.

Canning, George (1770–1827)
prime minister, 1827

The son of a barrister, Canning was educated at Eton and OXFORD UNIVERSITY; he entered PARLIAMENT in 1794. He served under William PITT, and on two later occasions he was foreign secretary (1807 and 1822). He favored liberal policies such as Catholic emancipation, and in foreign affairs he opposed the European autocracies that had been GREAT BRITAIN's allies against Napoleon Bonaparte. He supported the developing independent countries in Latin America as well as the movement for Greek independence. He clashed often with colleagues, even fighting a famous duel with Viscount CASTLEREAGH, a fellow CABINET member. He was made prime minister in April 1827 but died in August.

Canterbury

A main tribal center before the Romans, a regional capital during their occupation, and the capital of the pagan kingdom of Kent, this was the place where St. Augustine brought his mission in 597. It thus became the seat of the ARCHBISHOP of Canterbury, the senior primate of the English church. The cathedral was rebuilt in 1174 after a fire, and it became the destination for pilgrims visiting the shrine of Thomas Becket, the archbishop who was murdered there in 1170.

Cape Colony

The main British colony in SOUTH AFRICA, the Cape Colony was seized from the Dutch in 1795, returned and retaken, and finally ceded to GREAT BRITAIN in 1814. The original settlers, the Boers, could not accept British rule, particularly the antislavery policy adopted for the empire in 1833. The Great Trek into NATAL, and then the TRANSVAAL, and finally the ORANGE FREE STATE, demonstrated their determination to escape British control, seemingly settled by a war of independence (1880–81). However, the discovery of gold (1867) and diamonds (1886) brought further interference, leading eventually to the BOER WAR and the founding of the Union of SOUTH AFRICA, by which the Cape Colony and the republics were incorporated into a federal government in 1910.

capital punishment

Death, usually by hanging, was the routine sentence for a convicted felon or traitor until the 18th century. From the 17th century, transportation was an alternative punishment, first to the AMERICAN COLONIES and later to AUSTRALIA. The number of crimes punishable by death rose dramatically in the 18th century, which caused an increase in hangings, in transportation, and in jury acquittals. There was also growing support for reform of the CRIMINAL LAW, and in the 1840s the number of capital crimes was reduced

to four: murder, treason, piracy, and destruction of arsenals or dockyards. From 1868, executions were no longer in public, and the long debate over the death penalty resulted in the end of capital punishment for murder in 1965.

Cardigan, James Thomas Brudenell, seventh earl of (1797–1868)
army officer

A MEMBER OF PARLIAMENT (1818–37) before succeeding to his title, Cardigan was also a cavalry officer who rose to the rank of major general. He was the commander in the disastrous "charge of the light brigade" in the Battle of Balaclava (1854), an episode in the CRIMEAN WAR that made him famous. His name also was given to the wool jacket or sweater which became popular at the time.

Cardwell, Edward Cardwell, viscount (1813–1886)
secretary for war, 1868–1874

Son of a merchant in Liverpool, Cardwell attended Balliol College, OXFORD UNIVERSITY; and the Inner Temple (see INNS OF COURT). A MEMBER OF PARLIAMENT from the 1840s, he served as secretary for war under WILLIAM GLADSTONE, and he is known for abolishing flogging, ending the sale of officers' commissions, and implementing a general regimental reorganization. He also introduced shortened terms of enlistment and the subordination of the commander in chief to the secretary of state for war, the civilian head of the army.

Carlyle, Thomas (1795–1881)
historian, essayist

Carlyle attended the University of EDINBURGH, but did not take a degree. He worked as a schoolmaster and journalist, and he was instrumental in introducing the English to contemporary German literature ("Life of Schiller," *London Magazine*, 1824). He also wrote essays on many current subjects; his first collection was published as *Sartor resartus* (1833–34). After moving to London, he began writing historical works and moral essays. His history of *The French Revolution* appeared in 1837; his essay *On Heroes, Hero-Worship and the Heroic in History* in 1841. Essays on *Chartism* (1839) and *Past and Present* (1843) were vehicles for his critique of modern capitalist society. He also edited *Oliver Cromwell's Letters and Speeches* (2 volumes, 1845) and composed a massive study of *Frederick the Great* (6 volumes, 1858–65).

Carnarvon, Henry Howard Molyneux Herbert, fourth earl of (1831–1890)
colonial secretary

Lord Carnarvon was an advocate of colonial federation, within colonies and between them and Britain. He was colonial secretary when the British North America Act created the federal system in CANADA (1867). A similar effort for SOUTH AFRICA in the 1880s was a failure. He also tried to find this type of solution for IRELAND, when as lord lieutenant he had secret talks with IRISH HOME RULE leader Charles PARNELL.

Caroline of Brunswick (1768–1821)
wife of George IV

Caroline married George, Prince of Wales, in 1795; they separated the following year. She traveled widely and not too discreetly in Europe. When George came to the throne after his father's death in 1820, she was offered an allowance of £50,000 per year to stay abroad, but she returned to England and attempted to claim her title. The king sought a parliamentary divorce but failed; she in turn tried to enter WESTMINSTER ABBEY for the coronation in 1821, but was denied entry. These events were occasions for large demonstrations against the government, but there was no real danger, which was notable since there had recently been very serious concern raised by the PETERLOO MASSACRE (1819) and the CATO STREET CONSPIRACY (1820).

Carr, Robert   See SOMERSET, ROBERT CARR, EARL OF.

Carroll, Lewis (1832–1898)
author

Pseudonym of Charles Dodgson, author of *Alice's Adventures in Wonderland* (1865) and *Through the Looking-Glass* (1871). Dodgson had attended Rugby School and Christ Church, OXFORD UNIVERSITY. He lectured in mathematics there from 1855 to 1881. An ordained minister, he wrote occasional pamphlets on local subjects as well as mathematical works, the main one being *Euclid and his Modern Rivals* (1879).

Carson, Sir Edward (1854–1935)
lawyer, Ulster unionist

Born into a Protestant family in DUBLIN, Carson initially practiced law in IRELAND. He later moved to LONDON, where he became a MEMBER OF PARLIAMENT (1892–1921) and a leading figure in the CONSERVATIVE PARTY (solicitor general, 1900–06). He led the Ulster UNIONISTS in 1910, was active in organizing resistance to the third IRISH HOME RULE bill (1912–14), promoted the ULSTER COVENANT in 1912, and enlisted men in the Ulster Volunteers, a paramilitary group pledged to fight for ULSTER's continued union with GREAT BRITAIN. He became a member of the war cabinet in 1915 and helped to overthrow Herbert ASQUITH in 1916. By the time Carson resigned as unionist leader in 1921, Ulster had separated from the IRISH FREE STATE and achieved its goal of remaining in the UNITED KINGDOM.

Carte, Richard D'Oyly (1844–1901)
opera promoter

Carte composed operettas and ran a concert agency, produced GILBERT AND SULLIVAN's works (1875–89), and built the Savoy Theatre (1881) and the Royal English Opera House (1891). The last was not successful, and it became the Palace

Theatre of Varieties. The D'Oyly Carte Opera Company disbanded in 1982, no longer holding the monopoly on the Gilbert and Sullivan operas.

Cartwright, John (1740–1824)
political reformer

Known as the Major, Cartwright served for some years in the navy, but his rank came from a later position in the Nottinghamshire militia. He had a long career as an advocate of political reform, arguing that English tradition from Saxon times legitimized an open and democratic system. In his first publication, *Take Your Choice!* (1776), he advocated universal suffrage and annual parliaments. He founded the Society for Constitutional Information in 1780. Although he was out of step with the radicals of the 1790s, who were under the influence of the French Revolution, he returned to active radical politics in the early 19th century, founding the Hampden Club movement, which was made up of local groups discussing reforms. They evaded government interference (1812–17) as long as they were local. When a national meeting was called in 1817, they were suppressed.

Cartwright, Thomas (1535–1603)
Puritan intellectual

A fellow of Trinity College, CAMBRIDGE UNIVERSITY, in 1562, having been exiled in the reign of MARY I, Cartwright was involved in controversies over the proper position of BISHOPS, the correct vestments for the clergy, and other religious disputes in the reign of Queen ELIZABETH I. When he became the Lady Margaret Professor of Divinity (1569), his lectures advocated replacing bishops with a PRESBYTERIAN system. For his efforts he lost his posts and emigrated to Geneva. He returned to England in 1585, continued to support unorthodox views, was imprisoned twice, and retired to Guernsey in 1595. He was the foremost PURITAN intellectual of his time.

Casement, Sir Roger (1864–1916)
Irish nationalist

Born near DUBLIN, Casement had a distinguished career in the British colonial service. In both the Congo and the Amazon he reported on atrocities by Europeans against native workers, for which he was knighted in 1911. Returning to IRELAND at the height of the prewar agitation for IRISH HOME RULE, he joined the Irish Volunteers in 1913. When WORLD WAR I broke out, he traveled to Berlin and arranged for an arms shipment to Ireland. This was intercepted, and he was arrested in April 1916, on the eve of the EASTER REBELLION. He was tried for treason, convicted, and executed. Diaries attributed to him, with numerous homosexual passages, were circulated by the British Secret Service in order to buffer expected protests from Ireland and from Irish Americans.

castle

Fortified residence designed to defend an area, a route, or a town. Castle construction became increasingly elaborate and costly over the three centuries after the NORMAN CONQUEST in 1066. Early wooden structures were soon replaced with stone, with heavier walls and more elaborate design. Siege engines and mining techniques forced further improvements. Castles were the centers of government and the sites of treasuries, courts, jails, and places of official business. They retained their utility into the age of gunpowder, but apart from the CIVIL WAR of the 1640s, the need for these massive defense structures had passed, and for those who could or would build vast places of residence, they were replaced from the 16th century on by the country house.

Castlereagh, Robert Stewart, second viscount (1769–1822)
politician, foreign secretary

Lord Castlereagh began his career in the Irish Parliament in the 1790s and entered Westminster in 1794. He became a strong supporter of union between IRELAND and GREAT BRITAIN. As chief secretary for Ireland (1798–1801), he was responsible for gaining approval of the law creating the UNITED KINGDOM of Great Britain and Ireland. He served as secretary for war (1805 and 1807) and secured the duke of WELLINGTON's appointment as commander of British forces in Portugal. His greatest fame results from his service as foreign secretary (1812–22) as he crafted the alliance with Austria, Prussia, and Russia which defeated Napoleon Bonaparte. At the Congress of Vienna (1815) he helped to achieve a moderate settlement against France, and he kept the allies in a series of postwar meetings, known as the "congress system." When the autocratic states formed a "holy alliance" (Russia, Prussia, and Austria), he became discouraged at the failure of his diplomatic efforts. Seemingly exhausted, he committed suicide in 1822.

cathedral

The principal seat of a BISHOP or ARCHBISHOP. As the great centers of church governance and religious pageantry, cathedrals were usually important examples of the architecture of their period. From the Norman era, only a few elements of original buildings survive, the 12th-century nave of Durham being the most substantial. Parts of Wells cathedral date from the 13th century; Lincoln, Gloucester, and Salisbury from the 14th. Winchester, CANTERBURY, and York as well as others have all had reconstruction projects, the last (and largest) being in York in the 1970s. In the 17th century, the construction of ST. PAUL'S CATHEDRAL in LONDON was a unique effort for that period, arising from the general rebuilding in the capital after the great fire of 1666. From the late 19th century on, there was a revival of new construction (Truro, 1880; Liverpool, 1904; Guildford, 1936; Coventry, 1956). Roman Catholic cathedrals were begun at Westminster (1895), Liverpool (1962), and Bristol (1970).

Catherine of Aragon (1485–1536)
queen of England

The daughter of Ferdinand and Isabella of Spain, Catherine married Arthur, the eldest son of HENRY VII (1501); Arthur died five months later. The king obtained a dispensation to allow her to marry his younger son, but that wedding only took place after HENRY VIII came to the throne in 1509. Of their six children, only MARY I survived infancy. Moved by both his desire for a male heir and his love for Anne BOLEYN, Henry sought an annulment of the marriage, attacking the earlier dispensation as invalid. Catherine resisted, and her nephew, Emperor Charles V, put pressure on the pope to deny the annulment. Henry then acted unilaterally. They were separated formally in 1531, he married Anne in 1533, and Catherine lived the rest of her life deprived of her title and forbidden to see her daughter.

Catherine Howard See HOWARD, CATHERINE.

Catherine Parr See PARR, CATHERINE.

Catholic Association

A group organized in 1823 by Daniel O'CONNELL to pursue the goal of CATHOLIC EMANCIPATION. A mass organization, with dues of a penny a month, the Catholic Association prepared petitions, held public meetings, and brought some discipline to the disenfranchised Catholic majority in IRELAND. The Catholic community had begun to recover from the PENAL LAWS of the early 18th century by the 1770s, and this movement had the potential to complete that process. That was evident when O'Connell won the parliamentary election for County Clare in 1828. Though he was disqualified from sitting because of his religion, O'Connell had defeated a Protestant who favored emancipation, and there was every sign that he would continue to win in the future. Thus the government, led by the duke of WELLINGTON, bowed to the inevitable and allowed Catholic emancipation to become law in 1829. The emancipation act also called for the abolition of the Catholic Association, but this was an empty gesture, as the aim of that body had been achieved.

Catholic emancipation (1829)

This term meant removal of restrictions on Roman Catholics from full participation in political life. Laws that had severely limited legal, economic, and political rights dated from the 16th century and were fashioned into a code of PENAL LAWS in the early 18th century. But such legislation failed, and by the 1770s it was being modified. By 1800 the main remaining limit was denial of the ability to sit in PARLIAMENT or to hold civil offices. William PITT proposed to do away with this ban as part of the act of UNION in 1800, but GEORGE III refused, saying that it would violate his coronation oath as defender of the church. Both the WHIGS and the TORY Party were divided on the issue and loath to bring it forward, given the king's objections. The Catholic Relief Act of 1829 allowed Roman Catholics to sit in Parliament and to hold public offices, except those of regent, LORD LIEUTENANT, or LORD CHANCELLOR. This Act coincided with the end of the Tory Party's rule of the previous half-century.

Cato Street Conspiracy (1820)

A group of extreme radicals plotted to murder the members of the CABINET at dinner in 1820. The group had been infiltrated by government spies, and members were arrested at a meeting in a stable in Cato Street in London. Five members of the group were tried and executed.

Cavalier Parliament (1661–1679)

In 1660 the CONVENTION Parliament invited CHARLES II to return to the throne. That PARLIAMENT was irregular because it was not summoned by a king. Nevertheless it sat for the rest of 1660, and in the following year a new, legitimate parliament was elected. Because it contained a large number of royalists, many of whom had fought for the Crown in the CIVIL WAR, it was given the nickname "cavalier," the tag used for royalist supporters. This parliament remained in session (though prorogued many times) until 1679.

Cavell, Edith (1865–1915)
nurse

A native of Norfolk, Cavell was the matron of a Red Cross hospital in Brussels, Belgium, from where she helped a number of allied soldiers to escape during WORLD WAR I. The German authorities arrested her, and she was tried by court-martial and shot in October 1915. She thus became a national martyr.

Cavendish, Lord Frederick Charles (1836–1882)

The second son of William, seventh duke of Devonshire, and a graduate of Trinity College, CAMBRIDGE UNIVERSITY, Cavendish had been a MEMBER OF PARLIAMENT for the West Riding of Yorkshire since 1865. He served as private secretary to William GLADSTONE, who chose him to be chief secretary for IRELAND (1882). This was a critical point in relations with Ireland, as Gladstone had only recently made a deal with Charles PARNELL to reduce violent confrontations. The so-called KILMAINHAM TREATY allowed Parnell to be released from jail on condition that he order his followers desist from violent acts. That "treaty" led to the resignation of the chief secretary William E. FORSTER, thus requiring the appointment of a replacement.

When Cavendish arrived in DUBLIN on May 6, 1882, he met Thomas Burke, the undersecretary, and as the two walked through Phoenix Park in the center of the city, they were murdered in broad daylight by a gang of terrorists armed with surgical knives who called themselves "the Invincibles." They apparently had no connection with Parnell or his section of the IRISH HOME RULE movement, although that was hardly credible to the British public at the time.

The outrage led to a new Coercion Act, but it also put more pressure on Gladstone and Parnell to find solutions to the Irish problems.

Cavendish, Henry (1731–1810)
scientist

The grandson of the second duke, and a millionaire, he was a serious and brilliant scientific investigator. He presented a paper to the ROYAL SOCIETY in 1766 on the discovery of hydrogen ("inflammable air"). In 1784 he followed up with a demonstration that the product of hydrogen and oxygen was water. He studied the density of the earth and made experiments with electricity. The Cavendish Laboratory at CAMBRIDGE UNIVERSITY was founded in his memory.

Cavendish, Spencer See HARTINGTON, SPENCER CAVENDISH, MARQUESS OF.

Cavendish, Thomas (1560–1592)
sailor

Cavendish led an exploration of Carolina in 1585, his ship sailing under the command of Sir Richard Grenville. The next year Grenville planned to copy Sir Francis DRAKE's circumnavigation of the globe (1577–80), and though they captured a Spanish treasure ship, Cavendish squandered his wealth. He and John Davis set out for China in 1591, but they never reached the Pacific, and Cavendish died somewhere in the Atlantic.

Cavendish, William, duke of Devonshire See DEVONSHIRE, WILLIAM CAVENDISH, FOURTH DUKE OF.

Caxton, William (ca. 1422–1491)
printer

A merchant in Kent, Caxton engaged in trade with the Continent, learned the art of printing in Cologne, and had a printing shop in Bruges.

In 1476 he moved back to England, where he set up the first press in Westminster. He published nearly 100 titles ranging over many different subjects. While his printing was not deemed to be of high quality, his influence on English language and culture was enormous.

Cecil, Robert See SALISBURY, ROBERT GASCOYNE CECIL, MARQUESS OF.

Cecil, Sir Robert (1563–1612)
statesman

The son of William CECIL, Lord Burghley, ELIZABETH I's chief minister. He took over his father's role and was SECRETARY OF STATE from 1596 until 1608. He was an important figure in the smooth transition of government from Elizabeth to JAMES VI AND I. The king elevated him to the PEERAGE, and in 1608 made him lord treasurer. In that post Cecil had the unenviable task of trying to control the king's expenditures and raise his revenue. He put together a remarkable art collection and rebuilt Hatfield House as a palatial residence for his successors.

Cecil, William, See BURGHLEY, WILLIAM CECIL, FIRST BARON.

Celts

The name of the major ethnic group of central and western Europe, identified by Greek writers and mentioned by Julius Caesar. The Celts occupied the British Isles in the last days of prehistory, from about 500 B.C. into the time of the Roman occupation. They were a tribal people, led by a class of fierce warriors, worshipping a naturalist religion with Druid priests. The Romans subjugated the area approximating to modern ENGLAND, while WALES and SCOTLAND were not conquered but had garrisons controlling them. IRELAND, on the other hand, was untouched by Roman occupation. Thus there were different degrees of survival of Celtic traditions. The native languages, which scholars divided into *goidelic* (Irish and Scottish GAELIC, and Manx) and *brythonic* (Welsh, Cornish, and Breton), can still be seen in today's place names. However, from the time of the Norman Conquest onward, the spread of English colonization erased any political power among Celtic peoples, leaving varied levels of identity. The social and cultural traditions were preserved in Ireland and Wales, and the Christian church as formed in Celtic Ireland spread over much of Scotland and part of Northern England, while most of the South was being reconverted by Roman missions. The myths and traditions of these areas have had several revivals in the 18th, 19th, and 20th centuries. There is now strenuous effort to study and preserve the languages (Cornish and Manx have expired). There are periodic festivals and celebrations of ancient poetry and art, and archeologists have helped to fill a growing number of museum collections with artifacts since the 19th century. In sum, the tradition of the aboriginal inhabitants of the British Isles is now, belatedly, recognized as a matter of serious scientific, historical, and social value.

See also CLAN; EISTEDDFODAU; OSSIAN; PEARSE, PATRICK.

census

There were several attempts from the 17th century on to calculate the population of ENGLAND. In the course of the 18th century many European countries instituted a census as a tool of public policy. The debate over the matter went on, with opponents citing their concern for British liberty and fear of foreign influence. Only during the critical years of the French wars was the project deemed necessary. The Census Act of 1800, sponsored by Charles ABBOT, began the practice, and the census has been taken at 10-year intervals since 1801.

Ceylon

A large island south of INDIA, whose first European contact was with Portuguese and Dutch merchants. The EAST INDIA COMPANY took possession for the Crown in 1796 during the French wars. A plantation economy was developed, producing cinnamon, coconut, tea, coffee, and rubber. Political reforms came fairly early: a legislative council in 1912 and universal suffrage in 1931. Independence and Commonwealth membership came in 1948, and in 1972 the country gained full independence as the Republic of SRI LANKA.

Chadwick, Edwin (1800–1890)
reformer

A barrister and a social critic, associated with Jeremy BENTHAM and UTILITARIANISM, Chadwick served on the Poor Law Commission (1832) and the Factory Commission (1833). Probably his greatest contribution was his *Report on the Sanitary Condition of the Labouring Population of Great Britain* (1842), which led to the Public Health Act of 1848 and the Board of Health, on which he worked from 1848 to 1854.

Chalmers, Thomas (1780–1847)
churchman, social reformer

Chalmers entered St. Andrews University at age 11, and in 1823 he became professor of moral philosophy there. His main career was as a preacher and writer. His brand of EVANGELICAL Christianity had a strong element of social welfare, but through private charity, not the state. He was the minister of the Tron Church and of St. John's parish in Glasgow. In 1832, while professor of divinity at the University of EDINBURGH, he was made Moderator of the GENERAL ASSEMBLY of the CHURCH OF SCOTLAND. In 1834 he proposed what was called the Veto Act, a proviso that allowed a parish to reject a minister chosen by the patron. This became a major legal dispute, and when the court of SESSION ruled against such provisions, Chalmers led the secession movement, later known as the DISRUPTION, in 1843. He then became the Moderator of the new FREE CHURCH OF SCOTLAND.

Chamberlain, (Arthur) Neville
(1869–1940)

prime minister, 1937–1940

The son of Joseph CHAMBERLAIN, Neville Chamberlain had a successful career in manufacturing in Birmingham. He entered politics late, serving as mayor of Birmingham in 1915 and as a MEMBER OF PARLIAMENT from 1918. He held the post of Minister of Health (1923, and 1924–29), in which capacity he designed a new pension plan, promoted the construction of council housing, and supervised the dismantling of the old poor law. As CHANCELLOR OF THE EXCHEQUER in the National Government (1931–37), he abandoned FREE TRADE and adopted a general TARIFF which excluded the empire, a shadow of his father's IMPERIAL PREFERENCE scheme. In 1937 he succeeded Stanley BALDWIN as PRIME MINISTER, just in time to confront the growing threat of Germany, Italy, and Japan. He proposed to meet these threats with an active policy of APPEASEMENT, effectively buying off the aggressor states with concessions. This popular approach was expected to forestall fighting and provide more time for rearmament. The climax of the policy came in 1938 when Chamberlain flew to Munich to meet with Adolf Hitler, Benito Mussolini, and French premier Edouard Daladier. He conceded the Sudeten borderlands of Czechoslovakia to Germany, and in return he received a

British prime minister Neville Chamberlain making his "peace in our time" address, September 30, 1938 *(Hulton/Archive)*

written promise from Hitler that there would be no further aggression. Within six months, that promise was broken, and the British government ended appeasement by making an Anglo-Polish alliance in 1939. After WORLD WAR II broke out, Chamberlain was forced to resign in May 1940.

Chamberlain, Joseph (1836–1914)
politician

Chamberlain was a Birmingham manufacturer, successful in local politics, who applied progressive measures to the reform of the city. Elected to PARLIAMENT as a Liberal in 1876, he soon became a leader of the radical wing, a critic of the aristocracy, and a proponent of extensive reforms. But he was unhappy with what he saw as weak foreign and imperial policies in his own LIBERAL PARTY. He broke with William GLADSTONE over IRISH HOME RULE, leading the large LIBERAL UNIONIST faction toward eventual reconciliation with the TORY Party. He served in the Conservative CABINET of Lord SALISBURY as colonial secretary and was notably involved in the fruitless negotiations before the BOER WAR. He caused another major party split when in 1903 he opened a campaign for TARIFF reform, under the label IMPERIAL PREFERENCE, a scheme to draw the colonies and GREAT BRITAIN into ever closer ties in a unified trading system. The Conservatives divided on the issue and suffered a major loss in the 1906 election.

Chamberlain, (Joseph) Austen (1863–1937)
politician

The son of Joseph CHAMBERLAIN, Austen Chamberlain was a MEMBER OF PARLIAMENT from 1892 to 1937. He served in many ministerial posts, including CHANCELLOR OF THE EXCHEQUER, secretary of state for INDIA, and foreign secretary. In the last post he negotiated the 1925 Locarno Treaty, which normalized relations between France and Germany. This won him the Nobel Peace Prize.

chancellor of the exchequer

The CABINET minister responsible for fiscal and economic policy. He or she presents a BUDGET each year which embodies the government's main policy decisions. The office came from the ancient court of the EXCHEQUER, where from an early date a clerk of that body acted in the name of the high chancellor. That clerk was also a deputy to the lord treasurer, which post was the official base of the office of PRIME MINISTER in the 17th and 18th centuries. As that political role evolved, the responsibilities of the TREASURY board were delegated to the chancellor of the exchequer, who became the government's main financial officer.

Chancery, Court of

The chancery was the royal writing office, headed by the LORD CHANCELLOR. As he held the GREAT SEAL, he was responsible for the issue of WRITS, or royal orders of all kinds, including the original writs which initiated legal proceedings. The chancellor also saw all petitions to the Crown seeking royal justice; some were outside the jurisdiction of the COMMON LAW courts, and some might be from dissatisfied suitors in those courts. The chancellor began to act on these petitions, using what came to be known as EQUITY jurisdiction. By the end of the 15th century, this practice had produced an entirely new royal court, the Chancery.

See also COURTS OF LAW; JUDICATURE ACT; MASTER OF THE ROLLS.

Channel Islands

Located in the English Channel, at one point only 10 miles from France, the four major islands are Jersey, Guernsey, Alderney, and Sark. These possessions of the English Crown were retained when king John lost the duchy of Normandy to France in 1204. Jersey is the largest of the islands, and it forms one of two bailiwicks, with a lieutenant governor appointed by the Crown. Guernsey, with Alderney and Sark, form the other bailiwick. The islands have their own laws, courts, legislative assemblies, and currency.

charity schools

There was a long tradition of bequests to establish schools for the poor, a practice that accelerated in the 16th century. Along with some much older foundations, these often became the GRAMMAR or "public" schools which served the elite of society. At the end of the 17th century a movement began to establish schools for poor children, by subscription rather than endowment. There was a strong religious motive, namely to educate and catechize as many of the poor as possible. The SOCIETY FOR THE PROMOTION OF CHRISTIAN KNOWLEDGE (1698) was in the forefront of English school foundation. In SCOTLAND there was a statutory measure for parochial schools in 1696, rising from very similar motives. In WALES the schools of the Welsh Trust in the 1670s were a similar effort, as were the "circulating schools" of Griffith Jones in the 1730s. In IRELAND there were school ventures in the 18th century designed to promote Protestant faith at the expense of Roman Catholicism, and at the same time Catholic children were taught by itinerant schoolmasters in the so-called "hedge schools." These efforts were overtaken by more secular state-supported educational provision in the 19th century.

See also EDUCATION; SUNDAY SCHOOLS.

Charles I (1600–1649)

king of England, Scotland, and Ireland, 1625–1649

The second son of JAMES VI AND I, Charles became the heir apparent when his brother Henry died in 1612. The problems of his reign revolved around religious and constitutional issues which were evident long before he came to the throne. Where his father was in favor of compromising differences between Protestants and Catholics, even trying to take a middle ground during the bloody Thirty Years' War in Europe, Charles was decidedly in favor of more conservative policies, as reflected in his courtship of the Spanish Infanta and his marriage to the French princess Henrietta Maria, sister of Louis XIII. He also favored the positions and practice of the so-called ARMINIAN faction in the CHURCH OF ENGLAND, as opposed to the PURITANS, who were well-represented in PARLIAMENT. As for that body, Charles believed that his royal PREROGATIVE entitled him to full allegiance, and when Parliament refused financial support, he regarded this as something close to treason. He dissolved his first parliament (1625) when it failed to provide him with adequate funds; he dissolved the second when it attempted to impeach the royal favorite George Villiers, duke of BUCKINGHAM. The third parliament saw further battles result in the concession of the PETITION OF RIGHT (1628). Still more disputes led Charles to dissolve the body in 1629 and to govern without a parliament for 11 years.

During this period of personal rule, Charles used powerful and autocratic councillors: the earl of STRAFFORD as his chief officer, first in IRELAND and then in ENGLAND; and William LAUD, his ARCHBISHOP of CANTERBURY, as the principal agent of his religious policy. Their acts were seen as tending toward authoritarian rule—for instance, Strafford's policies of challenging land claims in Ireland and Laud's vigorous campaign against Puritans in England. In 1637 Charles authorized a new prayer book for SCOTLAND, which led to the BISHOPS' WARS. That conflict forced the king to summon a new parliament, though on the first occasion (April–May 1640) the SHORT PARLIAMENT did little more than harangue the king. He soon had to summon another, and when this LONG PARLIAMENT met, Charles had to accept many of its proposals because of his desperate financial need. In these circumstances of distrust, there was a rebellion in Ireland in late 1641, wherein a large number of Protestants were killed by Catholics in ULSTER. The question of raising an army underscored the fears of both sides and brought out further constitutional arguments in the GRAND REMONSTRANCE. In January 1642 the king ordered the arrest of five MPs, and he personally led a company of soldiers into the HOUSE OF COMMONS to apprehend them. They had escaped, but now the use of force had become inevitable.

The king withdrew from LONDON in 1642. Parliament made a series of even more radical demands limiting royal power in the NINETEEN PROPOSITIONS, and in August the king raised the royal standard at Nottingham, calling upon his loyal subjects to help him subdue his treacherous enemies. The CIVIL WAR—or, as some call it, the War of the Three Kingdoms—had begun. The rebels' armies defeated the king at the battles of MARSTON MOOR (1644) and NASEBY (1645), and the king surrendered in 1646. For the next three years he tried to bargain with allies in England and Scotland, and when royalist resistance led to uprisings and a brief campaign on his behalf, the army (see Oliver CROMWELL) and the radical Parliament leaders (see Sir Henry VANE the elder) decided to put Charles on trial. He was convicted of treason by an extraordinary HIGH COURT OF JUSTICE in 1649 and executed. His brave defense at trial and his dignified behavior on the scaffold were his finest moments. His two sons, CHARLES II and JAMES VII AND II, would later succeed him on the throne.

See also CLARENDON, EDWARD HYDE, EARL OF; MONTROSE, JAMES GRAHAM, MARQUESS OF; NEW MODEL ARMY; PYM, JOHN; RUPERT, PRINCE.

Charles II (1630–1685)

king of England, Scotland, and Ireland,
1660–1685

The eldest son of CHARLES I and Henrietta Maria, Charles II had been at the Battle of EDGEHILL at age 12. He held a nominal command in the west at age 15, and he went into exile the following year. At his father's death he was proclaimed king in EDINBURGH and DUBLIN; he was then 19. He commissioned the marquess of MONTROSE, who had served his father so well in the CIVIL WAR, to campaign for him, but he then made a pact with the Scottish COVENANTERS (who defeated and executed Montrose in 1650). Charles led a Scottish army into ENGLAND, was defeated by Oliver CROMWELL at Worcester (1651), and escaped to France.

In 1660, with the republicans at odds in England, Charles issued the declaration of BREDA, announcing his proposed settlement upon being restored to the throne. His return was met with general relief and some rejoicing. Charles did try to institute a tolerant policy, meeting with rival parties and issuing a DECLARATION OF INDULGENCE. But his CAVALIER PARLIAMENT would have none of it. They passed the series of laws known as the CLARENDON CODE, which imposed severe restrictions on DISSENTERS.

The economy of the RESTORATION era was expanding rapidly under the influence of trade and financial growth. The NAVIGATION ACTS were carried over from the 1650s and boosted trade in English ships. Financial reform was in some cases accelerated by the king's errors, for example the "Stop of the Exchequer" when he defaulted on royal loans in 1672. This made it necessary to base government borrowing on a more secure footing, and that eventually led to the establishment of the NATIONAL DEBT.

The king's religion was always a matter of concern. Charles had married the Catholic princess Catherine of Braganza, but they produced no heirs. Religion was also a diplomatic factor. Charles made a secret treaty with France in which he promised to foster a Catholic restoration. That this was possible may be doubted, but in any event, on his deathbed Charles received the last rites as a Catholic. The issue of religion intersected with the question of the constitution in the most serious crisis of the reign. It was known that the king's brother JAMES VII AND II was a Roman Catholic, and his succession was opposed by many Protestants. In 1679 there was a wild story of a POPISH PLOT to kill Charles and place James on the throne. Although this fabrication was exposed (after months of near panic), there was substantial opposition in PARLIAMENT, and a series of EXCLUSION bills were introduced to deprive James of the right to succeed his brother. These led to the dismissal of three parliaments

(1679–81) and the decision by Charles not to summon another one. The atmosphere was further heated by the abortive RYE HOUSE PLOT (1683) to seize the king. Thus, by the end of his reign Charles had seen politics and religion return to the state of explosive danger that he had witnessed during his father's rule.

See also DANBY, THOMAS OSBORNE, EARL OF; DOVER, TREATY OF.

Charles, prince of Wales (1948–   )
heir to the throne

The first son of Queen ELIZABETH II, Charles was created PRINCE OF WALES in 1958, and an elaborate investiture ceremony was held in Caernarfon Castle in 1969. He trained as a pilot after graduating from CAMBRIDGE UNIVERSITY, and he served in the NAVY (1971–76). He became an outspoken critic of modern architecture and made known his views on other subjects such as the environment. His public utterances and his private life have been thoroughly scrutinized by the press. He was married (1981–96) to Lady Diana Spencer (see DIANA, PRINCESS OF WALES), and they had two sons, William (1982) and Henry (1984). The couple separated in 1992, and they were divorced in 1996. Charles has risen in public esteem in recent years, and he will eventually succeed his mother to the throne.

Chartist movement

While moderate political reform had been achieved in the REFORM ACTS of 1832, those who did not qualify under the new property franchise still felt entitled to participate in the new political system. In 1836 William LOVETT organized the London Workingmen's Association and later drafted the People's Charter, which called for universal male suffrage, the SECRET BALLOT, equal electoral districts, an end to property qualifications for MEMBERS OF PARLIAMENT, payment of salary to MPs, and annual elections. Except for the last point, Lovett's proposals were a forecast of changes which would occur over the next

century. But at the time, such ideas were alien to the aristocratic society and government of GREAT BRITAIN. Local associations were formed, and the Chartists (as supporters of the People's Charter were called) held national meetings and presented petitions to PARLIAMENT in 1839, 1842, and 1848. These were all rejected, proving to many Chartists that only physical force would succeed. But riots in Birmingham, a violent clash in Newport (1839), and riots in northern England (1842) only proved to the establishment that the Chartists were dangerous ideologues. When a mass demonstration gathered to present the third petition in 1848, police and troops in LONDON were on alert, but the body dispersed peacefully. Despite its many conventions and assemblies, which some members hoped would become alternative legislatures, Chartism was fundamentally a nonrevolutionary form of protest, mixed with varied degrees of economic and social radicalism. The organization may have failed because it was constitutional; its agenda succeeded for the same reason.

See also CARLYLE, THOMAS; O'BRIEN, JAMES BRONTERRE; O'CONNOR, FEARGUS.

Chatham, first earl of   See PITT, WILLIAM, FIRST EARL OF CHATHAM.

Chesterfield, Philip Dormer Stanhope, fourth earl of (1694–1773)
diplomat, author

A member of PARLIAMENT before entering the PEERAGE (1726), Chesterfield was on good terms with GEORGE II but not the king's wife. He was a privy councillor and served as ambassador to the Hague (1728–32), LORD LIEUTENANT of IRELAND (1745), and SECRETARY OF STATE (1746). An accomplished classical scholar and a friend and patron of writers, including Alexander POPE, Voltaire, and Samuel JOHNSON, he wrote widely in periodicals of his day, chiefly on current political subjects. His *Letters to His Son* was published by his son's widow (1774). The book's letters were addressed to an illegitimate son and contained frank and witty advice on life in fashionable society.

Chichester, Sir Arthur (1563–1625)
lord deputy of Ireland

Chichester fought against the Spanish ARMADA and served in military expeditions. Knighted in 1597, he had command of a regiment in IRELAND and fought against insurgents as a provincial governor before he was appointed lord deputy in 1604. He was successful in weakening the loyalty of the native Irish to their leaders and promoting the settlement of Scottish Protestants in ULSTER. He advocated the translation of the prayer book into Irish. Replaced as deputy when he declined to resume the persecution of Catholics (1615), he was given the office of lord treasurer of Ireland (1616–25).

Child, Josiah (1630–1699)
merchant, writer

Child sold supplies to the NAVY, later becoming mayor of Portsmouth and a MEMBER OF PARLIAMENT. He was subsequently a director and governor of the EAST INDIA COMPANY. He wrote *New Discourse on Trade* (1663), which appeared in several editions. He argued for lower interest rates to stimulate trade and industry, and he was one of the exponents of MERCANTILISM.

Childers, Robert Erskine (1870–1922)
civil servant, author

A clerk in the HOUSE OF COMMONS, Childers volunteered to fight in the BOER WAR and wrote two books about his experiences. His most famous book was a novel, *The Riddle of the Sands* (1903), which described the discovery of German invasion plans by two yachtsmen. He became involved in the Irish nationalist movement, even carrying guns to IRELAND in his yacht (1914). He served in the Irish delegation to the ANGLO-IRISH TREATY conference (1921), but later he went over to the republican side, was captured, courtmartialed, and executed.

Chippendale, Thomas (1718–1779)
cabinet maker

Chippendale established a business in London in the 1750s, designing furnishings for the gentry and for their servants. He published *The Gentleman and Cabinet-Maker's Director* (1754), which was widely read and influenced styles in Europe and elsewhere. His work, particularly in mahogany, came to represent the major style of the mid-18th century.

chivalry

A code of behavior originating in the age of mounted knights, prescribing honor, loyalty, and courage. The code, which merged with ideals of the Christian church, was expressed in tournaments and in the creation of special orders, e.g., EDWARD III's Order of the Garter in 1348.

Churchill, John
See MARLBOROUGH, JOHN CHURCHILL, DUKE OF.

Churchill, Lord Randolph Henry Spencer (1849–1895)
politician

The younger son of the seventh duke of Marlborough, Churchill entered PARLIAMENT in 1874. He was at the forefront of the Conservatives who advocated "Tory Democracy," and he became the leader of the "Fourth Party" (1880–85), which sought to open the CONSERVATIVE PARTY to more local influence. He seemed to desert these causes when he joined Lord SALISBURY'S CABINET in 1885, first as secretary of state for INDIA, then as CHANCELLOR OF THE EXCHEQUER (1886). After a few months, he made an ill-timed tactical resignation which was accepted by the prime minister, and he never served in government again. He was taken ill and died an early death.

Churchill, Sir Winston Leonard Spencer (1874–1965)

prime minister, 1940–1945, 1951–1955

Son of Randolph CHURCHILL and Jenny Jerome, an American heiress, Winston Churchill was schooled at Harrow and Sandhurst. He served in the army in INDIA and AFRICA and was a war correspondent in SOUTH AFRICA when he escaped from the Boers. He entered PARLIAMENT in 1900 as a member of the CONSERVATIVE PARTY, but he joined the LIBERAL PARTY in 1904 on the question of FREE TRADE. He rose quickly in the Liberal ranks, serving as president of the board of trade (1908), home secretary (1910), and first lord of the ADMIRALTY (1911). In that post, during WORLD WAR I he was responsible for the disastrous GALLIPOLI campaign (1915), upon which he resigned from the CABINET and went to serve with the army in France (1916). He was returned to office at the ministry of munitions (1917), then was secretary for war and air (1919), and later colonial secretary (1921).

After a two-year hiatus, he returned to Parliament in 1924, once again as a Conservative. He was brought into Stanley BALDWIN's government as CHANCELLOR OF THE EXCHEQUER (1924–29), in which post he returned GREAT BRITAIN to the gold standard (1925); took a strong position against the GENERAL STRIKE in 1926; and, in 1928, introduced the "ten year rule"—the reduction of armed services expenditures on the expectation that there would be no war for 10 years. This last policy was a measure of the general view of foreign affairs in the 1920s, a time when there was great hope for the LEAGUE OF NATIONS, some expectation of general DISARMAMENT, and the lingering memory of WORLD WAR I and the onerous peace terms of the Treaty of VERSAILLES. Thus it was difficult for Churchill and others to raise the alarm over Nazi Germany's intentions, even when Adolph Hitler came to power in 1933.

With the failure of APPEASEMENT and the outbreak of WORLD WAR II, Churchill was asked to return to the admiralty in 1939. In his old post he moved quickly to take the initiative, and he launched a plan to invade Norway (to block Swedish iron-ore shipments to Germany), only to see it fail. But in this crisis, the blame was put on Prime Minister Neville CHAMBERLAIN, who resigned. Churchill replaced him as PRIME MINISTER just as Hitler launched his invasion of France in May 1940. Churchill was a gifted war leader who organized an all-party coalition; spurred the mobilization of society; and skillfully used radio and press coverage to inspire the people, especially in the wake of the evacuation of DUNKIRK and the fall of France. This was vital, because for over a year Britain was the sole target for Germany. The BLITZ and the Battle of the ATLANTIC against German U-boats were waged without the support of allies. The United States did produce LEND-LEASE and a gradual increase of submarine countermeasures. But it was the ROYAL AIR FORCE, the merchant NAVY, and the British fleet which bore the brunt of the assault. Churchill's response was to look for ways to take the offensive: bombing raids on Germany, attacks in the Mediterranean, and sorties against German warships.

When Hitler invaded the Soviet Union (June 1941) and Japan bombed Pearl Harbor (December 1941), a powerful alliance was formed which rescued GREAT BRITAIN. The United States, Soviet Union, and Britain held a series of wartime conferences at which they drew up strategy and also made plans for a postwar settlement. Churchill found himself becoming the more junior partner in these meetings, as the power of Joseph Stalin and Franklin Roosevelt became clear. On the home front, Churchill was not ready to endorse radical policies such as those of the William BEVERIDGE report, and thus he was defeated in the 1945 election. He stubbornly held on to the leadership of the party. Age and circumstances made him less effective, though he did lead the Tories to victory in 1951. He retired from government in 1955.

Churchill was a highly successful writer throughout his long and eventful career. Indeed, that career provided most of his subject matter. His early works were accounts of adventure (*The

Sir Winston Churchill *(Library of Congress)*

Malakand Field Force, 1898; *The River War,* 1899; *London to Ladysmith via Pretoria,* 1900). His history of World War I was *The World Crisis* (5 vols., 1923–31). He also wrote several autobiographical volumes (*My Early Life,* 1930; *Thoughts and Adventures,* 1932) and his major formal history, *Marlborough: His Life and Times* (4 vols., 1934–38). His best-selling works were the autobiographical *Second World War* (6 vols., 1948–54) and his imperialist overview, *A History of the English-Speaking Peoples* (4 vols., 1956–58).

See also AIR RAIDS; RADAR; ULTRA SECRET.

Church of England

The church as reorganized under its supreme head HENRY VIII in the ENGLISH REFORMATION. This was first a restructuring of the government of the church and later a revision of its creed and liturgy. When the king decided to procure his divorce from CATHERINE OF ARAGON, he feared losing the loyalty of the clergy. To prevent this, his servant Thomas CROMWELL conducted a systematic takeover of church authority by the Crown. The secular clergy had to join in a formal SUBMISSION to the king's authority. This was completed before the declaration of ROYAL SUPREMACY (1534) gave a parliamentary endorsement to the change. Because of doubts concerning the allegiance of the monastic clergy (monks, friars, and nuns), their establishments were terminated by DISSOLUTION.

The doctrine of the reformed church was settled by the THIRTY-NINE ARTICLES in 1563. This was the end result of efforts which began in the 1530s and were marked by frequent shifts and intermittent persecutions. At various dates, the observance of reformed doctrine was enjoined by acts of UNIFORMITY, applying the power of the state to enforce the observance of religion. The form and manner of worship was dictated by the BOOK OF COMMON PRAYER, which went through occasional revision.

This structure still exists, but since the beginning of the 18th century its legal dominance has eroded. Dissenters and catholics, and non-Christians somewhat later, have become accepted members of secular society. The established church still is headed by the monarch, who may not be of another faith. The BISHOPS of the church will retain seats in the HOUSE OF LORDS as long as it remains in its traditional form. But the Church of England now only claims about 2 percent of the population as regular communicants. On the other hand, the ANGLICAN communion—those churches outside ENGLAND which recognize the leadership of the ARCHBISHOP of CANTERBURY—has increased in size and formed ecumenical ties with other denominations.

Church of Ireland

In 1536 HENRY VIII ordered the rejection of Roman authority in IRELAND to parallel his action in ENGLAND. But the strength of the old church was far greater in Ireland, and the gulf between the Anglo-Irish and the native community assured the continued influence of Catholicism in spite of state sanctions. Indeed, the association of new colonial efforts with Protestantism assured that many of the "Old English" would also adhere to the traditional faith. For centuries the Church of Ireland was the church of the ruling class and only a small fraction of the total population. In 1800 the Act of UNION joined it to the CHURCH OF ENGLAND in order to give it greater security, but in 1869 the Church of Ireland was disestablished.

Church of Scotland

The church in SCOTLAND had been relatively unaffected by English rulers since the 14th-century wars of independence. The entry of Protestantism had been delayed, but by 1560, in the political crisis revolving around MARY, QUEEN OF SCOTS, there was a break from Roman authority. The distinctive feature in Scotland's church (or kirk) was that at several stages there was powerful *resistance* to royal power which shaped the church's history, first in 1560 against Mary, then in 1637–39 against CHARLES I, and then in 1689–90 against JAMES VII AND II. This resistance took the form of a PRESBYTERIAN system of church councils, in place of BISHOPS. Under the guidance of the GENERAL ASSEMBLY of the church, the Presbyterian doctrine and form of worship have been developed. This at times has been a turbulent process, and there have been major divisions in the church (1690, 1712, 1733, 1761, 1843) followed by a reunion of most of the Presbyterian denominations in 1929.

Cinque Ports

Five ports on the south coast of ENGLAND—Hastings, Romney, Hythe, Dover, Sandwich—which had special privileges from the Crown in return for providing ships to defend the coast and support cross-channel navigation. Their era of greatest importance was between the 11th and

16th centuries, but as the royal NAVY developed, their importance declined.

civil law

A law based mainly on Roman law, distinct from the church (or canon) law similarly derived; also a body of legal rules which it is the duty of the judges to follow and apply to cases before them. Such a pattern characterized Scots law, with its long exposure to continental legal systems; hence various compilations of rules (or "institutes") were composed in the 17th–19th centuries. These along with subsequent case law form the essence of the Scottish system. In ENGLAND the courts of admiralty followed the law of the sea, deriving from Roman law. Civilian principles were also adopted in ecclesiastical, matrimonial, and equity courts.

See also COURTS OF LAW.

civil service

The modern notion of the civil service is that of a corps of administrators paid by the state, recruited and promoted on merit rather than patronage, with a neutral position in regard to political parties. The civil servant is a servant of the Crown, paid by public funds appropriated by PARLIAMENT. In a sense, the long history of royal administrators is the prehistory of the civil service; in earlier times those were jobs obtained through connections and influence, there was faint distinction between government and private funds, and there was no pretense of political neutrality. In the early 19th century, with rapid growth in government business and the number of jobs, there was also a keen interest in reducing or eliminating corruption. Hence, by 1854 there were serious reforms in recruitment and the establishment of a Civil Service Commission (1855). The number of civil servants grew rapidly in the 19th century: in 1815 there were 25,000 and in 1900 about 80,000. The wars of the 20th century and the appearance of the WELFARE STATE and widened government

functions increased the numbers nearly tenfold by 1980. At the end of the century the numbers receded to a little over half a million.

Civil War (1642–1650)

In the 1640s the fighting that broke out between CHARLES I and the leaders of PARLIAMENT involved sharp religious differences (the ARMINIAN views of the court and the PURITAN positions of the rebels) and strong disagreement over the constitution (the king perceived his royal PREROGATIVE as above the law, Parliament viewed the government as a shared enterprise). In particular, there was violent dispute over the power of TAXATION (the king used arbitrary expedients such as FORCED LOANS, subsidies, and assessments; Parliament insisted that it alone had a traditional power to tax with the consent of the property owners it represented).

Actual warfare originated in two areas outside ENGLAND: the BISHOPS' WARS, in which Scottish invasion triggered English political crisis (1638–39); and the ULSTER rebellion (1641), which forced the question over ultimate control of the ARMY. In the early months of 1642, after Charles had personally entered the HOUSE OF COMMONS in an attempt to arrest its leaders, Parliament seized royal arsenals. The issue thus drawn, the king took up arms in August 1642. His greatest strength was in the North, whereas the rebels were strongest in LONDON and the South. In October 1642 the royalists advanced toward London, and the first major battle took place at EDGEHILL. There was no decisive result, but the king's army was prevented from advancing on the capital.

The next year saw a number of successful royalist attacks. Parliament was near defeat, but late in the year an alliance was made with the Scots (the SOLEMN LEAGUE AND COVENANT) whereby an army of 20,000 was sent to aid the rebels and Parliament promised to introduce a PRESBYTERIAN church government in England and IRELAND. The Scottish army led the victory over the king's forces at MARSTON MOOR in 1644, and after rebel losses in the Southwest, Parliament ordered the English army reconstituted as a NEW MODEL ARMY. No longer would the officers be taken from the aristocracy; army pay was to be reformed, and religious indoctrination was to be introduced. This renovated force was successful at the Battle of NASEBY and other battles in 1645, putting the royalists in retreat.

The king surrendered in 1646 and tried to exploit divisions among his enemies. When the rebel army was disbanded without its full pay, there was a revolt, and the insurgents seized the king and marched on London. In the unsettled circumstances, there was a year or so of unrest, uprisings, and an abortive invasion by yet another Scottish army, this one allied with the king. It was beaten easily, but the threat it represented led to the trial and execution of Charles in 1649.

The king's death brought the creation of a commonwealth, and it also meant the dispatch of armies to Ireland (1649) and Scotland (1650) to bring those areas under the control of the new government. With victories on those fronts, the battles of the Civil War were over.

See also CROMWELL, OLIVER; LONG PARLIAMENT; MANCHESTER, EDWARD MONTAGU, EARL OF; MONTROSE, JAMES GRAHAM, MARQUESS OF; RUPERT, PRINCE; ROUNDHEADS; SELF-DENYING ORDINANCE; WALLER, SIR WILLIAM.

Claim of Right

When WILLIAM III seized power in 1688, a convention of estates (a provisional parliament) was summoned in SCOTLAND, and that body composed a Claim of Right, the equivalent of the BILL OF RIGHTS drawn up in ENGLAND. This was more radical in several respects: it declared that JAMES II had been deposed (instead of abdicating), it abolished the office of BISHOP, and it demanded limits on judicial power. The terms were accepted by William and Mary with the offer of the Scottish crown.

clan

An extended family with autonomous authority over social, political, and military matters, par-

ticularly in the HIGHLANDS of SCOTLAND. Clans drew upon an old tradition of tribal or familial allegiance, and from the later medieval period they were used to maintain order in outlying areas, though they were often associated with disorder. As they evolved, clans included tenants and followers outside the main family group. Their leaders enjoyed special privileges and jurisdictions, owing to the weakness of royal authority. The dominant clan groupings were the Campbells in the West, Mackenzies in the North, and Gordons in the Northeast. As royal power grew, the function of the clan was increasingly restricted, but they continued to be a disruptive force in the circumstances of the 17th century. After the JACOBITE rebellion in 1745, the clans were dismantled by legislation which abolished the heritable jurisdictions, disarmed clansmen, banned the tartan, and forfeited large rebel estates. By 1782 the proscription of the clan tartan was lifted, and a romantic image of clan society was fostered, even as the remnants of some clans were being economically devastated in the HIGHLAND CLEARANCES.

Clapham Sect

In the London borough of Clapham, a group of EVANGELICAL reformers lived and/or met, among them Granville SHARP, William WILBERFORCE, Zachary Macaulay, James Stephen, Thomas CLARKSON, and the rector of Clapham parish, John Venn. They were instrumental in the ANTI-SLAVERY MOVEMENT, in efforts to send missionaries throughout the empire, and in the formation of societies to distribute BIBLES and evangelical literature in ENGLAND. They were most influential between 1785 and 1830.

Clarendon, Edward Hyde, first earl of (1609–1674)
lawyer, statesman

Lord Clarendon was an early opponent of royal policy, when in 1640 he challenged the authority of the prerogative courts, but he changed sides as the leaders of PARLIAMENT became increasingly radical in their demands. He was a key adviser to CHARLES I during the CIVIL WAR, going into exile in 1646. He drafted *The True Historical Narrative of the Rebellion* (published 1702–04). He became the major adviser to CHARLES II before the RESTORATION, and later he served that king as LORD CHANCELLOR. He was an advocate of toleration, and his views were not really those of the so-called CLARENDON CODE. His daughter Anne Hyde was the first wife of the king's brother JAMES VII AND II. After the loss of the second DUTCH WAR (1667), Clarendon was impeached and went into exile once again.

Clarendon Code

A series of laws, named after CHARLES II's first minister Edward Hyde, the earl of CLARENDON. A Corporation Act (1661) limited public office to members of the established church; an Act of UNIFORMITY (1662) ordered the use of the BOOK OF COMMON PRAYER (2,000 clergy resigned); a Conventicle Act (1664) banned some meetings for religious services; and a Five-Mile Act (1665) banned ministers of dissenting congregations from coming within five miles of their home towns and prohibited them from teaching school.

Clark, Kenneth Mackenzie, baron (1903–1983)

critic

Clark was born into a prominent Scottish thread-making family, whose members frequented yachting events, sporting estates, and casinos on the Riviera. He studied at Winchester and OXFORD UNIVERSITY and discovered a gift for artistic interpretation. He wrote a classic on *Leonardo* (1939) and important general works such as *Landscape into Art* (1949) and *The Nude* (1956). His career embraced a wide range of key positions, including director of the NATIONAL GALLERY (1934–46), chairman of the Arts Council of Great Britain (1953–1960), and chairman of the Independent Television Authority (1954–57). He

is best known for his television documentary *Civilisation* on the BBC (BRITISH BROADCASTING CORPORATION) in 1969, which was a powerful achievement in popularizing the history of art.

Clarkson, Thomas (1760–1846)

evangelical reformer

Cofounder of a committee for the suppression of the SLAVE TRADE (1787), Clarkson was active in the campaign for abolition. He wrote *The History of the Rise, Progress, and Accomplishment of the Abolition of the African Slave Trade by the British Parliament* (2 vols., 1808). He served as an officer of the Anti-Slavery Society in 1823 and worked in international campaigns after the abolition of slavery in the British Empire.

See also ANTISLAVERY MOVEMENT.

Clinton, Sir Henry (1730–1795)

general

Born in NEWFOUNDLAND, Clinton joined the British ARMY and fought in CANADA and Germany. In 1775 he fought at BUNKER HILL. He subsequently became second in command to General William HOWE and, after John BURGOYNE's surrender, commander in chief. He had a major victory over the rebels at Charleston, but after the surrender of General Charles CORNWALLIS, he resigned in 1782.

Clive, Robert (1725–1774)

soldier

Clive joined the EAST INDIA COMPANY in 1743 as a clerk. He entered the company's military service in 1751 and captured and defended the city of Arcot. Made governor of Madras in 1756, he led a force which recaptured CALCUTTA in 1757. Having returned to ENGLAND to enter politics in 1760, he was made governor of BENGAL in 1765. He gained great wealth, but made a number of enemies in GREAT BRITAIN, and he had to face a parliamentary inquiry into his affairs in 1772. He committed suicide in 1774.

Cliveden

The country home of Waldorf and Nancy ASTOR, Cliveden was the site of gatherings of many of the leading proponents of APPEASEMENT in the 1930s. Their number included Edward Wood, Lord HALIFAX, then the foreign secretary; and other MPs and journalists.

Cobbett, William (1763–1835)

radical journalist

Cobbett grew up on a farm in Surrey, served in the army, and tried to expose corruption in his regiment. He was forced to go into exile in France and in America, where he was an ardent defender of GREAT BRITAIN. At this stage he was a TORY, but when he returned to ENGLAND he became increasingly critical of top political figures. His newspaper *Political Register* (1802–35) attacked privilege and corruption and extolled traditional life. He was imprisoned (1810–12) for seditious libel when he opposed the flogging of militiamen. Regarded as a dangerous radical, he went into exile once more (1817–19). After his return he wrote journals of his travels, published as *Rural Rides* (2 vols., 1830). As a maverick journalist, he pioneered in the publication of parliamentary debates (1803), but the series was taken over by his publisher, T. C. Hansard, in 1812. He also published *Cobbett's Complete Collection of State Trials and Proceedings for High Treason* (38 vols., 1809–28), based on earlier collections and pamphlet literature.

Cobden, Richard (1804–1865)

radical politician

The son of a farmer, Cobden became a cloth manufacturer in Manchester. He was a leading advocate of FREE TRADE and a founder of the ANTI-CORN LAW LEAGUE. He entered PARLIAMENT in 1841 and used his position there and in League meetings to advance his proposals. Robert PEEL gave him considerable credit for the repeal of the CORN LAWS. In 1860 he negotiated the Cobden-Chevalier Treaty, which reduced French TARIFFS on British industrial imports in exchange for lower British duties on wines, brandy, and silk.

Cockburn, Henry (1779–1854)

Scottish advocate, judge

One of the founders of the *Edinburgh Review,* Cockburn was a prominent criminal lawyer, became solicitor general for SCOTLAND in 1830, a lord of session in 1834, and judge of the HIGH COURT OF JUSTICIARY in 1837. His posthumously published *Memorials of His Time* (1856) offers a vivid picture of 19th-century EDINBURGH. His account was continued in the *Journal of Henry Cockburn* (2 vols., 1874) and *Circuit Journeys* (1888).

Coke, Sir Edward (1552–1634)

lawyer, judge

Elected to PARLIAMENT in 1589, Coke served as SPEAKER of the HOUSE OF COMMONS (1593) and held the posts of solicitor general (1592) and attorney general (1594). He conducted the treason trials of Robert Devereux, earl of ESSEX; Sir Walter RALEIGH; and the GUNPOWDER PLOT conspirators (1601–05). He was made chief justice of the Court of COMMON PLEAS in 1606 and later chief justice of the Court of KING'S BENCH, but he was removed from that post in 1616 because of disputes with JAMES VI AND I. He entered parliament again in 1621 and became a leading opponent of royal policy, drafting the PETITION OF RIGHTS in 1628. Coke was a highly influential lawyer and a vigorous supporter of the COMMON LAW against its rival prerogative and civil courts. He published, in law French, *Les Reports de Edward Coke* (13 vols., 1600–15), and he stamped his imprint on the history and evolution of the common law with his *Institutes of the Laws of England* (1628–44).

Coke, Thomas, earl of Leicester (1752–1842)

agriculturalist

Known as "Coke of Norfolk" and "Coke of Holkham,"he used his estate at Holkham Hall as an agricultural exhibit, mostly for improvements already known but made more popular by Coke's talent for publicity and promotion. Fertilizing with manure or marl; rotating crops (turnips, grain, grasses); and improving breeding practices were among the methods he advocated, and he encouraged tenants to cooperate by granting them long leases. He held annual meetings at the estate to promote these methods and encourage improved farming (1778–1821). He had a seat in PARLIAMENT for most of the period from 1776 until 1832.

Colchester, Charles Abbot, first baron (1757–1829)
Speaker of the House of Commons
Abbot attended Westminster School and Christ Church, Oxford, and then studied law in the Middle Temple. He became a clerk in the court of KING'S BENCH (1794) and a member of PARLIAMENT (1795). He proposed the first CENSUS of the population in 1800. After serving briefly as chief secretary for IRELAND after the act of UNION in 1801, he was chosen SPEAKER OF THE HOUSE of Commons in 1802. At his retirement he assumed the title of baron Colchester.

Coleridge, Samuel Taylor (1772–1834)
poet
Educated at CAMBRIDGE UNIVERSITY, Coleridge printed a political and literary journal, the *Watchman,* in 1796. In 1798 he and William WORDSWORTH produced *Lyrical Ballads,* which included his "Rime of the Ancient Mariner," and they launched the period of English ROMANTICISM. The two traveled to Germany, where they gave lectures on philosophy and studied German writers; these experiences were reflected in Coleridge's future work. He wrote a critical study, *Biographia Literaria,* in 1817; a theological tract, *Aids to Reflection,* in 1825; and a summary of his latter-day conservatism in *On the Constitution of Church and State* in 1830.

Colet, John (1467–1519)
churchman, humanist
Educated in ENGLAND and in Europe, Colet taught at OXFORD UNIVERSITY from 1498. He met Erasmus in 1499 and was later a patron of the great scholar. Made dean of ST. PAUL'S CATHEDRAL

in 1504, he refounded the GRAMMAR SCHOOL there in 1509. His views on church reform caused some friction with other clergy. He was made a member of the king's council in 1516.

Collins, Michael (1890–1922)
Irish revolutionary
Collins fought in the EASTER REBELLION (1916) against British rule in Ireland. He was interned with other rebels, and when he was released he joined the reformed IRISH REPUBLICAN ARMY and became its director of intelligence. Elected a MEMBER OF PARLIAMENT in 1918, he sat in the DÁIL ÉIREANN, was finance minister of the provisional government, and was an active guerilla commander. He was alleged to have led a raid that killed 11 British intelligence officers in DUBLIN in 1920, and there was a £10,000 reward for his arrest. A member of the delegation that drew up the ANGLO-IRISH TREATY in 1921, he supported its ratification in 1922. When Eamon DE VALERA and other republicans rejected the agreement, Collins became the first prime minister of the IRISH FREE STATE and the commander in chief of the army. He was killed in an ambush by republicans in County Cork in August 1922.

colony
The authority to establish a colonial settlement and government was conveyed in several different ways. A *crown colony* was one chartered directly by the sovereign; a *proprietary colony* was one where the governing authority was vested in an individual or a group of proprietors. Other colonies were created after conquests of foreign settlements, or on the foundation of trading-company properties. They all shared the duty to obey the executive authority of the Crown, but they were given varying degrees of local power.

See also AMERICAN COLONIES.

Combination Acts
The "combinations" of workmen, precursors to TRADE UNIONS, were a source of alarm to employ-

ers and the government, who perceived them as potentially riotous and subversive. In fact such activity was illegal under COMMON LAW and older statutes, but in 1799, in the shadow of revolution in France, it was decided to expedite prosecutions by using summary trials. An amending act in 1800 provided for arbitration. In 1824, after a campaign by Joseph HUME and Francis PLACE, the Combination Acts were repealed, but a series of strikes brought new restrictions in 1825.

commission

Usually created by a royal WARRANT and issued under the GREAT SEAL, a commission conveyed the power of the royal PREROGATIVE to a person or group, enabling them to act in a particular capacity. Among the best known, from the 14th century the commission of the peace was issued to each county, naming JUSTICES OF THE PEACE who were empowered to act as local judges and administrators. The royal judges had commissions of OYER AND TERMINER, which gave them powers to act on the ASSIZE circuits. A commission of array was issued to enlist troops for royal service, and a parliamentary commission was issued to collect taxes. A commission was the source of authority for any number of (new) royal offices or courts, e.g., the Elizabethan Court of HIGH COMMISSION for overseeing ecclesiastical causes.

commission of inquiry

In the 19th century the increase in parliamentary oversight of the executive was reflected in the evolution of the commission of inquiry. There had been a long tradition of using investigative powers by committees of both houses of PARLIAMENT, both in the special area of official conduct (impeachment) and in SELECT COMMITTEES which prepared legislation. There were many cases after 1780 where government offices and procedures were being examined, from the 18th-century committees on finance to the 19th-century inquiries into government records, courts of law,

poor laws, and municipal corporations. Since these investigations might encroach on powers seen as immune from scrutiny, a *royal* commission of inquiry, embodying the power of the royal PREROGATIVE, provided sufficient authority to empower commissioners to summon witnesses, take testimony under oath, request documents, and report their findings to Parliament. The commission of inquiry continues to be used by governments to study, marshal evidence, and provide a basis for initiating legislation on any complicated or controversial question.

Committee of Both Kingdoms

In the early months of the CIVIL WAR, the English and Scottish rebels created a military alliance (the SOLEMN LEAGUE AND COVENANT), a forum for discussing a church settlement (the WESTMINSTER ASSEMBLY) and a joint executive body, called the Committee of Both Kingdoms. This body had to face the difficult task of planning strategy for the armies of England and Scotland while it tried to coordinate the many regional and local leaders from both countries. The latter problem could not be solved until the creation of the NEW MODEL ARMY in 1645. The joint direction of operations ended after CHARLES I surrendered in 1646 and tried to make a separate settlement with the Scots.

common law

The English legal system as it has functioned since the 13th century. Common law consists of the legal principles developed by the judges, who make decisions by referring to similar cases previously decided. The law was "common" in the sense that the king's courts superseded the numerous local jurisdictions from about 1170, and uniform justice became available in the king's courts. Suitors had access to a variety of WRITS that could be invoked, providing a hearing before the judges, in local and central courts. The counterparts to common law were statute law, made in PARLIAMENT; equity, or the law of the Court of CHANCERY; canon law, the law of the church; and its near relative, CIVIL LAW (Roman), which was used in ADMIRALTY courts.

See also COURTS OF LAW; LAW.

Common Market See EUROPEAN ECONOMIC COMMUNITY.

Common Pleas, Court of

The first royal court settled in a permanent meeting place was in Westminster in the early 13th century. Court rolls survive from 1223, and the first chief justice of the court was appointed in 1272. The court heard cases between the king's subjects, and these matters of property assured it of having more business than any other royal court. It had an appellate jurisdiction over local courts, but for a time it was subject to the authority of the Court of KING'S BENCH. The Serjeants-at-Law long had sole right of audience in the court. In 1873 the court was merged with other royal courts in the new HIGH COURT OF JUSTICE.

See also COURTS OF LAW.

Commonwealth of England

The republican government of England between the reigns of CHARLES I and CHARLES II (1649–60). In January 1649 PARLIAMENT declared that "the people are, under God, the original of all just power." After Charles I's execution, the monarchy was abolished along with the HOUSE OF LORDS, and in May a commonwealth was formally declared. Supreme power lay with the HOUSE OF COMMONS, which supplied 31 of the 40 members of the Council of State, the executive of the new government. The fact that military operations continued in IRELAND, SCOTLAND, and at sea meant that the ARMY's voice, and especially that of General Oliver CROMWELL, became dominant. After experimenting with the Independent Parliament (1653), Cromwell endorsed a PROTECTORATE, in which he assumed executive

powers. The Commonwealth constitution collapsed in 1659 amid feuds between army officers and members of Parliament, leading to the RESTORATION of Charles II.

Commonwealth of Nations See BRITISH EMPIRE AND COMMONWEALTH.

commutation

The conversion of feudal obligations (labor and payments in kind) to cash payment. The process varied from one MANOR to another, but it was completed by the 16th century.

Congregationalists

A major dissenting Protestant sect, committed to the autonomy of each individual congregation, also known as separatists or independents. Robert BROWNE, Henry Barrow, and John Penry were early leaders, and the last two were hung for their beliefs. They subscribed to the Calvinist concept of the priesthood of all believers. The Congregationalist sect grew during the period of the CIVIL WAR and the COMMONWEALTH OF ENGLAND. After a quiet period in the 18th century, there was rapid growth in the early 19th century, the creation of a number of theological colleges, and the formation of the Congregational Union of England and Wales (1831). In 1972 they joined with the Presbyterian Church of England to form the United Reformed Church.

Congress of Berlin See BERLIN, CONGRESS OF.

Connolly, James (1868–1916)
Irish union leader

Born in EDINBURGH, Connolly joined the British ARMY. After he organized the Irish Socialist Republican Party in 1896, he spent the years 1902–10 in the United States, where he established the Irish Socialist Federation. In 1910 he returned to IRELAND and set up the Irish Transport and General Workers' Union. He fought in the EASTER REBELLION, was badly wounded, and was strapped to a chair for his execution by a firing squad.

Conrad, Joseph (1857–1924)
writer

Born to Polish parents in the Ukraine, Conrad came to ENGLAND after a long career as a merchant seaman. In 1878 he landed in Suffolk with no knowledge of English. He became a naturalized British subject in 1886, and he retired from the sea to write in 1894. Among his works were *The Nigger of the "Narcissus"* (1897), *Lord Jim* (1900), his highly-regarded short story "The Heart of Darkness" (1902), *Nostromo* (1904), and *The Secret Agent* (1907). His great novel *Chance* (1913) was a triumph that marked him as a major modern author.

conscription

While other European states had long had large armies of conscripts, Britain prided itself on a volunteer force, and it relied on volunteers to fill the ARMY ranks until 1916, during WORLD WAR I. A bitter debate preceded enactment of the drafting of single men (January 1916) and married men (May 1916). Over 2 million were conscripted by 1918, but the law was not extended to IRELAND until the later year, and it only succeeded in worsening the already unstable political situation there. In 1939 conscription was enacted at the start of WORLD WAR II, and was extended to include unmarried women in 1941. Extended into the postwar period, the NATIONAL SERVICE program was only ended in 1960.

Conservative Party

Successor to the TORY Party (which still provides the nickname), the Conservative Party was formed in the 1830s after the REFORM ACT of 1832. Sir Robert PEEL led the aristocrats, gentry, and middle-class supporters of traditional institutions and values, who were afraid the recent reform measures might lead to others which would endanger the established institutions of the country. After Peel supported the repeal of the CORN LAWS in 1846, there was a period of realignment (1846–67) during which time a new LIBERAL PARTY began to form, and the Conservatives regrouped behind the leadership of Benjamin DISRAELI. When he and William GLADSTONE conducted their vigorous electoral and parliamentary debates (1865–80), they created or solidified the notion of a "two-party system," even though scholars will point out that such a "system" never existed, and that third parties—Irish, labour, and Social Democratic, for example—have been a constant feature. In the later 19th century Conservatives were joined by LIBERAL UNIONISTS—those who opposed IRISH HOME RULE—and by the turn of the century the party was renamed the Conservative and Unionist Party. As the franchise broadened, the party came to represent business leaders, middle-class shopkeepers, and professionals as well as aristocrats. In the later 20th century, after the dramatic performance of the LABOUR PARTY in the 1940s, Conservatives accepted the WELFARE STATE and allied measures, until the election of Margaret THATCHER in 1979. Her governments reversed much of the progressive agenda of the previous 30 years, and with John MAJOR succeeding her as PRIME MINISTER, her party remained in power for a record period of time (1979–97).

constable

Initially the name of the king's officer in charge of the military (lord high constable), the term was applied to local law enforcement as in the petty constable of a PARISH, the high constable of a hundred, or the military governor of a castle. In modern times, the POLICE constable is the basic rank of the professional police; the chief constable is the head of a police area, and constabulary is the inclusive term for county or regional forces.

Constable, John (1776–1837)

artist

A miller's son, raised in Sussex, Constable studied at the ROYAL ACADEMY, but his subjects were predominantly the landscapes he knew so well. He was not highly regarded in ENGLAND and had a better following in France, but today he is recognized as one of the premier English artists of the 19th century.

constitution

A set of rules for the operation of any government. The British constitution is unwritten, in the sense that there is no single master document containing all of the basic rules. There are, however, numerous documents and many unwritten CONVENTIONS that add up to a considerable body of rules. The former category contains all acts of PARLIAMENT and rulings of the COURTS OF LAW. Conventions include the rule that the monarch must act on the advice of ministers and that a government losing a VOTE OF CONFIDENCE in the HOUSE OF COMMONS is expected to resign or call a general election. Indeed, most facets of CABINET government, including ministerial responsibility, are conventions and have no force in law.

continental system

In 1806 Napoleon Bonaparte issued his Berlin Decrees, ordering all continental ports closed to British ships. The British retaliated in 1807 and said that the ports of France and her allies were closed, and that all ships were liable to seizure, even neutrals. While the latter point was the cause of the WAR OF 1812, the power of the British NAVY eventually broke the system.

conventicle

A meeting for worship in violation of acts of UNIFORMITY. A Conventicle Act was first passed in 1593. The better known act of 1664 was aimed at preventing the formation of congregations by ministers who left the church after the Act of Uniformity in 1662. Violators were subject to fine or imprisonment. The act was later suspended by the TOLERATION ACT of 1689.

convention

There are two basic meanings in British history: (1) a rule or practice accepted by long usage (see CONSTITUTION); (2) a formal meeting, either regular or irregular. In the first instance, there were bodies such as the Convention of Royal Burghs in SCOTLAND, dating from the 13th century. There were also "convention" parliaments which met in 1660 and 1689; as they were not summoned by a king, there being none present, they were convened by general consent, so their acts had to be ratified by a royally summoned PARLIAMENT. Finally, there were several occasions when radical groups met in convention, inspired by American and French examples, as in the meetings of UNITED IRISHMEN, UNITED SCOTSMEN, and CHARTISTS (1793–1848).

convocations

Meetings of the clergy of the provinces of CANTERBURY and York, containing the hierarchy and the lower clergy. The latter met separately, chaired by an elected member. The acts of convocation (canons) governed the church, but in 1532 the clergy submitted to HENRY VIII, surrendering independent authority. Because of controversy in early 18th-century convocations, they were dissolved in 1717. A revival of meetings began in the 19th century, with legal recognition in 1872. A General Synod was formed in 1970.

Cook, Captain James (1728–1779)

explorer

A seaman who rose in the ranks by his exceptional skills as a navigator, Cook provided charts aiding the campaign to take Quebec (1759). He took command of the *Endeavour* for its voyage to Tahiti in 1768, during which he charted the

Engraving of Captain James Cook, 1821 *(Library of Congress)*

coasts of NEW ZEALAND and AUSTRALIA. In his voyage in *Resolution* (1772–75) he disproved the idea of a great southern continent and discovered Tonga and the New Hebrides. On his last voyage he sailed the northwest coast of the Americas in search of the elusive NORTHWEST PASSAGE. He was killed in a fight with natives in Hawaii.

Cooper, Anthony Ashley See SHAFTES-
BURY, ANTHONY ASHLEY COOPER, FIRST EARL OF.

cooperative movement
Begun in the 19th century as a means to defend workers from the worst features of industrial capitalism, the cooperative movement was a plan to unite groups of working families in a common fund to provide necessities. It was actually one of the later projects of the radical Robert OWEN, whose more ambitious efforts had indifferent success in the 1820s and '30s. A shop in Rochdale, Lancashire, in 1844 was the first in which members paid a subscription and divided the profits from the sale of goods. The movement had phenomenal growth in the later 19th century, and it went beyond retailing into manufacturing and banking, then formed a union (1869) and a political party (1917).

See also SOCIALISM.

copyhold
A form of land tenure which originated on manorial estates. The tenant held a copy of the entry in the manorial roll describing his holding. This entitled him to hold the land on the terms prescribed, giving him much more security than a leasehold tenant. Most tenants held in this manner by 1500. From 1926 a copyhold became the same as a FREEHOLD, and copyhold tenure was abolished.

See also MANOR.

copyright
The ownership of works of art or literature and of the right to reproduce them. The first copyright act was in 1709, in which authors were given exclusive rights to books for 14 years, renewable for another 14. In 1814 and 1842 the term was extended, and other acts brought the protection to artwork, plays, and music. After further extensions, the term is now 70 years after an author's death.

corn laws
Laws that protected the domestic producers of grains in general (not just maize) by controlling or banning imports. These laws became a subject of serious concern during the wars with France (1793–1815), at which time ENGLAND had become a net importer of food. In 1815, with a

great deal of marginal LAND still under cultivation because of the high prices of wartime, PARLIAMENT enacted a law that banned imports until the price in the domestic market reached a certain level. In 1828 this was changed to a sliding scale of duties, which were lowered in later years of crisis. The law was nonetheless a hated symbol, the ANTI-CORN LAW LEAGUE campaigned against it, and the IRISH FAMINE ended it in 1846.

Cornwallis, Charles Cornwallis, first marquis (1738–1805)
soldier, administrator
A commander in the American war of independence, Cornwallis's surrender at YORKTOWN in 1781 was the final act of that conflict. He became the governor-general of INDIA in the wake of the scandals under Warren HASTINGS, and he introduced judicial and revenue reforms. He next took up the post of LORD LIEUTENANT of IRELAND in 1798 and put down the IRISH REBELLION of that year. He also helped to implement the Act of UNION in 1801. After negotiating the Peace of Amiens (1802), he returned to India and died there soon after.

corporation
A legal entity, either a corporation sole (an individual successively holding an office, such as a BISHOP) or a corporation aggregate (such as the group of persons forming a MUNICIPAL CORPORATION or the members of a company). A corporation can be created by the sovereign or by statute; it has a seal, it can sue or be sued, and it can hold property and make bylaws.

Cort, Henry (1740–1800)
iron manufacturer
Born to a mason in Lancaster, Cort went to LONDON at age 25 and became an agent for the NAVY. He purchased guns and developed a knowledge of ironmaking. He patented a method of "puddling" iron, using a coal-fired furnace to render it more malleable. Pig-iron production went from 40,000 tons in 1786 to 10 times that amount in 1820. Cort, however, did not profit from the boom, because his career was marred by illegal transactions with the navy, and by the time he was cleared, his patent rights had been lost. He later received a small pension from the government.

council
A body of advisers and administrators. The Crown kept a group of senior advisers, the *curia regis* under the Normans, the PRIVY COUNCIL under the TUDORS. The Crown also used special regional bodies, such as the Council of Wales and the Council of the North in the 16th century. The rebels in the 1650s used a Council of State as the executive power. The RESTORATION era saw the rise of the cabinet council, precursor to the modern CABINET, still in law a body of royal advisers.

The term *council* was borrowed for local government and other uses—e.g., county councils created by the Local Government Act of 1888, which displaced the governmental authority of JUSTICES OF THE PEACE. The Greater London Council was created by statute in 1965, abolished in 1986, and restored in 1999.

county
A territory within the countries of the British Isles, derived from older Celtic, Norse, or Anglo-Saxon kingdoms (e.g., Kent, Sussex, Essex). The basis for a county also might have been a fortified town or an earldom. The county formed the unit for TAXATION, law enforcement, the MILITIA, and administration. English counties had a SHERIFF who held a COUNTY COURT; his authority shifted to JUSTICES OF THE PEACE from the 15th century, and from 1549 the county was brought under closer royal control by a LORD LIEUTENANT, who was responsible for the county militia.

County units were introduced into WALES by the English Crown after the 13th century, and they extended to all of Wales by the acts of 1536 and 1543. In SCOTLAND the nobility were relatively more powerful in their localities, and counties were only slowly brought into any kind of central administrative network. Irish counties were similarly affected by English administrators, and both IRELAND and NORTHERN IRELAND still have county names deriving from the period of 16th and 17th century English conquest. The size and arrangement of those districts reflects the haphazard formation during years of conquest, and Irish local districts (baronies, parishes, and townlands) further complicate the picture.

Elected county COUNCILS were created in ENGLAND by an act of 1888, and there was a major redrawing of county boundaries by an act of 1972. In Wales some were rechristened with the names of old Welsh kingdoms, while the total of 13 was reduced to eight. The act for Scotland (1973) reduced 33 counties to nine regions and three island areas. Even more radical changes came in 1996, when counties in Wales and Scotland were abolished and replaced by "unitary authorities"—22 for Wales and 33 for Scotland. At the same time, England was divided into 34 administrative counties, six metropolitan counties, and 34 unitary authorities. New administrative districts have also been created in modern Ireland.

county court

After the Norman Conquest, each SHIRE was administered by a SHERIFF, who represented the Crown and held the shire moot, or county court. It was an important body, before the rise of itinerant justices on ASSIZE circuits and before the creation of JUSTICES OF THE PEACE. After the 14th century the courts fell into disuse, but there was a major revival in 1846. At first a set of 500 local small-debt courts, the county courts now hear cases up to £2,000 in value, and they exercise limited probate, matrimonial, and admiralty jurisdiction.

Court of Appeal   See APPEAL, COURT OF.

Court of Augmentations   See AUGMENTATIONS, COURT OF.

Court of Chancery   See CHANCERY, COURT OF.

Court of Criminal Appeal   See CRIMINAL APPEAL, COURT OF.

Court of King's Bench   See KING'S BENCH, COURT OF.

Court of Session   See SESSION, COURT OF.

court party

In general the term *court party* referred to the persons at the royal court who were close advisers of the monarch. In particular, in the wake of the upheavals of the CIVIL WARS and the GLORIOUS REVOLUTION in the late 17th century, the political system began to tolerate opposing views in government. The commonly used terms for the rival groups of politicians in that period were the *court party* and the *country party*. These terms coexisted with, and were less abrasive than, the labels WHIG and TORY, which came into use in the 1670s.

courts of law

There are six separate legal systems in the British Isles, each of them having a distinct set of courts with a limited amount of connection between the systems. In most systems there are central and local courts, and there are courts of special jurisdiction.

ENGLAND AND WALES

The royal courts date from the 12th century; the Court of COMMON PLEAS became the first court to emerge from the king's COUNCIL. In fact, it was declared in the MAGNA CARTA (1215) that the court should be in a fixed location rather than perambulatory, at a time when all royal servants still traveled with the king. In matters dealing with the Crown's rights, the Court of KING'S BENCH soon became the main venue, except for revenue cases, which were heard in the Court of EXCHEQUER. By the 15th century, the LORD CHANCELLOR heard cases in his Court of CHANCERY that fell outside the COMMON LAW. Thus was established the equity jurisdiction, which came to govern trusts, charities, mortgages, administration of infants and their estates, as well grants of relief in cases of fraud or accident. Appeals were taken from chancery to the HOUSE OF LORDS but the common law courts had no appellate procedure save the rarely used WRIT of error, a claim that there had been a flaw in process, which also could be heard in the Lords. The creation of the HIGH COURT OF JUSTICE in 1873 amalgamated all of the royal courts and added a Court of APPEAL, from which some cases might still go on to the judicial committee of the House of Lords. The English structure had absorbed Welsh jurisdiction by the acts of UNION of the 16th century.

The local jurisdictions passed from feudal and personal powers to local governmental divisions. Manorial and baronial courts as well as the old COUNTY COURTS, were supplanted, by the 15th and 16th centuries, by county JUSTICES OF THE PEACE sitting together in courts of QUARTER SESSIONS and in pairs in PETTY SESSIONS. They were paralleled by BOROUGH and municipal courts, some of them of ancient authority. In the 19th century the growth of population and advance of society produced some legal reforms. Thus by 1846 some 500 new county courts had been created to act in matters of small debts and other lesser cases. These were joined by growing numbers of lay MAGISTRATES in the 20th century, operating in somewhat the same fashion as the old justice of the peace, though petty sessions were renamed magistrates' courts (1949) and quarter sessions were abolished in 1971. Here also, the Welsh were brought into the anglicized system in the acts of 1536–43.

There have been many special jurisdictions with their own courts. In earlier times these courts had functional identities: church courts, military courts, courts of chivalry, and guild courts were but a few examples. Over time, these special functions tended to be absorbed by the more powerful central courts, though some of these ancient tribunals still exist. But in the 19th century, a new breed of special jurisdictions began to multiply: administrative tribunals were created by statute and endowed with legal authority to supervise different types of cases. Much of this work involved disputes between individuals and government departments, and in 1958 a Council on Tribunals was created to monitor the work of these courts.

In a special category, a parliamentary ombudsman (the term borrowed from Sweden) was created in 1965. Not a judge, but an investigator who might act at the request of a MEMBER OF PARLIAMENT, this Parliamentary Commissioner for Administration makes reports that serve to expose cases of maladministration.

SCOTLAND

The Scottish central courts have a unique structure, dating from the creation of the College of Justice in 1532. The lord president and 14 lords ordinary were the judges of the Court of SESSION, hearing civil cases. The court was reformed in the early 19th century, divided into an Inner and Outer House. The more junior judges serve in the Outer House, hearing cases in the first instance, with an appeal to the Inner House. From the early 18th century it was also possible to appeal from the Court of Session to the House of Lords. Central criminal jurisdiction had been in the office of the king's lord justice-general who appointed judges to hear cases; he and the lord justice-clerk, an assistant, were made judges of a new HIGH COURT OF JUSTICIARY in 1672, along with five lords of session. The offices of lord president and lord justice-general were merged in 1836. The lords of justiciary hear cases on circuit and in EDINBURGH, and they also hear appeals from the sheriff courts and the high court. There is no appeal from the Court of Justiciary to the House of Lords.

Local jurisdiction in SCOTLAND was very much a private affair until the 18th century. With a history of weaker central authority than England, aristocrats and CLAN leaders exercised hereditary powers over their tenants, and these were affirmed in the Act of UNION of 1707. But in the wake of the JACOBITE uprising in 1745, these powers were abolished, and revamped offices of SHERIFF depute and sheriff substitute were given statutory authority in 1747. This was the first instance of a salaried local judge, a step taken in the special circumstances to assure professional behavior and greater accountability. The sheriffdom was an old division, but now the sheriff court was reformed, and appeals would lie to the Court of Session. In criminal cases the appeal went to the Court of Justiciary. In Scotland there had also been attempts to develop an English-style Justice of the Peace (1587, 1609, 1708, 1718), but these attempts were not successful because they were seen as an alien intrusion and because they overlapped with existing authorities. The Scottish BURGHS had had special local authority since their origin. Royal burghs and burghs of barony were the main types, and other modern versions were created in the 19th century.

Scottish special jurisdictions include the same categories as the English system, although their histories differ. Church courts act at each level of the PRESBYTERIAN structure (kirk, presbytery, synod, and general assembly). Courts-martial are subject to the codes adopted by each service, are the same as the English, and are based on English criminal law. Some peculiar jurisdictions were unique to Scotland. Ancient Scottish offices such as the Marischal, the Constable, the Lyon King of Arms, the Admiral, and the Chamberlain had courts which heard cases in their peculiar jurisdictions. The recent expansion of social services has fueled the growth of tribunals in Scotland, some the same as the English, others peculiar to Scotland. In the first group are national insurance and national health. In the other are the Scottish Land Court (successor to the CROFTERS' commission) and the Mental Welfare Commission for Scotland. In addition, some Scottish tribunals are subject to the oversight of the Secretary of State for Scotland.

IRELAND

During the period of English rule (1171–1922), the central courts in IRELAND were a copy of the English courts, although the area of the country under English control fluctuated from a low point in the 15th century (the PALE around DUBLIN) to total coverage in the 18th and 19th centuries. Irish judges were often recruited from England until the end of the 18th century, after which time they were principally of Irish or, more properly, Anglo-Irish origin. Irish BARRISTERS were required by law to attend the INNS OF COURT in LONDON as part of their training, and English case law was cited in Irish courts. In 1887 an Irish Supreme Court was created, modeled on the English reform of 1873. After the establishment of the IRISH FREE STATE (1922), a brief experiment with "Dáil" courts and Celtic laws was abandoned, and English-style courts and proceedings were restored. Under a Courts of Justice Act in 1924, a new structure was put in place: at the local level, a district court and a circuit court; at the upper level, a high court, a court of criminal appeal, and a supreme court. These were affirmed by the constitution of 1937, under which Ireland became a republic governed by a written constitution.

The local courts, formerly those of justices of the peace (and in the 19th century paid resident magistrates), were replaced by district courts for minor civil and criminal cases. The circuit court, which replaced the county court, heard appeals from district courts and could hear serious criminal cases, subject to appeal to the court of criminal appeal.

Special jurisdictions were radically excised by the constitutional changes of 1922 and 1937. Earlier special courts were replaced by a collection of modern tribunals and boards, although in separate garb and styled to fit the Irish constitutions—e.g., land commission, employment tribunals, criminal injuries compensation. The idea of an ombudsman was adopted in acts of 1980 and 1984, and it has been replicated in selected areas outside government.

NORTHERN IRELAND

With the partition of Ireland brought about by the Government of Ireland Act of 1920 and the subsequent creation of the Irish Free State in 1922, a dominion government was created in BELFAST. A Supreme Court of Judicature copied that of England, and there was a Court of Appeal, from which decisions might be appealed to the House of Lords. Below the Supreme Court there is a Crown Court, which hears cases in different regions. Below that are county courts, and below them resident magistrates who try summary offenses. Because of the unrest in Northern Ireland (1969–98), some extraordinary features appeared in the law: judges may try terrorist offenses without juries ("Diplock" courts take their name from the English judge who led the inquiry recommending this change). Recent legislation restricted the right to silence for terrorists and made other important modifications in criminal law.

ISLE OF MAN

A self-governing dependency, technically not a part of the United Kingdom, the ISLE OF MAN has been under the protection of the Crown since the middle ages and was purchased by GEORGE III in 1765. The executive is the lieutenant governor; the legislature is Tynwald, composed of the governor, the Legislative Council, and the House of Keys (24 elected members). The high court has three divisions (common law, chancery, staff of government). The high court judges are the First and Second Deemsters, Clerk of the Rolls, and Judge of Appeal. Criminal cases are heard by the Court of General Gaol Delivery.

CHANNEL ISLANDS

The CHANNEL ISLANDS, Crown dependencies, are the inheritance of the Duchy of Normandy. They consist of the bailiwicks of Jersey and Guernsey as well as the latter's dependencies, Alderney and Sark. The royal court of Jersey and the royal court of Guernsey are presided over by a bailiff who hears cases with other judges (jurats). The court of Alderney consists of jurats appointed by the home secretary. Sark is a dependency of Guernsey and does not have a separate court.

See also ADMIRALTY; ASSIZE; CRIMINAL LAW; CROWN COURTS; ECCLESIASTICAL COURTS; GRAND JURY; JURY; LAW; MARTIAL LAW; PREROGATIVE, ROYAL; STAR CHAMBER.

covenant

One strand of REFORMATION theology emphasized the Old Testament idea of a covenant between God and his people. On some occasions this inspired covenants among Protestants against Catholics. In three cases the concept was central to Scottish 17th-century political history. The SCOTTISH NATIONAL COVENANT (1638), a document subscribed to by many Scots, pledged to maintain the true reformed kirk (church). The SOLEMN LEAGUE AND COVENANT (1643) was the treaty between ENGLAND and SCOTLAND against CHARLES I promising to extend the PRESBYTERIAN church to England and IRELAND. CHARLES II signed the covenant in 1650, perhaps not sincerely but surely adding to the hostility of those purged from the church after his RESTORATION in 1660. The term was also used in the 20th century by opponents of IRISH HOME RULE in NORTHERN IRELAND. They signed the ULSTER COVENANT in 1911–12, vowing to fight against the separation of Ireland from the UNITED KINGDOM.

Covenanters

The name applied to Scottish PRESBYTERIANS adhering to the COVENANTS of 1638 and 1643, which assured them of their form of church government. With the RESTORATION of 1660 they were outraged at the return of the rule of BISHOPS, and some resorted to field meetings and armed resistance in the 1660s and 1670s. Their actions brought brutal repression.

See also CAMERON RICHARD; JAMES VII AND II.

Coverdale, Miles (1488–1568)

churchman, translator

One of the early English Protestant reformers, Coverdale spent 20 years in exile. He worked from William TYNDALE's translation of the BIBLE to create an edition that was published in Zurich in 1535. Thomas CROMWELL convinced HENRY VIII to authorize the use of translations, and a revised edition by Coverdale, the "Great Bible," was printed in 1539.

Cranfield, Lionel (1575–1645)

lord treasurer

A merchant who was made surveyor general of the Customs in 1613, Cranfield entered PARLIAMENT in 1614 and rose to the position of lord treasurer in 1621. In that post he reduced spending, as the royal accounts were already in debt. His actions made a large number of enemies, and he was impeached, found guilty of corruption, and deprived of his offices in 1624.

Cranmer, Thomas (1489–1556)

archbishop of Canterbury

A member of the group of churchmen working to gain HENRY VIII's divorce, Cranmer was well positioned when ARCHBISHOP of CANTERBURY William Warham died in 1532 and was selected as his replacement. He annulled the king's marriage to CATHERINE OF ARAGON (1533) as he later did with Anne BOLEYN (1536). He worked with Thomas CROMWELL to advance the process of reform, which was erratic under Henry VIII but moved more decisively after his death. Cranmer was the principal author of the BOOK OF COMMON PRAYER of 1549 and 1552, and of the 42 (later 39) Articles of Religion (1553). He was put on trial for heresy under MARY I, and although he made several recantations, he later withdrew them and was burned at the stake in 1556.

cricket

The national sport of England, some form of cricket was probably played in very early times,

Cricket match, 1955 *(Hulton/Archive)*

but rules were not formulated until the 17th and 18th centuries. Two teams of 11 compete on a field, at the center of which are two wickets, 66 feet apart. The wicket consists of three stumps with wooden cross-pieces called bails. Batsmen from one team face a bowler from the other, whose object is to throw the leather-covered ball and dislodge the bails. The batsmen defend the wicket and attempt to strike the ball far enough to run to the other wicket, scoring a run, before a fielder can dislodge the bails. The sport has spread to many parts of the former empire, and international matches are played with AUSTRALIA, NEW ZEALAND, SOUTH AFRICA, the WEST INDIES, INDIA, and PAKISTAN.

Crimean War (1854–1856)

In British terms, the "Eastern Question" was a serious 19th-century foreign policy matter.

Would the decaying Ottoman Empire allow the advance of Russian power and influence into the Balkans and the Near East, and what should GREAT BRITAIN and the rest of Europe do to prevent that from happening? The question became urgent in 1853 when Russia occupied two Turkish provinces, claiming to protect the Moldavians and Wallachians from religious persecution. Turkey, with French support, declared war, and Britain entered the conflict months later. Both western powers landed forces on the Crimean peninsula in the Black Sea, aiming at the capture of Sevastopol. Both sides suffered very heavy casualties before the city fell. Meanwhile there were naval battles in the Baltic that destroyed Russian facilities and helped to bring a settlement via the Treaty of Paris (1856).

The war was a dramatic failure in two respects. While the British suffered far fewer deaths than the French or the Russians, at least four times as many men died of disease as were killed in battle. The work of nurses like Florence NIGHTINGALE could barely mitigate the appalling tragedy. As for the military performance, Lord CARDIGAN's futile "charge of the light brigade" at Balaclava and other examples of poor generalship were fuel for future ARMY reforms. Together these problems brought down the government of Lord ABERDEEN in 1855.

Criminal Appeal, Court of

Created in 1907, this court took over the work done previously by the Court of Crown Cases Reserved, a body created in the 19th century that was the first such court in ENGLAND. Previously there was no criminal appeal, only a writ of error (on matters of LAW) or petition for a royal pardon. The court would hear appeals on questions of law or (with the leave of the court) questions of fact or fact and law. The court could throw out a conviction and change the verdict or the sentence, but it could not order a new trial. Its decisions could be further appealed to the HOUSE OF LORDS. The court was abolished in 1966 when the jurisdiction was transferred to the Court of APPEAL.

criminal law

The traditional system of English criminal justice drew upon notions of royal justice known to the Anglo-Saxons, which were shaped into a centralized system by the Anglo-Norman kings in the 12th and 13th centuries. The major offenses were known as "pleas of the crown," or acts that violated the king's peace. Local grand juries were called upon to present criminal charges before royal justices; trials were soon conducted before a petty JURY, after the Lateran Council outlawed the use of the ordeal in 1215. Crimes were classified as treasons, felonies, or misdemeanors (until 1967). An accused person was not allowed to have counsel until 1837, and the judge was expected to be his adviser and protector. But the severity of criminal law, especially the increase in capital crimes in the 18th century, created a movement for reform. In 1842 the death penalty was restricted to the most serious felonies. In 1848 a limited form of appeal was created, but a court of criminal appeal had to wait until 1907.

See also CAPITAL PUNISHMENT; COURTS OF LAW; GRAND JURY; LAW.

Cripps, Sir Stafford (1889–1952)
Labour politician

A successful barrister before he joined the LABOUR PARTY, Cripps was appointed solicitor general in 1930. He became an ardent socialist, but his advocacy of a "popular front" with the communists led to his expulsion from the party in 1939. During WORLD WAR II he worked as ambassador to Moscow, and he was sent on a mission to INDIA to try to negotiate self-government. In Clement ATTLEE's government he served as president of the BOARD OF TRADE and as CHANCELLOR OF THE EXCHEQUER, where he implemented an austerity program and managed the devaluation of the currency.

crofter

A croft is a small holding in the HIGHLANDS and islands of SCOTLAND. Tenants had been forced into these uneconomical plots near the coast during the HIGHLAND CLEARANCES of large estates that began in the late 18th century. Crofters lived by harvesting kelp and fishing to augment their small farming output. In the 1880s their condition provoked some violent protest which led to an inquiry. The Crofter's Act of 1886 improved the terms of their tenancy, and a Crofters' Commission was established to guard their interests.

See also HIGHLAND CLEARANCES.

Cromer, Evelyn Baring, first earl of (1841–1917)

diplomat, administrator

Born into a banking family, Lord Cromer entered military service (1858–72), then became private secretary to the VICEROY of INDIA, Lord Northbrook. He went to EGYPT in 1877 as commissioner in charge of finances, eventually becoming consul general (1883–1907). During his term there were serious crises in the SUDAN, from General Charles GORDON's defeat at KHARTOUM (1885) to the diplomatic settlement of the FASHODA incident (1898). His *Modern Egypt* (2 vols., 1908) was an eyewitness account by an imperial consul.

Cromwell, Oliver (1599–1658)

general, lord protector

Born into a modest small gentry family, Cromwell was influenced by PURITANS at Cambridge and entered PARLIAMENT as a radical member for Cambridge in 1640. When the CIVIL WAR began he displayed a natural talent as a cavalry commander in the Eastern Association. His units played a key part in the victory at MARSTON MOOR (1644), but he was upset with the conduct of aristocratic leaders and helped to push through the SELF-DENYING ORDINANCE the following winter. This removed peers and MEMBERS OF PARLIAMENT (excepting himself and a few others) and reconstituted the ARMY as a NEW MODEL ARMY. It seemed to work, as the army routed King CHARLES I's forces at NASEBY, with Cromwell as second in command.

After the king's surrender in 1646, Cromwell became increasingly involved in the politics of revolution. He was a leader of the party of "independents" who opposed both the king's religion and that of the PRESBYTERIANS and their Scottish allies. He was also at the center of the political storm over the army's arrears of pay, its demand for indemnity, and its fears for a future religious settlement. In 1647 the army captured Charles I, marched on LONDON, and presented a constitutional manifesto, the "Heads of the Proposals." The still more radical army officers and men endorsed the LEVELLERS' document, the "Agreement of the People," and these contrasting views were debated in a public meeting at Putney, outside London, before the army council. These discussions were inconclusive, as Cromwell may have anticipated. But from late 1647 he took decisive action to stamp out a mutiny, put down royalist uprisings, and meet and crush an army coming from SCOTLAND in support of the king. Later in 1648 he had Colonel Thomas Pride purge the HOUSE OF COMMONS of its anti-army members, and the resulting RUMP PARLIAMENT went on to order the trial and execution of the king.

Cromwell led a campaign to conquer IRELAND in 1649 and then to Scotland in 1650–51. These conquests made him the obvious leader of the new military state, but he found it impossible to reconstruct a working constitution. First he fell out with the Rump; then a nominated PARLIAMENT, made up of independent ministers (1653) proved uncontrollable. After producing a new constitution, naming himself as "lord protector" (1654), he summoned further parliaments with similar results. The basic issues—religion, finance, and foreign policy—were the same ones that plagued the STUART kings. Cromwell's limited success as protector deserves some credit. He maintained army discipline; his limited toleration was a fundamental shift, however frustrating and incomplete; and his expenditure on the NAVY helped to set a foundation for future power. However, contemporary views of his rule were solidly negative. As a regicide, he could not produce a better scheme of government; as a general, he could only rule by force; and as spokesman for a "godly nation," he stoked the flames of religious discord. He died in September 1658, and his son

Richard succeeded him as lord protector, but the regime soon collapsed.

See also COMMONWEALTH OF ENGLAND; DROGHEDA; DUNBAR, BATTLE OF; INSTRUMENT OF GOVERNMENT; PRIDE'S PURGE.

Cromwell, Thomas (1485–1540)
king's secretary

Working for Cardinal WOLSEY, Cromwell was close to King HENRY VIII's divorce proceedings, and when Wolsey fell from office in 1529, he was able to move into the king's council. By 1534 he had become the king's secretary. During this period he played an important part in preparing the clergy of ENGLAND for the king's break with Rome. In 1532 he drafted the "Supplication of the Commons Against the Ordinaries," a petition reviewing flaws in the clerical courts. This was used to force the church to agree to the SUBMISSION OF THE CLERGY, conceding that canons were subject to secular review. He may have convinced Henry that statute law offered a viable direction to implement his next steps. He drafted the Act in RESTRAINT OF APPEALS (1533), which cut off legal appeal to Rome; and the Act of Supremacy (1534), which acknowledged the king as supreme head of the church in England (see ROYAL SUPREMACY).

Cromwell became Henry's chief agent in the new church, a position of precarious power. As vicar-general he took steps to promote reforms, including the DISSOLUTION of the monasteries; the 10 articles of religion and royal injunctions (1536, 1538); and campaigns against opponents such as Sir Thomas MORE. It was in this direction that Cromwell caused his own undoing. He used arbitrary acts of ATTAINDER to execute Anne BOLEYN, her household, and members of other high-ranking families. He also created a circle at court which was only too happy to overthrow him after he had promoted the disastrous marriage between Henry and ANNE OF CLEVES (1540). Declared a traitor by an act of attainder, he was executed in July 1540.

Crown See MONARCHY; PREROGATIVE, ROYAL.

crown colony See COLONY.

Crown Court

The first crown courts were created in Liverpool and Manchester (1956) and later absorbed in a national system of crown courts (1971) replacing the ASSIZE courts and QUARTER SESSIONS. They conduct trials on indictment, hear appeals from MAGISTRATES' courts, and have some civil appellate jurisdiction. Appeals lie to the Court of APPEAL (Criminal Division) and the HOUSE OF LORDS.

Crystal Palace

The Great Exhibition of 1851, planned by Prince ALBERT, was housed in a radical structure in Hyde Park: a giant iron-and-glass conservatory designed by Joseph Paxton. The building was several times the length of ST. PAUL'S CATHEDRAL, and it contained nearly 300,000 panes of glass. Itself one of the high points of the exhibition, at the end of the event it was dismantled and moved to Sydenham, in South LONDON. It was destroyed by fire in 1936.

Culloden, Battle of (1746)

In February 1746 the JACOBITES occupied Inverness, and as the duke of Cumberland advanced with an army of English and lowland Scots, they launched an unsuccessful surprise attack on the night of April 15. "Bonnie Prince Charlie" (Charles Edward STUART) chose to engage the duke's army the next day, on an open moor, five miles from the city. The rebel force numbered about 5,000, and the king's army 9,000 plus field artillery. That artillery shattered the Jacobite ranks, their subsequent advance was scattered, and the royal army routed them, losing only 50 men. The defeated prince fled to France; many of his men were pursued and, with the wounded, killed after the battle, earning the duke the nickname "the Butcher."

See also MACDONALD, FLORA; HIGHLANDS; MURRAY, LORD GEORGE; STUART, HOUSE OF.

Cumberland, William Augustus, duke of (1721–1765)

general

The third son of GEORGE II, William Augustus was trained for a naval career, but instead he became employed in the ARMY, gaining the rank of general in the War of AUSTRIAN SUCCESSION after fighting in the Battle of Dettingen (1744). In 1745 he took command of the army, repelling the JACOBITES' invasion. At the Battle of CULLODEN (1746) he led the royal forces to victory, and after the battle his troops relentlessly hunted down the rebels, gaining him the nickname "the butcher." PARLIAMENT, however, was quite satisfied with his performance, granting him a pension of £25,000 per annum. He returned to command forces on the continent but he was disgraced by a defeat at the hands of the French in 1757 and resigned from his posts.

Curragh mutiny (1914)

Curragh was the British ARMY station near DUBLIN, where in March 1914 some 57 officers of the third cavalry brigade declared that they would refuse orders to serve against ULSTER if it rejected the IRISH HOME RULE bill, set to become law momentarily. Sir John FRENCH, the army chief of staff, assured them that this would not be necessary. Herbert ASQUITH'S CABINET disagreed, and French and the war secretary J. E. B. Seely were forced to resign.

Curzon of Kedleston, George Nathaniel Curzon, first marquis (1859–1925)

(Viscount Scarsdale, Baron Ravensdale)

viceroy

An authority on the empire, especially Asia, Curzon was VICEROY of INDIA, 1898–1905, in which capacity he made a number of reforms.

After quarrels with General KITCHENER, commander of the Indian forces, he resigned. He later served in the CABINET as foreign secretary (1919–24), where he opposed the BALFOUR DECLARATION and supported a powerful British role in the Middle East.

customs and excise

The duties imposed on foreign and domestic products. Customs duties were levied at ports of entry as a tax or as a restraint on trade. The excise was a levy on classes of popular products, often alcohol and tobacco, but in earlier periods wool, salt, paper, glass, and other essential materials. Governments had to maintain increasing numbers of agents to collect these taxes, smuggling was a significant byproduct of the systems, and the incidence of such imposts added to the growth of support for FREE TRADE.

Cyprus

Island in the eastern Mediterranean, 60 miles west of Syria and 40 miles south of Turkey. A British PROTECTORATE was established in 1878; the island was annexed in 1914 and made a crown COLONY in 1925. The 80-percent majority Greek population demanded union with Greece, and rioting caused suspension of the legislative assembly in 1931. New constitutional plans were thwarted by a terrorist campaign. Talks were held (1957–60) that led to the foundation of the Republic of Cyprus in 1960. The Turkish minority set up its own assembly in northern Cyprus in 1970. In 1974 Turkish troops invaded, and a Turkish government was proclaimed in 1975. In 1983 a separate republic was declared. GREAT BRITAIN still supports reunification and has some troops stationed on the island along with United Nations peacekeepers.

D

Dáil Éireann

"Assembly of Ireland," the name given to the lower house of the Irish parliament (the *Oirechtas*), proclaimed in 1919 and recognized in the constitution of the IRISH FREE STATE. The 166 members or deputies are elected on a system of proportional representation.

Dalhousie, James Andrew Broun Ramsay, first marquis (1812–1860)

governor-general of India, 1848–1856

Lord Dalhousie was educated at Harrow and Christ Church, OXFORD UNIVERSITY. After briefly serving as president of the BOARD OF TRADE, he became governor-general of INDIA. He declared the Punjab a British province in 1849, and he was responsible for many improvements in roads, railways, ports, and schools. He made efforts to reduce the practices of suttee and female infanticide, as part of a campaign to remodel Indian culture. Under his direction, GREAT BRITAIN acquired territory in the Punjab, Oudh, and Lower BURMA. This was done by wars of annexation, sometimes exploiting the "doctrine of lapse" wherein the British assumed power when native rulers died without male heirs. Some critics blamed his policies for the tension that led to the INDIAN MUTINY (1857–58).

Dalrymple, James See STAIR, JAMES DALRYMPLE, VISCOUNT.

Danby, Thomas Osborne, earl of (1631–1712)

statesman

A MEMBER OF PARLIAMENT for York in 1665, Lord Danby rose to become lord high treasurer (1673) and CHARLES II's first minister. He built a court party by use of PATRONAGE, but he was caught up in contrary policies—for instance, the secret Treaty of DOVER with Louis XIV, which promised a French alliance versus the marriage between William of Orange (WILLIAM III) and Mary, the king's niece (MARY II), which suggested a pro-Dutch policy. At the time of the POPISH PLOT (1678), his involvement was exposed, and he was impeached and imprisoned (1679–84). After his release he enlisted with the opposition to JAMES VII AND II, and he served William III as chief minister from 1690 to 1695, at which time he was impeached for corruption.

Darby, Abraham (1677–1717)

iron founder

The son of a Quaker farmer, Darby became partner in a brass works, and he brought Dutch brass founders to Bristol. In 1708 he patented a process for casting cheap iron in sand. He later developed a method for smelting iron with coke instead of charcoal, allowing lighter castings for hollow pieces. His works at Coalbrookdale became famous, and the first cast-iron bridge was built there in 1777.

Dardanelles campaign See GALLIPOLI.

Darien

The name given to the isthmus of Panama by Scottish colonizers, who settled New Caledonia there (1698–1700) under the auspices of the Company of Scotland. The company wanted to break the English EAST INDIA COMPANY monopoly, but the scheme failed due to opposition from ENGLAND and Spain, as well as problems of funding and management. A very large share of SCOTLAND's wealth had been invested, and there was increased bitterness toward England, although ironically the crisis probably spurred the UNION of 1707 as a remedy for Scottish economic malaise.

Darnley, Henry Stewart, earl of (1545–1567)

father of James VI and I

A grandson of Margaret TUDOR, Darnley was married to MARY, QUEEN OF SCOTS, in 1565. Mary refused to share her throne, and the frustrated Darnley was implicated in the murder of her Italian adviser, David RIZZIO (March 1566). The couple's son James (later JAMES VI AND I) was born a few months later, but the relationship deteriorated. In February 1567 Darnley was strangled, and his lodging house was blown up. The queen and her new companion and later husband, James Hepburn, earl of BOTHWELL, were chief suspects.

darts

A game that probably began with throwing spears or arrows. The dartboard was only refined and standardized in the 19th century. When it was declared a game of skill in a court case in 1908, darts became a popular game in PUBS, as it was not subject to gaming laws. A National Darts Association was established in 1953, and the game has gained even greater popularity via television.

Darwin, Charles (1809–1882)

scientist

The grandson of Erasmus DARWIN and son of a successful physician, Charles Darwin studied in

Sir Charles Darwin *(Library of Congress)*

EDINBURGH and at CAMBRIDGE UNIVERSITY but turned away from a medical career. He began to collect specimens as his fascination with geology and botany increased. He took a place on the HMS *Beagle* for a voyage to chart Cape Horn, during which he collected specimens and made scientific observations (1831–36). He spent the following years analyzing his collections, and he wrote an essay in 1844 explaining his conclusions. However, it was only in 1859 that he published *On the Origin of Species by Means of Natural Selection,* which explained his theory of evolution. His even more controversial study *The Descent of Man* appeared in 1871, wherein he showed how man had evolved from primates. His work was of fundamental importance in providing a scientific explanation for evolution. This was a revolutionary idea in Victorian society, and it was widely denounced by churchmen and scientists alike. But Darwin did have his defenders, and the theory of evolution gained a solid foothold by the end of the century, while the concept of natural selection required several more generations for general acceptance.

See also HUXLEY, THOMAS HENRY.

Darwin, Erasmus (1731–1802)
physician, scientist

A doctor by training and zoologist by nature, Darwin was a leading 18th-century scientist. Declining an offer to become the royal physician to GEORGE III, he chose a career of study and writing. He organized a Philosophical Society in Derby and the Lunar Society of Birmingham. He wrote *The Botanic Garden* (1791) in verse, and his major prose work was *Zoonomia, or Laws of Organic Life* (1794–96), which studied and analyzed the evolutionary adaptations made by living organisms.

Davies, John (1569–1626)
lawyer, poet

Davies was a BARRISTER who became solicitor general for IRELAND (1603) and then attorney general (1606). He worked to advance the royal policy of PLANTATION, especially by removing the remnants of the Celtic legal system. He produced the first printed law reports in Ireland, and he wrote a tract on the subjugation of the Irish: *A Discoverie of the True Causes Why Ireland Was Never Entirely Subdued* (1612). He also published a number of poems in classical style but on contemporary subjects (published in a collected edition by Robert Krueger, 1975).

Davies, Richard (1501–1581)
bishop, translator

Born in North WALES, Davies studied at OXFORD UNIVERSITY and went into exile in the reign of MARY I, but after her death returned and was made BISHOP of St. Asaph (1560) and St. Davids (1561). He worked with William SALESBURY to translate the New Testament into Welsh (1567).

Davitt, Michael (1846–1906)
Irish nationalist

Born during the IRISH FAMINE, Davitt emigrated with his family to Lancashire. Working in a cotton mill there, he lost an arm in an industrial accident. He joined the FENIAN BROTHERHOOD and served time in jail. He decided that the Irish nationalist cause required the support of tenant farmers, and he formed the Irish Land League, with Charles Stewart PARNELL as president, in 1879. He favored LAND nationalization and IRISH HOME RULE, and he believed the latter cause was most likely to be achieved by the union with Parnell's parliamentary group. Their partnership was shaken by the Parnell divorce scandal, but Davitt served as a Parnellite MEMBER OF PARLIAMENT from 1895 to 1899. In his lifetime Davitt saw the IRISH LAND ACTS achieve much of the change he had fought for.

Davy, Sir Humphrey (1778–1829)
chemist

Davy discovered by electrolysis the metallic elements sodium and potassium (1807), as well as magnesium, strontium, and barium (1808). He proved that chlorine is an element, and he argued the presence of hydrogen in all acids. His invaluable practical invention was the miner's safety lamp for use in mines where methane was a safety hazard. He was a popular scientific lecturer, and he served as president of the ROYAL SOCIETY (1820–29).

Declaration of Independence (1776)

In July 1776 the Continental Congress of the AMERICAN COLONIES adopted the statement drafted by Thomas Jefferson (one of a committee of five) which contained a long indictment of GEORGE III, declaring that he was "a tyrant unfit to be the ruler of a free people." The text was written partly with an eye to attracting an alliance with France. The declaration concluded that because of the evils of colonial administration, the connection between GREAT BRITAIN and the colonies was "totally dissolved."

declaration of indulgence

A statement issued on several occasions by the later STUART kings, designed to suspend PENAL LAWS against Protestant dissenters and Roman Catholics (1662, 1672, 1687, 1688). The first attempt was withdrawn. The second was stoutly opposed as being illegal, and even though it was withdrawn, the TEST ACT was passed to ensure compliance with penal laws. The last two attempts precipitated the SEVEN BISHOPS' CASE (1688) and the GLORIOUS REVOLUTION (1688–89). The fundamental question in all cases was whether or not the king had any power to reject a duly enacted law. The definitive answer in 1689 was "no."

Declaration of Rights (1689)

After the flight of JAMES II, the prospective sovereigns WILLIAM III and MARY II were offered the crown by the Convention Parliament. That offer was accompanied by a declaration that stated grievances and terms for future conduct: frequent, freely elected parliaments; free speech and debate in PARLIAMENT; and power of parliament to tax, pass laws, and maintain an ARMY. When the Declaration of Rights was accepted by the king and queen, it was introduced into parliament as the BILL OF RIGHTS.

declaratory acts (1720, 1766)

On two occasions in the 18th century, PARLIAMENT felt compelled to set down a statement of its constitutional authority—a declaratory act—with respect to related governmental entities. In 1720, in the wake of a long property dispute in IRELAND in which the Irish House of Lords used its presumed power to hear the case on appeal, the declaratory act stated that all such appeals would go to the lords in Westminster and that the British parliament had full power to enact laws for Ireland. This act was repealed in 1782.

In 1766, when repealing the STAMP ACT for the AMERICAN COLONIES, Parliament felt it was necessary to underscore its fundamental power over the colonial governments and to deny the case made by the Stamp Act's opponents. This declaratory act was effectively repealed by the Revolutionary War, which began in 1776.

Dee, John (1527–1608)
astrologer, mathematician

Dee was prosecuted for sorcery under MARY I, but he became a scientific adviser to ELIZABETH I. He combined the study of mathematics and medicine with the more popular fields of astrology and alchemy.

Defence of the Realm Act (1914)

This act, which came at the very beginning of WORLD WAR I, gave the government "full power and authority" to conduct the war. This meant seizing property, imposing censorship, and controlling labor, all of which was backed by the power of courts-martial. This invasion of liberties was deemed necessary in the case of modern warfare. A peacetime version of the act was passed in 1920, while a wartime version was prepared in advance and quickly enacted in 1939 as WORLD WAR II broke out.

Defender of the Faith

Title conferred on HENRY VIII by Pope Leo X (1521) after the king had written a tract against Martin Luther entitled *Assertio septem sacramentorum,* or Defense of the Seven Sacraments. Since PARLIAMENT recognized the title in 1544, it has been borne by all British monarchs, apparently without any sense of irony. The title is represented by the initials "F.D." (*fidei defensor*) on British coins.

Defoe, Daniel (1660–1731)
author

A merchant and a dissenter, after some early adventures in politics (including an escape from Sedgmoor after MONMOUTH'S REBELLION), Defoe took up writing as a pamphleteer, a journalist, and then as a novelist. His mock-heroic *True-Born Englishman* (1701) poked fun at the emerging national identity of the English. His *Shortest Way with the Dissenters* (1702) satirized the bigotry of the high-church party and earned him time in prison for libel. His power as a writer was appreciated by political leaders who employed him as a propagandist. While he wrote *Review of the Affairs of France* (1704–13), he also reported on the progress of the act of UNION with SCOTLAND (1707). His works of fiction included *The Life and Surprising Adventures of Robinson Crusoe* (1719), *Moll Flanders* (1722), and *Journal of the Plague Year* (1722). He also wrote a remarkable guide book called *A Tour thro' the Whole Island of Great Britain* (1724–26).

de heretico comburendo (1382, 1401)

Statutes passed to punish the LOLLARDS, a group of reformers (i.e., heretics) who were followers of John WYCLIFFE. If convicted by the clerical courts, they would be handed over to civil authorities to be burned at the stake. Repealed in 1547, the act was revived briefly under MARY I (1554–59).

depression

An economic crisis marked by sharp declines in production, increases in unemployment, and widespread poverty and distress. When the economy grew beyond the level of local subsistence—that is, when it began to industrialize and engage in extensive overseas trade—this type of downturn in the business cycle became more dangerous. In the early years of industry there were many occasions of economic decline (1842, 1857, 1866) but historians have identified two periods that were of a magnitude beyond all others.

The years 1873 to 1896 have been called the "Great Depression," due to declining prices, increased unemployment, bank failures, and losses in overseas markets. While it is true that eco-

nomic growth faltered in the period, those workers with jobs actually experienced an increase in real wages, and many began to benefit from cheap food imports. The better description of this period is as one of economic contraction, a process that was more severe in some sectors of the economy than others.

The economic collapse of the 1920s and 1930s was truly a "Great Depression." For most of the earlier decade there had been a high level of unemployment, and there was only one brief period (1919–1921) of strong economic growth. WORLD WAR I had dislocated the world economy, and major industries like textiles, coal, steel, and shipbuilding were faced with shrinking markets and expanding competition. Unemployment, which had been around 10 percent, rose to more than twice that level after the Wall Street crash in 1929, and did not fall below 10 percent until WORLD WAR II. Governments were hampered by strict adherence to balanced budgets, but there were some attempts to alleviate distress and help industrial recovery.

Derby, Edward George Geoffrey Smith Stanley, 14th earl of (1799–1869)
prime minister, 1852, 1858–1859, and 1866–1868

A member of PARLIAMENT from 1822, Lord Derby served in the TORY governments of the late 1820s and was then chief secretary for IRELAND in the WHIG ministry of 1830–33. He later entered the Tory cabinet of Robert PEEL as secretary for war and the colonies, but he resigned over the repeal of the CORN LAWS. Leading the protectionist wing of the party, he worked with Benjamin DISRAELI to rebuild the CONSERVATIVE PARTY. He went to the HOUSE OF LORDS in 1851 on inheriting the earldom, and he was PRIME MINISTER in three minority governments, the last being the one that passed the second REFORM ACT in 1867.

Desmond, earls of See FITZGERALD, EARLS OF DESMOND.

Desmond Rebellion (1579–1583)

Gerald FITZGERALD, 15th earl of Desmond (1533–83), fought against the spread of English authority over family lands in southwest IRELAND. He had been imprisoned in ENGLAND for feuds with his stepson, James Butler, earl of ORMONDE, and he had sought aid from Catholic powers abroad. He was captured and executed, and his large estates were given to English settlers.

De Valera, Eamon (1882–1975)
Irish prime minister, 1932–1948, 1951–1954, 1957–1959

De Valera was the major figure in Irish republican politics for over half a century. Born in New York, he grew up in County Limerick and became a mathematics teacher. He joined the Irish Volunteers in 1913 and was an officer in the EASTER REBELLION. His death sentence for treason was commuted, and he was released in 1917. Elected as a SINN FÉIN member of parliament that year, he was head of the provisional government from 1919 to 1922 and led the party until 1926. He did not go to LONDON for the ANGLO-IRISH TREATY negotiations, deliberately insulating himself from what was bound to be a disputed settlement. When he withdrew from the government in 1922, he did not actively engage in the ensuing civil conflict. He resumed a leadership role in 1926 with the founding of the Fianna Fáil party. He became prime minister in 1932 and held the office until 1948, regaining it in 1951 and 1957. He was later elected to the ceremonial office of president of the IRISH REPUBLIC (1959–73). His singular achievement was the adoption of the constitution of 1937, which established the Republic of EIRE.

devolution

The transfer of limited powers from the central government to regional governments. This term has been used, especially in the 20th century, to describe plans and projects for sharing power within the UNITED KINGDOM. The first formal example was the creation of the separate gov-ernment for NORTHERN IRELAND (1921–72). There were lengthy debates and discussions from the 1960s on legislative assemblies for WALES and SCOTLAND, stimulated by rising nationalist parties in both of those countries. In 1969 a royal COMMISSION on the constitution made divided recommendations for elected assemblies in Scotland and Wales; referendums were held in those countries in 1979, and the schemes were defeated. The idea was revived by the Labour government in 1997, and assemblies were this time endorsed by the electorate and inaugurated in 1999. Ironically, the devolved government of Northern Ireland had been terminated during the sectarian violence of the early 1970s. However, after peace talks and an agreement in 1998, an unsteady truce saw an effort toward the reestablishment of a provincial government with devolved powers in BELFAST.

Devonshire, Spencer Cavendish, duke of
See HARTINGTON, SPENCER CAVENDISH, MARQUESS OF.

Devonshire, William Cavendish, fourth duke of (1720–1764)
prime minister, 1756–1757

Cavendish entered PARLIAMENT in 1741 and was LORD LIEUTENANT of IRELAND in 1754. He became first lord of the TREASURY in 1756, but he resigned the following year. He held the post of lord chamberlain of the household until 1762, when he was dismissed from the PRIVY COUNCIL

Diana, Princess of Wales (1961–1997)
wife of Prince Charles

Lady Diana Spencer was married to CHARLES, PRINCE OF WALES in a fairy-tale (televised) wedding in WESTMINSTER ABBEY in 1981. Their first child, Prince William, was born in 1982, and a brother, Henry, in 1984. The couple separated in 1992 and were divorced in 1996. "Princess Di" was known for her patronage of numerous charities, and her private life was vigorously followed by the press. She died in an automobile accident in Paris, and her funeral was an extraordinary public event, with public grief so massive that the royal family gave it full honors.

Dickens, Charles (1812–1870)
author

The son of a navy clerk imprisoned for debt, Dickens grew up in poverty and worked in a factory as a child. He later worked as a reporter in the law courts and in PARLIAMENT. Early articles were printed in his first book, *Sketches by 'Boz'* (1836), while he had begun to publish the monthly installments of what later appeared in a single volume as *Pickwick Papers* (1836–37). He was a hugely successful novelist who had a prodigious output and a highly tuned social conscience. *Oliver Twist* (1837–39), *Nicholas Nickleby* (1838–39), and *The Old Curiosity Shop* (1840–41) were in the first wave; the next surge included *Dombey and Son* (1848), *David Copperfield* (1849–50), *Bleak House* (1852–53), *Hard Times* (1854), *Little Dorritt* (1855–57), and *Great Expectations* (1860–61). In among these were sandwiched his historical novels of the GORDON RIOTS (*Barnaby Rudge,* 1841) and the French Revolution (*Tale of Two Cities,* 1859) plus his classic *A Christmas Carol* (1843), part of a series of Christmas books. Dickens was a prominent public figure, gave innumerable readings from his works, traveled to America, and was an active voice in many reform movements.

Dilke, Charles (1843–1911)
radical politician

A lawyer and member of PARLIAMENT, Dilke was a radical, a republican, and a champion of empire. His book *Greater Britain* (1868) espoused a belief in "Anglo-Saxondom," a worldwide race with its roots in ENGLAND. An advocate of radical domestic reforms, he held some CABINET posts, but after being cited in a prominent divorce case (1886), he was no longer considered cabinet material.

Dillon, John (1851–1927)
Irish nationalist

Forsaking his medical practice, Dillon entered politics and became a prominent nationalist. He was jailed three times for his support of the Irish Land League. He led the anti-PARNELL faction after that leader's famous divorce case, and he was overall leader of the nationalists in the 1890s, replaced by John REDMOND in 1900. He remained a MEMBER OF PARLIAMENT until 1918, when he had the distinction of being defeated in that year's election by Eamon DE VALERA while the latter was in prison.

disarmament

There have been three distinct methods of disarmament. Historically the most common was forced or involuntary denial of arms, typically imposed on a defeated enemy—e.g., Napoleonic France in 1815, Germany in 1919, or Japan in 1945. From the end of the 19th century, in reaction to the massive power of weapons of war, there has been a move toward voluntary surrender or limitation of arms. This has taken two forms: general disarmament and selective disarmament.

In international conferences in 1898 and 1907, the idea of general renunciation of weapons of war was discussed, and the gruesome toll of WORLD WAR I propelled this idea into world councils. The concept of voluntary surrender of arms by nations of the world was included in the covenant of the LEAGUE OF NATIONS, which was embodied in the Treaties of Paris, signed in 1920–1925. The process was very slow, as steps to organize a general disarmament conference only were taken in 1926, and the actual meeting did not take place until 1932. Whatever momentum there may have been in 1920 was replaced by the rise of aggressive states and the decline of internationalism, aided by the Great DEPRESSION. This concept has not been revived since the 1930s.

Selective voluntary disarmament has had a number of successes. In the wake of the First

World War, naval disarmament was discussed and launched in the WASHINGTON CONFERENCE in 1921–22. A 10-year holiday on ship construction was agreed to, and battleships were to be held to a set ratio between the major powers (GREAT BRITAIN, France, Italy, the United States, and Japan). Future meetings were supposed to impose limits on smaller classes of vessels, but those meetings fell victim to the same negative factors already noted. Meanwhile, talks in Geneva resulted in international agreements to ban the use of poison gas, and chemical and biological weapons generally (1925). This area was the subject of a convention on biological weapons in 1972. Meanwhile, a newer and more frightening menace had appeared with nuclear weaponry. From 1963 on, there have been treaties to limit testing (1963, 1974); production; deployment (outer space, 1967; undersea, 1971); and missile defense (1972). These treaties were mainly the work of the United States and the Soviet Union, whereas international involvement in nonproliferation treaties has been a more recent development, as the number of states possessing these weapons has continued to grow. Another recent effort, not generated by governments, was the Ottawa Convention to ban the use of antipersonnel land mines (1997).

disestablishment

The withdrawal of state legal and financial ties to the church. After the repeal of the TEST ACT and CATHOLIC EMANCIPATION (1828–29) came further reforms connected to tithes and church property. What was the legitimate extent of church authority? Was an established (i.e., state-supported) church still valid? In Catholic IRELAND, the case was weakest, and in 1869 William GLADSTONE put through a measure to disestablish the ANGLICAN church there. In WALES, with large numbers of dissenters, the cause was adopted by the LIBERAL PARTY in the 1890s, and disestablishment became law in 1914. No such action has occurred in ENGLAND or SCOTLAND.

dispensing power

Monarchs claimed an extraordinary power to dispense with laws as part of their royal PREROGATIVE. Somewhat like the royal pardon, this power allowed the king to relieve a subject from the force of a law. The STUART kings used the power freely, often to aid their Roman Catholic subjects. The right was upheld in the case of *Godden v. Hales* (1686), but it was declared illegal by the BILL OF RIGHTS.

See also DECLARATION OF RIGHTS; GLORIOUS REVOLUTION; SUSPENDING POWER.

Disraeli, Benjamin (1804–1881)
prime minister, 1868, 1874–1880

Disraeli was the son of an Anglo-Jewish writer; he was himself baptized in the CHURCH OF ENGLAND in 1817. His background impeded his entry into politics, but he enjoyed a successful career as a novelist, often using political subject matter (*Vivian Grey*, 1826; *Coningsby*, 1844; *Sybil*, 1845; *Tancred*, 1847). His first election to PARLIAMENT came in 1837, his first time in government office only in 1852. He had broken with Sir Robert PEEL and became a key supporter of the CORN LAWS in the later 1840s. He served as CHANCELLOR OF THE EXCHEQUER for Lord DERBY in his minority governments, and then became deputy leader in the 1860s, achieving his first great success in the second REFORM ACT (1867).

Disraeli was PRIME MINISTER for most of 1868, after Derby had retired. The CONSERVATIVE PARTY, which had struggled to regroup since the 1840s, was provided with a central organization in 1870. Disraeli also provided the party with a strong statement of purpose, what some called "Tory Democracy," but what to him was probably just good sound traditional conservatism. He supported the monarch, and indeed he cultivated a close bond with Queen VICTORIA. He was a strong imperialist, but then so were most of his colleagues. His manner of fostering empire was more colorful, as in his scheme of purchasing a large bloc of shares of the SUEZ CANAL (1875) or his creation of the title of empress of India for the

Benjamin Disraeli *(Library of Congress)*

queen (1876). These measures were highlights from his one long term in office, when he also asserted GREAT BRITAIN's role as a European power at the Congress of BERLIN in 1878. He retired having succeeded in reviving the Conservative Party and making it a viable alternative to the LIBERAL PARTY of William GLADSTONE.

disruption

A schism in the CHURCH OF SCOTLAND in 1843 came from debates over (1) whether a minister (selected by a patron) could be forced on an unwilling congregation, and (2) whether secular courts (e.g., the Court of SESSION) could interfere in church affairs. Both issues touched deep and long-standing arguments in the kirk, brought to a pitch by the charismatic leadership of Thomas CHALMERS. About 470 ministers (out of 1,200) joined with 40 percent of the members to form the FREE CHURCH OF SCOTLAND in 1843.

Dissenters

Refers to those Protestants who did not accept the doctrine or observe the rites of the CHURCH OF ENGLAND, as it was reestablished at the RESTORATION (1660–62). The term includes those of the BAPTIST, INDEPENDENT, PRESBYTERIAN, and QUAKER faiths. They were the targets of persecution until 1689, when a TOLERATION ACT exempted them from penalties, without prescribing religious freedom. The rise of METHODISM after the 1730s added a new and powerful body that only separated from the established church after John WESLEY died in 1790. The final repeal of the TEST ACT and Corporation Act in 1828 gave Dissenters equality before the LAW. Thereafter, the main issues of the next century turned on the reduction or elimination of privileges, the requirement to pay tithes, denial of university admission, and the basic legal position of the established church.

See also NONCONFORMISTS; PURITANS.

dissenting academies

Private schools for NONCONFORMISTS, which became numerous from the later 17th century, particularly in urban areas. They were operated on a fee-paying basis, and their curriculum usually contained a wider range of academic subjects than the classical GRAMMAR SCHOOL, including modern foreign languages, mathematics, and natural sciences. The advanced classes in some academies were comparable to advanced secondary and university levels. Both teachers and students were drawn from groups whose beliefs prevented them from taking the oaths required at OXFORD UNIVERSITY and CAMBRIDGE UNIVERSITY.

dissolution

The term has a specific and a general use. In the specific case, the dissolution of English and Irish monasteries took place in the 16th century. The earliest examples came before the REFORMATION. Authorities like Cardinal WOLSEY found it convenient to "dissolve" properties and convert their wealth to new purposes (schools, colleges, etc.).

One of the archbishop's former servants, Thomas CROMWELL, became a key official under HENRY VIII and conducted a survey of monastic properties (*VALOR ECCLESIASTICUS,* 1535). Later this was used as those houses were dissolved, i.e., pensions given to the clergy, and the property surrendered to the royal treasury (1536–40). Many foundations (churches, schools, almshouses, etc.) were reestablished on new terms with secular patrons. There was violent resistance to these measures, the most serious being the PILGRIMAGE OF GRACE in 1536. However, the process continued, and it was extended to IRELAND.

The other use of the term dissolution is in the realm of politics. A PARLIAMENT is dissolved by the monarch before a new election, on the advice of the PRIME MINISTER. When a parliament ceases to meet temporarily, it is prorogued (see PROROGATION). These royal powers were a focal point of the struggles of the 17th century, but from the 18th century they ceased to be contentious, as it became financially necessary to have Parliament meet on a regular basis. Thus the direct role of the sovereign declined.

divine right

From very early times the power of kings was seen as godlike; both Roman emperors and medieval rulers played upon this theme. The ROYAL SUPREMACY of the TUDORS brought an augmented form of power, and the STUARTS, beginning with JAMES VI AND I, made a point of stressing the divinity of kings. This emphasis was in response to secular political ideas of the RENAISSANCE and in reaction to the chaos of religious warfare (1560–1648). The king's divinity was a natural focus of the martyrdom of CHARLES I (1649), and it became an argument for unfettered royal succession under his sons. After the assertion of PARLIAMENT's power in the Act of SETTLEMENT (1701), no pretence of unfettered divine right could survive.

dominion

The term *dominion* originally had the loose meaning of a territory under the rule of the Crown. By the 19th century, it was applied to former colonies which achieved limited autonomy (CANADA, AUSTRALIA). After the experience of WORLD WAR I, and the evident growth of their power, dominions were defined by the IMPERIAL CONFERENCE of 1926 as "autonomous communities within the British Empire, equal in status, in no way subordinate to one another in any aspect of their domestic or external affairs, although united by a common allegiance to the Crown and freely associated as members of the British Commonwealth of Nations."

Donne, John (1572–1631)
poet

Donne came from a Catholic RECUSANT background, but in the course of his studies he moved toward the CHURCH OF ENGLAND. Dismissed by his patron when he married without consent of the bride's parents, he eventually found favor with JAMES VI AND I. After taking holy orders in 1615, he became a very successful preacher and was made dean of ST. PAUL'S CATHEDRAL (1621). Much of his poetry was written in his earlier career, and sermons and essays after his ordination.

Douglas, John See QUEENSBERRY, JOHN SHOLTO DOUGLAS, MARQUIS OF.

Douglas-Home, Sir Alec (1903–1995) (14th earl of Home, baron Home of the Hirsel of Coldstream)
prime minister, 1963–1964

A Conservative MEMBER OF PARLIAMENT from 1931, Douglas-Home had been Neville CHAMBERLAIN's private secretary (1937–40). He served in junior ministerial positions and, as earl of Home, was the leader of the HOUSE OF LORDS (1950–60) before becoming foreign secretary under Harold MACMILLAN (1960–63). He renounced his title when he was chosen to succeed Macmillan as PRIME MINISTER. The choice raised eyebrows because he was picked instead of the presumed heir, R. A. Butler. The manner of his selection, by apparent private influence and negotiation, played a large part in the decision to choose his successor as CONSERVATIVE PARTY leader by a ballot of the parliamentary party. Thus Edward HEATH was made leader in 1970. In 1974 he was created a life peer as baron Home of the Hirsel of Coldstream.

Dover, Treaty of (1670)

Created an Anglo-French alliance against the Dutch, England's late ally. CHARLES II agreed to a secret clause stating that he would announce his Catholic faith, and Louis XIV promised to provide a subsidy plus a force of troops to quell internal resistance.

Dowding, Hugh (1882–1970)
air marshal

A pilot and squadron commander in WORLD WAR I, Dowding was made head of Fighter Command in 1936. He was responsible for the victory of the Battle of BRITAIN in 1940 by careful development of aircraft, use of radar information, and tactical judgment. He was abruptly relieved of his command at the end of 1940 because of disputes with his superiors.

Downing Street

A small street in Westminster where the PRIME MINISTER's residence (No. 10) and that of the CHANCELLOR OF THE EXCHEQUER (No. 11) are located. Sir George Downing (1623–84) was secretary to the treasury commissioners, and he was involved in the early development of the street in the 1680s. The general location was once part of WHITEHALL palace, and from the 18th century prime ministers have resided in the neighborhood.

Drake, Sir Francis (1543–1596)
sailor, adventurer

An apprentice seaman, Drake sailed with Sir John HAWKINS, a relative, on voyages to Spain and the WEST INDIES. By 1569 he had his own command, and he made several excursions as a PRIVATEER to prey on Spanish treasure ships; one of these was his famous 1577–80 voyage around the world, by way of raiding in the Pacific. Now rich and famous, he led further anti-Spanish raids in the 1580s and became a figure in English politics before he died on a last voyage to the Indies.

Dreadnought

The *Dreadnought*, launched in 1906, was equipped with 10 large guns and capable of speeds up to 21 knots. Built in a single year, this ship revolutionized naval warfare, and an entire class of battleships was built with the designation Dreadnought. Because of the rate of competition between naval powers, there were even larger and faster vessels being built by the time of WORLD WAR I.

Drogheda

A garrison town north of DUBLIN, attacked by Oliver CROMWELL in 1649, defended by a small royalist force which refused to surrender. The English army broke through the walls, and Cromwell ordered that all men in arms should be put to the sword. By the next day there were as many as 3,500 dead, soldiers and civilians. The massacre was unusual in its ferocity, and Cromwell ensured its place in Irish historical memory by justifying it as retribution for the massacre of Protestants in 1641.

Drury Lane Theatre

Sir Thomas Drury had a house in this fashionable street (named after his family) in LONDON in the 16th century. While the neighborhood lost some of its social standing in the 17th century, it became the site of the first theater (managed by Thomas Killigrew) in 1663. The building has been destroyed by fire and restored on several occasions. The early 19th-century structure, built in 1812 with many subsequent additions, houses the present theater. Among the theater's better-known managers were David GARRICK and Richard Brinsley SHERIDAN.

Dryden, John (1631–1700)
poet, playwright, critic

The leading figure in RESTORATION literature, Dryden was the author of poetic tributes to Oliver CROMWELL and to CHARLES II. The latter were popular, as were his dramatic works. He was named POET LAUREATE in 1668, the same year that he published his great critical work *Of Dramatick Poesie.* He converted to Catholicism after the accession of JAMES VII AND II, and he was deprived of his offices after the GLORIOUS REVOLUTION.

Dublin

An important location on Ireland's east coast, Dublin was probably a church center when the Vikings captured the city in 841. Its priority remained when the Anglo-Normans invaded in 1170, and it was the capital of the English colony for the next 750 years. In the 18th century Dublin was probably the second city in the empire, but its political and economic importance declined in the 19th century because of political subordination under the UNION and the persistence of the Irish peasant agrarian economy. Its revival as a national capital (1922) was not paralleled by economic recovery until the 1970s and after.

Dudley, John See NORTHUMBERLAND, JOHN DUDLEY, DUKE OF.

duke

The highest rank of the PEERAGE was created in the 14th century. First used by EDWARD III to invest his son with the title of duke of Cornwall (1337), it was seldom used for persons outside the royal family until the 18th century, when nonroyal dukes were created. The last nonroyal duke was the duke of Westminster (1874).

Dunbar, Battle of (1650)

A Scottish effort to help CHARLES II claim his throne in 1650 was foiled by Oliver CROMWELL, whose army defeated a much larger Scottish force at Dunbar. This was in part because the latter had been purged of its "ungodly" elements, and because the leaders of the kirk (church) thought they were blessed with the ability to direct military affairs. Cromwell soundly defeated Alexander LESLIE's army, taking about 10,000 prisoners. He next defeated the Scots at Worcester (1651) and thus ended the royalist campaign.

Dundas, Henry See MELVILLE, HENRY DUNDAS, FIRST VISCOUNT.

Dundee, John Graham, first viscount (1648–1689)
soldier

Dundee served under William of Orange (later WILLIAM III) on the continent, then returned to Britain and led royal forces against COVENANTERS in SCOTLAND (1677–78). He led a Scottish force to aid JAMES VII AND II in 1688, but when the king fled, he returned to Scotland. He attended the CONVENTION parliament there in 1689, but withdrew and led an army of clansmen loyal to James at the Battle of KILLIECRANKIE (1689), where he was killed.

Dunkirk

Near the start of WORLD WAR II, the BRITISH EXPEDITIONARY FORCE had been sent to aid the French, but it was caught on the coast between Dunkirk and Ostend when the German invasion of May 1940 swiftly overran positions in Belgium and raced for the channel. Thanks to a rear-guard action, there was enough time to evacuate the trapped army. A fleet of 850 naval and small civilian vessels picked up 233,000 British troops and 113,000 others, leaving behind their heavy weapons and equipment. This escape gave a boost to morale, and it also raised the stakes for any German plan to invade GREAT BRITAIN.

Durham, John George Lambton, first earl of (1792–1840)

Whig politician

Lord Durham helped to draft the Great REFORM ACT of 1832, as a member of the government of his father-in-law, Earl GREY. Known as "Radical Jack," he later championed the ballot, triennial parliaments, and votes for all householders. After an embassy to Russia (1835–37), he led a mission to CANADA in the wake of a rebellion there. His famous "Report on the Affairs of British North America" (1839) recommended the union of Upper and Lower Canada and suggested that the colonial governors should be responsible to the local parliament. While the report was not adopted, it is seen in retrospect as the blueprint for Canada's eventual DOMINION status.

Dutch Wars

A series of 17th-century conflicts pitted the young English naval power against the Netherlands, its near neighbor and experienced maritime enemy of the Spanish, Portuguese, and French. The course of these conflicts had a great bearing on the direction of European and world affairs in the 17th and 18th centuries.

1. 1652–1654: There was a long history of friction between the two trading communities (see AMBOYNA MASSACRE). In 1651 the English republic enacted the first NAVIGATION ACT and claimed the right to seize Dutch vessels. Fighting in the Channel and the North Sea saw the Dutch take heavier losses, and they made concessions in the Treaty of Westminster.

2. 1665–1667: The root of this war was the trading rivalry, underscored by colonial clashes in Africa and America. After an early English victory, the Dutch, with aid from Denmark and France, inflicted a series of defeats. The Dutch were able to sail into the Thames and destroy ships in the royal dockyard at Chatham, sealing an embarrassing defeat.

3. 1672–1674: The war was the product of CHARLES II's Treaty of DOVER and his alliance with France. The naval actions were indecisive, and the major importance of the event for ENGLAND was in the realm of domestic (religious) affairs (see TEST ACT).

dynamite war

Name for a series of bombings by Irish sympathizers in the 1880s. These events alarmed the British government, bringing the passage of the first antiterrorist legislation (the Explosive Substances Act, 1883) and the establishment of special investigative departments within the metropolitan police (see SPECIAL BRANCH).

E

earl

The oldest title in the PEERAGE, the rank of earl comes from the period of the Anglo-Saxons and the Danes. At that time they were the king's officers in the shire, leaders of the *fyrd* (militia) and judges of the court. Earls came to have power over more than one shire, and so they were replaced at that level by the SHERIFF. The earl became a title of nobility in the 12th century, after the rank became hereditary. The titles of DUKE and MARQUESS were created in the 14th century as the uppermost ranks of the peerage.

Easter Rebellion (1916)

During WORLD WAR I the Irish Republican Brotherhood (IRB; see FENIAN BROTHERHOOD) planned to capitalize on GREAT BRITAIN's conflict with Germany by seeking arms and assistance from the enemy and by staging a national uprising. Both parts of the plan fell far short, but the "rising" of a small band of 2,000 in DUBLIN during Easter week 1916 did become an emotional symbol of the Irish quest for independence. Patrick PEARSE, James CONNOLLY, and the IRB war council planned the seizure of Dublin, taking over a number of buildings in the capital and proclaiming a provisional government. Within a week the British had crushed the rebels, executed 15 of the leaders, and interned about 2,000. The public had not supported the rising, but after the executions, general opinion began to shift. The oddest feature of the event was that although it was staged by the IRB, the British called it the SINN FÉIN Rebellion. This lent an aura of radical prestige to a previously constitutional-

ist national party and helped that party to become the foremost political force in IRELAND by the time of the 1918 election.

See also DÁIL ÉIREANN; DE VALERA, EAMON; GRIFFITH, ARTHUR.

East India Company

The first royal charter for the Company of Merchants Trading to the East Indies was issued in 1600. There would be many later editions as the economic and political importance of this enterprise grew. At first the company concentrated on the spice trade. By the 1630s it was engaged in trade in INDIA, and by the 18th century that project had evolved into a politico-military empire, and the company was pursuing trading ties with China. The trading monopolies the company enjoyed were ended in the era of FREE TRADE, and after the INDIAN MUTINY of 1857–58, power was vested in a government minister, the secretary of state for India. The company was abolished in 1873.

See also BENGAL; CALCUTTA; CLIVE, ROBERT; HASTINGS, WARREN.

ecclesiastical courts

In ENGLAND, the courts that administer canon law. The jurisdiction of ecclesiastical courts once extended beyond control over the affairs of clerics. They had wide authority in matters of tithes, testaments, matrimony, sexual conduct, and perjury. At the REFORMATION the secular courts began to encroach on their authority, although the church courts retained an important role through the 17th century, a role that was first augmented and then undermined by the ecclesiastical court of HIGH COMMISSION (1580–1641). The most extensive loss of jurisdiction came in the 19th century, especially with the end of probate and matrimonial jurisdictions in 1857.

In SCOTLAND after the reformation, the courts of kirk session, presbytery, synod, and GENERAL ASSEMBLY became major institutions of government in the new order. The Scottish Commissary Court (1564) had jurisdiction over matrimony and wills. Its work was absorbed by the Court of SESSION prior to its abolition in 1876.

Irish church courts were exclusively those of the Protestant CHURCH OF IRELAND until 1869. The four ARCHBISHOPS and 18 suffragan (i.e. assistant) BISHOPS held courts in their jurisdictions, but there were no ARCHDEACONS or rural deans, as in England, to provide a complete hierarchical structure. After the DISESTABLISHMENT, the Roman Catholic Church of Ireland provided clerical and canonical discipline in its hierarchy, which came to be central to the life of the community in the IRISH FREE STATE and the IRISH REPUBLIC. Meanwhile, in NORTHERN IRELAND the ANGLICANS and the more numerous PRESBYTERIAN congregations maintained their own church courts.

economical reform

Term applied to the efforts to regulate and reduce expenditure of government money to employ PLACEMEN. The use of patronage was the basic means of hiring and promoting officials in the age before the CIVIL SERVICE, but criticism became severe when heavy taxation for the American Revolution (1776–81) failed to produce victory. PARLIAMENT forced examination of public accounts, abolition of some offices, and limits on expenditure. Moreover, related discussion and petitions in the counties, particularly the ASSOCIATION MOVEMENT led by Christopher WYVILL, began a long process of parliamentary reform.

Eden, Anthony, first earl of Avon (1897–1977)
prime minister, 1955–1957

A conservative MEMBER OF PARLIAMENT from 1923 to 1957, Eden had a long and distinguished career in foreign affairs. He was foreign secretary (1935–38) but resigned over the APPEASEMENT policy of Neville CHAMBERLAIN. He served in Winston CHURCHILL's war cabinet as foreign secretary, 1940–45. He returned to that post in 1951 and had to deal with the postwar problems of communism and nationalism. When he finally succeeded Churchill as PRIME MINISTER, it was only to be faced with the SUEZ CANAL crisis (1956). Britain's invasion of EGYPT drew international opposition, and ironically Eden was forced to resign, the victim of a huge error in foreign policy.

Edgehill, Battle of (1642)

In the first major battle of the CIVIL WAR, the army of CHARLES I advanced toward LONDON and engaged the army of the earl of ESSEX near Banbury. Both sides numbered about 12,000. The royalist cavalry proved superior, but the PARLIAMENT's infantry fought well. Both sides claimed victory, but in fact the royalist advance was halted.

Edgeworth, Maria (1767–1849)
author, educator

Raised in Oxfordshire and schooled there and in Derby and LONDON, Edgeworth returned to the family home in County Longford, IRELAND, which became her source and her studio. She was a novelist and pioneer children's writer (*The Parent's Assistant,* 1796–1801; and *Moral Tales,* 1801). She coauthored *Practical Education* (1798) with her father. Her major novel was *Castle Rackrent* (1800), an original depiction of Irish life, which Sir Walter SCOTT considered a great inspiration. She enjoyed both commercial and critical success.

Edinburgh

The capital of SCOTLAND. Situated on a glacial ridge south of the Firth of Forth, the castle and the Old Town occupied a strong defensive position. It was a natural location for major institutions like the abbey of Holyrood (1128), where JAMES IV rebuilt the royal palace in 1501. The Scottish PARLIAMENT met in the city from the 15th century until its demise in 1707. The Court of SESSION was settled there in 1532; the university was founded in 1582. The city and its surrounding communities became an economic center, and in the late 18th century the New Town was built to offer accommodation for the growing wealthy class of Edinburgh society. It was set on high ground north of the Old Town and connected to it by bridges.

education

ENGLAND AND WALES

Until well into the 19th century, the provision of education was under the direction or influence of the churches. That tradition dated from the long period when there were only monastic and cathedral schools and the colleges run by and for the training of clerics. After the RENAISSANCE and REFORMATION, the purposes of education expanded. Later schools and UNIVERSITIES came to serve a wider clientele, as the GENTRY and nobility took to schools and colleges as part of their education, and as the "middling ranks" of society sought forms of training to parallel or supplant that of an APPRENTICESHIP. From the 16th through the 18th century there were manifold private efforts to reform or extend education in proprietary DISSENTING ACADEMIES and newly founded GRAMMAR SCHOOLS. The majority of this work addressed the needs of the elite, as in fact the whole of education had done throughout history.

The origin of a demand for elementary schooling for the population in general is hard to locate. It was not always a liberal idea. Popular education was a means of inculcating obedience, and it was so used in the authoritarian states of 18th-century Europe. There were early liberal expressions in the 17th-century revolutionary era, and there were efforts at the end of that century to broaden religious instruction, especially with the SOCIETY FOR THE PROMOTION OF CHRISTIAN KNOWLEDGE (1698). The growth of CHARITY SCHOOLS and SUNDAY SCHOOLS further stimulated the area of elementary education in the 18th century. The general religious orientation of schooling, which was a main source of strength, also retarded the growth of state support for schools. From the early 19th century, various attempts to launch broad programs of public education encountered sectarian obstacles: on the one hand, the systems of Andrew BELL and Joseph LANCASTER created rival groups, the latter's British and Foreign School Society (DISSENTERS) in 1808, and the former's National Society (ANGLICANS) in 1811. But they both agreed that secular schools were not to be trusted. For the next 60 years secular advances were confined to the so-called "ragged" or industrial schools, some of which were mandated by the FACTORY ACTS.

The middle of the 19th century saw some steps toward reform: a Committee of the Privy Council on education was formed (1839) with Sir James KAY-SHUTTLEWORTH as its secretary, several ROYAL COMMISSIONS examined the public schools and the universities, and there were studies of schooling in other countries, such as those of the school inspector Matthew ARNOLD. Finally, in 1870 a state system of elementary education was created, and attendance was made compulsory in 1880. At this stage the requisite amount of schooling was only to age 10; the leaving age was raised to 14 by the Education Act of 1918. Secondary education was provided for all under the Education Act of 1944 in grammar, secondary modern, and technical schools, the students' assignment to be determined by examination at "eleven plus." The leaving age was raised to 16 in 1973.

As schooling was being brought under state control, the mechanisms for that control were being fashioned: 2,000 local elected school boards in 1870; then a central board of education and an array of local education authorities (1902); then a ministry of education replaced the board in 1944. The aim of "comprehensive" education—the merging of the separate strands of secondary education—was pursued in the 1960s and '70s. The major flaw in the strategy was the continuing and influential presence of the old grammar (now private) schools. This long-established elite had grown very rapidly in the late 19th century. The most prestigious were united in the "Headmasters' Conference" (1869), an alliance of about 100 private schools.

The access of school graduates to the colleges and universities had been a source of contention in the 19th and early 20th centuries. The small number of places and the cost of tuition fostered a highly concentrated educational elite. After 1945, both of these elements changed dramatically. The growth of universities, which had begun in the 19th century, accelerated rapidly after 1945; the principle of government-supported tuition was adopted, making places open to applicants on merit. The national system of examinations (A-level and O-level) provided the basic screening for further education and employment.

For WALES the story of educational advance is complicated by its relation to ENGLAND. All education was affected by the bilingual nature of Welsh society, which only began to be fully addressed in the 1960s. Early schools in Wales were also limited in their resources, with some important reform efforts coming at the end of the 17th century, boosted by the rise of EVANGELICAL movements. There were few grammar schools, and Welshmen who sought university training went to OXFORD UNIVERSITY. Only in the 19th century did university-level education come to Wales, at first in denominational schools; by the end of the century there was a University of Wales. Where the 19th century had seen progressive change in England, the earliest inquiry into Welsh schools provoked a crisis. The inspectors reported that there was far too much Welsh spoken, and they gave the schools a very poor rating. This incident spurred the rise of Welsh national sentiment, and in a backhand fashion it may have also stimulated interest and effort in school reform.

SCOTLAND

A Scottish act of 1496 called for the compulsory education of the sons of BARONS, but in the 1560s the Book of Discipline set forth the objective of education for all believers. PARISH and BURGH schools were the objects of 17th-century legislation requiring landowners to pay for their operation, most notably a parish schools act in 1696. Greater prosperity in the 18th century made the goal more realistic. An act in 1803 enabled the CHURCH OF SCOTLAND to set standards, and it provided for the establishment of additional schools. The system was studied by the Argyll Commission (1864–67) and in 1872 there was a general overhaul. Rates were collected for education, government grants were instituted, and inspectors appeared for the new compulsory system, operated under the direction of 1,000 local boards and the "Scotch" Education Department—in London. The acts of 1918 and 1944 raised the leaving age and made secondary education generally available, as elsewhere in the UNITED KINGDOM.

The Scottish universities—Edinburgh, Glasgow, St. Andrews, and Aberdeen—dated from the later Middle Ages, and they had some features which were superior to the English, for instance in medical education. They too were in need of reform in the 19th century, and a Universities Act in 1889 modernized their organization and improved access. In the mid-20th century new universities were established in SCOTLAND, and increased general financial support was provided.

IRELAND

Schooling in IRELAND was adversely affected by the PENAL LAWS (ca. 1690–1770). The majority Catholic population was not served in any systematic fashion, though the tradition of the "hedge" schools says that itinerant teachers provided a source of elementary schooling, as did their cousins in Welsh "circulating schools." All that is known for certain is that there was no uniform national provision until the 1830s. Then a system was inaugurated, under English stimulus, of nondenominational schools. These were supposed to be for all children, to be managed jointly by Catholic and Protestant administrators. The scheme provided funds and rules, but the schools soon became denominational. In 1878 an Intermediate Education Act provided funds from the old church establishment to individual secondary schools. The allocations were based on examination results, a system that was replaced by a capitation method in 1924. By then the movement for Irish independence had made a major impact, especially in the revival of the Irish language, though the system's structure continued to be much like the days of English rule. Indeed, in NORTHERN IRELAND, that was a definite objective, as was a policy of discriminatory access to education and funding.

The oldest university in Ireland was Trinity College (University of Dublin) founded in 1592. There was no provision for Catholic university education until the 19th century, and then it was a source of controversy. A set of Queen's Colleges established in the 1840s (Cork, Galway, BELFAST) were intended to be interdenominational and therefore spurned by the Catholic hierarchy. A Catholic university was begun in 1879, but this was overtaken by the establishment of a National University of Ireland in 1908, with campuses in DUBLIN and Belfast, plus the Pontifical University at Maynooth, begun in 1886. Higher education grew much more in the 20th century, and there are now over 40 institutions, including a Dublin Institute of Technology, with regional centers and special branch schools.

With partition in 1922, the education system in Northern Ireland became separate from the rest of the island. It was linked to the U.K. education system, but there were some unusual features. Segregation was the main characteristic of the system. The government in STORMONT tried to pass an act providing a secular, publicly financed system of elementary education, but both Protestants and Catholics were afraid to surrender control. In the end a system was established in which a full government subsidy went to those schools that followed the Protestant curriculum. When state support was introduced for secondary education in 1947, there was only

limited assistance for Catholic schools. The imbalances in funding began to be corrected in the 1960s. In the 1970s efforts began to improve contacts between the two sectors, and these efforts gained funding from the government in the 1980s, with mandated programs for education for mutual understanding. Meanwhile a small number of integrated schools were created, although these only accounted for 1 percent of the school population in the early 1990s.

Edward III (1312–1377)
king of England, 1327–1377

The son of Edward II, Edward III succeeded that unhappy sovereign after the father was deposed by his queen and her lover, Roger MORTIMER. Edward assumed power in his own right in 1330 and had Mortimer executed. The successes of his reign mirrored the failures of his father's. He placated the BARONS and the merchants, chiefly by success in wars against SCOTLAND and France, in both of which he captured their kings and held them to ransom. His campaigns in France were initially victorious, at Sluys (1340), Crécy (1346), and Poitiers (1356). He was so certain of ultimate victory that he claimed the title of King of France (1340 and 1369), which would remain as part of the English royal style until the 19th century. But his victories had turned sour by the 1370s. French recovery after 1369, the drain of heavy expenditures, and the ineffective efforts of his son, the ailing Black Prince, all weakened the king's political position. He was confronted by the IMPEACHMENT of numerous royal servants and even his own mistress in the "Good Parliament" of 1376. When he died, he was succeeded by his grandson, RICHARD II.

Edward IV (1442–1483)
king of England, 1461–1470, 1471–1483

Edward IV was the eldest son of Richard, duke of YORK, and leader of that faction in the Wars of the ROSES. His first coronation came after the defeat of HENRY VI (Mortimer's Cross and Towton). He was only 18, his Lancastrian opponents were still strong, and he was himself still under the influence of the magnates in his own group, notably the earl of WARWICK, alias "the kingmaker." Warwick invaded ENGLAND in 1470 and forced Edward to flee into exile, but the king returned the following year, defeated Warwick at the Battle of BARNET, and then beat the Lancastrian forces at TEWKESBURY and reclaimed his crown.

In the second half of his reign, Edward succeeded in reestablishing the royal power which had been so depleted during the factional warfare since 1455. He did so by reviving a strong council of intimate advisers, taking control over government finance, and meeting and managing PARLIAMENTS. His greatest error, perhaps, was to die before his two sons had reached maturity, creating the opportunity that his brother RICHARD III was only too eager to seize.

Edward V (1470–1483)
king of England (uncrowned), 1483
Edward, prince of Wales and the son of EDWARD IV, was in Ludlow when his father died. While traveling to LONDON he was apprehended by his uncle Richard, who had himself proclaimed Protector and had the coronation delayed, first until June and then until November. In this period, Richard challenged the legitimacy of the king's sons and had himself declared King RICHARD III. The two princes (Edward and his younger brother Richard) were in the TOWER OF LONDON, where they were presumably murdered at Richard's command. Two boys' skeletons were discovered in the Tower in 1674; exhumed in 1933, the remains could not be positively identified.

Edward VI (1537–1553)
king of England, 1547–1553
The son of HENRY VIII and Jane SEYMOUR (who died giving birth), Edward VI was raised by Protestant tutors and a REGENCY council. Both of these influences were primarily responsible for ENGLAND's first decisive move into reformed theology with the BOOK OF COMMON PRAYER (1549

and 1552) and the Articles of Religion (1553). The young king was once set to marry MARY, QUEEN OF SCOTS (Treaty of Greenwich, 1543), but Anglo-Scottish warfare and French influence aborted that plan. By 1552 the king had become ill (smallpox and measles) and developed tuberculosis. He agreed to a plan to divert the succession from MARY I, his Catholic half-sister, to Lady Jane GREY, but that failed within weeks after his death.

Edward VII (1841–1910)
king of Great Britain and Ireland, 1901–1910
The son of Queen VICTORIA and Prince ALBERT, Edward VII was indolent and irresponsible in his early years. His overlong apprenticeship (he came to the throne at the age of 60), which included some romance and misbehavior, also schooled the king in public affairs and international diplomacy. He was able to elevate public esteem for the position of the Crown after its loss of energy in the old age of his mother. He was also keenly interested in the reforms of the ARMY and NAVY, where some find his influence important. The true test of his kingship could have come in the multiple crises of 1910—the reform of the HOUSE OF LORDS, IRISH HOME RULE, and the unrest among workers and women. He did not live to see their outcomes.

Edward VIII (1894–1972)
king of Great Britain and Ireland, 1936
The son of GEORGE V was created PRINCE OF WALES in 1911. He served as a staff officer in WORLD WAR I, making an effort to be a popular and approachable prince. He was also credited with a sensitive concern for the poor during the GENERAL STRIKE of 1926 and later in the DEPRESSION. He traveled throughout the BRITISH EMPIRE and was a successful emissary for the MONARCHY. His personal life was less successful. His affair with and desire to marry Wallis Simpson, a twice-divorced American whom he had known before her second divorce, shocked the government and the court. Edward was forced to abdicate in favor of his

brother, who took the throne as GEORGE VI and gave Edward the title of Duke of Windsor.

See also ABDICATION CRISIS.

Egypt

Egypt was under Ottoman Turkish rule when Napoleon's army was defeated there by a combined British and native force (1801). Throughout the 19th century, as Turkish power waned, the European states became increasingly involved in Egypt's fate. The French engineer Ferdinand de Lesseps led the construction of a canal across the Suez isthmus (1869), which transformed the country's strategic position. At the same time, this put European bankers in the forefront of local affairs. British involvement took a large step in 1875 when Benjamin DISRAELI purchased a bloc of SUEZ CANAL shares. In 1882 a rebellion was triggered by this European interference, leading only to greater control, and *de facto* British rule. A formal British PROTECTORATE was announced in 1914, but another rebellion broke out in 1919. The protectorate was terminated in 1922, and the last elements of British control were ended by treaty in 1936. During WORLD WAR II, Egypt was nominally neutral but gave support to the allies. After the rise of a nationalist movement in the 1950s and Egyptian seizure of the canal, Britain launched an invasion (with French support). The Egyptian government of Col. Nasser retaliated by sinking ships in the canal, and widespread international hostility forced the Anglo-French force to be withdrawn.

See also ABOUKIR BAY; ALAMEIN, BATTLE OF EL; ALEXANDER, HAROLD, EARL ALEXANDER OF TUNIS; CROMER, EVELYN BARING, EARL OF; EDEN, ANTHONY; NELSON, HORATIO, VISCOUNT.

Eire

The name of the IRISH REPUBLIC, established in the constitution of 1937. The office of governor-general was abolished, replaced by an elected president. Real political power resided in the office of prime minister (Taoiseach) and in the Irish parliament (Oireachtas). This constitution gave special priority to the Roman Catholic church, and it declared the national territory to be "the whole island of Ireland."

eisteddfodau

Meetings of bards (minstrels, poets, and chroniclers) were traditionally held at the seat of Welsh princes, at least from the 12th century but probably much earlier. The practice declined in the 17th century, but there was a Celtic revival from the late 18th century (Cymmrodorion Society, 1751; Gwynnedigion Society, 1771). The meetings became national in 1819, and a National Eisteddfod Association was formed in 1880. There are now annual national meetings as well as local and regional ones.

Eldon, John Scott, earl of (1751–1838)
lord chancellor

The son of a merchant, Lord Eldon studied law and rose, via politics, to the pinnacle of his profession. A MEMBER OF PARLIAMENT from 1783, he became solicitor general and attorney general during the period of intense political unrest connected with the French Revolution (1788–99). He was the prosecutor in the famous treason trial of Thomas HARDY, in which the jury voted for acquittal (1794). He was made chief justice of the Court of COMMON PLEAS in 1799 and LORD CHANCELLOR in 1801, serving in that post until 1827. With such a lengthy tenure on the eve of an era of reform, he was bound to be the target of political enemies who saw him as the embodiment of dilatory and corrupt judicial practices. This judgment seems to be off the mark, as the delays of CHANCERY proceedings were hardly his invention. A brilliant jurist, his reputation also suffered from his opposition to constitutional reform.

Elgar, Sir Edward (1857–1934)
composer

Elgar's father kept a music shop in Worcestershire, Elgar himself was a self-taught musician who for much of his early career taught and conducted in the local area. He went on to become the leading English composer of the early 20th century, his romantic compositions, both orchestral and choral, stand out. His first major work, *Enigma Variations* (1899), and his setting for the poem of Cardinal Newman, *The Dream of Gerontius* (1900), are on a par with his much-admired *Pomp and Circumstance* marches (1901–07). He was granted a knighthood in 1904 and the Order of Merit in 1911. He became Master of the King's Music in 1924.

Elgin, Thomas Bruce, seventh earl of (1766–1841)

Lord Elgin is remembered for the collection of marble sculptures, including parts of the frieze of the Parthenon, that he brought from Greece in 1812 and sold to the BRITISH MUSEUM in 1816. Defenders of his actions point out that Greece was then under Turkish rule, and the safety and preservation of the marbles were by no means guaranteed. Others argue that the pleas of Greek governments for their repatriation should be heeded. They are still on display in the British Museum.

Eliot, George (1819–1880)
(Mary Ann Evans)
novelist

George Eliot was born Mary Ann Evans into a family of EVANGELICAL Christians, but she was fascinated with the philosophy of positivism and became affiliated with a group of thinkers who included G. H. Lewes. Her liaison with the married Lewes was part of the reason she adopted a male pseudonym when she began to publish the novels on which her fame rests. These include *Adam Bede* (1859), *The Mill on the Floss* (1860), *Silas Marner* (1861), and *Middlemarch* (1872).

Eliot, Sir John (1592–1632)
politician

A MEMBER OF PARLIAMENT from 1614, Eliot was at first a supporter of the royal court. He turned against the duke of BUCKINGHAM when the duke was impeached, and he was imprisoned. He refused to pay the FORCED LOAN to the king in 1627 and was imprisoned again. He supported the PETITION OF RIGHT, and in the HOUSE OF COMMONS in 1629 he led the attacks on ARMINIAN policies and arbitrary taxation. He held the SPEAKER OF THE HOUSE in his chair so that debate could not be stopped, and once again he was sent to the TOWER OF LONDON, this time for the rest of his life. While there he composed a book on royal authority, which his political acts had done so much to undermine.

Eliot, T(homas) S(tearns) (1888–1965)
poet, playwright

Born in St. Louis, T. S. Eliot studied at Harvard, the Sorbonne, and OXFORD UNIVERSITY. His first major poetic work was *The Love Song of J. Alfred Prufrock* (1915). His reputation was secured with the publication of *The Waste Land* in 1922. Some of his later poems (*The Hollow Men, The Journey of the Magi, Ash Wednesday*) were signposts of his religious journey, but he also adapted his art to the stage, notably with *Murder in the Catheral* (1935) and *The Cocktail Party* (1950). He was the author of many important critical essays and books and winner of the Order of Merit and the Nobel Prize in literature. He also wrote a collection of children's verse, *Old Possum's Book of Practical Cats* (1939), which was adapted for the musical *Cats* in 1981.

Elizabeth I (1533–1603)
queen of England and Ireland, 1558–1603

The daughter of HENRY VIII and Anne BOLEYN, Elizabeth I was briefly the first in the line of royal succession, until her mother was executed and she was declared illegitimate (1536). Her half-brother EDWARD VI was born the next year, and an act of succession in 1543 restored her legitimacy and placed her in line after Edward and her half-sister MARY I. When Edward was dying, he agreed to the accession of Lady Jane GREY, bypassing both Mary and Elizabeth. Mary's supporters quickly assured her succession, and she began the process of Catholic restoration. Elizabeth was seen as a potential leader of a Protestant coup, and she was more than once put under guard. When Mary died in 1558, Elizabeth easily succeeded to the throne, though once there she had serious issues to face.

Her religious settlement was a compromise; the queen favored Protestant theology and feared Catholic enemies at home and abroad. She replaced Mary's BISHOPS, resumed the headship of the church, and by 1563 she had restored the prayer book and the articles of religion. Only diplomacy kept her from excommunication until 1570: Philip of Spain, her sister's widower, considered another English royal marriage while other powers sought alliances, and the papacy waited until these alternatives were exhausted. Meanwhile, MARY, QUEEN OF SCOTS had made her own claim to the English throne, but by 1568 she had been forced to flee to ENGLAND, becoming Elizabeth's uninvited guest and resident conspiracy suspect. A series of plots, ending with that of Anthony BABINGTON in 1586, forced the queen's decision to execute her cousin.

Elizabeth tried to preserve England's position in a Europe engulfed in religious hostility. She reluctantly supported some expeditions to aid Protestants (French and Dutch), and she allowed PRIVATEERS such as Sir Francis DRAKE to attack Spanish shipping. Then in 1588 she had to face the awesome threat of the Spanish ARMADA. Philip of Spain launched what was in effect a crusade against the heretic queen, one which might have ended in England's defeat. The English fleet, thanks to rough weather, enemy errors, and English maritime skill and determination, beat the invaders and forced a retreat. The victory became decisive when several later invasion attempts failed to reach English waters.

In her later career, Elizabeth, who had never married (mainly because of the incredibly complex diplomatic situation) was unwilling to name a successor. The logical candidate, whom she did eventually acknowledge, was the son of her cousin Mary, JAMES VI of Scotland. The queen's later years saw the extension of English power in

IRELAND, the affirmation of PARLIAMENT's role in the constitution, and the continued advance of English maritime power on the world stage.

Elizabeth II (1926–   )
queen of the United Kingdom of Great Britain and Northern Ireland

The daughter of George, duke of York, Elizabeth suddenly became the heiress to the throne with her father's coronation as GEORGE VI after the ABDICATION CRISIS in 1936. Her schooling was entrusted to governesses, and she spent the war years at Windsor. In 1947 she married her cousin Philip Mountbatten, and their first child, Prince CHARLES, was born in 1948. Her coronation in 1953 was the first to be shown on television, an augury for a reign that was always to be under media scrutiny. The press was a looming presence in a series of royal marriages and divorces, from those of Princess Margaret, her sister, to her daughter, Princess Anne, to Prince Charles and Lady DIANA. An attempt for more openness encouraged the prying of the public eye: the film *Royal Family* in 1966 and a number of television spectacles (the investiture of Charles as PRINCE OF WALES, 1969; the wedding of Charles and Diana, 1981) fed a growing public appetite. The press, having lost its inhibitions and found its audience for the sensational, became a threat to royal discretion and privacy. There was still very strong public support for the Crown, and especially for the queen, despite some murmurings of republican sentiments. In a poignant tragedy, a fire tore through WINDSOR Castle in 1992, and it opened the door to lengthy debate over royal finances: where was the boundary between the royal family's private finances and public funding for their activities? As a result, the queen accepted the need to pay tax on certain royal revenues, and she arranged to open part of BUCKINGHAM PALACE to tourists to help to defray the costs of repairs at Windsor. In her reign, Elizabeth has also presided over the shrinking BRITISH EMPIRE and over the successor Commonwealth, of which she remains the titular head.

Queen Elizabeth II *(Hulton/Archive)*

Emmet, Robert (1778–1803)
Irish rebel

Emmet joined the UNITED IRISHMEN in 1798, and when the rebellion of that year failed, he went to France and began to work on the reconstruction of the movement. He was convinced that the French would send aid to another Irish rebellion against British rule, and he led a small uprising in July 1803. It was easily crushed, there was no French aid, and Emmet was exe-cuted after a long state trial. His speech from the dock was published and became a classic text for Irish patriots.

enclosure

In medieval ENGLAND the typical form of LAND distribution was one of open fields—i.e., lands cultivated in common, with portions of waste and common land for general use by people of the PARISH. Portions of this land were later converted into private holdings, and at several periods there were extensive transfers. The first was in the 16th and 17th centuries, when large areas of land were taken by large landowners and converted to pasture to raise sheep. This activity aroused local opposition and sometimes brought government restriction. By the 18th century, with great demand for more efficient agricultural production, the government supported enclosures—dividing off common land into individually owned areas—by way of parliamentary acts. In the second half of the century there were thousands of private acts, converting perhaps 20 percent of the arable land. These acts deprived small tenants and laborers of traditional rights to common land. On the other side, the acts facilitated the transformation of English agriculture to more modern methods and greater productivity. By the later 19th century, the open fields had almost completely disappeared.

Engagement, the

In 1647 CHARLES I and some Scottish PRESBYTERIAN leaders signed a treaty known as The Engagement. The king, who was the captive of the Parliamentary army, promised to institute Presbyterian government in England for three years in exchange for an armed effort to restore him to power. The army of the Engagers was intercepted and beaten at Preston in 1648, ending the so-called "second civil war."

The term was also used in 1650 when the RUMP PARLIAMENT required an oath of allegiance to the republic from all men over 18. This caused a bitter controversy and led to purges of some local offices before the requirement was repealed in 1653.

England

England was the creation of its monarchs, its boundaries a function of those monarchs' interactions with Germans, CELTS, Scandinavians, and Frenchmen. Early Germanic invaders (Angles,

Saxons) established small tribal kingdoms in the sixth to eighth centuries. These in turn succumbed to Norse and Danish invasions in the ninth century, and the surviving kingdom of Wessex began a long process of recovery. That recovery saw an enlarged English kingdom emerging by the 10th century, a kingdom that was a target of further Danish rule (1016–35) and of the NORMAN CONQUEST (1066). But by that time the royal court, the social structure, and the system of administration and taxation were sufficiently entrenched so that the infrastructure was preserved—indeed, invaders coveted its revenue and other features.

The territory now known as England was the part of the British Isles settled by the Germanic invaders, contested in the west by the Welsh and the north by the Scots. The island of IRELAND was outside the orbit of early rulers and ignored by the Normans until the incursion of Henry II in 1171. A period of Anglo-French rule lasted until 1453. England was part of a larger European federation with continental territories such as Normandy, Anjou, Poitou, Brittany, and Gascony. Only with the end of the HUNDRED YEARS' WAR was the kingdom of England restricted to the island of BRITAIN, and in the next two centuries it became ever more entangled with its archipelago neighbors: conquest (1300) and annexation (1543) of WALES; invasion (1540) and conquest (1610, 1690) of Ireland; and dynastic (1603) and parliamentary union (1707) with SCOTLAND. Through this experience, the English constitution—the COMMON LAW and royal courts, the king's PARLIAMENT, and the royal administration—formed the essential core of government. The monarchs themselves came from varied origins: the Welsh line of the TUDORS, the Scottish ancestry of the STUARTS, the Dutch king WILLIAM III, and the Germans from HANOVER, beginning with GEORGE I. Yet their birthplaces were not an insurmountable problem in an age of aristocratic kingroups, which was also the age before the modern national state.

It was with the Tudor and Stuart dynasties (1485–1714) that modern England emerged:

with its own church, its precocious Parliament, and its maritime ambitions. The CHURCH OF ENGLAND, with the sovereign as supreme head, put a unique Protestant label on the country, one which many (even rulers) resisted, but no one (save Oliver CROMWELL) removed. The English Parliament, alone of like institutions in Europe, fought its way to a state of parity with the Crown by the end of the 17th century. It did so partly by means of warfare, but more effectively by means of indispensible fiscal power. That power was the central fact of the next 200 years of England's history.

Global commerce, industrial power, and a relatively open social and political structure marked the England of the 18th and 19th centuries. It was still England that dominated the British Isles and the BRITISH EMPIRE, although in retrospect it is easy to see major contributions from the Welsh, Scots, and Irish. The infrastructure of Crown, church, LAW, and administration was thoroughly anglicized, but it was in imperceptible decline. The crown of Queen VICTORIA, though the title "Empress of India" had been added, had lost any real political power between her accession in 1837 and her death in 1901. The church had always had rivals, but the 19th century saw them recognized in law while steps were taken to disestablish the church in Ireland and Wales (see DISESTABLISHMENT). Law and administration held more firmly to the English mold until the 20th century.

In the 20th century England and its UNITED KINGDOM engaged in two devastating world wars, which weakened the imperial structure and strengthened the identities of Ireland, Scotland, and Wales. The Irish separation and partition of 1920–22 was the first major blow. The political and administrative DEVOLUTION of Wales and Scotland (1945–99) were much less abrupt and not at all violent; however, they too marked the recession of the old, anglocentric federation. This did of course allow a clearer view of "England" at the end of the millennium: a kingdom, economy, and society which kept its precedence in the British Isles and struggled to

decide its relation to the EUROPEAN ECONOMIC COMMUNITY and its world role in ever-changing circumstances.

English language

The language of the Angles and Saxons was spoken in the fifth and sixth centuries. This initial form of Old English had little apparent interaction with Celtic languages. The early uses of the language were evident in legal documents and, from the time of Alfred the Great, in literature as well. In the ninth to 11th centuries there was very extensive interaction with Old Norse, introduced by Scandinavian invaders and settlers. Probably the similarities between them facilitated exchange. The influence of Norman and later French contact (on Middle English) was marked mainly in LAW and administration. English slowly regained prestige as a language of literature in the 14th and 15th centuries. The coincidental impact of the RENAISSANCE, the REFORMATION, and the advent of printing were powerful stimulants. Modern English was still a fluid language with numerous dialect variations, and the 17th and 18th centuries saw the beginning of standardization (i.e., the King James BIBLE, Samuel JOHNSON's *Dictionary*) At the same time, however, the language began to travel the globe and to add different forms even as it began to build an international base.

English reformation

The marital problems of HENRY VIII (or of his wives) sometimes overshadow the story of religious reform in ENGLAND. It is accurate to call the English experience of REFORMATION "erastian"— formed or directed by the state, as opposed to the experiences of Lutheran or Calvinist reforms growing out of preaching and proselytizing by churchmen. But the contrast is less than it seems. The king did try to annul his marriage (using biblical texts), he did coerce his clergy into obedience (see CROMWELL, THOMAS; SUBMISSION OF THE CLERGY), and he did have PARLIAMENT enact his ROYAL SUPREMACY. All of these things were done before he made any gestures toward reform of religion. But having taken these steps, the king was forced into an involuntary alliance with reformers, because honest Catholics (Thomas MORE, John FISHER) rejected his supremacy. Consequently, Cromwell, Thomas CRANMER, Miles COVERDALE and others became the king's religious advisers, and he was edged more and more into progressive public positions on the faith. His son EDWARD VI was schooled by Protestant tutors, and thus in 1547 there was a distinct move toward more advanced Protestant views. This trend was abruptly reversed by MARY I and then reversed again by ELIZABETH I. Thereafter the English church remained Protestant, despite periods of fear for its true nature, especially in the 17th century.

Enlightenment

A self-conscious movement of thinkers which extolled the power of human reason. The term is usually applied to the French, German, and Scottish authors of the 18th century (Voltaire, Diderot, Kant, and HUME, for example). They had in common a sense of liberating the intellectual world from the "darkness" of medieval tradition. Their work ranged from philosophy to politics to history and art. The roots of the movement lay in the 17th century, with the observations of Sir Isaac NEWTON, the rationalism of René Descartes, and the empiricism of Francis BACON.

entente

Because of GREAT BRITAIN's 19th-century policy of holding a BALANCE OF POWER, she discouraged any formal alliances. Meanwhile the great powers of Europe had drawn up a system of opposing groups: the triple alliance of Germany, Austria, and Italy against the dual alliance of France and Russia. Britain's status changed with the Anglo-Japanese alliance of 1902, but reaching agreement with one of the powers of Europe was bound to be more complicated. Since there was a naval arms race with Germany, and since there

had been steps toward accommodation with France (see FASHODA), the cross-channel neighbors were able to settle a number of issues and make an informal agreement short of an alliance in 1904—an "entente." A similar agreement with Russia in 1907 made Britain a quasi-member of the dual alliance. Further naval talks with France by 1912 made actual British commitments that pushed her toward full alliance but left her formal status unclear. Thus, in 1914 Britain's entry into WORLD WAR I and her alliance with France and Russia were only decided at the last minute.

Episcopal Church of Scotland

When the GLORIOUS REVOLUTION of 1688 was followed by the establishment of the Presbyterian CHURCH OF SCOTLAND in 1690, those who believed in a church governed by BISHOPS were forced to leave, especially the JACOBITES, supporters of the late king. They held secret consecrations of bishops, and by 1712 they were given the legal authority to preach, provided they took an oath to oppose the Jacobites. Most refused (see NONJURORS) and had to endure persecution until the dynastic cause was defeated. With the death of the last STUART pretender in 1788, the episcopal ministers gave their allegiance to GEORGE III, and in 1792 they were able to exercise their religion openly. Meanwhile, the Scottish bishops had played an important role in the history of the Episcopal church in the United States. In 1784 the Scottish bishops consecrated Samuel Seabury as the first bishop there, since the late rebellion prevented English bishops from doing so.

equity See COURTS OF LAW.

Erskine, Thomas (1750–1823)
lawyer

A BARRISTER who represented a number of controversial defendants, Erskine was counsel for Thomas PAINE, whose publication *The Rights of Man* was condemned in 1792. He was also the counsel for Thomas HARDY, the leader of the

London Corresponding Society who was acquitted in a famous treason trial in 1794. Erskine defended Queen CAROLINE OF BRUNSWICK at her trial in 1820. He was a MEMBER OF PARLIAMENT and briefly held the post of LORD CHANCELLOR in 1806–07.

esquire See SQUIRE.

Essex, earls of

1. Walter Devereux (1541–76) led a force to put down the NORTHERN REBELLION (1569). His expedition to ULSTER (1573) failed, but he became earl-marshal of Ireland in 1575.
2. Robert Devereux (1567–1601), a soldier who fought in the Netherlands, became a member of the PRIVY COUNCIL. He captured Cadiz in 1596 and led a mission to Ulster in 1599 but failed to defeat Hugh O'NEILL. When he returned to ENGLAND he was imprisoned. He tried to raise a rebellion in LONDON and was executed for treason.
3. Robert Devereux (1591–1646) commanded the forces of PARLIAMENT in the early years of the CIVIL WAR. He had served under the king but took the side of parliament, fought at EDGEHILL, and won the first Battle of Newbury (1644). He resigned his command after the SELF-DENYING ORDINANCE (1645).

European Community (EC)

Originating in the wake of WORLD WAR II, the European Community was the organization that included the European Coal and Steel Community (ECSC), the European Economic Community (EEC), and the European Atomic Energy Commission (EAEC). These bodies were consolidated in 1967, creating four main organs of government: a European Commission (in Brussels), a Council of Ministers, a European Parliament (in Strasbourg), and a European Court of Justice (in Luxembourg). In 1992 in the Treaty of Maastricht, the member states created a European Union, with a single market for free movement of goods and capital. In 1993 they planned a monetary union, which 11 countries entered in 1999, adopting the uniform currency known as the euro. After several false starts, Great Britain joined the EEC (or Common Market) in 1972, a move that was endorsed by a referendum in 1975. As of 2002, Britain had not adopted the euro.

evangelical

Refers to the Protestant belief in strict adherence to the teaching of the BIBLE, specifically the four gospels. The term has been applied to churches, to movements, and to individuals, but it is not theologically exclusive. Its forms in the life of the churches have at different times included PURITANS, ARMINIANS, and METHODISM.

exchequer

The royal financial and accounting office, so named because of the checked cloth on which the accounts of the SHERIFFS and other officials were tallied. The accounts were recorded in a roll of parchment. It was described in an account written in the 1170s, the *Dialogue of the Exchequer*. The office functioned both as a treasury and as a court of justice. The former activity moved to a separate office in the 17th century, and the judicial functions were terminated in the 1870s.

exclusion

Refers to the crisis in 1679–81 when PARLIAMENT passed bills in three successive sessions to exclude the duke of York (subsequently JAMES VII AND II) from the royal succession. CHARLES II finally decided not to summon another parliament when that body expressed fears that James would impose his Roman Catholic faith upon the country. These fears were enhanced by the concurrent POPISH PLOT and suspicions of the king's policy toward France, embodied in the Treaty of DOVER. The crisis was reminiscent of the events leading up to the CIVIL WAR, but this time the parties formed on both sides of the question did not go to war. The TORY element vowed their nonresistance to James, while the WHIGS actively pushed for his exclusion. Leaders of both would eventually invite William of Orange to replace James II in 1688; he became WILLIAM III.

excommunication

Removal by the church from the community of the faithful; persons declared excommunicate would be named in a WRIT issued to the SHERIFF for their arrest. The formal processes were abandoned in SCOTLAND in 1690 and in ENGLAND in 1813. The Roman Catholic church in IRELAND continues to have provision for excommunication, though it is seldom used.

extradition

The return of accused persons from one jurisdiction to another in which charges are pending. There were exchanges of criminal suspects between ENGLAND and SCOTLAND as early as the 12th century. There was a treaty between the United States and GREAT BRITAIN in 1794, and a major series of treaties involving Britain and European countries began in the 1840s. The early agreements were ineffective, and legislation of the 1870s and later treaties made the process more efficient. A person charged with political offenses is ordinarily exempt from extradition.

eyre

A circuit of courts which was attended by the justices of the royal court. The General Eyre probably dates from the reign of Henry I in the 12th century. The judges had very wide powers, in effect taking over a local court and holding the session in the king's name. This was superseded by the ASSIZE circuits in the 14th century.

F

Fabian Society

A group of intellectuals founded this organization in 1884 to pursue gradual socialist reform. They took their name from the Roman general Quintus Fabius, known for his cautious tactics in warfare. The society's early leaders—Sidney and Beatrice WEBB, George Bernard SHAW, and H. G. WELLS—fashioned programs and policies that were influential in the formative years of the LABOUR PARTY. The Fabian Society published essays, sponsored lectures and meetings, and became a continuing source of information and ideas for the party.

factory acts

The earliest and most influential form of legislative intervention, these were child-labor laws that expanded into general regulations for health, safety, and employment practices for a widening number of industries. The unsystematic process began in 1802 with the Health and Morals of Apprentices Act, which applied to PARISH apprentices, i.e., pauper children employed by factory owners. Their hours were limited, and they were to receive schooling. In 1819 an act applied limits to the working hours of all children and prohibited those under age nine from working in cotton mills. But it was only in 1833 that a factory act provided for inspectors and thus raised hope of better enforcement. It restated the limits of earlier acts and set limits for hours per week: children under age 13 could not work more than a 48-hour week, those ages 13–18 no more than 68 hours. This act was partly the result of the "ten hours movement," an ongoing reform effort which produced further acts in 1844, 1850, and after. The limits on hours were gradually extended to women, and much later to all workers. At the same time, added regulations were made to improve safety and health in the workplace.

Fairfax, Sir Thomas (1612–1671)
general

Fairfax attended St. John's, CAMBRIDGE UNIVERSITY, and Grays Inn (see INNS OF COURT). He fought for CHARLES I in the Netherlands and against SCOTLAND (1640), but he chose to serve as a parliamentary commander in 1642. During the CIVIL WAR he was one of the commanders at MARSTON MOOR, and he was made the lord general of the NEW MODEL ARMY, which he led to victory at NASEBY in June 1645. He was opposed to the capture of the king, tried to suppress the LEVELLERS, and urged PARLIAMENT to pay the arrears due to the ARMY. When nominated to serve on the HIGH COURT OF JUSTICE, which tried the king, he refused. Made commander in chief in 1649, he resisted the planned invasion of Scotland and resigned in 1650. He took little part in the later political events of the revolution, but he was one of the leaders who was sent to arrange the RESTORATION of CHARLES II.

Famine See IRISH FAMINE.

Fashoda

In 1898 a French expedition went to the fort at Fashoda on the White Nile, presumably to try to oust the British from the SUDAN. The crisis appeared to threaten war between the countries, but, weakened by the Dreyfus case and unable to rely on Russia for support, the French renounced their claim. This settlement was the prelude to the ENTENTE between Britain and France in 1904.

Fawcett, Dame Millicent (1847–1929)
suffragist

The younger sister of Elizabeth Garrett ANDERSON, Fawcett was the wife and secretary of Henry Fawcett, a blind MEMBER OF PARLIAMENT. She used her access and information to campaign for issues such as university EDUCATION and property rights for women. But her main cause was votes for women, and she became the president of the National Union of Women's Suffrage Societies in 1897. She opposed the militant tactics that came into use over the next decade, and she was often a supporter of conservative political views. Her personal account of the suffrage campaign is in her memoir, *What I Remember* (1924).

Fawkes, Guy (1570–1606)
conspirator

From a Protestant family, Fawkes converted to the Catholic faith and fought with Spanish forces in the Netherlands (1593). In 1605 he conspired with a number of disaffected Catholics in the GUNPOWDER PLOT to blow up the houses of PARLIAMENT while the king and the members were in session. He was to light the fuse, but an informer notified the authorities, and he was taken captive in the cellar beneath the HOUSE OF LORDS. He was subsequently tortured and executed. On November 5 every year, Fawkes's fate is celebrated by fireworks, bonfires, and the burning of his effigy.

Fenian Brotherhood

A secret society, organized in cells, founded in 1858 by James Stephens, a former member of YOUNG IRELAND and a rebel in 1848. The organization named itself after legendary Irish warriors, and it sought the establishment of an IRISH REPUBLIC. The Brotherhood's supporters were on both sides of the Atlantic, and it was responsible for an abortive invasion of CANADA and a failed uprising in IRELAND in 1867. The sequel to the latter event was a raid on a police van in Manchester to rescue two Fenians, in which a policeman was shot. There was also an explosion at LONDON's Clerkenwell Prison in another rescue attempt that killed 20 people. These events did dramatize the Irish "question" but probably did not gain support for the republicans. The Fenians were reconstituted as the Irish Republican Brotherhood in 1873.

feudalism

The system of LAND tenure in medieval Europe, in which a vassal held land (a *fief,* from the Latin *feodum*) from a lord in return for military service and other duties. Once thought to be a Norman import (1066), it now seems to have been a much more varied and widespread phenomenon. Feudal lordship in ENGLAND was centered on the king, whose tenants-in-chief were the main vassals in a complex hierarchy. The feudal lord exercised judicial authority and customary rights, which created conflict with royal power. Assertion of royal authority was one of the corrosive forces working on feudalism, as in the growth of royal courts and jurisdictions from the 12th century and the laws of Edward I, which barred further feudal lordships in the 13th century. The other element of the system was paid military service, which grew as an alternative to traditional vassalage, especially in the 14th century and after. This process was accelerated by the increasing cost of armor, weapons, and fortifications. Feudal arrangements across the British Isles varied, with Scottish vassals retaining much more in the way of hereditary jurisdictions, and Welsh and Irish lords generally evading the control of a VICEROY or governor.

Fielding, Henry (1701–1754)
author, magistrate

Born in Somerset, the son of an army officer, Fielding attended Eton. At age 19 he tried to elope with an heiress, and when that failed, he took up writing for the stage. His satires provoked the government to pass a Licensing Act, for theatrical productions, in 1737. He read for the bar, became a BARRISTER in 1740, and was a prolific journalist. His career as a novelist seems to have been a reaction to the work of Samuel Richardson, author of the epistolary novel *Pamela*. Fielding's novels included *Joseph Andrews* (1742), *Tom Jones* (1749), and *Amelia* (1751). He had practiced on the western ASSIZE circuit, and in 1748 he was appointed as a MAGISTRATE in Westminster, where he was noted for his aggressive efforts to fight crime and disorder (see BOW STREET RUNNERS).

Fifth Monarchy Men

A millenarian sect inspired by the execution of CHARLES I into a literal interpretation of the Book of Daniel. The Fifth Monarchy Men believed that the reign of Christ was to begin and would last for a thousand years, and it was their duty to purge the corrupt elements of government to pave the way. One of their leaders, Thomas Venner, led two uprisings (1653, 1661) before he was captured and executed.

Filmer, Sir Robert (unknown–1653)
political theorist

Born into a GENTRY family, Filmer went to Trinity College, CAMBRIDGE UNIVERSITY. Knighted by CHARLES I, he was a staunch royalist who lost much property and was imprisoned during the CIVIL WAR. He was the author of important works defending traditional ideas. In *The Freeholder's Grand Inquest* (1648) he held that PARLIAMENTS and laws owed their origin to royal authority. At the height of the EXCLUSION crisis his works were reprinted, along with *Patriarcha, or the Natural Power of Kings Asserted*, which had not been previously published. That work traced the rights of kings from Adam, and it was useful to the TORY Party in disputing the political theories of Thomas HOBBES and John LOCKE.

Finch, Daniel See NOTTINGHAM, DANIEL FINCH, EARL OF.

Finch, Heneage See NOTTINGHAM, HENEAGE FINCH, EARL OF.

Finch, Sir John (1584–1660)
judge

Finch was the SPEAKER OF THE HOUSE of Commons in 1629 who attempted to adjourn the meeting only to be held in his chair by Sir John ELIOT and others so that debate (and attacks on the Crown) could continue. He was later made chief justice of the Court of COMMON PLEAS, where he made the important judgment favoring the king in the SHIP MONEY case (1637). He was impeached by PARLIAMENT in 1640, went into exile, and returned at the RESTORATION.

Fire of London

A small fire in a baker's shop in Pudding Lane was fanned by high winds, spreading across the City of LONDON's closely packed wooden structures (September 2–6, 1666). Over 13,000 buildings were destroyed, including the Guildhall, ST. PAUL'S CATHEDRAL, and 87 parish churches. Royal commissioners were appointed to oversee the rebuilding of the city. The old street plan was kept, but new construction had to meet government specifications, including the use of brick instead of wood.

Fisher, John Arbuthnot Fisher, first baron (1841–1920)
admiral

Commander of the Mediterranean fleet from 1899 to 1902, Fisher was promoted to first sea lord in 1904 and began a remarkable series of reforms in administration, ship construction, and tactics. He supervised the building of the DREADNOUGHT and a new class of battle cruisers, which gave GREAT BRITAIN a brief advantage in the naval arms race with Germany. He retired in 1910, but was called back to duty by Winston CHURCHILL at the start of WORLD WAR I in 1914. He helped to spur wartime naval construction, but he proved to be a difficult colleague for Churchill. When they fell out over the conduct of the GALLIPOLI campaign, Fisher resigned and brought Churchill down as well.

Fisher, St. John (1469–1535)
bishop

Born in Yorkshire, the son of a mercer, Fisher attended the cathedral school in York and then Michaelhouse College, CAMBRIDGE UNIVERSITY. He later became a fellow and then master of the college at age 28. A chaplain to lady Margaret BEAUFORT and a friend of Erasmus, he became BISHOP of Rochester in 1504. He wrote in support of HENRY VIII's anti-Lutheran writings in the 1520s, but he vigorously opposed the king's arguments for a divorce, and he defended the church against the royal takeover in 1532. After the ROYAL SUPREMACY was declared and the royal succession was altered, Fisher refused to take the oath (1534), and he was arrested and executed (1535). He was canonized in 1935.

Fitzgerald, earls of Desmond

1. James Fitzjohn Fitzgerald (d. 1558), 14th earl, assumed the title in 1536. He allied with rebels but submitted to the lord deputy, Sir Anthony ST. LEGER, in 1540. Created lord treasurer, he served the Crown through the reign of MARY I.
2. Gerald Fitzjames (1533–1583), 15th earl, took the title in 1558, was sent to the TOWER OF LONDON in 1567, later conspired against ELIZABETH I, and in 1579 began the DESMOND REBELLION. He was captured and executed, and his head was displayed on Tower Bridge.

3. James (1570–1601), 16th earl, called "the Queen's earl of Desmond," was surrendered (as a hostage) by his mother in 1579, kept in the Tower for many years, and taken to Munster in 1600 to attempt to restore the allegiance of the family's followers. When this failed, he was returned to LONDON and died soon after.

Fitzgerald, earls of Kildare

1. Gerald (1457–1513), eighth earl, was a deputy to the LORD LIEUTENANT (who often was not in residence) and effective ruler of Ireland. He supported Lambert SIMNEL and perhaps Perkin WARBECK, but was pardoned by HENRY VII, possibly because he was the most useful governor of the PALE.
2. Gerald (1487–1534), ninth earl, known in Ireland as "Garrett Og" (Gerald the younger), was held hostage in England (1497–1503) during his father's escapades. HENRY VIII made him deputy. He was recalled on several occasions and imprisoned in the TOWER OF LONDON. On the last of these, in 1534, his son Thomas led an uprising.
3. Thomas (1513–1537), 10th earl (alias "Silken Thomas"), had been made deputy when his father was imprisoned in 1534. He was told that his father had been executed, and that triggered a revolt. In that uprising John Allen, the ARCHBISHOP of DUBLIN, was murdered. When Thomas was defeated and captured, he was promised a pardon, but in 1537 he and five of his uncles were executed. This ended the power of the house of Kildare.

Fitzgerald, Lord Edward (1763–1798)
Irish nationalist

Son of the duke of Leinster, Fitzgerald was raised in a wealthy Anglo-Irish family. After serving in the American Revolution and in CANADA (where he lived with an Indian tribe), he sat in the Irish House of Commons from 1783. Influenced both by his Whiggish family background and by a radical admiration for

France, he joined the UNITED IRISHMEN in 1796. As one of the leaders of that organization, he was the target of attempted arrests in early 1798. Wounded, he died in prison just as outbreaks of violence signaled the beginning of the IRISH REBELLION of 1798.

FitzRoy, Henry (1519–1536)
son of Henry VIII

The illegitimate son of HENRY VIII by Elizabeth Blount, FitzRoy was seen by many as the likely successor to the king. Among his various honors he was created duke of Richmond and appointed lord high admiral in 1525 and LORD LIEUTENANT of IRELAND in 1529. Acts of succession had declared his sisters (MARY I and ELIZABETH I) illegitimate, but the young duke died of consumption a year before EDWARD VI was born.

Five Knights' Case

When CHARLES I attempted to collect a FORCED LOAN in 1627, he was met with widespread resistance among the GENTRY, who recognized that he was trying to circumvent PARLIAMENT. Five gentlemen were arrested; they applied for a WRIT of HABEAS CORPUS, but the court denied their request. The court did not clearly decide the king's power to collect the loan, so the contested issue was addressed in the PETITION OF RIGHT in 1628. That statement said taxes could not be levied without parliamentary consent.

Fleming, Sir Alexander (1881–1955)
physician, researcher

Son of a farmer from Ayrshire, Fleming trained for a medical career at St. Mary's Hospital, LONDON. He worked in the hospital's inoculation department studying the treatment of syphilis. During WORLD WAR I he studied the infections of battlefield wounds, trying to learn why antiseptic methods were unsuccessful. After the war he discovered natural enzymes that fought bacteria. In 1928 he found that mold growing in a culture dish had killed the surrounding bacteria. His dis-

covery was only exploited years later when Howard Florey and Ernst Chain were able to purify the drug penicillin. The three men shared the Nobel Prize in medicine in 1945.

Fletcher, Andrew (1655–1716)
politician

Known as Fletcher of Saltoun, he was the son of Robert Fletcher of Salton in East Lothian, SCOTLAND. As a commissioner in the convention of estates (summoned, in emergencies, in lieu of Parliament) he opposed STUART policy, became an adviser to James Scott, the duke of Monmouth, but left the duke's ill-fated expedition and went to the continent. He returned to Scotland at the GLORIOUS REVOLUTION and regained his estates. He became a vocal supporter of Scottish institutions and independence, and he fiercely opposed the plan for an act of UNION. He was briefly imprisoned in LONDON in 1708, as it was thought that he was implicated in French invasion plans.

flight of the earls (1607)

In 1607 Rory O'DONNELL, earl of Tyrconnel, and Hugh O'NEILL, earl of Tyrone, were fearful of being arrested by the English, as the most prominent Catholic leaders in Ulster. The territory had been occupied, a new administration had been installed, and a large number of English and Scottish settlers were expected to be introduced. The two earls fled to the continent, ultimately to Rome, and their departure left the native Irish without any traditional leaders, thus facilitating the PLANTATION of the new colonists.

Flodden, Battle of (1513)

JAMES IV of SCOTLAND renounced his alliance with ENGLAND, invaded while HENRY VIII was campaigning in France, and suffered a resounding defeat. Though each side had roughly equal forces, England only lost about 1,500, while Scotland lost 10,000, including the king himself and many of the Scottish nobility.

football (soccer)

A game between opposing players, each attempting to strike a ball by foot into the opponents' goal; called soccer in the United States. In the early days the game was accompanied by considerable violence, and authorities tried to suppress it. Only in the 19th century were rules evolved which reduced violence on the field and made the game more respectable. The Football Association was formed in the 1860s, and a cup competition was begun in 1872. Originally an amateur sport, with extensive participation by university and club teams, professional teams dominated the game by the 1890s, forcing the organization of a separate amateur level. Several professional leagues were formed, including a Scottish and an Irish league in 1890. These fostered the tradition of "international" matches among the countries of the British Isles, which date from 1872. Genuine international competition grew in the years after 1918, and the World Cup was begun in 1930. Large crowds attended matches from an early date (111,000 at Crystal Palace in 1901; 126,000 at the new Wembley Stadium in 1923). A number of accidents in the late 20th century caused the loss of lives at football matches. A more intractable problem was the rise of football hooliganism—the riotous behavior of fans, particularly in international competitions. This has drawn the intervention of

Soccer player for England traps the ball as a player for Scotland comes in to tackle from the right (Hulton/Archive)

PARLIAMENT (Public Order Act, 1986) and threatened exclusion of English teams from European competition.

Forbes, Duncan (1685–1747)
Scottish judge

Studied law at Leiden, was SHERIFF of Midlothian (1709), a MEMBER OF PARLIAMENT (1722), and LORD ADVOCATE (1725). He became lord president of the Court of SESSION in 1737. Forbes was a strong supporter of the House of HANOVER, and he helped to maintain order in several incidents where there was unrest over English measures to raise taxes. He raised an army to fight in 1745 and led his troops to the west to divide the enemy CLANS. He thus was not present at the Battle of CULLODEN, although he later tried to mitigate the brutal treatment of the rebels.

forced loan

The Crown used its influence to extort funds at many points in history. The forced loan was one method, used often by the TUDORS. In the next century, when CHARLES I faced parliamentary opposition, he turned to the landowners and demanded their support. The loan of 1626 was actually an innovation, as it was applied to all taxpayers. Therefore the FIVE KNIGHTS' CASE was an appropriately innovative response. So too was the condemnation of such loans in the PETITION OF RIGHT (1628) and the outlawing of the practice in the BILL OF RIGHTS (1689).

Foreign Office

The government department responsible for relations with other countries, created in 1782. Formerly these affairs were handled by the two secretaries of state, for the Northern and Southern departments. The staff was very small for most of the 19th century. The first typist was hired in 1889, and the first telephone was installed in 1895. The office was one of the last to lose its elitist character, with limited examination for entry beginning in 1908. In 1968 it was joined to the remnants of the Colonial Office and the Commonwealth Relations Office, and is now known as the Foreign and Commonwealth Office.

See also SECRETARY OF STATE.

Forster, E(dward) M(organ) (1879–1970)
author

A student and later longtime lecturer at CAMBRIDGE UNIVERSITY, Forster was associated with the BLOOMSBURY GROUP. He wrote novels that gave penetrating analyses of the English, as in his early works: *Where Angels Fear to Tread* (1905), *The Longest Journey* (1907), and *A Room with a View* (1908). His novel *Howard's End* (1910) was a critical view of the social condition of England; his later work, *A Passage to India* (1924) was aimed at British imperialism. Forster was also a strong voice against censorship, and he was the first president of the National Council for Civil Liberties (1934).

Forster, William E. (1819–1886)
Liberal politician

The son of a QUAKER missionary, Forster entered PARLIAMENT in 1861. He was responsible for the Education Act of 1870, which created the first national system of elementary EDUCATION in ENGLAND. He also was a key figure in the passage of the BALLOT ACT (1872). He briefly served as chief secretary for IRELAND (1880–82), but resigned over the government's dealing with Charles PARNELL. His replacement was Lord Frederick CAVENDISH, who was murdered in Phoenix Park.

Fortescue, Sir John (1394–1476)
lawyer

A MEMBER OF PARLIAMENT and later chief justice of KING'S BENCH (1442), Fortescue was attainted when the Yorkists were victorious in 1461. He joined the Lancastrians again in 1471, only to be captured. He agreed to support EDWARD IV, and he went into exile. In this period he wrote *De laudibus legum angliae,* in which he praised the limited MONARCHY of ENGLAND (not printed until 1537). He also wrote *On the Governance of the Kingdom of England,* which was not published until 1714. His strong views on parliamentary authority awaited a larger following in the 17th century and after.

Fox, Charles James (1749–1806)
politician

The son of the politician Henry FOX, Charles Fox attended Eton and Hertford College, OXFORD UNIVERSITY. Indulged by his father, and with his influence, he entered PARLIAMENT in 1768, though he was underage. A champion of many liberal causes, he was an erratic colleague who had little success in ministerial positions. As a WHIG leader he opposed the policies of Lord NORTH and King GEORGE III toward the AMERICAN COLONIES. Briefly in government after the American war, he alienated the king further, and his coalition with his former enemy North was defeated in 1783. The young William PITT was the king's new choice, and Fox was cast as his adversary. There followed nearly two decades in sometimes lonely opposition, as Pitt proved to be highly popular, especially as the foe of the French Revolution, to which Fox had initially given his support. He was briefly foreign secretary and sought a peace with Napoleon, which was a failure (1806). Fox presented the resolution that brought the end of the British SLAVE TRADE (1807). He was a brilliant orator, but too inclined to improvisation. Despite a high intelligence and an ability to gain a following, he seemed to lack a serious commitment to the business of government. He was buried in WESTMINSTER ABBEY.

Fox, George (1624–1691)
founder of the Quakers

A Leicestershire apprentice shoemaker, Fox experienced a conversion by what he called an "inner light." Rejecting all church attendance, he set out to preach his faith, traveling through the British Isles and to the WEST INDIES, America, and the Netherlands. His message attracted many followers, perhaps as many as 40,000 by 1660, who took the name "Friends of Truth" and were also called QUAKERS. They were persecuted, Fox himself being imprisoned eight times.

Foxe, John (1516–1587)
Protestant writer

Educated at OXFORD UNIVERSITY and a fellow of Magdalen College, Foxe went into exile under MARY I. While on the continent he compiled his "Book of Martyrs," published first in Latin (1559) and then in an English edition as *Actes and Monuments* (1563). Dedicated to Queen ELIZABETH I, the book had vivid, illustrated depictions of the stories of hundreds of Christians, and particularly Protestants, who died for their faith. It was a best-seller and went through four editions in the 16th century.

fox hunting

The sport involves pursuit of a fox by mounted hunters (usually mounted) and a pack of foxhounds. Over the last half of the 20th century, there was growing opposition to the sport, especially from animal-rights activists. The season runs from November to April, and it is estimated that hunting kills some 12,000 foxes annually, whereas 10 times that number are killed by other means. Throughout the 1990s, legislation to ban fox hunting gained support, but it has been pointed out that the 200 or so packs of hounds and their hunters have provided livelihoods for thousands of workers in related trades and communities. These would be put at risk by a ban of the sport.

franchise

This term generally referred to "freedom" in medieval usage. Later it was applied to a specific legal jurisdiction, and at a still later time it came to mean the privilege of voting or the qualification thereto. The early franchise for parliamentary elections was stipulated in statute and in BOROUGH charters. Under a statute of 1429 the COUNTY freeholders who held property of an annual value of 40 shillings were able to vote. Their equivalent in a borough were regulated by the particular charter of the borough: votes might be given to all freemen, to the payers of local taxes, to owners of specific properties, or to local officials. Only in 1832 was the franchise made uniform, with a £10 property qualification for all boroughs. In 1867 all borough householders were allowed to vote; this was extended to all householders in the counties in 1884. In 1918 males age 21 and older and women over 30 were given the right to vote, and in 1928 all adults 21 and older were enfranchised.

Free Church of Scotland

The body formed at the DISRUPTION of the CHURCH OF SCOTLAND in 1843. Thomas CHALMERS was chosen as the moderator, and 470 ministers signed an Act of Separation. They split with the main body of the church over the matter of civil authority exerted over the spiritual, especially in issues of patronage. Because of the division, many new churches and schools had to be built. As the use of patronage declined, a process of reunion began toward the end of the 19th century, culminating in the reunited Church of Scotland in 1929.

freehold

A form of LAND tenure, from the medieval period "free" of feudal obligations, or rather, where those obligations had been converted into money payments. As the payments were fixed, over time they became negligible. In the 17th century, feudal tenures were abolished, making freehold a form of absolute ownership. In 1925 the COPYHOLD tenure was converted into freehold.

free trade

Trade that is free of TARIFFS and regulations. Advocated from the late 18th century by critics of MERCANTILISM, such as Adam SMITH, the doctrine of free trade gained an increasing following in the 19th century after the loss of the AMERICAN COLONIES, the beginning of industrial growth, and the expansion of trade. The battle over the CORN LAWS and their eventual repeal (1846) was followed quickly by the repeal of the NAVIGATION ACTS (1849). GREAT BRITAIN then entered a period of unrestricted trade that lasted until 1932, when a general tariff was imposed. Since WORLD WAR II, Britain has entered a variety of trade agreements aimed at limiting restrictions or creating specific free-trade arrangements.

French, Sir John (1852–1925)
field marshal

French served in the expedition to relieve KHARTOUM in 1884 and commanded cavalry in the BOER WAR. Made chief of the imperial general staff in 1912, he had to resign because of the CURRAGH MUTINY (1914). As WORLD WAR I broke out, he returned in 1914 to serve as commander of the BRITISH EXPEDITIONARY FORCE. Soon he was faced with the unexpected strategic challenge of trench warfare on the western front. His only tactic was to use increased artillery, and in 1915 he contributed to a panic over the short supply of shells. His several efforts to break through the stalemate were costly battles with poor results. He resigned as commander in chief and was replaced by Douglas HAIG in December 1915, upon which he took command of home forces. He was later LORD LIEUTENANT of IRELAND (1918–21).

friendly societies

A form of mutual benefit developed among workers as early as the 17th century. Known as friendly societies, they were recognized by statute in 1793. A small weekly contribution was paid into a common fund, and sickness and death benefits were paid out. Meetings, rituals, and ceremonies were part of their practice, and they were joined from the 1830s by growing numbers of cooperative societies and affiliated orders (Oddfellows, Ancient Britons, etc.).

Friends of the People

A society of radical WHIGS, mainly aristocrats, organized in 1792. Sympathetic to the French Revolution in its early stages, Friends of the People promoted parliamentary reform in ENGLAND. Leaders such as Lord John RUSSELL, Charles GREY, and Charles James FOX were among their number; the dues were high enough to prevent a surge of members who actually belonged to "the people." Other groups of radicals distrusted them, and within a few years, with growing danger on the military and political front, the society ceased to meet.

Frobisher, Martin (1539–1594)
explorer

Born in Yorkshire, Frobisher was brought up in the household of his maternal grandfather, who sent him on his first voyage to Guinea in 1554. He spent 15 years or so engaged in privateering, but his best-known efforts were his voyages to find a NORTHWEST PASSAGE to Cathay (1576–78). Though failing in the main mission, he discovered Baffin Island, near Labrador. He was vice-admiral in Sir Francis DRAKE's expedition to the WEST INDIES in 1586, returning to command a squadron in the battle against the Spanish ARMADA. In 1590 he sailed with the expedition of Sir John HAWKINS, again as vice-admiral.

Frost, John (1784–1877)
Chartist

A tailor and the mayor of Newport, South Wales, Frost represented Newport at the Chartist Convention (1839). After the Chartists' petition was rejected by PARLIAMENT, and in a climate of labor unrest in his region, he led an uprising in Newport (1839). It was suppressed, and he was sentenced to transportation for life to Van Dieman's Land (see TASMANIA). He was pardoned and allowed to return to WALES in 1856. In his later years he wrote and lectured on the experiences of convicts and the evils of transportation.

See also CHARTIST MOVEMENT.

Fry, Elizabeth (1780–1845)
prison reformer

Born into a family of wealthy QUAKER bankers who held moderate beliefs, Fry was able to study music and dance. She taught in a private school; married Joseph Fry, a strict Quaker; and moved to LONDON. There she was appalled at prison conditions when she visited NEWGATE PRISON in 1813. She founded an association to aid female prisoners, was a frequent visitor to convict ships, and helped convince the government to regulate the conditions for convict voyages to New South Wales. She campaigned in GREAT BRITAIN and in Europe, also working for improved hospital conditions and for accommodations for the homeless.

G

Gaelic

The Celtic languages spoken in IRELAND, SCOTLAND, and (until the 19th century) the ISLE OF MAN. They belong to the subgroup called Goidelic, or "q-celtic," to distinguish them from Welsh and Breton. The variations between the several areas are due to long periods of separate development and prolonged interaction with the encroaching English language. In Ireland, when the IRISH FREE STATE was declared, Gaelic was made the official language, with English as the second language. The western parts of the country had many more native speakers, and the region known as the Gaelthact has been given special support by the Irish government. Nevertheless, the use of Gaelic has declined. In Scotland the number of Gaelic speakers dropped sharply by the beginning of the 20th century, and strenuous efforts have been made to preserve the language there as well.

Gainsborough, Thomas (1727–1788)
painter

The son of a wool manufacturer, Gainsborough studied painting in LONDON, then married and lived in Ipswich (1746–60) and Bath (1760–74). He contributed paintings to the Society of Artists and was elected a founding member of the ROYAL ACADEMY. He exhibited at the academy in its early years, but after a dispute he withdrew all his works and exhibited at his own house in London. A landscape painter who developed a style of portraiture using landscape, he was one of the most popular of the 18th-century English artists. He enjoyed royal patronage and many of his portraits were of leading figures in the society of his day.

Gaitskell, Hugh (1906–1963)
Labour Party leader

Educated at Winchester and New College, OXFORD UNIVERSITY, Gaitskell taught economics at University College, LONDON, 1928–39. He joined the LABOUR PARTY during the GENERAL STRIKE, was in the CIVIL SERVICE during WORLD WAR II, and entered PARLIAMENT in 1945. A junior official at the TREASURY, he succeeded Sir Stafford CRIPPS as CHANCELLOR OF THE EXCHEQUER in 1950. In the contest for leadership after Clement ATTLEE's retirement (1955), he defeated Ernest BEVAN and Herbert MORRISON. After the SUEZ CANAL CRISIS in 1956, it was expected that Labour would win the next election. When they lost in 1959, Gaitskell was convinced that the party needed to be more appealing to the middle-class voter, and he tried to eliminate its commitment to NATIONALIZATION, which the Left regarded as the essential core of its socialist creed. He lost this battle but managed to reverse Labour's commitment to unilateral DISARMAMENT in 1960. He died suddenly in 1963 of a rare disease. Harold WILSON took over the party leadership and won the election of 1964, partly on the strength of Gaitskell's work.

Gallipoli (1915)

During WORLD WAR I the British and French tried to force their way through the straits of the Dardanelles (March 1915). They hoped to knock

Turkey out of the war and establish a supply line to their ally Russia. The naval assault on the straits failed, and it was followed by a landing on the Gallipoli Peninsula. The amphibious assault by 70,000 troops was a bold and desperate maneuver which resulted in very heavy casualties and ended in allied withdrawal in December. This defeat led to the resignations of Admiral John FISHER and First Lord of the ADMIRALTY Winston CHURCHILL.

Gambia, The

Surrounded by SENEGAL, The Gambia is a West African republic whose borders were created by Britain and France in 1889. Extending inland for 200 miles along the banks of the Gambia River, it had been a location for trading since the 16th century, with a British settlement established in the 17th century. It became a crown COLONY in the 19th century and achieved independence in 1965. The Gambia became a republic in 1970; a federation of Senegambia was established in 1982 but dissolved in 1989. In 1994 there was a military coup, and a new constitution was promulgated in 1996. By banning the parties of former national leaders, the military candidate won the first elections under the new regime.

Gandhi, Mohandas K. (1869–1948)
Indian nationalist leader

After studying law in LONDON, Gandhi practiced in NATAL in the expatriate Indian community, and in 1915 he returned to INDIA to lead the growing nationalist movement. After the AMRITSAR MASSACRE (1919) he spurred a nationwide nonviolent protest. He convinced the Indian National Congress to oppose British proposals and adopt his strategy of noncooperation. He did participate in the Round Table Conferences in London (1930–32), which failed to find a solution. Gandhi wanted revival of traditional village society, but he also preached toleration between Hindu and Moslem. That was radical

for the period of partition between India and PAKISTAN, which measure he opposed. India achieved independence in 1947, and Gandhi was assassinated in 1948 by a Hindu fanatic.

Gardiner, Stephen (ca. 1483–1555)
bishop

An influential church figure during the REFORMATION, Gardiner was secretary to Cardinal WOLSEY and assisted with HENRY VIII's efforts to obtain a divorce. In 1531 he became secretary to the king and BISHOP of Winchester in 1533. His book *De Vera Obedientia* (1535) supported the king's position on royal control of the church. In the reordering of the church, Gardiner reluctantly supported the changes in governance, but he opposed any change in doctrine. This made him the adversary of Thomas CROMWELL, whose policies he contested. In the Protestant period under EDWARD VI, Gardiner lost his place as bishop and was sent to the TOWER OF LONDON. On MARY I's accession, he was restored as bishop and made LORD CHANCELLOR. He officiated at Mary's marriage to Philip of Spain, and he worked to restore papal authority in ENGLAND.

Garrick, David (1717–1779)
actor

The son of an army officer and a student of Samuel JOHNSON, Garrick pursued the law, then the wine trade, and finally became an actor. His skill made him the nation's most popular stage figure for nearly 40 years, especially in his Shakespearean productions. He became the manager of the DRURY LANE THEATRE in 1747, where he introduced many innovations in staging and production.

gavelkind

A form of landholding in which the inheritance was partible—i.e., widows received half, and the remainder was shared among the male heirs—as opposed to the undivided inheritance under PRIMOGENITURE. Failing any male heirs, females shared equally under both systems. Gavelkind was the principal form of tenure in the county of Kent, and it also was followed in WALES and IRELAND. It was abolished in English law in 1925.

General Assembly

Created in the Scottish REFORMATION in 1560, the General Assembly was the senior body in the government of the CHURCH OF SCOTLAND. In its first version there were six ministers and 35 laymen. As the assembly represented the PRESBYTERIAN structure of authority, it frequently was in conflict with the royal policies of the STUART kings, JAMES VII AND I and CHARLES I in particular. In 1690 it became the supreme authority in the established Church of Scotland. The assembly now has over 1,200 clergy and laymen who meet under an elected moderator.

general election

The elections of members of the HOUSE OF COMMONS were once held only at times when PARLIAMENT had been summoned by the Crown. In 1694 statutory regulation called for an election every three years. The period was increased to seven years in 1716, and in 1911 it was reduced to five years, where it remains today. The term is a maximum, and the PRIME MINISTER is able to dissolve Parliament and call for a general election at any time before that limit. The election campaign is a combination of the efforts by the national parties to present a platform to attract the voter and individual campaigns in each single-member constituency. Campaigns are limited to three or four weeks, campaign spending is strictly regulated, and proportional television time is provided to major parties. The winning candidate is the person with the largest number of votes in the constituency, whether or not that is a majority. The leader of the party winning the most seats will be asked by the sovereign to form a government.

General Strike (1926)

A total stoppage of work was viewed in the labor movement as the ultimate weapon against the capitalist system. The one attempt to do this in GREAT BRITAIN was a failure. For nine days in May 1926, about 2.5 million workers from different unions went on strike in support of the miners' union. The government introduced emergency legislation, volunteers took up many critical positions, and the POLICE and ARMY remained loyal. The strike was called off, but the miners remained out for several more months, when they returned to work at lower pay. The following year an act was passed declaring such general strikes illegal, and union membership declined, though the act was repealed in 1946.

general warrant

An order issued by a SECRETARY OF STATE for the arrest of unspecified persons in connection with a specific act. The practice was authorized by a licensing act in 1662 for use against seditious publications. This usage was dramatized in 1763, when warrants were issued in connection with issue No. 45 of the *North Briton;* John WILKES and 48 others were arrested. Chief Justice Sir Charles Pratt declared the warrants illegal, and Wilkes later won a damage claim against the secretary for wrongful arrest (1769).

gentry

The general term for families of lesser aristocratic status, usually landowners, from the 16th to the 19th century. Ranks defined as gentry included BARONETS, KNIGHTS, esquires, and gentlemen. In the 15th and 16th centuries, the College of Heralds kept some control over the use of coats of arms, but by the end of the 17th century the number of claimants overwhelmed any such control. Some official titles carried this status: a JUSTICE OF THE PEACE was automatically an "esquire," but the minimum qualification of £100 for that office meant that over time the title might go to persons of less real wealth. In addition the unofficial label "gentleman" was increasingly appropriated without a legitimate claim. Meanwhile, among large landowners there were people with vast fortunes and no peerage. In an 1883 survey, over half the landowners with more than 10,000 acres were members of the gentry. By that date political reforms were beginning to erode the once dominant political position of the gentry.

George I (1660–1727)

king of Great Britain and Ireland, 1714–1727

George I was an accomplished soldier who fought under the duke of MARLBOROUGH. His mother, Electress Sophia of Hanover, had been named in the Act of Succession of 1701 as the heir to the throne, as she was the granddaughter of JAMES VI AND I and the nearest Protestant in the line of succession. She died weeks before Queen ANNE, and George took the throne peacefully in August 1714. He appointed a WHIG ministry and continued to manage the affairs of HANOVER. His divided attention did not endear him to his British subjects, but they did repel the JACOBITE rebellion in 1715. The king was generous with pardons for the rebels, but his political advice now came exclusively from the Whigs. The distractions of Hanover helped to reduce the king's role in British politics, while his chief minister Robert WALPOLE assumed more and more PATRONAGE and power.

George II (1683–1760)

king of Great Britain and Ireland, 1727–1760

A soldier like his father, George II was the last British king to lead troops in battle (Dettingen, 1743). As PRINCE OF WALES he was on bad terms with his father, who expelled him from the court in 1717. He created a rival court and worked with opposition WHIG leaders like Robert WALPOLE, who became PRIME MINISTER in 1721. He was retained in that post when George II came to the throne six years later. This continuity was also fostered by the persistent threat of JACOBITES' rebellion and the Whigs' policy of peace and economy. With the War of AUSTRIAN SUCCESSION (1740–48), the king used British forces in aid of his Hanoverian interests and found himself facing mounting parliamentary opposition. He had to summon ministers whom he disliked, especially William PITT, who became the hero of the SEVEN YEARS' WAR. In this generation there also was a father-son split: in 1737 Frederick, Prince of Wales (1707–1751), established a rival court, and his son, the future GEORGE III, grew up with a passionate distaste for the "Old Corps" Whigs who were then in power.

George III (1738–1820)

king of Great Britain and Ireland, 1760–1820

The grandson of GEORGE II and the first Hanoverian ruler born in GREAT BRITAIN, George III came to the throne determined to rid politics of corruption. His main tools were the exercise of royal power and the restoration of TORY politicians. He tried to act as his own PRIME MINISTER, but his reign showed an increase in the influence of PARLIAMENT, especially the HOUSE OF COMMONS, and furthermore saw the most severe internal and external crises. He ordered in troops to quell the GORDON RIOTS of 1780 when LONDON was ravaged by mobs for 10 days; he stubbornly pursued the war in the AMERICAN COLONIES, which ended with their independence; he faced the threat of revolutionary France (1789) but was no longer mentally competent at the time of WATERLOO (1815); and a dangerous rebellion in IRELAND required a new constitution for the UNITED KINGDOM (1801). The strains of his reign actually produced an entirely different form of government: not one of royal management but one of parliamentary management, ministerial responsibility, and a steadily growing stream of reform ideas—not to increase executive control, but rather to improve the process of choosing members of Parliament, so as to control the executive, and to control the rapidly expanding functions of government. This stream also had powerful whirlpools of radical unrest: Major John CARTWRIGHT's democratic ideas, William COBBETT's agrarian RADICALISM, Thomas

King George III *(Library of Congress)*

PAINE's American and French republican notions, the briefly ecumenical UNITED IRISHMEN, the fervent cause of CATHOLIC EMANCIPATION, and the array of working and middle-class radicals of the early 19th century. This unrest was not the cause of the king's recurrent mental problems. Modern diagnosis suggests that he suffered from a kidney disorder (porphyria) which brought on periods of apparent insanity. These episodes created REGENCY crises in 1765 and 1788. In 1810 George III went into a serious decline, accompanied by loss of eyesight and hearing. His son became regent in 1811, and the king died in 1820.

George IV (1762–1830)
king of the United Kingdom, 1820–1830
The eldest son of GEORGE III rebelled against his parents' strict upbringing and lived a life of fashion and immorality. George IV indulged extrav-

agant tastes, spent lavishly, and lived dangerously. He was secretly married to Maria Fitzherbert, a Roman Catholic, in 1785, a union that continued until 1811. During this period he formally married Princess CAROLINE OF BRUNSWICK in 1795 (while intoxicated), separated the following year, and tried to divorce her in 1820. He was not an effective ruler, and he was succeeded by his brother WILLIAM IV in 1830.

George V (1865–1936)
king of the United Kingdom, 1910–1936
The second son of EDWARD VII, George V had pursued a naval career until his older brother died in 1892. He became PRINCE OF WALES in 1901 and made tours of the empire as the heir apparent. When he came to the throne in 1910, the HOUSE OF LORDS was about to reject the BUDGET, and he promised to create enough new peers, if necessary, to allow it to pass. The peers relented, but their assertion of power brought on the PARLIAMENT Act of 1911, which permanently reduced their power. Meanwhile, an IRISH HOME RULE bill was introduced, and the king tried to soothe parties in that matter at a BUCKINGHAM PALACE conference in 1914. All of this was before the great calamity of WORLD WAR I. In that event, the king was clearly a figurehead, but to placate intense national feeling, he did order the royal family's name changed from Saxe-Coburg to WINDSOR in 1917. He was succeeded by his eldest son, EDWARD VIII.

George VI (1895–1952)
king of the United Kingdom, 1936–1952
George VI, the second son of GEORGE V, served in the NAVY and the air force in WORLD WAR I. He was the next in line when his brother EDWARD VIII abdicated in 1936 (see ABDICATION CRISIS). Though shy and afflicted with a stammer, he earned great respect, especially during WORLD WAR II, remaining in BUCKINGHAM PALACE during the BLITZ, touring sites of bombing, and visiting troops abroad. He was succeeded by his daughter ELIZABETH II.

Ghana

Located on Africa's western coast and known as the Gold Coast when British merchants first made contact in the 17th century, Ghana became a lucrative source of slaves. British control was only over coastal forts until later in the 19th century. A crown COLONY was proclaimed in 1874, with further extension in 1901. Independence for Ghana was granted in 1957.

Gibbon, Edward (1737–1794)
historian

Gibbon studied briefly at OXFORD UNIVERSITY and then on the continent, where he went after his conversion to Roman Catholicism forced him to leave Oxford. A journey to Italy inspired *The History of the Decline and Fall of the Roman Empire,* the first volume appearing in 1776. He was criticized for blaming the empire's fall on the influence of the Christian church, but his masterful survey (completed in 1787) was a major success. He was a MEMBER OF PARLIAMENT from 1774 and supported the ministry of Lord NORTH during the American Revolution.

Gibbons, Grinling (1648–1721)
woodcarver

Born in Rotterdam, Gibbons was working in ENGLAND by the 1660s. His carvings are found in WINDSOR Castle, ST. PAUL'S CATHEDRAL, and HAMPTON COURT PALACE. More of his work is found in the VICTORIA AND ALBERT MUSEUM and in country houses such as Petworth in West Sussex.

Gibraltar

With an area of 2.5 square miles, the smallest British COLONY was captured in 1704 and ceded to GREAT BRITAIN by treaty in 1713. The rock stands at the western entrance to the Mediterranean and retains its strategic significance. Spain's interest in retaking the area was shown when it closed the frontier in 1969, after residents had voted in a referendum in 1967 to remain British. In 1981 they were given British citizenship, and in 1985 Spain lifted restrictions on the colony's frontier.

Gilbert, Humphrey (1539?–1583)
explorer

Educated at Eton and OXFORD UNIVERSITY, Gilbert served in 1562 in an expedition to Le Havre. He wrote *Discourse on a Northwest Passage to India* in 1566. After going to IRELAND to assist in Elizabethan colonization there (1566, 1569), he made attempts on his proposed route for a NORTHWEST PASSAGE in 1579 and 1583. The first was a failure; the second landed in NEWFOUNDLAND, which he claimed for the Crown. He died in a storm on the return journey.

Gilbert, William S. See GILBERT AND SULLIVAN.

Gilbert and Sullivan

William S. Gilbert (1836–1911) and Arthur Sullivan (1842–1900) produced a unique and enduring series of comic operas which were a landmark in public entertainment in the later 19th century. Gilbert had practiced law with no great success and turned to writing librettos. Sullivan was an accomplished academy musician, composer of a symphony and lighter works. They met in 1871, and their first success was *Trial by Jury* (1875). Their lighthearted, satirical style was a sensation, and it continued with *The Pirates of Penzance* (1879), *The Mikado* (1885), and *The Grand Duke* (1896).

Girl Guides

Founded in 1910, the Girl Guides were inspired by the BOY SCOUT movement. In fact, Robert BADEN-POWELL's sister used her own funds to establish the group, which enlisted 8,000 girls in its first year. There was some reluctance to form a female organization, both from Baden-Powell himself, and from others who saw some connection to the SUFFRAGETTES and more generally to the WOMEN'S MOVEMENT. In 1914 a group for eight- to 11-year-olds was formed, known first as the Rosebuds, later as the Brownies. By 1915 Robert Baden-Powell assumed the leadership of the organization, and the first international conference met in 1920. By the end of the 20th century the movement had spread to 100 countries and enlisted more than 8 million girls.

Gladstone, William Ewart
(1809–1898)

prime minister, 1868–1874, 1880–1885, 1886, 1892–1894

Gladstone was a MEMBER OF PARLIAMENT from 1832 until 1895. At first a TORY, he held posts under Robert PEEL. He served as CHANCELLOR OF THE EXCHEQUER twice in the 1850s, left the CONSERVATIVE PARTY in 1859, and became leader of the fledgling LIBERAL PARTY in 1867.

Gladstone was noted for several key policy positions: fiscal frugality, rational reform of institutions, and support of nationalist movements. In his years as chancellor he reduced public spending, cut taxes, and expanded FREE TRADE. These were steps designed to promote prosperity and to fulfill the Liberal goal of reducing government intrusion in the economy. As he became a national leader, he left behind many of his earlier positions in both religion and politics. He firmly believed that there was a moral basis of politics and that it should manifest itself in toleration and integrity. He showed his support of nonconformity with policies such as abolition of church rates, the EDUCATION Act of 1870, and the disestablishment of the CHURCH OF IRELAND. The natural extensions of his views of economy and integrity were the reforms he sponsored in the army, the civil service, and the high courts (see JUDICATURE ACT).

Gladstone was also convinced of the moral value of national sentiment. In his day, the cause of nationalism aroused strong support as a means to combat the regressive autocracies of Europe, and national entities seemed to be the logical foundation for emerging international agreements (extradition, arbitration, law of the

William Ewart Gladstone *(Hulton/Archive)*

sea). Nationalists within the BRITISH EMPIRE were not, however, so equably perceived. Thus in the 1880s there were several incidents where he felt it necessary to use force against colonial populations: in SOUTH AFRICA (1881), in EGYPT (1882), and in The SUDAN (1885). In those same years he was struggling to work out a solution to the "Irish Question." His basic view was that legitimate aspirations could be met: the Catholic church could be appeased; the Irish tenant could be assisted; and above all, there was a valid demand for an Irish PARLIAMENT as part of a plan for IRISH HOME RULE. The last issue proved to be his undoing. In 1886 he pushed a bill that split his party and failed to pass. The second attempt in 1893 passed the HOUSE OF COMMONS but failed in the HOUSE OF LORDS. He resigned from office for the last time at age 84, one of the most influential leaders of the 19th century.

Glencoe massacre (1692)

WILLIAM III required Scottish CLAN leaders suspected of JACOBITE sympathies to take an oath recognizing his authority before January 1, 1692. The Macdonald chief presented himself and took the oath just after the deadline, but this was kept quiet. The authorities in EDINBURGH therefore dispatched a force to require the Macdonalds to submit; this force was made up of their rivals the Campbells. The Campbells accepted the hospitality of the Macdonalds, and then turned on them, killing 38 of their hosts. There was no punishment for the killers, even after a commission in 1695 had determined their guilt. The incident was condemned by the Scottish parliament and provided more fuel for Jacobite resistance.

Glendower, Owen (ca. 1355–ca. 1415)
Welsh prince and rebel

A landowner of princely descent on both sides of his family, he led the last major Welsh revolt against English rule (1400–08). He had trained in English law, served in the armies of RICHARD II, and chafed at the exploitation of the Welsh. He found allies in France and in the English aristocracy, he summoned parliamentary assemblies, and he planned for a native regime. However, English power eventually was too great, and his forces were defeated by 1408. Glendower admitted defeat in 1415; his end is unknown.

Glorious Revolution (1688–1689)

The replacement of JAMES VII AND II by WILLIAM III and his wife MARY II was named the Glorious Revolution because it was accomplished with such ease and so little loss of life (except in IRELAND). James had appeared to be intent upon a policy of Catholic restoration. He was revising BOROUGH governments and commissions of the peace, and he had called an election for a new PARLIAMENT, based on the altered FRANCHISES. He had issued a DECLARATION OF INDULGENCE and ordered it read from all pulpits, and he had put seven bishops on trial for SEDITION when they objected (see SEVEN BISHOPS' CASE). In June 1688

his wife gave birth to a son, ensuring that a Catholic heir to the throne would succeed him. At this point senior WHIG and TORY leaders joined in signing a letter to William of Orange, begging him to intervene. As there had been ample communication between William and English leaders, it is likely that the request came as no surprise. In any event, William prepared to invade, James hastily revoked many of his recent acts, and in November the Dutch prince landed in southwestern ENGLAND. Many of James's officers deserted, and he decided to flee to France, but he was captured on his first attempt. Once he was in exile, a CONVENTION Parliament was elected and began to negotiate with William. The sequels included the BILL OF RIGHTS in England, the CLAIM OF RIGHT in SCOTLAND, plus a war in Ireland, and King William's War against France (1689–97).

Gloucester, Humphrey, duke of (1390/91–1447)
protector of England

The youngest son of HENRY IV and brother of HENRY V, Gloucester served as protector after his brother's death in 1422, until HENRY VI assumed power in 1429. He was involved in bitter quarrels among the royal advisers, especially with Henry BEAUFORT, his uncle. The main disputes were about affairs in France. He lost influence, especially after his wife's trial for witchcraft (1442). He was accused of treason but died before his trial. He had been known as a patron of humanist scholars, and his library was donated to OXFORD UNIVERSITY, where it became the nucleus for the Bodleian Library (See BODLEY, SIR THOMAS).

Glyndwr, Owain   See GLENDOWER, OWEN.

Goderich, Frederick John Robinson, viscount (1782–1859)
(first earl of Ripon)
prime minister, 1827–28

Although he had the distinction of introducing one of the famous CORN LAWS (1815), Goderich served as president of the BOARD OF TRADE and CHANCELLOR OF THE EXCHEQUER in the 1820s, and he led the way toward reducing TARIFFS and removing NAVIGATION ACTS under the Liberal Tories. He was briefly PRIME MINISTER after the death of George CANNING, and he held office later under Charles GREY and Robert PEEL.

Godolphin, Sidney Godolphin, first earl of (1645–1712)
prime minister, 1702–1710

Lord Godolphin entered PARLIAMENT in 1668 and held numerous offices under CHARLES II, JAMES VII AND II, and Queen ANNE. He was lord treasurer (1702–10) and as such was responsible for financing ENGLAND's armed forces in a period of exceptionally costly fighting.

Godwin, William (1756–1836)
radical author

Born in Cambridgeshire, Godwin was the son of a dissenting minister. Raised with strict Calvinist beliefs, he attended Hoxton Academy. He was the pastor of a congregation at Stowmarket for five years, but he lost his faith and passed from this career into one as a writer. His *Enquiry Concerning the Principles of Political Justice* (1793) was an anarchist manifesto, deriving some inspiration from the events of the French Revolution and placing him in the pantheon of radicals. He also wrote novels, the best known being *Caleb Williams* (1794). He married Mary WOLLSTONECRAFT (1797), and their daughter Mary married Percy Bysshe SHELLEY.

Gold Coast See GHANA.

Golding, William (1911–1993)
novelist

Born in Cornwall, the son of a schoolmaster, Golding studied at Brasenose College, OXFORD UNIVERSITY. He taught school and served in the NAVY during WORLD WAR II. His first novel and probably his best work, *Lord of the Flies* (1954), was the story of shipwrecked boys trying to maintain a form of civilized life. He also wrote *The Inheritors* (1955), *Pincher Martin* (1956), *Free Fall* (1959), *The Spire* (1964), *Darkness Visible* (1979), and *Rites of Passage* (1980). He received the Nobel Prize in literature in 1983.

Goldsmith, Oliver (1728–1774)
author

Born near Longford, Goldsmith's father was a curate. At age eight he suffered a bout with smallpox and was badly disfigured. He attended Trinity College, DUBLIN, and then studied in EDINBURGH. Moving to LONDON, he wrote for the *Monthly Review*. His essays attracted the interest of Samuel JOHNSON, who helped him to publish *The Vicar of Wakefield* (1766). Goldsmith's greatest poetic work was *The Deserted Village* (1770). He also wrote two plays: *The Good-Natured Man* (1768) and *She Stoops to Conquer* (1773).

Goodall, Jane (1934–)
primatologist

Born in LONDON, Goodall left school and went to work with Louis Leakey in Africa. She began work with chimpanzees in 1960 at Lake Tanganyika, observing the animals in their habitat and noting their varied social behaviors. The world's leading authority on chimpanzees, she has continued to work extensively to protect the species. Goodall's books include *In the Shadow of Man* (1971) and *The Chimpanzees of Gombe* (1986).

Gordon, Charles George (1833–1885)
general

Gordon served in the CRIMEAN WAR and later led the defense of Shanghai during the Taiping Rebellion (1863–64). In the service of the government of EGYPT, he was engaged in the administration of the SUDAN (1873–80). He was sent back in 1884 to evacuate an Egyptian garrison from KHARTOUM and was besieged there by forces of the Mahdi (a Muslim holy warrior named Mohammed Ahmed). He was killed two days before a relief force arrived, much to the embarrassment of William GLADSTONE's government.

Gordon, George Hamilton See ABERDEEN, GEORGE HAMILTON-GORDON, EARL OF.

Gordon Riots (1780)

Lord George Gordon (1751–93) was a Scottish MEMBER OF PARLIAMENT who became president of the Protestant Association, a group violently opposed to the concessions to Catholics that had been initiated in 1778. He led a large crowd presenting a petition to PARLIAMENT on June 2, 1780, and the mayhem that followed resulted in a week of rioting and looting. At first Catholic chapels were attacked, and Catholic homes were destroyed. Breweries, taverns, and distilleries became targets, and a more sinister development saw the release of inmates from prisons. The ARMY was called in, several hundred deaths resulted, and some 59 rioters were convicted, but not Gordon, who was acquitted of high treason.

Government of Ireland Act (1920)

The movement for IRISH HOME RULE had agitated Irish and British politics for more than 30 years. The debate was centered on the means of granting some form of autonomy to IRELAND within the UNITED KINGDOM. Any such step frightened the PROTESTANT majority in NORTHERN IRELAND, as it would put power in the hands of the overall CATHOLIC majority in Ireland. Successive Home Rule bills had failed in 1886, 1892, and 1912. But the last bill finally passed in 1914, just as war broke out in Europe. The war was an excuse to put the measure aside temporarily. The 1914 bill had provided for two governments: one for the six northeastern counties, the other for the 26 counties of the south and west. Limited powers were delegated to each of these governments, and a council was created to deal with matters

pertaining to all of Ireland. The south rejected the 1914 act and accepted in its stead the ANGLO-IRISH TREATY of 1921. Meanwhile, PARLIAMENT passed the 1920 act, which restated the terms of 1914, enabling a separate parliament to be formed in the north and providing for the partition of Ireland. King GEORGE V went to Belfast to preside over the opening of the new parliament on June 23, 1921.

Graham, James See MONTROSE, JAMES GRAHAM, MARQUESS OF.

Graham, Sir James (1792–1861)
politician

Graham entered PARLIAMENT in 1818 and held office under Charles GREY and Robert PEEL. He supported CATHOLIC EMANCIPATION and parliamentary reform. First lord of the ADMIRALTY in grey's cabinet in 1830, he helped to draft the Great Reform bill. In the 1840s he served as home secretary during the CHARTIST MOVEMENT disturbances and helped Peel with repeal of the CORN LAWS. He was again at the admiralty (1852–1855) during the CRIMEAN WAR.

Graham of Claverhouse, John See DUNDEE, JOHN GRAHAM, VISCOUNT.

grammar schools

Historically those schools teaching the rudiments of Latin were usually endowed for the education of future clerics and sometimes established by individuals or institutions. Some older foundations achieved special status as "public schools"— that is, they were of superior social standing if not academic prowess (Winchester, 1382; Eton, 1440; St. Paul's, 1509; Westminster, 1560; Shrewsbury, 1552; Merchant Taylors', 1561; Rugby, 1567; Harrow, 1571; Charterhouse, 1611). A royal commission was appointed to examine them in 1861, due to continued comments on their shortcomings. During the 19th century a number of newer and more modern grammar schools were established to cater to a much larger and socially ambitious middle class. Schools had been encouraged to broaden curricula since an act of 1840, and they began to admit girls in 1870. A major turn came after the 1902 act, which called for locally supported secondary, or "grammar," schools. This produced a large number of schools, many of which were merged into the newer "comprehensive" schools in the 1950s and 1960s.

See also EDUCATION.

grand jury

Originally a group of 12 called to report crimes and suspects to the justices in EYRE and later to the ASSIZE judges. The grand jury later came to number 23 persons, chosen from a panel named by the SHERIFF, and was the place where indictments were examined and approved for trial. It became redundant in the 19th century as MAGISTRATES took over this function with pretrial hearings, and the grand jury was terminated in 1933.

Grand Remonstrance

In November 1641, with increasing tension between CHARLES I and PARLIAMENT, and with some faltering in the latter group, John PYM and other leaders prepared a summary indictment of the king's actions. They demanded that his councillors be approved by Parliament, that the BISHOPS' authority be limited, and that the church be reformed. The Grand Remonstrance only passed by a small margin, the king rejected it, and the hostility between sides escalated further.

Grattan, Henry (1746–1820)
Irish politician

Trained in LAW, Grattan was elected to the Irish parliament in 1775 and was soon one of its leading speakers. He led the debates for Irish liberty at the time of the American Revolution. He suc-

ceeded in obtaining the repeal of POYNINGS' LAWS and the DECLARATORY ACT OF 1766, which gave legislative independence to the Irish parliament (known commonly as "Grattan's Parliament," 1782–1800). He protested against the Act of UNION in 1800, but later served in the PARLIAMENT of the UNITED KINGDOM, where he was an advocate of CATHOLIC EMANCIPATION.

Graves, Robert Ranke (1895–1985)
poet, critic

From an Anglo-Irish family, Graves studied at Charterhouse and at St. John's College, CAMBRIDGE UNIVERSITY. A prodigious author, he produced over 120 volumes of poetry, fiction, and criticism. Among his best-known works are his autobiography of the war years, *Goodbye to All That* (1929); his historical novels *I, Claudius* and *Claudius the God* (both 1934); his critical masterpiece *The White Goddess: A Historical Grammar of Poetic Myth* (1948); and his *Collected Poems* (1975). He held the position of professor of poetry at OXFORD UNIVERSITY, 1961–66.

Great Britain

The term *Great Britain* applies to the largest island of the British Isles, sometimes in contrast to "Little Britain," or Brittany. As a political term, it refers to the joint sovereign entity of ENGLAND, WALES, and SCOTLAND. This only became a political reality in 1603, with the accession of JAMES VI AND I to the English throne. The English PARLIAMENT was not inclined to accept the name then, but the king had it proclaimed and used in official documents and on the coinage. The name was recognized in the Act of UNION in 1707.

Great Exhibition (1851)

Prince ALBERT inspired the convening of this International Exhibition of the Industrial Works of All Nations, which served to display the primacy of English manufactures. The central structure was the CRYSTAL PALACE in Hyde Park. There were tens of thousands of exhibits, and the event attracted over 6 million visitors. Profits from the exhibition went to acquire land for the future sites of the VICTORIA AND ALBERT MUSEUM, Science Museum, Natural History Museum, the Albert Hall, the Royal College of Music, and the Imperial College of Science and Technology.

Great Famine See IRISH FAMINE.

Great Reform Act (or Bill) See REFORM ACTS.

great seal

The symbol for authenticating royal orders. A great seal has been designed for each sovereign since Edward the Confessor. At the end of a reign, the old seal is broken as the new one is prepared. A round, double-sided metal casting, it is used to imprint the design in the melted wax appended to a document: a WRIT, a PROCLAMATION, a royal letter, or a treaty. The seal is kept by the LORD CHANCELLOR, and the use of the seal is directed by means of a WARRANT with the king's or queen's PRIVY SEAL or the SIGNET.

Greene, (Henry) Graham (1904–1991)
novelist

Born in Berkhamstead, Greene studied at Balliol College, OXFORD UNIVERSITY. He worked as a journalist, and his early work included an account of his travel across Liberia, *Journey Without Maps* (1936); and a study of the church in Mexico in the 1930s, *Lawless Roads* (1939). A political reporter and film reviewer, Greene found ample material for his fiction in his daily work. His first success was the historical thriller *The Man Within* (1926). He found even more success with themes of crime and politics: *Brighton Rock* (1938), *The Power and the Glory*

(1940), *The Heart of the Matter* (1948), *The Third Man* (1949), *The Honorary Consul* (1973), and *Monsignor Quixote* (1982). He was also the author of nine movie scripts.

Grenville, George (1712–1770)
prime minister, 1763–1765

Grenville was elected to PARLIAMENT in 1741, was a lord of the ADMIRALTY in 1744, and served in the government of his brother-in-law, William PITT. After Pitt's resignation he remained as first lord of the admiralty. In 1763 he was picked as the successor to Lord BUTE as first lord of the TREASURY, or PRIME MINISTER. But there was a suspicion that Bute was still being consulted by GEORGE III, who disliked Grenville. Soon after the passage of the STAMP ACT (1765), Grenville was dismissed. His policies of more strict fiscal management were widely supported, but he lost power due to friction with the king.

Gresham, Thomas (1519–1579)
financier

Gresham was a LONDON merchant who was engaged in the cloth trade and adept in international finance. He became ambassador to the Netherlands (1559) and helped arrange loans to the Crown from Flemish merchants. He established the ROYAL EXCHANGE in London in 1566; endowed Gresham College there (1575); and, having no children, gave his wealth to other charitable uses. He is often credited with "Gresham's Law," the saying that bad money drives out good.

Grey, Charles Grey, second earl (1764–1845)
prime minister, 1830–1834

A WHIG political leader, Grey was an ally of Charles James FOX and a longtime supporter of parliamentary reform. He was a member of the FRIENDS OF THE PEOPLE, and he introduced a FRANCHISE reform bill in 1797. These early measures were futile, as was the Whig opposition generally until the 1820s. When the duke of WELLINGTON refused to consider parliamentary reform in 1830, WILLIAM IV invited Grey to form a government. His first reform bill was defeated, and he called an election, convincing the king to create enough peers for it to pass the HOUSE OF LORDS. Under this threat, the REFORM ACT passed in 1832, as did measures for SCOTLAND and IRELAND. A uniform franchise was created, allowing householders with property worth £10 to vote and eliminating a large number of ROTTEN BOROUGHS.

Grey, Sir Edward (1862–1933)
foreign secretary

A MEMBER OF PARLIAMENT since 1885, Grey was made foreign secretary in 1905, in time for a crisis in Morocco, when Germany opposed a French protectorate there. At this point, Grey reassured France in secret military staff discussions, leading the French to expect support in any future conflict with Germany. He soon obtained an ENTENTE with Russia (1907), which paralleled the earlier one with France (1904). However, on the naval arms race with Germany, he was unsuccessful in reaching any accommodation. In 1914, as WORLD WAR I loomed, the ambiguity of his policies allowed Germany to hope that GREAT BRITAIN would remain neutral and encouraged France and Russia to hope that she would be an active ally. He remained at the foreign office until 1916 and later became president of the LEAGUE OF NATIONS Union (1918) and ambassador to the United States (1919). He wrote a valuable account of British diplomacy in his memoir, *Twenty-Five Years, 1892–1916* (2 vols., 1925).

Grey, Lady Jane (1537–1554)
queen of England, 1553

The granddaughter of HENRY VIII's sister Mary, Lady Jane Grey was married to the son of the earl of NORTHUMBERLAND, adviser to EDWARD VI. Northumberland tried to retain power prior to the young king's death by arranging for him to settle the succession on her. She was proclaimed queen when Edward died, but within days she was ousted by forces loyal to MARY I, Henry's eldest child. Lady Jane was spared at first, but when further plots arose, she and her husband were executed.

Griffith, Arthur (1872–1922)
founder of Sinn Féin

A journalist and printer involved with the GAELIC revival and the Irish nationalist movement, Griffith helped to publish a weekly paper with the resonant name of *The United Irishman* (1899–1906). He founded SINN FÉIN in 1905, with the object of forming an autonomous government of IRELAND, possibly along the line of the dual monarchy in Austria-Hungary. He was elected to the DÁIL ÉIREANN in 1919, and he gave up the leadership of Sinn Féin to Eamon DE VALERA. He joined the delegation which negotiated the ANGLO-IRISH TREATY, and in 1922 he briefly held the presidency of the IRISH FREE STATE after de Valera's resignation. Griffith died of a stroke shortly before the renewed civil war broke out that summer.

Grindal, Edmund (1519–1583)
archbishop of Canterbury

Born in Cumberland, son of a farmer, Grindal went to CAMBRIDGE UNIVERSITY at age 15, and he later became a fellow of Pembroke College. By the time he was ordained, he was adopting Protestant views. He had been a chaplain to EDWARD VI, and he went into exile during the reign of MARY I. While in Germany, his Protestant beliefs were strengthened. On returning he became BISHOP OF LONDON (1559), then ARCHBISHOP of York (1570) and CANTERBURY (1575). He was unwilling to suppress the PURITAN practice of "prophesying" (meetings in which individuals made personal interpretations of scripture). For his disobedience he was suspended from office by Queen ELIZABETH I (1577).

guild

A type of voluntary association, traced from the Anglo-Saxon period, which took many different forms. Members of a PARISH formed devotional groups, and townsmen formed groups of merchants or craftsmen who joined together to regulate their economic activity. The latter controlled production, markets, and APPRENTICE-SHIPS. With time these bodies gained sufficient power to assert themselves in local government. By the 17th century the power of guilds was being challenged by the capitalist form of production. They were eventually superseded by TRADE UNIONS.

Guilford, earl of See NORTH, FREDERICK NORTH, EIGHTH BARON.

Gunpowder Plot (1605)

A group of extremist Roman Catholics were incensed by the policies of the English government under JAMES VI AND I. Led by Robert Catesby, the group planned to destroy the entire government by blowing up the HOUSE OF LORDS while the king was attending the opening of PARLIAMENT. They put 30 barrels of gunpowder in a cellar under the house, and they planned to have the explosion signal a rebellion in the country. Their plans were exposed, however, and the plotters were arrested, tortured, and executed.

See also FAWKES, GUY.

Gurkha

A ruling clan in NEPAL who engaged the British in battle in the early 19th century and successfully defended their homeland. Impressed by their valor and fighting ability, the British recruited Gurkhas to fight in the British ARMY. They did so, both in INDIA and in other colonies and in the two world wars of the 20th century. In 1914 there were 10 Gurkha regiments that fought in Europe, Mesopotamia, and PALESTINE. In WORLD WAR II their units fought in Europe, AFRICA, and Asia. At the time of Indian independence, some regiments went into the new Indian army, and a brigade was incorporated into the British army.

H

habeas corpus

A COMMON LAW writ, of which the opening words in Latin mean "you have the body." It was directed to SHERIFFS or other custodians, ordering them to present a prisoner before the court. By the 16th century the order was being used by common law courts to challenge detentions by other authorities. By the 17th century it was being used to contest the power of royal councillors to commit, and it was a key element in the FIVE KNIGHT'S CASE and the PETITION OF RIGHT. A statutory rule was laid down for protection against arbitrary imprisonment in the STAR CHAMBER act of 1641. A further law made rules for administering the WRIT in the Habeas Corpus Act of 1679. The writ only applied to criminal cases until it was extended to civil cases in 1816. The 19th-century reforms of MAGISTRATES' powers and procedures tended to bypass the writ in most cases, and in the 20th century it was used chiefly in cases of extradition and deportation.

Haggard, H(enry) Rider (1856–1925)
novelist

Son of a Norfolk squire, Haggard lived in SOUTH AFRICA and wrote widely on South African history and agriculture. His most popular work was in adventure stories, some 34 novels in all. His first novel, *Dawn* (1884), was followed by *King Solomon's Mines* (1885) and *She* (1887). His work incorporated African custom and myth, giving vivid pictures to an audience eager for the tales of the colonial frontier.

Haig, Douglas Haig, first earl (1861–1928)
general

Born in EDINBURGH into the well-known family of whisky distillers, Haig attended Brasenose College, OXFORD UNIVERSITY. At SANDHURST he graduated first in his class. He served in INDIA, then fought in The SUDAN and in the BOER WAR. He was with the BRITISH EXPEDITIONARY FORCE in France in 1914, fighting at Mons, the Marne, and Ypres. In 1915 he was made commander in chief of the British armies, replacing Sir John FRENCH. Haig was criticized for his leadership in the battles of the SOMME (1916) and Ypres (1917) which resulted in very heavy casualties. He led the successful campaign of 1918, but the earlier and bloodier battles of WORLD WAR I stand as his main memorial.

Hailsham, Quinton McGarel Hogg Hailsham, baron of Saint Marylebone (1907–2001)
(second viscount Halisham)
lawyer, politician

A Conservative who entered PARLIAMENT in 1938, Hailsham was a TORY social reformer who served in the cabinets of Anthony EDEN and Harold MACMILLAN. He gave up his PEERAGE (second viscount Halisham) in 1963, hoping to become party leader, but he was unsuccessful. He was made a life peer when he took the post of LORD CHANCELLOR in 1974, and he was reappointed in 1979.

Hakluyt, Richard (1551–1616)
geographer

An orphan, Hakluyt was taken in by a cousin who was a BARRISTER and grew up in Herefordshire. He attended Westminster and Christ's Church, OXFORD UNIVERSITY, where he studied geography and collected narratives of voyages. He became a major promoter of exploration and engaged in several colonizing schemes, such as Sir Walter RALEIGH's Roanoke. He published *Principall Navigations, Voiages, Traffiques and Discoveries of the English Nation* in 1589, as well as a much-enlarged version in 1598–1600.

Haldane, Richard Burdon Haldane, viscount (1856–1928)

politician

Haldane studied at Edinburgh Academy, the University of Edinburgh, and Göttingen University. He also studied at Lincoln's Inn, became a BARRISTER in 1879, and made Queen's Counsel in 1890. Elected to PARLIAMENT as a Liberal in 1885, he became secretary for war in 1905. He introduced a set of ARMY reforms, creating a general staff, reorganizing forces into a home or "territorial" force, and forming an expeditionary force. Raised to the PEERAGE in 1911, he became LORD CHANCELLOR in 1912. However, because of his fondness for Germany and for German philosophy, he was dismissed in 1915. He was chancellor again in the first LABOUR PARTY government, formed in 1924. He was also active in EDUCATION, a cofounder of the London School of Economics in 1895 and president of Birkbeck College in the University of London, 1919–28.

Hale, Sir Matthew (1609–1676)

judge, author

Born in Gloucestershire, Hale attended Magdalen Hall, OXFORD UNIVERSITY, and Lincoln's Inn. He was one of the counsel to ARCHBISHOP William LAUD and an eminent jurist who had the distinction of serving under the COMMONWEALTH OF ENGLAND and then under CHARLES II. He headed a reform commission which examined the COMMON LAW in 1652, and he became chief justice of the Court of COMMON PLEAS in 1654. He played an important role in the Convention Parliament (1660), and he was chief justice of the Court of KING'S BENCH in

1671. He was also a prolific author in the fields of science, theology, and the LAW. His legal works were mostly unpublished in his lifetime, but his *History of the Common Law* (1713) and *History of the Pleas of the Crown* (1736) were important landmarks, and he collected a great quantity of sources for medieval legal history.

Halifax, Charles Montagu, earl of (1661–1715)

politician, financier

As a lord of the TREASURY from 1692, Halifax was responsible for the introduction of the NATIONAL DEBT (1693) as part of the terms of a £1 million loan to the government. A similar loan in 1694 was the occasion for the founding of the BANK OF ENGLAND. By then Halifax was CHANCELLOR OF THE EXCHEQUER, and in 1697 he became first lord of the treasury. He was forced to resign in 1699, and he was impeached and acquitted in 1701. He returned to power under GEORGE I in 1714 but died the following year.

Halifax, Edward Frederick Lindley Wood, earl of (1881–1959)

statesman

Halifax studied at Eton and Christ Church, OXFORD UNIVERSITY, and was also a Fellow of All Souls, Oxford. He was a MEMBER OF PARLIAMENT from 1910 until 1925. As Lord Irwin he was VICEROY of INDIA (1925–31), and he had some success in discussing constitutional reform for INDIA with Mohandas GANDHI. As foreign secretary (1938–41) he was a supporter of APPEASEMENT. When Neville CHAMBERLAIN was ousted, Halifax was a candidate for PRIME MINISTER, but Winston CHURCHILL was picked instead, and he sent Halifax as ambassador to the United States (1941–46), where he was a very successful intermediary.

Halley, Edmond (1656–1742)

astronomer

The son of a wealthy London manufacturer, Halley attended St. Paul's School and Queen's College, OXFORD UNIVERSITY. A fellow of the ROYAL SOCIETY in 1678, he was its assistant secretary, 1685–93. He led a scientific expedition for the ADMIRALTY to study magnetic compass variation (1698–1700). He is best known for identifying the comet which bears his name. Observing it in 1682, he calculated that it was the same one that had been seen in 1456, 1531, and 1607, and he correctly predicted its return in 1758.

Hamilton, James, first duke of (1606–1649)
Scottish royalist

Born into one of the great landowning families in Scotland, Hamilton attended Exeter College, OXFORD UNIVERSITY. He became master of the horse (an office at Court) in 1628. He commanded British forces in Germany (1631–34) with little success. He tried to negotiate on behalf of CHARLES I with the COVENANTERS in 1638, but then and later he was suspected of treachery. Imprisoned by the king (1644–46), he later negotiated the ENGAGEMENT with the Scots, and he led the army that was defeated at Preston by Oliver CROMWELL. He was captured and executed.

Hamilton, James, fourth duke (1658–1712)
Jacobite leader

Hamilton's father was a supporter of WILLIAM III, but he remained loyal to JAMES VII AND II. He entered the Scottish parliament in 1700, and he was an advocate of the Act of Security (1704), which asserted the Scots' right to declare the successor to their throne. He then supported the motion to ask Queen ANNE to appoint commissioners to negotiate a UNION, but he later strongly opposed the terms. He was chosen as a Scottish representative peer in 1708, but had to struggle to gain admission to the HOUSE OF LORDS. He was killed in a duel in Hyde Park.

Hamilton-Gordon, George See
ABERDEEN, GEORGE HAMILTON-GORDON, EARL OF.

Hampden, John (1594–1643)
politician

Born in LONDON, Hampden was the son of a wealthy landowner. He attended Magdalen College (OXFORD UNIVERSITY) and the Inner Temple (see INNS OF COURT). He was elected to PARLIAMENT in 1621, and he became a leading opponent of CHARLES I. He was one of the FIVE KNIGHTS imprisoned for refusing to pay the king's FORCED LOAN in 1627. His refusal to pay the SHIP MONEY tax in 1635 led to a famous court case and helped to spread resistance to the tax. He played a conciliatory role at the beginning of the LONG PARLIAMENT, in debates on the GRAND REMONSTRANCE, and in opposing the IMPEACHMENT of Lord STRAFFORD. He raised a regiment to fight the king, and he was killed in a skirmish after the Battle of EDGEHILL. As a reform hero, he was the namesake of the Hampden Clubs founded by Major John CARTWRIGHT in the 1790s.

Hampton Court Conference (1604)

When JAMES VI AND I took the English throne, he had to reconcile the churches of England and Scotland. The ANGLICAN church as settled by Queen ELIZABETH I still kept BISHOPS and used ceremonies that offended PURITANS. The English Puritans believed that James, coming from PRESBYTERIAN Scotland, would be receptive to change. They addressed a petition to him, and the king summoned Puritans and bishops to meet at Hampton Court for a theological debate. James did not accept Puritans' proposals, and he was loath to do away with bishops. The conference did endorse a new translation of the Holy BIBLE, which became known as the King James Version, completed in 1611.

Hampton Court Palace

A royal palace on the Thames River near Richmond in Middlesex. Built by Cardinal Thomas WOLSEY in 1515, it was taken in 1529 by HENRY VIII, who expanded it. There are excellent examples of Tudor architecture from this period. Further major additions to the palace were made in the time of WILLIAM III, designed by Christopher WREN. GEORGE I was the last monarch to live in the palace, and in Queen VICTORIA's reign the buildings were opened to the public. Parts of the palace were seriously damaged by fire in 1986.

Handel, George Frederick (1685–1759)
composer

Born in Saxony, Handel was the court composer for GEORGE I when the latter was Elector of HANOVER. In 1710 he came to LONDON, where he composed 35 operas, a number of oratorios (including his *Messiah,* 1741), and two orchestral works for the royal court: *Water Music* (1717) and *Music for the Royal Fireworks* (1749).

Hankey, Maurice Pascal Alers Hankey, first baron (1877–1963)
cabinet secretary

Hankey was born in Biarritz; his father became a sheep farmer in Australia. He attended Rugby School and the Royal Naval College, he served as a naval intelligence officer, and then became secretary to the Committee of IMPERIAL DEFENCE (1912–38). Working in the War Cabinet in 1916, he helped create the CABINET secretariat, the structure of which was carried over into peacetime government. This was the first formally organized administrative staff for the cabinet, and Hankey continued to serve there until 1938. Meanwhile he had also been secretary to the British delegation to the Paris Peace Conference (1919), and he served in the same capacity at many of the major interwar conferences. Hankey also worked in the wartime cabinets from 1939 to 1942. He published several works based on his experience: *Government Control in War* (1945); *Diplomacy by Conference* (1946); *The Science and Art of Government* (1951); and his much-edited WORLD WAR I memoirs, appearing in two volumes in 1961: *The Supreme Command, 1914–1918.*

Hanover

A German state, also known as Brunswick-Lüneberg, granted electoral status within the Holy Roman Empire in 1705. A century earlier, Elizabeth, the daughter of JAMES VI AND I of ENGLAND, had married Prince Frederick, the Elector Palatine. Their daughter Sophia married the Elector of Hanover, and their son was GEORGE I. The Act of SETTLEMENT (1701), which vested the succession in this family, placed many restrictions on the monarch: PARLIAMENT had to approve any war in aid of Hanover, no Germans were to be appointed to British offices, and the king's visits to his homeland were to be approved by Parliament. The dynastic tie with a small continental state was a dubious asset for the British, and its major contribution was to enable the passing of the Crown to a Protestant heir.

Hansard family (1752–1828)
printers

Born in Norwich, Luke Hansard established a printing business in LONDON, and in 1774 he began to print the *Journals of the House of Commons.* His son Thomas (1776–1833) took over the printing of parliamentary debates for William COBBETT, and he was a codefendant with Cobbett on SEDITION charges, for which he was imprisoned. At this point Cobbett was forced to sell the debate publication business to Hansard. The firm maintained the work for a century, but in 1909 the HOUSE OF COMMONS shifted to an official report of the debates, prepared by the stationery office. The name "Hansard" is still used to refer to the series.

Hanway, Jonas (1712–1786)
philanthropist

A merchant in Portugal, then with the Russia Company, Hanway published accounts of his travels, and he founded the Marine Society (1756), which trained poor boys to become sailors. In 1758 he became a governor of the Foundling Hospital, and he helped to found the Magdalen Hospital for penitent prostitutes. He supported a number of other causes, including providing wet-nurses for parish children, protecting chimney sweeps, and promoting prison reforms and SUNDAY SCHOOLS.

Harcourt, Sir William (1827–1904)
politician

A BARRISTER and a leading figure in the LIBERAL PARTY, Harcourt served in PARLIAMENT from 1868 to 1898. He was home secretary under William GLADSTONE (1880–85), and he was also CHANCELLOR OF THE EXCHEQUER in 1886 and 1892–95. In the latter period he was famous for the introduction of death duties (inheritance tax) in 1894, when he used the unduly alarming words: "We are all socialists now!"

Hardie, (James) Keir (1856–1915)
Labour leader

A coal miner as a child in Lanarkshire, Hardie was expelled as an agitator and blacklisted by the mine owners. He became the secretary of the Scottish Miners' Federation in 1886, and the next year he headed the Scottish Labour Party. Elected to PARLIAMENT as an independent Labour candidate in 1892, he founded the INDEPENDENT LABOUR PARTY in 1893. He helped to organize the Labour Representation Committee in 1900, and in 1906 he became the first leader of the LABOUR PARTY.

Hardy, Thomas (1840–1928)
novelist

Born into a family of stonemasons, Hardy trained as an architect, but his true craft was writing. His novels were set in his native Dorset ("Wessex" in the books). His major works were *Under the Greenwood Tree* (1872), *Far From the Madding Crowd* (1874), *Tess of the D'Urbervilles* (1891), and *Jude the Obscure* (1895). His books gained a hostile reception, and he returned to poetry, where his artistry was even more evident. He produced eight volumes of poetry and over 40 short stories.

Hargreaves, James (1720–1778)
inventor

A craftsman and weaver in Lancashire, Hargreaves who invented the spinning jenny (1764). His device allowed a spinner to produce several threads at once. Hand spinners were alarmed at this change, and his house was attacked by an angry mob. His patent for the machine was ruled illegal because he sold several models prior to seeking the patent. This innovation was the first of many that were instrumental in England's INDUSTRIAL REVOLUTION.

Harley, Robert, first earl of Oxford (1661–1724)
prime minister, 1710–1714

From Herefordshire, Harley was a student at a DISSENTING ACADEMY. His first election to PARLIAMENT was in 1689. At first a supporter of the WHIGS, he switched his allegiance at the accession of Queen ANNE. He was made SPEAKER OF THE HOUSE (1702–05), became SECRETARY OF STATE (1704–08), and then was chancellor and lord treasurer (1710–14). In 1713 he negotiated the treaty of UTRECHT with France. He was suspected of sympathizing with the JACOBITES, and he was impeached and imprisoned for two years, but eventually he was acquitted. He had a large collection of books and manuscripts, and the Harleian collection became part of the nucleus of the BRITISH MUSEUM library.

Harmsworth, Alfred See NORTHCLIFFE, ALFRED HARMSWORTH, VISCOUNT.

Harmsworth, Harold See ROTHERMERE, HAROLD HARMSWORTH, VISCOUNT.

Harrington, James (1611–1677)
philosopher

Born into an aristocratic family, Harrington attended Trinity College, OXFORD UNIVERSITY. He was not involved in the CIVIL WAR, but he was a personal friend of CHARLES I. He published *The Commonwealth of Oceana* (1656), which argued that the nature of the state derived from the manner in which property was distributed within it: a single owner is an absolute monarch, a small group produces a tight aristocratic order, and a large body of landowners ought to be governed by a republic. Harrington also formed the Rota Club, a forum for political discussion.

Harris, Arthur Travers (1892–1984)
Royal Air Force commander

As the head of ROYAL AIR FORCE bomber command, he pushed for strategic bombing of Germany during WORLD WAR II. His nickname "Bomber" Harris denoted his fanatical commitment to what was known as "area bombing," i.e., the indiscriminate bombing of military and civilian targets with the goal of demoralizing the enemy. The most frightful example was the bombing of Dresden, which took an estimated 100,000 lives. After the war, Harris was not honored as other military leaders were, because of the growing odium attached to his tactics, although they had been supported by many while the fighting was going on, and in any event he had been following government policy.

Harrison, John (1693–1776)
clockmaker

The son of a carpenter in Barrow-on-Humber, Harrison learned about clocks by repairing them. He began making clocks with his brother, trying to build more and more precise mechanisms. When he heard of the great prize (£20,000) created by PARLIAMENT for the most accurate measurement of longitude, he set to work devising frictionless parts for a clock that was seaworthy. He obtained a LONDON patron and submitted his designs to the Board of Longitude while continuing to work on perfecting his designs. Many years later he was finally, grudgingly, awarded the prize, but not without the direct intervention of GEORGE III.

Hartington, Spencer Cavendish, marquis of (1833–1908)
politician

Heir of the duke of Devonshire, Hartington was known for most of his career by his courtesy title, Marquis of Hartington. He sat in the HOUSE OF COMMONS for most of the period from 1857 to 1891 and served as secretary for war and SECRETARY OF STATE for INDIA in LIBERAL PARTY cabinets. He was briefly the leader of the Liberals (1875–80), but he opposed William GLADSTONE over IRISH HOME RULE in 1886 and was one of the leaders of the LIBERAL UNIONISTS who broke from the party over this issue.

Harvey, William (1578–1657)
physician

Harvey was born in Folkestone to a wealthy merchant. After King's School, Canterbury, he attended Caius College, CAMBRIDGE UNIVERSITY. Later he studied in Padua, Italy, and he became physician to JAMES VI AND I. He was also at the court of CHARLES I. His dissections and anatomical studies proved the circulation of the blood, which he explained in *De Motu Cordis* (1628). He also studied embryology and developed a theory of the gestation of animals from eggs.

Haselrig, Sir Arthur (1600–1661)
politician

A staunch PURITAN, Haselrig denounced the king's ministers Lord STAFFORD and William LAUD in the House of Commons. One of the five MPs CHARLES I tried to arrest in 1642, he was a successful commander of rebel forces, but he became alienated during the PROTECTORATE. He helped with the RESTORATION, but he was arrested and died in the TOWER OF LONDON.

Hastings, Warren (1732–1818)
colonial administrator

Born in Oxfordshire, Hastings was orphaned at an early age. His uncle sent him to school, and he joined the EAST INDIA COMPANY in 1750. In

1772 he was appointed governor of BENGAL and the next year he became the first governor-general of INDIA. He was responsible for many administrative and legal reforms, and he also dealt harshly with a number of enemies. On his return to ENGLAND he faced charges of murder and extortion, and he was impeached in 1788. The trial lasted until 1795, when he was acquitted, but by then he was impoverished, though he was made a privy councillor and received other honors.

Hawking, Stephen (1942–)
physicist

An outstanding figure in theoretical physics, Hawking is afflicted with motor neuron disease and uses a voice synthesizer. His project has been to join quantum mechanics and relativity theory to explain "black holes" and the "big bang." His major work was *The Large Scale Structure of Space-Time,* with G. F. R. Ellis (1973). A shorter book, *A Brief History of Time* (1988), was an international best-seller.

Hawkins, Sir John (1532–1595)
sailor

A merchant and shipowner, Hawkins began the English SLAVE TRADE (1562), violating the laws of Spain which barred foreigners from trade in their empire. Later a MEMBER OF PARLIAMENT and a NAVY official, he was also an efficient and gallant commander in the fleet that defeated the Spanish ARMADA. He died on an expedition to the WEST INDIES.

Hazlitt, William (1778–1830)
essayist

Born in Maidstone, the son of an Irish Unitarian minister, Hazlitt trained first for the ministry and then tried his hand as a painter. He found his true vocation as a writer—critic, travel writer, and biographer. He was theatre critic for *The Times* in 1816. He also wrote *Characters of Shakespeare's Plays* (1817), *Lectures on English Poets* (1818), *English Comic Writers* (1819), and *Dramatic Literature of the Age of Elizabeth* (1821).

Heath, Sir Edward (1916–)
prime minister, 1970–1974

Born into a lower-middle-class family with no political background, Heath found his calling when he became president of the Union at OXFORD UNIVERSITY. He entered the HOUSE OF COMMONS in 1950 and became chief WHIP by 1955. He was a TORY who supported social reform and advocated European unity. In 1965 he was elected to the CONSERVATIVE PARTY leadership, the first such election in the party's history. He won the general election of 1970 but immediately faced a major crisis in NORTHERN IRELAND, a serious clash with the miners union, and the OPEC oil embargo of 1973. The main achievement of his government was the entry into the EUROPEAN ECONOMIC COMMUNITY in 1973, although this was an issue on which there were divisions in both major parties. The Conservatives lost two general elections in 1974, and in 1975 Heath was ousted as leader and replaced by Margaret THATCHER.

Henderson, Arthur (1863–1935)
Labour politician

Born in Glasgow and raised in poverty, Henderson was nine years old when his father, a laborer, died. An apprentice at age 12, he converted to METHODISM, which was a powerful force in his career. Elected to PARLIAMENT in 1903 as a candidate of the Labour Representation Committee, he was one of the organizers of the first parliamentary LABOUR PARTY, serving as chief WHIP (1906–14) and as party secretary (1911–34). He joined Herbert ASQUITH's government in 1915 and became a member of the War Cabinet in 1916. He helped to draft the constitution of the Labour Party in 1918, and he served as foreign secretary in the Labour government of 1929–31. He was chairman of the World Disarmament Conference under the auspices of the LEAGUE OF NATIONS in 1932.

Henry IV (1367–1413)
king of England, 1399–1413

Known as Henry Bolingbroke, he was banished by RICHARD II in 1398. The next year, when Henry's father, John of Gaunt, died, the king seized his estates. In order to reclaim his patrimony, Bolingbroke returned to England, defeated Richard, and took the throne as Henry IV. The new reign was troubled with rebellions and financial weakness. The revolt of Owen GLENDOWER in WALES, aided by the Percys of Northumberland (former supporters of Henry), caused intermittent fighting for nearly a decade. The king's declining health and his son Henry's ambition marked his last years.

Henry V (1387–1422)
king of England, 1413–1422

The son of HENRY IV became PRINCE OF WALES in 1400, and he was deeply involved in the warfare which kept that principality in the control of the Crown. He gained experience in the royal council to the point where he may have tried to exercise too much authority in his father's last years. After his coronation as Henry V, he planned and carried out an impressive invasion of France in order to reassert the claims to that throne. He captured the port of Harfleur and won the famous victory of AGINCOURT in 1415. He had control of the north of France, and after conquering Normandy in 1419, he gained his objective in the Treaty of TROYES in 1420: he was recognized as heir to the French throne, and he married the daughter of King Charles VI of France, Catherine of Valois. However, soon after, still campaigning, he fell victim to dysentery and died. A heroic figure to the English, he promoted the use of the native language, the worship of English saints, and the exalting of national identity.

Henry VI (1421–1471)
king of England, 1422–1461, 1470–1471

The infant son of HENRY V and Catherine of Valois became king of ENGLAND at the age of nine months upon his father's death. When his maternal grandfather died a month later, he was proclaimed king of France. Henry VI would manage to lose both crowns in the course of a bizarre half-century. He had little of the martial or governing skills of his father, he was beset by conflicts between his advisers, and he suffered from bouts of insanity. His first major defeat was in France, where his coronation in 1431 was no match for the appearance of the Maid of Orleans, Joan of Arc, who inspired a French revival. Meanwhile the factions in his court feuded over policy and patronage and squandered England's position on the continent. By 1453 they had lost Normandy and Aquitaine, and the HUNDRED YEARS' WAR was over. At this low point, the king lost his sanity, and Richard, duke of YORK, asserted a claim to be lord protector. He was soon ousted, beginning the long-running duel known as the Wars of the ROSES (1455–71, 1485). After the Yorkist victory in 1461, Henry was deposed by EDWARD IV, was restored briefly in 1470, and captured in 1471 and murdered.

Henry VII (1457–1509)
king of England, 1485–1509

Henry TUDOR was the son of Edmund, earl of Richmond, and Margaret BEAUFORT. He spent part of his early life in WALES, the land of his father, and part in exile in France. His weak claim to the throne, through his mother's descent from EDWARD III, was made stronger by the treachery of RICHARD III and the elimination of eligible royal heirs. He led a small force from France to Wales in 1485, and upon entering ENGLAND he defeated Richard at the Battle of BOSWORTH and seized the Crown. He had to put down pretenders to his title (Lambert SIMNEL and Perkin WARBECK), but by the end of the century, with two male heirs of his own, he had established the Tudor family on the English throne. Henry was an able and efficient ruler, shrewd in finance and diplomacy. He married his eldest son to CATHERINE OF ARAGON, thus sealing an alliance with Spain, Europe's strongest power. He brought the Welsh into a close alliance with England and married his daughter Margaret to JAMES IV of SCOTLAND, thus bringing a union of BRITAIN closer than it had ever been. When his son Arthur died, he arranged for the Spanish marriage to be renewed by his second son, HENRY VIII. He also left an unprecedented surplus in the royal treasury.

Henry VIII (1491–1547)
king of England, 1509–1547; king of Ireland, 1541–1547

The second son of Henry TUDOR was a total contrast to his father: outgoing, brash, and energetic, he saw himself as a RENAISSANCE prince. He did fulfill his father's wish that he marry his brother's widow CATHERINE OF ARAGON, but he pursued costly and wasteful foreign adventures which HENRY VII would have deemed pointless. Henry saw ENGLAND as a rival to the powers of France and Spain, and he pursued policies designed to fulfill that image. He fought with France (1512), defeated a Scots invasion (1513), negotiated a treaty in 1518 that appeared to ratify England's power, and made a sham alliance with France (1520). In much of this his trusted and able adviser was Thomas Cardinal WOLSEY. It was he who became the king's agent in the next diplomatic enterprise: the quest for annulment of Henry's marriage. As an experienced ecclesiastical politician, Wolsey should have been able to gain what many aristocrats often needed—a convenient clerical license to remarry. However, Catherine's nephew, Charles V, was the Holy Roman Emperor, and his army was then occupying Rome. His presence made any papal action against Catherine unthinkable. This proved to be an insuperable obstacle for Wolsey, and thus he was dismissed (1529) and replaced by his secretary Thomas CROMWELL. The ENGLISH REFORMATION began as Henry pursued his romance with Anne BOLEYN, and he ordered the clergy in England to be brought under his firm control, so as to enforce the unilateral decision to divorce his wife.

Henry's marital history became the most scandalous feature of his reign. Anne was his wife for only three years (1533–36) before she was accused of adultery and executed. Jane SEYMOUR (1537) bore him the son he so desperately wanted, but she died in childbirth. ANNE OF CLEVES (1540) proved to be unattractive and was rejected. Catherine HOWARD (1540–42) was also unfaithful and shortlived. Catherine PARR married Henry, was a comfort to him in his last years, and died in 1548, one year after him.

Henry's three children all came to the throne: EDWARD VI (1547–53), MARY I (1553–58), and ELIZABETH I (1558–1603). Their religious differences emphasized the impact of the peculiar REFORMATION under their father. Henry was a loyal son of the church into the 1520s. He was not inclined to accept any reform theology beyond the assertion of his ROYAL SUPREMACY in the church in England. So he only reluctantly endorsed the issue of articles of religion, the translation of the scriptures, and the alteration of the liturgy. It was his son (and his advisers) who propelled the Protestant cause, his eldest daughter who tried to restore the Catholic faith and church government, and his second daughter who tried to strike some balance between royal government and Protestant belief.

Henry's other achievement was to alter the form and power of royal government. Cromwell was one engineer of this transformation. The DISSOLUTION was one exercise of a royal administration becoming more comprehensive and centralized. The royal NAVY was in its early formative stage, and the conduct of PARLIAMENT was altered by the king's decision to involve it in the creation of his supremacy. Finally, as the strongest ruler in the British Isles, Henry tried to cement English control over its neighbors. He succeeded in annexing WALES by statutes (1536, 1543) which brought it into the English parliamentary structure and introduced English laws. He planned a dynastic marriage between Edward and Mary of SCOTLAND (later MARY, QUEEN OF SCOTS), which did not occur, though he invaded Scotland in an effort to enforce his will. He also had himself proclaimed king of IRELAND (1541) after a period of rebellion and reaction to his antipapal policies. Thus he advanced by force the policy pursued diplomatically by

HENRY VII, a policy which showed that England was ready to assert its primacy over the whole of the archipelago.

Hepburn, James   See BOTHWELL, JAMES HEPBURN, EARL OF.

Hertford, earl of   See SOMERSET, EDWARD SEYMOUR, EARL OF HERTFORD AND DUKE OF.

High Commission, ecclesiastical courts of

The power of the royal PREROGATIVE was used to issue COMMISSIONS to enforce clerical discipline in the 16th century. In 1559 this power was recognized in statute, and it was exercised in individual dioceses and in the provinces of CANTERBURY and York. The latter became regular courts, using secret proceedings, oaths *ex officio* (where one was compelled to answer), and no juries. Known as ecclesiastical courts of High Commission, they were denounced by common lawyers in the 17th century and abolished in 1641.

See also COURTS OF LAW; ECCLESIASTICAL COURTS.

High Court of Justice

The title of the combined courts created under the JUDICATURE ACT of 1873. The High Court of Justice included the courts of CHANCERY, COMMON PLEAS, KING'S BENCH, EXCHEQUER, ADMIRALTY, probate, divorce, and the London court of bankruptcy. At first the court was arranged in several divisions, out of respect for tradition, but the court's jurisdiction was unified, and each judge could act in any division. Together with the Court of APPEAL and the CROWN COURT, they constitute the Supreme Court of Judicature. Ironically, the court created by the army and the RUMP PARLIAMENT which tried CHARLES I for treason in January 1649 was also known as the High Court of Justice.

See also COURTS OF LAW.

High Court of Justiciary

The highest criminal court in SCOTLAND was formally established in 1672. It took over the work which had been done previously by judiciaries and irregularly appointed royal commissioners. The new court consisted of seven judges: the lord justice general, the lord justice clerk, and five lords of session. In 1830 the lord president of the Court of SESSION was designated to succeed the lord justice general, merging the two highest offices of the College of Justice. In 1887 a law provided that all lords of session would be lords commissioners of justiciary. The court has general criminal jurisdiction, and it hears criminal appeals. There is no appeal beyond this court in Scottish criminal law.

See also COURTS OF LAW.

Highland clearances

The clearances were evictions or forced removals of large numbers of the Gaelic-speaking population of the Scottish Highlands in the 18th and 19th centuries. This agrarian society had large estates that were leased to middlemen (tacksmen) who in turn collected rents from the poor farmworkers. In the decade before the AMERICAN REVOLUTION, large numbers of these workers immigrated to North America rather than pay high rents. A generation later, as sheep-farming spread widely, lowland farmers acquired large holdings and, particularly on the holdings of the countess of Sutherland in the far north, forced poor tenants to leave their land, resettling them on small holdings (crofts) on the coast, where they eked out a living gathering kelp (seaweed) and raising a few animals. In the later 19th century more Highland estates were cleared to open land for deer hunting.

See also CROFTER, HIGHLANDS.

Highlands

Geographically the Highlands occupy the area west of the line connecting the Clyde estuary and the town of Stonehaven on the east coast of SCOTLAND. Historically the interior portion of that zone, plus the Hebrides, constituted a GAELIC cultural and linguistic community, with political and social structures provided by CLANS into the 18th century. After the rebellion of the JACOBITES in 1745, acts were passed ordering the disarming of the clans, prohibiting the wearing of clan tartans, and abolishing old heritable jurisdictions. Large-scale forfeiture of estates and transformation of LAND use uprooted the old society. In the last quarter of the century, with higher rents and consolidation of holdings, many people were evicted or chose to emigrate. These "clearances" continued into the 19th century, with the extension of sheep farming and large hunting estates. All of these movements contributed to the growth of the CROFTER population.

See also CULLODEN, BATTLE OF; FORBES, DUNCAN; HIGHLAND CLEARANCES; SHERIFF.

Hill, Octavia (1838–1912)
reformer

The daughter of a banker who lost his fortune in the crash of 1840, Hill worked in a shop and developed business skills. She joined with Christian Socialists to create better housing for the poor. With a loan from John RUSKIN she purchased slum properties in LONDON, and with close supervision and reinvested income, she created some 6,000 homes. She also campaigned for preservation of open space, and to that end she cofounded the NATIONAL TRUST in 1895.

Hill, Sir Rowland (1795–1879)
inventor of the penny post

The son of a Unitarian schoolmaster in Birmingham, Hill and his brothers created and taught a modern curriculum in a school with small, separate classes. An inventor and administrator, he proposed a postal system based on prepayment at standard rates, with the use of adhesive stamps. His system was implemented in 1840, and he was put in charge, but he was removed from office because of disputes with his staff. He returned in 1846 as secretary to the postmaster general, in which post he remained until 1864.

Hillary, Sir Edmund (1919–1995)
mountaineer

Born in NEW ZEALAND and experienced in climbing in the Himalayas, Hillary was part of a 1953 expedition to climb Mt. Everest. He and Sherpa Tenzing were selected to make the final stage of the climb, becoming the first men to ascend the world's highest mountain.

Hitchcock, Alfred (1899–1980)
film director

Born in LONDON, Hitchcock worked in many jobs in film before becoming a director. He made the first British talking picture, *Blackmail,* in 1929. His trademark was the thriller, and some early examples were *The Man Who Knew Too Much*

Alfred Hitchcock *(Hulton/Archive)*

(1934) and *The 39 Steps* (1935). He went to the United States in 1939 under contract with David O. Selznick. His early American films included *Rebecca* (1940), *Shadow of a Doubt* (1942), and *Strangers on a Train* (1951). The height of his career came with *Rear Window* and *To Catch a Thief* (both 1954), *Vertigo* (1957), *North by Northwest* (1959), and *Psycho* (1960).

Hoadly, Benjamin (1676–1761)
churchman

The son of a schoolmaster, Hoadly became a Fellow of Catherine Hall, CAMBRIDGE UNIVERSITY. One of the more outspoken low-church divines of the early 18th century, he was attacked by Francis ATTERBURY for advocating the right to resist rulers. Hoadly was appointed a royal chaplain and later made BISHOP of Bangor. His view that private conscience was more powerful than episcopal authority so incensed the high-church party that it caused furious debate in the church CONVOCATION, leading to the dismissal of that body. He went on to several other bishoprics (Hereford, Salisbury, and Winchester), having no trouble accepting the fruits of an established order which he belittled.

Hoare, Samuel John Gurney, See
TEMPLEWOOD, SAMUEL JOHN GURNEY HOARE, FIRST VISCOUNT.

Hobbes, Thomas (1588–1679)
philosopher

Born in Wiltshire, the son of a clergyman, Hobbes was educated at OXFORD UNIVERSITY. He traveled on the continent as a tutor to the future earl of Devonshire, William Cavendish. On his travels he met Galileo and Descartes. He was in exile in Paris during the CIVIL WAR (1640–1650). His famous *Leviathan* was published in London in 1651, in which he held that human nature was essentially brutal, and the only security could be found in granting absolute power to a governor. He was thus not surprised by the events of the INTERREGNUM. After returning to ENGLAND in 1651, Hobbes remained and was given a royal pension after the RESTORATION.

Hobhouse, John Cam (1786–1869)
politician, writer

Hobhouse was a radical, friend and traveling companion of Lord BYRON, and MEMBER OF PARLIAMENT from 1820 to 1851. He was secretary at war (1832), chief secretary of IRELAND (1833), and president of the India Board (1835–41), which maintained liaison between the government and the EAST INDIA COMPANY. He is credited with coining the phrase "His Majesty's Loyal Opposition." He wrote *Recollections of a Long Life* (1865).

Hobson, John Atkinson (1858–1940)
economist

Hobson's father was a newspaper editor in Derby. He studied at OXFORD UNIVERSITY and then taught school, but inherited wealth enabled him to become a full-time writer. His work was well ahead of its time. In 1889 he wrote *The Physiology of Industry,* with A. F. Mummery. This work tried to undermine LAISSEZ FAIRE economics by pointing to tendencies to overproduction and unemployment. His further argument was that industrial states compensated for their economic weaknesses by aggressive imperial schemes. This analysis was presented in his *Imperialism: A Study* (1902).

Hogarth, William (1697–1764)
artist

Hogarth's family was from the north of ENGLAND, but he was raised in poor circumstances in LONDON, and his early life gave intense feeling to his work. He learned engraving and produced many of his own satirical and moral paintings, which works were extremely influential. His *Harlot's Progress* (1732), *A Rake's Progress* (1733–35), and *Marriage a la Mode* (1743–45) were biting commentaries on contemporary society. *Gin Lane* (1751) was an important contribution to the awareness of the problem of excessive gin consumption.

Holinshed, Raphael (1520–1581)
chronicler
Probably born in Cheshire, Holinshed worked in LONDON as a translator for a printer, Reginald Wolfe, who was preparing a *Universal History.* When Wolfe died, Holinshed finished the work, changing the title to *Chronicles of England, Scotlande, and Irelande* (1577). His work was not critical and contained a multitude of fanciful as well as accurate materials. A later and larger edition in 1587 proved a valuable source for playwrights like William SHAKESPEARE.

Holland, Henry Fox, baron (1705–1774)
politician
Fox entered PARLIAMENT in 1738; he became secretary for war (1746–54), SECRETARY OF STATE (1755–56), and paymaster general (1757–65). His experience and positions enabled him to become a master of political patronage and a very wealthy man. His cynical manipulation of power was typical of the old WHIGS, despised by GEORGE III and seen as corrupt by the new generation of politicians, which included his son Charles James FOX.

Holles, Denzil, baron (1599–1680)
politician
A MEMBER OF PARLIAMENT and opponent of CHARLES I and the duke of BUCKINGHAM, Holles was one of the members who restrained the SPEAKER OF THE HOUSE in 1629. He was imprisoned but was elected again in 1640. He was among the five MPs whom Charles tried to arrest in 1642, but after he fell out with the ARMY and radical leaders, he was out of political life until the RESTORATION. He was given a PEERAGE in 1661, but he drifted into the opposition

again in the 1670s. He wrote tracts on the constitutional questions of his day, including one on *The Grand Question concerning the judicature of the House of Peers* (on the case of Thomas Skinner) in 1669. His *Memoirs* were published in 1699.

Home, Alexander Frederick, 14th earl of See DOUGLAS-HOME, SIR ALEC.

Home, Henry See KAMES, HENRY HOME, LORD.

Home Office
There were two secretaries of state until 1782, dividing the functions into the Northern and Southern departments. The duties were realigned into a home office and a foreign office in that year. The home secretary is responsible for public order, a portfolio which has grown dramatically since the 19th century. Supervision of POLICE forces, prisons, civil defense, IMMIGRATION, and broadcasting have swollen a department which once had a dozen civil servants into a massive enterprise employing many thousands.

See also SECRETARY OF STATE.

home rule See DEVOLUTION; IRISH HOME RULE.

Hong Kong
The island of Hong Kong offered a valuable deep-water port which GREAT BRITAIN seized during the OPIUM WARS. The possession was ratified by treaty in 1842, and the COLONY was expanded by acquisition of the Kowloon peninsula and the New Territories. The latter were leased for 99 years from the government of China in 1898. By the later 20th century, Hong Kong had become an extremely wealthy commercial and industrial center. When the colony's lease was due to expire, arrangements were made to return all of the territories to the People's Republic of China in 1997.

Hood, Samuel (1724–1816)

Admiral

Hood's father was the rector of a PARISH in Somerset. Both Hood and his brother Alexander were sent to sea in 1741, and both would become admirals. Samuel served in the SEVEN YEARS' WAR, and in 1767 he was made commander in chief on the North American station. In the 1770s he was stationed at Portsmouth and later had commands in the Battle of the Chesapeake (1781) and at Toulon (1793) and Corsica (1794). He also sat in PARLIAMENT for Westminster and was a lord of the ADMIRALTY (1788).

Hooke, Robert (1635–1703)

scientist

Son of a clergyman in the Isle of Wight, Hooke attended Westminster School and OXFORD UNIVERSITY. In 1665 he published *Micrographia,* a work on the nature of combustion. He invented marine barometers and was the first to use a spiral spring to regulate watches. He was the curator of the ROYAL SOCIETY, became the Surveyor of LONDON in 1667, and worked with Robert BOYLE on gases and Sir Isaac NEWTON on optics and astronomy.

Hooker, Richard (1554–1600)

theologian

Hooker was born in Exeter to a family with modest means. With the help of the BISHOP of Salisbury, he went to Corpus Christi College, OXFORD UNIVERSITY, and he became a fellow of the college in 1577. His great work, *The Laws of Ecclesiastical Polity,* was composed near the end of his life; the first part was published in 1593. This work was a stout defense of the Episcopal order against the independent claims of PURITANS. Hooker described the Elizabethan state as a joint community in which church and state were under the authority of the monarch, subject to the consent of the people, as embodied in the laws, civil and ecclesiastical. They were derived from the law of God, as interpreted by human reason.

House of Commons

The first parliaments were not divided into "houses." They were meetings of the king's great council (see HOUSE OF LORDS) which were from time to time supplemented by members chosen from the communities (i.e., "commons") of shires (see COUNTY) and then BOROUGHS in the 13th century. The summons to attend a PARLIAMENT was a burden, for the main task that awaited the members was to approve measures of TAXATION. That function, however, gave the commons their special and increasingly important role. They met separately, at first by reason of their marginal role in matters of state, and increasingly because they found added strength in their representative function. The group elected a SPEAKER OF THE HOUSE from 1376, though he was for several centuries a servant of the Crown, not the legislature. In 1547 they were given St. Stephen's Chapel in Westminster for their meetings, and the house began to record its proceedings in a continuous *Journal.* In that same generation, HENRY VIII inadvertently enhanced the power of Parliament by using it to endorse the reform of the church and to adjust (many times) the royal succession. But still the members were not free to resist the power of the Crown. That only came about as a result of the struggles of the 17th century. The STUART monarchs held themselves above Parliament, but they were not able to govern without the fiscal support of the legislature. As a result, after the long parliamentary absence of 1629–40, the CIVIL WAR of 1642–50, and the *coup d'etat* of 1688–89, Parliament won the right to free speech, free and frequent elections, and control over taxation. The last power fell particularly to the Commons, where it had been *de facto* for a long time and by 1700 was clearly its province alone.

In the 18th century the Commons played a part in further development of the CABINET system and the place of the PRIME MINISTER, as Robert WALPOLE (in the 1730s and '40s) and William PITT (in the 1780s and '90s) sought the support of majorities in the lower chamber as their authority to lead the country. As the turn of the century came, that authority was sullied

Houses of Parliament, London, England *(Library of Congress)*

by the archaic and corrupt nature of the electoral FRANCHISE. ROTTEN BOROUGHS—those that sent MPs who had either bought their place or were given it by a patron—had clearly become a political machine from an earlier time. By 1832 the demand for reform was met by creating a uniform borough franchise (one for the counties had existed since 1429). The idea of property ownership still held sway as a basis for the vote, and it was expanded in 1867 and 1884.

Only in 1918 did the vote become a right belonging to all adult citizens. By that time the superior place of the House of Commons in the constitution had been recognized. In 1910 the House of Lords had rejected a BUDGET, an act which had not been attempted since the later 17th century. This violation of convention created a crisis, two elections were held, and the governing LIBERAL PARTY emerged with the narrowest of majorities. Now the government advanced a plan to reform the Lords, formally denying them power to veto money bills and limiting them to two vetoes of any other bill. The Parliament Act of 1911 thus gave superior power to the House of Commons. The next major development saw the power of the Commons come more and more under the control of ministers, due to wartime centralization and to political party organization. Individual MPs had once been able to propose and obtain important legislative acts. That ceased to be the case during the 19th century. The nature of business and the complexity of modern industrial society account for some of the change. Other changes stem from a more centralized, bureaucratic state and the existence of two very powerful centralized political parties.

The size of the House of Commons fluctuated considerably over 700 years, but the ratio of members to the total population fell dramatically. In 1295 there were about 290 members; in 1510 there were 296, but the size swelled to 469 in 1601 and 551 in 1689. Although 45 Scottish members were added in 1707, the total in 1790 was just 558. Union with IRELAND in 1801 added 100 members, and the total in 1900 was 670. At the end of the 20th century it was 630. This number represented a population of 58 million, compared with an estimated 3 million in 1300.

See also ACT OF PARLIAMENT; MEMBER OF PARLIAMENT; REFORM ACTS.

House of Lords

The king's council and the nobility of the realm were often called to meet with the sovereign. It was out of these meetings that the idea of a PARLIAMENT grew, so called when it was enhanced by the attendance of commoners. There was no distinct "house" of lords, and even the phrase was not used until there was a separate meeting place for the HOUSE OF COMMONS. The members of this ephemeral house were those of the PEERAGE who had been summoned individually by the king, including the BISHOPS and ARCHBISHOPS (the spiritual peers). Their numbers were relatively small: as few as 50 in the early TUDOR period, rising to 220 by the end of the 17th century. The House of Lords was briefly abolished, 1649–60. The Lords surrendered the power of TAXATION shortly after they were restored, but they retained the power to influence the election of MPs, to control the PRIVY COUNCIL and the later CABINET, and to manage the legislative agenda. After the RESTORATION, a flood of petitions came to the Lords and triggered the growth of judicial appeals, and the house became the nation's highest appellate court. Thus, a major share of power remained with the Lords, at least until the 19th century.

Scottish representative peers (16) were added by the Act of UNION of 1707; Irish representative peers (32) were added in the Act of Union of 1801. Life peerages were introduced for appellate judges (1876) and extended to laymen in 1958. But as the numbers of peers increased (590 in 1900; over 1,000 in 1970; and 1,290 in 1999), their powers diminished. The Parliament Act of 1911 took away any role in money bills and limited the Lords to two "suspensive" vetos (the third successive passage of a bill by the Commons meant it would become law). The latter was changed to a one-year delay in 1949. Consequently, for most of the 20th century the Lords have become a senior advisory and debating chamber. The greatest indignity was perhaps the recognition that the PRIME MINISTER could no longer sit there. The last peer to be prime minister was Lord SALISBURY, who left office in 1902. When Lord CURZON seemed the obvious candidate for the post (1923), he was passed over. When Lord Home (Alec DOUGLAS-HOME) was chosen in 1963, he had to renounce his title before taking office. The final indignity was the proposal to abolish the House of Lords, made by the LABOUR PARTY government of Tony BLAIR in 1997. The process of abolition began by reducing the peers' numbers in 1999, and the main issue of what might replace the house remained in limbo at the beginning of the new millenium.

JUDICIAL COMMITTEE

Whatever happens to the legislative function of the house, there will undoubtedly be a continuing appellate body which functions in the legal system (see COURTS OF LAW). Originally, the house had several specific legal powers: to adjudge peerage claims, to hear charges against peers for treason or felony, and to sit as a court in IMPEACHMENTS. The house also had become the court for hearing writs of error from COMMON LAW courts. This power broadened in the late 17th century, when the house took appeals from the Court of CHANCERY (1660s) and then from the Scottish Court of SESSION (1709) and from the courts in IRELAND (1720). This appellate power became more cumbersome by the 19th century, due to a large quantity of Scottish appeals. In addition, by the 1840s it was established that lay peers could not vote on appeals. Only the LORD CHANCELLOR, who presided in the house, and fellow judges who sat there were expected to deliberate. Due to a shortage of qualified peers, there was an attempt to create a life peerage for a judge in 1856. This was rebuffed by the house, but in 1876 an act allowed the creation of two lords of appeal with life peerages. The number of law lords has increased, and the house now divides them into committees to hear civil and criminal appeals. The lords' decisions were formerly held to bind the lords themselves (*stare decisis*) but this was overruled in 1966.

Howard, Catherine (1521–1542)
queen of England

The niece of Thomas HOWARD, the duke of Norfolk, Catherine Howard was the fifth wife of HENRY VIII. After their marriage in 1540 there were rumors of her adultery, and she confessed to prenuptial unchastity. Those implicated with her were arrested, two were sentenced to death, and she and her cousin, Lady Rochford, were convicted by act of ATTAINDER and beheaded in the TOWER OF LONDON.

Howard, Charles   See NOTTINGHAM, CHARLES HOWARD, FIRST EARL OF.

Howard, Henry   See SURREY, HENRY HOWARD, EARL OF.

Howard, John (1726–1790)
prison reformer

As the high SHERIFF of Bedfordshire, Howard was disturbed by the conditions of confinement and the treatment of prisoners by their jailers. He tried to convince his fellow MAGISTRATES to pay a salary to jailers instead of letting them extort fees from the prisoners, but his idea was too radical. He compiled a report on *The State of the Prisons of England and Wales* in 1777 which served as a prime mover for prison reform. He

made many journeys and surveyed conditions elsewhere. He died after he was stricken with jail fever on a tour in Russia.

Howard, Thomas   See NORFOLK, THOMAS HOWARD, THIRD DUKE OF.

Howard, William, baron (1510–1573)
admiral

Howard conducted diplomatic missions to SCOTLAND and to France in the 1530s. He was convicted of concealing the treason of his niece Catherine HOWARD but was pardoned. As lord high admiral under MARY I, he helped put down Thomas WYATT's rebellion in 1554. He subsequently served ELIZABETH I as lord chamberlain (1558–72).

Howe, Richard (1726–1799)
admiral

The son of an Irish peer, Howe went to sea at 14 and sailed in George ANSON's circumnavigation. He was a key figure in the American Revolution with his brother William HOWE. He was unable to subdue the American privateers, and when France joined the rebels, British naval superiority was threatened. In addition to his service at sea, he sat as a MEMBER OF PARLIAMENT for Dartmouth (1758–82) and served as first lord of the ADMIRALTY (1783–88). He was the commander at the "Glorious First of June" victory over the French in the English Channel (1794), and he played a major role in ending the SPITHEAD MUTINY in 1797.

Howe, William (1729–1814)
general

The brother of Richard HOWE, William Howe served in several military campaigns and was a MEMBER OF PARLIAMENT for Nottingham (1758–80). He served in the SEVEN YEARS' WAR, returned to the AMERICAN COLONIES, and took part in the Battle of BUNKER HILL (1775). He was made commander in

1775, and took New York and Philadelphia. He resigned after General BURGOYNE lost the Battle of Saratoga (1778). He and his brother sought and obtained a parliamentary inquiry into the conduct of the war.

Hume, David (1711–1776)
philosopher

Hume was born in EDINBURGH and attended the university there. Though from a PRESBYTERIAN background, he became noted for his scepticism and his empiricism, which probably kept him from academic appointments. He was librarian for the Faculty of Advocates (1751–63) and he traveled extensively in ENGLAND and France. He wrote *Treatise of Human Nature* (1739–40) and *Enquiry Concerning Human Understanding* (1748), which gave him a solid claim as a leader of the Scottish ENLIGHTENMENT. He also wrote *History of England* (1754–62), the work that gave him the greatest notoriety in his own time.

Hume, David (1757–1838)
professor of law

The nephew of the philosopher of the same name, Hume was an advocate and professor of Scots Law at EDINBURGH University (1786–1822). His *Commentaries on the Law of Scotland Respecting Crimes* (1797–1800) was the first major treatise on that subject since the 17th century. He based it on research in the records of the High Court of JUSTICIARY, and it remains a classic in Scottish criminal law. His *Lectures* on the laws of SCOTLAND (published by the Stair Society in six volumes, 1939–58) gave a vivid picture of contemporary law and practice. Hume was later a judge of the Scottish Court of Exchequer, and he published a collection of *Reports of Decisions*, 1781–1822.

Hume, Joseph (1777–1855)
radical politician

Hume was very young when his father, a Scottish seaman, died. His mother worked as a shop-keeper to raise the children, and he was apprenticed to a surgeon-apothecary at age 12. Later he went to INDIA as a surgeon with the EAST INDIA COMPANY, and there he earned enough to start a political career. A follower of Jeremy BENTHAM, he sat in PARLIAMENT between 1812 and 1855 and was a tireless advocate of REFORM ACTS. Although he was first elected as a TORY, he supported a broad array of reform ideas: extension of the vote, repeal of the COMBINATION ACTS, CATHOLIC EMANCIPATION, FREE TRADE, and reduction of government spending were all very high on his list. When he shifted his allegiance to the radicals (ca. 1818) he represented various Scottish BURGHS in Parliament.

Hundred Years' War (1337–1453)

The term is applied to the intermittent warfare between ENGLAND and France from 1337 to 1453. The expression was first used in the later 19th century, and it has become the conventional, if inaccurate, label for periodic invasions by which English rulers from EDWARD III on sought to assert a claim to the throne of France.

The main line of succession to the French throne was broken in 1328, but it was only in 1340 that Edward asserted his modest claim through his mother Isabel of France. He was prompted to do so by the confiscation of Gascony and French threats to his interests in Flanders. The first phase of fighting saw notable English victories at Sluys (1340) and Crécy (1346), and the crushing defeat at Poitiers (1356), where the French king was captured and held for ransom.

French revival began by 1370, with victories over RICHARD II leading to a treaty and two decades of peace after 1396. In the new century, France experienced a civil war, and the conditions invited the aggressive campaign of HENRY V, who won the Battle of Agincourt (1415) and went on to secure the Treaty of TROYES (1420), which recognized him as the heir to the French throne. Henry's death in 1422 passed the claim to his infant son, and HENRY VI was crowned in Paris in 1431. But the final French recovery had already begun, with the heroic relief of the siege of Orleans by Joan of Arc in 1429. Between 1450 and 1453 the English were driven out of Gascony and Normandy, amid the escalating domestic turmoil in England that preceded the Wars of the ROSES. One way of viewing this long and tortuous experience is that an English state, taken by the Normans in 1066, had been a rival to the French monarch as overlord of various dominions on the continent, and only such a long and complex struggle could resolve the contest. In the end, England lost all continental holdings except CALAIS, which was controlled by the Crown until 1558. Although English kings continued to style themselves "king of France" until 1802, England was henceforth a government which had to focus on its island territories.

Hunt, Henry (1773–1835)
radical politician

A gentleman farmer from Wiltshire who became one of the most important figures in the struggle for FRANCHISE reform, Hunt was in favor of universal suffrage and the ballot. He emerged as a prominent figure in the post-Napoleonic period and a main speaker at the mass demonstrations at SPA FIELDS in 1816 and 1817. He presided at the meeting in St. Peter's Fields near Manchester in 1819 (see PETERLOO MASSACRE) and was imprisoned for two and a half years as a result. Known as the "Orator," Hunt was a formidable agitator, who believed that the power of large public demonstrations would force the government to accept reform. Ironically, when he himself entered PARLIAMENT (1830–33), he could not support the reform bill of 1832, a measure which, he correctly observed, did nothing for the working class.

Huskisson, William (1770–1830)
Liberal Tory

The son of a squire in Warwickshire, Huskisson went to live with a relative in Paris because his family's means were limited. He became private secretary to Lord Gower, the ambassador, and returned when he was recalled in 1792. He was made under secretary for war in 1795, before his election to PARLIAMENT in 1796. He became an advocate of FREE TRADE, and his most important work was at the BOARD OF TRADE in the 1820s, where he promoted the reform of the CORN LAWS, the opening of colonial trade, and relaxation of the NAVIGATION ACTS. He attended the opening of the Liverpool-to-Manchester railway in 1830 and was tragically run down by the locomotive, the *Rocket*.

husting

A platform constructed for a parliamentary election, from which candidates would address the electors, and upon which the SHERIFF or other officers would take the poll. In the event that the voice vote was not conclusive, each voter would come forward and declare his choice (until the BALLOT ACT in 1872). The term *hustings,* in common usage, came to stand for election proceedings in general.

Huxley, Aldous (1894–1963)
novelist, mystic

The grandson of T. H. HUXLEY, Aldous Huxley graduated with distinction from OXFORD UNIVERSITY, and he published a volume of poems in 1917. His early novels *Crome Yellow* (1921) and *Antic Hay* (1923) addressed the conditions of postwar Britain. His more important works were *Point Counter Point* (1928) and *Brave New World* (1932). Later works included *Apes and Essence* (1948), *Devils of Loudoun* (1952) and his utopian *Island* (1962).

Huxley, T(homas) H(enry) (1825–1895)
zoologist

A prominent Victorian scientist who studied medicine and served as a naval surgeon, Huxley became famous as the defender of Charles DARWIN's *Origin of Species.* In one notable debate at OXFORD UNIVERSITY with Bishop Wilberforce, he said he would rather be descended from an ape than from a BISHOP. Huxley coined the term "agnostic" as a way of describing his own religious beliefs.

Hyde, Edward   See CLARENDON, EDWARD HYDE, EARL OF.

Hyndman, Henry   (1842–1921)
socialist

A wealthy businessman and heir to a West Indian fortune, Hyndman was a convert to Marxism. He composed a summary of *Das Kapital* that he called *England For All* (1881), and he convened a conference to form what became the SOCIAL DEMOCRATIC FEDERATION. Karl MARX himself was not pleased that Hyndman failed to acknowledge his authorship of the ideas that were now being touted to English would-be socialists. The federation was but one of the vocal bodies of intellectual socialists that, with others like the FABIAN SOCIETY, joined with the trade unionists to form the Labour Representation Committee in 1900 and begin the electoral construction of a workingman's socialist political party.

I

immigration

For most of its early history, Britain was inhabited by large numbers of immigrants, and there has always been movement between parts of the British Isles and the nearby parts of the European continent. But in the modern era, when the BRITISH EMPIRE was growing in the 18th and 19th centuries, the movement of population was mainly outward, and only since the end of the empire, in the second half of the 20th century, has there been sizeable movement of former colonial peoples into GREAT BRITAIN. That has created a multiracial community in many large cities, a condition that appears to be utterly new, but in reality it is a throwback to a much earlier time.

impeachment

A trial before the HOUSE OF LORDS on articles presented by the HOUSE OF COMMONS. The method was pioneered in the 14th century in order to challenge the king's ministers. It fell into disuse but was revived in the 17th century and used on a number of occasions (1621–1710). The last cases (Warren HASTINGS, 1788, and Henry DUNDAS, 1806), like most of their predecessors, ended in acquittals. However, the accusers may have been just as interested in the intimidation which the procedure could produce as in convictions.

See also BACON, FRANCIS, VISCOUNT ST. ALBANS; CLARENDON, EDWARD HYDE, EARL OF; CRANFIELD, LIONEL; DANBY, THOMAS OSBORNE, EARL OF; LAUD, WILLIAM; SACHEVERELL, DR. HENRY; STRAFFORD, THOMAS WENTWORTH, EARL OF.

imperial conference

The idea of an imperial conference arose from a movement for closer coordination within the BRITISH EMPIRE, or an imperial federation. At Queen VICTORIA's golden JUBILEE in 1887 there was a pioneer gathering, a "colonial" conference, followed up in 1894 and 1897. At the latter, it was agreed to hold regular meetings of prime ministers. At the 1911 meeting the name was changed to "imperial conference," and at the 1926 meeting the new definition of the British Commonwealth was drafted, later incorporated in the Statute of WESTMINSTER (1931). From 1944 the meetings became Commonwealth conferences. The meetings became annual in 1969, and they were no longer exclusively in LONDON.

Imperial Defence, Committee of

The British government formed a committee (1902) to oversee strategy for the BRITISH EMPIRE. It was chaired by the PRIME MINISTER, and it recommended allocation of resources. This advisory body was absorbed by a CABINET committee in 1947. It should not be confused with the Imperial War Cabinet, a body created by David LLOYD GEORGE in 1917, which was designed to coordinate the DOMINIONS during the late stages of WORLD WAR I and the postwar peace conferences. That body was disbanded in 1918.

imperialism

The term *imperialism* developed in the later 19th century, although for ENGLAND the history behind it reaches back to the 16th century. The basic definition is extension of power over other peoples and territories; the means might be military, economic, or cultural. Victorian political leaders of all parties were enthusiastic supporters of England's mission to spread Anglo-Saxon civilization. The vehicle was powered by the economic resources of empire: raw materials, markets, and investment opportunities. The last features were harshly criticized in J. A. HOBSON's *Imperialism: A Study* (1902), which was taken further in V. I. Lenin's *Imperialism as the Highest Stage of Capitalism* (1915). The main solvent of imperialism was not Marxist ideology, though it was often invoked. The desire for independence drove more and more colonies (as it had the DOMINIONS before them) to seek self-rule. After the WORLD WAR II, the oldest of the former colonies, the United States, pressed GREAT BRITAIN to allow the process to accelerate.

imperial preference

In the 1890s some of GREAT BRITAIN's leaders were shaken by the economic problems of the Great DEPRESSION and worried by the developing naval arms race with Germany and the race for colonial power in AFRICA and Asia. Joseph CHAMBERLAIN and others felt that the policy of FREE TRADE was harming Britain's interests, and that a policy of TARIFF protection, jointly applied by the BRITISH EMPIRE, would solve their problems. The debate at first went in favor of free trade, and the LIBERAL PARTY won a huge majority in the 1906 general election. But a form of imperial preference was in fact adopted during the depression of the 1930s, and it remained the basic British policy for 40 years until Britain entered the EUROPEAN ECONOMIC COMMUNITY in 1972.

Inchiquin, Murrough O'Brien, earl of (1614–1674)
Irish soldier

An Irish Protestant commander in the CIVIL WAR, O'Brien fought for CHARLES I against the Catholic confederacy in Munster (1642–44), then switched his allegiance to PARLIAMENT. He rejoined

the royalists in 1648 and left IRELAND when Oliver CROMWELL invaded. During exile in France, he converted to the Catholic faith. He returned to Ireland in 1663.

income tax

Tax on individual income was first used in 1799, as an emergency wartime measure, and it was abolished in 1816. As TARIFFS were reduced, and the approach of FREE TRADE seemed inevitable, the income tax was revived in 1842. It was portrayed as a temporary measure, but continued expenses and changing policies assured its survival. It became a major revenue source by 1900, it was crucial to the funding of the wars of the 20th century, and by 1950 it was a critical support for the expanding WELFARE STATE.

See also TAXATION.

independent

A term to describe the opponents of the king in the 1640s. It applied to the religious reformers who rejected central authority, whether of an ANGLICAN type or even the PRESBYTERIAN order promoted by the Scots. These independents were kin to the PURITANS of Massachusetts, and were forerunners of 19th-century CONGREGATIONALISTS. The political label of independent applied to Oliver CROMWELL and many of the men in the NEW MODEL ARMY and the Council of State, who were equally suspicious of political authority.

Independent Labour Party (ILP)

In 1893 Keir HARDIE convened a conference in Bradford, Yorkshire, at which delegates from Scotland and northern England formed a workers' socialist party, called the Independent Labour Party. At this point, the only workers to be elected to PARLIAMENT had run as LIBERAL PARTY candidates (sometimes called "Lib-Labs"), and the leaders of most TRADE UNIONS were not interested in the new plan. But by 1900, as the unions lost some major court decisions (see TAFF VALE CASE), they joined with the socialists to form a

Labour Representation Committee to pool their resources and coordinate campaigning. This grouping led to the birth of the LABOUR PARTY (1906), though until 1918 the only political party through which individuals could support labor was the ILP. After membership in the Labour Party was opened, the ILP declined, and its last MEMBER OF PARLIAMENT lost his seat in 1959.

India

The home of ancient civilizations, Hindu and Buddhist, India saw waves of invasions, first from the north by Islamic rulers, notably the Mogul emperors in the 16th century. Europeans followed—Portuguese, Dutch, French, and English—during the 16th and 17th centuries. For more than three centuries the ties between GREAT BRITAIN and India were woven into a complex bond at the center of the BRITISH EMPIRE, a bond which had powerful effects in both countries. The connection was born in trade, it evolved through political transformations, and it made profound impressions on the respective cultures. The bond was finally broken by a powerful nationalist movement that brought independence, and partition, in 1947.

TRADE

The EAST INDIA COMPANY originally set out to develop trade in spices, not looking to the subcontinent until conflicts with the Dutch pushed them in that direction. Because English goods were not in demand in Asia, the early trade had to be supported by the export of bullion, in opposition to the dictates of MERCANTILISM. By the 18th century, many English merchants were making great fortunes in India, less from trade than from their dealings with local princes. The pattern of trade soon involved China, with opium and other goods from India, for tea and other Chinese exports to Britain. The great expansion in British cotton production found a ready market in 18th century India, and in the next century a series of industrial exports, notably railroad construction, offered further profits for British investors, and employment for Indian workers.

POLITICS

The government of India was in the hands of Mogul emperors at the beginning of the 18th century, but internal weaknesses in that empire and encroaching European power broke the subcontinent into a collection of principalities. The East India Company became a military-political organization as it expanded its activities from the trading centers of Bombay, CALCUTTA, and Madras. As the company power expanded, especially in BENGAL, the British government intervened and established a governor-general (1773) and a board of control (1784). That intervention guaranteed a continuing British interest in institutions, frontier disputes, and consolidation of power.

At the end of the 18th century, Charles CORNWALLIS became governor-general and inaugurated a number of reforms that led to the formation of the Indian Civil Service, a better-regulated body of administrators which operated in a structure with reformed revenue collection, new laws on land tenure, and a new penal code. During the early 19th century there was progressive expansion of British authority in the interior of India, and there were continuing skirmishes across the vast and rugged frontiers: in Nepal (1815); in BURMA (1823, 1856, annexation in 1886); in the AFGHAN WARS (1838, 1878, 1919); the Punjab (1845–49, leading to annexation); and in Tibet (1904).

The role of the British government grew during the 19th century. In the first place, the East India Company was brought under closer supervision, by acts limiting its authority (1784, 1813, 1833, 1853). The company's role ended in 1858, after the INDIAN MUTINY. From that point it was the direct responsibility of the British government to manage the affairs of the COLONY. This was not something easily done, as the colorful creation of Queen VICTORIA's title "Empress of India" seemed to imply. A long series of attempts were made to adjust India's government, and the role of Indians in it. Councils were created (1861) and modified (1892, 1909). Reformers seemed sure that self-government would come, but no one knew how or when.

CULTURE

The biggest stumbling block to progress was a cultural chasm that blocked the path to political reform. First the elemental racial differences prevented most British in India from understanding and accepting autonomy for the native peoples of India. This gap was vividly seen in the British efforts to stamp out Indian customs like *suttee* (widow burning) and *thuggee* (ritual murder). The more effective level of cultural engagement came with the English language and English-style schooling. For a deeper level of penetration, strenuous efforts were made to bring wholesale reform by an impartial legal system, with the codes of Thomas MACAULAY and James Stephen. (It should be noted that codification was never successful in ENGLAND in the 19th century; nevertheless, it was judged appropriate for India.) Another area of incomprehension which may have surpassed the rest was in the gulf in religious belief between the Christian colonizers and their Hindu, Muslim, and Buddhist hosts. It is fair to say that Europeans and Englishmen gained more understanding of these religions in the 19th century, and that while missionaries tried to convert, there were also serious students and admirers of the alien faiths. But for the vast majority of imperialists, understanding came very slowly. Finally, the cultural differences did produce varied forms of artistic and literary expression, much of it emphasizing the blending and interaction which was taking place: James MILL's *History of India* (1817) was an early attempt to comprehend the rich past of this exotic region; Rudyard KIPLING's stories and poems at the end of the century illuminated the imperial servants' work and knowledge of India and the special identity they derived from that. But at the end of the 19th century, powerful forces were beginning to change the colonial condition.

INDIAN NATIONALISM

An unauthorized Indian National Congress met in Bombay in 1885, and the idea quickly spread across other regions. The general object of the members was greater self-government, and there were slow and grudging reforms in that direction. The Indian Councils Act in 1909 brought in both Hindu and Muslim elected members. In the aftermath of WORLD WAR I and the AMRITSAR MASSACRE, 1919 saw the creation of a bicameral Indian legislature. But the move to self-rule was much too slow, and at this point Mohandas GANDHI's passive resistance campaigns greatly expanded the involvement of the population in the reform effort. The next major stage came with the Government of India Act in 1935, much delayed by resistance in PARLIAMENT and division among Indian communities. This promised a form of DOMINION status, but the slow implementation and then the advent of WORLD WAR II, allowed time for a strong separatist Muslim movement to develop. When independence came after the war in 1947, the hurried partition into India and PAKISTAN led to violent clashes between Hindus and Muslims and the deaths of as many as 500,000. The tragic end of British rule in India also marked the first successful colonial independence movement in the 20th century.

The new states, with Pakistan being divided into West and East Pakistan (the latter became BANGLADESH in 1971), decided to remain within the British Commonwealth, and when they were later declared republics, that membership was continued.

Indian Mutiny (1857–1858)

In what appeared to be a violent reaction to westernizing influence, soldiers in the army of India mutinied in 1857 at Meerut, and the revolt spread to Delhi and other parts of BENGAL. A Mogul emperor was proclaimed, and English colonists were captured and massacred, but there were sufficient loyal army units to put down the rebels by July 1858. Within weeks the government of INDIA was transferred to the Crown. The EAST INDIA COMPANY was stripped of its authority, and a new secretary of state for India was created to govern the COLONY.

Industrial Revolution

This term was coined in the 19th century to describe the massive changes that transformed the British economy and society from the middle of the 18th century on. For some reason or reasons, this process happened first in GREAT BRITAIN and then spread to Europe and America. The possible explanations are that a fairly advanced system of finance with banking and credit existed beside a well-developed trade network and colonial markets, and at home there was the right combination of raw materials, especially coal, iron, and wool. A number of other characteristics have been cited (enterprise connected with nonconformity, stability of political regime) but whatever predisposed Britain to this modernizing change, there is more agreement about what it was. There have been many ways of presenting the elements of industrial development, but any explanation must take account of the roles of power, capital, and transportation.

The use of coal, whether in the coking process, which produced better iron, or in the fuel for the steam engine (first used to pump out mines, later as a power source for looms and locomotives) captures the sense of the industrial transformation. The development of fuel-driven engines was a slow and erratic process. The early mine engines were at work in 1710, the first power loom only went into operation in 1806, the locomotive in 1830. Nevertheless they each used this new source of energy, which seemed to have unbounded potential.

The other "engine" that drove industry was the accumulated capital (from farming, finance, and most of all commerce) which was invested in factories. The new power and new production methods (spinning, weaving, engineering) required new workplaces of a size and structure unknown outside of a few older operations (mines, shipyards, breweries). The most dramatic change was from the cottage spinner to the large cotton factory, but the pattern was applied many times over, and it required investment on a large scale.

The final element in this equation was transport—that is, the ability to move the product to markets and a capacity to move the workers to the new workplace. There were connected transport revolutions in the 18th and 19th centuries: a canal-building boom beginning in the 1770s brought new waterways for the shipment of heavy cargoes from most points of production to the ports of Britain. There soon followed rapid improvement and expansion of ROADS, especially turnpike roads. These served to move goods and people more efficiently by about 1800. It was much later, around 1840, that a boom in railroad building began, and an entirely new, power-driven transport revolution propelled the industrial era further. The movement of workers came from displaced agricultural workers and from IMMIGRATION, mainly from IRELAND.

The impact of industry was felt in many ways. In society it had the twin results of fostering a larger middle class and a newly conscious working class. The latter was exploited in many of the new factories, but at the same time, industrial concentrations helped workers to form groups that could eventually exercise greater influence, whether in unions or in other efforts like the COOPERATIVE MOVEMENT. In social geography, industry transformed whole regions of Britain: the Clyde around Glasgow, the midlands of England around Manchester and Birmingham, and the region of South WALES all were radically changed from agrarian to urban-industrial communities. These shifts had positive and negative effects, and sometimes those were interdependent. The affected areas all experienced great increases in wealth and population. Many also suffered the consequences of rapid growth and intermittent economic distress. The new cities had neighborhoods which were the worst slums imaginable, but those conditions attracted sufficient concern to cause reformers to campaign for public health measures, and these produced significant advances in that area by 1850.

injunction

In church affairs, an instruction to the clergy from the Crown or BISHOPS regarding visitation or more general conduct (the latter were used especially in the 16th century). In secular courts, an injunction is an order to perform or desist from an act; it may be temporary or permanent.

Inns of Court

Collegiate institutions in medieval LONDON, where lawyers lived and worked. They became the central training and licensing bodies for BARRISTERS. Only a small number of the original inns survive: Middle Temple, Inner Temple, Lincoln's Inn, and Gray's Inn. They are unincorporated bodies controlled by the senior members, or benchers.

inquest

An inquiry, always held by a coroner, to determine the cause of a death. Typically held before a jury, witnesses are called to give evidence, and the resulting findings are held to be a judicial decision. This does not prevent the findings being overturned by subsequent legal action.

Instrument of Government (1653)

The constitution drafted by the Council of State which reconstituted the government, creating the PROTECTORATE of Oliver CROMWELL. He was designated Lord Protector, and he governed with elected PARLIAMENTS which had members from ENGLAND, WALES, SCOTLAND, and IRELAND.

interregnum

The term *interregnum* is used to denote a period of interrupted monarchic rule. The best-known example in English history was the period from the execution of CHARLES I and the abolition of the monarchy (1649) to the RESTORATION of CHARLES II in 1660. Monarchists believed that the eldest son inherited the title and position of the father at the moment of the sovereign's death. Therefore, Charles II dated all his acts as if the first year of his reign were 1649. Implicit in this practice, and in the term *interregnum,* is a denial of any legitimacy to the rule of those who usurped royal power.

Intolerable Acts (1774)

These laws, passed after the Boston Tea Party closed the port of Boston until there was compensation for the tea destroyed, revoked the charter of Massachusetts, allowed the quartering of British troops in the COLONY, and provided for trials of British troops outside the colony.

Ireland

The history of Ireland is often told in terms of the English occupation, but it is clear that an ancient civilization occupied Ireland before the Romans built their empire, and the Irish developed unhindered until the arrival of the Anglo-Normans in the 12th century. Those 16 or 17 centuries were much longer than the period of English invasion and occupation, and many would argue that the period of Ireland's early autonomy was far more significant in European and world history. This sketch begins with that period and then traces the main stages of the English occupation, with highlights treated in detail afterward.

CELTIC IRELAND

CELTS had entered the British Isles centuries before the Romans, and Celtic Ireland was untouched by that later invasion, at least in military and political terms. Indeed, the Celts were part of a well-developed civilization, one which had spread to central Europe, to Gaul, and to the Iberian peninsula. Celtic peoples had mastered the use of iron, and they had applied that to their warrior culture, developing weapons and chariots. Their culture was tribal and pastoral, their gods were of human form and superhuman abilities. Though illiterate, their bards and lawmen kept an oral tradition that recorded their genealogies, history, and tribal customs.

There may have been missionaries who reached Ireland before St. Patrick, but his work and his life are so well-recorded and revered that he deserves to be identified with the foundation of Christian Ireland. A young boy who was captured in BRITAIN and enslaved in Ireland, he escaped and went to the continent to study, was ordained, and vowed to return and save the souls of his captors. Sometime in the fifth century he reached Ireland, and he succeeded in converting many and in establishing a highly successful mission church, reputedly based at Armagh. A century later there were missions from Ireland to northern Britain, and the establishment of the monastery of Iona by St. Columba (563) was followed by mission work among the Picts and Scots and the establishment of the monastery at Lindisfarne (634), whence came several bishops of the church in Northumbria. It is in this period that Irish legend and history were first transcribed by monks who preserved a great deal of classical culture. This was retransmitted along with their knowledge of Christian tradition, in the course of their later missions, both to Britain and to the continent.

At the end of the eighth century the same monasteries that were the pride of the Celtic church became the first targets of the deadly assaults of the Norsemen. The Viking raiders were only interested in plunder on these raids, but it was not long before others had landed on the Irish coast and settled, creating trading towns in DUBLIN, Limerick, Wexford, Waterford, and Cork. In the 10th century there was a joint kingdom of Dublin and York, which only lasted for a generation. In the early 11th century at the famous Battle of Clontarf (1014), the Irish high-king was killed, but the Norsemen were defeated and confined to their coastal towns.

MEDIEVAL IRELAND

Two years after Clontarf, LONDON fell to the Danes, and ENGLAND became part of a short-lived Danish Empire, only to be succeeded by the Norman Conquest a half century later. These events had little immediate impact in Ireland. The Norman influence in England created a geopolitical orientation to the east, toward France. Indeed,

the Normans had created garrisons on the Welsh border, making that the limit of their westward expansion. A century after the conquest, though, an Irish king sought aid from Henry II and inadvertently began the process of English conquest. Dermot McMurrough (king of Leinster) petitioned Henry for aid, and he was allowed to solicit help from some of the king's vassals. One of them, the earl of Pembroke (alias Strongbow), fought for Dermot and was promised the title to Dermot's kingdom. This prospect was too alarming to the English king, who led an army to Ireland in 1171 to discipline his wayward vassal. Henry also brought a papal bull which gave him the lordship of Ireland. He received the submission of his English vassals and of most of the Irish rulers.

The actual "conquest" of Ireland took place over the next four centuries, and for much of that time the progress was invisible. Henry had received pledges from the Irish rulers and had recognized their subordinate authority in quasi-feudal terms. Henry's son John was made "lord of Ireland," and as such he visited in 1185 (he went again as King in 1210), and there were formal extensions of English law and legal procedures. Meanwhile, a process of colonization had begun, with eager lords and GENTRY seeking estates on the cheap. Much of Ireland appeared to be under English control by 1300. However, the next two centuries saw a considerable recession in that control, with a remarkable resurgence of Irish culture and an absorption of the colonists into it. This was not supposed to happen. In 1366 the Statutes of KILKENNY ordered the English not to use the Irish language or to intermarry or to allow the Irish into any church properties or patronage or to deal in horses or armor with the Irish or even to play Irish games. The fear of cultural assimilation was clear in these laws; their efficacy in retarding the process is doubtful. After another century, the only part of Ireland under the control of the king's deputy was the PALE, a territory around Dublin, which varied in size, but by 1500 it extended about 50 miles north of Dublin and 30 miles inland. Furthermore, a deputy like Gerald FITZGERALD, earl of Kildare (1457–1513), was often a law unto himself. It was this shrunken area that the Irish PARLIAMENT, which passed POYNINGS' LAWS in 1494 (taking effect in 1495), was representing.

EARLY MODERN IRELAND

The tide began to turn with the reign of HENRY VIII. The futile revolt of Silken Thomas FITZGERALD (1513–1537) and the extension of the king's reformed church brought major changes, symbolized by Henry's creation of the title "King of Ireland" in 1541. English power was hereafter exercised much more vigorously, through PLANTATION of colonists, military campaigns, and administrative control. But Ireland remained impossible to govern as an English province. The majority support for the Catholic Church; the alienated aristocrats who found allies in Rome, in Spain, and in other parts of the British Isles; and the widespread resistance to many measures of colonial government boiled over during the period of CIVIL WAR in England. The rebellion in ULSTER in 1641 pushed the English crisis into armed conflict, and the fighting in Ireland, especially Oliver CROMWELL's campaign of 1649, was some of the bloodiest of the period. The particular significance for Ireland was that many English soldiers were promised grants of Irish LAND as payment for their fighting; as one leader put it, they needed another Ireland to have enough land to fulfill all the promises.

Between 1660 and 1690 there were further convulsions as the English Crown became a prize in the battle between Protestant and Catholic claimants. The result for Ireland was another invasion and the imposition of a stronger Protestant regime. This time the government used the infamous PENAL LAWS to support Protestants against their Catholic neighbors, barring them from land ownership, schooling, and other rights. The government of Ireland was the preserve of Protestants and their English sponsors. A LORD LIEUTENANT, a PARLIAMENT, a set of COURTS OF LAW, and an established church were all copies of the English model, but they were operated in Ireland by and for the Anglo-Irish minority. Yet even this privileged class felt oppressed by English colonial rule, and in the wake of rebellion in America, they pressed for and obtained a degree of autonomy: Poynings' laws were repealed, the DECLARATORY ACT of 1720 was repealed, and the Irish parliament enjoyed 20 years of something like autonomy (1782–1800). This era was marked by a rising demand for more freedom, both from colonial rule and from the power of the landed aristocracy. The UNITED IRISHMEN joined others, influenced by revolutionary ideas from France, to begin a long period of radical and violent resistance to English rule. The first major explosion came in 1798. A disorganized series of uprisings ended with many Irishmen dead, many more in prison, and a firmer union being forged with Britain: the UNITED KINGDOM of GREAT BRITAIN and Ireland, which came into existence in 1801.

MODERN IRELAND

The new structure incorporated the Irish into the British Parliament, but otherwise left institutions in Ireland much as they had been. In other words, a colonial executive, colonial courts, and a colonial church were operating beside a joint legislature managed by an imperial cabinet. More important, since the late 18th century the penal regime had been crumbling. Catholics were freed of many penal restrictions (1778), allowed to vote (1793), and finally, by 1829, allowed to sit in Parliament. After achieving this "emancipation," Daniel O'CONNELL formed a large successor organization aimed at repeal of the Act of UNION. He managed to rouse wide support for this effort, but it was blunted by demographic disaster. The most profound event of the 19th century was the IRISH FAMINE. When more than a million people died (1845–50) because of the successive failures of the potato crop (1846–48), the whole society suffered a massive blow. Its effects were seen in several stark facts: emigration rose and stayed high for the rest of the century, the population declined from over 8 million to about 4 million by the end of the century, and the total failure to provide elementary security fundamentally damaged the government's credibility. The responses came in the form of radical outbursts by YOUNG IRELAND (1848) and by the FENIAN BROTHERHOOD (1867); lawful political organization for IRISH HOME RULE (from 1870); and a mixture of violent and peaceful efforts to change the structure and economy of Irish land (see IRISH LAND ACTS).

The debate over Irish Home Rule occupied the British parliament for almost half a century. The consequences were quite far-reaching. Charles PARNELL organized his supporters well enough to be able to filibuster and disrupt proceedings in the HOUSE OF COMMONS. This led to the adoption of means to cut off debate, known as the "guillotine," which shocked contemporaries. The alliance between Parnell and Michael DAVITT of the Land League seemed to be giving terrorists a role in politics. This was vividly portrayed by the Phoenix Park murders of 1882, when the chief secretary and his under secretary were killed in broad daylight by a group calling themselves the "Invincibles." The killers were never found, but their actions were taken as a symbol of the depths Irish radicals might reach. Some years later there was a scandal when *The Times* claimed to have letters proving that Parnell was linked to the crime—letters which turned out to be forged. But a real scandal developed shortly afterward: Parnell had been living with another man's wife, and the effect of this revelation and the ensuing divorce proceeding ruined his career and severely shook the leadership of his movement.

More important to Ireland's future was the increasing commitment to reform the system and the structure of Irish landholding. By the 1880s there was a general acceptance that land law needed reform, and out of that came a series of Irish Land Acts to provide subsidies to tenant farmers to help them to buy land from their landlords. This brought a major shift by the early 20th century, and the absentee English landowner began to disappear as a figure on the Irish scene. He was replaced by another factor in the years before the war.

There was serious opposition to Home Rule in the province of ULSTER, the nine northeastern counties that were heavily PROTESTANT in composition. The resistance to constitutional reform

had been evident from the time of the first Irish Home Rule bill in 1886, and opinion was only more inflamed as the cause of Home Rule seemed to move closer to realization. In 1912 a new Home Rule bill was likely to become law, because the HOUSE OF LORDS could not stop it, due to the ACT OF PARLIAMENT of 1911. Therefore, Sir Edward CARSON and others organized the Ulster Volunteers and promoted the signing of the ULSTER COVENANT (1912). Their activity included shipping arms to Ulster, drilling units of volunteers, and forming what appeared to be a rebellious organization, one which some ARMY officers at the Curragh army station were going to refuse to fight. War in Europe intervened in 1914, and home rule was put on hold; and when fighting did come over home rule, it came to the South. The EASTER REBELLION in 1916 was a failure, but it ignited a larger movement for separation. The election of 1918 was a victory for SINN FÉIN and independence, though the civil war (1919–21) brought a DOMINION government in the form of the IRISH FREE STATE.

The British government had passed a Government of Ireland Act in 1920, which anticipated the partition of Ireland into southern and northern regions. While the civil war went on in the south, political leaders in the north took steps to consolidate their position, and King George V went to Belfast in 1921 to preside over the opening of the parliament of Northern Ireland, making the division of the country more permanent.

After the government of the Irish Free State defeated its internal rivals, it had to pull together the divided community of the 26 southern counties of Ireland. That process was accelerated in the 1930s, and in 1937 a new constitution was adopted for a virtual republic, one that was officially proclaimed in 1948. The leader of this movement was Eamon DE VALERA, a hero of 1916, leader of the provisional government in 1919, but an enemy of the 1921 ANGLO-IRISH TREATY who only returned to normal politics in 1926.

Ireland's break with Britain was epitomized by her decision to be neutral in WORLD WAR II. This decision was highly unpopular in Britain, as was the continued activity, albeit low profile, of the IRISH REPUBLICAN ARMY. But in 1969 the questions that had been ignored for 50 years were suddenly revived. Should Ireland continue to be partitioned? Should British troops serve in Ireland? Was the British commitment to the North really firm? There were nearly 30 years of terrorist violence in Ulster, and a ceasefire reached in the late 1990s was meant to be the start of renewed, interdenominational, peaceful "dominion" government. Meanwhile, the republic had matured, its constitution and institutions were well established, its role in Europe advancing with membership in the EUROPEAN ECONOMIC COMMUNITY in 1972, and its official view of partition making it a vital partner in the accommodations reached in the late 1990s.

Ireton, Henry (1611–1651)
soldier

Born in Nottinghamshire, to a PURITAN GENTRY family, Ireton went to Trinity College, OXFORD UNIVERSITY, and to the Middle Temple (see INNS OF COURT). The son-in-law of Oliver CROMWELL, he fought at EDGEHILL and Newbury, and he commanded cavalry at the Battle of NASEBY. He played a major role at the Putney Debates in 1647, defending the side of the landowners against the radicals. He signed the death warrant of CHARLES I, and he accompanied Cromwell during his campaign in IRELAND, remaining there as his deputy. He died during the siege of Limerick.

Irish Famine

The population of IRELAND grew rapidly in the early 19th century, passing 8 million in 1840. The agricultural laborer was heavily dependent on the potato, a highly efficient food source for the small plot which supported a typical family. In 1845 a deadly fungus destroyed three-quarters of the crop, causing great distress; but in 1846 there was a total crop failure, and most of the seed potatoes for the next year were eaten. In 1847 the area planted was reduced from 2 million acres to about 300,000, and so the harvest was far too small. Then in 1848 there was

another general failure. These disastrous years saw over 1 million die from starvation and disease, and a larger number emigrated. There were strenuous government efforts at relief, with public-works projects and soup kitchens which fed up to 3 million a day in 1847. But these efforts were insufficient. Lower birth rates and continued emigration meant a declining Irish population until the 1920s. The famine also produced a searing indictment of British rule.

Irish Free State

In order to quell the violence of the postwar years, the ANGLO-IRISH TREATY of 1921 reached an agreement between the British government and the leaders of the Irish resistance. The IRISH FREE STATE was constituted as a DOMINION of the Crown, with its own political institutions and virtual independence. This was not enough for the more radical republicans, and the anti-treaty forces fought against the new government. The fighting lasted for over a year, and the more conservative forces won. The new government, covering 26 counties of IRELAND, was inclined to conservative social policy, protectionist economics, and GAELIC revival. Nonetheless, much of the English-style institutional framework was retained. The return of Eamon DE VALERA to politics in the 1926 brought a keener edge to Irish constitutional issues. The Free State was effectively terminated by the adoption of a new republican constitution in 1937, which declared EIRE to be a "sovereign, independent democratic state." The formal end of the Free State came with the Republic of Ireland Act of 1948.

Irish Home Rule

The main strand of constitutional opposition to British rule in IRELAND comes under the heading of home rule. In contrast to the radical designs of YOUNG IRELAND or the FENIAN BROTHERHOOD, the home-rule objective was always a form of autonomy under imperial rule, more or less a DOMINION solution. In 1870 the Protestant BARRISTER and politician Isaac BUTT founded the

Home Government Association, which became the Home Rule League in 1873. Increasing numbers of Irish MPs backed the effort, which gained support after the BALLOT ACT of 1872, and even more strength during the economic crisis of the later 1870s. In that setting, Charles Stewart PARNELL emerged as a more effective leader, uniting with the radical Land League and taking more assertive positions in PARLIAMENT. Parnell was implicated in many episodes of agrarian violence, but his strategy seemed successful when William GLADSTONE introduced a Home Rule bill in 1886. That measure failed, as did another in 1893. The third bill came after the crisis of the Parliament Act of 1911, but it was shelved in 1914. By the end of the war, two separate parliaments were foreshadowed in the Government of Ireland Act of 1920. The government of NORTHERN IRELAND was founded on this law, and the IRISH FREE STATE was the southern version, adopted in 1922 after several years of fighting.

Irish Land Acts

Landholding in IRELAND was a major source of unrest. The rights of landlords, tenant farmers, and agricultural laborers were always in competition, but in the economic and political climate of the later 19th century, the clashes became more serious. Irish tenants wanted "the three Fs"—fair rent, free sale, and fixity of tenure. They resisted arbitrary rent increases, lack of compensation for improvements they made when property was sold, and liability to sudden eviction. William GLADSTONE's government in 1870 passed an act that limited the absolute rights of landowners, but its enforcement was problematic. Fuller guarantees came in the Land Act of 1881, but by then the focus had shifted to providing subsidies to tenants so that they could buy out their landlords. This began in 1883 and was greatly extended over the next two decades. Tenants were eager to gain this kind of ownership, landlords were often eager to sell during a time of falling land values, and politicians believed that such a large transfer of ownership would blunt the IRISH HOME RULE movement.

Joseph CHAMBERLAIN called it "killing home rule with kindness."

Irish Rebellion (1798)

Under the influence of the French Revolution, the organized efforts of the UNITED IRISHMEN posed a threat to British rule, and the government responded with harsh repressive measures, especially after a failed French invasion attempt in 1796. In early 1798 there were disjointed rebel assaults in several provinces, the most serious being in Wexford, with others in ULSTER and County Mayo. By the end of the year, between 20,000 and 30,000 were dead and thousands more were arrested and interned or transported to AUSTRALIA. The British government therefore decided to form a constitutional union, the UNITED KINGDOM of 1801.

See also CORNWALLIS, CHARLES; TONE, WOLFE.

Irish Republic

The goal of the FENIAN BROTHERHOOD and their successors was achieved in the constitution of 1937 and declared in the Irish Republic Act of 1948. The effective sovereignty of the republic was made clear by its decision to remain neutral in WORLD WAR II. The Irish constitution claimed the authority to govern the whole island (articles 2 and 3), and this claim made relations between GREAT BRITAIN and IRELAND uneasy, particularly during the unrest in the North, 1969–97. However, relations were improving, as evident in the countries' joint entry into the EUROPEAN ECONOMIC COMMUNITY (1972) and the improved contacts between LONDON and DUBLIN from the 1980s, culminating in the peace agreement for NORTHERN IRELAND in 1998.

Irish Republican Army (IRA)

The IRA grew out of the Irish Volunteers, organized in 1913 to confront their northern counterparts in the IRISH HOME RULE crisis of 1911–14. After the EASTER REBELLION of 1916, triggered by dissident members of the Volunteers, the units were reorganized. In 1919 the force became the agent of the provisional government, engaged in guerilla warfare which went on until 1921. The organization split over the ANGLO-IRISH TREATY, and those who did not agree with it began a savage civil war (1922–23). The IRA revived during the troubles in the North after 1969, though at first its ineffectiveness was mocked in graffiti which said "IRA = I ran away." By the mid-1970s there was serious terrorist activity, in both NORTHERN IRELAND and GREAT BRITAIN, aimed at forcing the end of British rule. The most dangerous element called itself the Provisional IRA, and there were various splinter groups. By the 1990s the IRA had agreed to a cease-fire, and lengthy negotiations began to bring peaceful political activity, including the group's political arm SINN FÉIN. The main outstanding question was "decommissioning" of IRA arms stockpiles, which was supposed to begin under international supervision in 2000.

Isaacs, Rufus   See READING, RUFUS ISAACS, MARQUIS OF.

Isle of Man
Located in the Irish Sea, midway between IRELAND and north WALES, and only 20 miles from SCOTLAND, the Isle of Man is only 10 miles wide and 30 miles long. Settled by Norse invaders in the ninth century, its institutions bear the marks of that history. Briefly in Scottish possession (1266), it was taken by the English (1333), made a lordship of the earls of Derby (1406), purchased by the British government in 1765, and given to the Crown. Tynwald is the legislature, the lower house the House of Keys. The Manx language, a Celtic tongue, was spoken until the 19th century.

See also COURTS OF LAW.

J

Jacobites

The supporters of the deposed and exiled JAMES VII AND II, derived from the Latin for his name, "Jacobus." There was a series of uprisings on behalf of James and his heirs. The first was in SCOTLAND in 1689, ended by the Battle of KILLIECRANKIE. The next was the invasion of IRELAND under James himself (1689–91), which was halted by his defeat at the Battle of the BOYNE in 1690. In 1715, after the accession of GEORGE I, an uprising in Scotland and ENGLAND was put down. An invasion attempt in 1719 and a plot in 1722 were crushed easily. The final rebellion came in 1745, when "Bonnie Prince Charlie" (Charles Edward STUART) led a French and Scottish force on an ill-starred invasion of Northern England. Forced to retreat to the north of Scotland, he was beaten at the Battle of CULLODEN. The last of the Stuart line died in 1807.

Jamaica

Island in the WEST INDIES seized from Spain in 1655. It became a sugar colony employing large numbers of slaves. The island was also a center for pirates and legitimate traders. Significant economic problems ensued from the abolition of slavery (1833). An insurrection in 1865 was followed by savage punishments, and Governor Edward Eyre was sharply criticized but not charged with any wrongdoing. The island became independent in 1962.

James I (1394–1437)
king of Scots, 1406–1437

Captured by the English as he was being sent to safety in France (1406), James I succeeded his father Robert III, but he remained in captivity until 1424. When he did return to his realm, he introduced many new laws and new taxes. He also took vengeance on those nobles whom he thought had been disloyal. He in turn was murdered by conspirators, but he left a six-year-old son to succeed him.

James II (1430–1460)
king of Scots, 1437–1460

In his early years the young King James II was beset with rival noble factions, but in 1449 he destroyed the power of the Livingston family and over the next decade he eliminated other dangerous noblemen. An avid soldier, he was besieging Roxburgh castle in 1460 when one of his cannons exploded and killed him.

James III (1451–1488)
king of Scots, 1460–1488

During his minority (1460–69) James III married the daughter of the king of Denmark and was able to gain the lordships of ORKNEY and Shetland. He had been kidnapped by one noble family and was antagonized by others, leading to a series of conflicts in the 1480s. He was ultimately killed by a large force of angry nobles, led by his son and heir JAMES IV, at the Battle of Sauchieburn.

James IV (1473–1513)
king of Scots, 1488–1513

An aggressive and intelligent ruler, James IV was able to rule with a strong hand and to extend the power of the Crown without seriously alienating his more powerful subjects. While penitent for his crime of patricide, he earned a considerable amount of noble support for that very act. He traveled around his kingdom, bringing a much enhanced image of royal authority to many parts. He launched ill-advised invasions of ENGLAND, first in support of the pretender Perkin WARBECK in 1496 and then in the disastrous campaign which led to his death and the major defeat at the Battle of FLODDEN in 1513. In between he had married Margaret, the daughter of HENRY VII, and their infant son JAMES V succeeded him on the throne.

James V (1512–1542)
king of Scots, 1513–1542

James V's long minority was troubled by disputes between rival factions of nobles. The Scottish PARLIAMENT granted him full powers in 1524, but it took him several more years to assert his authority. He chose a French alliance over one with ENGLAND, and he married the daughter of the king of France in 1537. When she died six months later, he married the French princess, MARY OF GUISE. James worked to strengthen the Scottish kingship, creating the College of Justice in 1532, reclaiming disputed property from noblemen, and wringing revenues from the church. But despite a promising start, his reign came to a sudden end after the English defeated him at the Battle of Solway Moss in 1542. The king was not present, but he died shortly afterward of unknown causes. His two sons had died in 1541, making his infant daughter MARY, QUEEN OF SCOTS the heir to the throne.

James VI and I (1566–1625)
king of Scots, 1567–1625, and king of England and Ireland, 1603–1625

The son of MARY, QUEEN OF SCOTS and Henry, Lord DARNLEY, James was only 13 months old when his mother abdicated the throne of SCOTLAND. As a result, he endured a long minority, marked by the predictable infighting among fac-

tions at Court, intensified now by the clash between Protestants and Catholics. He was a highly intelligent young man, tutored by George BUCHANAN, who tried to teach him that kings were servants of the people. The young sovereign rebelled at this lesson, and as soon as he assumed full power, he pursued a different ideal of kingship. In 1586 he made the Treaty of Berwick with ELIZABETH I, which provided him a pension and recognized his claim to succeed her, provided he made no trouble for her. This may explain his acceptance of his mother's execution the following year and his neutrality during the invasion of the Spanish ARMADA in 1588. James played the religious factions in Scotland against one another, endorsing a PRESBYTERIAN church in 1592 while battling Catholic noblemen, and then promoting the restoration of BISHOPS to combat the more zealous Presbyterians like Andrew MELVILLE. He spelled out his autocratic theory of kingship in his book *Trew Law of Free Monarchies* (1598) and in the guide he wrote for his son Henry, *Basilikon Doron* (1599).

When James succeeded Elizabeth, he hoped to establish a union of the two governments, not merely a union of crowns. His plans ran aground on the resistance of the English PARLIAMENT, suspicious of this autocrat who seemed to misunderstand the political and legal traditions of ENGLAND. For the church, the new king summoned a conference at Hampton Court (1604), where it became clear that the English PURITANS, expecting an ally from Presbyterian Scotland, found instead a ruler whose slogan was "no bishop, no king"—that is, he insisted on the retention and strengthening of church hierarchy. He evoked serious religious antagonism from discontented Roman Catholics, the most violent being the ones who plotted to blow up the entire government (see GUNPOWDER PLOT).

James continued to try to balance his enemies. He married his daughter to the elector palatine, a Protestant prince; his son CHARLES I was meant to marry a Spanish princess, but ended up with a French one instead. If the royal policy was shrewd, its cleverness did not sit well with the English Parliament. Likewise, the king's demands for revenue and his refusal to accept Parliament's interference in royal finance were points of friction. This reign was once seen as the origin of the future clash between king and Parliament, with the HOUSE OF COMMONS "winning the initiative" in government affairs. Now historians see James as a less antagonistic figure, an intelligent, well-meaning ruler who shared a mutual incomprehension with his new subjects in their very different form of government.

James VII and II (1633–1701)
king of England, Scotland, and Ireland, 1685–1688

Going into exile as a boy, witnessing the terrible fate of his father CHARLES I, and serving in early adulthood in Spanish and French armies, gave James, an heir to the throne, a decidedly authoritarian view of the demands of kingship. At the RESTORATION he was made lord high admiral, and he fought in the wars against the Dutch. He resigned this post in 1673 after the TEST ACT had imposed anti-Catholic oaths on all royal officials. It thus became known that he had converted to the old faith in the late 1660s. This brought a major complication into English politics: a potential Catholic heir to the throne meant a likely restoration of the Catholic faith, with all of the religious, social, political, and diplomatic consequences that would entail.

Meanwhile, James had married Anne Hyde (daughter of Lord CLARENDON) in 1660, and they had two daughters, MARY II and ANNE, both raised as Protestants. As his brother CHARLES II had no legitimate male offspring, James was the next in line of succession. Most ardent Protestants, and those who did not accept divine right (as in the new political group called WHIGS), wanted James excluded from the royal succession. Those with a TORY viewpoint, who believed that kingship, and the succession to it, were above the power of men to intervene, insisted that James should be king regardless of his religious faith. Three parliaments in quick succession argued over the

issue, but the EXCLUSION crisis (1679–81) ended when Charles declined to summon any more parliaments. When James did become king in 1685, he was met by a very pliant parliament, which voted him substantial revenues. However, in a few years he had alarmed many by his campaign to reconstruct the political system and restore Catholics to public life. Thus, in 1688 a group of Whig and Tory leaders urged Mary's husband, WILLIAM III of Orange, to invade, bringing about the GLORIOUS REVOLUTION.

James was forced into exile, but he found enough assistance from Louis XIV of France to invade IRELAND in 1689 in a campaign to regain his throne. With defeat there, he returned to France. For the next decade he continued to plan on a restoration, keeping in touch with disaffected English leaders and hoping to collect a large enough force to make another invasion. His son James, born in 1688, and known as the Old Pretender, was recognized by JACOBITES as James III on his father's death, but he was unsuccessful in two attempts to invade and restore the STUART line (1708, 1715).

Jameson Raid (1895)

In December 1895 a force of almost 500 men invaded the TRANSVAAL, led by Dr. Leander Starr Jameson, an official of the British South Africa Company. They were part of a plan to overthrow the government of Paul Kruger, a plan approved by Cecil RHODES and probably also by the colonial secretary Joseph CHAMBERLAIN. The coup failed, Jameson was arrested, Rhodes resigned, and the worsening relations led to the BOER WAR. Jameson later became the premier of the CAPE COLONY (1904–08).

Jane Seymour See SEYMOUR, JANE.

Jarrow March (1936)

During the DEPRESSION there were numerous marches of unemployed workers, staged in order to draw attention to their plight; to ask for relief; and, in some cases, to exploit the poverty of the workers to advance political prospects for communist and other political groups. Jarrow, in Northern ENGLAND, was one of a number of pockets of very severe unemployment. The Labour MEMBER OF PARLIAMENT, Ellen Wilkinson, led 200 workers on a nonpolitical march to LONDON. They attracted sympathetic publicity, but their petition to PARLIAMENT did not gain any notable response.

Jeffrey, Francis, Lord (1773–1850)
lawyer, critic

Lord Jeffrey was called to the Scottish bar in 1794, but his WHIG political affiliation prevented him from attracting clients. He turned to literature and edited the new *Edinburgh Review* (1802–29). Under his direction, the *Review* was probably the most influential progressive publication in GREAT BRITAIN. He resigned as editor in order to take the post of LORD ADVOCATE when the Whigs came to power in 1830. He went on to become a lord of session in 1834, but his reputation was made in literature rather than the law.

Jeffreys of Wem, George Jeffreys, first baron (1648–1689)
judge

A lawyer sympathetic to the cause of JAMES VII AND II, Jeffreys was recorder of LONDON in 1677, and he was an aggressive prosecutor in trials connected to the POPISH PLOT. In 1683 he became chief justice of the Court of KING'S BENCH, and he presided at the trials of Titus OATES, Algernon SIDNEY, and Richard BAXTER. When MONMOUTH'S REBELLION broke out in 1685, Jeffreys led the judges who presided at the famous BLOODY ASSIZES. The 1,300 prisoners were tried in a summary fashion, and most were transported, but 250 were executed with the full grisly fate of being drawn and quartered. The punishments were carefully spread out over the west country, and they had a very strong impact, especially on

Jeffrey's reputation. Later LORD CHANCELLOR for James, he was captured after the GLORIOUS REVOLUTION and died in the TOWER OF LONDON.

Jellicoe, John Rushworth Jellicoe, first earl (1859–1935)
admiral

Jellicoe assumed command of the Grand Fleet at the beginning of WORLD WAR I. At the Battle of JUTLAND he was severely criticized for not destroying the German fleet, though he ensured it never again sought a major conflict. He was transferred to the ADMIRALTY and the post of first sea lord, where he introduced the concept of convoy tactics against the submarine.

Jenkins' Ear, War of (1739–1748)

British merchants had complained of Spanish mistreatment throughout the WEST INDIES. Captain Robert Jenkins had an ear cut off in a skirmish with the *guarda-costas* in 1731. Mounting complaints in Parliament, made more vivid by the sight of the now-famous ear, caused WALPOLE's government to declare war on Spain. The British were actually attempting to break down the Spanish imperial monopoly, and enough of these encounters would guarantee an armed conflict. British squadrons had a mixed record, most notably capturing Porto Bello in 1739. This war merged with the war of AUSTRIAN SUCCESSION in 1740.

Jenkinson, Robert See LIVERPOOL, ROBERT JENKINSON, EARL OF.

Jenner, Edward (1749–1823)
physician

Jenner worked at St. George's Hospital, LONDON, before deciding to practice in his native Gloucestershire. There he worked with local medical groups, and he studied the best method for protection against smallpox. He believed that the injection of cowpox matter was more effective than the current practice of inoculation with smallpox material. He wrote and published *An Inquiry into Cow-Pox* (1798). He slowly gained support for his idea and then was honored as a pioneer. His aim of eradicating the disease was only accomplished in 1978.

Jervis, John, earl St. Vincent (1735–1823)
admiral

Served with General James WOLFE at Quebec (1759); led expeditions to relieve GIBRALTAR (1780–82); and took command in the WEST INDIES, where he captured Martinique and Guadeloupe (1794). His fame rests on victories in the Mediterranean. In 1797 he led the fleet in defeating Spain off Cape St. Vincent. He was first lord of the ADMIRALTY in 1801–04. In this role his inquiries into misuse of funds in the dockyards helped to bring on the impeachment of Henry DUNDAS, Lord Melville.

Jesuits

The Society of Jesus, founded by St. Ignatius Loyola in 1534, was dedicated to combating the heresy of the Protestant REFORMATION. Though not allowed into ENGLAND by MARY I, the order infiltrated successfully by the time ELIZABETH I was excommunicated (1570). Some, like Edmund CAMPION, were apprehended and tortured. Others were involved in plots tied to MARY, QUEEN OF SCOTS, as well as the GUNPOWDER PLOT. By the 18th century, secular governments were wary of their reputation, and Pope Clement XIV dissolved the order in 1773. Restored by Pius VI in 1814, they returned to England in 1829 and have since assumed a pastoral and educational role.

Jinnah, Mohammed Ali (1876–1948)
Muslim nationalist

Trained as a BARRISTER, Jinnah is known as the "father of PAKISTAN." He joined the Muslim League in 1913 and was a leading critic of colonialism. He organized campaigns of resistance to parallel the Indian National Congress (Khilafat movement), but parted from them when he perceived Hindu nationalists were unlikely to allow minority rights. Demands for a separate Pakistan were made at the League's Lahore Conference in 1940, and in the negotiations in 1947 he insisted on partition. He became the first governor-general of independent Pakistan in 1947.

Johnson, Samuel (1709–1784)
lexicographer, author

After an abbreviated period of schooling and a short career as a teacher, Johnson went to LONDON and wrote for *The Gentleman's Magazine.* From 1747 to 1755 he worked on his *Dictionary of the English Language,* which became a landmark of prose and erudition for the 18th century. Author of numerous essays, of the novel *Rasselas*

Engraving of Samuel Johnson *(Library of Congress)*

(1759), and of *The Lives of the Most Eminent English Poets* (1779–81), Johnson was also a founder of the famous Literary Club. His life and many of his opinions are known today through the writing of James BOSWELL, his frequent companion, and that author's *Life of Johnson* (1791).

Johnston, Archibald, baron Warriston (1611–1663)

statesman

One of the authors of the SCOTTISH NATIONAL COVENANT, Johnston led the Scottish PRESBYTERIANS attending the WESTMINSTER ASSEMBLY (1643), where the participants tried to work out a settlement of religion as promised in the SOLEMN LEAGUE AND COVENANT (1643) between ENGLAND and SCOTLAND. He was deprived of his offices when Oliver CROMWELL defeated the Scots in 1650, but that English leader appointed him lord clerk register in 1657 and gave him a PEERAGE. He fled at the RESTORATION, was apprehended, convicted of TREASON in EDINBURGH, and hanged.

Jones, Inigo (1573–1652)

architect, designer

After travel abroad, Jones applied what he had learned of classical design, first to the decoration of masques (see Ben JONSON) and later to buildings. He held the post of Surveyor of the King's Works (1615–44), and while he designed at least 45 architectural projects, only a small number survive, including the Whitehall Banqueting House; the Queen's House at Greenwich; and St. Paul's Church, Covent Garden.

Jones, William (1746–1794)

orientalist, judge

A lawyer and a linguist, Jones was appointed judge of the High Court of Calcutta in 1783. He was a leading scholar of oriental law and languages, and with his understanding of Sanskrit he translated Indian classics and published digests of Indian law.

Jonson, Ben (1572–1637)

poet, playwright

Jonson composed masques for the Court, staged with Inigo JONES. His more durable works include *Volpone* (1605), *The Alchemist* (1610), and *Bartholomew Fair* (1614). Once imprisoned for a scurrilous play, *The Isle of Dogs,* he acted in some of SHAKESPEARE's plays and was jailed for killing a fellow actor.

Jowett, Benjamin (1817–1893)

scholar

Professor of Greek (1855) and master of Balliol College, OXFORD UNIVERSITY (1870), Jowett is credited with being a major influence in the lives of many leaders of the late 19th century. In his scholarly work he translated Plato (1871), Thucydides (1881), and Aristotle's *Politics* (1885).

Joyce, James (1882–1941)

novelist

Born in DUBLIN, which he used as a background, Joyce was a pioneer of modern literary style. His early *Dubliners* (1914) and his *Portrait of the Artist as a Young Man* (1916) were composed before his extended exile on the continent. He later wrote his experimental works *Ulysses* (1922) and *Finnegan's Wake* (1939), which challenged the critics and the censors.

jubilee

The length of Queen VICTORIA's reign, the growth of her empire, and the sense of British power (augmented by its challenges from abroad) made the 50th anniversary of her accession an important date. In 1887 the Golden JUBILEE was celebrated with a review of the fleet, erection of statues, and a service in WESTMINSTER ABBEY. Ten years later the Diamond Jubilee brought together an even larger fleet, a massive parade of troops from around the empire, and many other demonstrations of loyalty. But due to her age, the queen attended few events, the main one being a short service outside ST. PAUL'S CATHEDRAL, which she attended in an open carriage. In 2002 her great-great granddaughter, ELIZABETH II, also celebrated a Golden Jubilee.

Judicature Act (1873)

By 1873 the medieval English court system had long been recognized as archaic. Their rules, their jurisdictions, and their procedures had all been subject to piecemeal reform in the 19th century, but a more general overhaul was needed. In the Judicature Act, a single HIGH COURT OF JUSTICE was created, combining the ancient courts of KING'S BENCH, COMMON PLEAS, EXCHEQUER, and CHANCERY, along with the ADMIRALTY and the newer Probate and Divorce courts. The new high court retained divisions with the old names, mainly to ease the transition. The judges of the new court were meant to act in any of the areas, and all of them came under the review of the Court of APPEAL and, later, the judicial committee of the HOUSE OF LORDS.

See also COURTS OF LAW.

Junius

The pen name of an anonymous author who wrote 69 letters to the *Public Advertiser* between 1769 and 1772. The letters were attacks on ministers and on the king. In a set of sensational trials on one letter criticizing GEORGE III, the juries refused to convict for libel. There has never been a definitive identification of the author.

jury

In addition to the GRAND JURY, which presented criminal charges, the trial or petty jury was an early medieval institution. In English law 12 persons were chosen from a panel and sworn to give a verdict based on evidence presented to them. The practice of using juries in civil cases dates from 1179 and in criminal cases from about 1222, after the Lateran Council of 1215 had abolished the use of the ordeal. At first it was assumed that jurors would have knowledge of the matter of the case, but over time their proximity to the issue dwindled, and their role became that of assessors of evidence. Verdicts were supposed to be unanimous, but that rule was changed to majority vote in 1967, which had long been the practice in SCOTLAND. By this time the number of cases using the trial jury was greatly outnumbered by summary proceedings.

Justice, High Court of See HIGH COURT OF JUSTICE.

Justice of the Peace (JP)

The JP was the principal local official of the English Crown for many centuries. The office, which originated in the 13th and 14th centuries, was filled by an unpaid royal servant who was charged with keeping the peace. He was named in a COMMISSION of the peace for the COUNTY, and he would meet four times a year in QUARTER SESSIONS with his fellow justices to try criminal offenders. The duties of the JPs began to expand, especially from the 16th century, as work connected to the POOR LAW and other aspects of government was assigned to them. In the 19th century the administrative functions were taken from them, and local government was entrusted to county and borough councils. In the 20th century the Quarter Sessions were abolished (1971), but JPs are still named in commissions, and each commission area is divided into PETTY SESSION areas. The modern JP, or MAGISTRATE, sits in courts of two or more, and the magistrates' court exercises civil and criminal jurisdiction. The vast majority of modern legal business is done in these courts, as was the case with their predecessors. The JP was introduced at various times in SCOTLAND, but there the office had to compete with other local authorities. In IRELAND the JP had a role similar to that of ENGLAND, but in the 19th century much of the work of local judicial administration fell to stipendiary magistrates, sometimes known as resident magistrates, or RMs.

Justiciary, High Court of See HIGH COURT OF JUSTICIARY.

Jutland, Battle of (1916)

The meeting of the two fleets of GREAT BRITAIN and Germany was the climax of the feverish preparations dating back to the naval arms race of the 1890s. The smaller German fleet had been held in the Baltic, but the British tempted them into the North Sea in May 1916. The British fleet under Admiral John JELLICOE found that its gunnery and signals were deficient, and in the engagements between the two, more British ships and men were lost. However, the German ships retired to port and never emerged in force for the rest of WORLD WAR I. Thus the tactical victory went to Germany, the strategic victory to Britain.

K

Kames, Henry Home, Lord (1696–1782)

judge, author

Tutored at home and having no formal education, Lord Kames went to work in a law office and studied independently before being called to the bar in 1723. He was a member of a group of EDINBURGH intellectuals which eventually became the Edinburgh Philosophical Society, of which he was president from 1769. But his primary vocation was the LAW. He became a lord of session in 1752, taking the title Lord Kames. He made important contributions in the publication of court decisions, first with a short volume, *Remarkable Decisions* (1728) and then two folio volumes, *Decisions of the Court of Session . . . in the Form of a Dictionary* (1741). His original compositions included an important collection of *Historical Law Tracts* (1759), which showed great interest in the comparative aspects of English and Scots law. Kames's talents ranged widely, as he also wrote *Essays Concerning British Antiquities* (1747), *Essays on the Principles of Morality and Natural Religion* (1751), *Principles of Equity* (1760), the widely read *Elements of Criticism* (1762), and *Sketches of the History of Man* (1774).

See also COURTS OF LAW; SESSION, COURT OF.

Kay, John (1704–ca. 1780)

inventor

Manager of a woolen workshop, Kay invented devices for the manufacture of cloth, the most notable being the "flying shuttle." This enabled one person to work wider fabrics, which previously had required two workers. The device became very popular, though not with workers who were unemployed. Kay's efforts to protect his patent were costly and unsuccessful, and he went to France, evidently to continue his work there, but there is no record of his death.

Kay-Shuttleworth, James (1804–1877)

physician, education reformer

Trained in medicine at the University of EDINBURGH, Kay-Shuttleworth worked in Manchester and became involved in the reform of public health and EDUCATION. In Manchester he was secretary to the Board of Health, and he later served as an assistant POOR LAW commisioner. In 1839 he became secretary to the Committee of the Privy Council on Education, and he made significant contributions by founding a training college for pupil-teachers and helping to institute a system of school inspectors.

Keats, John (1795–1821)

poet

Apprenticed to an apothecary-surgeon, Keats gave up that career for poetry. In 1817 his first volume of poems was published, followed in the next few years by a remarkable output: *Endymion* (1818), "The Eve of St. Agnes," "Ode to a Nightingale," "Ode on a Grecian Urn," which with others were published in 1820, as was his *Hyperion*. He went to Italy at the end of the year, hoping to recover from tuberculosis, but he died in Rome early the following year. He was one of the main figures in English ROMANTICISM.

Kenya

Called British East Africa in the late 19th century and managed by a company of that name, Kenya was made a PROTECTORATE in 1893 but became a COLONY only in 1920, when its name was changed to Kenya. In the 1950s the Mau Mau rebellion, a series of terrorist attacks on settlers, forced the pace of liberation. Kenya became independent in 1963, and in 1964 it was made a republic, remaining in the Commonwealth.

Keppel, Augustus Keppel, viscount (1725–1786)

admiral

Keppel sailed with George ANSON's voyage around the world (1740) and was involved in the SEVEN YEARS' WAR. He entered PARLIAMENT in 1761 as a supporter of the Rockingham WHIGS. In the American Revolution he commanded the fleet, but he was court-martialed for his conduct against the French at Ushant (1779). The charges, brought by a subordinate, alleged failure to take action and cowardly retreat. Keppel was acquitted and was made first lord of the ADMIRALTY in 1782.

Keynes, John Maynard (1883–1946)

economist

A scholar and government servant, Keynes's pronounced influence on economic policy spanned nearly half a century. He was at the TREASURY during WORLD WAR I and went to the Paris Peace Conference, where he disputed plans for REPARATIONS and resigned from the delegation. He went to write *The Economic Consequences of the Peace* (1919), which deplored the policy of making Germany pay for war damages. Returning to his research, Keynes wrote important books on economic theory, including his *Treatise on Money* (1930) and *The General Theory of Employment, Interest, and Money* (1938). The thrust of his work was to encourage government intervention in the economy in order to stimulate growth and full employment. He

was chief British delegate to the 1944 Bretton Woods Conference, which established the International Monetary Fund and the World Bank. His ideas influenced the policies of many industrial countries down to the 1970s.

Khartoum

The capital of The SUDAN. In the 19th century Khartoum was the settlement which General Charles GORDON was supposed to evacuate in the face of the forces of the Mahdi and his zealous followers. After Gordon's death, the city was destroyed. When it was retaken by General KITCHENER in 1898, it was made the base for the government of The Sudan until 1956.

Kidd, William (1645–1701)

pirate

A PRIVATEER with a commission to seize pirates (1695), "Captain Kidd" turned to piracy himself. He was arrested in 1699 and claimed that he was innocent. Sent to ENGLAND for trial in 1701, he was found guilty of murder and piracy and was executed.

Kildare, earls of See FITZGERALD, EARL OF KILDARE.

Kilkenny, Confederation of

Irish government established in 1642 by the Old English and their GAELIC fellow Catholics. The Confederation wrote a provisional constitution, raised armies, and sent ambassadors to other states and to Rome. The government negotiated with CHARLES I, eventually proposing to send him an army in exchange for a Catholic government of IRELAND. When these terms were discovered, the king suffered a major propaganda defeat; moreover, the promised army never reached him. The Confederation was the *de facto* government of Ireland until its forces were destroyed by Oliver CROMWELL in 1649.

Kilkenny, Statutes of (1366)

There was a widespread revival of GAELIC culture in 14th-century IRELAND, and a PARLIAMENT in 1366 passed a series of laws designed to prevent further dilution of English culture and influence. Intermarriage, adoption of Irish dress and customs, and observance of Irish laws were among the proscribed items. Known as the Statutes of Kilkenny, the laws only applied to the areas under English control, they were not easily enforced, and in 1613 they were repealed.

Killiecrankie, Battle of (1689)

Scottish JACOBITES under Viscount DUNDEE fought with troops of WILLIAM III in the summer of 1689. The king's army was caught in a pass and badly defeated, but Dundee was killed. Over the next month the royal army overcame the loss and secured SCOTLAND for the Crown.

Kilmainham Treaty

Charles Stewart PARNELL, the Irish nationalist leader, was imprisoned in Kilmainham jail in DUBLIN in 1881 for making speeches inciting violence. An agreement was reached (April 1882) between Parnell and WILLIAM GLADSTONE's government for his release, and in the Kilmainham Treaty he agreed to try to prevent further violence in exchange for concessions to Irish tenants. When Parnell was released from prison, the chief secretary of IRELAND (the British government's representative) resigned in protest. His replacement was Frederick CAVENDISH, who with his undersecretary was assassinated in Phoenix Park, Dublin, in May 1882, a brutal comment on the wisdom of the treaty.

King, Gregory (1648–1712)
statistician

An early student of political arithmetic, King developed methods of extrapolating population from tax records, and he made estimates of income and other economic measurements. He published his *Natural and Political Observations . . . on the State and Condition of England* in 1696.

King's Bench, Court of

One of the early COMMON LAW courts, the Court of King's Bench met "before the lord king" as he traveled around his kingdom. The first record of a chief justice is in 1268, and over the next two centuries the court's location became fixed, it kept a set of rolls to record decisions, and it began to extend its original criminal jurisdiction. It used legal fictions to claim authority in many cases, and it took appeals from other royal courts. In 1873 it was merged with the other royal courts to form the HIGH COURT OF JUSTICE. The court is referred to as the *Queen's Bench* when the monarch is female.

See also COURTS OF LAW.

king's evil

The disease scrofula, believed to be cured by the touch of royalty. The custom was revived by the house of STUART, and CHARLES II was estimated to have touched as many as 90,000 sufferers. The ceremony not coincidentally reinforced beliefs in the divinity of kings. It was last practiced by Queen ANNE.

king's friends

A term used to describe influential friends of GEORGE III, pictured by some politicians as the sinister tools of the court who undermined conventional party government. The characterization was popularized by Edmund BURKE's *Thoughts on the Present Discontents* (1770).

kingship See MONARCHY.

Kingsley, Charles (1819–1875)
clergyman, novelist, reformer

A leader of the Christian Socialist movement of the mid-19th century, Kingsley wrote for radical publications. Two of his books—*Yeast* (1848) and *Alton Locke* (1850)—presented sympathetic pictures of the conditions of the poor. Kingsley also wrote historical novels, including *Westward Ho!* (1855) and *Hereward the Wake* (1866). His children's books were well-liked: *The Heroes* (1856) and *The Water Babies* (1863).

Kinsale, Battle of (1601)

When Spanish aid arrived for Irish rebels in 1601, it was at the wrong end of IRELAND. The port of Kinsale on the southwest coast was the site where 4,000 Spanish troops landed. They were besieged by ELIZABETH I's commander, Lord MOUNTJOY. Hugh O'NEILL, the ULSTER rebel leader, was forced to march across the country to attempt to aid them, but the Spaniards surrendered, and O'Neill had to return to Ulster, the effort having been so costly as to undermine his chances of victory.

Kipling, Rudyard (1865–1936)
writer

Born in INDIA, Kipling was first a journalist, but his best-known works were composed after he moved to ENGLAND in 1889. He became an important figure after publishing his "Recessional" for the Diamond JUBILEE in 1897. Major works included *Barrack Room Ballads* (1892), *The Jungle Book* (1894), *Kim* (1901), and *Just So Stories* (1902). He was awarded the Nobel Prize in 1907. A resonant voice of empire, his view of "the white man's burden" did not wear well in the 20th century.

Kitchener, Horatio Herbert Kitchener, first earl (1850–1916)
soldier

Lord Kitchener served in PALESTINE and CYPRUS in the 1870s and in The SUDAN in the 1880s, where he was able to restore imperial authority. As chief of staff to General Frederick ROBERTS in the BOER WAR, he succeeded to command and

Lord Kitchener *(Hulton/Archive)*

implemented the concentration camp policy which broke the Boers' resistance. He then served in INDIA as commander in chief (1902–09). In 1914 he was made secretary for war, and he created a "new" ARMY of 70 divisions of volunteers, anticipating the long conflict that eventually materialized as WORLD WAR I. He died in 1916 when his ship sank on a mission to Russia.

knight

The mounted medieval warrior customarily paid by a "fee," or land granted on condition of military service and various other prescribed duties. Landowning brought the knight into the framework of government and administration, and he played an important role as a member of the growing GENTRY class. The practical utility of the knight declined by the late medieval period, there being only a few hundred by the 15th century, from about 2,000 in the 13th century. Orders of knighthood, heraldic symbols, and concepts of CHIVALRY outlived the military value of the knight, and the title became primarily a social distinction.

Knox, John (ca. 1505–1572)
Protestant reformer

Educated at St. Andrews, Knox was ordained as a Catholic priest but became a Protestant under the influence of George WISHART. In 1547 he was preacher in the Protestant garrison at St. Andrews castle, and though he was probably not involved in the murder of Cardinal BEATON there, he was captured by the French when they seized the castle, and he was made a galley slave.

After his release in 1549, he went to ENGLAND and a few years later went to Geneva to join the exiles from MARY I's government. There he wrote his intemperate attack on female rulers: *The First Blast of the Trumpet Against the Monstrous Regiment of Women* (1558) aimed at Mary I and MARY OF GUISE, but sure to be read by their successors, ELIZABETH I and MARY, QUEEN OF SCOTS. Knox returned to SCOTLAND, became one of the leaders of the REFORMATION there, and was one of the authors of the *First Book of Discipline* (1559). He was minister of Edinburgh in 1560, but he had no part in the downfall of Mary, Queen of Scots, and his role overall was somewhat less than he claimed in his *History of the Reformation of Religion within the Realm of Scotland* (1587).

L

Labour Party

The efforts of workingmen to enter political life began with the CHARTIST MOVEMENT in the early 19th century and culminated in the formation of workers' political parties at the beginning of the 20th century. The largest and most durable of these, Labour became one of the major parliamentary parties by the 1920s. The obstacles to worker participation—voting rights, property qualifications for MEMBERS OF PARLIAMENT (MPs), no pay for legislators, and lack of voter organization—were the product of a system that never expected workers to become involved. Thus there was no solid principle of opposition to the removal of most of the restrictions. In 1858 the property qualification for MPs was abolished. By 1885 some coal miners had been elected under the banner of the LIBERAL PARTY. In the next decade the electorate was widened and reorganized into equal districts. By then the growing TRADE UNION and small but vocal socialist groups (e.g., the FABIAN SOCIETY) made increasing demands for full (male) participation in politics. In 1893 Keir HARDIE organized the INDEPENDENT LABOUR PARTY. In 1900 these disparate groups formed a joint Labour Representation Committee to coordinate their parliamentary campaigns and conserve their limited resources. They won 29 seats in the 1906 election and formed an official parliamentary party, together with 25 MPs affiliated with the Liberal Party.

In 1911 MPs were granted small salaries, a sign that politics was becoming more open. Another sign was the addition of the Labour Party to the wartime coalition formed in 1915. In 1918, when the vote was granted to all adult men (and some women), a new constitution for the party was written. Local constituency parties were formed, and membership was opened to individuals. Perhaps the most significant item in the revised constitution was the fourth clause, which called for "common ownership of the means of production," a central tenet of the socialist membership. This was to be one of several internal points of friction, as the party now grew beyond its working-class base and took in more and more middle-class members. By 1924 the party had formed its first government, when a minority CONSERVATIVE PARTY government fell. But that only lasted nine months. The next Labour CABINET took office in 1929, this time with 288 seats. In the economic crisis of 1931, the Labour PRIME MINISTER Ramsay MACDONALD resigned and formed a coalition government. This so outraged his colleagues that he was expelled from the party. The conflict contributed to a fall to only 52 Labour seats in the 1931 election. But the effects of DEPRESSION and war brought a rebound in 1945, when the party won with 393 seats, a majority of 146. This enabled Labour to implement the reforms of the WELFARE STATE: full employment, NATIONAL INSURANCE, a NATIONAL HEALTH SERVICE, and nationalized industry. In subsequent elections, Labour held power in 1964–70, and 1974–79, alternating with the Conservatives. There followed the long era of Margaret THATCHER (1979–90), followed by John MAJOR, with the next Labour victory in 1997.

See also ATTLEE, CLEMENT; BLAIR, TONY; GAITSKELL, HUGH; LANSBURY, GEORGE; WILSON, SIR HAROLD.

laissez faire

The body of thought and policies which opposed government intervention in economic affairs. The term *laissez faire* was adopted from French authors of the 18th century who promoted FREE TRADE. These authors inspired the school of "classical economists," such as Adam SMITH, David RICARDO, and others who argued that individuals should be free to pursue their own interests, and the government should be restrained in its powers of TAXATION, imposing TARIFFS, and regulation. The debates on this subject still continue, although a majority of economists would probably agree that there are limited areas which require some regulation. These include the legal power to secure property and enforce contracts, and general taxation to support EDUCATION and public health. Such exceptions help to explain the coexistence in 19th-century Britain of a dominant laissez-faire philosophy and a wide range of social reforms (factories, sanitation, poor laws, education).

See also BRIGHT, JOHN; COBDEN, RICHARD.

Lamb, William See MELBOURNE, WILLIAM LAMB, VISCOUNT.

Lambert, John (1619–1684)
soldier

A successful and popular commander in the parliamentary armies, Lambert was involved in battles at MARSTON MOOR (1644), Preston (1648), and Worcester (1650). He helped to compose the INSTRUMENT OF GOVERNMENT (1653) setting up the PROTECTORATE of Oliver CROMWELL (1654), but when he opposed greater authority for the Lord Protector in 1657, he was dismissed. He returned to command the ARMY in 1659, but failing to gain power with it, he was arrested and spent the rest of his life in prison.

Lambton, John See DURHAM, JOHN LAMBTON, EARL OF.

Lancaster, house of

The descendants of John of Gaunt, duke of Lancaster, ruled England from 1400 to 1461: HENRY IV, HENRY V, and HENRY VI. The last was the leader of the Lancastrians in the Wars of the ROSES, against the forces of the house of YORK.

Lancaster, Joseph 1778–1838
education reformer

The son of a soldier, Lancaster was intended for the ministry but joined the NAVY. After one voyage he became a QUAKER and started teaching. He opened a school in LONDON, and offered free tuition to those who could not pay, organizing the teaching under older boys, called monitors. In this fashion his school taught up to 1,000 pupils. The Royal Lancasterian Society was established in 1808 to manage a group of schools on his plan. The CHURCH OF ENGLAND adopted a similar plan under the inspiration of Andrew BELL. Lancaster quarreled with the trustees and emigrated to America, where he continued to promote his teaching methods.

land

Until the end of the 19th century, landowning was the dominant form of wealth, the main gauge of social standing, and the basis for the political system. Thus it was naturally the subject of extensive legislation, litigation, and economic transactions. This general description was equally true of all parts of the British Isles, while there were differences in detail.

In theory all land was held from the Crown, originally by various feudal tenures. These fell out of use and were abolished at the time of the RESTORATION in 1660. COPYHOLD, leasehold, and FREEHOLD were the main English forms of tenancy. The first came from the manorial system (see MANOR), and it was abolished in 1925. The second was subject to many variations: leases for lives, fixed terms, or merely the will of the landlord. Freehold was full ownership, the term originally indicating freedom from feudal obligations.

There were numerous other forms of tenure specific to SCOTLAND and IRELAND, also of medieval origin, and often of greater endurance than their English counterparts.

The customary rules came from feudal law and were subject to legislative alteration and judicial interpretation. Generally speaking, for the modern era, an English estate was supposed to be free of binding limits. However, the lawyers devised a strict settlement, a will with conditions that preserved an estate intact. Scottish law, on the other hand, permitted entails—a binding limit on an inheritance—and an act of 1685 endorsed and regulated these devices.

There was an inherent conflict between the preservation of an estate and the sale of property, which tended to deplete the inheritance. The growth of commerce and industry in the 18th century put pressure on older, static landholding. Because of urban development, new factories, and the demand from a large new class of aspiring landowners, selling was made easier. There were very large transfers of land in all parts of the British Isles in the later 19th century, with many Irish peasant proprietors gaining land from former landlords (IRISH LAND ACTS). At the same time, English and Scottish estate owners were beginning to feel the effects of increased progressive TAXATION, and they were forced to liquidate large holdings.

Taxation of land was introduced in ENGLAND to pay for the French wars of the 1690s. The primary source of government revenue for the 18th century, it was levied on assessed values and began at four shillings in the pound (20 percent), but the calculation was changed to a fixed sum for certain areas. In Scotland there was an older tradition of the tax, or cess, levied on property.

From time to time the issue of landowning dominated economic and political life in different parts of the islands. For instance, the CLAN structure of the HIGHLANDS was a central issue in the 17th and 18th centuries, playing a part in the JACOBITES' unrest. In the 19th century the special circumstances of Ireland—its many Anglo-Irish landowners, its large class of tenants, and adverse economic conditions—energized the Irish "land question," a struggle to redefine the relation of Irish landlords and tenants. In general, the questions surrounding land, urban as well as rural, were and remain vital to the social and economic well-being of all parts of the archipelago.

See also COMMON LAW; COURTS OF LAW; GENTRY; LAW.

Lansbury, George (1859–1940)
Labour politician

A highly-principled Christian socialist and pacifist, Lansbury preferred the arena of local politics. He gave up his seat in PARLIAMENT in 1912 to campaign in a BY-ELECTION on a women's suffrage platform. He was a leader of the protest by the BOROUGH council of Poplar against taxes by the London County Council, for which he was sent to prison. In the later 1920s he was in Parliament and served in Ramsay MACDONALD's government. When the LABOUR PARTY split in 1931, Lansbury was chosen as leader of the wrecked organization. His pacifist opposition to sanctions on Italy, after Mussolini invaded Ethiopia, caused his fall as party leader in 1935, and he was replaced by Clement ATTLEE.

Lansdowne, Henry Petty-Fitzmaurice, marquis of (1845–1927)
politician

Heir to an Irish PEERAGE and a LIBERAL PARTY member, Lansdowne opposed William GLADSTONE's Irish policies, became a leader of the LIBERAL UNIONISTS and later a member of the CONSERVATIVE PARTY. He served as governor-general of CANADA (1883–88) and VICEROY of INDIA (1888–94). As foreign secretary (1900–05) he arranged the Anglo-Japanese alliance (1902) and the Anglo-French ENTENTE (1904).

Larkin, James (1876–1947)
Irish union leader

Born in Liverpool, Larkin went to IRELAND to organize the dock workers. He founded the Irish Transport and General Workers' Union in 1908.

A believer in syndicalism—the use of union power to disable the economy—he led a DUBLIN tramway strike in 1913, but it failed. Although he became a Marxist and was expelled from his own union, he was elected to the DÁIL ÉIRANN in the 1920s and 1930s.

Laski, Harold (1893–1950)
theorist, professor

An OXFORD graduate, Laski taught at Harvard University, where he became a friend of Oliver Wendell Holmes (1916–20). While there he wrote *Studies in the Problem of Sovereignty* (1917) and *Authority in the Modern State* (1919). Thereafter he taught political science at the London School of Economics, and he served as chairman of the LABOUR PARTY. His shifting political thought is reflected in *A Grammar of Politics* (1925), *Parliamentary Government in England* (1938), and *Reflections on the Constitution* (1950).

Latimer, Hugh (1485–1555)
bishop

From humble origins, Latimer became a renowned preacher and a strong spokesman for church reform. He was made BISHOP of Worcester in 1535. He resigned in 1539 to protest the adoption of the conservative Six Articles of Religion. Under EDWARD VI he was free to preach, but with MARY I's accession, he was examined for heresy and burned at the stake in 1555.

latitudinarian

The early 18th-century theological and liturgical reaction to controversies of the 17th century: a lax attitude toward UNIFORMITY, and a toleration of different shades of ANGLICAN belief. This naturally excited criticism from "high church" members.

Laud, William (1573–1645)
archbishop of Canterbury, 1633–1645

The son of a clothier, Laud was born in Reading and attended St. John's College, OXFORD UNIVER-

SITY. A royal chaplain, then councillor, and finally ARCHBISHOP, he was the key architect of the religious policy of CHARLES I. An enemy of Calvinist influence, hence described as ARMINIAN, he tried to bring the church into uniform belief and practice using the courts of STAR CHAMBER and HIGH COMMISSION. His enemies portrayed him as a crypto-Catholic, though he was undoubtedly nothing of the sort. When a new prayer book drafted by Scottish bishops was imposed there in 1637, the public reaction was swift and violent. Laud became a target for the king's enemies, and in 1641 he was arrested, impeached, and executed in 1645 at the order of PARLIAMENT.

Lauderdale, John Maitland, duke of (1616–1682)
secretary of state

A royalist, a signer of the SCOTTISH NATIONAL COVENANT, and a negotiator of both the SOLEMN LEAGUE AND COVENANT and the ENGAGEMENT with King CHARLES I, Lauderdale was at the center of 17th-century politics. After the RESTORATION he was the chief Scottish agent for CHARLES II (1660–80). He was feared as the promoter of restored episcopal authority and the scourge of the PRESBYTERIANS.

law

The many varieties of law in the British Isles since the later Middle Ages are valuable guides to the histories of the several communities. Understanding the different systems of law begins with two questions: what were the sources of legal rules, and who enforced them?

Custom is what people have done in like circumstances in the past; the memory of a judge or a jury was both source and enforcer. The customary law of a MANOR or BOROUGH or GUILD was later written down, and the variety of customs was remarkable.

The COMMON LAW practiced in the king's courts was common to the realm as a whole. Judgments followed prevailing legal rules, as found in decided cases. These were recorded in rolls or

LAW REPORTS. ENGLAND had the premier system, and it was mandated for WALES in 16th-century statutes. The Scots drew upon their own recorded cases, but also upon major treatises called "institutes." The Irish courts emulated the English, borrowing heavily from their precedents.

Even as the royal courts developed in different countries, Roman law (or CIVIL LAW) was applied in areas such as the ADMIRALTY (mercantile and maritime disputes). The laws of the church were preserved in *canons*, which also drew upon civilian tradition. Prior to the 16th century the canons were those of the universal church, and later the national churches of England and Scotland and (for the Catholic Irish) the church of Rome. The canons governed the affairs of the clergy and the enforcement of moral law, including marital and testamentary cases.

The CRIMINAL LAW was one of the most ancient legal functions, and one in which there had long been public involvement in apprehension, accusation, and trial. Until the 19th century, trials were typically done in a day, before the king's judges on circuit, or in their central courts. The criminal law was the accumulation of custom and practice before the judges; only very lately was it written down and collated in the form of digests. The practice of recording and arranging the decisions of courts (criminal or otherwise) was a private venture, done by judges, BARRISTERS (or advocates), or their clerks.

From the origin of parliaments until the 19th century, *statute* law was a small part of the legal process. Yet as early as the 16th century, the statements of law made by "the king in parliament" were accorded the highest authority. By the 18th century, legislation had become much more prominent, and by the 20th century it became the main source of law. This trend reflected an expanding electorate and a sense that the judges should not (or could not) make law in the modern world. The legislators assumed the power to collect, inscribe, and formulate laws for the modern age.

See also ACT OF PARLIAMENT; COURTS OF LAW.

Law, Andrew Bonar (1858–1923)
prime minister, 1922–1923

A Conservative MEMBER OF PARLIAMENT from 1900 to 1923, Law was born in CANADA and raised in SCOTLAND. He succeeded Arthur BALFOUR as a compromise choice for CONSERVATIVE PARTY leader in 1911. Leading the opposition to the IRISH HOME RULE bill, he supported extreme measures of resistance. In WORLD WAR I, he entered a coalition government under Herbert ASQUITH in 1915 and rose to a more important position when that CABINET was replaced by one under David LLOYD GEORGE in 1916. He continued to support Lloyd George in the 1918 election, but in 1922 he assumed party leadership and won a brief term in office before he was forced to retire because of ill health.

Law, John (1671–1729)
financier

A Scot, Law was an early proponent of deficit spending. He was allowed to establish a bank in France that issued paper currency, and at first the effect was to help to revive business (1716). But Law also gained a monopoly on foreign trade and sold shares in his Mississippi Company, which experienced a speculative boom and then collapsed in 1720.

Law, William (1686–1761)
religious writer

Born in Northamptonshire, the son of a grocer, Law graduated from Emmanuel College, CAMBRIDGE UNIVERSITY, where he was made a fellow. However, he was deprived of the fellowship after refusing to take the oath to George I. He defended NONJURORS, and he wrote *Three Letters to the Bishop of Bangor* (1717–19), disputing the ideas of Benjamin HOADLY. He was the author of the most popular devotional work of the 18th century, *A Serious Call to a Devout and Holy Life* (1728). Law also wrote *The Case of Reason* (1732), which disputed the rational and deistic ideas of the day.

Lawrence, D(avid) H(erbert) (1885–1930)
novelist

A miner's son, D. H. Lawrence went to university and became a teacher. His novels were explicit and sometimes autobiographical; he was prosecuted for obscenity for *The Rainbow* (1915). He and his wife Frieda spent much of their lives abroad, as he wrote *Women in Love* (1920) and *Lady Chatterley's Lover* (1928), both privately published. The latter work could not be published in its original form in Britain until 1960, because of the obscenity laws.

Lawrence, T(homas) E(dward) (1888–1935)
soldier, arabist

Known as "Lawrence of Arabia," T. E. Lawrence had studied in the Middle East and was drawn into intelligence work at the beginning of WORLD WAR I. He assisted in the rebellion of the Arabs against Turkish rule in 1917. At the peace conference in 1919 he tried unsuccessfully to gain support for Arab independence. In 1921 Winston CHURCHILL took him into the Colonial Office to organize a new Middle East department. Lawrence's celebrated account of his experience in the Arab revolt was *Seven Pillars of Wisdom* (1926).

law reports

The nature of the COMMON LAW demanded a written record of proceedings, arguments, and decisions, as the basis for study, debate, and future adjudication. As odd as it might seem today, much of the practice of recording and arranging the decisions of COURTS OF LAW was a private venture done by judges, BARRISTERS (or advocates), or their clerks. The clerks made formal entries in the official court rolls for each case. These were augmented by the notes on arguments in the medieval YEAR BOOKS, which were cumulated and printed in the 16th century. By then new forms of reports were being published under the names of the reporters, each working for a certain period in a particular court. There was little standardization until the 19th century. Regular reporting in the Scottish courts began in the 18th century and in Irish courts in the 19th century.

League of Nations

The idea of an international organization of states had become current from the end of the 19th century, and it was embodied in the treaties signed at the end of WORLD WAR I. Formed in 1920, the League of Nations had 53 member states, and it met in Geneva, where there was an assembly of all members and a council with permanent and rotating members. The constitution of the League, the covenant, was part of each of the postwar treaties. It called for international DISARMAMENT, the peaceful resolution of all disputes, and a long list of rules for international behavior. The League was hampered by lack of participation. The United States never ratified the Versailles Treaty and so never became a member state. GREAT BRITAIN and France were the only major powers who belonged to the League throughout its existence, 1920–46. There was no enforcement machinery available to the League, only the threat of economic sanctions. Thus when aggression threatened world peace in the 1930s, there was little to fear from the League.

Leicester See COKE, THOMAS, EARL OF LEICESTER.

Leicester, Robert Dudley, earl of (1532–1588)
courtier

A favorite of Queen ELIZABETH I, Leicester was an ardent Protestant and a member of the queen's council. He was involved in the plot his father (John Dudley, duke of NORTHUMBERLAND) engineered for Lady Jane GREY and had been under a death sentence. There were rumors of his involvement in the death of his first wife. He led a disastrous expedition to the Netherlands and was recalled in 1587. He died as the preparations for the Spanish ARMADA were being made.

lend-lease

As GREAT BRITAIN fought alone against Germany in 1940–41, her supplies and her sources of cash and credit were badly depleted. The American government was still neutral, but the U.S. Congress passed the Lend-Lease Act in March 1941. The act offered material and supplies to countries which were the victims of aggression, to be paid for at the end of WORLD WAR II. In all Britain received about $30 billion in aid, or about 60 percent of the total, with the rest going to the Soviet Union and other countries.

Lennox, Esmé Stuart, duke of (1542–1583)
politician
A Frenchman, invited to SCOTLAND by JAMES VI, his cousin, in 1579, Lennox made a powerful impression on the young king. He helped in the removal of the regent, the earl of MORTON (executed for the murder of Lord DARNLEY). When James was kidnapped by radical Protestants (the RUTHVEN RAID) in 1582, he was obliged to order Lennox to leave the kingdom.

Leslie, Alexander (1580–1661)
soldier
As with many professional British soldiers, Leslie served on the Continent, in his case, for 30 years with the Swedish army. In 1639 he took command of Scottish forces in the BISHOPS' WARS. At the Battle of MARSTON MOOR he led the Scottish army against the king, and he received CHARLES I's surrender in 1646. Within a few years he had changed sides, and he led the Scottish army against Oliver CROMWELL at Worcester (1650). After his defeat there, he was imprisoned by the English (1651–54).

Lesotho

The former COLONY of BASUTOLAND became independent in 1966. A constitutional monarchy and member of the Commonwealth, Lesotho is surrounded by SOUTH AFRICA. In its farming economy, many people have to find work in South Africa, while in the 1970s and 1980s, the country was a haven for political refugees. These factors have created instability, and there have been several forcible changes in the succession.

Levant Company

A merchant company trading in the Mediterranean, the Levant Company was preceded by the Turkey Company (chartered in 1581) and the Venice Company (1583). The two merged in 1592, and the Levant Company was chartered in 1605 for trade with ports of the Ottoman Empire. The main exports were cloth and metals, and the imports included spices, currants, wine, and silk. The company's monopoly was surrendered in 1825.

Levellers

A radical faction that emerged late in the CIVIL WAR, with a few extremist members of PARLIAMENT and a large number of soldiers in the NEW MODEL ARMY. The Levellers' outspoken leader was John LILBURNE, who with others produced a tract called *The Agreement of the People* (1647). This called for manhood suffrage, removal of social distinctions, religious toleration, and biennial parliaments. The terms were debated at Putney and rejected by the army officers, but the soldiers continued to press their case, and in some cases there were mutinies. Whether or not these were the doing of the Levellers, they provided the government with an excuse to suppress the group.

Liberal Party

The party formed in the 1860s by former WHIGS, TORY followers of Robert PEEL, and an assortment of radicals. The general goals of the party were individual liberty, social reform, and FREE TRADE. The electoral reform of 1867 and the BALLOT ACT of 1872 seemed to galvanize the elements of the emerging party. William GLADSTONE was the standard bearer, and his government from 1868 to 1874 was one of the foremost reforming administrations of the century. Naturally, as the movements to reform intensified by the 1880s, there were fewer Whig aristocrats who were comfortable in this organization. The IRISH HOME RULE bill of 1886 became a defining moment, one when a large number of aristocratic and conservative members seceded and formed the LIBERAL UNIONISTS. Over the next two decades, the Liberals were mostly in opposition and were increasingly identified with the middle and lower classes and with progressive reform. This was clear in the Newcastle Programme of 1891, which called for DISESTABLISHMENT, land law reform, and workmens' compensation.

In 1906 the Liberals won their last and greatest electoral victory. The party by then had two clearly divergent groups: the progressive faction with David LLOYD GEORGE and others who wanted extensive social reform; and the Liberal Imperialists, like Herbert ASQUITH, who were more pragmatic and moderate. During WORLD WAR I, Prime Minister Asquith was forced to form a coalition (1915), and continued internal divisions resulted in his replacement by Lloyd George as PRIME MINISTER in 1916. This act of treachery was the cause of a split in the party that never healed. After the war, the coalition stayed in power until 1922. Then in a series of elections, Liberal power melted away, while the LABOUR PARTY emerged as the second major party. By 1924 the Liberals only had 42 seats, and their strength never recovered. Since then they have formed a small third party, and in the 1970s they began a series of reformations, the successor party becoming the Social and Liberal Democrat Party in 1988.

Liberal Unionists

The name of the splinter group that seceded from the LIBERAL PARTY over IRISH HOME RULE in 1886. An astonishing 93 Liberal MPs defected over this issue. A faction led by Joseph CHAMBERLAIN and one headed by the marquis of HARTINGTON formed a National Liberal Union in 1889, and in 1895 they won 70 seats. In 1912 the unionists joined the CONSERVATIVE PARTY, and that party changed its name to the Conservative and Unionist Party.

Lilburne, John (1615–1657)

Leveller leader

Born into a gentry family in Sunderland, Lilburne came to LONDON in 1630 and was apprenticed to a clothier. Punished by the Court of STAR CHAMBER for distributing PURITAN tracts (1638), he was an officer in Oliver CROMWELL's cavalry and fought until 1645. He then resigned, refusing to swear to the SOLEMN LEAGUE AND COVENANT. An outspoken critic of the ARMY and PARLIAMENT, he was one of the leading figures among the LEVELLERS, and he was jailed many times. After attacking the COMMONWEALTH OF ENGLAND in *England's New Chains Discovered* (1649), he was tried for treason and acquitted but banished in 1651. He returned in 1653, spent more time in prison, and latterly joined the QUAKERS.

Limerick, Treaty of (1691)

The treaty ending the siege of Limerick and the war between JAMES VII AND II and WILLIAM III in 1691. Under the terms of the military agreement, the soldiers defending Limerick were allowed to go to France. The civilian articles called for toleration of Catholics and security for their land. The Protestant Irish PARLIAMENT did not ratify the treaty until 1697, and by then it was in a substantially different form. Moreover, they soon began to enact the intolerant system of PENAL LAWS.

limited liability

Investors in companies had been exposed to the loss of their property when a company failed.

After a series of acts (1855–62), the investor was only liable to the extent of the shares he owned. This added security contributed to increased investment and industrial growth.

Lister, Joseph Lister, first baron (1827–1912)
surgeon

Lister was born in Upton, Essex; his father was a QUAKER. He studied at University College, London, and with James Syme of the University of EDINBURGH. Lister became a leader in antiseptic surgery, adopting ideas of Louis Pasteur. He was professor of surgery at Glasgow University (1860–69), the University of Edinburgh (1869–77), and King's College, London (1877–92). He used carbolic acid for disinfectant and later adopted the method of Robert Koch of Germany to sterilize with steam.

Liverpool, Robert Jenkinson, earl of (1770–1828)
prime minister, 1812–1827

Liverpool grew up in Oxfordshire; his father was a BARONET. He attended Charterhouse and Christ Church, OXFORD UNIVERSITY. A grand tour afterward was eventful, and he was present at the fall of the Bastille in Paris in 1789. A member of the HOUSE OF COMMONS from 1790, he went to the HOUSE OF LORDS in 1803. His apprenticeship was varied, as he was foreign secretary in 1801–03, home secretary in 1804 and again in 1807, and secretary for war from 1809 to 1812. When he took over as PRIME MINISTER in 1812, the concluding phase of the NAPOLEONIC WARS had begun, and he presided over the final victory. His government took a firm line against domestic protest, as in the SPA FIELDS RIOT and PETERLOO MASSACRE. Liverpool was an effective leader, and though opposed to major reform (CATHOLIC EMANCIPATION, FRANCHISE reform), he brought in more liberal members of his party in the 1820s and showed flexibility on TARIFFS and CRIMINAL LAW. After suffering a stroke, he resigned in 1827.

Livingstone, David (1813–1873)
explorer, missionary

Born in Blantyre, SCOTLAND, Livingstone trained as a medical missionary in Glasgow. After his medical education and ordination, he went to AFRICA to work for the London Missionary Society. Beginning in Southern Africa, he moved into the central part of the continent. His expeditions there brought significant results with the discoveries of Lake Ngami, the Victoria Falls, and Lake Nyasa. In 1866 he set out to find the source of the Nile, and he was not heard from until the famous encounter with the journalist Henry Morton STANLEY at Lake Tanganyika (1871), when the legend has it that he was greeted with the phrase "Dr. Livingstone, I presume?"

Lloyd George, David (1863–1945)
prime minister, 1916–1922

Born in Manchester, Lloyd George was raised in WALES by his mother and his uncle. After working as a SOLICITOR he entered politics, and in 1890 he was elected a Liberal MEMBER OF PARLIAMENT for Caernarfon, which seat he held until his death. Lloyd George was a flamboyant speaker and an advocate of radical policies. An outspoken critic of the BOER WAR, he held his first CABINET post in 1905, and in 1908 he was made CHANCELLOR OF THE EXCHEQUER. In this office he startled everyone with his "People's Budget" of 1909, which called for greatly increased revenues to pay for more ships and more social programs. This measure precipitated the HOUSE OF LORDS' rejection of the BUDGET, leading to the Parliament Act of 1911.

During WORLD WAR I Lloyd George served as Minister of Munitions. In 1916 his maneuvers led to the ouster of Herbert ASQUITH, and he became PRIME MINISTER with the support of the Conservatives and many in his own LIBERAL PARTY. He led the government during the final stages of the war, and he called an election immediately afterward, at the head of the wartime coalition. After victory in the 1918 election, he led the British delegation to Paris for the

David Lloyd George *(Hulton/Archive)*

1670s. On his return in 1689, much of the work which Locke had written earlier was published. He wrote a *Letter Concerning Toleration* (1689), which argued for individual religious liberty and toleration (except for Catholics and atheists). His *Two Treatises of Government* (1690), some of which was composed around 1680, argued against divine right and in favor of the government resting on consent of the governed (or at least those who owned property). His main philosophical work, *An Essay Concerning Human Understanding* (1690), extolled the role of experience in finding truth. He also wrote *Some Thoughts Concerning Education* (1693) and *The Reasonableness of Christianity* (1695), which together with his earlier works reorganized the field of discussion of politics, society, and religion for the 18th century.

Lollards

A nickname for the followers of John WYCLIFFE, they held the heretical belief that the bread and wine of the eucharist did not become (by transubstantiation) the body and blood of Christ. Lollards also criticized the worldliness of the clergy, and they believed that the scriptures should be available to all, hence they used English for preaching and in their translation of scripture. At first they enjoyed at least tacit support from some of the ruling classes. But in the turbulence of the early 15th century, the church and the government reacted sharply to this challenge, enacting laws condemning heretics (1401) and banning their BIBLE (1407). After an abortive revolt (1413–14), the Lollards lost support, and some went underground. There is a theory that they influenced the early stages of the REFORMATION in the 16th century, but there is no conclusive proof for this.

See also *DE HERETICO COMBURENDO.*

peace conference. While he was considered successful in his efforts there, the conditions of postwar politics were unsettled: the electoral reform of 1918 and other measures for EDUCATION and housing were offset by problems in demobilization, violence in IRELAND, and scandals over the sale of knighthoods and other honors. When the CONSERVATIVE PARTY withdrew its support for him in 1922, his reign was ended.

Locke, John (1632–1704)
philosopher

Locke was born in Wrington, Somerset, where his father was an attorney who owned a small amount of land. A student and then teacher at Christ Church, OXFORD UNIVERSITY, he was in the household of Lord Ashley Cooper, later first earl SHAFTESBURY, whom he followed into exile in the

London

The capital of ENGLAND and later GREAT BRITAIN and then the UNITED KINGDOM, London was a center of importance from Anglo-Saxon times.

Its location on the river Thames, its protected anchorage, and its access to the interior were all factors in its favor. Its size and wealth acted like a magnet for all of the British Isles, and the medieval City of London became the core of an enlarging metropolis. Around 100,000 in the 14th century, the population grew to 600,000 by 1700 and to 1 million by 1800. By the middle of the 20th century the population had peaked at 9 million, and it began to decline due to suburban migration.

The government of London was complicated. Early royal charters acknowledged the rights and customs of the city. A mayor and aldermen were in evidence from the late 12th century, but the old city was soon outgrown by surrounding BOROUGHS, and the royal precincts of Westminster, the estates of great noblemen, and church PARISHES with overlapping boundaries defied any simple form of government. Further growth of area and population led to the formation of new boroughs, and by the late 19th century, metropolitan forms of government were created. A London County Council was established in 1889, and a new Greater London Council in 1965. This body was abolished in 1985, because of resistance to the Conservative government by the radical Council chairman Ken Livingstone. The resurrection of the city government in 1998 found Livingstone running for office, now opposed by the LABOUR PARTY's official candidate, and winning the newly created post of mayor.

Long Parliament

In 1640 CHARLES I was forced to summon a PARLIAMENT to meet the costs of fielding an ARMY to face the Scots. His first attempt in April only produced wrangling over the demands of the members for attention to their grievances. The parliament was dissolved after three weeks, but the king's financial necessity did not go away. In November he summoned another parliament, this one destined to remain in existence, in some form or other, until 1660. Hence the two were known as the SHORT PARLIAMENT and the Long Parliament.

The latter was able to wring some concessions from the king but ultimately waged a CIVIL WAR against him (1642–50). It was reduced to a radical RUMP PARLIAMENT in PRIDE'S PURGE of 1648, and that remnant was terminated by Oliver CROMWELL in 1653. The surviving members were recalled in 1659, and they voted to dissolve the body and call an election to form a CONVENTION Parliament, which brought CHARLES II to the throne in 1660.

lord advocate

The chief legal officer for SCOTLAND; senior public prosecutor and political adviser. During the abeyance of the office of SECRETARY OF STATE for Scotland (1746–1885), the lord advocate was the principal manager of Scottish administrative affairs as well.

lord chancellor

This officer was the king's secretary, the custodian of the GREAT SEAL, and eventually the judge of the Court of CHANCERY as well. Until the 16th century the post was usually held by a clergyman. The chancellor presides in the HOUSE OF LORDS, and he is the president of the judicial committee sitting for the house as the final court of appeal. As the chief legal officer, the lord chancellor is a member of the CABINET.

lord chief justice

The senior judge in the English system, this title was informally given to the chief justice of the Court of KING'S BENCH. With the reorganization of the courts in 1873, the title was formally given to the chief justice of the Queen's Bench division (as it was known under Queen VICTORIA) of the new HIGH COURT OF JUSTICE. This position is strictly professional and not political.

lord lieutenant

County officers appointed first during the reign of EDWARD VI to command the militia and assist the Crown in maintaining order. The office was retained and strengthened in the reign of ELIZABETH I, and it became a pivotal office in local government. The lieutenants advised the LORD CHANCELLOR on appointments of JUSTICES OF THE PEACE, and they retained their military function until 1871. Soon after, the functions of county government were vested in elected county COUNCILS, and now the post has become a ceremonial one.

In IRELAND the lord lieutenant was the king's chief representative and a member of the British CABINET. Usually a peer, he was the VICEROY, the ceremonial head of the administration. His deputy in charge of actual government operations was the chief secretary, whose duties were like those of the SECRETARY OF STATE in GREAT BRITAIN.

lords of the congregation

The Scottish Protestant noblemen who constituted themselves as a ruling COUNCIL in the early days of the REFORMATION. The lords of the congregation signed a bond to oppose the REGENCY of MARY OF GUISE in 1557, and they invited John KNOX to return from exile. They formed an army, signed the Treaty of Berwick with Queen ELIZABETH I, and forced the French to leave SCOTLAND. They then summoned the PARLIAMENT of 1560 and forced the enactment of Scottish church reforms.

lorry

The name for flatbed wagons used on early rail and tramways, now a common name for freight-carrying motor vehicles.

Lovett, William (1800–1877)

Chartist

Raised in Cornwall, Lovett moved to LONDON and worked as a cabinet maker. He took part in the early COOPERATIVE MOVEMENT, and after Robert OWEN's attempt to form a national trade union failed, he founded the London Working Mens' Association in 1836. This became the nucleus of the CHARTIST MOVEMENT. A principal author of the People's Charter, he was among the moderate "moral force" faction, which encouraged cooperation with middle-class radicals like Francis PLACE. Lovett clashed with F6argus O'CONNOR, the Irish leader of the more militant "physical force" faction, and Lovett's role in the movement declined after 1842.

Luddites

Workers who protested against the introduction of machinery, especially handloom weavers and framework knitters. Luddites raided shops and destroyed machines, sometimes leaving a note signed by "General Ned Ludd," a legendary figure. The disturbances turned to rioting in some cases, and in 1813 some 17 men were executed at York. Historians have disputed whether these were late examples of an old tradition of communal violence or an early sign of organized working-class protest against industrialization.

Ludlow, Edmund (1617–1692)

soldier

A leader in the ARMY seizure of power in 1648 and signer of CHARLES I's death warrant, he was opposed to Oliver CROMWELL as lord protector. He returned to PARLIAMENT in 1659, but had to flee to the continent at the RESTORATION. He tried to return in 1689, but had to flee again. His memoir, *A Voyce from the Watch Tower,* was published in 1698.

Lugard, Frederick John Dealtry Lugard, first baron (1858–1945)

colonial administrator

Lugard served in Afghanistan, The SUDAN, and BURMA in the 1880s. In 1890 he led a force into UGANDA to intervene in religious wars there. The British PROTECTORATE was established in 1894.

Later Lugard became British commissioner in northern NIGERIA, where he developed his ideas of "indirect rule," a system designed to govern native peoples according to their own principles rather than those of the British colonists. He wrote an explanatory work, *The Dual Mandate in British Tropical Africa* (1922), and he was a member of the LEAGUE OF NATIONS Permanent Mandates Commission (1922–36).

M

Macadam, John (1756–1836)
road engineer

Born in Ayr, SCOTLAND, Macadam grew up in America and made a fortune there. Returning to ENGLAND, he worked at the ADMIRALTY and traveled extensively. He bought an estate in Scotland and became a MAGISTRATE and a road trustee in Ayrshire, where he experimented in building ROADS. In 1811 he presented some of his ideas to PARLIAMENT. He was made surveyor of roads in Bristol in 1815, and his methods of compacting layers of small stones over the subsoil produced water-resistant, smoother surfaces. His success led to further appointments, and his roads were an important element of improvement in TRANSPORTATION.

Macaulay, Thomas Babington (1800–1859)
politician, historian

The son of Zachary Macaulay, one of the leading EVANGELICALS, Thomas Babington Macaulay was a prodigy. Educated at CAMBRIDGE UNIVERSITY, he passed the bar and made valuable contributions to the *Edinburgh Review.* Elected to PARLIAMENT, he became a brilliant orator, but his major work was done outside the HOUSE OF COMMONS. In the 1830s he worked in INDIA and drafted a new penal code. He published his major poetic work, *Lays of Ancient Rome,* in 1842. His most durable work was a *History of England,* intended to provide an uplifting account of the English past from 1688 to 1820. It only reached the year 1702 in the first five volumes (published 1849–61). The work was very popular, and it reestablished the school of WHIG historiography, which approach was dominant well into the 20th century.

MacDonald, Flora (1722–1790)

MacDonald helped "Bonnie Prince Charlie" escape after the Battle of CULLODEN (1746). She obtained a passport for herself and her servants, Charles STUART being disguised as an Irish girl. When this became known, she was arrested and briefly detained in the TOWER OF LONDON. Her story was later the source of romantic legend.

MacDonald, (James) Ramsay (1866–1937)
prime minister, 1924, 1929–1935

The illegitimate son of a Scottish servant girl and a farm laborer, Ramsay MacDonald was a journalist in London, secretary to a Liberal MEMBER OF PARLIAMENT, and then became active in the INDEPENDENT LABOUR PARTY in the 1890s. As secretary of the Labour Representation Committee (1900–05) he managed the coordination of electoral campaigns which produced the LABOUR PARTY breakthrough in 1906. He himself was elected that year and became party leader in 1911. His opposition to WORLD WAR I meant the loss of that post, but he regained it in 1922. In 1924 MacDonald became the first Labour PRIME MINISTER (and also foreign secretary). Though only in office for nine months, he proved to contemporaries that Labour was capable of running the government. He returned to power with a majority in 1929, but immediately encountered the Great DEPRESSION. His party

Ramsay MacDonald *(Hulton Archive)*

rejected his decision to reduce unemployment benefits to balance the BUDGET. When he formed the national government in 1931, he was expelled by the party but remained as prime minister until 1935. He was succeeded by Stanley BALDWIN, and he retired in 1937.

MacDonald, Sir John (1815–1891)
prime minister of Canada, 1867–1873, 1878–1891

Born in Glasgow, MacDonald grew up in CANADA, where he became a BARRISTER and a

leader of the movement for a Canadian federal government. He had served in the colonial assembly, and he became the first PRIME MINISTER under the DOMINION created by the British North America Act of 1867.

Mackenzie, Sir George, of Rosehaugh (1636–1691)
lawyer, author

A lawyer and king's advocate, Mackenzie persecuted COVENANTERS. The English government dispatched CHARLES II's brother, James, duke of York (later JAMES VII AND II), to conduct raids on the dissidents, who called this period "the killing time." Mackenzie's aggressive tactics, including torture and vigorous prosecution, were widely despised, earning him the nickname "Bloody Mackenzie" (1679–86). He is also remembered as the founder of the library of the Faculty of Advocates (1689) and author of *Laws and Customs of Scotland in Matters Criminal* (1674) and the much shorter *Institutions of the Laws of Scotland*, a valued text for many years. In addition to other legal works, Mackenzie wrote *Aretina, or the Serious Romance* (1661), possibly the first novel written in SCOTLAND.

Mackenzie, William Lyon (1795–1861)
journalist

Mackenzie migrated to CANADA from his native SCOTLAND in 1820. He published a journal called the *Colonial Advocate*, in Toronto, became a member of the legislative assembly, and was the first mayor of Toronto in 1834. He led a failed insurrection in 1837. After a short imprisonment he was pardoned in 1849, and he sat in the legislature of the united provinces, 1850–58.

Mackintosh, Charles Rennie (1868–1928)
architect

Born and educated in Glasgow, Mackintosh created the winning design for the Glasgow

School of Art competition in 1894. His work in furniture and interior design was exhibited widely in Europe, where he was more influential than in Britain, as a leader in the art nouveau school. In his later life he was a watercolor painter.

Mackintosh, Sir James (1765–1832)
lawyer, politician, writer

Educated at Aberdeen and EDINBURGH (in medicine), Mackintosh moved to LONDON and wrote for literary journals. His *Vindiciae Gallicae* (1791) was a reply to Edmund BURKE's *Reflections on the Revolution in France*. In 1795 he became a BARRISTER, and he went to INDIA as recorder of Bombay. After his return, he was elected to PARLIAMENT in 1813, and in 1818 he became a professor at Haileybury, the school for future Indian civil servants. Among his written works were *Dissertation on the Progress of Ethical Philosophy* (1830), *The History of England* (1830), and *History of the Revolution in England in 1688* (1834).

Macmillan, Harold (1894–1986)
prime minister, 1957–1963

Member of the publishing family, Macmillan was educated at Eton and OXFORD UNIVERSITY. He was injured in WORLD WAR I, and he entered politics in the 1920s as a progressive TORY. Macmillan was against APPEASEMENT and in favor of social reform. In 1938 he published his views in *The Middle Way,* which anticipated the active government intervention of the next decade. He held several important posts in the 1950s, and he assumed the CONSERVATIVE PARTY leadership after Anthony EDEN's resignation in 1957. He rebuilt the party's strength enough to win the election of 1959, but his health forced him to resign in 1963, even as a mounting list of foreign and domestic problems confronted him. His successor was Alec DOUGLAS-HOME.

mad cow disease See B.S.E.

magistrate

A lower court judge. *Stipendiary* (paid) magistrates were appointed, first in SCOTLAND (1747), then in IRELAND (1822), and finally ENGLAND (1839). They were departures from the unpaid JUSTICES OF THE PEACE and a move toward modern, salaried officials. But the earlier form has persisted in England, even after the BOROUGH and COUNTY councils took over the administrative work of JPs in the 1880s. The judicial function of the unpaid magistrate is still carried on in today's magistrate's courts. Normally there are two lay justices, and they have petty jurisdiction in civil cases as well as criminal jurisdiction in summary (i.e. non-jury) proceedings.

Magna Carta (1215)

Although composed centuries ago, the Magna Carta has had a resonance through all of later British history. King John (1199–1216) had lost Normandy and most of the continental holdings of the Crown, and he was regarded as a rapacious and unreliable ruler. In the great crisis of his reign, the clergy, the nobility, and the citizens of LONDON all rebelled against him. His reply was to issue charters of liberties, or statements of the customary rights which he formally recognized. The most famous of these was the Great Charter (Magna Carta) of 1215, which John sealed in the presence of his barons at Runnymede, near WINDSOR. In it he promised to honor the practices of the feudal order. The 63 articles also contained more general promises, i.e., that "no free man shall be taken or imprisoned . . . except by the lawful judgment of his peers or by the law of the land" (article 39); or "to no one will we sell, to no one will we deny or delay right or justice" (article 40). But John immediately appealed to his overlord, the pope, to annul this grant, given under duress, and that was done later in the year. Nevertheless, the charter was a precedent, and there were many reissues, in one form or another, over the next few centuries. These acts created a tradition of royal accountability and general liberty. This tradition was what the 17th-century PARLIAMENT leaders Edward COKE, John HAMPDEN, and John PYM relied on (even if they exaggerated it). The charter has ever since been seen as a symbol or a source of English constitutional government.

Maitland, Frederic William (1850–1906)
historian

Maitland was a leading historian of medieval ENGLAND, particularly through his examination of LAW and legal records. After a short career in the law, he found his vocation in editing medieval plea rolls and parliamentary records. He and others founded the Selden Society in 1886 for the purpose of editing major texts and records of English legal history. He became Downing Professor of the Laws of England at CAMBRIDGE UNIVERSITY in 1888. His main work was *The History of English Law before the Time of Edward I* (2 vols., 1895), coauthored with Frederick Pollock, though Maitland wrote the majority of the work. He also wrote numerous works of legal history, including *Justice and Police* (1885), *Domesday Book and Beyond* (1897), and *Roman Canon Law in the Church of England* (1898). His lectures on the *Constitutional History of England,* and *Equity,* and *The Forms of Action* were also published, both separately and in later collected editions.

Maitland, John Maitland, baron (1545–1595)
royal councillor

Brother of William MAITLAND and keeper of the privy seal in SCOTLAND (1567), Baron Maitland had been an ardent supporter of MARY, QUEEN OF SCOTS, and he was out of favor during the 1570s. In 1583 he was made a privy councillor, and he became one of the most influential advisers to JAMES VI in the early years of his reign. A friend of the PRESBYTERIANS, he was responsible for the "Golden Act" of 1592, which established the kirk on a Presbyterian basis.

Maitland, John, duke of Lauderdale
See LAUDERDALE, JOHN MAITLAND, DUKE OF.

Maitland, William (1528–1573)
royal adviser, ambassador

Brother of John MAITLAND and secretary to MARY OF GUISE in 1558, Maitland switched his allegiance to the English in 1559, and his negotiation with ELIZABETH I led to the Treaty of Berwick and French withdrawal from SCOTLAND. He was retained as ambassador in order to present MARY, QUEEN OF SCOTS' claim to be Elizabeth's successor. He continued to be a close adviser to the Scottish queen, even holding EDINBURGH Castle for her until 1573. He died in prison.

Major, John (1943–   )
prime minister, 1990–1997

Major served as foreign secretary in 1989 and then CHANCELLOR OF THE EXCHEQUER in 1989–90, during which time GREAT BRITAIN joined the exchange rate mechanism (ERM) of the EUROPEAN ECONOMIC COMMUNITY (EEC). He won election as the CONSERVATIVE PARTY leader after the resignation of Margaret THATCHER. The difficult issues around the EEC, the POLL TAX, and the NATIONAL HEALTH SERVICE were overcome in his successful bid for election in 1992. But these issues and internal wrangling within the party weakened his grip. He lost the next election, in 1997, to Tony BLAIR.

major generals, the rule of the

After a royalist uprising in 1655, Oliver CROMWELL divided ENGLAND and WALES into 11 districts, each commanded by a major general. The military nature of the government was perhaps less annoying to the GENTRY—the natural rulers of society—than their demotion. The new PARLIAMENT of 1657 refused to supply the funds for this scheme, and a new constitution had to be written.

Malawi

An independent central African republic in the Commonwealth, formerly called Nyasaland. The area was reached by British missions in the mid-19th century, and later the British South Africa company developed its resources. After 1945 there was growing agitation for self-rule. Dr. Hastings Banda became the first premier, and independence was proclaimed in 1964, with Banda elected president in 1966. He soon took dictatorial power, but in 1993 a referendum on the constitution led to democratic elections in 1994.

Malaysia

An elective monarchical federation within the Commonwealth, Malaysia includes the 11 states of the Federation of Malaya plus Sabah and Sarawak. Each state has a separate ruler and constitution, but the rather powerful federal system (established in 1963) has a leader chosen from among the 13 state leaders, alternating every five years. The major exports are rubber and tin.

Malta

The island of Malta, only 58 miles from Sicily, is a republic and a member of the Commonwealth. The medieval rulers were Normans, but the Knights of St. John established a government that lasted from 1530 to 1798. British annexation came during the NAPOLEONIC WARS (1814), and the island became a major base for the British fleet. Self-government was granted in 1947, and after much unrest, independence was granted in 1964.

Malthus, Thomas (1766–1834)
economist

Malthus was the second son of a gentleman who was a follower of philosopher Jean-Jacques Rousseau. Taught by tutors, he attended Warrington Academy and then Jesus College, CAMBRIDGE UNI-

VERSITY. After ordination, he became a Fellow of the college. He took a post as professor of history and political economy at the EAST INDIA COMPANY's college at Haileybury in 1805. Prompted by William GODWIN's *Political Justice*, Malthus argued that human perfectibility would be limited by an increase in population. His *Essay on the Principle of Population* (1798) established him as a pioneer in demography. His basic argument, that population grew geometrically and food supply only arithmetically, was later refined somewhat. But the thrust of it was that only preventive checks (fewer births) or positive checks (famine, war) could adjust the balance. This grim prospect helps to explain the 19th-century view of poor relief as a source of population pressure. Although Malthus opposed contraception, his name was used by the Malthusian League (1861), which advocated birth control. As he failed to see, improving living standards were going to exercise a strong restraining influence on family size.

Man, Isle of See ISLE OF MAN.

Manchester, Edward Montagu, earl of (1602–1671)
general

A leader of the parliamentary armies in the early stages of the CIVIL WAR, Manchester commanded at the Battle of MARSTON MOOR (1644), but his tactics and temperament were too moderate for the increasingly radical ARMY leaders. He was denounced by Oliver CROMWELL and forced to resign by the SELF-DENYING ORDINANCE of 1645. He retired, but later assisted at the RESTORATION of CHARLES II and served in that king's court.

Manchester school

The economists and politicians noted for their support of LAISSEZ FAIRE and FREE TRADE in the 1840s. The name was coined by Benjamin DISRAELI, with a touch of scorn for the northern manufacturing towns and their residents. Among the members of the group were John BRIGHT and Richard COBDEN.

Manning, Henry, Cardinal (1808–1892)
archbishop of Westminster, 1865–1892

Manning's father was a MEMBER OF PARLIAMENT and a governor of the BANK OF ENGLAND. Manning was educated at Harrow and Balliol College, OXFORD UNIVERSITY. Ordained in 1833, he was persuaded by much of the work of John NEWMAN, and he was appalled at the increasing amount of state interference in the government of the church. He converted to Roman Catholicism in 1851, and he was a major supporter of papal infallibility at the Vatican Council in 1869–70. An active champion of the poor and a strong advocate of IRISH HOME RULE, Manning was made cardinal in 1875.

manor

The typical unit of property and jurisdiction in medieval and early modern ENGLAND. Once thought to be a Norman institution, manors probably existed earlier and were given the new name after 1066. The property was held by a lord, and it might include his own land, that of his tenants, and some common land and one or more villages. It would also have courts and officials responsible to the lord of the manor. It was their job to regulate the economy and supervise the residents, both serfs or villeins (unfree) and free tenants. New manors were not created after the 13th century, and existing manors declined in importance from the 16th century, but many of their features were visible down to the 19th century. The title "lord of the manor," though no longer of any practical significance, is still in use today.

Mansfield, William Murray, earl of (1705–1793)
chief justice of King's Bench, 1756–1788

Born at Scone, the ancient capital of SCOTLAND, Lord Mansfield was the son of a minor JACOBITE peer. He came to ENGLAND in 1718 and studied as Westminster School and Christ Church, OXFORD UNIVERSITY. Called to the bar in 1730, he became one of the leading BARRISTERS of his day. As solicitor general (1742) and attorney general (1754), he had a seat in the HOUSE OF COMMONS, and he was an important member of the duke of NEWCASTLE's government. A powerful and controversial judge, Mansfield retained a seat in the CABINET after his elevation to the bench, causing some of the attacks on his conduct, especially in the letters of JUNIUS. His judicial work was of the greatest importance because he reformed procedures and developed bodies of precedent in the fields of commercial law, copyright, patents, and contract.

Mar, John Erskine, earl of (1675–1732)
politician

A leading Scottish politician, Lord Mar helped to achieve the UNION of 1707, and he was one of the representative peers chosen under that new constitution. But he soon changed his mind and proposed repeal of the union. Dismissed by GEORGE I, he returned to Scotland, where his ineffective leadership played a part in the failure of the JACOBITES' uprising in 1715.

March, earls of   See MORTIMER FAMILY.

marches

The term *march* denotes a border area, particularly ENGLAND's northern border with SCOTLAND and its western frontier with WALES. On the Anglo-Scottish border the counties of Northumberland, Cumberland, and Westmorland had wardens appointed by the Crown to control incursions from either side. The Scottish border counties also had special officers. These marches were abolished with the union of the kingdoms under JAMES VI AND I in 1603.

In Wales the marches and their marcher lords separated English shires from Welsh tribal kingdoms. The Welsh marcher lordships were numerous and fluctuated in area. A Council of the March was established under EDWARD IV, and the lordships were aborted into English-style counties by the Acts of Union of 1536 and 1543. Yet marcher lords continued to hold their lands and to exercise authority, though in a new framework.

Margaret of Anjou (1430–1482)
queen of England, 1445–1460

Married to HENRY VI, Margaret of Anjou faced the dual challenge of a weak husband and her own French ancestry, neither of which were great assets in the final stages of the HUNDRED YEARS' WAR with France. The birth of her only son, Prince Edward, in 1453 coincided with the king's mental collapse and the opening maneuvers of the Wars of the ROSES. She became the leader of the court faction opposing Richard of YORK, who claimed the protectorate on behalf of the ailing king. Fighting in the next few years led to her defeat, the capture of Henry, and the seizure of the throne by Richard of York's son, EDWARD IV. Margaret thereafter was in exile, briefly returning in 1470–71, when her son was killed in the Battle of TEWKESBURY (1471), and she was imprisoned. She was allowed to return to France in 1476.

See also ST. ALBANS, BATTLES OF.

Margaret Tudor See TUDOR, MARGARET.

Marlborough, John Churchill, duke of (1650–1722)
general

A courtier and soldier, Marlborough's career rose under the patronage of JAMES VII AND II, especially after he routed the rebels under the duke of Monmouth in 1685 (see MONMOUTH'S REBELLION). Nevertheless, he was responsible for many of the defections among the officers of the king in 1688. He served WILLIAM III well in IRELAND in 1690, but he was dismissed in 1691. Recalled in 1700, he took command of British forces in the low countries (today's Netherlands and Belgium), and his

authority was affirmed by Queen ANNE in 1702. He won a remarkable series of battles (BLENHEIM, 1704; RAMILLIES 1706; Oudenarde, 1708; and Malplaquet, 1709). With her allies, GREAT BRITAIN had defeated France and was rewarded at the Treaty of UTRECHT (1713), but Marlborough had been dismissed again in 1711, the victim of party feuds. He was reinstated by GEORGE I, supervised the defeat of the JACOBITES, and resigned in 1718.

Marlowe, Christopher (1564–1593)
dramatist

The son of a shoemaker, Marlowe was educated at King's School, CANTERBURY; and Corpus Christi College, CAMBRIDGE UNIVERSITY. His curious career included working as a government spy, but his lasting fame rests on powerful dramatic works that probed the human psyche: *Tamburlaine* (1587), *Edward II* (1594), and *Doctor Faustus* (1604) were published after his death. He was killed in a tavern brawl.

marprelate tracts (1588–1589)

Essays written from an extreme PURITAN viewpoint, attacking the episcopal hierarchy. The anonymous author's aim was to "mar" the "prelates" by satirical attacks. Suspected authors were tortured, several were executed, but the real author was probably Job Throckmorton, who was never punished.

marquess (marquis)

The title of marquess (or marquis) ranks second in the PEERAGE, behind that of DUKE. It was the last of the new creations, used for the first time in 1385. Employed sparingly, it was introduced to the Scottish peerage a century later.

Married Women's Property Acts

In English law a woman's property was merged with her husband's at marriage. In an act of 1870, married women could retain earnings from property, and in 1882 they were entitled to keep property held prior to or after the marriage. These measures were part of the WOMEN'S MOVEMENT toward legal equality.

Marshalsea

A London prison in Southwark, serving the court of the same name, which had jurisdiction over cases in the royal household. Marshalsea was one of the prisons attacked in the Peasants' Revolt (1381) and in CADE'S REBELLION (1450). It subsequently became a debtor's prison and closed in 1842.

Marston Moor, Battle of (1644)

In the largest battle of the CIVIL WAR, King CHARLES I's forces, under Prince RUPERT, were caught in Yorkshire between the Scottish army of Alexander LESLIE and the armies of PARLIAMENT under General Thomas FAIRFAX, his cavalry commander Oliver CROMWELL, and the earl of MANCHESTER. The royalists lost 4,000 men, and the king lost control of Northern ENGLAND.

martial law

Originally the law administered by the court of the king's CONSTABLE and the marshal. It means the law enforced by military authorities, either in occupied territory or, under extreme conditions, in the state during war, rebellion, or civil unrest. Today the term does not mean the law applied to the armed forces (as it did at first). That term is now "military law." The other modern equivalent is "emergency powers," a status much more likely to be enacted by PARLIAMENT.

Martineau, Harriet (1802–1876)
writer

Martineau was from a Huguenot family in Norwich. Her father's clothmaking business collapsed at the end of the war in 1815. She began a career as a writer, and her first success was a set of 24 stories based on the ideas of classical economists, *Illustrations of Political Economy* (1832). After she traveled to America, she published *Society in America* (1837). She also wrote a *History of England during the Thirty Years' Peace, 1816–1846* (1849). In later life she wrote children's books and adult novels. Her work covered a very wide range, and her *Autobiography* was published in 1877.

Marx, Karl (1818–1883)
political theorist

Born in Germany, the author of *Communist Manifesto* went into exile in ENGLAND in 1849 and lived the rest of his life there. Studying and writing in the BRITISH MUSEUM, Marx produced his master work *Das Kapital,* which described the capitalist system and its flaws, arguing that it would undermine itself and give way to SOCIALISM and then communism. Personally Marx was not a major political figure, and his main political activity was in organizing the unsuccessful International Working Men's Association (1864–72). Further, he and his work had little impact on British politics in his lifetime. Indeed, since his work was not translated until 1887, the earliest impact came from Henry HYNDMAN's borrowed rendition (*England for All,* 1881) and his SOCIAL DEMOCRATIC FEDERATION. Marxism became very influential in the 20th century, less so in GREAT BRITAIN than in revolutionary regimes in Europe and elsewhere.

Mary, Queen of Scots (1542–1587)
queen of Scots, 1542–1567

Sent to France in 1548, the daughter of JAMES V and MARY OF GUISE was married to Francis I, the heir to the French throne, in 1558. He succeeded a year later and died a year after that. Mary returned to her native country, a confirmed Roman Catholic and one who had spent most of her life outside of SCOTLAND. She had to confront a hostile Protestant faction, which with English help had ousted her mother and the occupying French advisers. But Mary was probably driven by her hope of succeeding ELIZABETH I on the English throne. If that was her objective, the path she chose could hardly have been more unlucky. Her marriage to Henry Stewart, Lord DARNLEY,

Mary, Queen of Scots, in a romanticized 19th-century engraving by Alexander Hay Ritchie after a painting by J. B. Wandesforde *(Library of Congress)*

did produce a son, the future JAMES VI AND I, but it was otherwise a disaster. He was involved in the murder of her Italian courtier, David RIZZIO, in 1566. In February 1567, Darnley was murdered, and Mary was soon in the company of one of his assassins, the earl of BOTHWELL. They were married later in 1567, and that act cost Mary much of her support. She was forced to abdicate, and she chose to flee to ENGLAND. There she was taken into custody, and from that point was suspected as a Catholic plotter intent on seizing the throne. After a series of incidents, she was accused of treason, tried, and executed in 1587.

Mary I (1516–1558)

queen of England and Ireland, 1553–1558

The daughter of HENRY VIII and CATHERINE OF ARAGON, Mary was declared illegitimate when her parents' marriage was annulled in 1533. Continued loyalty to her mother and devotion to her faith meant that she was not only out of favor but in some danger, especially during the reign of her brother, EDWARD VI. Before he died, he designated Lady Jane GREY as his successor, but this plan fell apart, and Mary was able to quickly take power. Her main objectives were to reconcile ENGLAND to the Roman Catholic church and to marry and produce an heir. To achieve the first, she removed BISHOPS like Thomas CRANMER and Nicholas RIDLEY and restored Stephen GARDINER and other loyal Catholics. She also acknowledged the authority of Rome, and she began the work of removing the statutes on which the CHURCH OF ENGLAND rested. Her second policy produced the plan to marry Philip II of Spain, which in turn triggered Sir Thomas WYATT's rebellion. The supression of rebels led to harsher policy against Protestants and eventually the execution of about 300, which earned the queen the nickname "Bloody Mary." But both of Mary's plans failed, as a phantom pregnancy in 1558 turned out to be stomach cancer. At her death, Princess Elizabeth became Queen ELIZABETH I and reversed the Catholic restoration.

Mary II (1662–1694)

queen of England, Scotland, and Ireland, 1689–1694

Mary was the eldest daughter of James, duke of York (later JAMES VII AND II), and Anne Hyde, his first wife. When her brother died in 1671, she became heir to the throne after her father. In 1677 her uncle CHARLES II arranged her marriage to William of Orange (later WILLIAM III). The couple had no children. When William invaded ENGLAND in 1688, the succession passed to Mary and William jointly. Mary acted as regent on her husband's continental expeditions, but she died of smallpox in 1694. Her sister ANNE succeeded William to the throne in 1702.

Mary of Guise (1515–1560)

queen of Scots, 1538–1542

Married to JAMES V in 1538, Mary of Guise bore him three children, but only the princess Mary survived, and she was born a week before her father died in 1542. The queen was thus placed in the position of trying to manage the realm for her daughter, being formally made regent only in 1554. She sponsored the marriage of her daughter to Francis I (1558), but his untimely death in 1560 coincided with rising Protestant opposition in SCOTLAND supported by English intervention. Mary was besieged and died in EDINBURGH Castle.

Massachusetts Bay Company

The company chartered in 1629 to supervise the PURITAN settlement in New England (North America). The government was altered locally to favor the dominant religion, and it produced offshoots in Connecticut and Rhode Island. The charter was revoked in 1684 and replaced in 1691. Massachusetts, with its tradition of vigorous independence, was a leading center of rebellion in the AMERICAN COLONIES in the 18th century.

Master of the Rolls

An assistant to the LORD CHANCELLOR, in charge of the records kept on rolls of parchment. The Master of the Rolls became the second judge in the court of CHANCERY, and is now a judge in the Court of APPEAL.

Maugham, (William) Somerset (1874–1965)
writer

Maugham's father was a lawyer in the British embassy in Paris. Orphaned at 10, the young Maugham was taken to ENGLAND, where he attended King's School, CANTERBURY. He then studied in Germany before being educated as a physician at St. Thomas' Medical School (1897). His autobiographical *Of Human Bondage* (1915) made him famous. His other notable works include *The Moon and Sixpence* (1919), *Cakes and Ale* (1930), and *The Razor's Edge* (1944). He was also a successful playwright, his better-known works including *Our Betters* (1917), *The Circle* (1921), *The Constant Wife* (1926), and *For Services Rendered* (1932).

Mau Mau See KENYA.

Maurice, (John) F. D. (1805–1872)
social reformer

Born in Suffolk, the son of a UNITARIAN minister, F. D. Maurice attended Trinity College, CAMBRIDGE UNIVERSITY, but did not take a degree as he declined the oath. In 1830 he entered OXFORD UNIVERSITY and was ordained in 1831. Living in London, he began a writing career, producing an autobiographical novel, *Eustace Conway* (1834), and editing the *Athenaeum.* He became professor of literature at King's College, London and then professor of theology (1846). On publication of his *Theological Essays* (1853) he was forced to resign his professorship. He helped to found the Christian Socialist movement, and he founded the Working Man's College in London (1854).

Maxwell, James Clerk (1831–1879)
physicist

Born in EDINBURGH and educated there and at CAMBRIDGE UNIVERSITY, Maxwell was noted for his study of electromagnetic waves. He taught at Aberdeen, LONDON, and Cambridge. In the latter school, he was the Cavendish professor and supervised the new Cavendish laboratory. Known for his experiments with light, radio waves, and gases, Maxwell brought together the work of the 19th century on electricity and developed a general theory of electromagnetic radiation, from which later applications like radio, radar, and television were derived.

Mayhew, Henry (1812–1887)
journalist

Founder of *Figaro in London* (1831–39) and cofounder of *Punch* (1841), Mayhew wrote novels and plays, but his most memorable contribution was the multivolume *London Labour and the London Poor* (1851). These articles had originally appeared as letters to the *Morning Chronicle,* and they gave vivid descriptions of the life of the underclass. Together with later works, *The Criminal Prisons of London* (1862) and *London Children* (1874), his writing helped to build public support for social reforms.

Maynooth, St. Patrick's College

Seminaries were closed during the French Revolution, and the British government gave permission to open one at Maynooth in IRELAND (1795). The government gave annual grants to support the school, but in 1845 a proposal by Robert PEEL to increase the grant caused a political crisis and William GLADSTONE's resignation from the CABINET.

mechanics institutes

The wave of educational reform of the early 19th century featured efforts for adult EDUCATION, such as mechanics institutes (programs and lectures for tradespeople and artisans). These institutes appeared in Scotland in the first decade, in London by 1823, and then spread to the provinces. Spurred by Henry BROUGHAM's *Observations upon the Education of the People* (1825), the movement was part self-education and part an engine for spreading social responsibility. By 1860 the enrollment in such institutes had grown to 200,000.

Melbourne, William Lamb, viscount (1779–1848)
prime minister, 1834, 1835–1841

Lord Melbourne's father was a peer, his mother a society hostess, and rumors swirled around his true parentage. He went to Eton; Trinity College, CAMBRIDGE UNIVERSITY; and Glasgow. A WHIG who entered PARLIAMENT in 1806, he was one of those who supported the moderate TORY government of George CANNING, and he served as chief secretary for IRELAND (1827 and 1828). He resigned from the duke of WELLINGTON's government and was chosen to be home secretary in the Whig cabinet of Charles, Earl GREY (1830–34). In that post Melbourne had to deal with a variety of radical disturbances, and he was effective in so doing. He became the new PRIME MINISTER upon Grey's resignation but resigned himself shortly thereafter because his ministers were not united. In 1835 he formed a government that had to struggle with strains in the economy and the discontent of the CHARTIST MOVEMENT and the ANTI-CORN LAW LEAGUE. He was a sage political advisor to the young Queen VICTORIA for the first four years of her reign.

Melville, Andrew (1545–1622)
Presbyterian leader

After studies at Aberdeen and at Paris and a period of teaching in Geneva, Melville became principal of Glasgow University, then Aberdeen, and then St. Andrews (1574–80). His extreme views on PRESBYTERIAN order were reflected in the Second Book of Discipline, adopted when he was moderator of the GENERAL ASSEMBLY in 1578. This put him at odds with the moves by JAMES VI to restore royal and episcopal authority in the kirk. In 1599 he was deprived of his post at St. Andrews. In 1607 he was called before the PRIVY COUNCIL and sent to the TOWER OF LONDON. On his release in 1611, he went into exile in France.

Melville, Henry Dundas, first viscount (1742–1811)
Scottish politician

A Scottish advocate, son of the lord president of the Court of SESSION (Lord Arniston), Dundas sat in PARLIAMENT from 1774 until 1802. He held a number of CABINET posts, but his principal role was as right-hand man and manager of Scottish affairs for Prime Minister William PITT. He was made first lord of the ADMIRALTY in 1804 but was impeached in 1806 over irregularities in the NAVY accounts. This was the last use of IMPEACHMENT, and Melville was acquitted in the HOUSE OF LORDS.

member of parliament

Term referring to elected members of the HOUSE OF COMMONS, often abbreviated "MP." It does not include the peers of the realm, who are members of the HOUSE OF LORDS.

Menzies, Sir Robert (1894–1978)
prime minister of Australia, 1939–1941, 1949–1966

A BARRISTER in Victoria, AUSTRALIA (1918), and a prominent Nationalist member of the Victoria parliament, Menzies served as attorney general before becoming a member of the Commonwealth House of Representatives (1934–66). He led the government that joined GREAT BRITAIN in declaring war (1939–41) and attended CABINET meetings in LONDON in 1941. There was great anxiety about whether Australia would be protected from Japanese aggression, and this helped to build support for a more American-oriented foreign policy. A Labour government succeeded Menzies in office, and he in turn led a victorious antisocialist coalition in 1949. He supported the U.S. involvement in Korea (1951) and in Vietnam (1965).

mercantilism

The prevailing economic orthodoxy of the 16th and 17th centuries which saw national wealth in terms of precious metals. The object of trade was to increase the reserves of gold bullion, and to this end the laws regulating colonies and trade were seen as vital as a means of preserving and enhancing the nation's wealth. In the 18th and 19th centuries, this economic policy was replaced by FREE TRADE.

Merchant Venturers

Early advances in English overseas trade were made under various royal grants and monopoly privileges such as the "staple" towns for export of wool and woolen cloth. In this same spirit, merchants banded together to utilize mutual protection and reduce risk. They were, after all, trying to compete with well-established German, Italian, Dutch, and Iberian commercial enterprises. The London Merchant Venturers were formed in the later 15th century, and they received a royal charter in 1486. They were intent upon breaking foreign monopolies—and maintaining their own over other English merchants. They lost this monopoly in 1689, and the company was dissolved in 1809.

Merthyr Rising (1831)

In South WALES the serious incidence of poverty and industrial decline coincided with the first national campaign for political reform in 1831. Coal miners and ironworkers in Merthyr Tydfil seized control of the town for several days. Troops were ordered in, and in a confrontation 16 of the workers were killed. In the aftermath of the Merthyr Rising, as it was called, one of the leaders (Richard Lewis, *alias* Dic Penderyn) was charged with wounding a soldier, and he was executed. There was no disciplinary action against the soldiers.

Mesopotamia

The part of the Ottoman empire corresponding to present-day Iraq, Mesopotamia was the location of vital oil supplies. During WORLD WAR I, in 1914 and 1915 there was a British advance toward Baghdad, with a major setback in 1916

and final victory in 1917. Nearly 300,000 men were committed to the campaign, and British backing for King Faisal meant the area supported British interests in the interwar years.

Methodism

A religious revival movement, begun by a group at OXFORD UNIVERSITY in the 1720s, including and later dominated by John WESLEY. The name referred to the devout and methodical behavior of members. Through extensive travel and field preaching, Wesley, his brother Charles, and George WHITEFIELD built up a large following, mainly of the lower ranks of society. The group was organized in "classes" of 10 or 12 members, meeting weekly, while the church as a whole held annual conferences from 1744. Their EVANGELICAL faith stressed individual salvation through the love of God. While they remained within the CHURCH OF ENGLAND at first, the group seceded after Wesley's death in 1790, and it began a process of subdividing which lasted for much of the 19th century. There was a continuing effort to reunite the separate groups (Wesleyan, New Connection, Primitive, Bible Christian), and a major reunion came in 1932.

Methuen, John (1650?–1706)
ambassador to Portugal

A BARRISTER who was also a CHANCERY master, Methuen was chosen as an envoy to Portugal in 1691 and returned there as ambassador in 1702 and 1703. He concluded a commercial treaty with that country (the Methuen Treaty). English wool was to be imported freely in exchange for a reduced duty on Portuguese wines. The consumption of port was increased at the expense of French wines. The treaty was terminated in 1836.

MI 5

A division of the British Directorate of Military Intelligence, organized in 1905, which is responsible for surveillance of subversive groups and for counterespionage. MI 5 reports to the home secretary, but its activities are secret. It has no powers of arrest, and therefore relies on the SPE-CIAL BRANCH of Scotland Yard for such authority.

MI 6

This foreign intelligence service began operation in 1911. It was superseded by other intelligence operations in WORLD WAR II, but MI 6 became a key agency working on Soviet intelligence after 1945. High-level defectors were recruited by both sides.

See also BLUNT, ANTHONY.

Midlothian campaign (1879–1880)

William GLADSTONE emerged from semiretirement to contest the seat for Midlothian, the region around EDINBURGH. He was motivated particularly by the foreign policy of Benjamin DISRAELI. Gladstone addressed large crowds on at least 20 occasions, denouncing TORY policy and laying out his own principles for foreign and imperial policy. While not completely original, this campaign of public elaboration of policy for the electorate, which exploited the LIBERAL PARTY leader's oratorical skill, seemed to contemporaries to be a major step in opening up the political process. Gladstone won the election and once again became PRIME MINISTER.

militia

Armed force of ordinary citizens, drafted by virtue of custom, edict, or statute LAW. Nominal volunteers, the militia were in fact required, under some Anglo-Saxon rules and by the Assize of Arms (1181), to serve in defense of their region. There were many alterations over the next few centuries, and in the 1660s a set of statutes regulated the militia. It became a symbolic counterweight to a standing ARMY, though in practice it was never a significant military force in modern times. In 1907 it was absorbed into the Territorial Army.

Mill, James (1773–1836)
philosopher

Born and educated in SCOTLAND, Mill went to LONDON to work as a journalist. One of the disciples of Jeremy BENTHAM, he helped to form the "philosophic radicals," the exponents of the body of thought known as UTILITARIANISM. Mill wrote on a wide range of topics, and his works include *History of India* (1818); *Essay on Government* (1820); *Elements of Political Economy* (1821); and *Analysis of the Phenomenon of the Human Mind* (1829).

Mill, John Stuart (1806–1873)
philosopher

The son of James MILL, John Stuart Mill was also a follower of Jeremy BENTHAM and a utilitarian, but he later wrote an extensive new version of that philosophy (*Utilitarianism*, 1861). Among his most influential works were *Principles of Political Economy* (1848); *On Liberty* (1859); *Considerations on Representative Government* (1861); and *The Subjection of Women* (1869). Through these works he became the most prominent advocate of individual liberty and democratic government in the Victorian era.

Milner, Alfred, viscount (1854–1925)
colonial administrator

Born in Germany, the son of a physician, Lord Milner studied at King's College, LONDON; and Balliol College, OXFORD UNIVERSITY, where he was a student of Benjamin JOWETT. Also a student at the Inner Temple (see INNS OF COURT), he became a BARRISTER in 1881 and worked briefly on the *Pall Mall Gazette*. In 1884 Milner became private secretary to Viscount Goschen, who helped him get a post as a financial administrator in EGYPT. After this he wrote his book *England in Egypt* (1892). He was then chairman of the Board of Inland Revenue (1892–97), before he became high commissioner in SOUTH AFRICA (1897–1905). His criticism of the Boer republics played a part in the origin of the BOER WAR. He returned to GREAT BRITAIN in 1905 and later served in the wartime and postwar CABINET of David LLOYD GEORGE (1916–21).

Milton, John (1608–1674)
poet

Born in LONDON, Milton went to Christ's College, CAMBRIDGE UNIVERSITY, where he began preparing for the ministry but became increasingly devoted to poetry. Without having established any career, he was drawn into the swirl of political events in the 1640s, and he was the author of numerous radical pamphlets attacking the power of BISHOPS, advocating the freedom to divorce, championing freedom of the press (*Areopagitica,* 1644), and arguing for the right to depose a monarch (*The Tenure of Kings and Magistrates,* 1649). He held a post under the government of the COMMONWEALTH OF ENGLAND, and his own views became more radical. During the same period, his eyesight failed. Briefly imprisoned at the RESTORATION, he returned to writing the epic poetry which had been his lifelong objective. In 1663 he completed *Paradise Lost,* and in 1671 *Paradise Regained* and *Samson Agonistes.*

monarchy

The institution of monarchy has proven to be the most flexible and durable part of British government. Kingship was common to early peoples in all parts of the British Isles. The English monarchy had its roots in the Anglo-Saxon period, with an English state emerging by the 10th century. The progress of Scottish monarchs was similar, the earliest amalgamation coming in the ninth century. Irish and Welsh rulers remained in greater numbers with more localized authority. In all cases, ancestry was traced to the earliest times, though there was a point where legend replaced fact in any ancestral line. The earliest kings ruled on the basis of tribal custom and crude collections of written law, while their Christian clergy became ever more impor-

tant advisers and administrators. The major difference between ENGLAND and its neighbors was the relative rate of centralization: a single English king had emerged clearly by the 10th century. The king of Scots was also above his petty rivals, but in WALES and IRELAND there was much less consolidation. In most cases, the rates of change were governed by external invasions, and the most emphatic of all came to 11th-century England: first the Danish conquest by Sweyn and his son Cnut (1014–35) and then the conquest by William of Normandy (1066). These events set the English kingdom apart, bringing its nobility under the control of a powerful central ruler, providing him with a strong council, royal judges, and tax collectors.

In the early Middle Ages, kings traveled constantly. Their officials were members of their household, and it was only in the 12th and 13th centuries that offices came to have fixed locations in England. Over time the monarch extended his influence through the majesty and solemnity of coronation, investiture, and formal meetings and proclamations, as well as by daily instruments of royal communication: charters, WRITS, and letters.

The idea of monarchy was more carefully defined by the 13th century. The king was a sacred figure, anointed at his coronation, enjoying the divine sanction of the church. With this connection came the potential for conflict between royal and papal power, clearly visible in the reigns of the Anglo-Norman kings (1066–1272). From this religious source, and from imperial ideas rooted in Roman law, the king was said to possess a comprehensive legal authority, the royal PREROGATIVE. It was, however, subject to limitation in special situations, as with the MAGNA CARTA (1215); and in the ordinary course of business by the COMMON LAW. The latter was a unique English development, stemming from the work of royal judges, in central and ASSIZE courts, making and preserving decisions and precedents that became the rules of royal justice.

English medieval kings kept power by adopting the feudal relationship, making themselves the overlords of all their territory, with each vassal being dependent on their lordship. At the same time, a contractual relation was established, one in which the obligatory councils of royal subjects would eventually come to check the absolute power of the Crown. Kings of SCOTLAND were also feudal overlords, without nearly as much central control, and when Irish or Welsh rulers introduced feudal ties, it was usually as the vassals of England. The most important outcome of this relationship was the emergence, in the 13th century, of more or less regular meetings of the king and his COUNCIL, enlarged to contain KNIGHTS and BURGESSES from all parts of the realm. These PARLIAMENTS were used to approve statutes (see ACT OF PARLIAMENT) and to endorse TAXATION. They thus acquired the essential quality of a legislative body, though without any independent power. Such bodies were common in medieval Europe, and they appeared in Scotland and in Ireland, though not in Wales.

The end of the Middle Ages brought a "new" monarchy—or so many historians once described the later 15th and early 16th centuries. This description was linked to more modern finances, military power, trade, and exploration, all transforming the English monarch's power, especially with the reigns of HENRY VII and HENRY VIII. While this explanation is now less fashionable, and many "new" features are seen prefigured in earlier periods, there was clearly a new cast to the monarch's role in the 16th century:

1. The English sovereign became the sole regal authority, annexing Wales (1536–43), declaring kingly rule in Ireland (1541), and achieving the personal union of the English and Scottish crowns (1603).

2. The 16th-century challenge to papal authority in the REFORMATION resulted in expanded royal power as the head of the several PROTESTANT churches in England, Scotland, and Ireland.

3. Due to dramatic inflation and economic strains, royal governance was ever more dependent upon Parliament's taxation power, which turned into a brake on royal authority in the 17th century.

The modern monarchy was the creation of the civil wars and revolutions of the 17th century. While the execution of CHARLES I in 1649 was certainly not a sign of popular rejection of the Crown, it was just as certainly a sign of the dangers of unlimited exercise of royal power. No later ruler was likely to test the limits; nor indeed did many later radicals attack the institution of monarchy. The Crown was restored in 1660, and a form of resolution came in 1689. When WILLIAM III and MARY II accepted the DECLARATION OF RIGHTS, they endorsed a "balanced constitution," one in which the king, the lords, and the commons shared political power. Indeed, the king was still extremely powerful: he was the commander in chief of all forces (though there was a careful watch kept on his "standing army"), he appointed judges and bishops, he had the power to create peers, and he selected leading ministers of state who managed the now annual sessions of Parliament.

The next stage of constitutional development was the product of personal and political changes in the 18th and 19th centuries. The essential alteration was in the loss of royal power to name ministers at will, and the necessity to name ministers who had the confidence of Parliament's HOUSE OF COMMONS. This change began during the time of William PITT the younger (1783–1801, 1804–06) and it was complete by the middle of the reign of Queen VICTORIA (ca. 1870). Once this change was settled, it was the electorate who decided the political leadership of the country. In the words of Walter BAGEHOT, the monarch had "the right to be consulted, the right to encourage, the right to warn" (*The English Constitution*, 1867). He did not say the right to govern.

In the 20th century, the Crown retained an important symbolic role, and the sovereigns in time of war were vital rallying figures and the embodiment of imperial power. That power of course dwindled after 1945, though the queen was still the head of the Commonwealth (see BRITISH EMPIRE AND COMMONWEALTH), a valuable international body. At the end of the century, despite a troubled familial scene, Queen ELIZABETH II still occupied the central place in the constitutional order: sovereign, head of the established church, leader of the government, in whose name and service all official acts were performed.

See also CABINET; HOUSE OF LORDS; PRIME MINISTER; and individual rulers.

monasticism

Monasticism had its roots in the third century, with holy men who lived as hermits in the desert. In the fourth century, communal forms of withdrawal from the world evolved, and these became the main form of monastic life. Men and women devoted themselves to a religious life for the greater glory of God. They lived according to a rule such as that of St. Benedict in the fifth century. They took vows of poverty, chastity, and obedience. This distinctive element of the Christian church enabled it to spread across Europe. Monastic, or "regular," clergy were the counterpart of the secular clergy, who managed the public functions of the church: PARISH and diocesan ministry and clerical aid to the government (councillors, judges, and administrators).

The earliest order in BRITAIN was the Benedictine, brought first to Southern ENGLAND by St. Augustine and later to Northern England by St. Wilfrid. In IRELAND the solitary monastic life was preserved beside centers of learning and communal worship in the Celtic church. In addition, through missionary work, the influence of Celtic Christians spread across the British Isles and Europe: Celtic monks were reaching Scotland, England, and the continent from the sixth century, and the missions of Boniface and Alcuin became ministers and teachers in European courts in the eighth and ninth centuries. This work coincided with the terrible visitations of Norse and Danish raids from the end of the eighth century. While many monasteries were destroyed, there was a revival in the 10th century, followed by the introduction of the newer orders of Cistercians (1098), Franciscans (1209), and Dominicans (1215). Each of the orders established monastic houses, endowed by patrons and supported by alms and bequests as well as by their own productive enterprise. After the 13th century there were few new foundations, and from the late 14th century the economy of monasteries declined, as they suffered from general economic weakness due to plague, inflation, and war. Whether or not the monasteries deteriorated in spiritual terms was and remains an unresolved question. What is sure is that they were dissolved by the order of HENRY VIII, beginning in 1536.

Monck, George, first duke of Albemarle (1608–1670)
general

Born into a landed family in Devonshire, Monck was engaged in the duke of BUCKINGHAM's expeditions to Cádiz (1625) and La Rochelle (1627). He fought for the Crown in the CIVIL WAR until he was captured in 1644. By 1647 he had joined forces with the parliamentary army and was a MAJOR GENERAL in ULSTER. He later assisted Oliver CROMWELL in the Scottish campaign (1650), and after their victory, Cromwell installed Monck as commander in chief in SCOTLAND. Given a command in the NAVY, he was victorious in the first Dutch War (1652–54). After Cromwell died, Monck brought his army from Scotland and arranged the election of the CONVENTION Parliament, thereby ensuring the RESTORATION of CHARLES II. For this he was made a DUKE, and he continued to serve the Crown.

Monmouth's Rebellion (1685)

James Scott, the duke of Monmouth, was one of the illegitimate sons of CHARLES II. A successful general, he became the figurehead for extreme opponents of the succession of JAMES VII AND II to the throne. At Charles's death, Monmouth led an small uprising in the south of England. His group of 3,000–4,000 captured the town of Taunton, but did not move toward the larger target of Bristol. Monmouth issued a proclamation as rightful king, but when his untrained force met the royal army at Sedgmoor, they were quickly defeated.

Monmouth was taken to LONDON, where he was executed. The surviving rebels were tried at the BLOODY ASSIZES by justice George JEFFREYS, and many of them were executed.

Montagu, Charles See HALIFAX, CHARLES MONTAGU, EARL OF.

Montagu, Edward See MANCHESTER, EDWARD MONTAGU, EARL OF.

Montgomery, Bernard, viscount (1887–1976)
field marshal

The son of an ANGLICAN bishop, Montgomery served in WORLD WAR I and was wounded at Ypres in 1914. He commanded the Third division in the evacuation at DUNKIRK (1940), and he was given the command of the Eighth Army in EGYPT in 1942. There he won the Battle of EL ALAMEIN, and in 1943 his army joined the invasion of Sicily and Italy. Later that year he was appointed the commander of land forces for the invasion of Normandy in 1944. A contentious figure, his personality clashed with most of his colleagues and superiors, but his record on the battlefield was impressive. He commanded occupying forces in Germany in 1945 and was made chief of the imperial general staff in 1946. He later served as deputy supreme commander of the NORTH ATLANTIC TREATY ORGANIZATION (1951–58).

Montrose, James Graham, fifth earl and first marquis of (1612–1650)
general

The son of the fourth earl of Montrose, James Graham had sided with the COVENANTERS in 1639, but by 1643 he was in the service of CHARLES I. In 1644 he led a brilliant campaign across the north of SCOTLAND, using Irish and Highland troops. There was little support for him in the Lowlands, and he was defeated at the Battle of Philiphaugh in 1645. He had raised hopes among the royalists, but in fact his army was small and had little chance of rescuing the fortunes of the king. In 1650 he was defeated at Corbiesdale, betrayed after the battle, taken to EDINBURGH, and executed.

Moore, Henry (1898–1986)
sculptor

The foremost English sculptor of the 20th century, Moore came from a family of coal miners in Yorkshire. He studied in Leeds, LONDON, and Paris, and taught at the Royal College of Art and the Chelsea School of Art. His massive figures were startling to traditionalists, his style one of energetic abstraction. From the 1940s his commissions increased, and he produced a large number of works.

Moore, Sir John (1761–1809)
soldier

Moore was the son of a Scottish doctor and writer who took him on a long tour of the continent to learn languages. On returning, he joined the British ARMY at age 15. Known for development of light-infantry tactics, he served in the American Revolution, returned to GREAT BRITAIN, and was elected to PARLIAMENT (1784–90). In the wars with France after 1790, he fought in Corsica, the WEST INDIES, Ireland, Holland, and Egypt. He commanded the British forces in the Iberian Peninsula, fighting against French occupation, and he was killed at Corunna after directing a dangerous and successful retreat (1809).

Moray, James Stewart, earl of (1531–1570)
regent

The illegitimate son of JAMES V and half-brother of MARY, QUEEN OF SCOTS, Lord Moray was a leader in the provisional government of 1559–60, and he helped to arrange Mary's return from France to take the throne. He became a leading figure in her regime, promoting a friendly policy toward ENGLAND. He opposed the marriage to Lord DARNLEY, led an abortive rebellion, and went into exile.

When he returned in 1567, he became regent for JAMES VI, but he was assassinated in 1570.

More, Hannah (1745–1833)
writer
The daughter of a Norfolk gentleman and school-master, More ran a school with her sisters but also wrote for the stage and became acquainted with the literary circle of Samuel JOHNSON. Her interests turned toward EVANGELICAL causes, and she used her talent to support religious and conservative ideas as an antidote to the RADICALISM inspired by the French Revolution. Her *Cheap Repository Tracts* (1795–98) encouraged loyal and dutiful behavior by the lower orders. She also established FRIENDLY SOCIETIES and SUNDAY SCHOOLS.

More, St. Thomas (1477–1535)
lord chancellor, 1529–1532
More's father was a judge, and he was educated in LONDON and Oxford. A renowned humanist, the author of *Utopia* (1516), and friend of Erasmus, More studied LAW at Lincoln's Inn, where he began a very successful career. A MEMBER OF PARLIAMENT by 1504, he became a royal councillor in 1517, and he was made chancellor of the duchy of Lancaster in 1525. After the fall of Cardinal WOLSEY, he became LORD CHANCELLOR. As HENRY VIII's efforts to rid himself of CATHERINE OF ARAGON increased, the measures he took to dominate the church were anathema to More. He resigned as chancellor in 1532, but the king was determined to silence his famous critic. When More refused to take the oath of succession, denying papal authority, he was imprisoned. Although he refused to openly deny the king's authority, his interrogators claimed that he had done so. He was executed, and in 1935 he was canonized.

Morgan, Sir Henry (1635–1688)
buccaneer
Morgan's uncle, lieutenant governor of JAMAICA, was killed in 1665, and Morgan led an expedition that captured Porto Bello and slaughtered the Spanish garrison. He also raided Cuba and Panama. Charged with piracy, he was returned to ENGLAND (1671) but was acquitted and later became lieutenant governor of Jamaica.

Morley, John Morley, viscount (1838–1923)
writer, politician
Editor of the *Fortnightly Review,* a liberal journal, Morley became a MEMBER OF PARLIAMENT in 1883. One of the authors of the Radical Programme in 1885, he favored IRISH HOME RULE and opposed the British engagement in the BOER WAR. He wrote *The Life of William Ewart Gladstone* (3 vols., 1903). In the LIBERAL PARTY governments (1905–1914), as secretary for INDIA, he drafted reforms that increased Indian participation in government (1909). He resigned in protest at the declaration of war in 1914.

Morris, William (1834–1896)
poet, socialist
Educated for a career in the church, Morris renounced that and studied art and architecture. His interest in craftsmanship paralleled his socialist view of industrial society, and he became a highly influential designer, printer, and writer. He established a company to produce his designs for decoration and stained-glass windows. He also founded the Kelmscott Press, through which he had great influence on typography and book design. A founder of the Socialist League (1885), an offshoot of the SOCIAL DEMOCRATIC FEDERATION, he also launched the journal *Commonweal.*

Morrison, Herbert (1888–1965)
Labour politician
Born into a working-class family in London, Morrison rose through the ranks of LONDON politics and became LABOUR PARTY secretary, mayor of Hackney, and member of the London County Council prior to his election to the HOUSE OF COMMONS in 1923. He served in the first Labour governments and was an unsuccessful candidate for

party leader in 1935. In WORLD WAR II he was Winston CHURCHILL's home secretary (1940–45), responsible for air-raid precautions and emergency services. In the postwar government he was the leader of the House of Commons, and in 1955 he was again defeated for the post of party leader.

Mortimer family

In the 13th century the Mortimer family held great estates in the Welsh marches. Roger Mortimer (1231–82) was an important BARON who fought against Welsh princes and defeated the rebel Simon de Montfort at the Battle of Evesham in 1265. Thenceforth he was a strong supporter of Edward I (king of England, 1272–1307).

Roger, first earl of March (1287–1330), was called the virtual ruler of England. As the lover of Edward II's estranged queen Isabella, he organized an invasion in 1326, bringing with him the king's son Edward, who was crowned after Mortimer had arranged his father's deposition and murder. He was made EARL in 1328, but EDWARD III had him arrested and hanged in 1330.

Edmund, third earl of March (1351–81), married Philippa, daughter of Lionel, duke of Clarence and son of Edward III. The house of YORK's claim to the throne came from this union.

Roger, fourth earl of March (1374–98), was a ward of the Crown and the heir presumptive by virtue of his descent from Lionel, younger son of Edward III. He died while serving as LORD LIEUTENANT of IRELAND.

Edmund, fifth earl of March (1391–1425), was the ward of the king after his father died in 1398. Although there were uprisings on his behalf in 1405 and 1415, he was loyal to the Crown. His son Richard, duke of York, inherited his claim to the throne.

Morton, James Douglas, earl of (1525–1581)

regent of Scotland

Lord Morton's three predecessors as regent had died suddenly, but he fared slightly better. As LORD CHANCELLOR to MARY, QUEEN OF SCOTS (1563), he was involved in the murder of David RIZZIO and that of Lord DARNLEY. He was regent from 1572 to 1578 but was later condemned for Darnley's murder and executed.

Mosley, Sir Oswald (1896–1980)

British fascist leader

Mosley was born in LONDON, and his parents separated when he was five. He attended Winchester, then Sandhurst, where he was expelled in his first year (1914). When WORLD WAR I broke out, he was able to obtain a commission. He applied for the Royal Flying Corps, but he was injured when he crashed his plane while testing for his pilot's license. He was elected to PARLIAMENT as a member of the CONSERVATIVE PARTY in 1918, later as an independent (1922), and then as a LABOUR PARTY candidate (1926). Not satisfied with any of the parties, he chose to found his own British Union of Fascists (1932). His oratory was tinged with antisemitism, and his rallies often provoked violent demonstrations. The group's activities prompted the Public Order Act of 1936, which banned uniforms and created the power to ban marches deemed dangerous. The party was proscribed in 1940, and Mosley was interned. He had a brief career in postwar politics, advocating IMMIGRATION controls.

Mountbatten of Burma, Louis Mountbatten, first earl (1900–1979)

admiral, viceroy of India, 1947

The great-grandson of Queen VICTORIA, Lord Mountbatten served in the NAVY in WORLD WAR I. In 1942 he was made commander of combined operations, then allied commander in southeast Asia (1943). As the last VICEROY of INDIA, he was in charge of the surrender of power, and after independence he served as governor-general for 10 months. He resumed his naval career and was first sea lord and then chief of the defense staff (1955–65). In 1979 he was assassinated in IRELAND by the IRISH REPUBLICAN ARMY.

Mountjoy, Charles Blount, baron (1563–1606)

soldier

Mountjoy served ELIZABETH I in IRELAND as lord deputy and LORD LIEUTENANT (1601–03). He took over after the aborted mission of Robert Devereaux, earl of ESSEX, defeated Hugh O'NEILL at the Battle of KINSALE, and then took his surrender in 1603. This signified the end of Irish resistance and the seemingly "final" conquest of Ireland.

MP See MEMBER OF PARLIAMENT.

municipal corporations

The government of towns was no less antiquated than representation in PARLIAMENT around 1830. Existing BOROUGHS had chartered governing bodies which in some cases were old and corrupt. Some new industrial cities were without adequate government institutions. The Municipal Corporations Act of 1835 created governments elected by ratepayers, with councils, alderman, and mayors operating on a standard pattern. There were many boroughs that fell outside the new system, and another act in 1882 extended the reforms to most of them.

Murray, Lord George (1690–1760)

Jacobite general

Murray fought in the 1715 JACOBITE rebellion and escaped to France. He joined the invasion of 1719 and was later pardoned. In 1745 he served Bonnie Prince Charlie (Charles Edward STUART) as the actual commander of his forces, and he was responsible for the early victories (Prestonpans, Clifton, Falkirk). At CULLODEN he was not in favor of the plan of battle, though he fought well. He died in exile in the Netherlands.

Murray, William See MANSFIELD, WILLIAM MURRAY, LORD.

Mutiny Act

First passed in 1689, and then only for a six-month term, the Mutiny Act provided the authority for military discipline. The articles of war (for the NAVY and the ARMY) were confirmed and given force by this law. Its required renewal, later extended to 12 months, was the method of ensuring PARLIAMENT's safety from the threat of a standing army under the control of the Crown. This law was replaced by the Army Discipline and Regulation Act of 1879, and then the Army and Air Force (annual) Acts in 1917.

Myanmar See BURMA.

N

nabob

A nickname used for wealthy returnees from 18th century INDIA, from the word *nawab*, a title for a princely ruler. Their wealth was often a target of criticism, as they used it to buy their way into the aristocracy.

Namibia

Once a German colony, this territory in Southwest AFRICA was governed under a mandate by SOUTH AFRICA until 1966, after which time control was contested between South Africa and the South-West African People's Organization (SWAPO), which took over after independence in 1990. The country's economy depends on mineral resources (diamonds, copper, and uranium).

Napier, Sir Charles (1782–1853)

soldier

Napier served in IRELAND in 1798, in the Peninsular campaign (1809), and in the war of 1812 before taking a post in Greece. In 1839 he was in command of crown forces in the north of ENGLAND during the CHARTIST MOVEMENT disturbances. Sent to INDIA in 1841, he commanded the conquest of Sind (reportedly sending back the telegraphic message "peccavi"—"I have *sinned*").

Napier, John (1550–1617)

mathematician

Born at Merchiston Castle near EDINBURGH, Napier was educated at St. Andrews. He invented logarithms, simplifying complex calculations with exponential numbers; his invention of logarithmically calibrated rods (called "Napier's bones") was the basis for the slide rule.

Napoleonic Wars (1803–1815)

The continuation of warfare between France and her European neighbors, which had begun in 1793. Napoleon Bonaparte had become the leading French general by 1799, and his campaigns to conquer Italy and Egypt, while having mixed results, were the foundation for his consolidation of imperial power in France, where he became consul (1799) and then emperor (1804). In the interim, a brief peace (1802–03) was ended when GREAT BRITAIN declared war in 1803. There was a plan to invade ENGLAND, but that was no longer possible after the British under Admiral Horatio NELSON won the Battle of TRAFALGAR (1805). A third coalition was formed (Britain, Austria, Russia, and Sweden) in 1805. Napoleon crushed his continental enemies in the next two years, and with his "Continental System" he tried to close the ports of the continent to British trade. The reply was a blockade of the ports under French control. Meanwhile Napoleon installed puppet regimes in European states under French supervision. He invaded Russia with an army of 500,000 men in 1812, but this was the turning point. When Napoleon entered Moscow, the city was burned to the ground. He was forced to retreat, and the retreat became a rout. The coalition was revived, and a series of victories forced Napoleon out of power in 1814. He returned from exile in 1815 to lead a futile effort to restore French power, and he was finally defeated by the duke of WELLINGTON at the Battle of WATERLOO.

See also ABOUKIR BAY; MOORE, SIR JOHN; VIENNA, CONGRESS OF.

Naseby, Battle of (1645)

The decisive battle of the CIVIL WAR. In May 1645 Prince RUPERT had captured Leicester, and the rebel army, which had been besieging Oxford, marched to engage the royalists. At first Rupert had some success with his cavalry, but the NEW MODEL ARMY under Thomas FAIRFAX and Oliver CROMWELL badly defeated the much smaller royalist force. About 5,000 men were taken prisoner, and CHARLES I's hopes of victory were crushed. The king's private correspondence was captured, and its publication proved embarrassing, as it exposed his plan to use a Catholic army from IRELAND.

Nash, John (1752–1835)
architect

The foremost English architect of the early 19th century, Nash was the son of a millwright in LONDON. In the first stages of his career, he suffered financial problems and moved to WALES, where he built a number of country houses until he was able to return to London and reestablish himself there. The prince regent (later GEORGE IV) employed him to rebuild much of the west end of London, including Regent Street and Regent's Park as well as Trafalgar Square and St. James's Park. He also made additions to BUCKINGHAM PALACE and contributed to the rebuilding of the Brighton Pavilion.

Natal

British traders settled at Port Natal (later Durban) in SOUTH AFRICA as early as 1824. A colony was declared in 1843, and settlement of British colonists was encouraged. This was part of an ongoing British effort to gain control at the expense of Dutch Afrikaners and native peoples.

The economy of the colony was based on sheep farming and sugar cultivation. In 1910 Natal was made a part of the Union of South Africa.

National Assistance

A major part of the WELFARE STATE. In 1948 the National Assistance Act provided cash benefits for those in need, referred to as a "safety net" for the poor. This marked the end of the old POOR LAW, and it was the beginning of a system of targeted benefits that later included supplements to income and housing and emergency grants.

national debt

Government borrowing, backed by the security of PARLIAMENT's power of TAXATION. The national debt was first formally recognized in the 1690s. The term also stands for the accumulated excess of expenditure for which loans must be obtained. The debt around 1900 was about 10 percent of national income. It rose to nearly 50 percent in WORLD WAR II, and at the end of the 20th century the debt was about 8 percent of national income.

National Gallery

The British government acquired several private collections of paintings at the beginning of the 19th century, and they were housed in a building constructed on Trafalgar Square in 1838. With government and private support, the National Gallery has become one of the major collections in the world. National galleries were also established in EDINBURGH (1859) and DUBLIN (1864).

National Health Service

There had been considerable discussion of the provision of health care from the 1920s onward, and the subject was a theme of William BEVERIDGE's wartime report. The service was to provide free medical care for all, and in order to implement such an ambitious plan, there were protracted negotiations between the government and the medical profession and hospitals. When it began in 1948, local authorities, panels of physicians, and nationalized hospitals were the main administrative groups. The costs of the service were much higher than expected, and when charges for prescriptions, dentures, and spectacles were introduced in 1951, Aneurin BEVAN, the minister responsible for the act, resigned. Since then, the service has been plagued with rising medical costs and peppered with assorted reform proposals, but it has retained wide public support.

National Insurance

As early as 1911 there was legislation to insure those who were victims of economic distress. Based on contributions from employers and employees, the early acts were limited to specific occupations. An act in 1946 made the system national: contributions provided insurance for unemployment, sickness, maternity benefits, widowhood, and old age.

nationalization

The LABOUR PARTY set out the objective of compulsory purchase of private enterprises from their owners in its constitution in 1918. Several public enterprises were created in the interwar years (Central Electricity Board, 1926; BRITISH BROADCASTING CORPORATION, 1927; London Passenger Transport Board, 1933; British Overseas Airways Corporation, 1939). This type of public corporation became the model for nationalized industry. The first state purchase was the BANK OF ENGLAND in 1946. The coal, gas, electricity, railway, and road haulage businesses were next. But the iron and steel industry proved to be a challenge. The CONSERVATIVE PARTY victory in 1951 returned that industry to private hands, though it was renationalized in 1967. There were few other changes until the series of privatizing efforts of the 1980s under Margaret THATCHER. Nationalized industries were gone by 1996.

National Service

Compulsory military service which was continued from WORLD WAR II. The National Service Act of 1947 ordered all males over 18 to report for military service. At first the term was 12 months; this was increased to two years by 1950. The intake was reduced in 1957, and no one was called after 1960, due to cutbacks in the military and general reductions in public expenditure.

National Trust

A private voluntary organization, founded in 1895. Conservationists like Octavia HILL, who led the effort, were concerned about the deteriorating environment, and their first effort was to preserve the cliffs around Cardigan Bay. Other natural sites were soon joined by houses and other buildings as part of the inventory. The body is funded by private and corporate gifts; by fees; and, since 1946, by state support. The National Trust now owns some 350 stately homes. The National Trust for Scotland was established in 1931.

navigation acts

These were the legislative expression of MERCANTILISM. The first act in 1651 required goods shipped to ENGLAND to be in English ships, or those of the cargo's country of origin. This was clearly aimed at Dutch shipping (see DUTCH WARS). The next act in 1660 said that colonial goods had to be carried in English ships. A ban on foreign vessels in all colonies was passed in 1663, and further acts placed restrictions on specific articles. The acts were not fully enforced, but they were still an irritant to colonial merchants. The structure of trade regulation was attacked by FREE TRADE supporters, and the navigation acts were repealed in 1849 and 1854.

navy

The peoples of island communities can hardly avoid developing maritime skills. Consequently, from the earliest times the inhabitants of BRITAIN and IRELAND took to the sea for fishing, trading, and travel. A navy, an organized fleet of ships under the command of the sovereign, was unknown until the 17th century. There were earlier occasions when the Crown commanded the owners of vessels to serve. There were special provisions for supplying those ships, as with the CINQUE PORTS during the Middle Ages, and the demands for SHIP MONEY in times of emergency. By the time of HENRY VIII there was at least the germ of a naval establishment. But ELIZABETH I's victory over the Spanish ARMADA was still the work of a temporary assembly of ships. The twin forces that drove naval organization into the modern era were the rapid expansion of trade and the increasing size and armament of vessels. In Oliver CROMWELL's time the organization developed under an ADMIRALTY board. After the RESTORATION there was further improvement in organization, growth of the royal dockyards, and a steady increase in the size and number of ships. By the end of the 18th century, GREAT BRITAIN had created the world's most powerful fleet. This force surpassed its rivals until the end of the 19th century, when the growth of naval power in Germany, Japan, and the United States began to overtake the British superpower.

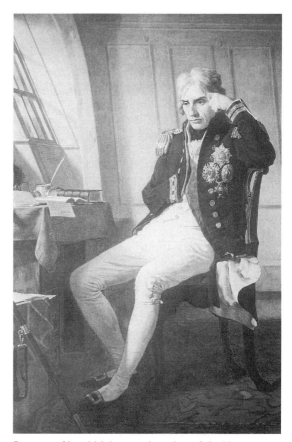

Painting of Lord Nelson in the cabin of the *Victory* *(Library of Congress)*

Nehru, Jawaharlal (1889–1964)
prime minister of India, 1947–1964

Son of a leader of the Indian National Congress, Nehru was educated in ENGLAND and trained in the LAW. A follower of Mohandas GANDHI, though a socialist, he became the Congress's president in 1929. Active in the negotiations for British withdrawal, he approved the partition of INDIA and PAKISTAN. The first prime minister of India, he was reelected several times. He wrote *Glimpses of World History* (1934–35), *Autobiography* (1936), and *The Discovery of India* (1946).

Nelson, Horatio Nelson, viscount (1758–1805)
admiral

Entering naval service at the age of 12, Nelson sailed to the Arctic and the WEST INDIES. His first command was during the American Revolution. In the war against revolutionary France, he lost his right eye in battle in 1794, his right arm in 1797. In 1798 he pursued the French fleet across the Mediterranean, where he won the Battle of ABOUKIR BAY (Battle of the Nile). He defeated a rebellion in Naples, where he became the lover of Lady Emma Hamilton, wife of the British ambassador. As second in command in the Baltic, in 1801 he won the Battle of Copenhagen, disregarding his orders and defeating the Danish fleet. Taking command in the Mediterranean, Nelson blockaded the French fleet in Toulon (1803–05). When it escaped, he pursued it to the West Indies and back, finally engaging and destroying the enemy at the Battle of TRAFALGAR. He was killed by musket fire as his flagship *Victory* engaged the enemy. Nelson is buried in ST. PAUL'S CATHEDRAL.

Neville, Richard   See WARWICK, RICHARD NEVILLE, EARL OF.

New Brunswick

Coastal province of CANADA, settled by the French in the 16th century. New Brunswick is part of Acadia, which the British took and renamed NOVA SCOTIA. This part was detached and renamed when thousands of American loyalists came to settle in 1783. Self-government was granted in 1848, and the territory was a key battleground in the formation of the Canadian federation in the 1860s.

New Caledonia   See DARIEN.

Newcastle, Thomas Pelham-Holles, duke of   (1693–1768)

prime minister, 1754–1756, 1757–1762

One of England's wealthiest peers, Newcastle supported the house of HANOVER and was a leading member of the WHIGS, holding high government office for over 40 years. He was an eccentric figure who devoted himself to the details of political patronage rather than lofty statesmanship. A SECRETARY OF STATE from 1724, he was a supporter of Robert WALPOLE, the chief minister from 1721 to 1742. With his brother Henry PELHAM, he led what was called a "broad bottom" administration—one that included members of most factions (1743–1754). When his brother died, Newcastle became sole leader but proved to be ineffective. In 1756 he resigned after a series of military defeats by the French. But soon he was back, in a coalition with William PITT, who directed the victorious campaigns of the SEVEN YEARS' WAR, while Newcastle managed PATRONAGE. That skill was less

admired by the new king, GEORGE III, who preferred the services of Lord BUTE, and Newcastle resigned in 1762.

Newcomen, Thomas   (1663–1729)

inventor

An ironmonger in Devon, Newcomen became the partner of Thomas SAVERY, whose steam engine (patented 1698) was an elementary boiler and piston. Newcomen made significant improvements to the design, producing an atmospheric self-acting engine. These engines were adopted for pumping water from coal mines and a variety of other uses. Up to 50 of them were in use by the 1730s.

New Delhi

New Delhi was made the capital of British INDIA (in place of CALCUTTA) in 1912. Located next to the old capital of the Mogul empire, it was continued as the capital of the new republic of India in 1947.

Newfoundland

The easternmost province of CANADA, discovered by John CABOT in the 1490s. The territory was claimed for the English Crown in 1583 by Humphrey GILBERT, but control was disputed by the French, and both countries had extensive fishing operations. An elected assembly was created in 1832 and the province became self-governing in 1855. Union with the new federal government was rejected in 1869. With a desperately poor economy, Newfoundland reverted to colonial status in 1933. In 1949, after a close vote, it became the last province to join the DOMINION OF CANADA.

Newgate Prison

First located in one of LONDON's city gates in the 12th century, Newgate Prison was rebuilt twice, after the FIRE OF LONDON in 1666 and after the GORDON RIOTS in 1780. Notorious for the corruption of its officers and the conduct of its inmates, Newgate was the site for public executions, from 1783 to 1868. In 1902 the prison was torn down, and the Central Criminal Court (the OLD BAILEY) was built on the site.

Newman, John Henry (1801–1890)
cardinal

The son of a London banker, educated in Ealing and at Trinity College, OXFORD UNIVERSITY, Newman became a Fellow of Oriel College and vicar of St. Mary's, the university church (1828–43). He gained a reputation as a compelling preacher, and he was the leading figure in the OXFORD MOVEMENT. In the 1830s high church leaders were mobilized by the interference of government in church affairs. This added fuel to an existing revival of Anglo-Catholic sentiment. Newman was editor of a series of essays called *Tracts for the Times,* in which the positions of the ANGLICAN church were compared with those of the Roman Catholic church. He left the CHURCH OF ENGLAND in 1843 and converted in 1845. After that he established religious communities in ENGLAND and a Catholic university in DUBLIN. He was made cardinal in 1879. His spiritual autobiography, *Apologia pro vita sua,* was published in 1864.

New Model Army

In the course of the CIVIL WAR, there was discontent in the LONG PARLIAMENT with the performance of its armies, and the SELF-DENYING ORDINANCE was passed in 1645. This removed most of the aristocratic officers and allowed the reorganization of the army, with unified command under Thomas FAIRFAX. This body of 20,000 was more professional in its behavior and more EVANGELICAL in its faith. The army defeated CHARLES I at the Battle of NASEBY and in ensuing battles, bringing him to surrender in 1646. The new army was more formidable in politics as well as in battle, and it played a central role in government through the interregnum. After the RESTORATION, most of its units

disbanded, the rest becoming part of the new royal standing army.

See also CROMWELL, OLIVER.

Newton, Sir Isaac (1642–1727)
mathematician, scientist

Born in Lincolnshire and raised by his mother, Newton was educated at King's School, Grantham; and Trinity College, CAMBRIDGE UNIVERSITY. He became professor of mathematics at Cambridge in 1669. His first scientific paper explained that white light consisted of all colors. He devised laws of motion, including a universal law of gravitation, described in his *Philosophia naturalis principia mathematica* (1687). He was also the inventor of differential and integral calculus. His own religious views were probably deistic, but he received a dispensation to hold a university post without being in holy orders. He was twice elected MEMBER OF PARLIAMENT for the university, and he was master of the royal mint.

New Zealand

An archipelago 1,000 miles east of AUSTRALIA, in which the two main islands together are somewhat larger than the UNITED KINGDOM. The native Maori mainly inhabited the North island, and their numbers rapidly declined as colonists brought new diseases and guns into their simple culture. The small English settlement in the 1830s was built up by IMMIGRATION, and British sovereignty was recognized after the Treaty of Waitangi (1840). A form of responsible government was set up in 1846 and a federal constitution in 1852. Democracy came with votes for men (1879) and women (1893). New Zealand became a DOMINION in 1907. Meanwhile, the Maori were decimated by a series of wars (1860–72). Discovery of gold in the 1850s accelerated immigration and heightened interest in the colonial economy. By the 1880s refrigeration allowed export of meat to GREAT BRITAIN. In the 20th century New Zealand was a stout supporter of Britain in time of war, and in 1947 the country became an independent member of the

Commonwealth. New Zealanders fought beside the Americans in Korea and in Vietnam. In the 1990s the population of 3.6 million included 400,000 Maori, who had been thought to be nearing extinction in 1900. As with other former colonies, the matter of land rights for indigenous peoples became a major item on the political agenda at the end of the 20th century.

Nigeria

Contact with this former COLONY in West AFRICA began with slave traders, and forts were established by the Royal African Company in the 1670s. After Britain's activity in that enterprise ended, explorers and missionaries came in the 1840s. GREAT BRITAIN's first colonial government was in Lagos and the south. Other regions were contested by French and German interests. In the north there were native Muslim princes, with other forms of tribal rule in the south. A federation was created under British authority in 1914, and after independence in 1960, a federal scheme was implemented. But in 1966 the government was overthrown in the first of many military takeovers. Ethnic violence caused the breakup of the federation with the secession of the eastern region of Biafra. The successive military regimes seemed to create more and more subordinate states, and the instability spread to the once-successful oil industry, which was disrupted in the 1990s. With 115 million people in 2000, Nigeria's population was twice as large as any other African state, its resources were abundant, but its social and political fabric was in tatters.

Nightingale, Florence (1820–1910)
nurse, reformer

Born into a wealthy family, Nightingale prevailed upon her father to allow her to enter the then lowly profession of nursing. After she founded a women's clinic in LONDON, she heard of deplorable conditions in the hospitals in the Crimea. She led a team of nurses there (1854),

Florence Nightingale *(Hulton/Archive)*

and through hard work and efficient organization they radically reduced the death rate among injured soldiers. She herself was taken ill and returned in 1856. But she remained a tireless campaigner for reforms: in the army medical service, in nursing education, and in hospital construction. She founded a school of nursing at St. Thomas's Hospital, London, in 1860, and thus launched the modern nursing profession in GREAT BRITAIN.

Nile, Battle of the See ABOUKIR BAY.

Nineteen propositions

In June 1642 PARLIAMENT presented these 19 demands to CHARLES I. They wanted to control the selection of ministers, to reform the church, and to control the MILITIA. The king parried with a plausible rejection of the terms, and the CIVIL WAR began in August.

nisi prius

The essential feature of the ASSIZE system: where at one time juries were brought to trials before the Court of COMMON PLEAS, in 1285 a statute said that trials would be held in Westminster, "unless before that" (*nisi prius*) the trial was held before a judge at assizes. This endorsed the circuit system which meant more efficient and regular judicial proceedings, while it also insured more consistent and uniform judicial practice.

nonconformists

Protestants not conforming to the doctrine or practice of the CHURCH OF ENGLAND. The earliest PURITANS sought to remodel the established church, but they were punished under acts of UNIFORMITY, causing them to separate from the main body of the church. Those who continued to dissent were disciplined more severely in the reign of CHARLES I (BAPTISTS, INDEPENDENTS) and CHARLES II (QUAKERS, PRESBYTERIANS). In the 18th century there was less systematic persecution, but there was continuing deviation from the established church, by UNITARIANS and later by followers of METHODISM. In 1828 the old laws against dissenters were repealed, but many other disabilities were only slowly dropped over the rest of the 19th century. Because of their status as outsiders, nonconformists tended to align with the LIBERAL PARTY, and they were one of that group's main bodies of support.

nonjurors

The ANGLICAN clergy and laymen who refused to take the oath supporting WILLIAM III and MARY II in 1689. Their position was that this oath violated their earlier oath to JAMES VII AND II. If not JACOBITES, they were typically high-church anglicans who did not approve of the new WHIG regime. Archbishop William SANCROFT, six BISHOPS, and some 400 other clergy maintained this position, and for several generations nonjurors held their own consecrations. Eventually they were reabsorbed into the established church.

nonresistance

A doctrine calling for obedience to authority, even if it was exercised unjustly. The concept was advocated in the reign of CHARLES I, but it took on special strength after the regicide and INTERREGNUM, in the reigns of CHARLES II and JAMES VII AND II. Oaths of nonresistance were required in 1661 as a result of the corporation Act. However, such oaths were declared to be unnecessary in 1689, and the act was repealed in 1719.

Norfolk, Thomas Howard, third duke of (1473–1554)
politician
Howard served at sea, operating against Spanish corsairs in 1511. He became lord admiral in 1513, and in the same year he fought at the Battle of FLODDEN and was ennobled. He was LORD LIEUTENANT of IRELAND in 1520, and he led raids on France in 1521 and 1522. The uncle of Anne BOLEYN and Catherine HOWARD, he was a constant royal servant, a strong supporter of the more conservative elements in government, and himself a lifelong Catholic. He was imprisoned in 1546, saved from execution by EDWARD VI's death, and later released by Queen MARY I.

Norman Conquest (1066)
The forces of Duke William of Normandy landed in southern England in October. King Harold of Wessex, who had just defeated an invading force under Harold of Norway, marched south to confront the new threat. At the Battle of Hastings, the Normans defeated the Saxons, killing Harold and a large part of the English nobility. William

marched around LONDON, seized the capital city, and held his coronation in the new church of the late English king, Edward the Confessor, WESTMINSTER ABBEY. The conquest brought in a new ruling class and created an unusually centralized medieval kingdom. These events also created a royal connection between England and the continent that lasted until the 15th century.

North, Frederick North, eighth lord
(1732–1792)
(earl of Guilford)
prime minister, 1770–1782

After education at Eton and Trinity College, OXFORD UNIVERSITY, Lord North entered PARLIAMENT in 1754. A supporter of NEWCASTLE, he held office under the elder William PITT. In 1767 he became CHANCELLOR OF THE EXCHEQUER and in 1770 first lord of the TREASURY. The early years of his administration were very successful in establishing stable government and making reforms in government finance. But North was destined to be the man to face rebellion in the AMERICAN COLONIES. It began innocently with the conciliatory removal of many customs duties, except that on tea. The angry colonial response, especially the Boston Tea Party, provoked coercive action. What the colonists termed INTOLERABLE ACTS were needed to restore order, at least from the British perspective. But with mobilization proceeding on both sides, North was forced to pursue military action and thus to lead in circumstances for which he was not well qualified. On a number of occasions he tried to resign, but GEORGE III would not allow it, mainly because North was such a skillful manager of the HOUSE OF COMMONS. Only when his majority there had dwindled did the king allow him to resign in 1782. He briefly returned in 1783 in a coalition with Charles James FOX, but that unnatural union only lasted for nine months. Increasingly blind, North slowly withdrew from politics, an unlucky symbol of defeat, though a highly skilled parliamentarian. He succeeded to the earldom of Guilford two years before his death.

North Atlantic Treaty Organization (NATO)

The alliance formed in 1949 to oppose the threat of the Soviet Union, especially in regard to occupied Germany. An attack on any of the treaty nations was to be considered an attack on all. The original members were the United States, CANADA, GREAT BRITAIN, France, Italy, and Portugal, plus Norway, Iceland, Denmark, Belgium, Luxembourg, and the Netherlands. Greece and Turkey joined in 1952. West Germany became a member in 1955 and Spain in 1985. The organization maintained a military force in Europe, with a joint-command structure and under the protection of American strategic nuclear weapons. With the demise of the Soviet Union in 1989, NATO's role was revised. On the one hand it became involved in peacekeeping in Bosnia and Kosovo, and on the other it began to extend its influence into central and eastern Europe by inviting new states to join.

North Briton

The journal published by John WILKES, satirizing another titled the *Briton,* by Tobias Smollett, which supported the government of Lord BUTE. Wilkes only published the weekly for about 10 months from 1762 to 1763, but he outraged his readers with attacks on the peace treaty with France and on Bute. In issue number 45, he alleged that a statement in a speech given by the king was a lie. For this he was prosecuted for seditious libel, and the GENERAL WARRANT issued to arrest him and seize his papers became the focus of the celebrated decision that such WARRANTS were illegal.

Northcliffe, Alfred Harmsworth, viscount (1865–1922)
newspaper publisher

Lord Northcliffe formed a publishing house with his brother Harold Harmsworth, viscount ROTHERMERE, in 1887. They acquired the *Evening News* and launched the *Daily Mail* (1896) and the *Daily*

Mirror (1903). They later bought the *Observer* and, in 1908, *The Times.* Northcliffe used the papers to express his own political views, which unsurprising behavior earned him criticism. He was made a BARON in 1905 and a VISCOUNT in 1918.

Northern Ireland

The partitioned state formed under the Government of Ireland Act of 1920, ratified by the ANGLO-IRISH TREATY of 1921; also known as ULSTER, the name of the ancient province of the northeast. In fact, the modern state has only six of the nine counties from the area of the old province, which decision was made in order to guarantee a Protestant majority in the new state. The constitution included a PARLIAMENT with authority over domestic matters, and a small delegation to Westminster, where authority remained for foreign affairs. The UNIONIST majority steadfastly opposed separation from the UNITED KINGDOM, and there was a single-party Protestant government from 1921 until 1972. The Catholic minority had boycotted the political system of the North, and because of this sectarian division, local government, police, public housing, and schools were riddled with discriminatory features. It was the attempt to moderate these conditions, by Prime Minister Terence O'NEILL's government, which helped bring about a rapid rise in protests and demonstrations in the late 1960s. These civil-rights protests, and the unionist reactions, escalated into confrontations between demonstrators and the Royal Ulster Constabulary, and when these grew serious, the British ARMY was called in.

The army presence was intended to provide protection for Catholics. But with provocation, especially from the IRISH REPUBLICAN ARMY (IRA), a more dangerous instability soon appeared. Extremist attacks and reprisals involving the army, the IRA, and Protestant loyalist paramilitaries dominated the next three decades (1969–98). British authorities were at a loss to counter the violence. In 1972 they dissolved the government and restored direct rule. There were several attempts to reinstitute local government,

and in 1998 a truce and negotiated settlement brought one more effort to establish a joint Protestant-Catholic provincial government.

Northern Rebellion (1569)

There was widespread hostility to the settlement of the ANGLICAN Church by Queen ELIZABETH I in the 1560s. The opposition was particularly strong in the more remote parts of ENGLAND. Thus, when MARY, QUEEN OF SCOTS fled to northern England in 1568 and surrendered to Elizabeth, the CATHOLIC earls of Northumberland and Cumberland hatched a plot to free the Scottish queen and arrange her marriage to the duke of Norfolk. The rebels mustered a small army, destroyed symbols of the reformed church, took over Durham Cathedral, and held a traditional mass. In 1570 the rebels fled to Scotland, their leaders disgraced and punished. The rebellion probably was most important in affirming Elizabeth's PROTESTANT settlement.

North Sea oil

Discovery of oil in the North Sea in 1969 dramatically changed Britain's stock of energy resources. Having seen her coal industry decline for much of the 20th century, with extensive pit closures from 1970 onwards, the new resource came none too soon. The oil began to be extracted by 1975, and there were positive effects on the economy in general, and greater impact on Northeast SCOTLAND (Aberdeen in particular), where the base facilities to support oil rigs were located. By the mid-1980s GREAT BRITAIN was an exporter of oil. Although the level of production is expected to slowly decline, this source may remain important well into the 21st century.

Northumberland, Henry Percy, earl of (1341–1408)

Northumberland fought in France with John of Gaunt and was made EARL by RICHARD II (1377), and he became the dominant leader in the northern MARCHES (the Scottish borders). He and his son "Hotspur" (Sir Henry PERCY) rebelled in 1403 against HENRY IV, and allied with OWEN GLENDOWER in Wales. When their plans failed, Northumberland had to flee to SCOTLAND. He invaded ENGLAND again in 1408 and was killed at Branham Moor.

Northumberland, John Dudley, duke of (1502–1553)

politician

Northumberland's father Edmund, an adviser of HENRY VII, was attainted and executed in 1510. A soldier, Northumberland helped to put down the PILGRIMAGE OF GRACE (1536). He was warden of the Scottish MARCHES (borders) in 1542, and he led the capture of Boulogne from the French in 1544. Gaining influence within the COUNCIL of the new king EDWARD VI, he was lord president from 1549, created DUKE in 1551, and responsible for pushing Protestant reforms. As the king became seriously ill, Northumberland convinced him to issue letters patent denying the succession to MARY I or ELIZABETH I, and recognizing Lady Jane GREY instead. He arranged Jane's marriage to his son, but the coup failed, and he was executed.

Northwest Passage

A long-sought arctic water route from the Atlantic to the Pacific—dubbed the Northwest Passage—attracted the explorers Martin FROBISHER and Henry Hudson, among others. In the 18th century PARLIAMENT offered a cash prize for its discovery. Several attempts were made in the 19th century, and the first successful navigation was a three-year journey by the Norwegian Roald Amundsen, completed in 1906. The first single-season passage was made in 1944.

Nottingham, Charles Howard, first earl of (1536–1624)

admiral

The son of William, first Lord Howard of Effingham, and grandson of Thomas HOWARD, duke of

Norfolk, Charles Howard served at sea from 1554. In the reign of ELIZABETH I he was both a successful courtier and sailor. Lord high admiral from 1585 to 1618, he commanded the fleet that defeated the Spanish ARMADA. In 1596 he joined Robert Devereaux, earl of ESSEX, in the raid on Cadiz, which prevented another armada. He was in charge of suppressing Essex's rebellion in 1601, and he led the negotiations for an Anglo-Spanish treaty in 1604.

Nottingham, Daniel Finch, earl of (1647–1730)

Tory politician

The eldest son of Heneage Finch, earl of NOTTINGHAM, was educated at Westminster school; Christ Church, OXFORD UNIVERSITY; and the Inner Temple (see INNS OF COURT). A leading figure in the later STUART era, Nottingham supported CHARLES II during the EXCLUSION crisis (1679–81). He was one of three commissioners sent to negotiate with William of Orange in 1688, and he became a SECRETARY OF STATE under WILLIAM III. He was also in a TORY cabinet in 1702–04 under Queen ANNE.

Nottingham, Heneage Finch, earl of (1621–1682)

lord chancellor

Born in Kent, Nottingham was the son of the recorder of LONDON. After education at Westminster school; Christ Church, OXFORD UNIVERSITY; and the Inner Temple (see INNS OF COURT), he entered PARLIAMENT in 1660. As solicitor general he was the prosecutor of the regicides (those who had participated in murdering CHARLES I). He was attorney general in 1670 and LORD CHANCELLOR in 1674. As an equity judge he developed principles in several areas of CHANCERY practice, and he was able to regularize the procedure of that court.

Nova Scotia

Southeastern province of CANADA, disputed by French and British settlers. The area, called

Acadia by the French, was ceded to GREAT BRITAIN at the Treaty of UTRECHT (1713). The modern name comes from the Scottish colonization attempts from the 17th century. A capital was founded at Halifax in 1749, an assembly was created in 1758, and with the conquest of the city of Louisbourg in that year, French hopes were crushed. The Acadian population had been deported in 1755, and the immigration of American loyalists in the 1780s created a strong British orientation.

nuclear energy

A team of American and British scientists developed the ATOM BOMB during WORLD WAR II. In the 1950s it became possible to produce electrical power using nuclear reactors. At the same time, reactors produced plutonium for weapons, which was probably the primary purpose of the first British reactor at Calder Hall (1956). In any event, a system of energy-producing reactors was built in the 1960s. They seemed to have significant advantages in efficient energy production and cost savings, and further construction programs were launched in the 1970s, as an oil crisis heightened concerns about available energy. A series of accidents combined with growing environmental fears to slow down the growth of nuclear energy in the 1980s, and at the same time new information showed that the costs of this form of energy were greater than had been thought.

Nyasaland See MALAWI.

O

Oastler, Richard (1789–1861)
reformer

An estate manager in Yorkshire, Oastler was a TORY radical—a staunch supporter of the established church, opponent of universal suffrage, and champion of workers. He campaigned vigorously for limiting working hours in factories and against the new POOR LAW of 1834. So active was he that his employer dismissed him, and he was imprisoned for debt. While in prison he composed *Fleet Papers* (3 vols., 1841–43).

Oates, Titus (1649–1705)
instigator of the popish plot

The son of a parson, Oates was expelled from Merchant Taylor's school and attended two Cambridge colleges without taking a degree. He managed to be ordained, and he was so obsessed with the threat of the Catholic church that he feigned a conversion to that faith, entered a JESUIT seminary on the continent, and made himself familiar with the inner workings of the order. In 1678 he spread rumors of a plot to murder CHARLES II and install his Catholic brother James (JAMES VII AND II) on the throne. In the hysteria that followed, nine Jesuits were executed, and a total of 35 lost their lives, including Oliver PLUNKETT, the Catholic ARCHBISHOP of IRELAND. Oates's testimony was later discredited, and he was convicted of perjury, flogged, and imprisoned in 1685. He was released in 1689.

See also EXCLUSION.

O'Brien, James Bronterre (1805–1864)
Chartist

An Irish BARRISTER, O'Brien became one of the most outspoken leaders of the CHARTIST MOVEMENT. He was editor of the *Poor Man's Guardian* (1831–34) and later wrote for the *Northern Star.* The movement's leading thinker, he was called "the schoolmaster of Chartism." By the 1840s he had disowned revolutionary violence in favor of gradual socialist reform. He founded the National Reform League in 1850.

O'Brien, Murrough See INCHIQUIN, MURROUGH O'BRIEN, EARL OF.

O'Brien, William (1852–1928)
Irish nationalist

The editor of *United Ireland* (1881–82) and supporter of the Land League, O'Brien was imprisoned for his radical activities on three different occasions. Elected to PARLIAMENT in 1883, he was returned several times until 1918. He chose not to run in that election, and he declined to serve in the provisional government because he opposed partition.

O'Brien, William Smith (1803–1864)
Irish rebel

A member of the Protestant GENTRY, educated in ENGLAND, O'Brien entered PARLIAMENT in 1828. By the 1830s his nationalist position was clear when he became a member of YOUNG IRELAND

and advocated the repeal of the union. In 1848 he was involved in some violent incidents, the last being an attack upon a group of police. He received a death sentence, commuted to TRANS-PORTATION, and he spent six years in TASMANIA.

O'Casey, Sean (1880–1964)
Irish playwright

A self-educated workingman, O'Casey joined Irish nationalist groups when he was in his 30s. He also began to write plays, the earliest being about the troubled period of Irish history in the 1920s: *The Shadow of a Gunman* (1923), *Juno and the Paycock* (1924), *The Plough and the Stars* (1926).

Occasional Conformity Act (1711)

NONCONFORMISTS had found it possible to avoid penalties under the acts of UNIFORMITY, and even to hold public office, by taking communion in an ANGLICAN church once a year. The Occasional Conformity Act was a sign of the exasperation of TORY partisans, for it imposed a fine on those who attended a dissenting chapel after taking the oath of office. The law was repealed in 1719.

O'Connell, Daniel (1775–1847)
Irish nationalist

Educated in Irish schools and in the Catholic seminaries of St. Omer and Douai, O'Connell became the leading champion of CATHOLIC EMANCIPATION. A highly successful BARRISTER, his extensive practice enabled him to create a network that served as the basis for the CATHOLIC ASSOCIATION, formed in 1823. The group was dedicated to political reform, land reform, and emancipation, and some have called it the first modern political party. The British government tried to ban the organization, but it was quickly reconstituted. The use of petitions, mass meetings, and peaceful public pressure proved irresistible. In 1828 O'Connell won the parliamentary election in County Clare, but he was barred from taking his seat.

Daniel O'Connell *(Library of Congress)*

When it became evident that he would be reelected, the duke of WELLINGTON and Robert PEEL opted to allow an emancipation act to become law to avoid widespread Irish protest and violence. In 1829, amid great rejoicing, O'Connell took his seat at Westminster. His tactics were employed by other radical groups, but his next great venture, the Repeal Movement, had nothing like his earlier success. He wanted to remove the Act of UNION, a far more serious target and one which his National Repeal Association (1841) could not achieve. The campaign was sidetracked by the IRISH FAMINE in 1845 and the more radical nationalism of YOUNG IRELAND.

O'Connor, Feargus (1794–1855)
Chartist leader

O'Connor was the son of a Protestant landowner who had belonged to the UNITED IRISHMEN. An

Irish BARRISTER, he was elected to PARLIAMENT in 1832 as a follower of Daniel O'CONNELL. He gravitated toward the new CHARTIST MOVEMENT in the later 1830s, becoming its most colorful and vigorous leader. He edited the *Northern Star,* the main newspaper of the movement, and piloted a land nationalization scheme (1845–51). In 1847 he was elected to Parliament again, and he presented the last petition for the People's Charter to the HOUSE OF COMMONS in 1848.

O'Donnell, Hugh Roe, lord of Tyrconnel (1571–1602)
Irish leader

The grandson of a deputy governor of Tyrconnel, O'Donnell escaped from imprisonment by the English authorities (1591) and joined the revolt led by Hugh O'NEILL. After the defeat at KINSALE, he left for the continent and died there. His brother Rory O'DONNELL assumed his place as chief.

O'Donnell, Rory, earl of Tyrconnel (1575–1608)
Gaelic chief

Brother of Hugh O'DONNELL, Rory O'Donnell had also fought in the Hugh O'NEILL revolt. He submitted to the English and was made an earl by JAMES VI AND I in 1603. Facing encroaching English power in ULSTER, he joined O'Neill in leaving IRELAND in 1607, the so-called FLIGHT OF THE EARLS.

Oglethorpe, James (1696–1785)
philanthropist

Educated at Corpus Christi College, OXFORD UNIVERSITY, Oglethorpe became an ARMY officer and a MEMBER OF PARLIAMENT. In 1729 he led an inquiry into the conditions on debtors' prisons. Believing that the plight of the impoverished might be relieved in a colonial setting, he and others obtained a charter for the COLONY of Georgia in 1732. His decision to abolish slavery there aroused great opposition. He also had problems with the mission work of John WESLEY and George WHITEFIELD. He returned to ENGLAND in 1743.

O'Higgins, Kevin (1892–1927)
Irish nationalist

A member of SINN FÉIN, elected to PARLIAMENT in 1918, O'Higgins represented the provisional government at the ANGLO-IRISH TREATY talks in 1921. He became minister of justice in the new IRISH FREE STATE government, establishing a new police force and judicial system. He was assassinated by republicans in 1927.

Old Bailey

The name of the central criminal court, established in 1834. The name was taken from the street on which it is situated in the City of LONDON. Built on the site of the former NEWGATE PRISON, the court tries cases for the Greater London area.

Olivier, Laurence Kerr, baron Olivier of Brighton (1907–1989)
actor, director, producer

The son of a clergyman, Olivier was born in Dorking, Surrey. He attended drama school at age 17, and by the late 1920s he was appearing in West End theaters. He was in Noel Coward's *Private Lives* and Olivier made his first film, *Too Many Crooks,* in 1930. Olivier went on to make highly successful films, some with director Alfred HITCHCOCK. In the 1930s he did a large number of Shakespearean roles. During WORLD WAR II he directed filming of *Henry V,* and in the postwar era he and his actress wife Vivien Leigh starred in many productions. As director of the Old Vic theater, he performed regularly until 1973.

O'Neill, Con
See TYRONE, CON O'NEILL, EARL OF.

O'Neill, Hugh
See TYRONE, HUGH O'NEILL, SECOND EARL OF.

O'Neill, Owen Roe (1590–1649)
soldier

The nephew of Hugh O'NEILL served for 30 years in the Spanish army. He returned to IRELAND in 1642 to lead Irish forces in the North. He won the Battle of Benburb in 1646, defeating the Scots and their ULSTER allies. He fell out with other Catholic leaders and was declared a traitor in 1648. He died shortly afterward.

O'Neill, Sir Phelim (1604–1653)
rebel leader

A leader in the ULSTER rebellion of 1641, O'Neill was in command of Ulster forces before the arrival of Owen Roe O'NEILL. They fought together, but in 1650 he was forced to surrender to English forces, and he was executed.

O'Neill, Shane (1530–1567)
Gaelic chief

The son of Con O'NEILL and his rightful heir, Shane O'Neill was forced to fight for his title, drove his father from his territory, killed his half-brother, and held off the English. He visited ELIZABETH I in 1562 and seemed to secure his hold on authority when he returned to IRELAND. He attacked the PALE in 1566, took refuge with some of his rivals, and was assassinated in 1567.

O'Neill, Terence (1914–1990)
prime minister of Northern Ireland, 1963–1969

Leader of the UNIONISTS in ULSTER, O'Neill wanted to promote modernization and increased toleration between the Catholic and Protestant communities. He succeeded in stimulating loyalist fears and Catholic ambitions. He hosted a visit from the PRIME MINISTER of the IRISH REPUBLIC in 1965, and in 1968 he authored a reform program that promised to reduce discrimination against Catholics. These moves met with opposition within his party, which in turn encouraged protests by civil-rights groups and led to violent confrontations.

Open University

Combining radio, television, and tutorials, this modern degree-granting body began in 1971. Its clientele were mainly adults pursuing further education, its faculty was drawn from a wide spectrum of academics, and it sponsored extensive publication of course materials and related works.

Opium Wars (1839–1842, 1856–1860)

British merchants in INDIA developed a lucrative trade in opium in China. In 1839 the authorities in Canton confiscated the shipments of opium and demanded that the British turn over two sailors who were suspects in the murder of a Chinese. Gunboats from the EAST INDIA COMPANY bombarded Canton, and the British seized HONG KONG. The Treaty of Nanking recognized that acquisition plus other "treaty ports." The deadly Taiping rebellion (1850–64), in which millions of Chinese died, created a power vacuum that European states used to extend their authority in port cities such as Shanghai and Port Arthur.

Orange Free State

Afrikaners (Boers) who emigrated from the CAPE COLONY in the "Great Trek" settled along the Orange River in 1836. Their territory was annexed by GREAT BRITAIN (1848), then granted independence in 1854 as the Orange Free State. It was annexed once more during the BOER WAR (1900). As the Orange River Colony, it became independent in 1907 and joined the Union of SOUTH AFRICA in 1910.

Orange Order

A loyalist Protestant organization, the Orange Order takes its name from the hero of northern Irish Protestants, William of Orange (King WILLIAM III.) In the 1790s a combination of agitations—for Catholic relief, for republican reform, and LAND reform—created rival groups. The Catholic "Defenders" inspired the Protestant Orange Order, which was run in the manner of masonic lodges. Its members were well repre-sented in the YEOMANRY and the ARMY. There was a critical examination of the Order by PAR-LIAMENT in the 1830s, and it was disbanded. In the later 19th century it revived to lead oppo-sition to IRISH HOME RULE. In the 20th century the order remained a prominent force behind ULSTER unionism. Its annual marches celebrat-ing William III's victory at the BOYNE (July 12) have been regular occasions for sectarian con-frontation.

order in council

Order issued by the Crown, on the advice of the PRIVY COUNCIL, either on the authority of the royal PREROGATIVE or under the powers given by statute to ministers to issue regulations.

Ordnance Survey

The mapping of the British Isles was found to be seriously deficient in the 18th century. At the time of the rebellion of 1745, a survey in SCOT-LAND was the precursor to further mapping. A national survey was undertaken in 1791, with triangulation of the whole of GREAT BRITAIN, sup-plemented with local surveying. The operation was under the Master General of the Ordnance, the office in charge of explosives and artillery. By the middle of the 19th century there had been systematic mapping of ENGLAND, WALES, Scotland, and IRELAND.

Orford, first earl of   See WALPOLE, ROBERT, FIRST EARL OF ORFORD.

Orkney

The northernmost islands, long held by Scandi-navian rulers and part of SCOTLAND since the marriage of Margaret of Denmark to JAMES III (1469). Agriculture and fishing were principal employments before the development of NORTH SEA OIL. Some of the most important stone-age sites (Skara Brae dwellings, Maes Howe burial cairns) are located on the islands.

Ormonde, dukes and earls of

James Butler, first duke (1610–88), became LORD LIEUTENANT of IRELAND and led royalist forces in the CIVIL WAR. He returned from exile at the RESTORATION and resumed office, then resigned in 1685.

James Butler, 2nd duke (1665–1745), heir to the title (1688), supported WILLIAM III. He served as LORD LIEUTENANT, opposed the succession of GEORGE I, and participated in JACOBITE rebellions in 1715 and 1719.

Piers Butler, eighth earl (1467–1539), lord deputy of IRELAND (1521) and lord treasurer (1524), helped to suppress rebellion by the Irish.

Thomas Butler, tenth earl (1532–1614), was a loyal supporter of queen ELIZABETH I. His author-ity in Southwestern IRELAND was increased after the defeat of the DESMOND REBELLION (1583).

Orwell, George (1903–1950)
author

Born Eric Blair, Orwell was the son of an official in the government of INDIA. He worked in BURMA and then at odd jobs in France and ENGLAND. His early works were based on these experiences. In 1937 he was commissioned to write a study of unemployment, and his *Road to Wigan Pier* (1937) was followed by an account of his experience in the Spanish civil war (*Homage to Catalonia,* 1938). His best-known works are the satirical account of totalitarian rule, *Animal Farm* (1945), and *Nine-teen Eighty-Four* (1949).

Osborne, Thomas   See DANBY, THOMAS OSBORNE, EARL OF.

Osborne judgment (1909)

W. V. Osborne was the secretary of a branch of the Amalgamated Society of Railway Servants.

He filed a suit objecting to the forced contribution to the LABOUR PARTY from his union. The Judicial Committee of the HOUSE OF LORDS decided that a union could not use its funds for political purposes. The party suffered a serious loss of funds, but an act in 1913 made union contributions lawful and gave individuals the ability to opt out. The temporary loss of funds was a factor in the introduction of salaries for MPs in 1911.

Ossian

James MacPherson caused a stir in literary circles with the publication (1762–63) of what he said were the poems of an ancient GAELIC bard named Ossian. From the time of their publication, doubts have been expressed about their authenticity. Probably they are a mixture of fragments of oral tradition and the editor's imagination. In any event, the works exploited a growing sense of Gaelic revival and national sentiment.

Ottawa Conference (1932)

An imperial conference on economic matters, at the height of the DEPRESSION. In response to CANADA's need to protect wheat prices, GREAT BRITAIN agreed to a set of preferential TARIFFS with and between the DOMINIONS, a policy that ended the era of FREE TRADE.

Owen, Robert (1771–1858)

social reformer

Born in WALES, Owen worked in cotton factories, and he helped to reorganize the mills at New Lanark in SCOTLAND. There a model community was set up, and it became something of a sensation in reform circles. His book *A New View of Society* (1813) espoused the theory that environment governed social development, and he advocated planned communities in connection with industry. He also had ideas about cooperative communities, leading to experiments in various locations in both the United States and the UNITED KINGDOM. In a more worldly effort, he organized the Grand National Consolidated Trades Union (1834), which proved to be too ambitious for its time. Owen was a visionary, and his work was one source of inspiration for the very practical and successful COOPERATIVE MOVEMENT of the 19th century.

Oxford and Asquith, earl of See

ASQUITH, HERBERT HENRY, EARL OF OXFORD AND ASQUITH.

Oxford movement

The religious reform movement within the ANGLICAN church, launched in 1833 by John Keble (1792–1866). His sermon on "National Apostasy" sought to turn the church toward its prereformation roots. He and other OXFORD UNIVERSITY dons were hostile to recent interference by the civil government in church affairs. *Tracts for the Times* (1833–41) were essays written by the movement's leaders, J. H. NEWMAN, R. H. Froude, and E. B. Pusey. The result of the movement was the emergence of a strong Anglo-Catholic segment, one which came to predominate within the church in the 20th century.

Oxford University

Because of the disputes between Henry II and his French overlord, students could not attend the University of Paris. Scholars therefore had gathered in this English town and trade center to form a new academic community. When a quarrel between townsmen and scholars erupted in 1209, the pope intervened and issued what amounted to a charter in 1214. The Dominican and Franciscan orders made Oxford a base for their movements in the 1220s, and naturally the degree in divinity was the principal field of study. Wealthy benefactors endowed colleges, several in the 13th and in the 14th centuries. There were six new foundations (added to the existing 10) in the 16th century, two each in the 17th and 18th centuries, eight in the 19th, and 12 in the 20th century. At various times the university was associated with different religious orientations: it was the base for John WYCLIFFE in the 14th century and a haven for humanists in the 16th century, but then it became the high church center, under the revised statutes of Archbishop William LAUD in 1636. It was a main retreat of JACOBITES in the 18th century and the focal point of the OXFORD MOVEMENT in the 19th century. With CAMBRIDGE UNIVERSITY, Oxford experienced major reforms from the middle of the 19th century, admitting dissenters and women and adding modern curriculum and facilities.

oyer and terminer

Literally, to hear and determine—the instruction to justices in their commission to visit the shires and hear charges against criminal suspects. These were the central commissions of the ASSIZE system, which operated in ENGLAND from the 12th century until its abolition in 1971.

P

Paine, Thomas (1737–1809)
revolutionary author
From a Norfolk QUAKER family, Paine worked for the Excise until dismissed for publishing a pamphlet demanding higher pay. He emigrated to America in 1774 and was caught up in the independence movement there. In 1776 he wrote his famous essay *Common Sense,* and he was made secretary to the congressional committee on foreign affairs. He went on diplomatic missions to France and returned to ENGLAND in the early days of the revolution. He wrote *The Rights of Man* (part I) in 1791; the second part was published in 1792. His famous rebuttal to Edmund BURKE's *Reflections on the Revolution* made him the hero of British radicals and the nemesis of the establishment. It also earned him a trial for seditious libel, at which he was convicted *in absentia.* Meanwhile, he had returned to France, where he was elected to the national convention. When he opposed the execution of the king, he was dismissed and imprisoned. In 1794 he published *The Age of Reason.* He returned to America in 1802.

See also RADICALISM.

Paisley, Ian (1926–)
politician, clergyman
A vigorous anti-Catholic and UNIONIST politician, Paisley has led the Democratic Unionist Party since 1971. He joined with the Ulster Workers' Council in 1974 to organize a strike to disrupt a power-sharing agreement. He won decisive victories in European elections in ULSTER (1979, 1984). Having a seat in the Westminster PARLIAMENT, he resigned in 1985 to protest the Anglo-Irish agreement of that year. He was an outspoken opponent of the "Good Friday" peace agreement of 1998, and he led the opposition in the Northern Ireland Assembly, which was constituted as a result of that agreement.

Pakistan
The Islamic Republic of Pakistan was formed in the bloody partition of newly independent INDIA in 1947. The Muslim minority wanted separate control, and the partition resulted in two separate units, East and West Pakistan. M. A. JINNAH was the leader of the Muslim League, the main body advocating separation, and it is unlikely that the result of partition was what he aimed for. There were serious tensions between India and Pakistan, unstable internal politics with a number of military regimes, and the eastern part declared independence as the state of BANGLADESH in 1971.

Pale
The area around DUBLIN where the English were able to maintain authority in the medieval and early modern period. Its size was drastically reduced around 1500 to an area of about 30 by 50 miles, but over the following century, the TUDORS steadily expanded into the areas of native control, achieving a form of conquest by the end of ELIZABETH I's reign.

Palestine
The area between the Mediterranean and Jordan, which, after the diaspora of the Jewish people in A.D. 70 was inhabited by Arabic peoples. The location of holy places for Christians and

Arabs as well as Jews, the region was for many years under the government of the Ottoman Turks. When it was captured in 1917, the British promised in the BALFOUR DECLARATION to allow establishment of a homeland for the Jewish people, the long-sought objective of Zionists. Palestine became a mandate of GREAT BRITAIN under the LEAGUE OF NATIONS in 1920. After WORLD WAR II, with increasing pressure for Jewish immigration and terrorist activity on both sides resulting in a civil war, Britain withdrew in 1948. The state of Israel was proclaimed at the same time, and after a series of wars with Arab neighbors (1948–73), the Jewish state was established, its relations with EGYPT and Jordan were settled by treaties, but its internal peace with Palestinians remained elusive.

Palmer, Roundell See SELBORNE, ROUNDELL PALMER, EARL OF.

Palmerston, Henry Temple, viscount (1784–1865)

prime minister, 1855–1858, 1859–1865

Palmerston was educated at Harrow, Edinburgh, and CAMBRIDGE UNIVERSITY. As an Irish peer, he was not allowed to sit in the HOUSE OF LORDS, but he was able to hold a seat in the HOUSE OF COMMONS, and did so for 58 years. For most of that time he held government office, most notably as foreign secretary for most of the 1830s and 1840s. He was a TORY at first, but changed to the WHIGS in 1830. His foreign policy was pragmatic, supporting British interests wherever possible and usually favoring liberal constitutional regimes, but not on ideological grounds. He took office as PRIME MINISTER when the Aberdeen ministry fell during the CRIMEAN WAR. His decade of leadership is often seen as the time of gestation of the LIBERAL PARTY, and he did support FREE TRADE, reduced government expenditure, and the establishment of a unified Italy. However, Palmerston did not favor further reform in the FRANCHISE or in economic and social areas.

Pankhurst family

Christabel, 1880–1958, eldest daughter of Emmeline, studied law at Manchester, but she was denied entry to Lincoln's Inn in 1904 because she was a woman. She founded the Women's Social and Political Union with her mother in 1903, and she edited *The Suffragette.*

Emmeline, 1858–1928, married Richard Pankhurst and with him joined the FABIAN SOCIETY and the INDEPENDENT LABOUR PARTY. But the latter group was opposed to women's suffrage, and she and her daughter Christabel decided to found their own organization, the Women's Social and Political Union (1903). From a base in Manchester, this grew to a national body, inspired by protests, imprisonments, and clumsy government reactions. At the start of the war, activity was suspended, and she and Christabel became supporters of the war effort.

Emmeline Pankhurst *(Library of Congress)*

Sylvia, 1882–1960, daughter of Emmeline, was an artist and a socialist. She was involved with the Women's Social and Political Union, but her views were more radical, favoring a wide range of rights for women of all classes. She continued to press her views during WORLD WAR I, and in 1920 she went to Moscow to attend the Third International.

See also SUFFRAGETTES; WOMEN'S MOVEMENT.

parish

The local area under the direction of a priest, having an endowment and an income from the TITHES of property owners. Parish churches were often built by the principal landowner(s), the affairs of the local church were managed by a vestry led by a churchwarden. The priest (rector, vicar, or curate) was subject to the visitation of the BISHOP of the diocese. A parish also had a civil identity as a unit of local government, e.g., for the administration of the POOR LAW and the upkeep of highways.

Parker, Matthew (1504–1575)
archbishop of Canterbury, 1559–1575

Born in Norwich, Parker attended Corpus Christi College, CAMBRIDGE UNIVERSITY. He became a Fellow, and though he lost his university posts under MARY I, he was called by ELIZABETH I to become ARCHBISHOP of CANTERBURY. His moderate positions helped to find a middle ground in the THIRTY-NINE ARTICLES of 1563. He sponsored the translation known as the "Bishops' Bible," in 1568, but he was obliged to support the queen's views. He provoked PURITAN hostility when he published the *Advertisements* (1566), which called for use of formal clerical vestments.

Parliament

ENGLAND

Parliament's origins were with royal COUNCILS, which were summoned by the king. A great council was an occasion when all of the king's officials were assembled. In the 13th century these meetings were augmented with the "commons"—KNIGHTS and BURGESSES. They were present to endorse TAXATION and from time to time to present petitions to the Crown, which formed the basis for legislation. Such legislative acts were very few in number before the modern period. The move toward more powerful statutes began with the REFORMATION and its attendant laws regarding the established church and the royal succession. After the CIVIL WAR and revolutions of the 17th century, Parliament became a regular part of government, its leaders (and their followers) divided into parties, which vied for the management of the king's affairs. Their title to do so came to depend on the support of the electorate. As the number of enfranchised voters grew in the 19th century, it became clear that they, not the sovereign, would choose the party and the leaders who would govern. Meanwhile the internal structure of Parliament and its operations had also evolved, and the HOUSE OF COMMONS slowly (1660–1911) became the superior branch. From the 18th century both the HOUSE OF LORDS and the Commons conducted business with an elaborate system of committees. Operations of government departments grew, and CABINET ministers had their business organized by a cabinet secretariat and in their separate areas by a large body of civil servants (see CIVIL SERVICE).

SCOTLAND

The kings of Scots had their royal councils, noted from as early as the 13th century in meetings (colloquia) to make policy and render legal judgments. In the next century there were knights and landholders called to meetings, along with representatives of BURGHS. This was, as in ENGLAND, to approve taxation, but the opposition in these bodies seemed to be more vigorous than in the English Parliament. Other differences were that the Scottish Parliament was managed by an elected committee, called the Lords of the Articles, and the Scots maintained a more typical European unicameral legislature of three estates: clergy, barons, and burgh commissioners. The estates became more powerful in the 17th century, just as the English houses did, but in SCOTLAND's case that development was aborted by the UNION of 1707. Election of Scottish members to both English houses replaced the distinctive Scottish legislature, and only in 1999 was a form of purely Scottish representation recreated in a new Scottish Parliament.

IRELAND

A parliament in IRELAND can be traced to the 13th century, but it was peculiar in that it was not intended to include the "mere Irish," the GAELIC majority population (until 1542). Also, the forms and procedures were English imports, and as of 1494, under POYNINGS' LAWS, the acts of these parliaments were to be approved by the English government before becoming law. There were long periods with no parliament, and until 1768 a parliament was meant to last for an entire reign (of the English sovereign). The period of Henry GRATTAN's Parliament (1782–1800) was an anomaly in that a certain amount of Irish initiative was granted; however, the power of government had not been surrendered. Moreover, in reaction to the rebellion of 1798, the Act of Union ended the Irish Parliament in 1801. In 1920 the Government of Ireland Act began the process of restoring an Irish parliament, actually two parliaments. The southern body became a republican institution by 1937, the northern became a one-party, UNIONIST institution, which was dissolved in 1972 and not replaced for the rest of the century.

WALES

There was no continuing parliamentary tradition in WALES, though undoubtedly there was consultation between Welsh princes and their councils. In 1404 and 1405 Owen GLENDOWER summoned men from all districts to meet in parliaments, but no tradition grew from this rebellious precedent. Welsh members were sent to English parliaments, and from 1536 this was on a regular basis. In 1999 a WELSH ASSEMBLY was created.

Charles Stewart Parnell *(Library of Congress)*

Parnell, Charles Stewart (1846–1891)
Irish nationalist

Born into an Anglo-Irish landowning family, Parnell attended Westminster School and Magdalene College, CAMBRIDGE UNIVERSITY. He entered PARLIAMENT in 1875 and joined the more extreme wing of the IRISH HOME RULE party, which he soon came to dominate. As the first president of the Irish Land League he allied the parliamentary movement with a popular organization agitating for LAND reform. He employed the influence of both—through filibusters in Parliament and agitation in IRELAND—to gain more favorable terms in legislation. By 1885 the 85 Irish nationalist MPs held the balance of power between the LIBERAL PARTY and Conservative Party, and this may have inspired William GLADSTONE to introduce the first Irish Home Rule bill in 1886. That measure was defeated by the secession of the LIBERAL UNIONISTS, and in the next few years Parnell had to defend himself from spurious charges based on forged letters (he won) and real charges in a divorce suit (he lost). The latter ended his leadership, and he died soon after.

Parr, Catherine (1512–1548)
queen of England

The sixth wife of HENRY VIII (1543), Catherine Parr had been married twice before. Her age and experience brought stability to the relationship, and she was active in overseeing the upbringing of the princesses, Mary and Elizabeth. She acted as regent while the king campaigned in France in 1544, but she was not allowed to take that post when the young EDWARD VI became king.

Paterson, William (1658–1719)
banker, economist

Born in Dumfriesshire, SCOTLAND, Paterson came to ENGLAND as a youth, and he had a successful career in trade, especially in the WEST INDIES. He participated in the scheme to found the BANK OF ENGLAND, but he quarrelled with other directors and resigned. He also was a principal in the formation of the Bank of Scotland, and he promoted the DARIEN scheme for a Scottish company to trade in Central America (1698–1700). He went to the site of the new COLONY, where there was great loss of life (including that of his wife) and a general failure, due in part to English opposition to investment in the scheme.

patronage

In Roman law the patron was the former master of a freed slave, and as such had legal responsibilities to his client. The term was adapted to the church in two senses: that there were patron saints who were special guardians, or that a person had the patronage, or right to name successors to a benefice. Patronage later came to be used generally in respect of the arts and of politics. In the former case, patrons provided resources for artistic projects. In the latter case, persons in positions of power were able to bestow titles, offices, and incomes on their followers.

Pearse, Patrick (1879–1916)
Irish nationalist

Trained as a BARRISTER, Pearse worked as a writer and schoolteacher. A member of the Gaelic League, he became disenchanted with IRISH HOME RULE and joined the Irish Republican Brotherhood (IRB) and the Irish Volunteers (1913). He believed that a blood sacrifice was necessary to mobilize sentiment for an Irish republic. His opportunity came when the IRB council planned the EASTER REBELLION in 1916. Pearse read the proclamation of the Irish Republic from the steps of the General Post Office after it was seized by the rebels. He took the position of president of the provisional government, but five days later he was forced to surrender. A few days after that he was executed. The rebellion was futile, the British response was brutal, and the cause of the republic was greatly enhanced.

Peasants' Revolt (1381)

The first and largest popular uprising in English history was caused by a conjunction of critical events: effects of the repeated appearance of the plague, or BLACK DEATH; government efforts to enforce wage controls in the Statute of Labourers; losses in the wars with France; and, finally, imposition of a POLL TAX. Groups of peasants protested in Essex, Kent, and later in other counties. Rebel armies marched on LONDON, and one of their leaders was the renegade priest John BALL. They executed the ARCHBISHOP of CANTERBURY and the lord treasurer, as well as other officials. The anger of the rebels was not directed at the 13-year-old king, RICHARD II, who promised to abolish serfdom when he met the rebels at Smithfield. But after the rebels withdrew, the king renounced his concession, and rebel leaders were rounded up and executed. Although the revolt seemed to be a failure, the poll tax was abandoned.

Peel, Sir Robert (1788–1850)
prime minister, 1834–1835, 1841–1846

Son of a wealthy cotton manufacturer in Lancashire, Peel was educated at Harrow and Christ Church, OXFORD UNIVERSITY, where he excelled in classics and mathematics. He entered PARLIAMENT in 1809 for a seat in IRELAND. An unusually able politician, he was made chief secretary for Ireland in 1812. In 1822 he became home secretary and was responsible for reform of the CRIMINAL LAW and the establishment of the metropolitan POLICE (1829). Although a staunch opponent of FRANCHISE reform, once the act of 1832 was passed, Peel recognized the change as permanent, and in his TAMWORTH MANIFESTO (1834) he made the case for a CONSERVATIVE PARTY. After a brief term in office, he made his mark as PRIME MINISTER in the 1840s. He had become a supporter of FREE TRADE and TARIFF reforms, and even the repeal of the CORN LAWS in 1846. This step split his party, as the protectionist wing (led by Benjamin DISRAELI) refused to support him. Peel was thus forced to resign.

peerage

From the earliest times there have been ranks of nobility, from the Anglo-Saxon EARL to the Norman BARON. By the 14th century, due to the emerging HOUSE OF LORDS and an ambitious body of aristocrats competing in war with their French cousins, some further definition became necessary. The ranks of DUKE (1337), MARQUESS (1385), and VISCOUNT (1440) were established with that order of precedence, followed by the earls and barons. The numbers were small—about 50 English peers by 1600. The STUART dynasty inflated the peerage to about 130 by 1641. The English peerage continued to grow, and peers of SCOTLAND (in 1707) and IRELAND (in 1801) were added to the HOUSE OF LORDS. The size of that body (which also included spiritual peers—BISHOPS and ARCHBISHOPS) was inflated further by the creation of life peers, especially after 1958. There were well over 1,200 at the end of the 20th century, just before the announced "reform" or demise of the House of Lords.

Pelham, Henry (1696–1754)
prime minister, 1743–1754

A MEMBER OF PARLIAMENT from 1717, brother of the duke of NEWCASTLE, and supporter of Robert WALPOLE, Pelham was secretary at war in 1724 and paymaster of the forces in 1730. After Walpole's fall, Pelham became first lord of the TREASURY in 1743. When GEORGE II tried to replace the Pelhams in 1746, they and their supporters resigned, and the king was forced to take them back, as no other group could manage PARLIAMENT. This was an important stage in the developing conventions of CABINET government. Pelham was a very successful first minister, proven by the political turmoil which followed his sudden death in 1754.

Pelham-Holles, Thomas   See NEWCASTLE, THOMAS PELHAM-HOLLES, DUKE OF.

penal laws

1. A number of laws penalizing Roman Catholic worship were enacted in the 16th and 17th centuries. The adherents to the old faith (RECUSANTS, i.e., those who would not take the oaths of UNIFORMITY) were driven underground, forced to practice their faith in secret and risking charges of treason. Enforcement tended to fluctuate, and the last severe episode coincided with the rebellions of the JACOBITES. From about 1770 there was progressive relief from the laws.
2. The laws to "prevent the growth of popery" (1695–1727), mainly directed at Irish Roman

Catholics, were the tools of a more extensive campaign to exclude them from political life and deprive them of economic and social capacities. Catholics were disarmed, prohibited from owning horses worth more than £5, from buying or inheriting land, teaching schools, pursuing professions, and of course from being served by their own clergy (priests were liable to TRANSPORTATION). By the third quarter of the 18th century, these laws were falling out of use and relief acts were passed to repeal them (1778, 1792, 1829).

Penn, William (1644–1718)
Quaker
Born in LONDON, Penn studied at OXFORD UNIVERSITY and at Lincoln's Inn, and he became a leader and spokesman for the QUAKERS. To repay a debt to his father (a former admiral), CHARLES II gave him a grant in 1681 for land in America, on which Penn founded the COLONY of Pennsylvania. His constitution for the colony provided for religious toleration, and it was initially very prosperous, although French and Indian incursions later affected it adversely.

People's Charter See CHARTIST MOVEMENT.

Pepys, Samuel (1633–1703)
naval administrator, diarist
Born in LONDON, the son of a tailor, Pepys was educated at St. Paul's School and Magdalene College, CAMBRIDGE UNIVERSITY. While he was a member of PARLIAMENT and president of the ROYAL SOCIETY, he is best known in his role as a naval administrator and a revealing diarist. He was made a clerk to the NAVY board in 1660 and first secretary of the ADMIRALTY in 1673. Throughout the 1660s he kept a detailed diary in shorthand, only deciphered and published in six volumes in 1825. It contains detailed descriptions of events such as the FIRE OF LONDON and the plague of 1666, and he provides innumerable minor insights into life in the RESTORATION era.

Perceval, Spencer (1762–1812)
prime minister, 1809–1812
The younger son of Lord Egremont, Perceval was educated at Harrow and Trinity College, CAMBRIDGE UNIVERSITY. A BARRISTER and an EVANGELICAL Christian, he entered PARLIAMENT in 1796. A strong TORY and an effective speaker, he was appointed solicitor general in 1801 and attorney general in 1802. Perceval became CHANCELLOR OF THE EXCHEQUER in 1807 and PRIME MINISTER in 1809. He maintained financial stability despite the costs of the French war. He was assassinated in the lobby of the HOUSE OF COMMONS in 1812 by a deranged bankrupt merchant.

Percy, Henry, earl of Northumberland
See NORTHUMBERLAND, HENRY PERCY, EARL OF.

Percy, Sir Henry (1364–1403)
soldier
The son of Henry Percy, earl of NORTHUMBERLAND, Sir Henry Percy fought in France and on the Scottish border, where his daring and bravery earned him the nickname "Hotspur." Both he and his father served as warden of the MARCHES (Scottish borders), and they defeated a Scottish invasion at Homildon Hill in 1402. They joined in the rebellion of Owen GLENDOWER, and Hotspur was en route to meet the Welsh leader when HENRY IV intercepted and killed him at the Battle of Shrewsbury.

Peterloo massacre (1819)
In the aftermath of the Battle of WATERLOO, social and political unrest combined with economic distress to produce a series of large demonstrations and apparent threats to public order. Plans were made to hold a mass meeting at St. Peter's Fields outside Manchester, and more than 60,000 people assembled there on August 16, 1819. The authorities decided to arrest Henry "Orator" HUNT as he was about to address them. In the confusion and clamor, the mounted yeomanry, plus a unit of Hussars, drew their sabres

and moved into the unarmed crowd; 11 men and women were killed, and hundreds were wounded. Disgusted radicals satirized this "victory" of British forces. The frightened government in Westminster responded by passing the repressive SIX ACTS in December 1819.

Petition of Right (1628)

The confrontation between CHARLES I and the HOUSE OF COMMONS came to a head when the king tried to collect a FORCED LOAN in 1627, and the FIVE KNIGHTS' CASE upheld his power to do so. A petition of right was an ancient legal device, and here it was used to state the grievances against the king: that PARLIAMENT had the right to consent to TAXATION, and that there should be no arbitrary imprisonment, no billeting of troops, and no MARTIAL LAW. Charles accepted the petition, claiming that he was merely recognizing existing rights.

Petty, Sir William (1623–1687)
statistician

Petty studied in ENGLAND and on the continent, earned doctorates in physics and medicine, and taught at OXFORD UNIVERSITY. When he took the post of physician to the ARMY in IRELAND, he also became involved in the problematic redistribution of LAND there, especially to the Cromwellian soldiers. He proposed and conducted a topographical survey, and in the course of this work, he became fascinated with what he called "political arithmetic," or what is known today as statistics. A founding member of the ROYAL SOCIETY, Petty wrote *Natural and Political Observations upon the Bills of Mortality* (1662), *Political Arithmetic* (1690), and *The Political Anatomy of Ireland* (1691).

Petty, William See SHELBURNE, WILLIAM PETTY, EARL OF.

Petty-Fitzmaurice, Henry See LANS-DOWNE, HENRY PETTY-MAURICE, MARQUESS OF.

petty sessions

A meeting of two or more JUSTICES OF THE PEACE during the intervals between QUARTER SESSIONS. The meeting is held for less serious judicial and administrative business, e.g., minor offenses, licensing, or POOR LAW settlements. This is now the work of the MAGISTRATES' courts.

Pilgrimage of Grace (1536)

When the initial phase of DISSOLUTION of the monasteries began, it was aimed at smaller monastic houses, most of which provided essential welfare for their rural communities. Across the north of ENGLAND, from Lincolnshire through Yorkshire, groups of YEOMAN farmers and GENTRY formed protests. Lawyer Robert ASKE emerged as a leader of what became known as the Pilgrimage of Grace, but the large and dangerous rising was disorganized. King HENRY VIII at first promised concessions and pardons, but after new disturbances in 1537, leaders were arrested and executed. The disorder demonstrated the weakness of royal power, and in 1537 a Council of the North was created in an attempt to remedy the problem.

Pitt, William (1759–1806)
(Pitt "the younger")
prime minister, 1783–1801, 1804–06

The second son of William PITT, earl of Chatham, Pitt "the younger" entered Pembroke College, CAMBRIDGE UNIVERSITY, at age 14. Later he was admitted to Lincoln's Inn and called to the bar in 1780, but his career was destined to be in politics. In PARLIAMENT from 1781, he was a critic of Lord NORTH and a proponent of parliamentary reform and ECONOMICAL REFORM. In 1783, when GEORGE III dismissed the coalition of North and Charles James FOX, Pitt took office as the youngest PRIME MINISTER in British history (age 24). His reform ideas had varied fates. A parliamentary reform bill in 1785 was defeated, and he did not pursue the matter. On the other hand, he did continue to reduce the number and value of government places, especially as a way of reducing expenses later during the war years.

In 1788 there was a crisis as the king's illness created demand for a REGENCY. Pitt resisted the demands, and he was rewarded with staunch support from the recovered king in 1789. That year saw the outbreak of revolution in France, which Pitt at first did not see as a threat to peace and stability. But when the French monarchy was overthrown and radical ideas seemed to penetrate all parts of the islands, he became a stout enforcer of the establishment and a determined adversary of France. War came in 1793, and Pitt put together a series of coalitions, none of them fully satisfactory. Meanwhile, in domestic affairs he made increasingly tough policy choices: outlawing political assemblies (1793), suspending the HABEAS CORPUS act (1794), and imposing MARTIAL LAW in IRELAND (1796). When rebellion broke out in Ireland in 1798, it was crushed easily, but the circumstances of war made it seem necessary to have a formal UNION of GREAT BRITAIN and Ireland, for strategic purposes and for public order. Part of Pitt's plan called for the full participation of Catholics in the new regime, as they might be valuable allies against the atheistic French and even grateful companions in a newly constituted Ireland. But George III refused, saying that his coronation oath to support the established church would be violated by any such concessions. Pitt resigned in 1801. He returned in 1804 and created a new coalition against Napoleon, but when it was beaten at Austerlitz, Pitt, seemingly exhausted by his efforts, died in January 1806.

Pitt, William, first earl of Chatham (1708–1778)
prime minister, 1766–1768

Pitt's grandfather had made a fortune in INDIA, and William went to Eton and OXFORD UNIVERSITY before he entered PARLIAMENT in 1735. He was a longtime MEMBER OF PARLIAMENT and a critic of Hanoverian influence on British affairs, and so he only latterly rose to a position of political power. After the early losses of the SEVEN YEARS' WAR, Pitt joined the government of the duke of NEWCASTLE and was an extremely successful war minister

(1757–61). When he proposed to launch attacks on Spain, the CABINET balked, and Pitt resigned. The new king GEORGE III preferred Pitt to any of his other ministers, and in 1766 he made him earl of Chatham and head of the government. Unfortunately, by this point Pitt was suffering from mental stress or illness, and after a short term of ineffective government, he resigned in 1768. The rest of his political life was spent in intermittent attacks on the government's policy in America. He collapsed and died during a debate in the HOUSE OF LORDS in May 1778.

Place, Francis (1771–1854)
radical

The son of a LONDON baker, Place was apprenticed to a maker of breeches. He organized a strike of these workers in 1793, which was the beginning of his involvement in the reform movements of the early 19th century. A member of the London Corresponding Society in his early days, he was later a key figure in the repeal of the COMBINATION ACTS (1824), which helped to foster the growth of TRADE UNIONS. He was an active campaigner for the reform bill in 1832, and he supported the CHARTIST MOVEMENT. His general view was that workers ought to become well-informed defenders of their interests, but that they should ally with the middle class to achieve political goals more quickly.

placemen

The holders of pensions or positions in the gift of the Crown or the government. There was a long history of attempts to limit the placemen's numbers and influence, dating from the later years of the 17th century. As government continued to grow, the source of this complaint did likewise. While it was never sure that places were payment for future loyalty instead of rewards for past service, the placemen's influence was a constant source of suspicion of undue influence on political behavior. Place acts in the early 18th century required any holder of such a position who was elected to PARLIAMENT to resign and stand for reelection. This practice lasted until 1926. Patronage was an essential part of government, but by the end of the 18th century it was being reduced, and by the middle of the 19th century it began to be superseded by a professional CIVIL SERVICE.

Plaid Cymru

The Party of Wales, established in 1925, first as an effort to protect Welsh language and culture and then as a political movement for Welsh independence. Plaid Cymru's first successful parliamentary candidate was Gwynfor Evans in 1966. By 1974 it had three seats and was behind the DEVOLUTION measure adopted by the LABOUR PARTY in 1979. But the referendum of that year was a blow, with only 20 percent of those voting supporting a WELSH ASSEMBLY. The party continued to press for language education and other measures, somewhat increasing its number of seats in the 1990s and seeing a Welsh Assembly become a reality in 1999.

plantation

Term used to describe the deliberate settlement of English and Scottish colonists in IRELAND in the 16th century. The aim was to neutralize or remove the cultural and religious influence of the native Irish and the gaelicized anglo-Irish. The earliest attempts in the 1540s (Leix and Offaly) were followed under MARY I with the creation of Queen's County and King's County. ELIZABETH I's efforts in Munster and Leinster continued the policy. Finally, the ULSTER plantation under JAMES VI AND I (1608–12) was the largest concerted settlement plan, and it was accompanied by smaller efforts in Wexford, Longford, and Westmeath. Later in the 17th century, there were further introductions of English and Scots, as soldiers claimed lands promised to them during the civil wars.

The colonial plantations were a natural borrowing of the term from the late TUDOR period (Roanoke, Virginia, and Plymouth). Thus it was also natural that the PRIVY COUNCIL's agency for overseeing these ventures in the 17th century was called the BOARD OF TRADE and Plantations.

Plunkett, St. Oliver (1629–1681)
archbishop of Armagh

A Roman Catholic prelate, Plunkett had a good relations with the VICEROYS of IRELAND. He had managed to improve conditions for his flock, but after the TEST ACT (1673), he went into hiding. During the POPISH PLOT he was arrested in DUBLIN, taken to LONDON, tried for treason, and executed. It was alleged that he was preparing to support a French invasion of Ireland, but there was no reliable evidence of any such plot. He was canonized in 1975.

pluralism

The holding of more than one church benefice (post) at a time, a practice which was often encountered where the value of the livings was small or the venality of church leaders was great. Pluralism was prohibited by ACTS OF PARLIAMENT from 1529, the most effective one being passed in 1838. It is also a product of a shortage of clergy, which has been the typical problem of the 20th century.

poet laureate

A poet chosen by the Crown, receiving a nominal salary as a member of the royal household. Originally he was responsible for writing odes for the Court. The first poet laureate in the modern era was Ben JONSON. Others have included William WORDSWORTH and Alfred, Lord TENNYSON.

Pole, Reginald (1500–1558)
cardinal, archbishop of Canterbury

Pole was the son of Sir Richard Pole and his wife Margaret, countess of Salisbury and niece of EDWARD IV. Pole thus carried the Yorkist claim to the English throne. He was educated at Magdelen College, OXFORD UNIVERSITY; and the

University of Padua. An opponent of HENRY VIII'S ROYAL SUPREMACY, he went abroad in 1532. He wrote an attack on the king's policies in 1536, and he received the cardinal's hat. These events caused his family to be in great danger, and several of them were executed. He returned when MARY I came to the throne, and he became ARCHBISHOP of CANTERBURY. He died within hours of the queen.

Pole, William de la, fourth earl and first duke of Suffolk (1396–1450)
royal councillor

Pole served HENRY VI, fought in the wars in France, returned, and became a great manager of royal PATRONAGE. He was deeply involved in intrigues among court factions, was impeached and banished by the king, and captured and beheaded while attempting to cross the English Channel.

police

Law enforcement was the job of local and private CONSTABLES and parish watchmen down to the 19th century. Constables were usually accountable to JUSTICES OF THE PEACE, who might have more or less ability to control public order, but there were few incentives and no guidelines. In 1829 Robert PEEL (who had created a paid constabulary in IRELAND in 1822) introduced legislation to create the Metropolitan London Police, and a centralized force of 1,000 was formed. Other towns and counties adopted similar measures in the 1830s and '40s, and in 1856 an act required all districts to have a police force. These were organized under chief constables who were locally accountable. Various powers were given to the HOME OFFICE (a Criminal Investigation Department in 1878, a SPECIAL BRANCH in the 1880s). General reorganization by the Police Act of 1964 began the consolidation of 200 police forces into 42 regional authorities. With much independence and some supervision by the Home Office, they remain a decentralized force.

poll tax

A tax levied on every person. One such was the immediate cause of the Peasants' Revolt in 1381. In 1989 the government of Margaret THATCHER announced a similar tax, called a "community charge," which was to consolidate the sources of funding for local government. Its introduction in SCOTLAND brought protests and riots which contributed to her removal from office.

polytechnics

Schools of higher education that were begun in the 1960s, with technical and practical curricula. The distinction between the polytechnics and the UNIVERSITIES was eliminated in 1993.

poor law

The general system of public support for relief of poor and indigent persons, replacing the TITHES and alms of PARISH members by a state-mandated system. The poor law's most familiar form dates from the time of Queen ELIZABETH I. Each parish, under the supervision of JUSTICES OF THE PEACE (JPs), collected rates and these were managed by overseers of the poor. The system was susceptible to error: the poor migrating to wealthier parishes; the JPs, overseers, or ratepayers failing in their duties; and the forces of economic distress or development placing undue burdens on all parties. There were innumerable experiments within the system: combining parishes into (more affluent) unions; revising the organization and regulation of workhouses and houses of correction; rewriting laws on vagrancy; and, in times of great distress, allowing the overseers to dispense aid directly to the poor ("outdoor relief"). The latter was an object of great complaint as the total expenditure on poor rates soared in the early 19th century. The answer was found in the 1834 enactment of a new poor law that cracked down on outdoor relief and required residence and labor in deliberately unappealing workhouses. This drew scornful and hostile reactions from workers, particularly in large industrial towns, and especially when the business cycle put many out of work. The poor laws were thoroughly investigated at the beginning of the 20th century, and in 1929 the old system was ended. Local councils were responsible for the poor, but already a new trend was visible with the old-age pensions act of 1908, the NATIONAL INSURANCE Act of 1911, and increased unemployment benefits from the 1920s. In 1945 a new national system of relief and assistance was created under the WELFARE STATE.

Pope, Alexander (1688–1744)
poet

The son of a Roman Catholic, Pope suffered from curvature of the spine due to tuberculosis. A self-educated man, his poetry gained him an entry into the circles of literary figures. His *Pastorals* (1709) gave him the first taste of fame. He wrote *Essay on Criticism* in 1711 and *Rape of the Lock* in 1712. He was an associate of Jonathan SWIFT and John Gay, and he became adept at political satire, which was particularly pungent in *The Dunciad* (1728).

popish plot

In 1678 Titus OATES and others swore to the existence of a plot to kill King CHARLES II and place his brother (the future JAMES VII AND II) on the throne. There was already some amount of fear over the king's own religious faith, the known Catholicism of his brother, and rumors of French invasion or intervention. The London MAGISTRATE who took the depositions was later found murdered, and the plotters' stories suddenly became more believable. The HOUSE OF COMMONS resolved that there was "a damnable and hellish plot" and proceeded to examine witnesses. A number of trials produced convictions and 35 executions, notably Lord Stafford and Oliver PLUNKETT. Oates was later exposed as a liar, convicted of perjury, and imprisoned (1685).

Porteous riots (1736)

After the execution of a smuggler in EDINBURGH, the town guard was pelted with stones, and troops fired on the crowd, killing six people. Captain John Porteous insisted that he had not ordered them to fire, but he was arrested, tried, and sentenced to death. The LONDON government granted a reprieve, and a mob of several thousand broke into the jail and lynched Porteous. An official inquiry ordered sanctions against the city (1737), and Robert WALPOLE found himself dealing with an aroused Scottish opposition in PARLIAMENT. The incident was one of a number of examples of tension in the early years of the Anglo-Scottish UNION.

Poynings' laws (1494)

Sir Edward Poynings (1459–1521) was the lord deputy sent to IRELAND by HENRY VII in 1494. The laws he put through the Irish PARLIAMENT stated (1) that English law applied to Ireland, and (2) that a meeting of an Irish parliament or any law enacted therein had to have prior approval of the king's COUNCIL. These measures were modified in their impact over time, but they were stoutly restated in the DECLARATORY ACT of 1720, which was repealed in 1782 but effectively reenacted by the UNION of 1801.

praemunire

Laws which forbade the exercise of papal jurisdiction in ENGLAND without royal license. They were first enacted in 1351 to prevent the use of papal decrees to void the acts of royal courts, usually in cases of the disposition of clerical benefices. The word is a corruption of *praemonere* ("to forewarn").

prerogative, royal

The powers and rights, theoretically unlimited, pertaining to the Crown. Lawyers hesitated to suggest any limits to these powers, and the TUDOR and STUART sovereigns encouraged the belief that there were few or none. The result of the strife of the 17th century, however, was to place the king, lords, and commons in a balanced constitution, one which clearly implied that the still extensive prerogative powers were in fact limited and exercised by the joint authority of the "king in parliament."

Presbyterian

A Protestant faith that disputes the biblical authority for BISHOPS. The Calvinist view was that church government was meant to be by a hierarchy of courts: kirk session, presbytery, synod, and GENERAL ASSEMBLY. Theologically, the church consists of God's elect, those who are predestined to be saved. The Presbyterian church was strongest in SCOTLAND and later in NORTHERN IRELAND. A number of followers in ENGLAND hoped that the joint action during the 1640s, particularly the SOLEMN LEAGUE AND COVENANT (1643) and the WESTMINSTER ASSEMBLY (1643), would produce a joint Anglo-Scottish Presbyterian establishment. The RESTORATION in 1660 was followed by talks on church settlement in the SAVOY CONFERENCE (1661), but there was no agreement. In 1690 the establishment of the CHURCH OF SCOTLAND on a Presbyterian model was confirmed.

press gang

The Crown had an ancient right to conscript men into sea service, noted in statutes as early as the 14th century and as a corollary to the power to commandeer merchant vessels for royal service. The work of rounding up seamen was done by groups of sailors from warships and, late in the 18th century, by an Impress Service. The practice declined in the 19th century, as the NAVY retained personnel on longer terms of service.

Price, Richard (1723–1791)
dissenter, economist

The son of a Welsh Calvinist minister, Price was educated in dissenting academies. He became an important contemporary author, with works on moral questions, economics, and politics. The latter area drew the most attention, especially in his *Observations on the Nature of Civil Liberty, the Principles of Government, and the Justice and Policy of War with America* (1776). His sermon before the Revolution Society ("On the Love of our Country," 1789) commended the radicals in France and drew the withering reply of Edmund BURKE's *Reflections on the Revolution in France.*

Pride's purge (1648)

Colonel Thomas Pride led a detachment of troops that prevented the army's opponents from taking their seats in the HOUSE OF COMMONS in December 1648. This act created the RUMP PARLIAMENT.

Priestley, Joseph (1733–1804)
scientist, dissenter, radical author

Son of a Yorkshire cloth dresser, Priestley attended a grammar school and a dissenting academy, but he was largely self-taught. He was a PRESBYTERIAN minister for a time, but his faith moved toward the UNITARIAN position. An amateur investigator, he identified the properties of oxygen and he experimented with electricity. In religion he challenged conventional views in works such as the *History of the Corruptions of Christianity* (1782) and *History of Early Opinions concerning Jesus Christ* (1786). His political views were expressed in his *Essay on the First Principles of Government* (1768) and *The Present State of Liberty in Great Britain and Her Colonies* (1769). A sympathizer with the French revolution, he wrote a response to Edmund BURKE, and afterward his house and laboratory in Birmingham were destroyed by an angry mob (1791). He emigrated to Philadelphia, where he spent the rest of his life.

prime minister

The king's advisory COUNCILS were often dominated by a single minister, though there was no formal acknowledgment of such a position. With the major changes after 1688—the reliance on the HOUSE OF COMMONS for financial support, the corresponding need for annual sessions of PAR-

LIAMENT, and the concurrent emergence of political parties—there was a new political landscape. A minister, especially one who could manage finances and could put together an effective majority in the Commons, could control affairs. But the idea of such individual power was not yet acceptable. Thus Robert WALPOLE, often regarded as the first prime minister (1721–42), objected to being called one. By the end of the century, William PITT (1783–1801, 1804–06) was equally effective and not shy about his title. The prime minister from this point on took over more and more powers formerly exercised by the sovereign: the power to install and remove ministers, to call elections, and to prepare the political agenda.

The prime minister is almost always the party leader of the majority party, the principal exceptions occurring during periods of coalition government. In early days party leadership was obtained by consultation among leaders and with the Crown. Now it is by election—the CONSERVATIVE PARTY by election of MPs since 1965; the LABOUR PARTY, once by election of MPs but now through an electoral college (MPs, union leaders, and constituency parties) since 1981.

Primrose, Archibald   See ROSEBERY, ARCHIBALD PRIMROSE, EARL OF.

prince of Wales

The earliest use of this title by Welsh princes appears to be in the middle of the 13th century. When Edward I (1272–1307) conquered WALES, he deemed it advisable to display his power through the creation of his eldest son as Prince of Wales, and the title was bestowed in 1301. Since then, the title has usually been given to the heir apparent to the English throne.

privateer

Owner or captain of a private vessel commissioned to attack enemy shipping. The WARRANT for such operation was a royal authority called a letter of marque. When the ship captured another, the prize was shared with the government. This activity was widespread in the 18th and early 19th centuries, but it was banned by the Peace of Paris in 1856.

privy council

The royal council consisted of members who were in daily contact doing the king's business, as well as those who were of a certain rank and hence entitled to attend the king. It was natural for this body to expand, and therefore it became less efficient. In the early TUDOR period, a smaller body emerged, called the privy (i.e. private) council. By 1540 it had a clerk and a minute book, and its functions were vital for the next century and a half. By then it too was growing in size, and it was superseded by a cabinet council, and then the modern CABINET. The privy council and its committees (Trade and Plantations, Judicial Committee, etc.) were effective until the 19th century. Although it still retains some important powers, it has now become largely a formal body.

privy seal

The private seal of the monarch, used in lieu of the GREAT SEAL to authenticate documents of more limited or private nature. A keeper of the privy seal, later lord privy seal, was its custodian. Thomas CROMWELL inaugurated the use of the seal on the documents of the PRIVY COUNCIL.

proclamation

A royal declaration, issued in writing, which had the force of law but was not superior to STATUTE. Proclamations were widely used during the reigns of the TUDORS and STUARTS, but their legal status was clarified in 1610 when it was settled that they could not create new offenses. Through the rest of the century the power of statute became clearly superior, but the use of proclamations was still valuable. Today they are used for summoning or dissolving PARLIAMENTS, declaring war or states of emergency, and announcing public holidays.

prorogation

Suspension of a session of PARLIAMENT, formerly decided by the sovereign but now usually decided by the PRIME MINISTER. All business except legal action is halted, and bills must be reintroduced. The full termination of a parliament is a DISSOLUTION.

protectorate

1. The period of republican rule (1653–59) when Oliver CROMWELL dismissed the RUMP PARLIAMENT and governed under a series of constitutions which made him Lord Protector and allowed for parliaments and other institutions equivalent to their predecessors under the Crown.
2. A territory under the protection of the Crown. This form of colonial status was the result of a negotiated agreement between the British government and a local authority.
3. Rule on behalf of an underage or incompetent sovereign (e.g., HENRY III, HENRY VI, EDWARD VI).

Prynne, William (1600–1669)

Puritan pamphleteer

The son of a gentleman, Prynne was born near Bath, attended the grammar school there, and went to Oriel College, OXFORD UNIVERSITY; and Lincoln's Inn (see INNS OF COURT). He began to write PURITAN pamphlets in 1626. He published one that criticized the stage plays much beloved by the queen (*Histriomastix*, 1633), for which he was punished by the STAR CHAMBER, having his ears cropped. While imprisoned he continued to write, now taking the BISHOPS as a target. Again before the court in 1637, his ears were further trimmed. He was almost equally critical of the ARMY and other regimes in the 1640s and '50s. He later became royal archivist in the TOWER OF LONDON.

pub

The public house was an institution before it was set apart in English law as a licensed establishment during the 17th century. The inn had been a way station for travelers. The ale house and the tavern were more devoted to casual trade and were followed in the 19th century with a proliferating number of less-regulated beer houses. All these were licensed by local MAGISTRATES. In the 19th century many pubs had dining rooms, meeting rooms, and locations set aside for entertainment. Brewers acquired pubs to dispense their product, and those became known as "tied" houses. At the time of WORLD WAR I, the hours of operation were limited so as to assist the war effort, and afternoon closing was only lifted in the later years of the century. In 1998 there were more than 77,000 pubs in GREAT BRITAIN.

public school   See GRAMMAR SCHOOL.

Purcell, Henry (1659–1695)

composer

A choirboy in the chapel royal at Westminster, Purcell was later the organist at the abbey. He composed anthems and odes for special occasions, as well as the opera *Dido and Aeneas* (1689). His work drew on Italian and French styles, and he was the foremost English composer of his time.

Puritans

Those Protestants who would "purify" the faith and practice of the CHURCH OF ENGLAND. Many had been exiles in the reign of MARY I and returned from the continent with hopes of making ELIZABETH I's reign one in which their beliefs were accepted as orthodox. Puritans wanted to purge all traces of Catholic ceremony, ritual, and belief. Elizabeth, however, wanted a traditional church order without papal authority and little Puritan theology. In later years, under ARCHBISHOP William LAUD, the term was used more widely to include all who opposed royal religious policy. But there was no coherent body of Puritans, as was clear at the RESTORATION and after the TOLERATION ACT was passed in 1689. Numerous sects had always existed under that banner, united by their resistance to official uniformity of religious practice.

See also BROWNE, ROBERT; BUNYAN JOHN; DISSENTERS; PRYNNE, WILLIAM; WENTWORTH, PETER AND WENTWORTH, PAUL; WINTHROP, JOHN.

Pym, John (1584–1643)

politician

Born in Somerset, where his family had held land for generations, Pym attended OXFORD UNIVERSITY and was admitted to the Middle Temple (see INNS OF COURT). He was a member of the PARLIAMENTS of the 1620s and thereafter became a strong adversary of royal policy. He had taken part in the IMPEACHMENT of Lord BUCKINGHAM (1626), drafted the petition asking the king to summon a parliament in 1640, and led the drive to impeach Lord STRAFFORD and Archbishop LAUD. He pursued even more radical legislative measures, and he was named as one of the five members CHARLES I wanted to arrest in January 1642. He helped to organize the finances for war and to arrange the alliance with the Scots, and thus he was a major figure in the parliamentary victory that came after his death.

Q

Quakers

A sect that originated in the 1650s, the name either derived from visible reactions to preaching or from the admonition of George FOX to a judge that he should "tremble at the word of the Lord." They called themselves "Friends of Truth" and rejected professional ministry, refused to pay TITHES, swear oaths, or recognize social distinctions. Their "inner light" was a substitute for liturgy and sacraments, and despite persecution, they were admired for their philanthropy, sobriety, and diligence.

quarter sessions

The regular meetings of the JUSTICES OF THE PEACE of a county, required by a statute of 1362. At quarter session meetings the justices heard presentment of suspected criminals, and from the 16th century they discussed and acted on other matters. Under the TUDORS they came to deal with laws governing prices and wages, roads and bridges, jails and alehouses. In short, they were unpaid agents of local government, and they kept those functions and others until the 19th century. The quarter sessions were abolished in 1971.

Quebec Act (1774)

This law was passed at the time of the INTOLERABLE ACTS, which was a response to the BOSTON Tea Party. The fall of Quebec in 1759 had left a number of issues to be resolved in CANADA. In this act, the British recognized the Catholic church, acknowledged the use of French civil law in the territory, and extended the boundary of the province to the Ohio River. Each of these terms caused great resentment in the neighboring AMERICAN COLONIES, thus contributing to the outbreak of the American Revolution.

Queen Anne's Bounty

A fund established by Queen ANNE in 1703. The revenues came from the "first fruits and tenths," or the first year's income from church livings, traditionally owing to the papacy (until 1532) and then to the Crown. The money was to be disbursed to poor clergy, at first those who held livings worth less than £10 per annum. This also helped to pay for 50 new parish churches in LONDON. The fund was augmented by parliamentary grants from 1809.

Queen's Bench See KING'S BENCH, COURT OF.

Queensberry, John Sholto Douglas, marquis of (1844–1900)
sportsman

A Scottish peer and an amateur boxer, the marquis of Queensbury helped to draw up the Queensberry Rules for that sport (1867). His personal life was very troubled, one element being the friendship that his son, Lord Alfred Douglas, cultivated with Oscar WILDE, which led to Wilde's conviction for homosexual practices.

quo warranto

A legal proceeding, first used by Edward I in 1272. A WRIT beginning with these words (meaning "by what warrant?") was sent to holders of private courts, obliging them to prove the validity of their jurisdiction. The device was used by CHARLES II and JAMES VII AND II to recall the charters of BOROUGHS, so that they might be reissued in such a way as to alter the parliamentary electorate. Such usage was denounced in the DECLARATION OF RIGHTS in 1689.

R

radar

Radar (the name comes from *r*adio *d*etection *a*nd *r*anging), is used to detect the range and bearing of distant objects, including ships and aircraft. The system was developed by Sir Robert Watson Watt and a team of British scientists. A network of radar stations was begun along the east and south coast of GREAT BRITAIN in 1936, and this device was an extremely important tool in the victory over the Luftwaffe in the Battle of BRITAIN.

radicalism

The pursuit of fundamental change in institutions—political, economic, or social—by constitutional means. Such an agenda emerged toward the end of the 18th century, when American and French upheaval stimulated critical views of institutions. The strand of political REFORM ACTS (meaning the reform of parliamentary FRANCHISES) came first. Proposals for modest changes in franchises (by William PITT, Christopher WYVILL, and others) were followed by the sweeping critiques of John CARTWRIGHT, Thomas PAINE, and Henry HUNT. They helped to widen the agenda to include a free press and other civil liberties. By the 1830s there were political unions in most large towns advocating reform. The Great Reform Act of 1832 created many new voters and new constituencies, but the population at large was not satisfied, and radicals such as William LOVETT and Feargus O'CONNOR supported the People's Charter as a way of further expanding the electorate and the political process. Its goals were largely met by the early 20th century, even before the final chapter of parliamentary reform—universal suffrage for men (1918) and women (1928).

In economics, radicals wanted markets free of government controls (Adam SMITH, David RICARDO), campaigned for the abolition of slavery (Thomas CLARKSON, William WILBERFORCE), and soon ventured into the workplace to demand regulation of factories and working hours. Meanwhile, the MANCHESTER SCHOOL (Richard COBDEN, John BRIGHT) continued the campaign to reduce the role of government, promoting free trade and, in particular, fighting for repeal of the CORN LAWS.

The radical view of society was best captured by the "philosophic radicals," those followers of Jeremy BENTHAM (including James MILL, Henry BROUGHAM, John Stuart MILL) whose credo of utility brought a new and rational bearing to social questions. That view was reflected in the analysis of Thomas MALTHUS and in the ideas of Joseph HUME and others.

The radicals were contemporary with, but alien to, the early socialists, and the ideas of the latter would overtake and supplant radicalism toward the end of the 19th century. Thus Robert OWEN, Thomas Spence, and Charles KINGSLEY were advocates of even more fundamental change, to whom the thoughts and plans of radicals were mild, middle class remedies which did not cure the real ills of society.

See also CHARTIST MOVEMENT.

radio

With James Clerk Maxwell's discovery of electromagnetic waves, wireless communication became possible, and by 1901 there were radio transmissions across the Atlantic. The invention of a means to use radio waves for voice communication came before WORLD WAR I, and it was developed significantly during the war. Regular radio programming began in the 1920s, and the BRITISH BROADCASTING CORPORATION (BBC; initially the British Broadcasting Company) was created in 1922. The BBC dominated radio in GREAT BRITAIN until the 1960s, when pirate stations began competing, and in the 1970s new stations were authorized under an Independent Broadcasting Authority. Radio marked the first of the communications revolutions of the 20th century.

Raffles, Sir Thomas Stamford (1781–1826)
founder of Singapore

Raffles joined the EAST INDIA COMPANY in 1795. He was sent to Penang, an island in the straits of Molucca, in 1805. When in 1810 he was assigned to the Malay states, he began to prepare an invasion of Java. When that succeeded, he became lieutenant governor there until 1815. He had to return to GREAT BRITAIN to undergo an inquiry into his administration, but when he returned he convinced the Company to acquire SINGAPORE island, then only thinly inhabited, and began its development into one of the major ports and stations in Asia. A prominent oriental scholar and zoologist, Raffles founded the Zoological Society in LONDON (1825).

railways

The steam locomotive was developed in 1804 by Richard TREVITHICK, but the first railway opened to the public only in 1825 (Stockton to Darlington). Turnpike ROADS and canals had been improving transportation for over 50 years, but this new addition was a giant step forward. Spurts of railway construction (1836, 1840, 1844) brought hazards: a maze of competing companies, no uniform gauge of track, and a host of safety concerns came along with the

7,000 miles of rail track laid by the 1850s. But this development transformed travel, linking all the major cities of the UNITED KINGDOM with a peak mileage of 21,000 by the 1920s. The challenge of the LORRY and motor car reduced that number to 12,000 in 1970. The railway was a natural target of government regulation and intervention, and, in the years after 1945, a period of nationalization until the 1990s.

Raleigh, Sir Walter (1554–1618)
courtier, explorer

An enterprising courtier of Queen ELIZABETH I, Raleigh sailed in a number of colonizing ventures in America. When he married one of the queen's principal ladies, Elizabeth expelled him from the Court. A few years later Raleigh launched an expedition in search of Eldorado (in Guiana), and he participated in an attack on Cádiz. But he was out of favor with JAMES VI AND I and convicted of

Sir Walter Raleigh *(Library of Congress)*

being a part of a plot against the king. In the TOWER OF LONDON until 1617, Raleigh wrote his *History of the World* (1614). When released, he made one more voyage to find Eldorado, in the course of which he destroyed a Spanish settlement, and on his return he was executed.

Ramillies, Battle of (1706)

During the War of SPANISH SUCCESSION, the duke of MARLBOROUGH was campaigning against Louis XIV in the Spanish Netherlands when he intercepted a French army, killing 15,000 (and losing 5,000 of the British and Dutch force). Most of the rest of the province then surrendered. The French threat to the Netherlands was ended, and the British had gained the initiative.

Ramsay, James See DALHOUSIE, JAMES RAMSAY, MARQUIS.

Reading, Rufus Isaacs, marquis of (1860–1935)
lawyer, politician
Isaacs began life in East London; his father was a fruit merchant. He tried various business careers before reading law. Called to the bar in 1887, he became a successful BARRISTER. He was elected to PARLIAMENT in 1904, became solicitor general and then attorney general (1910–11). He was made LORD CHIEF JUSTICE in 1913, served as ambassador to the United States in 1918–19 and then as VICEROY OF INDIA (1921–26). He served as foreign secretary in 1931.

Rebecca riots (1838–1844)
In West WALES there were attacks on turnpike toll houses as distressed farmers and others claimed they were being ruined by the high toll charges. Blackening their faces and wearing women's clothes, the protesters called themselves the "daughters of Rebecca," probably referring to the passage in Genesis which said,

"the seed of Rebecca shall possess the gates of her enemies." There were also attacks on workhouses, and after an official inquiry, the government ordered a reduction in tolls.

recusants
The Catholics (and some Protestants) who refused to attend the services of the CHURCH OF ENGLAND—called recusants—were required to pay a fine under the acts of UNIFORMITY (1552, 1559, 1662). More severe penalties were enacted (fines, forfeitures, and imprisonment and possible execution for treason) and enforced at times of the greatest tension. By the later 17th century, such punishments were reduced, first by DECLARATIONS OF INDULGENCE, then by the TOLERATION ACT (1689), which excluded Catholics but brought de facto toleration. The age of uniformity ended with CATHOLIC EMANCIPATION in 1829.

Redmond, John (1856–1918)
Irish nationalist
Redmond joined the Irish nationalists in PARLIAMENT in 1881, became the leader of the Charles PARNELL faction after that leader's fall (1890), and reunited the party in 1900. He supported IRISH HOME RULE, but he was outflanked by the events that followed the introduction of the third home rule bill in 1912. The Ulster Volunteers challenged the basic policy, and in the South the Irish Volunteers were a militant force which Redmond had to try to control. At the same time he was obliged to support the war in 1914, and in the next few years, especially after the EASTER REBELLION in 1916, that loyal position became untenable. His party shrank and was overtaken by SINN FÉIN by 1918.

reform acts
While the term is widely used to encompass many areas and specific measures of reform, the most common usage refers to the major statutes that opened up the electoral system in 1832,

1867, and 1884–85. The first act came after several years of agitation, a general election, and a promise by the king to create enough peers to put it through the HOUSE OF LORDS. The Great Reform Act created a uniform FRANCHISE: those who held property of £10 annual value were entitled to vote. The act removed a large number of ROTTEN BOROUGHS (where there was a tiny electorate or none at all) and gave representation to a number of large new industrial towns. In all it meant a 50 percent increase in the size of the electorate. There was a companion measure for SCOTLAND and one for IRELAND. The Scottish act resulted in the largest increase (from 4,500 voters to 65,000), while the Irish act made little numerical change, as the number of voters there had been reduced when CATHOLIC EMANCIPATION was granted. In 1867 the electorate was increased from a little over 1 million to 2 million. In boroughs all £10 householders and renters could vote; in counties leaseholders (£5) and occupiers (£12) were admitted. In 1884 county householders were added, increasing the total from 3 million to 5 million. In 1885 all districts were made single-member and redistributed to equalize the number of votes in each. From this point, the ultimate democratic goal was clear: in 1918 all males aged 21 could vote (13 million) as well as women over 30 (8.5 million). In 1928 women 21 years or older (an added 5 million) completed the process. In 1969 the voting age was lowered to 18, adding another 3 million. In addition to these changes, there were many related reforms. To note only the most significant, in 1872 the SECRET BALLOT was introduced; and in 1883 a strict ban on corrupt and illegal practices put controls on election expenditure. Besides the reform of PARLIAMENT, progressive changes also reformed the election of local authorities between 1835 and 1894.

Reformation

In the 16th century the European movement to reform the Roman Catholic Church grew out of humanist and anticlerical criticism, sometimes manipulated by heads of state, and ended with the secession of large numbers of "protestant" heretics/reformers. In ENGLAND, HENRY VIII was quite hostile to reformers, but his desire for a divorce from CATHERINE OF ARAGON triggered a royal takeover of the church in England, which in turn was part of the reason for annexing WALES (1536), dissolving monasteries (1536), and proclaiming a royal title in IRELAND (1541). The same acts made a statement of ROYAL SUPREMACY necessary, which engaged PARLIAMENT in important constitutional definitions and in many ways altered the course of English politics.

In SCOTLAND, reformation was a very different story. In a country that was firmly Catholic until 1560, the turmoil which saw the end of French occupation, the intrusion of English influence, and the return of MARY, QUEEN OF SCOTS, created a fluid situation in which a group of Scottish nobles and reformers began to lay the foundation for a PRESBYTERIAN church—that is, a Protestant church made in a near vacuum of royal authority. JAMES VI tried very hard to overcome this tendency by restoring episcopal authority, but the Presbyterian core was preserved, emerging with force in the 1630s and '40s and becoming the new establishment in 1690.

In Ireland, the Reformation was always the project of the ruling minority. Most native Irish and some old English were Catholic, and they remained so despite efforts to apply an English-style settlement. Thus the wars of the 17th century became Ireland's wars of religion, and they ended with a stern system of PENAL LAWS imposed on the majority. The papacy was not idle in these times, with church councils promoting a Counter Reformation, fostering the work of militant orders such as the Society of Jesus (JESUITS) to recapture lost heretic communities.

In general, the Reformation brought out the worst in both sides—persecuting laws, systems of uniformity, and brutal punishments for the enemy. There can be no accurate tally, but it seems that the TUDORS killed thousands of enemies, political and religious. The STUARTS and their rebellious subjects gave many more lives in decades of skirmishes, pogroms, and CIVIL WAR. In the end, the Reformation produced a multiplicity of established churches and dissenting sects which grudgingly accepted a peace of exhaustion in the 18th century.

See also ENGLISH REFORMATION.

regency

In the event of minority or illness or incapacity of the sovereign, a regent might rule in his/her stead. Henry III (1216) succeeded at nine months of age, RICHARD II was only 10 years old (1377), HENRY VI suffered a mental collapse in 1453, EDWARD V was only 12 when he was presumably murdered by his uncle (and "protector") RICHARD III, and EDWARD VI was a minor in 1547. GEORGE III suffered a series of illnesses, and his son George became prince regent from 1811. The latter gave his name to the "regency period" (1811–20), which was marked by the contrast between the prince's elegant world of high fashion and the agonies of the soldiers and sailors fighting France as well as people at home struggling to survive economic distress.

Reith, John Reith, baron (1889–1971)
director general of the BBC
Lord Reith was the first manager of the British Broadcasting Company (1922), then director general of the BRITISH BROADCASTING CORPORATION (1927). He oversaw the development of the BBC as a national institution, maintaining its political neutrality and its educational function. After brief service with British Overseas Airways, he held posts in Winston CHURCHILL'S wartime cabinet from 1940 to 1942.

Renaissance

The rebirth of art and literature, beginning in 14th-century Italy and expanding across western Europe, generating a period and movement of heightened intellectual creativity inspired by classical Greece and Rome. GREAT BRITAIN'S Renaissance came rather later on the time scale of the continent, generally in the 16th century. Important pioneers included the earliest patron, Humphrey, duke of Gloucester (1390–1447); the

early linguists William Grocyn and Thomas Linacre; and the model humanists John COLET and Thomas MORE. In drama, poetry, and the arts, the era of Queen ELIZABETH I contained the greatest number of figures, many of them migrants or exiles from the continent.

reparations

At the end of WORLD WAR I, the deep revulsion at the loss of life and the destruction of property created a vengeful demand for compensation. In the Treaty of VERSAILLES in 1919, Germany was forced to accept a clause in which she admitted guilt for beginning the war, and that became the basis for the assessment of reparations. The amounts sought were subject to complex calculation, which in fact was only completed by the Reparations Commission in 1921. The total arrived at was £6.6 billion, but it soon became apparent that the postwar German economy could not pay such an astronomical amount. After reductions in 1924 and 1929, the payments were canceled in 1932. Nevertheless, the whole experience managed to create profound hostility on all sides. Following WORLD WAR II, in 1945 the western powers decided to emphasize reconstruction, whereas the Soviet Union stripped its zone of occupation in Germany of a large quantity of capital equipment.

Restoration

CHARLES II was returned to his thrones in ENGLAND, SCOTLAND, and IRELAND in 1660. This settlement was made possible by the breakdown of authority in England after Oliver CROMWELL'S death and the failure of the political groups there to produce a viable government. Thus, when George MONCK led his army from Scotland in 1660, he was able to enter LONDON and collect enough support to summon a meeting of the surviving members of the LONG PARLIAMENT. It dissolved itelf, calling for the election of a CONVENTION Parliament. That body was assured by the declaration of BREDA that there would be no retribution, and it invited Charles to return. When he arrived in May 1660, there was a very general acceptance of the monarchy. All institutions, except the courts of STAR CHAMBER and HIGH COMMISSION, were restored, and at the end of the year the king issued WRITS for the election of a new PARLIAMENT.

Restraint of Appeals, Act in (1533)

HENRY VIII authored this act, which declared that no legal appeals could be taken from ENGLAND to Rome. This terminated papal authority in England, and it allowed the king's divorce from CATHERINE OF ARAGAON to proceed. This was also part of the foundation for ROYAL SUPREMACY, which would be declared in the following year.

See also CROMWELL, THOMAS.

Reynolds, Sir Joshua (1723–1792)
painter

Reynolds was born in Devonshire; his father was a clergyman and a schoolmaster. He was apprenticed to Thomas Hudson, a leading painter, and he later studied in Italy (1748–51). The leading portrait painter of the 18th century, Reynolds became the first president of the ROYAL ACADEMY in 1768. His nearly 2,000 portraits included most of the notable figures of his time. A number of those were members of the Literary Club, a group he had formed in 1764 that included Samuel JOHNSON, Edmund BURKE, Adam SMITH, and Edward GIBBON.

Rhodes, Cecil John (1853–1902)
imperialist

The son of a vicar, Rhodes went to SOUTH AFRICA for health reasons, and he subsequently made a fortune in the diamond fields of Kimberley. After returning to study at OXFORD UNIVERSITY he went back to Africa and founded the De Beers company (1880). He then entered the gold business and began to look beyond to political horizons. His British South Africa Company received a charter for extensive lands (1889) which became RHODESIA. Rhodes was prime minister of the CAPE COLONY in 1890, but he had to resign the post

Cecil John Rhodes *(Library of Congress)*

after the JAMESON RAID (1895) had raised the possibility that he was fomenting rebellion in the Boer Republics. When he died he endowed a group of 170 scholarships at Oxford for Americans, Germans, and British colonists.

See also BOER WAR.

Rhodesia (Zimbabwe)

Part of southern AFRICA, bordering BECHUANALAND, Congo, TANGANYIKA, and Mozambique, Rhodesia was first controlled by the British South Africa Company. The northern part became ZAMBIA (1964), and the remainder—Rhodesia—attempted to maintain all-white rule, departing from the Commonwealth in 1965. The black majority gained control of the new state of Zimbabwe in 1980.

Ricardo, David (1772–1823)
economist

The younger son of a Dutch Jew who had been a successful LONDON businessman, Ricardo went to work in his father's business at age 14. He prospered and later became a highly important economic theorist. He conceived the law of rent, which explained the relation of capital, labor, and profits in land. His theory of comparative advantage was the essential underpinning of the arguments for FREE TRADE. In his *Principles of Political Economy and Taxation* (1817), Ricardo explained the labor theory of value, an argument that was to play a central role in the theoretical work of Karl Marx and others.

Richard II (1367–1400)
king of England, 1377–1399
Son of Edward, the Black Prince, and grandson of EDWARD III, Richard came to the throne as a boy of 10. He was under the tutelage of his uncle John of Gaunt, and his reign was marked by severe internal and external problems. In 1381 the PEASANTS' REVOLT was triggered by a POLL TAX, rebels marched on the capital, and the boy king showed great courage in going before them and demanding their loyalty. The rebellion was dispersed, and the leaders were executed. However, Richard did not fare so well with his noblemen. He was overly generous with PATRONAGE to his close advisers, and he was not careful to balance the factions at court. In 1386 his favorites were attacked by PARLIAMENT and outlawed. Richard waited until 1397 to exact vengeance by executions and banishments. The son and heir of Gaunt was Henry of Lancaster (later HENRY IV). Richard confiscated his estates in 1399, forcing Henry to act. He led an invasion while Richard was in IRELAND, captured the king, and forced him to abdicate.

Richard III (1452–1485)
king of England, 1483–1485
The younger brother of EDWARD IV, Richard had been a loyal and powerful leader in the north of ENGLAND. When the king died, he left two sons, Edward and Richard. Their uncle made himself protector of the young EDWARD V (age 12), but soon after he had the two princes imprisoned in the TOWER OF LONDON and seized the throne for himself. The princes were probably later murdered at Richard's order; certainly he executed leaders of hostile factions and defeated a revolt by the duke of Buckingham, who was also executed. However, Henry Tudor (later HENRY VII) led an army from France and WALES which defeated Richard at the Battle of BOSWORTH. The TUDOR dynasty was established, and it was in their interest to portray Richard as evil personified (as in the works of Thomas MORE, Polydore Vergil, and William SHAKESPEARE). His career made their task fairly easy.

Ridley, Nicholas (1500–1555)
bishop
One of the leading Protestant reformers in the reign of EDWARD VI, Ridley had been one of the drafters of the BOOK OF COMMON PRAYER in 1549, and he promoted the more extreme prayer book of 1552. BISHOP of Rochester and then LONDON, he was a supporter of Lady Jane GREY. After MARY I's accession he was deprived of office. With fellow reformers Thomas CRANMER and Hugh LATIMER, he entered a disputation at OXFORD UNIVERSITY against Catholic churchmen, and after the inevitable defeat he was burned for heresy.

Ridolfi plot (1571)
Roberto Ridolfi was an Italian banker who lived in LONDON. He conspired with English Catholics and with Spain to free MARY, QUEEN OF SCOTS, and place her on the throne; the heretic queen ELIZABETH I, who had just been excommunicated, would be murdered. Agents of Lord Burghley (William CECIL) uncovered the plot, and one of the plotters, Thomas HOWARD, duke of Norfolk, was executed. Ridolfi escaped and was never punished.

Riot Act (1715)
In fear of JACOBITE resistance, PARLIAMENT enacted this law to strengthen the authorities. The

Riot Act stated that when a JUSTICE OF THE PEACE ordered a crowd to disperse, those who did not do so within an hour were guilty of a felony and thus liable to the death penalty. "Reading the riot act" became a common expression, though in practice it was very difficult to implement. The act also indemnified officials—that is, it promised them immunity from future legal action for their conduct in these circumstances. The repressive potential of the law was seldom realized, as MAGISTRATES, and troops who might be called upon to shoot at rioters, were often reluctant to act. The Riot Act was last used in 1919, and it was repealed in 1967.

Ripon, Frederick John Robinson, first earl of   See GODERICH, FREDERICK JOHN ROBINSON, VISCOUNT.

Rizzio, David (1533–1566)
court musician, secretary

Rizzio was an Italian musician who came to SCOTLAND in 1561 as a member of a diplomatic mission. He became a servant to MARY, QUEEN OF SCOTS, and later her secretary. He was also the object of suspicion for a group of Scots nobles, led by Henry Stewart, Lord DARNLEY, the queen's husband. In 1566 he was seized by Darnley and others in the presence of the then-pregnant queen, dragged away, and stabbed to death.

roads

The first system of roads in BRITAIN was built by the Romans. They allowed fairly rapid movement from the center in LONDON over a network of about 5,000 miles of roadways. Some of these still survive, and until the 18th century they were the best overland routes available. Little had been done to develop road transport for over a millenium, not only because the skills were lost and the costs were prohibitive, but also because the island made extensive use of coastal shipping and river traffic. However, the rise of industrial towns and the need to move heavy loads of coal and iron stimulated the rise of TURNPIKE trusts in the 18th century, which provided 15,000 miles of roadways by 1770. The engineering work of Thomas TELFORD and John MACADAM fostered a period of extensive road improvement and the growth of coach travel in the early 19th century. This was overtaken by the RAILWAY boom, but in the early 20th century the motor car inspired yet another burst of activity. Speed limits rose from four mph in 1865 (for steam-driven vehicles) to 14 mph in 1896 to 20 mph in 1903. In the 1920s there was a rapid increase in traffic and further extension of paved roads. The period after 1945 saw the greatest growth yet, and by the 1960s the limited-access motorways triggered a quadrupling of passenger miles traveled between 1950 and 1990.

Roberts of Kandahar, Frederick Sleigh Roberts, first earl (1832–1914)
field marshal

The son of an Anglo-Irish general, Lord Roberts served in INDIA for most of the period 1851–93. He fought in the INDIAN MUTINY and the second AFGHAN WAR and then commanded forces in India, and later in IRELAND (1895). He took the post of commander in chief of the forces in SOUTH AFRICA in 1900, where he captured the Boer capitals of Bloemfontein and Pretoria during th BOER WAR. After turning over his command to Herbert KITCHENER, he returned and assumed the post of commander-in-chief of the British ARMY (1901–04).

Robin Hood

The legendary hero first appears in William Langland's *Piers Plowman* (1377), and other English and Scottish sources pick up the story in the early 1400s. Robin allegedly lived during the time of Richard I, in the 1190s, when his brother John was governing, or misgoverning, ENGLAND. There is a record of a fugitive in Yorkshire named Robin Hood in a pipe roll of 1230, but the most common locale of the stories is Sherwood Forest in Nottingham. The tales emerge from the period of wide peasant unrest in the later 14th century, and they evoke a sense of rough justice against oppressive aristocrats.

Rochdale Pioneers

Workers who opened a cooperative shop in Toad Lane, Rochdale, in 1844. They distributed profits to themselves in dividend payments. The origin of the idea has been ascribed to Robert OWEN and to the advocates of self-help like Samuel SMILES and George Holyoake, who lectured to workers. This example was adopted in growing numbers of shops and in larger enterprises over the next few decades.

See also COOPERATIVE MOVEMENT.

Rockingham, Charles Wentworth, marquis of (1730–1782)
prime minister, 1765–1766, 1782

A WHIG leader who succeeded George GRENVILLE as PRIME MINISTER, Rockingham opposed the war with the AMERICAN COLONIES. His government repealed the STAMP ACT, but it also authored the DECLARATORY ACT in 1766. Leader of the opposition to Lord NORTH, he again took office at the end of the American war. He had begun peace negotiations, had arranged concessions to Henry GRATTAN'S PARLIAMENT in IRELAND, and he was introducing the ECONOMICAL REFORMS proposed by Edmund BURKE and others when he died in office.

Rodney, George (1719–1792)
admiral

Born in LONDON, Rodney attended Harrow, but at the age of 14 he joined the NAVY. He became a captain at 23, and during the SEVEN YEARS' WAR he captured St. Lucia and Grenada (1762). During the American Revolution he led a relief force to GIBRALTAR, and he won the Battle of Cape St. Vincent (1780). He then saved the COLONY of JAMAICA by his victory in the Battle of the Saints (off Dominica), where the British destroyed several French ships, caused several thousand casualties, and captured the French admiral François, comte de Grasse.

Roebuck, John Arthur (1801–1879)
radical

Born in Madras and educated in CANADA, Roebuck became a BARRISTER, and he served as agent in ENGLAND for the house of assembly of Lower Canada. He regarded himself an independent member, which was appropriate as his causes did not fit into neat categories. One of the followers of Jeremy BENTHAM, he proposed state schools, endorsed the new POOR LAW, and was a party to the drafting of the People's Charter (see CHARTIST MOVEMENT). He was a supporter of CIVIL SERVICE reform and a foe of the FACTORY ACTS and TRADE UNIONS. A critic of the CRIMEAN WAR, he promoted colonization and became a supporter of Benjamin DISRAELI's imperialism. He became a privy councillor in 1878.

romanticism

Artistic and intellectual movement from around 1770 to 1830. In reaction to the neoclassical period of the 18th century, romanticism explored the world of nature, emotion, and imagination. Some of its sources were medieval romance literature and the supernatural, as well as the aspirations of revolutions in America and France and national movements in Europe. Early figures of the romantic movement in Britain were William WORDSWORTH, Samuel Taylor COLERIDGE, William BLAKE, and Robert BURNS. Later, Lord BYRON, Percy Bysshe SHELLEY, and John KEATS seemed to live out careers reflecting the passion of the movement.

Romilly, Sir Samuel (1757–1818)
law reformer

Romilly was born into a Huguenot family; his father was a jeweler. Thanks to an inheritance from a relative, Romilly was able to study LAW. Called to the bar in 1783, he was a champion of enlightened ideas on the law, and he wrote tracts promoting CRIMINAL LAW reform in the 1780s. As his early support for the French revolution faded, he became solicitor general in 1806 and entered PARLIAMENT. He continued to advocate criminal law reform and supported slavery abolition and CATHOLIC EMANCIPATION. He was able to get statutes passed to remove the death penalty from some offenses. He wrote *Observations on the Criminal Law of England as it relates to Capital Punishment* (1810). When his wife died in 1818, he committed suicide.

Rosebery, Archibald Primrose, earl of (1847–1929)
prime minister, 1894–1895

A wealthy peer from SCOTLAND, Lord Rosebery rose to the leadership of the LIBERAL PARTY under William GLADSTONE, whom he served at the HOME OFFICE. He helped with the creation of the Scottish office and later was foreign secretary. When he replaced Gladstone as party leader and PRIME MINISTER in 1894, he encountered serious divisions within the party and was unable to overcome them. He resigned after a defeat in the HOUSE OF COMMONS in 1895.

Roses, Wars of the (1455–1485)

The struggles between aristocratic factions—the house of YORK (white) and the house of LANCASTER (red)—for the succession to the English throne in the later 15th century. The name was given by Sir Walter SCOTT in the 19th century. There was in fact a series of skirmishes: first a struggle over the failing rule (and mental capacity) of HENRY VI (1455–61), which ended in his deposition and the installation of EDWARD IV (York). Then in 1469–71, that king was ousted by his former allies and the late queen (MARGARET OF ANJOU), but he returned and destroyed his enemies at the Battle of TEWKESBURY. A third phase might be seen between the coup of RICHARD III (1483) and the establishment of HENRY VII (1487). In this period of three decades

there was probably less than a year and a half of fighting, involving modest casualties and limited loss of property in the aggregate. But the deaths of many aristocrats and the absence of law and order boosted support for the TUDOR king, HENRY VII, a Lancastrian who married the daughter of EDWARD IV, thus uniting the two lines and resolving this cause of civil warfare.

Rothermere, Harold Harmsworth, viscount (1868–1940)
newspaperman

The brother of Lord NORTHCLIFFE, Lord Rothermere was the financial manager of the Amalgamated Press. He produced LONDON's first illustrated Sunday paper, the *Sunday Pictorial* (1915). In WORLD WAR I he was the head of the Ministry for Air in 1917. When his brother died in 1922, he assumed control of the Associated Newspapers. He freely expressed his fascist sympathies in writing for the *Daily Mail*.

Rothschild, Lionel Nathan, baron de (1808–1879)
banker

The first Jew to be elected to PARLIAMENT (1847), Rothschild was not allowed to take his seat as he would not take the parliamentary oath "on the true faith of a Christian." He was reelected five times and finally seated in 1858, when the law changed. Nathan, baron Rothschild (1840–1915), was his son, and he became the first Jewish member of the HOUSE OF LORDS (1885).

rotten borough

The term applied to those parliamentary BOROUGHS which over time had either been depopulated or had become the sole property of a landowner, who thus had the nomination of the borough in his pocket. They were thus also called "nomination," or "pocket" boroughs. William PITT the elder had called them "the rotten part of the constitution."

Roundheads

The slur used by royalists to describe the rebels in the parliamentary army and, more generally, all of those who opposed CHARLES I. The name apparently came from the PURITAN style of haircut close around the head, as opposed to the long, flowing hair favored by royalists (aka "cavaliers").

Rowntree, Benjamin Seebohm (1871–1954)

social reformer

Born into a QUAKER family, chocolate manufacturers in York, Rowntree conducted a detailed survey, published as *Poverty: A Study of Town Life* (1901). He identified primary poverty as the lack of basic requirements of food, fuel, shelter, and clothing; secondary poverty as the lack of further essentials such as medicine. In his study he found that over 9 percent were in the first category and nearly 18 percent in the second. He made later studies of York in 1936 and 1950. Meanwhile he ran the welfare department of the Ministry of Munitions (1915–18), wrote *The Human Needs of Labour* (1918), and campaigned in the 1920s and '30s for improved policies on social welfare.

Royal Academy

British artists had complained of the lack of support for their profession compared to other countries, and in 1768 GEORGE III approved the founding of an academy for painters, sculptors, and architects. A free school of art, annual exhibitions which used proceeds to support indigent artists, and regular meetings of the 40 elected members were prescribed in the founding charter. The Royal Academy has been housed in Burlington House, Piccadilly, since 1869.

Royal African Company

Chartered in 1662, the company consisted of traders who transported slaves as well as gold, ivory, and redwood. Its monopoly was under attack by 1700, and it lost the right to trade slaves with the Spanish empire to the South Sea Company in 1713. It was ended in 1821.

See also SOUTH SEA BUBBLE.

Royal Air Force (RAF)

The military use of aircraft was developed rapidly in the first years of the 20th century, and the Royal Flying Corps and the Royal Naval Air Service were among the earliest bodies involved. The RAF was formed in 1918, at first as a merger of its predecessors. They were not immediately dispersed, and indeed the RAF had to struggle for recognition from the older services. By the 1930s it had built a bomber force, and in the later '30s it developed fighter defense and radar. As WORLD WAR II began, the force was outnumbered and outclassed at first by the larger Luftwaffe of Germany. The advantage of a defensive role, plus the premature launch of the BLITZ against the civilian population, contributed to a remarkable victory in the Battle of BRITAIN. Once that was achieved, however, there was an even greater task of mounting effective air power over the far-flung fields of battle, from AFRICA to Asia to the European continent, especially Germany. With massive support from the United States, British planes began to inflict great damage on German forces and German factories. In the postwar period, the RAF became a major element of defense, with deployment of jet aircraft armed with nuclear weapons.

royal commission

Broadly, this refers to any royal order to act on behalf of the Crown. Specifically, it denotes a body commissioned by the ministers of the Crown to inquire into a particular area of activity (charities, POOR LAWS, TRADE UNIONS, municipal corporations, public health, public schools, and UNIVERSITIES were some of the early 19th-century examples). The commission is addressed to a group of experienced persons, and powers are granted to summon witnesses, collect information, and make reports. The reports are directed to the leaders of the government, who in turn decide whether and how to use them. The inquiries have only the influence which their prestigious members, the collected evidence, and the prevailing climate of opinion may lend to them. Only the government of the day will determine which of them is to have a meaningful outcome.

Royal Exchange

The first Royal Exchange, a meeting place for merchants, bankers, and traders, was opened by Queen ELIZABETH I in 1571. Located in the city of LONDON, it was modeled on the exchange of Antwerp. Destroyed by fire (1666 and 1838), it was rebuilt. It is now the location of the financial futures market.

Royal Irish Constabulary

A centrally controlled POLICE force was first developed in IRELAND under the direction of Robert PEEL, the chief secretary. The Peace Preservation Force was a body of constables, led by a paid magistrate, sent to areas afflicted with agrarian violence (1814). These forces were first paid for by the local authorities, and in 1822 they were followed by a new County Constabulary. In 1836 the Irish Constabulary was created; it was given the designation "royal" in 1867. This force was a mainstay of law and order until 1922, when it was disbanded in the South but found a successor force in NORTHERN IRELAND in The Royal Ulster Constabulary.

Royal Society

With its charter dating from 1662, the Royal Society is the oldest scientific body in the world. Discussion of religion and politics were excluded—no mean task in its early period—and the society began to publish a journal, *Philosophical Transactions*, which still continues. Some of its prominent early members were Christopher WREN and Isaac NEWTON. However, most of its members were, until the later 19th century, amateur scientists and gentlemen. Then it became a more formal body, with parliamentary grants for research. The society also provides advice to governments on scientific matters.

royal supremacy

The centerpiece of the REFORMATION in ENGLAND was HENRY VIII's assertion of the king's supreme power, or royal supremacy, in church and state. The power was implied in the SUBMISSION OF THE CLERGY (1532) and in the ACT in RESTRAINT OF APPEALS to Rome (1533). In 1534 the king's authority was "confirmed" by the Act of Supremacy. This was repealed by MARY I in 1554 and reinstated by ELIZABETH I in 1559.

rugby

This variant of FOOTBALL appeared in the early 19th century. Players picked up the ball and ran with it, until they were stopped by opponents. Definition and rules followed, particularly at the time of the founding of the Football Association (1863). A Rugby Football Union was formed in 1871, and Scottish, Irish, and Welsh unions soon followed. A breakaway group formed the Rugby Football League in 1922, introducing a number of variations in the rules. Later in the 20th century the sport became professionalized.

Rump Parliament (1648–1653)

The derogatory name for the remnant of the LONG PARLIAMENT (1640–60) which remained sitting after PRIDE'S PURGE in 1648. Colonel Pride had prevented the entry of those members who supported reinstating the king. Some 231 members were excluded, and the remaining 70 MPs worked with the ARMY to conduct the trial and execution of CHARLES I and establish the institutions of the COMMONWEALTH OF ENGLAND.

Rupert, Prince (1619–1682)
royalist commander

The son of Elizabeth of Bohemia, daughter of JAMES VI AND I. Prince Rupert was the leading royalist cavalry commander, famous for lightning raids and impressive movements of cavalry units. He held the overall command at the Battle of NASEBY, and later he surrendered Bristol to the rebel forces. That angered the king, and Rupert left the country. Later he served as a naval commander and eventually led British forces in the DUTCH WARS of 1665 and 1672.

Ruskin, John (1819–1900)
art critic

The son of a wealthy wine merchant, Ruskin was the most influential art critic of the 19th century. He was appalled at the cultural influence of industrial development, and in reaction he extolled the art of the Middle Ages, called for a return to older values, and wanted art to be seen as an expression of moral values. He wrote *The Seven Lamps of Architecture* (1849) and *The Stones of Venice* (1851–53). He was a professor at OXFORD UNIVERSITY, and he endowed the drawing school there. His private life was unhappy, and he suffered bouts of mental illness later in life.

Russell, Bertrand Arthur William Russell, third earl (1872–1970)
philosopher, pacifist

The grandson of Lord John RUSSELL, Bertrand Russell was a brilliant mathematician, and in 1911 he published, with Alfred North WHITEHEAD, *Principia Mathematica*. The following year he published *The Problems of Philosophy*. Russell was deprived of his post at CAMBRIDGE UNIVERSITY in 1915 because of his opposition to WORLD WAR I. His continued support of conscientious objectors led to imprisonment in 1918 for seditious writings. He was in America during WORLD WAR II, and he published his very successful *History of Western Philosophy* in 1945. He was awarded the Order of Merit in 1949 and the Nobel Prize in literature in 1950. In his last great cause, he cofounded the CAMPAIGN FOR NUCLEAR DISARMAMENT in 1958, was its first president, and was jailed in 1961.

Russell, Lord John (1792–1878)
prime minister, 1846–1852, 1865–1866

Third son of the duke of Bedford, Russell entered PARLIAMENT in 1813 and was an early advocate of REFORM ACTS. He drafted the reform bill in 1831 for Earl GREY's WHIG ministry. He also served as home secretary and colonial secretary (1834–41). When Robert PEEL resigned after the repeal of the CORN LAWS, Russell became PRIME MINISTER (1846–52). He later served twice as foreign secretary, and one more time as prime minster. Ironically, in that last office, he was the author of further parliamentary reform which was defeated, only to be surpassed by the 1867 reform act, carried by his TORY opponents.

Russell, William (1820–1907)
journalist

Born into a poor Irish middle-class family, Russell worked for *The Times,* and he was sent to cover the CRIMEAN WAR. His reports took 10 days to reach London, but they exposed many of the shortcomings of the British ARMY there, and they had a great political impact. He also reported on the INDIAN MUTINY, the American Civil War, the Prussian wars of 1866 and 1870, and the ZULU war. Russell pioneered modern journalistic coverage of world conflicts.

Rutherford, Ernest Rutherford, first baron (1871–1937)
scientist

Born in NEW ZEALAND, Rutherford worked at McGill University in CANADA, where he discovered radioactivity, winning the Nobel Prize in chemistry in 1908. Meanwhile he had moved to Manchester, ENGLAND, in 1907, and then became professor of experimental physics and director of the Cavendish Laboratory at CAMBRIDGE UNIVER-

SITY in 1919. There in 1932 it was discovered that the uranium atom could be split, producing enormous amounts of "atomic" energy.

Ruthven raid (1582)

The intense rivalry between factions of Scottish nobles resulted in the kidnapping of the 16-year-old JAMES VI by the Protestant earl of Gowrie (William Ruthven) and his colleagues. They were afraid of the influence of the current favorite, the king's Catholic cousin Esmé Stuart, the duke of LENNOX. The king was held captive for 10 months, and Lennox fled to France, but when James escaped, he took revenge on his captors. Gowrie was executed in 1584, and the king developed a lifelong dislike for Protestant extremism.

Rye House plot (1683)

In the wake of the EXCLUSION crisis, a plot was discovered in which CHARLES II and his brother James (the future JAMES VII AND II) were to be captured (and possibly executed) at Rye House on their return from the races at Newmarket. Their return was earlier than expected, foiling the plot, but the occasion was used to arrest many of the WHIG opponents of the Crown, and it led to the trial and execution of Algernon SIDNEY and William Russell (1683), and the forced exile of others.

Ryswick, Treaty of (1697)

The end of King William's War (also known as the Nine Years' War, 1688–97) saw Louis XIV of France accept the terms of his coalition opponents (England, Holland, the Holy Roman Empire, and Spain). He surrendered most captured territory, acknowledged WILLIAM III as king of ENGLAND, and withdrew his support for JAMES VII AND II, the former king. The peace was short, as it was only four years until the start of the War of the SPANISH SUCCESSION.

S

Sacheverell, Dr. Henry (1674–1724)
political preacher

Sacheverell was a high-church ANGLICAN and Fellow of Magdalen College, OXFORD UNIVERSITY, who preached a pair of angry sermons against DISSENTERS, leading to his IMPEACHMENT and trial. Those events provoked riots in LONDON in 1710, in which half a dozen dissenting chapels were destroyed. He was suspended from preaching for three years, but upon the WHIG administration being dismissed, he was reinstated by the TORY government.

St. Albans, battles of

May 22, 1455: Regarded as the first battle of the Wars of the ROSES, this battle was actually a skirmish in the town, after Richard, duke of YORK's, protectorate had ended. Several of the leading Lancastrian noblemen were killed, HENRY VI was captured, and the aristocratic rivalry turned into civil war.

February 17, 1461: Queen Margaret (see MARGARET OF ANJOU) attacked, following her victory at Wakefield, and rescued HENRY VI from yet another period of captivity. However, the new Yorkist leader reached LONDON first and was proclaimed as EDWARD IV.

St. Albans, viscount See BACON, FRANCIS, VISCOUNT ST. ALBANS.

St. John, Henry See BOLINGBROKE, HENRY ST. JOHN, VISCOUNT.

St. Leger, Sir Anthony (1496–1559)
lord deputy of Ireland, 1540–1548

St. Leger worked for Thomas CROMWELL and led a commission to IRELAND for him. When he became lord deputy in 1540, it was his task to begin to assert royal authority more firmly and extensively (1540). The plan involved declaring HENRY VIII's kingship of Ireland (1541) and converting Gaelic chiefs to royal vassals with a policy called "surrender and regrant," wherein the Irish leaders surrendered native titles in exchange for Anglo-Irish noble rank. This was done in a general atmosphere of conciliation, but it was only partly successful. St. Leger returned for two more short terms as deputy (1551 and 1553), but there was much opposition to his strategy and it was overtaken by more aggressive methods on both sides.

St. Paul's Cathedral

The site of this LONDON landmark had a cathedral in the Anglo-Saxon period, rebuilt several times before a great edifice was built in the Norman period. That gothic structure was a main location for royal ceremonies, but after the REFORMATION it was allowed to deteriorate. During the CIVIL WAR it was used as a cavalry barracks. Destroyed by the great FIRE OF LONDON (1666), it was rebuilt by Sir Christopher WREN (1705–11). The cathedral became the resting place for military heroes (NELSON, WELLINGTON), and it served as the locale for important state occasions.

St. Vincent See JERVIS, JOHN, EARL ST. VINCENT.

Salesbury, William (1520–1584)
Welsh scholar

An OXFORD UNIVERSITY graduate and student of LAW, Salesbury converted to Protestantism and devoted himself to writing in Welsh. He composed a Welsh-English dictionary in 1547, and the same year he published a collection of proverbs. These were the first books printed in Welsh. Queen ELIZABETH I commissioned him to translate the BIBLE and the BOOK OF COMMON PRAYER into Welsh. Together with Bishop Richard DAVIES, he completed the prayer book and the New Testament by 1567. Later scholars produced better translations, but his work was vital in the history of the Welsh language.

Salisbury, Robert Gascoyne Cecil, marquis of (1830–1903)
prime minister, 1885–1886, 1886–1892, 1895–1902

Conservative leader and staunch defender of established institutions, Lord Salisbury served in PARLIAMENT for half a century. In the HOUSE OF COMMONS for 15 years before he inherited the title, he was especially interested in imperial and foreign affairs. He was secretary for INDIA twice and was foreign secretary before becoming PRIME MINISTER. His first time as premier was as head of a minority government; in the latter terms he had the support of LIBERAL UNIONISTS, which gave him a majority but also restricted his policy making. For most of his time as prime minister, Salisbury was also the head of the FOREIGN OFFICE. His area of expertise was in diplomacy, where GREAT BRITAIN, without any formal allies, tried to maintain a leading position in Europe and to retain world authority through the BRITISH EMPIRE AND COMMONWEALTH. The imperial role was seriously injured by the events of the BOER WAR (1899–1902), in which Britain appeared to be bullying two small colonial states in SOUTH AFRICA, employing excessive force and barbaric treatment (concentration camps in particular). The war was "won" by the British, and an enlarged Union of South Africa was created. Meanwhile, at home Salisbury had resisted IRISH HOME RULE (as leader of the opposition in the HOUSE OF LORDS, he smashed the second home rule bill by a vote of 419–41 in 1893). When in office, he grudgingly accepted reforms in local government, education, and Irish land purchase, in order to maintain his majority.

Salvation Army

William BOOTH had founded the Christian Revival Association in 1865, in Whitechapel (LONDON). Initially a mission community, it took its new name of Salvation Army and its militaristic organization in 1878. "General" Booth and his wife used open meetings, brass bands, and banners to energize their EVANGELICAL message. Forsaking sacramental religion, they promoted temperance, abstinence, and social action. The CHURCH OF ENGLAND was moved to copy them by organizing a "church army" in 1882. The movement spread to other countries, especially to the United States, where it had great success.

Samuel, Herbert Louis Samuel, first viscount (1870–1963)
Liberal Party leader

Lord Samuel sat in PARLIAMENT from 1902, serving in minor offices, and he was at the HOME OFFICE in 1916 at the time of the EASTER REBELLION. He resigned when David LLOYD GEORGE replaced Herbert ASQUITH as PRIME MINISTER. In 1920 Samuel took the post of high commissioner of PALESTINE. On his return in 1925, he headed a commission to investigate the coal industry. Its recommendations touched off the GENERAL STRIKE in 1926. Samuel returned to Parliament in 1929, had a role in forming the national government of 1931, and was the LIBERAL PARTY leader. His PEERAGE was bestowed in 1937, and he led his party in the HOUSE OF LORDS, 1944–55.

Sancroft, William (1617–1693)
archbishop of Canterbury, 1678–1689

A man of conviction, Sancroft was ejected from his fellowship at CAMBRIDGE UNIVERSITY by the

COMMONWEALTH OF ENGLAND regime. Having been royal chaplain and dean of ST. PAUL'S CATHEDRAL, he was made archbishop in 1678. He officiated at the coronation of JAMES VII AND II, but he declined to sit on the court of HIGH COMMISSION. He later led the SEVEN BISHOPS in opposing the reading of the king's DECLARATION OF INDULGENCE in 1688. They were committed to the TOWER OF LONDON but acquitted by a LONDON jury. After the GLORIOUS REVOLUTION, Sancroft refused to take an oath of allegiance to WILLIAM III, thus becoming a NONJUROR.

See also SEVEN BISHOPS' CASE.

Sandhurst

The original Royal Military Academy was established at Woolwich in 1741 by GEORGE II, the last British sovereign to serve in battle. In 1799 a Royal Military College was created on land in Windsor Forest that William PITT sold to the government. Sandhurst was designed as a school for junior officers of infantry and cavalry, a need keenly felt in the ARMY during the NAPOLEONIC WARS. The college was merged with the academy at Woolwich in 1946.

Sandwich, John Montagu, fourth earl of (1718–1792)
politician

Sandwich served as first lord of the ADMIRALTY several times, including the period of the American Revolution. He is thought to be the inventor of the sandwich—in one version as a means of sustenance while spending long hours at the gaming table; in the more flattering version, as a form of nourishment during less exciting hours of work at his office.

Savery, Thomas (1650–1715)
inventor

Born in a mining area of Devon, Savery served as a military engineeer and developed the first STEAM ENGINE, a vacuum pump for removing water from coal mines (1698). This design was the basis for Thomas NEWCOMEN's improved design, and under the terms of the original patent they formed a partnership and began to produce the new engines.

Savoy Conference

In an attempt to resolve differences between ANGLICANS and PRESBYTERIANS after the RESTORATION, a meeting was called in April 1661 at the Savoy Hospital in LONDON. The 12 delegates from each side could not agree on a revised prayer book, and the conference broke up in July. The aftermath saw the return of BISHOPS to the HOUSE OF LORDS, the resignation or removal of a thousand Presbyterian ministers, and the adoption of the CLARENDON CODE.

Scapa Flow

A large natural harbor in the ORKNEY islands, Scapa Flow was used as a royal NAVY base in both world wars. In 1918 the German high seas fleet was interned there at the end of the war. In June 1919, after the Treaty of VERSAILLES was signed, all 74 ships were scuttled by their crews rather than be turned over to British control.

Scone

The site of the palace and the abbey in which the "stone of destiny," or stone of Scone, was kept. Tradition has it that Scottish kings, from Kenneth MacAlpin in A.D. 850, sat on this stone when they were crowned. The stone was seized by Edward I in 1296 while he was asserting English authority over the Scots. Placed in WESTMINSTER ABBEY, it was put under the coronation chair used by English sovereigns. As a protest by Scottish nationalists, the stone was stolen in 1950, but it was recovered and replaced. In 1996 the stone was returned to SCOTLAND and put on display in EDINBURGH Castle.

Scotland

The names "Scotia" and "scot" were originally used by Romans to describe IRELAND and its inhabitants. Migrations and missions from Ireland brought growing numbers of "scots" into the north of BRITAIN from the sixth century. There they cohabited with the Picts in the North, Britons in the Southwest, and incoming Angles in the Southeast. The kingdom formed by Kenneth MacAlpin in the ninth century took the name of the prevailing immigrant people. This kingdom was able to consolidate its rule over the eastern part of modern Scotland, thanks in part to the concurrent invasions of Danes. Those migrations took over much of the island hinterland in Shetland, ORKNEY, and the Hebrides. Royal consolidation continued, somewhat in parallel with the English to the south. But in 1066 the Normans did not take power in Scotland. The kingdom of the Scots maintained a separate existence, sharing culture, institutions, and a turbulent frontier with ENGLAND. When the Scottish line of succession failed in 1290, the English king Edward I tried to control and incorporate the northern kingdom. This was foiled in the Wars of Independence (1308–28), as the Scots resumed their own royal line with Robert the Bruce. Yet this realm, with its limited resources and divisions of culture and terrain, was no match for its neighbor. When an English dynasty next tried to control Scotland, HENRY VII arranged a dynastic marriage, that of his daughter Margaret TUDOR to JAMES IV. Then HENRY VIII tried to bring Scotland under English control but failed, even with armed force. In the end, ELIZABETH I recognized the descendant of her aunt's marriage as her rightful heir, and JAMES VI of Scotland came to the English throne as James I in 1603. This union was only constitutional, as the later wars of the 17th century made clear. But in 1707 a parliamentary UNION was achieved, and the United Kingdom of GREAT BRITAIN was formed. Scotland has ever since been a part of a larger, English-dominated entity, now the UNITED KINGDOM of Great Britain and NORTHERN IRELAND. However, Scottish nationalism, which began its modern career in the 19th century, has led to the formation of a new Scottish PARLIAMENT, giving a limited form of "home rule" for the northern realm at the end of the 20th century.

Scott, Sir Walter (1771–1832)
poet, novelist

The son of a writer to the signet (Scottish attorney), Scott was born in EDINBURGH. Trained for the Scottish legal profession, he was an advocate and practiced law throughout his life. His first literary success came with narrative poems (especially *Lay of the Last Minstrel,* 1805, and *Marmion,* 1808). *Waverly* in 1814 was his first novel, and it was followed by two dozen more over the rest of his life. His authorship was only acknowledged in 1827, when he was entangled in the financial ruin of a publishing house, and he was obliged to settle very large debts. Scott's literary output went far beyond these works, with many essays, plays, and critical works. His patriotic and romantic subjects made an indelible mark in European literature.

Scottish National Covenant (1638)

When CHARLES I ordered the adoption of a new prayer book in SCOTLAND in 1637, it received a very rude welcome. A service at St. Giles Cathedral in EDINBURGH was the occasion of angry disturbance and hurled prayer cushions. A number of noblemen and clergy drafted a COVENANT in 1638, in the form of a pledge to protect the "true reformed kirk." This document recited the legal and statutory record of the church at length. It was signed by an estimated 300,000 people and became the manifesto for PRESBYTERIANS for many generations.

Scottish National Party (SNP)

There were varied groups and individuals expressing nationalist sentiment in SCOTLAND, particularly during the high tide of IRISH HOME RULE in the 19th century. Yet none of these created a durable political grouping. The first two small parties, the National Party of Scotland (1928) and the Scottish Party (1930), merged in 1934 to form the SNP. Its first electoral victory came in 1945, and the next in 1967. By 1974 there were 11 MPs, as the Westminster government attempted to arrange a form of DEVOLU-

TION. In a referendum on a Scottish Assembly in 1979, the measure was defeated, and the SNP went into decline. But the government of Margaret THATCHER revived it in 1989. She proposed a POLL TAX as a new method of financing local government. It was set to be levied in Scotland a year before the rest of the UNITED KINGDOM and thus was a natural lightning rod for discontent. Riots and demonstrations brought the end of the tax, but also a revival of the nationalists. When the LABOUR PARTY government of 1997 instituted a Scottish PARLIAMENT, the SNP was split over the probable effect: would it dampen or increase national sentiment and the desire for independence?

Seanad Éireann

The upper house of the legislature (Oireachtas) of the IRISH REPUBLIC was created in 1922 and modified in 1937. This body has the general appearance of an "upper" chamber, but it is indirectly elected and its powers are severely restricted. Under the 1937 constitution it is inferior to the DAIL ÉIRANN, which alone can initiate money bills and can overrule the Seanad on other measures.

secretary of state

The title secretary was applied to minor officials until the 16th century. Thomas CROMWELL, as HENRY VIII's secretary, combined several older posts into a position of a more modern and consequential nature. The Elizabethan secretaries, William and Robert CECIL, cemented the importance of the office. Under JAMES VI AND I it became the convention to appoint two secretaries. After the RESTORATION, the two divided affairs into northern and southern departments (dealing with Protestant and Catholic countries respectively). In 1782 this was changed to the more rational division between a HOME OFFICE and a FOREIGN OFFICE. In the 19th century additional secretaryships were created for war and colonies, for INDIA, and for SCOTLAND. In the 20th century the number has multiplied to include industry, EDUCATION, employment, and environment. The secretary of state is a member of the CABINET, the head of a department, and is assisted by a minister of state, one or more parliamentary undersecretaries (political appointees), and a permanent undersecretary (a civil servant).

secret ballot

The BALLOT ACT of 1872 introduced a secret ballot for parliamentary elections, one of the demands in the People's Charter (see CHARTIST MOVEMENT). The old system had the sheriff call for a voice vote, and if that proved indecisive, he would take a poll: each voter came forward and stated the candidate of his choice. This leant itself to intimidation of tenants, workers, or others dependent on the good will of candidates, patrons, and landlords. Indeed there were many incidents of this type after the election of 1868, prompting some to call for reform. The secret ballot was probably most important in Irish elections, where the pressure put on tenants by landlords could no longer affect the outcome directly.

sedition

The crime of acting, speaking, or publishing with the intent of causing contempt or disaffection toward the institutions of government, or inciting a disturbance of the peace, or promoting hostility between classes of subjects. The sweeping definitions were useful in apprehending suspects whom the authorities considered dangerous, as they embraced anything tending toward, but not amounting to, TREASON. After the 18th century the courts defined sedition more narrowly, and it lost its value as a weapon to silence government critics.

Selborne, Roundell Palmer, earl of (1812–1895)

lord chancellor

After OXFORD UNIVERSITY and Lincoln's Inn, Selborne entered PARLIAMENT in 1847. Made solicitor general in 1861 and attorney general in 1863, he became LORD CHANCELLOR in 1872. Holding the office until 1874 and again from 1880 to 1885, he played a pivotal role in drafting the JUDICATURE ACT of 1873. That act fused LAW and equity and merged the old royal courts into the HIGH COURT OF JUSTICE.

Selden, John (1584–1654)
lawyer, historian

Selden studied at OXFORD UNIVERSITY, and the Inner Temple (see INNS OF COURT), and he was called to the bar in 1612. He was a student with vast interests, from ancient languages to oriental scholarship to antiquities, both British and international. His major works were a *History of Tythes* (1617), a study of the law of the sea; *Mare Clausum* (1636); and *Fleta* (1647), a study of the influence of Roman law in England. He was deeply involved, as a MEMBER OF PARLIAMENT and as a lawyer, in the controversies of the reign of CHARLES I, including the FORCED LOAN, HABEAS CORPUS, and the taxing power of PARLIAMENT. He was imprisoned (1629–31), and he supported the parliamentary side in the CIVIL WAR. The Selden Society, established by Frederic MAITLAND for the support of legal history, was named for him.

See also LONG PARLIAMENT; SHORT PARLIAMENT.

select committee

As opposed to standing committees, select committees are groups appointed by the HOUSE OF LORDS or the HOUSE OF COMMONS to investigate and report on specific matters. Having no more than 15 members, they take written and oral evidence, report to the house, and when their work is finished, they are terminated.

See also PARLIAMENT.

self-denying ordinance (1645)

The discontent with the performance of the armies of PARLIAMENT led to this measure, which required officers in both houses of PARLIAMENT to resign their commissions. It was aimed particularly at Robert Devereaux, earl of ESSEX and Edward Montagu, earl of MANCHESTER; and more generally at the aristocracy. Since members of the HOUSE OF COMMONS could resign their seats, they could avoid the impact of the law, but peers were eliminated. This also paved the way for general reorganization in the NEW MODEL ARMY.

See also ARMY; CIVIL WAR; STANDING ARMY.

Senegal

West African country first explored by the Portuguese in the 15th century and then by the French, who established a trading post in 1659. With a 250-mile coastline on the Atlantic Ocean, the country is bordered by Mauritania (north), French Sudan (east), French Guinea (southeast), and Portuguese Guinea (southwest). In WORLD WAR II Senegal was aligned with the Vichy regime until 1942 and thereafter with the Free French. In 1946 Senegal became part of the French Union, thus giving French citizenship to the inhabitants and granting them representation in the French National Assembly. Senegal received its own assembly in 1952, and it became a republic in 1958. Independence followed in 1960.

Septennial Act (1716)

The life of a PARLIAMENT had been three years since 1694, and the result was constant electioneering and some amount of instability. The JACOBITE rebellion of 1715 gave an excuse to prolong the life of Parliament, from three to seven years by means of the Septennial Act, which did tend to promote more stability—and less accountability. The seven-year term was reduced to five years by the Parliament Act of 1911.

Session, Court of

The Scottish king's council heard legal disputes, but a settled court structure only emerged in the

15th century. In 1532 JAMES IV established the College of Justice, a body of 14 lords, half clergy and half laymen, with a lord president. They did most of their judicial work as a single body. The system was reformed in the early 19th century, when the court was divided into smaller units and some old procedures were changed. At the same time the court assumed some other jurisdictions (admiralty, commissary, exchequer), and members sat in courts of special jurisdiction. All the lords of session also sit as judges in the HIGH COURT OF JUSTICIARY.

Settlement, Act of (1701)

If WILLIAM III and Queen ANNE had no heirs, the exiled Catholic Stuarts (JAMES VII AND II and his son) had the best claim to the throne. This act designated a Protestant line of succession through Elizabeth, the daughter of JAMES VI AND I, who had been queen of Bohemia. Her daughter Sophia, the current electress of HANOVER, was the prospective successor, though in the event Sophia's son, GEORGE I, was the beneficiary of the act. The measure also provided that PARLIAMENT had to approve any foreign wars, that only British subjects could hold office, that only parliament could remove judges, and that royal pardons had no power over IMPEACHMENTS. Thus the British prepared themselves to welcome another sovereign from abroad.

See also JACOBITES.

Seven Bishops' Case (1688)

In 1687 JAMES VII AND II issued a DECLARATION OF INDULGENCE using a tactic employed several times earlier—namely to promote religious freedom for Catholics by tying their liberties to those of Protestant DISSENTERS. Prompting the Seven Bishops' Case were the most sweeping changes yet tried, waiving acts of UNIFORMITY under the king's assumed SUSPENDING POWER. The declaration was to be read from all pulpits. Archbishop William SANCROFT and six of his colleagues sent a petition requesting that they be excused from this command, and for their impertinence they were charged with seditious libel. They were acquitted, but the king had managed to galvanize his opponents.

Seven Years' War (1756–1763)

Often called the first "world" war, this conflict involved the far-flung interests of GREAT BRITAIN and France in North America, the WEST INDIES, INDIA, the Mediterranean, and Europe. In America, the fighting began two years earlier, in 1754, and was known as the French and Indian War. On the continent, Britain and France switched allies in a "diplomatic revolution," with Prussia joining Britain and Austria joining France in 1756. The largest battles were in Europe, where Prussia suffered heavy losses at first. The French took the naval base at Minorca in the Mediterranean, and Britain's fortunes seemed to be slipping. However, by 1759 the tide had turned: preceded by Robert CLIVE's great victory at Plassey (1757) and the capture of Louisbourg (1758), the British and German forces defeated France at the Battle of Minden, while British arms seized Quebec in CANADA and won decisively in India and the West Indies. By 1760 Britain had gained command of the seas, so that even when France made an alliance with Spain, Britain soon had further victories in the West Indies. The Treaty of Paris in 1763 gave Britain control of Quebec, Florida, islands in the West Indies, Minorca, and parts of India. These victories came at the cost of doubling the national DEBT and intensifying internal political battles.

Seymour, Edward See SOMERSET, EDWARD SEYMOUR, EARL OF HERTFORD AND DUKE OF.

Seymour, Jane (1509–1537)
queen of England, 1536–1537

Jane Seymour had served in the court of CATHERINE OF ARAGON and Anne BOLEYN. She was courted by HENRY VIII after Anne was arrested, and they were married two days after her predecessor's execution. She gave birth to EDWARD VI in 1537 but died soon after. Henry was buried beside her at Windsor 10 years later.

Seymour, Thomas, baron (1508–1549)

The brother of Jane and younger brother of Edward SEYMOUR, Thomas Seymour gained influence at Court, and after the death of HENRY VIII, he married the king's widow, Catherine PARR. She died in childbirth (1548), and soon it was rumored that Thomas was planning to marry Princess Elizabeth (later ELIZABETH I). He was accused of conspiring against his brother, condemned by an act of ATTAINDER, and executed.

Shaftesbury, Anthony Ashley Cooper, first earl of (1621–1683)

politician

A long and tangled political career marked one of the early WHIG leaders of the "country" party—i.e., those who opposed the policies of the Court in the later 17th century. Lord Shaftesbury supported the Crown at the outset of the CIVIL WAR, switched and became a leader in the COMMONWEALTH OF ENGLAND, but then joined the opposition in 1654. Pardoned by CHARLES II, he served that monarch as CHANCELLOR OF THE EXCHEQUER and LORD CHANCELLOR. In the 1670s he resisted the pro-Catholic policies of the king and was dismissed. He returned to office during the EXCLUSION crisis, continued to rouse opposition to royal policies, and was charged with TREASON. He went into exile in the Netherlands in 1682 and died a year later.

Shaftesbury, Anthony Ashley Cooper, seventh earl of (1801–1885)

reformer

Shaftesbury was a powerful EVANGELICAL leader who campaigned vigorously for the reform of working conditions and the relief of the plight of the poor. He led the fight for a Ten Hours Bill to limit working hours; he supported FACTORY ACTS mandating improved working conditions; and he campaigned for the Mines Act of 1842, which prohibited the employment of women and children in mines. His deep religious convictions were allied with TORY political principles, and he opposed democratic political reform.

Shakespeare, William (1564–1616)

poet, dramatist

Born in Stratford-upon-Avon, son of a glove-maker and later mayor, Shakespeare married Anne Hathaway in 1582. He migrated alone to LONDON, where he began an acting career and then became a playwright and, eventually, a theatrical legend. He wrote nearly 40 plays—comedies, histories, and tragedies. The extant texts of these works are not the original versions but come from the *First Folio,* which was published in 1623, seven years after his death. In addition to the plays, he wrote sonnets (a compilation published in 1609) and other poems. The body of his work had enormous influence on the English language and on the culture of ENGLAND and of Europe.

Shakespeare's early career is not well documented. As a player and then writer in the theatrical companies of the 1580s and 1590s, he was evidently an early success. When the plague struck LONDON in 1593, the theaters were closed, and the companies were dispersed. At this time Shakespeare published his first volumes of poetry. When performances resumed, Shakespeare worked with The Queen's Men, the major London players, and his history plays (*Richard II, Richard III, Henry IV, Henry V*) seem to come from this period as did his *Romeo and Juliet.* The move to the new Globe Theater coincided with his rise in the theatrical world and the appearance of some of his most important plays: *Julius Caesar, As You Like It, Twelfth Night, Hamlet,* and *All's Well That Ends Well.* He worked with The King's Men, the major company authorized by JAMES VI AND I, and he produced *Othello, King Lear, Macbeth, Antony and Cleopatra,*

William Shakespeare, engraved by Benjamin Holl from a print by Arnold Houbraken *(Library of Congress)*

and *Coriolanus.* He went into semiretirement at Stratford in 1610. His plays had not been published, as their value was realized in performances and the resulting profit to the company, in which Shakespeare was a partner. The many later editions of his work—and their innumerable performances and adaptations—recognize Shakespeare as a figure of genius and a national treasure.

Sharp, Granville (1734–1813)
antislavery reformer

Born in Durham, where his father was a prebendary (clergyman) in the cathedral, Sharp was sent to London at age 15 and apprenticed to a linen draper. He found a post in the ordnance office in 1758. Having met a runaway slave and tried without success to protect him in court, Sharp studied the subject and published an antislavery tract in 1769. His work was thought to have influenced the decision in the SOMERSET CASE (1772), which said that slavery was not recognized in English law. President of the Society for the Abolition of the Slave Trade (1787), he helped with the formation of a COLONY for freed slaves (SIERRA LEONE) and the establishment of the abolitionist African Institution. In politics he supported the American Revolution, the Irish movement for an independent PARLIAMENT, and the cause of parliamentary reform. In matters of religion, he founded the Society for the Conversion of the Jews (1808) and the Protestant Union, which opposed CATHOLIC EMANCIPATION (1813).

See also ANTISLAVERY MOVEMENT.

Shaw, George Bernard (1856–1950)
dramatist

Born in IRELAND, Shaw came to ENGLAND in 1876. His attempts at novel writing were not successful, and he became a critic and then a playwright. As a member of the FABIAN SOCIETY, he was a vigorous exponent of SOCIALISM, women's rights, and free thought. His plays were unsettling to the Victorian audience, but they brought wit to the stage while they raised social consciousness. His best-known are *Arms and the Man* (1894), *The Devil's Disciple* (1897), *Mrs. Warren's Profession* (1902), *John Bull's Other Island* (1904), *Pygmalion* (1913), and *St. Joan* (1923). He won the Nobel Prize in 1925.

Shelburne, William Petty, earl of (1737–1805)
prime minister, 1782–1783

A follower of William PITT the elder, Lord Shelburne served as a SECRETARY OF STATE (1766–68), but his desire for conciliation of the AMERICAN COLONIES forced him to resign. At the end of the war, he was again secretary of state under Lord ROCKINGHAM, and when that PRIME MINISTER died, Shelburne took office briefly. He negotiated the treaty ending the war, but his views in favor of FREE TRADE worried his colleagues, and his government fell.

Shelley, Percy Bysshe (1792–1822)
radical poet

Son of a Sussex BARONET and MEMBER OF PARLIAMENT, Shelley was raised with a conventional education at Eton and University College, OXFORD UNIVERSITY. He became increasingly rebellious and eloped two times with three women (Harriett Westbrook, 1811; and Mary WOLLSTONECRAFT with her stepsister Jane, 1814). His writing reflected an extreme radical and atheist position: *Queen Mab* (1813), *Alastor* (1816), *The Mask of Anarchy* (1819) and *Prometheus Unbound* (1820). He settled in Italy, where he died in a boating accident.

Sheridan, Richard Brinsley (1751–1816)
dramatist, politician

The son of an Irish actor and dramatist, Sheridan wrote successful comedies (*The School for Scandal,* 1777, being the best-known). As manager of the DRURY LANE THEATRE he had an income and an entrée into polite society. He entered PARLIAMENT in 1780, was a follower of Charles James FOX, and held several minor government offices. While he was a noted orator, Sheridan was too extreme in his political views, and he had a disorderly private life, both of which prevented him from having greater political success.

sheriff

The "reeve" was an Anglo-Saxon officer, and by the 11th century kings had begun to appoint a reeve for each shire (see COUNTY), responsible for collecting taxes and keeping order. Their powers were augmented after the Norman Conquest, as the "shire reeve" was a useful royal agent. Those powers came to be seen as excessive, and other local officials (e.g., the JUSTICE OF THE PEACE) were created, eventually diminishing the role of the sheriff. In SCOTLAND the same office existed, but it was less powerful. In the 18th century the Scottish sheriff became a district judge and remains so today.

ship money

The medieval tax levied on port towns in wartime to finance the naval forces required for their protection. CHARLES I used this tax to raise revenues while no PARLIAMENT was in session (1634–40). The extension of the levy to inland towns was resisted, but in the case of John HAMPDEN, the courts validated the king's right to do so (1637). Parliament declared the practice illegal in 1641.

shire See COUNTY.

Short Parliament (1640)

In April 1640 CHARLES I was forced to summon a PARLIAMENT, his first in 11 years, because he needed funds to field an army to resist the Scots. However, members of the HOUSE OF COMMONS were more interested in airing their accumulated grievances over religion and TAXATION. After three weeks the king dissolved this unruly body; yet the problems remained, and he summoned another Parliament in November. That body was not formally dissolved until 1660—hence the respective names of the "short" and "long" parliaments.

See also LONG PARLIAMENT.

Shrewsbury, Elizabeth Talbot, countess of
See "BESS OF HARDWICK."

Sidmouth, viscount
See ADDINGTON, HENRY, VISCOUNT SIDMOUTH.

Sidney, Algernon (1622–1683)
republican

Sidney fought at the Battle of MARSTON MOOR and served in the Council of State (1652, 1659). He remained abroad after the RESTORATION. When pardoned, he returned in 1677 and supported the WHIG opposition. He was arrested in 1683 and convicted of conspiring in the RYE HOUSE PLOT. The manuscript of his *Discourses Concerning Government,* which approved tyrannicide, was used in evidence against him, and he was executed. The book was later published in 1698.

Sidney, Sir Henry (1529–1586)
lord deputy of Ireland

Sidney grew up at the court of EDWARD VI, served on diplomatic missions, and went to IRELAND in 1556, returning as deputy in 1565. Meanwhile he had been made lord president of the Council in the Marches of Wales, which post he held until his death. While in Ireland he put down the rebellion of Shane O'NEILL, but he resigned in 1571. Recalled in 1575, he again faced rebels and the famously stingy government of Queen ELIZABETH I. He was the father of Sir Philip SIDNEY.

Sidney, Sir Philip (1554–1586)
soldier, poet

The son of Sir Henry SIDNEY, Philip Sidney held a variety of posts in Elizabethan government. His Protestant zeal showed in his strong views on Queen ELIZABETH I's suitors, in his activity in colonial projects, and in his support for Protestants in the Netherlands. It was there, as the governor of Flushing, that he was mortally wounded in the siege of Zutphen (1586). His written work (all published posthumously) included *Arcadia* (1590); a sonnet sequence, *Astrophel and Stella* (1592); and *Defense of Poetry* (1595).

Sierra Leone

A COLONY on the west coast of AFRICA, originally designed to be the home of freed slaves. The British abolitionists organized the Sierre Leone Company (chartered in 1790) and established Freetown. Colonial status came in 1808. When the colonists expanded inland, the hinterland was made a PROTECTORATE in 1896. Independence was granted to the colony and protectorate in 1961. A republic was proclaimed in 1971, and it became a one-party state in 1978. A military coup in 1992 launched a period of instability and internal warfare.

signet

A small royal seal, appearing in the early 14th century, used to authenticate warrants for the PRIVY SEAL and the GREAT SEAL. Intended to give the king or his advisers more control over business, it was kept by secretaries and later by secretaries of state.

Simnel, Lambert (1475–1535)
pretender

Simnel claimed to be Edward, earl of Warwick, the nephew of EDWARD IV. He was crowned in DUBLIN in 1487, recognized by many Yorkist followers, and led a force to ENGLAND. This plot had a fatal flaw: the true nephew was a prisoner of HENRY VII and thus easily shown to the public to foil the plot. The king's forces defeated the insurgents at the Battle of Stoke, and Simnel, regarded as harmless, was pardoned and put to work in the royal kitchen.

Simon, Sir John, viscount (1873–1954)
Liberal politician

Born in Manchester, Simon's parents were Welsh. He attended Fettes College and Wadham College, OXFORD UNIVERSITY. Called to the bar in 1898, he entered PARLIAMENT in 1906. He was made solicitor general in 1910, attorney general in 1913, and home secretary in 1915. He resigned from the CABINET in 1916 over conscription and joined the Royal Flying Corps in France. Returning to parliament in 1922, he led a major inquiry into the constitution of INDIA (1927–30). He also served in the National Government as foreign secretary (1931–35), home secretary (1935–37), CHANCELLOR OF THE EXCHEQUER (1937–40), and LORD CHANCELLOR (1940–45).

Singapore

This COLONY was established in 1819 by Sir Stamford RAFFLES. Its economic value was shown in the rapid increase of trade, and it was made a crown colony in 1867. A major naval base was established in 1921 as the strategic value of Singapore's rubber, tin, and oil became clear. The base was easy prey to Japanese invasion in 1942. The colony received a constitution in 1955 and separate government in 1959. Briefly part of the Federation of MALAYSIA, it became fully independent in 1965.

sinking fund

A reserve established to pay off interest and principal of the national DEBT. The sinking fund was conceived by Robert WALPOLE and first employed in 1717. It did reduce the debt somewhat, but some of the fund was diverted to other uses. In 1786 a new version was established, in which dividends were used to pay off debt and controls were more strict. But the high cost of borrowing during the war years (1789–1815) actually made the debt grow. Similar plans were also used later (1875 and 1923).

Sinn Féin

An organization aimed at Irish autonomy; the GAELIC expression is translated as "we ourselves," or "ourselves alone." Arthur GRIFFITH was the founder of Sinn Féin (1905), and at first it was not a very radical group. One of his proposals for Irish government was the establishment of a dual MONARCHY, like that of Austria-Hungary. But with the events of the next decade, especially the EASTER REBELLION (1916), the hopes for some sort of constitutional

home rule were in decline. Moreover, the British authorities mistakenly christened the events of 1916 as the "Sinn Féin rebellion," when in fact that group had no responsibility for the uprising. However, the organization obliged by taking the cue, winning the 1918 election, and forming a provisional government in DUBLIN. In the fighting that followed (1919–21) the IRISH REPUBLICAN ARMY took the lead, and Sinn Féin became its political agency. This placed it outside the government of the IRISH FREE STATE, when the republicans rejected the ANGLO-IRISH TREATY of 1922 and began a bloody civil war. A split occurred in 1926, with a large bloc of the party returning to normal political action as the Fianna Fáil party. Sinn Féin remained a marginal group until the "troubles" in NORTHERN IRELAND (1969–98) gave it a stage on which to revive the old themes of republicanism. Arguably the party was much more successful in ULSTER than it had been in the republic, and at the end of the 20th century it was poised to be a part of a new government in the North.

Six Acts (1819)

After the PETERLOO MASSACRE, the government was afraid of the public reaction and the prospect of more mass meetings or other disturbances. Thus it cracked down with measures known as the Six Acts, which prohibited meetings of more than 50 people, allowed JUSTICES OF THE PEACE to search homes for arms, banned military drilling by civilians, toughened penalties for SEDITION, limited the rights of accused persons, and increased stamp duties on newspapers. The measures were an overreaction, especially since improving economic conditions soon reduced support for the radicals.

slave trade

Traffic in African slaves was probably a long-standing practice in AFRICA itself. Of course slavery had been known in the British Isles, among Celtic peoples, Roman occupiers, and their descendants down to the 12th century. But it was with European colonization that a new phase began. The demand for a workforce increased steadily, first for the Portuguese and the Spanish and later for British and French colonies. By the 18th century GREAT BRITAIN's role in this barbarous commerce was booming. Some estimates put the number at 2.5 million carried in British ships, out of a total trade of more than 6 million. British colonies in North America took about 350,000 and in the WEST INDIES close to 1.5 million during the 18th century. The production of sugar, tobacco, rice, and latterly cotton provided the demand. By the end of the 18th century, the ANTISLAVERY MOVEMENT to end the trade was gathering strength in Britain, and it was abolished in 1807.

Slim, William Joseph Slim, viscount (1891–1970)
field marshal

Educated at King Edward's School, Birmingham, Slim was commissioned in 1914. After serving in the Middle East (1915–16), he was transferred to INDIA. He occupied staff positions there between the wars, and in 1940 he commanded Indian units fighting in AFRICA, the Middle East, and ultimately in BURMA. There he captured Rangoon in 1945 and he was made commander in chief of forces in Southeast Asia. He became field marshal and chief of the Imperial General Staff in 1948, and later served as governor-general of AUSTRALIA.

Smiles, Samuel (1812–1904)
writer

A successful popularizer of Victorian ideals, Smiles had been a doctor and a journalist. His most successful book was *Self-Help* (1859), which gave "illustrations of character, conduct, and perseverance" drawn particularly from the individual efforts of successful entrepreneurs. He argued that institutions "can give a man no active help" and that man must be independent—something that "has in all times been a

marked feature in the English character." Smiles wanted to instill industry, thrift, and high moral standards in his middle- and lower-class audience. He also wrote the very popular *Lives of the Engineers* (1861–62).

Smith, Adam (1723–1790)
philosopher, economist

After his education at Glasgow University, Smith studied at OXFORD UNIVERSITY and returned to Glasgow as professor of logic and later professor of moral philosophy. His first book, *The Theory of Moral Sentiments* (1759), established him as a major figure. As a tutor he traveled in France and Switzerland, and on his return he was elected to the ROYAL SOCIETY (1767). The work that gave him a lasting reputation was *An Inquiry into the Nature and Causes of the Wealth of Nations* (1776). This analysis of economic relationships discredited mercantile regulation and advocated FREE TRADE, within certain limits, in order to maximize economic potential. His work has been seen as the basic text for modern economics. He became a government adviser and commissioner of customs, and in 1787 he was chosen rector of Glasgow University.

Smith, Frederick Edwin, earl of Birkenhead See BIRKENHEAD, FREDERICK EDWIN SMITH, FIRST EARL OF.

Smith, Reverend Sydney (1771–1845)
essayist, clergyman

Educated at Winchester and OXFORD UNIVERSITY, Smith took holy orders in 1794. While serving as a tutor, he traveled to EDINBURGH, where he joined Francis Jeffrey and Henry BROUGHAM in founding the *Edinburgh Review*. He wrote extensively for that journal over the next three decades while also holding a variety of church places, eventually becoming a canon of ST. PAUL's CATHEDRAL. Smith was a brilliant wit and a progressive thinker. His *Letters of Peter Plymley* (1807) argued for religious liberty, attacking the opponents of CATHOLIC EMANCIPATION. He was an enemy of the SLAVE TRADE and a supporter of parliamentary reform.

Smith, W(illiam) H(enry) (1825–1891)
newsagent, politician

Building on his father's newspaper business, Smith acquired a monopoly of outlets in railway stations from 1849. He entered PARLIAMENT in 1868 and held office under Benjamin DISRAELI (first lord of the ADMIRALTY, 1877) and Lord SALISBURY (first lord of the TREASURY and leader of the HOUSE OF COMMONS, 1886). His firm of W. H. Smith flourished, becoming a leading retailer in the 20th century.

Smuts, Jan Christian (1870–1950)
soldier, statesman

After studying law in ENGLAND, Smuts returned to his native SOUTH AFRICA and fought in the BOER WAR. He was a major figure in the formation of the Union of South Africa (1910). A member of the British war CABINET (1917–18) and a delegate to the Paris Peace Conference, he became prime minister of South Africa (1919–24). He served again in 1939 and took the country, against considerable protest, into WORLD WAR II. A member of Winston CHURCHILL's war cabinet (1940–45), he resigned as premier in 1948 and was replaced by Afrikaner leadership, which introduced the policy of "apartheid," the systematic separation of races and oppressive regimentation of black people.

Snowden, Philip Snowden, first viscount (1864–1937)
Labour politician

A self-taught radical socialist from Yorkshire, Snowden was a publicist for the INDEPENDENT LABOUR PARTY and became its national chairman in 1903. Entering PARLIAMENT in 1906, he was an advocate of pacifism and temperance, and he pushed for higher TAXATION, believing that

wealth should be "conscripted" to pay for war. Soon recognized as the leading Labour financial expert, he served as CHANCELLOR OF THE EXCHEQUER in 1924, producing a BUDGET that might well have come from the Liberals. In 1929 he again served as chancellor, his economic views still in an orthodox mode. When the DEPRESSION came, he was unprepared to condone government spending. He joined Ramsay MACDONALD in the newly formed National Government of 1931 and criticized his former colleagues. He resigned in 1932 when the government abandoned FREE TRADE at the OTTAWA CONFERENCE.

Soane, Sir John (1753–1837)
architect

Educated as an architect in the school of the ROYAL ACADEMY, Soane traveled in Italy and developed a neoclassical style, employed in the construction of several country houses. He won the competition for the design of a new BANK OF ENGLAND (1788), and he was given commissions by PARLIAMENT and Chelsea Hospital for new buildings. He became professor of architecture at the Royal Academy in 1806. Little of his work survives, except the rebuilt Dulwich Picture Gallery and his house in Lincoln's Inn Fields, which now contains the Sir John Soane Museum.

Social and Liberal Democrat Party See LIBERAL PARTY.

Social Democratic Federation (SDF)

Henry HYNDMAN, a wealthy Marxist convert and a writer for the *Pall Mall Gazette*, founded the Democratic Federation, a small and contentious group of socialists, in 1881. Hyndman's *England for All* (1881) was a derivative work which MARX thought to be plagiarized from his *Das Kapital*, and thus there was little chance of a working relationship between the two. The organization also experienced defections, like that of William MORRIS in 1884. About this time the "social" was added to the organization's name. A small but vocal group, it organized demonstrations of the unemployed, and through association with others such as the FABIAN SOCIETY, it nurtured the theory of a workingman's political party. Distrusted by TRADE UNIONS, the SDF was a group of energetic activists who made a small contribution to the birth of the LABOUR PARTY. By the 1920s the group had been superseded by the Communist Party of Great Britain.

socialism

The political theory and policy that the state should intervene in economic affairs for the purpose of redistribution of wealth. The term "socialism" was probably used first by Robert OWEN, who led experiments in forming "utopian" communities and cooperative societies in the early 19th century. The central concept was developed by Christian Socialists (see Charles KINGSLEY, F. D. MAURICE) in the middle of the century. By the 1880s there were competing strands of socialism: the more militant ideas of social revolution, fostered by Henry HYNDMAN and the SOCIAL DEMOCRATIC FEDERATION, inspired by the work of Karl MARX; the gradual plans of social reform sponsored by the FABIAN SOCIETY; and the practical political organization of workers and middle-class allies, such as the INDEPENDENT LABOUR PARTY (1893) and eventually the LABOUR PARTY (1918). There was never a mass movement, nor a genuinely revolutionary party set upon seizing property and making a general redistribution. Instead, most of the varied British socialist groups promoted constitutional and progressive reform through mandated programs such as NATIONAL INSURANCE, the NATIONAL HEALTH SERVICE, and NATIONALIZATION.

See also COOPERATIVE MOVEMENT.

Society for the Promotion of Christian Knowledge (SPCK)

Founded in 1698, the SPCK was designed to provide better education for laymen and ministers. Thomas Bray, one of the founders, had experienced the dearth of devotional material in the colonies, and the organization set out to supply cheap editions of BIBLES, prayer books, and other literature in large quantities, in addition to promoting CHARITY SCHOOLS and other endeavors. Though an ANGLICAN body, the SPCK was friendly to old DISSENTERS and to Christian missionary work. In 1701 a branch of the group called the Society for the Propagation of the Gospel in Foreign Parts was founded to pursue the mission of the church in the colonies. The SPCK opened its first bookshop in 1835, and it continues as a religious publishing house. When it was founded, this sort of semiprivate association was a pioneer effort, one which had a considerable and lasting impact.

Solemn League and Covenant (1643)

This agreement between the Scottish estates and the English PARLIAMENT promised to reform the church in ENGLAND and IRELAND along PRESBYTERIAN lines, to preserve the constitutional liberties of the two legislatures and to make provisions for them to work together. To seal the agreement, the Scots promised an army of 20,000 to fight against the king. The military side was decisive in defeating CHARLES I, but the religious and constitutional agreements proved to be more difficult to implement. The Westminster Assembly (1643–53) did compose the Westminster Confession (1647), still the standard for the Presbyterian Church. But the adoption of the new faith in England and Ireland was never ratified.

solicitor

Agents for legal business in English courts of equity (e.g., court of CHANCERY) were given this name by the 15th century. They were comparable to the attorneys who practiced in the COMMON LAW courts. In 1728 a law regulated the admission to both professions. When the Law Society was chartered in 1831, it took control of examinations for admission. A solicitor must pass this examination and be articled to a practicing solicitor for a period of time. The solicitor does general legal work (property, wills, trusts, commercial cases). The solicitor in SCOTLAND has similar functions but has been known under varied older titles (e.g., writers to the signet, solicitors in the Faculty of Procurators [Glasgow], or solicitors to the Society of Advocates [Aberdeen]). These titles were collected and modernized in 1933.

See also COURTS OF LAW.

Somaliland, British

Made a PROTECTORATE in 1885, this area in the Horn of AFRICA was the scene of a holy war against the British from 1900 to 1920. During WORLD WAR II it was occupied by Italian forces and later merged with Italian Somaliland. The area gained independence as the Somali Republic in 1960.

Somers, John Somers, baron (1651–1716)
(John Sommers)
lawyer, politician

The son of an attorney, Somers attended Worcester Cathedral School; Trinity College, OXFORD UNIVERSITY; and the Middle Temple (see INNS OF COURT). He was called to the bar in 1676. One of the counsel for the SEVEN BISHOPS' CASE in 1688, he was elected to the CONVENTION Parliament in 1689, was involved with the drafting of the DECLARATION OF RIGHTS, and became solicitor general. His advance up the ranks was steady: attorney general (1692), lord keeper (1693), and LORD CHANCELLOR (1697). As a leading WHIG he was dismissed in 1700. Not favored at first by Queen ANNE, he later became an adviser on the Anglo-Scottish UNION in 1707.

Somerset, Edmund Beaufort, second duke of (1406–1455)
soldier

Somerset served in France and was made lieutenant general there in 1447, but he saw the loss of Normandy over the next three years. For this he was accused of treason by Richard of YORK, but was still King HENRY VI's favorite adviser. He put down an uprising by York in 1452, was imprisoned when that duke became protector in 1454, and died in the first Battle of ST. ALBANS. Their feud began the Wars of the ROSES.

Somerset, Edward Seymour, earl of Hertford and duke of (1500–1552)
lord protector

Seymour's sister Jane SEYMOUR married HENRY VIII in 1536. Seymour himself fought in the king's forces in the wars against SCOTLAND and France. Shortly after Henry's death, he assumed the PROTECTORATE of his nephew EDWARD VI and became duke of Somerset. His policies provoked rebellions by continuing wars, debasing the coinage, and pressing religious reforms. His brother Thomas SEYMOUR appeared to challenge his authority, and Edward had him executed. He was imprisoned, released briefly, but then executed by his enemies in the COUNCIL.

Somerset, Robert Carr, earl of (1586–1645)
courtier

A favorite of JAMES VI AND I, Carr had served in the Scottish court; was in the entourage that traveled to London in 1603; and became the favorite of the king, with whom he allegedly had a homosexual relationship. He subsequently received titles and honors from the king. He was involved in the murder of Sir Thomas Overbury, a former friend. Carr and his wife were found guilty of poisoning Overbury, but the king granted him a pardon.

Somerset case (1772)

The best-known of a series of cases concerning the right of slaveholders to seize and remove their slaves from ENGLAND. James Somerset became a public figure, his trial a closely followed event.

With the help of Granville SHARP, he had obtained a WRIT of HABEAS CORPUS, which granted him a hearing in the Court of KING'S BENCH before Chief Justice MANSFIELD. There were eight sessions, long arguments on both sides, and a controversial decision. Mansfield said that the power to take Somerset out of England had to be based on LAW, and "such a claim is not known to the laws of England." Mansfield's decision did not declare slavery illegal, did not free any slaves then held in England, and did not prevent the seizure of other slaves and their return to America. However, the decision was misunderstood by contemporaries and by historians, and more important, it became a beacon of hope for abolitionists.

Somme, Battle of the (1916)

A joint Anglo-French offensive was launched against entrenched German positions, in the hope that a massive assault might break through and end WORLD WAR I. General Douglas HAIG's plan failed miserably. Nearly 60,000 British soldiers died on the first day of battle (July 1, 1916), and the attack continued until November. In the end, British and German losses stood close to 400,000 each, while the French lost 200,000. During the operation, tanks had been used for the first time, but with little effect. The farthest advance of the allies was about eight miles; the impact of this terrible loss of life was incalculable, and it tarnished Haig's reputation and deepened the public despair over the war's direction.

South Africa

British entry into southern AFRICA began with the capture of the Dutch CAPE COLONY during the NAPOLEONIC WARS. The clashes between the Afrikaners (or Boers) and the British resulted in migrations and settlements of other colonies: NATAL, TRANSVAAL, and the ORANGE FREE STATE. There was a continuing British desire to incorporate these colonies, and that was vastly increased with the discoveries of diamonds (1868) and gold

(1886). Those resources required outside capital and labor to exploit them, and thus there was escalating contact and eventual conflict. The BOER WAR (1899–1902) resulted in a British victory, the establishment of autonomous colonies, and an eventual union of the four states. Membership in the BRITISH EMPIRE was supported at first, but by the 1930s a strong Afrikaner resistance was developing. In 1948 the National Party won the elections and introduced a comprehensive policy of racial separation and discrimination—apartheid—which in turn produced protests and violent repression by the emerging police state. South Africa resigned from the Commonwealth in 1961, becoming an independent republic. Over the next generation, mounting hostility from neighboring countries, increasing international ostracism, and persistent internal resistance brought the nation to reject the apartheid regime and install democratic institutions in 1991. The longtime leader and symbol of resistance, Nelson Mandela, was the first elected president of the new government.

Southey, Robert (1774–1843)
poet, historian

The son of a draper in Bristol, Southey was expelled from Westminster school. He wrote radical plays at OXFORD UNIVERSITY, and he and Samuel Taylor COLERIDGE invented a scheme for a utopian settlement in America (which they called "Pantisocracy"). From the 1790s his poetic output surged in a variety of forms, but his RADICALISM had vanished by 1810. In 1813 he was made POET LAUREATE. In addition, he wrote extensively for the *Quarterly Review,* and he published *Life of Nelson* (1813), *History of Brazil* (3 vols., 1810–19), *Life of Wesley* (1821), *History of the Peninsular War* (1823–32), and *Lives of the British Admirals* (1833).

South Sea Bubble

The South Sea Company was organized as a joint-stock venture in 1711, receiving trading privileges in South America in exchange for loans to the government, on a basis similar to the BANK OF ENGLAND and the EAST INDIA COMPANY. In 1713, as a result of the Treaty of UTRECHT, the company received the contract to supply slaves to Spanish colonies. When it proposed to take over 60 percent of the national DEBT in 1719, a speculative boom drove its shares up by more than 1,000% in six months. When the bubble burst, there was panic, and the price of the company's stock fell rapidly. Robert WALPOLE devised a scheme to transfer some of the stock, and in the process shielded some members of the royal court from embarrassing evidence of corrupt and improper dealings. The company continued to pay dividends on government securities, gave up its trading privileges, and was eventually dissolved in 1854.

Spa Fields Riot (1816)

After the NAPOLEONIC WARS there were serious economic problems in GREAT BRITAIN, and widespread distress made radical feeling run high. In LONDON a demonstration was to be addressed by Henry HUNT on behalf of parliamentary reform when a part of the crowd attacked gunsmiths' shops and tried to organize a march on the TOWER OF LONDON. In the trial of some of the participants, a government spy named Castles proved to be a tainted witness, and the rioters were acquitted.

Spanish Succession, War of (1702–1713)

When Louis XIV claimed the throne of Spain for his grandson, Philip of Anjou (1701), in violation of previous treaty commitments, he also invaded the Spanish Netherlands and recognized the son of the late King JAMES VII AND II as "James III." This led WILLIAM III to form an alliance with the United Provinces and Austria, and later Prussia and other German states. The campaigns on the continent saw the duke of MARLBOROUGH win a series of great battles (1704–08) on the Rhine, the Danube, and the frontiers of the Netherlands. In Spain the allies

were less successful. Political and financial stress at home led to Marlborough's removal, and soon negotiations for peace began. The Treaty of UTRECHT (1713) recognized Philip as king, but he had to renounce any claim to the French throne. Spanish influence was removed from the Netherlands, and Louis said he would no longer support the STUART pretender.

Speaker of the House

At first the Speaker of the HOUSE OF COMMONS in the 14th century was chosen to address the Crown and express the opinions or decisions of the house. Soon this post came under the influence of the king, until the 17th century, when it became independent. Indeed, by the 19th century, the speaker became a strictly impartial figure, one who enforced the rules of the House (especially the rules governing debate and amendments to bills). Today the speaker receives a salary, pension, office space, and a life PEERAGE upon retirement. In the HOUSE OF LORDS the same function is carried out by the LORD CHANCELLOR.

Special Branch

The London Metropolitan POLICE first created a "Fenian Office" in 1881 to combat Irish terrorism. The Special (Irish) Branch was then used to track and record the activities of terrorists when a series of bombings created a scare in the DYNAMITE WAR of the 1880s. The activities of this office came to include aliens of all descriptions prior to 1914 and subversives in the 1920s and '30s as well as after 1945. The Special Branch operated beside the military intelligence unit, MI 5. That group operated within GREAT BRITAIN, conducting surveillance and counterespionage, but it had no powers of arrest and relied on the Special Branch for that service.

Speenhamland system

Due to economic distress and the high price of bread, the Berkshire JUSTICES OF THE PEACE meeting in Speenhamland in 1795 decided on a scale of poor relief for working families, linked to the price of bread. The system was widely copied in southern ENGLAND, and it was criticized for having the effect of depressing wages and pauperizing the workers. There is no doubt that it caused rapid increases in poor rates, and in turn the increases brought debates and inquiries, and ultimately a revision of the POOR LAW in 1834.

Spencer, Charles See SUNDERLAND, CHARLES SPENCER, EARL OF.

Spencer, Herbert (1820–1903)
philosopher, sociologist
The son of a nonconformist schoolmaster in Derby, Spencer became a student of society and its relation to government. He worked as a schoolteacher, a railway engineer, and an editor for *The Economist*. The theme of his work was that the state should have a limited role, that individuals ought to be responsible for decisions, and that their combined efforts would advance society along an evolutionary path. He wrote *The Proper Sphere of Government* (1842); developed his philosophy in *Social Statics* (1851); and proceeded to the general systematic works *Synthetic Philosophy* (14 vols., 1860–96) and *Descriptive Sociology* (8 vols., 1881). His work ran into a rising tide of collectivist thinking, but the later 20th century saw some revival of interest in his writing.

Spencer, Robert See SUNDERLAND, ROBERT SPENCER, EARL OF.

Spenser, Edmund (1552–1599)
poet
Born in LONDON, Spenser was publishing poems while still at CAMBRIDGE UNIVERSITY, joined the household of the earl of LEICESTER, and met Sir Philip SIDNEY, to whom he dedicated his *Shephearde's Calender* (1579). In 1580 he went to IRELAND in the household of Lord Grey de Wilton, the lord deputy. While working there he com-pleted the early volumes of his masterpiece *The Fairie Queene* (1590–96). During a rebellion in 1598, his castle at Kilcolman was destroyed, and he had to flee to ENGLAND. Regarded as the finest of the Elizabethan poets, his other major works included *Epithalamion* (1595) and *Prothalamion* (1596). He also wrote *A View of the Present State of Ireland* (1597), a plea for strict government of the barbarous Irish.

Spithead Mutiny (1797)
The British fleets, by now the most powerful in the world, subjected their sailors to miserable living conditions, arrears of pay, and grievances about discipline. These exploded in a set of mutinies in 1797, which in some cases raised fears of French revolutionary influence. The channel fleet at Spithead on the south coast of ENGLAND was the first to mutiny, and its grievances were met with concessions and pardons (April). A second outburst at Plymouth (May) resulted in limited violence, but when the North Sea fleet mutinied at the Nore (in the Thames estuary), the government resisted, and the mutineers tried to blockade LONDON. By mid-June, that mutiny was broken, and its leader, Richard Parker, was executed along with 36 others.

squire (esquire)
Originally a young man who attended a KNIGHT, the esquire was later entitled to bear his own coat of arms. By the 16th and 17th centuries, squire had become a term for a landowning gentleman. The 19th century spoke of the squirearchy, meaning the landed GENTRY in general. The title "esquire" also came to be given to SHERIFFS, JUSTICES OF THE PEACE, and BARRISTERS.

Sri Lanka
The COLONY of CEYLON was granted independence in 1948. After independence, the government stripped Tamil workers, who constituted a large minority of Indian descent, of their civil rights. In the 1950s the Sinhala language was made the

official tongue, touching off widespread civil unrest on the part of the Tamil population. The friction escalated, with a revolt in 1971 that was crushed, leading to a new constitution in 1972 and the proclamation of a republic. In 1977 a presidential system was instituted, based loosely on that of France. The Tamil and Sinhalese conflict continued. During a state of emergency in 1983, Indian troops intervened, but violence continued, and eventually the withdrawal of Indian forces was negotiated in 1990. Serious violence, with a number of assassinations of national leaders, continued into the 1990s.

Stair, James Dalrymple, first viscount (1619–1695)
Scottish jurist

Born in Ayrshire, SCOTLAND, Lord Stair attended grammar school and then Glasgow University (1633–37), where he earned his M.A. He had no formal education in Scots LAW, as none was then available. He became an advocate in 1648, served as a commissioner for administration of justice under the PROTECTORATE of Oliver CROMWELL, and continued in office after the RESTORATION. He became lord president of the Court of SESSION in 1671, but he resigned and went into exile in 1681, refusing to take an oath on the TEST ACT. He returned in 1688 and was reappointed as lord president. In 1681 he published his *Institutions of the Law of Scotland,* the leading example of the major juristic works which form one pillar of Scots law. Stair's work derived legal rules from their sources in Roman, canon, and feudal law, and it remains a leading authority in cases where no later rule has been adopted.

Stamp Act (1765)

This act was designed to apply an established method of raising revenue in Britain to the AMERICAN COLONIES. Prime Minister George GRENVILLE needed revenue to provide added military forces for the extended colonial frontiers after 1763. But the colonists reacted violently with public demonstrations, attacks on tax col-

lectors, and a Stamp Act "Congress" to complain about the new internal TAXATION. Meanwhile, British merchants also protested, and the new administration of Lord ROCKINGHAM repealed the tax, but only after PARLIAMENT had passed the DECLARATORY ACT (1766), which affirmed its power to enact such laws.

standing army

A permanent armed force, as opposed to a MILITIA. The modern army of GREAT BRITAIN traces its origins to the NEW MODEL ARMY of 1645, part of which was retained under CHARLES II. This force was very small; its purpose was to garrison outposts overseas and, from time to time, to be augmented and used in continental wars. Because of its origins, there was great distrust of a standing army and its possible use to overawe the king's subjects. Thus the MUTINY ACT was conceived as a way to give PARLIAMENT control over the ARMY. In 18th- and 19th-century Britain, this tradition also meant that there would be no large conscript army like those in continental European states. This void was offset by large colonial forces, especially the army of INDIA. Thus the British experience as WORLD WAR I broke out in 1914 was unique, with the country relying on a call for a vast volunteer force—in effect, a national militia. Conscription was not found necessary until 1916. In the 20th century, with its new strategic conditions and the completed transition to democracy, a regular army has become accepted, though the later 20th century saw it revert to a small volunteer force.

Stanhope, James Stanhope, first earl (1673–1721)
soldier, politician

Stanhope fought in the wars against the French under WILLIAM III, commanded forces in Spain, and was taken prisoner. He held various offices from 1702 to 1718; helped to suppress the JACOBITE rebellion of 1715; and was a leading diplomat, arranging the Triple Alliance of 1717 and the Quadruple Alliance of 1718.

Stanhope, Philip See CHESTERFIELD, PHILIP STANHOPE, EARL OF.

Stanley, Edward See DERBY, EDWARD GEORGE STANLEY, EARL OF.

Stanley, Sir Henry Morton (1841–1904)
journalist, explorer

Born in WALES, Stanley emigrated to the United States and worked as a writer for the *New York Herald,* with a specialty in British imperial affairs. He was sent to find David LIVINGSTONE in 1871, and he led further expeditions, especially for King Leopold of Belgium, establishing the bounds of the Congo Free State (1879–84).

staple

A location that was licensed for the controlled trade in wool. Begun in the 14th century, the staple improved the Crown's ability to tax and regulate this vital trade. At first it was a single town on the continent, subject to change; later a number of home staples were created, and as many as 15 towns were licensed. The port of CALAIS was the revived site of the staple from 1392 until 1558. The system was also applied to other commodities such as leather and tin. By the 17th century the staples were no longer useful to commerce and ceased to be used.

Star Chamber

A meeting of the king's COUNCIL, sitting as a court of law. The name came from the room in the palace of Westminster (with stars on the ceiling) that was used for its meetings. Created in the late 15th century and used by the TUDORS to deal with problems of public order, the court was not bound by the rules of the COMMON LAW courts. At first popular, as it was able to tame "overmighty subjects," it was used by the STUART kings to enforce their unpopular civil and religious policies. PARLIAMENT abolished the court in 1641.

Stationers Company

A guild of scriveners, bookbinders, and stationers (booksellers), formed in 1403 and granted a charter to control printing in 1557. Any publisher thus had to obtain the Stationers Company's license before printing. The exclusive right so awarded seems to have been the origin of modern copyright. The Stationers' Register recorded all works published, while the new charter of 1694 recognized authors' rights in published books. Those rights were further addressed in legislation in the next century, and gradually the company's role declined.

statute

A statute, or ACT OF PARLIAMENT, is the highest legal authority in the UNITED KINGDOM. A statute is created by the passage of a bill through both houses of PARLIAMENT and the granting of the royal assent. Due to the increased complexity of government, in 1890 Parliament began to allow ministers to create statutory rules and orders to supplement legislation. This adjunct form of law became known as statutory instruments in 1948. The preparation of statutory instruments is under the supervision of a joint committee of Parliament that examines the texts and calls the attention of Parliament to any apparent defects.

Stead, William Thomas (1849–1912)
journalist

Editor of the *Pall Mall Gazette* (1883–90), Stead collaborated with Josephine BUTLER to expose the problem of child prostitution in *The Maiden Tribute of Modern Babylon* (1885). He was a spiritualist and a pacifist, and in his own profession he was regarded as a sponsor of sensationalism before the dawn of the modern British press. He died aboard the *Titanic.*

steam engine

The first practical steam engine was the atmospheric engine developed by Thomas SAVERY in 1698; the improvements made by Thomas NEWCOMEN (1712) brought it into wider use in mines. The addition of a condenser and a rotary flywheel by James WATT (1769, 1782) allowed many more applications. At the same time, improved machine making increased the engine's efficiency, and it was applied to factories and to locomotive devices on land and sea. Continued improvements in the 19th century provided a significant advantage for British manufacturing and transport industries.

Steele, Richard (1672–1729)
writer, politician
The son of an Irish attorney, Steele was educated at Charterhouse School and Merton College, OXFORD UNIVERSITY. He served in the Life Guards and later became a playwright. In 1709 he began the *Tatler* with Joseph ADDISON, and they published the *Spectator* in 1711–12. Steele was elected to PARLIAMENT in 1713 and became propaganda writer for the WHIGS.

Stephenson, George (1781–1848)
engineer
Stephenson was born in Northumberland, where his father was an engineer who worked with colliery engines. He developed a locomotive design which, when wooden rails were replaced with iron, could reach unprecedented speeds. He was the engineer for the Stockton to Darlington Mineral Railway (1825). In 1829 he built the *Rocket,* which was clocked at the amazing rate of 27 mph. Stephenson's engine was adopted for the Liverpool to Manchester Railway in 1830, the first passenger line in ENGLAND.

Stewart, Henry See DARNLEY, HENRY STEWART, LORD.

Stewart, Robert See CASTLEREAGH, ROBERT STEWART, VISCOUNT.

Stormont
A castle outside BELFAST, the site of the PARLIAMENT of NORTHERN IRELAND (1932–72). The name was used as a synonym for ULSTER unionist government. It was chosen as the site of meetings for the reconstituted government in 1999.

Stow, John (1525–1605)
antiquary
Stow worked as a tailor, but he was an avid collector of manuscripts and chronicles. He produced *Chronicles of England* (1580), a revised edition of the medieval historian Holinshed's *Chronicles* (1585–87), and his own *Survey of London* (1598).

Strachey, (Giles) Lytton (1880–1932)
biographer, critic
Educated at Liverpool and then Trinity College, CAMBRIDGE UNIVERSITY, Strachey was the son of a longtime soldier and administrator in INDIA. Indeed, he was named after a VICEROY, but his career moved in a decidedly different direction. A conscientious objector during WORLD WAR I, he turned to writing as a career. His *Eminent Victorians* (1918) contained witty essays on Cardinal MANNING, Florence NIGHTINGALE, Thomas ARNOLD, and General Charles GORDON. He wrote an unflattering but sympathetic life of *Queen Victoria* (1921). His last major work was *Elizabeth and Essex: A Tragic History* (1928) for which he used some Freudian analysis and earned some negative criticism.

Strafford, Thomas Wentworth, first earl of (1593–1641)
politician
At first an opponent of royal policies, Strafford became head of the king's COUNCIL in the north, then his deputy in IRELAND (1633), where he carried out a ruthless policy of exploiting Crown resources and manipulating Irish factions, arousing the general enmity of all. Recalled by

CHARLES I in 1639 to be the chief adviser, he became a target for revenge by PARLIAMENT. He was impeached but defended himself ably, and Parliament resorted to an act of ATTAINDER which declared his guilt and ordered his execution. The king made the tactical error of allowing the execution to proceed. The King's decision did not satisfy the radicals, rather, it added fuel to their complaints.

Stuart, Charles Edward (1720–1788)
Stuart pretender

The "Young Pretender," also known as "Bonnie Prince Charlie," Stuart was the grandson of JAMES VII AND II. He was born and raised in Italy. He was summoned to lead a French expedition to GREAT BRITAIN in 1744, but that venture was canceled. The prince led a small group to SCOTLAND in 1745, hoping to raise a rebellion and induce the French to support it. He landed in the Hebrides in July, and he was in EDINBURGH by September. His small army marched into ENGLAND, getting as far as Derby by December. The French aid did not come, and in fear of being cut off, the JACOBITES' force retreated into Scotland and was defeated at the Battle of CULLODEN in April 1746. The prince retreated and spent months hiding in the HIGHLANDS, escaping to France with the help of Flora MACDONALD. He was now an embarrassment to the French, who were trying to negotiate a peace, so he was expelled and sent to the papal state of Avignon. When his father died in 1766, no European court recognized his title, and he died without heirs, leaving a brother, Henry, who declined to claim the throne. The Stuart line was said to have expired, but a recent claimant has argued that it did not (see Prince Michael, *The Forgotten Monarchy of Scotland,* 1998).

Stuart, house of

The Stuart monarchy was created by the failure of the direct TUDOR line. In 1503 HENRY VII's daughter Margaret TUDOR married JAMES IV of SCOTLAND. Their granddaughter was MARY, QUEEN OF SCOTS, and Queen ELIZABETH I recognized JAMES VI, Mary's son, as her rightful successor. James and his son CHARLES I ruled ENGLAND, WALES, Scotland, and IRELAND until 1649. After Charles's execution in 1649, an INTERREGNUM lasted until 1660. The two sons of the late king, CHARLES II and JAMES VII AND II then ruled until 1688. The GLORIOUS REVOLUTION brought the rule of WILLIAM III, nephew and son-in-law of James II, and his wife MARY II. William was followed by his sister-in-law Queen ANNE, James's second daughter and the last of the Stuart rulers.

Submission of the Clergy (1532)

In 1532 the powers of the clergy to hold courts, make canons, and enjoy certain immunities from secular power were surrendered at the command of HENRY VIII. This came on the heels of statutes critical of clerical misconduct, and it preceded the king's declaration of his ROYAL SUPREMACY (1534).

Succession, Acts of

HENRY VIII had to alter the line of royal succession in view of his series of marriages and the resulting heirs of those unions. When he divorced CATHERINE OF ARAGON, he used an ACT OF PARLIAMENT to declare his daughter Mary illegitimate (1534). After the execution of Anne BOLEYN, an act was used to declare Princess Elizabeth illegitimate (1536). Finally, in an act of 1543 Henry recognized Prince Edward as his successor, providing that if he died without heirs, Mary and Elizabeth would succeed him, in that order. This frequent tinkering with the succession not only revealed Henry's obsession, it also contributed to an increasing sense of statutory authority.

Sudan, The

The largest country in AFRICA, The Sudan stood at the junction of black African and Muslim cultures. Islamic rule had been enforced since the

16th century, and in the early 19th century Egyptian authority was extended into the area, recognized by the Convention of London in 1840. The affairs of EGYPT later came under the control of France and GREAT BRITAIN, while The Sudan was taken over in a holy war by Muhammad Ahmad al-Mahdi. The attempt by General Charles GORDON to hold KHARTOUM against the Mahdi resulted in his death (1885), which was later avenged by Herbert KITCHENER, who recaptured the city (1898). While British and Egyptian governments tried to control the area, it was beset with revolts in the early 20th century, in one of which the British governor was killed (1924). Further efforts at control were ineffective, and the country gained self-government in 1956. Competing groups kept the country in a state of civil war for most of the rest of the 20th century. The great-grandson of the Mahdi, Sadeq al-Mahdi, was elected president but was overthrown by a military coup in 1991, and The Sudan was plunged into more fighting between the Islamic North and the Christian animist South.

Suez Canal

The great engineering project, led by the French builder Ferdinand de Lessups, was completed in 1869. The 100-mile waterway between the Mediterranean Sea and the Red Sea (and thus the Indian Ocean) shortened the voyage from GREAT BRITAIN to INDIA from three months to three weeks. The Khedive of EGYPT sold 40 percent of the canal company shares to the British government in 1875, as he was nearly bankrupt. Benjamin DISRAELI saw this as an opportunity to ensure Britain's rights in this vital route. Free navigation was guaranteed by international convention, and British troops provided protection from 1883 until 1956. But a crisis struck when Egyptian nationalists seized the canal. The British and French governments then made a secret agreement with Israel whereby the Israelis would attack Egypt, providing a pretext for the Europeans to intervene. Opposition from the

United States and the United Nations forced an end to the operation and resulted in the resignation of the government of Anthony EDEN.

Suffolk, Charles Brandon, duke of (1484–1585)
royal official

Suffolk was a member of the court of HENRY VIII who, as Viscount Lisle, fought for the king in France in 1513. A year later he was made duke of Suffolk. He married the king's sister Mary, queen of France (1515), and managed to calm Henry's anger at this apparent power play. He was given many royal offices, from earl marshal to lord president of the council to lord steward, over the next 30 years. He commanded troops for Henry against the PILGRIMAGE OF GRACE, and he fought in another French campaign in 1544.

Suffolk, duke of See POLE, WILLIAM DE LA, DUKE OF SUFFOLK.

suffragettes

Those feminists who employed militant tactics in the campaign for votes for women (1903–14). The name was coined to distinguish them from the "suffragists" who had campaigned since the 1860s by constitutional means to attain the same objective. By demonstration, disruption, and damage to property, the Women's Social and Political Union, under the PANKHURSTS' leadership, sought to dramatize the cause and speed its resolution. But whether the numerous arrests, imprisonments, hunger strikes, and forced feedings had this effect is impossible to tell. Because they were opposed to organized labor, they failed to elicit support from the bulk of the female population. In any event, there was no progress in PARLIAMENT before 1914, and then the leaders suspended their action and joined recruiting drives instead. The Representation of the People Act of 1918 provided the first breakthrough, giving votes to 8.4 million women over

30 years of age. The suffragettes probably had less influence on this than the thousands of women who had joined the workforce, served as nurses, or otherwise aided in the war effort.

Sullivan, Arthur   See GILBERT AND SULLIVAN.

Sunday schools

Schooling was not generally available to children of working parents, and those children were themselves often employed six days of the week. The 17th- and early 18th-century CHARITY SCHOOLS and the schools of the SOCIETY FOR THE PROMOTION OF CHRISTIAN KNOWLEDGE had reached many of these children. Yet there was still a large portion of children with no educational opportunity. In 1780 a journalist in Gloucester, Robert Raikes, gathered a group of children and taught them on Sunday. The effort included elementary reading and writing as well as religious instruction. As the idea caught on, DISSENTERS and ANGLICANS worked together at first, but eventually they set up separate establishments. Some estimates suggest that 250,000 children were being taught by 1795 and almost 6 million in the 1880s. By the 20th century the Sunday schools had been superseded by the state elementary schools.

Sunderland, Charles Spencer, third earl of (1674–1722)
Whig leader

Lord Sunderland entered PARLIAMENT in 1695, married the daughter of the duke of MARLBOROUGH, and was high in the councils of the WHIGS. SECRETARY OF STATE in 1706 (despite QUEEN ANNE's dislike of him), he was a leader of the government from 1708 to 1710. Removed from office over the IMPEACHMENT of Dr. Henry SACHEVERELL, he returned under GEORGE I and became first lord of the TREASURY in 1718. Implicated in the SOUTH SEA BUBBLE collapse, he was replaced by Robert WALPOLE.

Sunderland, Robert Spencer, second earl of (1640–1702)
politician

After an early career as an ambassador, Sunderland became SECRETARY OF STATE in 1679, but he was dismissed for supporting EXCLUSION. After reconciliation with CHARLES II, he became the principal minister (1683–88). He supported JAMES VII AND II more fully and for a longer period than any other leading politician. In spite of this, he was called upon by WILLIAM III as a principal adviser, but one who could not be appointed to a major office because of his past. He thus was a "minister behind the curtain," a role that would become unconstitutional over the next century.

Surrey, Henry Howard, earl of (1517–1547)
soldier, poet

A favored member of the court of HENRY VIII, Surrey fought against the Scots and the French in the 1540s and was governor of Boulogne in 1545. He wrote lyric verse and introduced the sonnet form into ENGLAND from Italy. His arrest and trial on the charge of "treasonable ambition" was apparently because he had the arms of Edward the Confessor quartered on his coat of arms. Presumably this "crime" was reported to the king by the Protestant rivals of this representative of a leading Catholic family. Surrey was executed on Tower Hill in 1547.

suspending power

The use of the royal PREROGATIVE to suspend the operation of a statute. Such a power had a logical basis when PARLIAMENTS met at irregular intervals. But the STUARTS used DECLARATIONS OF INDULGENCE (1672–87) to abort the operation of the religious legislation of their parliaments, thereby raising a more fundamental question about their respective powers. The suspending power was declared illegal in the BILL OF RIGHTS (1689).

Swaziland

A southern African territory once under the control of Transvaal. British administration was installed after the BOER WAR, but no separate government was put in place until the 1950s, when the apartheid regime of SOUTH AFRICA made a new arrangement seem necessary. The tribal king Sobhuza II was granted independence in 1968. The economy had been heavily dependent on South Africa, but iron, coal, and sugar production were developed in order to provide a measure of autonomy.

Swift, Jonathan (1667–1745)
clergyman, writer
Born in DUBLIN to English parents, Swift attended school in Kilkenny and then Trinity College, Dublin. At first a WHIG pamphleteer, his ANGLICAN positions drew him to the TORY Party, and he became a persuasive publicist and satirist in their service. His *Conduct of the Allies* (1711) was a powerful defense of Tory peace proposals. He was made dean of St. Patrick's Cathedral in Dublin, and he wrote a number of works that defended Irish causes. His *Drapier's Letters* (1724) attacked the plan for an altered Irish coinage; *Modest Proposal* (1729) scornfully satirized English views of Irish poverty. Swift's best-known work was *Gulliver's Travels* (1726), which satirized human nature more generally.

T

Taff Vale Case (1901)

The strike of the Amalgamated Society of Railway Servants against the Taff Vale Railway brought an INJUNCTION to stop the action. This was overruled, then appealed to the HOUSE OF LORDS and upheld. The union was subsequently sued for damages and lost, its bill coming to more than £40,000. The exposure of union funds to liability for damages threatened the entire TRADE UNION movement and brought an increase in support for the fledgling LABOUR PARTY. This legal position was reversed by the Trades Disputes Act of 1906.

Talbot, Elizabeth See "BESS OF HARDWICK."

Talbot, Richard See TYRCONNEL, RICHARD TALBOT, EARL OF.

Tamworth Manifesto (1835)

In the aftermath of the REFORM ACT of 1832, Robert PEEL issued an election manifesto in his Parliamentary borough of Tamworth, Staffordshire, which called the act "a final and irrevocable settlement." In other words, the TORY leader accepted the fundamental change, which had so divided the country, and he set forth a vision of maintaining "established rights" while being ready to correct "real grievances." This statement has been regarded as the foundation of the modern CONSERVATIVE PARTY.

Tanganyika

Formerly German East Africa, Tanganyika was taken after WORLD WAR I and made a British mandate in 1920. Its lack of resources meant a fairly quiet development toward independence in 1961. It became a republic in 1962 and joined with ZANZIBAR in 1964 to become TANZANIA.

Tanzania

The union of TANGANYIKA and ZANZIBAR in 1964 created the state of Tanzania. Zanzibar kept a separate assembly, and its political system was controlled by President Julius Nyerere until his retirement in 1985. His successor authorized multiparty politics in 1992. The country relies on exports of coffee, tea, cotton, and diamonds.

Taoiseach

The GAELIC name for the prime minister of the IRISH REPUBLIC. He is appointed by the president but must come from and have the support of the DÁIL ÉIRANN. He advises the president on the selection of ministers and judges, and he decides when to dissolve PARLIAMENT and hold elections.

tariff

Duty imposed on international commerce. Tariffs are used either to raise revenue or to protect domestic producers by excluding or restricting imports. The tariffs of the second category are the particular target of advocates of FREE TRADE. Tariffs have been a source of contention from the revolt of the AMERICAN COLONIES to the agitation over the CORN LAWS to the battle for IMPERIAL PREFERENCE at the beginning of the 20th century. In recent times, the EUROPEAN ECONOMIC COMMUNITY and the World Trade Organization have preempted individual governments in this area.

Tasmania

At first called Van Dieman's Land by its Dutch discoverer Abel Tasman, Tasmania was the second area in AUSTRALIA to serve as a penal colony (1804). The treatment of convicts there as well as the extermination of the aboriginal population by 1876 made the colony a byword for cruelty. In 1856 the name was changed, but the economy, based on wood and agricultural products, weakened, and there was population decline due to the discovery of gold in Victoria (1851). Some economic recovery came with mineral discoveries in the later 19th century, but this smallest of Australian states still needs significant financial aid from the government in Melbourne.

taxation

Amounts assessed on persons, property, businesses, and exchanges of goods and services used for funding government operations. Formerly most taxation was incidental, i.e., imposed in order to meet specific needs, such as payment of debts incurred in wars or other crises. Permanent forms of taxation were widely used by the 17th century: indirect taxes on land; direct (excise) taxes on ale, salt, glass; and customs duties on all manner of trade. Further innovation came with taxes on incomes in the 19th century and taxes on sales and then on production (value added tax) in the 20th century.

　See also CUSTOMS AND EXCISE; FORCED LOAN; INCOME TAX.

Tay Bridge

The estuary of the river Tay on the east coast of SCOTLAND was a challenge to engineers. In 1879 a two-mile railway bridge was opened, but parts of it collapsed in a storm, and 74 train passengers and crewmen died. An improved bridge was built and opened in 1887, and a road bridge was built in 1966.

tea

The beverage brewed from the leaves of a bush found in East Asia (*thea sinensis*). First imported from China to Europe by the Dutch (1600), tea was in use in GREAT BRITAIN in the later 17th century and reached the AMERICAN COLONIES about the same time. In the 19th century tea cultivation began in INDIA and then in CEYLON (SRI LANKA). By the late 19th century tea had become the British national drink.

Telford, Thomas　(1757–1834)
engineer

A Scottish stonemason, Telford moved to LONDON and was employed in a number of building projects. He then became a builder of ROADS, canals, and bridges. In the first quarter of the 19th century he built 1,200 miles of road on the principles of carefully packed foundations. He supervised construction of the Ellesmere Canal (1805), the Caledonian Canal (1823), and the Menai suspension bridge (1825). He also helped to found the Institute of Civil Engineers (1828).

Temple, Henry　See PALMERSTON, HENRY TEMPLE, VISCOUNT.

Temple, Sir William　(1628–1699)
diplomat, author

Temple negotiated alliances with the Netherlands and Sweden in the 1660s as well as the marriage of Princess Mary (later MARY II) to William of Orange (later WILLIAM III) in 1677. He wrote *Observations upon the Netherlands* (1672) and *The Advancement of Trade in Ireland* (1673) and published several volumes of essays. Jonathan SWIFT was employed as his secretary (1689–94).

Templewood, Samuel John Gurney Hoare, first viscount (1880–1959)
politician

A Conservative MEMBER OF PARLIAMENT from 1910 to 1944, Hoare served in many different posts. He is best known for the Hoare-Laval Pact (1935), made when he was foreign secretary. A secret deal was made with his French counterpart to settle the crisis caused by the Italian invasion of Ethiopia. They were meant to be arranging the sanctions to be imposed by the LEAGUE OF NATIONS, but instead they proposed to give Benito Mussolini two-thirds of the country. The outcry caused by this gesture of APPEASEMENT forced him to resign. He returned to office and held a number of important positions over the next decade.

Tennyson, Alfred Tennyson, first baron (1809–1892)
poet

The son of a clergyman who was disinherited by his father, Lord Tennyson was educated at Trinity College, CAMBRIDGE UNIVERSITY. His poems gained an audience slowly; the first volume was not a success (1830), but with succeeding volumes he became highly popular. In 1850 he was made POET LAUREATE, and that same year *In Memoriam* was published. Much of Tennyson's work was based on history and tradition: *Morte d'Arthur* (1842); *The Charge of the Light Brigade* (1854); *The Idylls of the King* (1859); and the dramas *Queen Mary* (1875), *Harold* (1876), and *Becket* (1884).

test act

An act requiring a prospective office holder to pass a religious "test." One example is the act of 1673, where a holder of an office had to take communion in the ANGLICAN church at least once a year, take the oath of supremacy and allegiance to the Crown, and subscribe to a declaration against transubstantiation. These were the requirements which forced CHARLES II's brother James (later JAMES VII AND II) to resign as lord high admiral. This act and later versions (1678 for ENGLAND and 1681 for SCOTLAND) were reversed by the CATHOLIC EMANCIPATION act in 1829.

Tewkesbury, Battle of (1471)

EDWARD IV had been removed from the throne in 1470 by an alliance led by his former supporter, the earl of WARWICK. Edward killed Warwick at the Battle of BARNET, just as the Lancastrian forces landed in the West. Edward's army intercepted the invaders, led by Queen MARGARET OF ANJOU and her son Edward, and defeated them at Tewkesbury (1471). This resulted in his restoration to the throne, and it was the most critical battle of the Wars of the ROSES.

Thackeray, William Makepeace (1811–1863)
novelist

Son of a minor EAST INDIA COMPANY official, Thackeray worked as a journalist and was forced to produce in great quantities by serious financial burdens. He was a contributor to *Punch* and *Fraser's Magazine,* and he wrote the novel *Barry Lyndon,* serialized in 1840; *Book of Snobs* (1846); and his major social satire, *Vanity Fair* (1847). These were followed by *Pendennis* (1848), *Henry Esmond* (1852), and *The Newcomes* (1853–55). He also published lectures on *The English Humourists of the Eighteenth Century* (1851) and *The Four Georges* (1855–57).

Thatcher, Margaret (1925–   )
prime minister, 1979–1990

The first woman to be PRIME MINISTER, Thatcher led the CONSERVATIVE PARTY to a series of three electoral victories (1979, 1983, and 1987). She was first elected to PARLIAMENT in 1959, having completed a degree at OXFORD UNIVERSITY and qualified as a BARRISTER. By 1975 she had become leader of the opposition in the HOUSE OF COMMONS, defeating Sir Edward HEATH for the party leadership. Her policies were much more conservative than his: monetarist economic policies, strong law-and-order and defense policies, and stout resistance to TRADE UNIONS were marked with her signature style of an abrasive and assured sense of righteousness. Her victory in the Falklands War (1982) against Argentine occupation of the tiny islands in the South Atlantic was a patriotic success and an echo of imperial days.

Thatcher achieved a constructive relationship with U.S. president Ronald Reagan and Soviet leader Mikhail Gorbachev, appearing to keep Britain in an important position in international affairs. Her relation with the EUROPEAN ECONOMIC COMMUNITY was marked by a desire to participate combined with a basic distrust of the continental machinery of government. Her internal policies were generally based on a rejection of postwar governmental remedies, and thus she began the privatization of many sectors of the economy. In 1990, facing debates over her POLL TAX (alias "community charge") and European currency, and having a revolt within her own CABINET, she confronted an election for the leadership of the party. While taking the most votes, her margin was slender, and she chose to resign. She was succeeded by John MAJOR as party leader and prime minister.

Thirty-nine Articles (1563)

The statement of doctrine of the CHURCH OF ENGLAND. The articles of 1563 were a modified form of an earlier 42 articles (1553), those being preceded by assorted prescriptions from the 1530s onwards. The articles were debated and affirmed in the convocations of the clergy, and rendered as a statute in 1571.

Titanic

Then the world's largest steamship, over 46,000 tons, the *Titanic* was built in Belfast in 1912. The "unsinkable" vessel collided with an iceberg on her maiden voyage in April that same year. A fleet of ships responded to her distress calls, but over 1,500 passengers and crew were lost. The

wreck was located by a robot submarine in 1985, two and a half miles below the surface. Salvage operations began in 1987, and in 1996 a crew managed to lift a section of the hull almost two miles off the bottom, but the flotation device failed, and the section sank.

tithe

One-tenth of earnings or annual produce, owed to the PARISH church. This formula was used in the early church, but tithes of a parish were often assigned to monastic and college foundations, and in the DISSOLUTION they were taken over by laymen. Tithes were owed by all, regardless of denomination, and thus they became a source of friction in later years. Tithes were sometimes changed to rent-charges (commutation). General acts were passed for this purpose for ENGLAND and WALES (1836) and IRELAND (1838). Redemption of these charges began in 1918 and was completed by 1996. In SCOTLAND the tithe was called a *teind*, payable on similar terms until legislation in 1925 revised the system and substituted fixed monetary values.

Tizard, Sir Henry (1885–1959)
scientist
Tizard served in the Royal Flying Corps (1915–17), and as a student of chemistry he worked with aviation fuels. He went on to work in government research departments, and in 1934 he headed the Aeronautical Research Committee (1933–43) and the Air Defence Committee (1935–40). The latter was in charge of developing RADAR, but Tizard resigned because of a feud with Frederick Lindemann, one of Winston CHURCHILL's close advisers.

Toleration Act (1689)

This act relieved DISSENTERS of the restrictions of the CLARENDON CODE. They were allowed to have their own teachers, preachers, and places of worship. They were not, however, allowed to serve in public office until 1828, and UNITARIANS and

Catholics did not benefit from the act. Nevertheless, this first formal toleration of dissent did establish a legal precedent and the official acceptance of differences in religious belief.

Tone, (Theobald) Wolfe (1763–1798)
Irish patriot

The son of a coachmaker in DUBLIN, Tone attended Trinity College there and the Middle Temple (see INNS OF COURT) in LONDON. Though a Protestant Dublin lawyer, he supported Catholic relief and wrote an *Argument on behalf of the Catholics of Ireland* (1791). A founder of the UNITED IRISHMEN, he became a radical supporter of an Irish republic. In exile in France, he sought military help for the Irish cause, but the two efforts made by the French were abortive (1796 and 1798). Tone was arrested and convicted of TREASON (1798), but he committed suicide before his trial.

Tory

From an Irish word for outlaw, the name was a slur used in the 1670s to refer to the supporters of James, the Duke of York (JAMES VII AND II), and his Catholic and royalist supporters. They were divided by the GLORIOUS REVOLUTION of 1688, some giving support to the new regime of WILLIAM III, the more orthodox refusing to allow the deposition of a rightful ruler. The name Tory has remained in use until today as a casual reference to the CONSERVATIVE PARTY.

Tower of London

The stone castle beside the Roman wall of LONDON erected (1077–1097) by William the Conqueror was one of the major Norman forts in ENGLAND. Added enclosures were built over the next six centuries. The White Tower is the only part remaining from the original castle, with

Tower of London and Tower Bridge, England (1880–1900) *(Library of Congress)*

other traces of later structures. The Tower was used as a royal residence into the 17th century, and it has also been used as a prison, a mint, and an armory. Today it is still an ARMY fort and home to the Crown Jewels.

Townshend, Charles (1725–1767)
politician

Grandson of Charles "Turnip" TOWNSHEND and a WHIG member of PARLIAMENT, Townshend studied at Clare College, CAMBRIDGE UNIVERSITY, and later at Leyden and at Lincoln's Inn. He held a number of offices and became CHANCELLOR OF THE EXCHEQUER under William PITT in 1766. He proposed a series of new duties on American trade (lead, glass, paper, and tea), partly to offset his failure to get Parliament to approve a land tax at a sufficient level to meet expenses. The duties met with widespread resistance in the AMERICAN COLONIES, and Lord NORTH repealed all but the duty on tea in 1770.

Townshend, Charles Townshend, second viscount (1674–1738)
diplomat, agriculturalist

Lord Townshend's father had been ennobled by CHARLES II. Townshend was educated at Eton and King's College, CAMBRIDGE UNIVERSITY. A secretary of state under Robert WALPOLE, his main interest was in foreign affairs. He was LORD LIEUTENANT of IRELAND in 1717, then took office as Walpole's main assistant in foreign policy (1720–30). Upon retiring from government, he spent his time on his Norfolk estate, devoting himself to agricultural improvements. He studied livestock breeding, soil culture, and crop rotation. His experiments with turnips in rotation with other crops earned him the nickname "Turnip" Townshend.

Trades Union Congress (TUC)

The large number of TRADE UNIONS had relatively little voice in political affairs, as they were small and separate bodies. Union councils were organized in several cities, and in 1868 a group of 34 delegates met in Manchester to form the Trades Union Congress, a national coordinating body. At first there was no organizational structure, only an annual meeting. In 1871 a parliamentary committee was formed to lobby on behalf of unions. As the new industrial unions grew, so did the size of the TUC and its constituent body. The group joined the Labour Representation Committee in 1900, to help co-ordinate election plans, and this led to the formation of the LABOUR PARTY. Some 2.5 million workers were connected to the TUC by 1914, and it was useful that the organization adopted a "strike truce" for the duration of the war. The TUC continued to grow, and its political role, except for the disaster of the GENERAL STRIKE (1926), also grew. In the decades after the WORLD WAR II, it was a major political force. In the 1980s, however, as membership fell and the government took a harder line against unions, the political influence of the TUC declined.

trade union

An organized group of workers, usually in a single trade, the union superseded the older craft GUILD as a means of protecting common interests. Trade unions appeared in the 18th and early 19th centuries, perhaps as a byproduct of industrial growth and rising urban population. They were distrusted by employers and property owners, who saw the union as a source of political and economic conflict. Trade unions were slow to gain legal recognition: the COMMON LAW prohibited a "combination" in restraint of trade, and this injunction was reinforced by statutes in 1799 and 1800. The COMBINATION ACTS were repealed by 1825, and over the rest of the 19th century, progressive legislation improved working conditions, and the unions themselves gained legal status in the Trade Union Act of 1871. Until this time, union activity was led by relatively small groups of skilled workers.

By 1868 unions had come together to form the TRADES UNION CONGRESS, a lobbying organization. Also in the last quarter of the century, larger unions of miners, dockworkers, railwaymen, and general laborers formed a new and militant segment of the movement. In this period the earlier fears of political danger were heightened by the idea of syndicalist general strikes and union intimidation. In the end, however, union members found a political outlet in the new LABOUR PARTY or other socialist groups, and there was but one instance of a GENERAL STRIKE, in 1926. Union membership rose from 4 million (1914) to over 8 million (1920). There was a steep decline during the DEPRESSION, and the number passed 8 million again in 1945. A new high of 13.5 million (1979) represented about 58 percent of the workforce, but then the numbers fell again, partly in response to the antiunion measures of the Margaret THATCHER era.

Trafalgar, Battle of (1805)

Admiral Horatio NELSON led the British fleet in a daring and unconventional attack on the combined French and Spanish fleets as they were heading from Cadiz to the Mediterranean. In fighting off Cape Trafalgar, which lasted for an afternoon, the British sailed into the enemy fleet at a right angle to their course, broke the line, and engaged the ships at close quarters. Some 18 French ships were captured, and none of the British ships were lost. There were about 2,000 enemy sailors killed to 500 of the British. Nelson himself died in the battle, having been shot by a sniper in the French flagship. The victory was the decisive naval engagement of the NAPOLEONIC WARS, and it assured GREAT BRITAIN's maritime supremacy.

tram

Urban passenger railways were first used for horse-drawn, then steam-powered, and finally electrical vehicles. The latter were developed in the years after 1860, and by 1910 there were some 3,000 miles in operation. Called trams, they declined from the 1920s, in competition with motor coaches, and in 1952 the last tram in LONDON was scrapped. However, by the end of the century, several cities such as Manchester and Sheffield had rebuilt systems of light railways.

transportation

Convicts sentenced to death might be pardoned on condition of being transported to overseas possessions, penal colonies or otherwise. The practice began in the early 17th century, with the AMERICAN COLONIES serving as the original destination. After the loss of those colonies, AUSTRALIA was used for this purpose, as was TASMANIA. In the 19th century this method of punishment was terminated, first in New South Wales (1840), then Tasmania (1853), and Western Australia (1868).

Transvaal

The Transvaal was established as an independent republic by the Boer or Afrikaner settlers of SOUTH AFRICA when they moved north from the CAPE COLONY in the early 19th century to escape British control. Britain annexed the Transvaal in 1877, but restored its autonomy in 1881. Over the next decade gold was discovered in the territory, and that brought an influx of foreign (mainly British) miners and prospectors. These alien *uitlanders* were discriminated against by the government of the republic, and the situation was used as a pretext for renewed British intervention, which led to the BOER WAR and the eventual annexation of the republic as part of the Union of South Africa (1910).

treason

The crime of plotting against the king was always seen as the most serious offense. By 1352 the statute of treason defined the crime as plotting the death of the king; violating the queen (or the king's eldest daughter, or his eldest son's wife);

or, as added crimes, counterfeiting the GREAT SEAL or the king's coin; or killing his chancellor, treasurer, or judges. Many more crimes were added, the TUDORS alone creating 60 new treason offenses. The Treasonable Practices Act of 1795 expanded the definition of treason to include any kind of intimidation of the monarch or PARLIAMENT. The classic punishment was to hang the criminal until almost dead, cut him down and disembowel him, and then cut off all his limbs—"drawing and quartering"—so that they might be taken to different parts of the kingdom and displayed to his Majesty's subjects. In the early 19th century the punishment was reduced and it was made the same as murder by 1870.

treasury

The royal repository of precious metals, jewels, and other valuables. All kings had such an office, and in the early Middle Ages the treasurer presided over the EXCHEQUER, a combined court and financial office. These two functions were separated by the early modern period, and the lord high treasurer wielded growing power as the Crown's chief minister. The treasury was converted to a board of commissioners in the 17th century, its work becoming much more complex as the government and economy grew. These lords of the treasury were headed by a first lord, a position of major importance and hence the one typically held in the 18th century by the emerging PRIME MINISTER. The treasury was generally responsible for raising and managing revenues, and its manager, the CHANCELLOR OF THE EXCHEQUER, became the primary official in charge of the BUDGET. Increasing public spending and heightened concerns over monetary and fiscal policy make the modern treasury the central department of state.

Trenchard, Hugh (1873–1956)
air marshal

A major in the ARMY, Trenchard joined the Royal Flying Corps in 1912, commanding the force in Western Europe during WORLD WAR I. As chief of the air staff (1919–29), he established a bomber force that was vital to Britain's security.

Trevithick, Richard (1771–1833)
locomotive inventor

Trevithick's father was a mining engineer, and in the process of working with mine engines, Trevithick developed the first steam carriage (1801) and locomotive (1804). This work laid the foundation for modern RAILWAYS. He also experimented with many other devices (iron ships, screw propellers, and other boilers and engines). He was not successful with the business side of his ventures and died penniless.

Triple Alliance

The term has been applied to several diplomatic alignments. In 1668 an Anglo-Dutch alliance was joined by Sweden to oppose France. In 1716 GREAT BRITAIN and France were joined by the United Provinces in a settlement whereby each offered security to the others in terms of their dynastic problems. In 1882 Germany, Austria-Hungary, and Italy joined in a military alliance, though in 1914 Italy did not fight against Britain, France, and Russia.

Troyes, Treaty of (1420)

After HENRY V's resounding victories in France, he negotiated an agreement—the Treaty of Troyes—whereby he stood to inherit the crown of France, and he was wed to Princess Catherine, the daughter of Charles VI, the reigning French king. With Henry's death in 1422, his titles passed to his infant son, HENRY VI.

Tudor, house of

The origins of this English dynasty came, on one side, from Welshmen; on the other, from King EDWARD III, through John of Gaunt. That line had been declared illegitimate during the dynastic Wars of the ROSES, but it was later re-legitimized. The widow of HENRY V, Catherine, married Owen

Tudor, and their son Edmund married Margaret BEAUFORT (the great-granddaughter of Gaunt). Edmund was created earl of Richmond. His son, later HENRY VII, grew up in WALES and in France before leading a small army in 1485 to defeat RICHARD III at the Battle of BOSWORTH. Henry and his four successors restored royal authority, which had been diminished during the Wars of the ROSES. They further exalted the power and sovereignty of the Crown. The REFORMATION, the modernization of government, and the enhanced power of PARLIAMENT were all parts of their success. Part of their legacy was the concentration of English, Welsh, Irish, and Scottish realms into a (more or less) united regime by 1603.

See also EDWARD VI; ELIZABETH I; HENRY VIII; MARY I.

Tudor, Margaret (1489–1541)
queen of Scots, 1503–1513

Daughter of HENRY VII, Margaret married JAMES IV of SCOTLAND in 1503. Of their six children, only JAMES V survived. Her husband was killed in the terrible defeat at FLODDEN (1513), and Margaret involved herself in the political struggles around her young son's REGENCY. She married Archibald Douglas, the earl of Angus (1514), but was forced to give up the regency in 1515. After a time in ENGLAND, she returned to Scotland, divorced Angus, and married Henry Stewart, Lord Methven in 1527. It is through her first marriage that the claim to the English throne passed to her great-grandson JAMES VI AND I.

Turner, J(oseph) M(allord) W(illiam) (1775–1851)
painter

A brilliant student at the ROYAL ACADEMY (1789), Turner was elected to the academy in 1802 and a professor there in 1807. His landscapes were a paramount example of romantic influence in art, his choice of subjects emphasizing the power of nature. His early work was mainly in watercolor, and he began to work in oil in 1796. He made many sketching tours of GREAT BRITAIN and the continent. He left his massive collection (300 oils and 19,000 watercolors) to the nation, but only in 1987 was a Turner Gallery established at the Tate Gallery in LONDON.

turnpike

A tollgate on early improved roads. Turnpike trusts were established in the 18th century to manage toll ROADS, often under authority of local acts of PARLIAMENT. There was a boom in such road building in the later 18th century, paralleled by the expansion of canals and later RAILWAYS. These were all important elements of the industrial growth of ENGLAND, SCOTLAND, and WALES.

Tweedsmuir, Baron See BUCHAN, JOHN, BARON TWEEDSMUIR.

Tyburn

The site of public executions in LONDON, a hill near the Tyburn, a tributary of the Thames. The location is near the present-day Marble Arch, at the northeast corner of Hyde Park. Executions were moved to NEWGATE PRISON in 1783.

Tyndale, William (1494–1536)
translator of the Bible

Tyndale began an English translation of the BIBLE without royal or church authority. He was forced to move to Germany, where he completed the New Testament in 1525. Copies were smuggled into ENGLAND, and he was thereafter a marked man, despite his published support for temporal power in religious matters (*The Obedience of a Christian Man*, 1528). He attacked HENRY VIII's divorce scheme in *Practice of Prelates* (1530). He was captured and burned as a heretic in Flanders.

Tyrconnel See O'DONNELL, HUGH ROE, LORD OF TYRCONNEL; O'DONNELL, RORY, EARL OF TYRCONNEL.

Tyrconnel, Richard Talbot, earl of (1630–1691)
lord lieutenant of Ireland

An Irish gentleman who escaped from the siege of DROGHEDA in 1649, Tyrconnel served with James, duke of York (later JAMES VII AND II), and was made a colonel (despite his Catholic faith) in 1672. He was imprisoned during the POPISH PLOT (1678). When James acceded to the throne, Tyrconnel was made an earl, commanded the army in IRELAND, and was made LORD LIEUTENANT (1687). He fought in the battles after the GLORIOUS REVOLUTION, and he died at Limerick.

Tyrone, Con O'Neill, earl of (1484–1559)
Gaelic chief

A leader in ULSTER, O'Neill fought the English in the 1520s and '30s. In 1542 he went to ENGLAND, visited HENRY VIII at Greenwich, and renounced his title of chief in exchange for the anglicized earldom. He recognized his illegitimate son Matthew as his successor, and in the 1550s his legitimate son Shane O'NEILL disputed the title, and Con was forced to seek refuge in the PALE.

Tyrone, Hugh O'Neill, second earl of (1550–1616)
Gaelic chief

Raised in ENGLAND, O'Neill was sent to IRELAND in 1568, with hopes that he would take the leadership among quarreling family members. For a time this seemed to work, and his title as EARL was confirmed in 1585, but in 1594 he rebelled against the English, found allies among European states, and won a famous victory at the Yellow Ford. He was finally defeated by Charles MOUNTJOY in 1603. He made his peace with JAMES VI AND I, but in 1607 he fled to the continent with Rory O'DONNELL, earl of Tyrconnel.

See also FLIGHT OF THE EARLS.

U

Uganda

A British PROTECTORATE in East AFRICA (1894–1962), during which time native monarchs continued to rule. Self-government was achieved in 1962. In 1971 Idi Amin Dada established a dictatorship which expelled some 30,000 people of Asian origin. An estimated 300,000 deaths have been attributed to the regime. In 1976 a hijacked plane landed in Entebbe, and an Israeli commando raid rescued hundreds of hostages there. Amin invaded TANZANIA in 1978, but a counterattack caused him to flee into exile. There were elections in 1980, and Dr. Milton Obote became president. He was ousted in a coup in 1983, and Yoweri Museveni took power. In the early 1990s AIDS became the country's most relentless killer (about 100,000 deaths by 1993). In 1993 a constituent assembly was elected to draft a new constitution. Tribal monarchs were restored to limited power, and Museveni was able to get international loans to begin to stabilize the economy.

Ulster

The ancient province of northeastern Ireland. Ulster posed stout resistance to Norse, Danish, and Norman invaders. It was the last region to be subdued by the English, and that process included the settlement of large numbers of English and Scottish settlers in the Ulster PLANTATION (1609–13). This process of colonization created the distinctively Protestant culture of the region, preserved in the 20th century by the partition of Ireland in 1920–22.

Ulster Covenant (1911–1912)

When the passage of IRISH HOME RULE became inevitable in 1911, Protestant loyalists composed a covenant, or pact, which vowed to resist the establishment of a home-rule PARLIAMENT, "by all means necessary." Some 237,000 signed the covenant, and many joined the newly formed militia, the Ulster Volunteers, established to fight against home rule (1912).

Ulster custom

The traditional rights of tenants, including security of tenure (if rent was paid up) and a title to compensation for improvements, in the event tenanted land was sold. These were actually rights found in various parts of IRELAND and not always found in ULSTER. Nevertheless, in the course of debates on landlord-tenant relations in the 19th century, the term came to stand for preferred status, sought for all tenants, in the various IRISH LAND ACTS of the later 19th century (1870–1903).

Ultra secret

The German "Enigma" encoding machine was used for top-secret diplomatic and military transmissions in WORLD WAR II. British agents had seized a machine and had been able to decipher many messages. "Ultra" was the codename for the intercepted and decoded traffic, which was only made available to a select number of high-ranking leaders. The decoding operations were conducted at the intelligence center at Bletchley Park. All personnel were required to take an oath not to reveal any information regarding their work. The existence of the Ultra secret was not made public until 1978.

uniformity, acts of

Legislation used to establish the liturgy and doctrine of the CHURCH OF ENGLAND and thereby empower courts to enforce obedience. The acts of 1549, 1552, 1559, and 1662 coincided with the issue of a BOOK OF COMMON PRAYER, the use of which was to prescribe proper religious worship and belief.

Union, Acts of

Wales: In 1536 and 1543, laws annexed WALES to ENGLAND, created shires (see COUNTY), gave them members in the English PARLIAMENT, and extended the COMMON LAW to Wales, along with the use of English for official business and a new court structure.

Scotland: In 1707 a treaty between English and Scottish commissioners was ratified by the English and Scottish parliaments. It created the UNITED KINGDOM of GREAT BRITAIN, abolished the Scottish parliament, and added Scottish members to the HOUSE OF LORDS (16) and HOUSE OF COMMONS (45) of England. The act kept separate the two countries' church establishments and legal systems, but it made provisions to integrate their economies and administrations.

Ireland: In 1801 the United Kingdom of Great Britain and IRELAND was created. The parliament of Ireland was abolished, and 32 peers and 100 commoners were sent from Ireland to the Parliament in Westminster. A plan for CATHOLIC EMANCIPATION was rejected, but otherwise inclusive measures were made for the economy, religion, and administration of Ireland.

Unionists

The political label for Protestants in NORTHERN IRELAND who support the continued union with GREAT BRITAIN. The term emerged in the 19th century as a description of those who opposed IRISH HOME RULE, and it was applied to the main Northern Ireland political party after the creation of the separate PARLIAMENT there in 1920. For the next half-century, that party governed without opposition, due to the Catholic boycott of the institutions created in the 1920s.

Union of South Africa See SOUTH AFRICA.

Unitarians

DISSENTERS who deny the trinity and the divinity of Christ. A sect formed in the course of the REFORMATION, Unitarians only appeared in significant numbers in ENGLAND in the 17th century, forming congregations in the 18th century. Prominent rationalists and deists like Joseph PRIESTLEY helped to bring about the legalization of the group in 1813.

United Irishmen

A nonsectarian radical group formed in 1791, promoting parliamentary reform and religious equality. Increasingly influenced by the French revolution, the United Irishmen moved toward revolutionary republican ideas, and thus hostility to English rule. This trend was paralleled by sectarian division in the later 1790s. They had joined with like-minded reformers and radicals in GREAT BRITAIN (1792–95), but their "conventions" were suppressed, and many were tried for SEDITION. Their role in the IRISH REBELLION of 1798 led to the suppression of the group.

United Kingdom

The United Kingdom of Great Britain and Northern Ireland is the official name of the British state since 1921, when the IRISH FREE STATE was created. With that alteration in the name of the United Kingdom of Great Britain and Ireland (formed in 1801), a dual administration was created, with a PARLIAMENT and a

PRIME MINISTER in NORTHERN IRELAND. That region continued to send elected members to the Parliament in Westminster, along with those from ENGLAND, WALES, AND SCOTLAND. In addition, separate administrative offices and COURTS OF LAW characterized the different regions, and over the course of the later 20th century, those distinctions tended to increase. The most recent extension was the creation of separate national assemblies for Wales and Scotland (1999) and the attempted reestablishment of a Catholic/Protestant legislative assembly in Northern Ireland.

United Scotsmen

A group that imitated the UNITED IRISHMEN (1793–99), the United Scotsmen grew out of the repressive atmosphere of the early 1790s, and a small uprising of republicans in 1797 brought arrests and suppression acts. These were further strengthened after the IRISH REBELLION in 1798, and the group was terminated by an act of 1799.

universities

The 12th century institutions were no more than communities of scholars, teaching small groups of students, mainly prospective members of the clergy. They grew into elite institutions for the aristocracy by the 17th century. When OXFORD UNIVERSITY and CAMBRIDGE UNIVERSITY were finally joined by a new university in LONDON (1828), an entirely different trend had begun. The education of an expanding middle class demanded more capacity, and in the 19th century the "red brick" universities began to appear. There were several types: university colleges, municipal colleges, an extension movement to provide courses for women, all active before 1914. A lull followed, but after 1945 there was renewed growth, with new institutions and promotion of many others to university rank.

The University Grants Committee was established in 1919 "to inquire into the financial needs of university education in the United Kingdom" and further to advise on the distribution of "grants that might be made by parliament." Government grants were added to fees and gifts and endowments. After 1945 government policy was generous in adding to the funding for what became nearly 100 university-level institutions by 1990. But in the 1980s a new and stringent policy was applied, and funding was shifted to a new Higher Education Funding Council more directly under ministerial control.

utilitarianism

The central tenet of the philosophic radicals, followers of Jeremy BENTHAM, that society should afford the "greatest happiness for the greatest number," which they called the principle of utility. The idea was an important factor in the many reform efforts of the 19th century, and it was defined more fully in John Stuart MILL's essay *Utilitarianism* in 1861.

Utrecht, Treaty of (1713)

The settlement of the War of the SPANISH SUCCESSION, the Treaty of Utrecht recognized the house of HANOVER as rulers of GREAT BRITAIN. In addition, Philip V of Spain renounced his claim to the French throne, parts of the low countries (present-day Belgium and the Netherlands) were ceded by Spain to the Holy Roman emperor, and Britain took some French territories in North America, plus Gibraltar and Minorca from Spain. This first international treaty was composed in French rather than Latin.

V

vaccination

Edward JENNER developed the process of injecting a small dose of cowpox, which gave humans immunity to smallpox. The first successful use was in 1796. Free vaccination was made available after 1840, and compulsory use was decreed in 1853. The last smallpox epidemic was in 1871, and the disease was declared eradicated in 1979.

valor ecclesiasticus

The record of church property required by an act of 1534. It was aimed at determining the amounts owed to the Crown when it took over the annates (first year's profits from a benefice) payable to Rome. The document was used as a guide by the Crown's agents in the DISSOLUTION of the monasteries.

Vane, Sir Henry, the elder (1589–1655)
councillor

One of the councillors of CHARLES I, Vane took part in the IMPEACHMENT of Lord STRAFFORD, lost the confidence of the king, and was thereafter a supporter of the revolution. He sat in the RUMP PARLIAMENT and was a member of the COMMITTEE OF BOTH KINGDOMS, an Anglo-Scottish executive established in 1644.

Vane, Sir Henry, the younger (1613–1662)

Son of Sir Henry VANE, the elder, Vane was a PURITAN and governor of Massachusetts (1636–37), but he resigned in a religious controversy and returned to ENGLAND. A member of the LONG PARLIAMENT, he opposed Oliver CROMWELL's grasping for power, but remained an important figure during the COMMONWEALTH OF ENGLAND. He was excepted from pardon in 1660 and executed in 1662.

Vaughan Williams, Ralph (1872–1958)
composer

A leading figure in 20th-century British music, Vaughan Williams used folk music and that of early English composers as material for his compositions. His major works included *Fantasia on a Theme of Thomas Tallis* (1909), his song cycle *On Wenlock Edge* (1909), nine symphonies, and a number of film scores.

Vauxhall Gardens

A park or "pleasure ground" in South LONDON, opened in the RESTORATION era and closed in 1859. A place of entertainments, decorated walks, and buildings, entry cost one shilling from 1730, a rather high figure. Nevertheless, it became a site of rowdy behavior, and after it was shut down, the area was used for new construction in the later 19th century.

Vernon, Edward (1684–1757)
admiral

Vernon fought in the war with Spain in 1739, capturing Porto Bello in Panama and thus becoming a national hero. Entering PARLIAMENT on his return, he became a loud critic of the ADMIRALTY. He led a fleet to block French aid to the JACOBITES in 1745, but his continued criticism caused him to be dismissed from the service in 1746.

Versailles, Treaty of (1919)

The Paris Peace Conference composed five treaties with the defeated powers of WORLD WAR I. The Versailles treaty was the principal agreement, settling the terms on Germany. It was designed to prevent Germany from starting another war: she surrendered Alsace and Lorraine to France, accepted the demilitarization of the Rhineland, and ceded eastern lands to the new state of Poland. Rearmament was prohibited, and REPARATIONS were to be paid to the victims of German aggression.

vicar

A parish priest appointed to perform parochial duties, while the revenues went to the rector. In cases where a monastery or college had the TITHES of a PARISH, a vicar was appointed to conduct services and minister to the parish.

viceroy

Acting governor of a country, province, or region, under the authority of the Crown. The title was used in imperial government, especially for the Crown's agents in IRELAND and in INDIA. It had intimations of royal authority beyond the more mundane executive rank of governor-general.

Victoria (1819–1901)

queen of Great Britain and Ireland, 1837–1901

The daughter of the fourth son of GEORGE III, the duke of Kent, Victoria succeeded her uncle WILLIAM IV in 1837. Her father had died when she was an infant, and she was raised in her German mother's female household in Kensington Palace. She was tutored in politics by her uncle, King Leopold of Belgium; and by Lord MELBOURNE, her first PRIME MINISTER. In 1839 her uncle sent a visitor—Prince Albert of Saxe-

Queen Victoria *(Hulton/Archive)*

Coburg. The cousins quickly became engaged, married in 1840, and soon had the first of their nine children. Their clan would become occupants of many of the thrones of Europe. In GREAT BRITAIN, the royal pair took an active part in government, but after Albert's death in 1861, Victoria went into prolonged mourning, even declining to attend opening sessions of PARLIAMENT. When she emerged in the 1870s, it was to a much-diminished role in government, though a greatly enhanced role as a ceremonial figure. Her creation as empress of INDIA (1877) and her JUBILEE (1887 and 1897) were powerful symbols of the place of the British sovereign and the power of her public persona. Victoria was at the center of the world's greatest empire, she restored the dignity of the royal family, and she lent her name to a period of prosperous, proper, and proud achievement.

Victoria and Albert Museum

Built with the profits of the GREAT EXHIBITION of 1851, the Victoria and Albert Museum has been located in South Kensington since 1857. A new structure was opened in 1908. First arranged by crafts, it was reorganized to display exhibits in chronological sequence in 1948. It stands as one of the world's leading collections of industrial artifacts.

Vienna, Congress of (1814–1815)

This meeting at the conclusion of the NAPOLEONIC WARS redrew the map of Europe after its convulsions in the previous quarter-century of warfare. One guiding principle was the restoration of legitimate rulers (as opposed to upstart dictators). Another was compensation from France, to be assured by an army of occupation. GREAT BRITAIN received a number of additional colonies (CEYLON, Trinidad, Tobago, MALTA). The major powers (Britain, Prussia, Austria, and Russia) formed a Quadruple Alliance to meet regularly and maintain European peace. Although the congress had begun in September 1814, Napoleon's return to France temporarily disrupted the proceedings. After his defeat at the Battle of WATERLOO, the congress completed its work in November 1815.

viscount

The rank in the peerage below EARL and above BARON. The name derived from the county official, a deputy to an earl (Latin: *vicecomes*). In 1440 the first of the peers by this title was created.

vote of confidence

In CABINET government, when a ministry wishes to affirm its control of the legislature, it will announce that a particular vote will be taken as a vote of confidence in the ministers. This calls upon supporters to vote with their leaders in order to keep them in power. When such a vote fails, or the margin is uncomfortably close, the PRIME MINISTER will resign and either form a new government (for example, Ramsay MACDONALD in 1931), defer to another to do so (Neville CHAMBERLAIN in 1940), or call an election (Edward HEATH in 1974).

v-weapons

The German rockets (V-1 and V-2) launched against GREAT BRITAIN and liberated France in 1944 and 1945. About 1,600 V-1 unmanned aircraft were used, and a large proportion were shot down. But the V-2 had a longer range, carried more explosives, and could not be intercepted. About 2,000 of these primitive missiles were fired at Britain in the last six months of the war.

W

Wade, George (1673–1748)
general

Wade fought in the wars of WILLIAM III and the War of the SPANISH SUCCESSION. He took command in SCOTLAND in 1724 and was effective in disarming CLANS of the HIGHLANDS and building a network of 250 miles of ROADS. He took command of the ARMY in face of the JACOBITE revolt in 1745, but when the rebels successfully invaded ENGLAND, he was replaced by the king's son, WILLIAM AUGUSTUS, the duke of Cumberland.

Wakefield, Edward Gibbon (1796–1862)
colonial reformer

A troubled early life was marked by scandal, especially when Wakefield abducted and eloped with an heiress. After a three-year jail term, he was sent to AUSTRALIA. When he became involved in colonial administration, he opposed the policy of free land grants, advocating what he called "systematic colonization." He helped to found South Australia, and he served with Lord DURHAM in CANADA, where he was a major influence in the drafting of the Durham Report on responsible government. Becoming agent for the NEW ZEALAND Land Company in 1839, he emigrated to that territory in 1852, preceded by two brothers who were important figures in early colonization there.

Wales

Western region of GREAT BRITAIN populated by Celtic tribes, speaking a dialect common to Northern Britain but different from IRELAND. The Roman occupation had limited impact here, the Saxon migrations almost none. At the Norman Conquest, the border between ENGLAND and Wales was entrusted to "marcher lords," powerful vassals of the king, who were granted large tracts of LAND and extensive lordship rights, in exchange for keeping the frontier secure. Native rulers in Wales were in frequent conflict, with each other and with English rulers. Edward I of England imposed his authority on Wales at the end of the 13th century, and he created a large, western region as a "principality" of the Crown, the remainder of the lands being held as marcher lordships. The authority of native Welsh princes was thereby extinguished. At the same time, Edward invested his son and heir with the title PRINCE OF WALES. A council was created to be the governing authority in Wales and the marches (border lands), either under the English prince or an agent of the Crown. After the experience of Owen GLENDOWER's rebellion (1405–10), and spurred by the events of the REFORMATION, the government of Wales was annexed to that of England under HENRY VIII (1536–43). Lordships were merged into counties, represented in PARLIAMENT. English law and language were prescribed, and Wales became—from the Crown's point of view—a part of England. But the Welsh language remained, and indeed it was fostered by its use to translate scripture in the 16th century. Customs and communities were preserved, even through the upheavals of the 17th century.

Wales was a center of Methodist revival in the 18th century and industrial development in the 19th century, both colored by the unique culture of the region. The special features of Welsh life did not find full expression in a nationalist movement until the 20th century, by which time heavy English immigration and powerful centralizing forces in society and government in Britain prevented any strong effort for home rule. But by the end of the 20th century there was a Welsh Office (1964), the language was being used in legal proceedings and legal documents, and a WELSH ASSEMBLY was created (first elected in May 1999).

Waller, Sir William (1598–1668)
general

Son of the lieutenant of Dover, Waller was educated at Magdalen College, OXFORD UNIVERSITY. He fought in the Thirty Years' War on the continent (1618–48), then served in the parliamentary army during the CIVIL WAR, winning several battles in the west country. Nicknamed William "the conqueror," he later suffered defeats at Roundway Down (1643) and Cropredy Bridge (1644), and he was forced to resign by the SELF-DENYING ORDINANCE (1645). He became a strong PRESBYTERIAN supporter, and the ARMY ordered his imprisonment (1648–51). He was involved with a royalist plot in 1659, and he sat in the CONVENTION Parliament of 1660.

Wallis, John (1616–1703)
mathematician

Wallis's father was a clergyman in Kent, and Wallis was educated at Felsted School and Emmanuel College, CAMBRIDGE UNIVERSITY. Professor of geometry at OXFORD UNIVERSITY, he decoded messages for the PARLIAMENT forces during the CIVIL WAR, and he served as secretary to the WESTMINSTER ASSEMBLY. He helped to found the ROYAL SOCIETY in 1660 and wrote books on geometry, algebra, and mechanics, also translating some works of Archimedes.

Walpole, Horace, fourth earl of Orford (1717–1797)
writer

The youngest son of Robert WALPOLE, Horace Walpole served in PARLIAMENT (1741–68) without distinction. He rebuilt a villa, Strawberry Hill, outside LONDON, in a Gothic style. He installed a printing press there and published editions of classic works plus his own writing, which included *Anecdotes of Painting in England* (1762); a novel, *The Castle of Otranto* (1764); and *Historic Doubts on Richard III* (1768). His *Memoirs* were published posthumously (1822, 1845), and his voluminous correspondence appeared in a massive 42-volume edition (1937–81).

Walpole, Robert, first earl of Orford (1676–1745)
prime minister, 1721–1742

One of 19 children born into a family of Norfolk GENTRY, Walpole was educated at Eton and King's College, CAMBRIDGE UNIVERSITY. Although he sometimes renounced the title, he was seen as the first PRIME MINISTER, and he was clearly the most durable of the leading 18th-century politicians. He was a MEMBER OF PARLIAMENT from 1701. A Whig, he was secretary at war (1708) and treasurer of the NAVY (1710). When the TORY Party came into office, he was impeached for corruption, imprisoned, and expelled from PARLIAMENT. This was not entirely unusual for this period of intense party warfare, and when the WHIGS returned after the HANOVER succession (1714), Walpole was restored. By 1715 he had become first lord of the TREASURY. There followed a period of party maneuvering, after which he emerged as sole leader in 1721. Probably some earlier leading figures were eligible for the label of "prime" minister, but Walpole's financial acumen plus his durability over two decades and two reigns (GEORGE I and GEORGE II) gave him a strong claim on the title. Walpole combined administrative ability and political skill, and he is credited with the evolution of the CABINET system. He also reinforced the importance of the HOUSE OF COMMONS, declining a PEERAGE until after his resignation from office. His policy was generally to avoid foreign wars and thus reduce or restrain taxation. On occasion he faced serious opposition: an EXCISE scheme in 1733; unrest in SCOTLAND in 1736; and the developing War of JENKINS' EAR (1739), which ultimately led to his downfall in 1742.

Walsingham, Sir Francis (1532–1590)
royal secretary

The son of a Kentish gentleman who died when he was an infant, Walsingham went to King's College, CAMBRIDGE UNIVERSITY. He was a councillor and secretary to Queen ELIZABETH I, a firm Protestant, and an adviser on European diplomacy. He managed the queen's security, using agents and informants to penetrate and expose plots against her. He uncovered the RIDOLFI PLOT and that of Anthony BABINGTON, leading eventually to the conviction of MARY, QUEEN OF SCOTS.

Warbeck, Perkin (1474–1499)
pretender

Warbeck assumed the identity of Edward, earl of Warwick, nephew of EDWARD IV, and then in Ireland in 1491 claimed to be Richard, the second son of the late king, allegedly murdered in the TOWER OF LONDON. Prompted by Irish noblemen and supported by JAMES IV of SCOTLAND and European rulers, Warbeck was a pawn in efforts to unsettle the reign of HENRY VII. When Warbeck came to ENGLAND with an invading force in 1497, he was captured and imprisoned. Upon attempting to escape, he was caught and executed.

wardrobe

The treasury of the royal household, where funds for the king's immediate use were kept. In the 13th and 14th centuries the wardrobe had authority for military expenses, and there was conflict between it and the EXCHEQUER over financial authority. This was not finally resolved until the wardrobe was abolished in 1782, at which time household financial functions passed to the lord chamberlain.

Wards, Court of

Wardship was one of the ancient feudal dues owed by a vassal to a lord; when an underaged heir succeeded to a title, his lord assumed wardship over the estate during the minority. After the practice of subinfeudation (creation of new, subordinate lordships), was outlawed in 1290, feudal titles tended to revert to Crown control. This court was set up in 1540 to administer wardships and ensure that the Crown received all ancient rights due to it. The court was abolished in 1656 during the COMMONWEALTH OF ENGLAND.

War of 1812

During the NAPOLEONIC WARS Britain enforced trade restrictions to weaken the French, but these also resulted in disruption of the trade of neutral countries like the United States. American ships were denied access to continental ports, and American seamen were impressed (forced to serve on British ships). The United States Congress declared war in June 1812, and American invasion of Canada was thwarted, while the British retaliated by occupying Washington and burning the White House. After American victories at sea and on the Great Lakes, the Treaty of Ghent (1814) ended the conflict, but none of the original causes was settled.

War Office

The government office in charge of ARMY administration. Created in 1661, its roots can be traced back to a war council of 1620 and earlier royal councils. It was headed by the secretary *at* war, which post was later overtaken (1794) by the secretary of state *for* war (and colonies, 1801). The office asserted civilian control over the army, though that was contested well into the 19th century. It was merged into the Ministry of Defence in 1964.

warrant

A written order, issued by an officer of the Crown, e.g., a councillor or a JUSTICE OF THE PEACE. The warrant directs a certain action to be taken (search, arrest, detain) or conveys a grant of authority. Originally a warrant could only be executed in the area of the issuing jurisdiction, hence the warrants of justices had to be endorsed ("backed") by others in case a suspect was found at a distance from the place of issue. Since 1925 this was no longer necessary in ENGLAND and WALES.

See also GENERAL WARRANT.

Warriston, Archibald Johnston, baron

See, JOHNSTON, ARCHIBALD, BARON WARRISTON.

Wars of the Roses See, ROSES, WARS OF THE.

Warwick, Richard Neville, earl of (1428–1471)

rebel aristocrat

Known as "the kingmaker," Warwick was a very powerful aristocrat who helped EDWARD IV take the throne in 1461, only to rebel and depose him in 1470. His revenues from extensive lands in the North of ENGLAND made him a key figure, but his allegiance faltered before his ambition. He was killed at the Battle of BARNET in 1471.

Washington Conference (1921–1922)

In the wake of WORLD WAR I, with oversized fleets and reduced budgets, the great naval powers met, at the invitation of the U.S. government. The main agreement was a treaty that imposed a 10-year moratorium on warship construction, along with the acceptance of a ratio of capital ships between GREAT BRITAIN, the UNITED STATES, and Japan of 5:5:3, with France and Italy at 1.5. Besides this unique disarmament treaty, there was an agreement to respect the status quo in the Pacific (Britain, France, Japan, and the United States), which supplanted the Anglo-Japanese alliance of 1902. There was also a third pact (adding the Netherlands, Portugal, Belgium, and China), a nine-power agreement that pledged to honor China's independence and territorial integrity.

Waterloo, Battle of (1815)

After a year in exile, Napoleon Bonaparte returned to power in France in March 1815. This famous battle occurred in Belgium, Napoleon attacking the army of the duke of WELLINGTON. After several French attacks were repulsed, the British advanced and linked up with the Prussian general Blucher's forces to destroy the French army. There were very heavy casualties on both sides, about 25,000 French (of 72,000); 15,000 of Wellington's 68,000; and 8,000 of Blucher's 45,000. Napoleon was again sent into exile (at a safe distance in St. Helena), and the allies resumed the negotiations at the Congress of VIENNA.

Watt, James (1736–1819)

engineer

An instrument maker at Glasgow University, Watt devised an important improvement to Thomas NEWCOMEN's engine by adding a condenser. He continued to work with the steam engine, setting up a partnership with the English manufacturer Matthew BOULTON in 1774 to manufacture the engines in Birmingham. Watt's further patented improvements increased the efficiency and application of the engine. In all, his work made a critical contribution to the INDUSTRIAL REVOLUTION.

Waugh, Evelyn (1903–1966)

novelist

After OXFORD UNIVERSITY and a stint as a schoolteacher, Waugh began to write satirical novels based on his own experiences. These included *Decline and Fall* (1928), *Vile Bodies* (1930), *Scoop* (1938), *Brideshead Revisited* (1945), and his *Sword of Honour* trilogy (1962).

Wavell, Archibald Percival Wavell, first earl (1883–1950)

general

Lord Wavell commanded forces in the Middle East (1939–1941). Though victorious against Italian armies in 1940 and 1941, he was ordered to defend Greece against German attacks and was defeated. He was relieved by Claude AUCHINLECK and assigned to command in INDIA, and then overall command in the South Pacific. With small forces, he struggled to stop Japanese advances in BURMA. Made VICEROY of India in 1943, he did all he could to bring about a peaceful settlement, being replaced at the last minute by Lord MOUNTBATTEN in 1947.

Webb, Beatrice (1858–1943) and Webb, Sidney (1859–1947)
social reformers

Charter members of the FABIAN SOCIETY, Sidney and Beatrice Webb were married in 1892. Their socialist philosophy was reflected in extensive social research and publications, plus a busy public life: Sidney was a LONDON county councillor (1892–1910) and a Labour MEMBER OF PARLIAMENT (1922–29); Beatrice served on the Royal Commission on the Poor Laws (1905–09). They wrote *The History of Trade Unionism* (1894); *Industrial Democracy* (1897); and a mammoth history of *English Local Government* (9 vols., 1906–29), based on years of research. They were also notable for other major contributions: joining in the founding of the London School of Economics and Political Science (1895); founding the *New Statesman* (1913); and drafting the new constitution of the LABOUR PARTY in 1918, its policy outlined in *Labour and the New Social Order.* They also naively praised the regime of Josef Stalin in their *Soviet Communism: A New Civilization* (1935).

Wedgwood, Josiah (1730–1795)
manufacturer

Wedgwood was the youngest of 13 children of a Staffordshire potter. He set up his own pottery factory in 1759, surpassing his competitors with excellent design and clever salesmanship. He also had a keen interest in social questions, and his radical views showed in his support for American independence, French revolution, and slavery abolition. He produced for both the luxury and ordinary markets. Most notable was his

952-piece service, made for Catherine the Great, displayed in the Hermitage Museum in St. Petersburg. Although he gave generously to charities, he still left a fortune of over £500,000.

welfare state

The idea of state-supported comprehensive social insurance developed in the first half of the 20th century, and the experience of two world wars and the Great DEPRESSION propelled the nation toward this goal. The term "welfare state" was coined in the 1930s, and the major steps to achieve the idea were taken by the 1945 LABOUR PARTY government. The concept of social insurance was as old as 18th-century benefit clubs, early TRADE UNIONS, and FRIENDLY SOCIETIES. The entry of government came at the end of the 19th century with the enactment of workmen's compensation insurance in 1897. Soon after, there were schemes for old-age pensions (1908) and a NATIONAL INSURANCE Act (1911), which protected a limited number of workers from lost wages. Over the next decades, increases in unemployment insurance, provision of public housing, and other programs were added, while the old POOR LAW was reformed and then dismantled (1929). During WORLD WAR II, the BEVERIDGE report presented the first general scheme for social insurance (1942). It included social-security measures; a full-employment policy; and support for health, EDUCATION, and housing. In the 1940s most of the proposals were put into law, and in later decades there were additions made to the forms of assistance, while a broad consensus across parties supported the general idea. By 1990 some 40 percent of government spending was directed toward the social-welfare provisions, and that figure was responsible for shifting views on the affordability of the welfare state.

Wellington, Arthur Wellesley, first duke of (1769–1852)
general; prime minister, 1828–1830

Born into an Anglo-Irish noble family, Wellington entered the ARMY, fought in Flanders (1794),

Arthur Wellesley, the first Duke of Wellington
(Hulton/Archive)

and was transferred to INDIA, where his older brother was governor-general. There he had his first major military victories, defeating native forces in two important battles. For a brief period he served in government, as a MEMBER OF PARLIAMENT and chief secretary for IRELAND (1807–09). Then he took a command in Portugal, where British forces were trying to stop French conquest of the peninsula. After an early set of failures and a recall for a government inquiry, he returned to Portugal, made a successful defense against the French, and ultimately pursued their army back into France. He was attending the first session of the Congress of VIENNA in 1815 when

Napoleon Bonaparte returned to Paris. Wellington was made commander of the British forces, and he led his army to victory at the Battle of WATERLOO. After the war he commanded the army of occupation in France (1815–18).

Returning to ENGLAND, Wellington again entered PARLIAMENT in Lord LIVERPOOL's administration, and he became PRIME MINISTER in 1828. Conservatives expected him to stoutly defend the established order, and when he accepted CATHOLIC EMANCIPATION in 1829, it was regarded by some as treachery, when in fact it was a pragmatic, tactical retreat. He did firmly oppose political reform, but with a divided party, he had to resign, and the government of Earl GREY took office. In the reform-bill debate, Wellington eventually led a large group of TORY peers in abstaining, rather than see the HOUSE OF LORDS swamped with new peers to pass the bill. From this point he became an elder statesman, a highly regarded national hero for many, a symbol of an unloved old order for others.

Wells, H(erbert) G(eorge) (1866–1946)
writer

After studies in science, Wells wrote a series of science-fiction works: *The Time Machine* (1895), *The Island of Dr. Moreau* (1896), *The War of the Worlds* (1898), and *The First Men on the Moon* (1901). He was active in the FABIAN SOCIETY, and his novels were often written with an eye on social questions: *Tono-Bungay* (1909), *Ann Veronica* (1909), *The History of Mr Polly* (1910), and *The New Machiavelli* (1911). In 1914 he wrote *The War That Will End War,* which probably led to his service as Minister of Information. After WORLD WAR I he turned to history, but in his own unique manner, with *The Outline of History* (1920), which promised to distill the lessons of history for the "salvation" of mankind.

Welsh Assembly

WALES was the only region of the British Isles without a native legislature. The matter had been discussed and debated for much of the 1960s, and a referendum on the issue had failed to carry in 1979. A similar measure passed in 1997, by a very small majority. The newly formed Welsh Assembly convened for its inaugural session on May 26, 1999.

Wentworth, Charles See ROCKINGHAM, CHARLES WENTWORTH, MARQUIS OF.

Wentworth, Thomas See STRAFFORD, THOMAS WENTWORTH, EARL OF.

Wentworth, Peter (1530–1596) and Wentworth, Paul (1533–1593)

The Wentworth brothers were outspoken PURITAN members of PARLIAMENT under Queen ELIZABETH I. Peter was imprisoned on several occasions for his blunt comments on Crown influence in Parliament, on the ROYAL SUPREMACY, and on the royal succession.

Wesley, John (1703–1791) and Wesley, Charles (1707–1788)

pioneers of Methodism

The Wesley brothers were both ANGLICAN priests who worked together. Charles formed the Holy Club at OXFORD UNIVERSITY in 1729. John had a conversion in 1738, which was followed by his sensational career of EVANGELICAL preaching. He began to address large, outdoor meetings in 1739, and over the next 50 years he traveled more than 25,000 miles and gave over 40,000 sermons. Charles was a masterful composer of hymns, writing more than 6,000 in his career. The Wesleys considered themselves Anglicans who were reforming the church from within; however, their followers—and the establishment—saw them as leaders of a breakaway movement. That in fact was what followed after John's death. He had built a network of lay preachers organized into sessions and regular

meetings, a structure that could not easily be accommodated in the established church.

West Indies

The islands of the Caribbean, first settled by Europeans after the voyage of Christopher Columbus. Spain was followed by English, French, and Dutch colonists in the 17th century. The earliest English colonies were St. Kitts (1623), BARBADOS (1627), and the Bahamas (1629). JAMAICA was conquered in 1655, and many other islands were taken by GREAT BRITAIN in the wars of the 18th century. The Europeans had imported slaves to work the sugar plantations, and the islands were sources of considerable wealth as well as centers for piracy. In the 19th and 20th centuries the islands lost their economic value but gained their political independence. Spain lost its presence in 1898, the United States asserting control over Puerto Rico and a protectorate over Cuba. Britain tried to form an island federation in 1958, but rivalries within it caused a breakup, and in the next 25 years most of the islands became independent.

Westminster, Statute of

Several acts of PARLIAMENT have had this designation, beginning in the reign of Edward I. That king had three major acts containing statements or restatements of LAW on many issues (1275, 1285, and 1290). In the modern era, the name was applied to an act of 1931 which formalized the British Commonwealth (see BRITISH EMPIRE AND COMMONWEALTH), recognizing the DOMINIONS as "autonomous communities within the British Empire, equal in status, in no way subordinate to one another."

Westminster Abbey

In 1065 Edward the Confessor began enlarging the small chapel at Thorney Island, which became the present Westminster Abbey and was completed just in time for his own death (1066).

Because of its new importance, William the Conqueror became the first monarch to be crowned there. He has been followed by all of his successors, and there are 16 monarchs buried there as well. Very little of the original structure remains, and the present abbey was begun by Henry III in 1245. The palace of Westminster—that is, the complex of buildings adjoining the abbey—was used by royalty for many centuries. It contained a hall begun by William II which was the site of PARLIAMENT's meetings for three centuries before the REFORMATION. At that time the monastery was spared the fate of most religious houses, and eventually it became the home of one of the great public schools, Westminster. The abbey has been rebuilt several times; the towers of the western front were designed by Nicholas Hawksmoor in the 18th century. It is the burial site of many of the greatest figures in British history: Edmund SPENSER, Isaac NEWTON, Samuel JOHNSON, and William PITT. The British pantheon was declared full in the 20th century, but plaques are still placed to commemorate war dead.

Westminster Assembly (1643)

As part of PARLIAMENT's effort to reform the English Church, an assembly was convened to consider possible changes. Some 30 members of both houses plus 121 ministers were invited, including representatives from Scotland. Despite severe disagreements, the assembly produced a *Directory of Worship,* which replaced the BOOK OF COMMON PRAYER (1645). The assembly also drafted a statement of doctrinal beliefs called the Westminster Confession (1646), which remained a standard in PRESBYTERIAN churches for many years. Meetings of the assembly ended in 1653.

Whigs

Derived from a derogatory name for Scottish COVENANTERS ("whiggamore"), Whig was used as a label to mark the opponents of James, duke of York (later JAMES VII AND II), during the EXCLU-SION crisis (1679–81). The core beliefs of the Whigs were that political authority derived from a social contract (see John LOCKE), and if the king violated this implied agreement, it was lawful to resist him. This was made explicit in the GLORIOUS REVOLUTION by the DECLARATION OF RIGHTS (1689). The Whigs were divided over the means and methods of governing, a court party favoring the more traditional royalist style and a country party that opposed government growth, TAXATION, and war. Some of the latter found a home in the TORY Party, which, however, was marginalized after 1715, because it was identified with the JACOBITE rebellion. Whig politicians dominated political life from 1715 to 1760, but with GEORGE III the political lines blurred again. The king wanted loyal ministers, and he had low regard for party labels. There was a long period of Tory dominance, from 1784 to 1829, followed by a Whig revival (1830–60) and a transition to the modern LIBERAL PARTY. The term "Whig" was still used for the more aristocratic members of that party, until they migrated to the Tories at the end of the 19th century. Since then there has been little or no use for the term in party politics.

whip

A PARLIAMENT member whose duty it is to assure the attendance and participation of others. The name came from the fox hunt, where a "whipper in" kept the hunting dogs from straying. Today the government and the opposition each have a chief whip. They arrange the order of business, and they each have a number of assistants. The whip is also the name of the weekly schedule, sent to members by each chief, in which each item is underlined one, two, or three times, indicating the degree of importance of the members' attendance.

Whiteboys

Agrarian secret societies in IRELAND, which opposed enclosures, TITHES, and evictions. Their protests were especially violent in the 1760s, as groups rode at night, dressed in white shirts, destroying houses and property.

Whitefield, George (1714–1770)
Methodist evangelist

Whitefield joined John and Charles WESLEY at OXFORD UNIVERSITY as a member of the Holy Club. He, like John, went to Georgia as a missionary, returned to ENGLAND, and began to preach to large open-air meetings. He disagreed with Wesley on doctrine, but he continued to preach and to travel in the British Isles and America.

Whitehall

This palace in LONDON had been rebuilt by Thomas WOLSEY, and it was taken by HENRY VIII in 1529. Whitehall replaced the royal residence in Westminster Palace lost by fire in 1512. After reconstruction by JAMES VI AND I it was used as a royal residence during the 17th century, but another fire in 1698 destroyed many of the buildings. The space began to be taken over by government offices in the 18th century. The street of the same name in Westminster was occupied by government offices in the 19th century, and hence the name came to be used as a general term for the government bureaucracy.

Whitehead, Alfred North (1861–1947)
mathematician, philosopher

Born into a family of churchmen, Whitehead studied at Sherborne School and Trinity College, CAMBRIDGE UNIVERSITY. A Fellow there in 1884, one of his students was Bertrand RUSSELL. They collaborated on *Principia Mathematica* (3 vols, 1910–13). He resigned in 1910 and moved to University College, LONDON, and then he took a chair in applied mathematics at Imperial College (1914–24). He devoted increasing effort to philosophy, writing *The Concept of Nature* (1920) and *The Principle of Relativity* (1922). In 1924 he left

for Harvard University and taught there until 1937, working on a synthesis of metaphysics and science: *Adventures of Ideas* (1933) and *Modes of Thought* (1938).

Whitgift, John (1530–1604)
archbishop of Canterbury, 1583–1604

Born in Grimsby, where his father was a merchant, Whitgift studied at CAMBRIDGE UNIVERSITY. Later he became professor of divinity at Cambridge and master of Trinity College, and he was made BISHOP of Worcester in 1577. In 1583 he was named ARCHBISHOP of CANTERBURY after Edmund GRINDAL had been dismissed. He was instrumental in the enforcement of Queen ELIZABETH I's acts of UNIFORMITY. A staunch Calvinist, he allowed no PURITAN deviations from the established order.

Wilberforce, William (1759–1833)
evangelical leader

Born to a wealthy merchant from Hull, Wilberforce was educated at St. John's College, CAMBRIDGE UNIVERSITY. A MEMBER OF PARLIAMENT from 1780, he was converted to EVANGELICAL beliefs in 1784. This led him to found and join public associations for worthy causes: the Society for the Abolition of the Slave Trade (1787); the Proclamation Society, which prosecuted vice and blasphemy (1787); the Society for Bettering the Condition of the Poor (1796); the Church Missionary Society (1799); and the Bible Society (1804). He and his like-minded members of the CLAPHAM SECT (James Stephen, Zachary Macaulay, Henry Thornton) were powerful voices for rectitude in public life and public policy.

Wilde, Oscar (1854–1900)
playwright

Born in DUBLIN, where his father was a surgeon, Wilde was educated at Trinity College, Dublin, and at OXFORD UNIVERSITY. He wrote *Poems* (1881), short stories, and a novel, *The Picture of*

Oscar Wilde *(Library of Congress)*

Dorian Gray (1891), but his true craft was writing for the stage. Among his works were *Lady Windermere's Fan* (1893), *An Ideal Husband* (1895), and *The Importance of Being Earnest* (1895). In the latter year he was tried and convicted for homosexual acts and sentenced to two years' hard labor. After his release he went into exile in France, where he died a few years later.

Wilkes, John (1727–1797)
radical politician

A flamboyant and provocative personality, Wilkes produced several significant political crises. As the son of a wealthy distiller, he entered PARLIAMENT in 1757, supported William PITT the elder, and thus was opposed to the ministry of Lord BUTE. In 1762 Wilkes began a journal called the *North Briton*, which he used to attack the king's first minister. He was arrested on a GENERAL WARRANT for the contents of issue 45. Eventually he won his case on the illegality of the WARRANT, but meanwhile he was condemned and expelled by Parliament. He fled to France but returned in 1768 and was imprisoned on the earlier libel charge. Nevertheless, he campaigned to regain his seat. He became a popular hero, and mobs were brought out to demonstrate on his behalf. After several elections and rejections, Wilkes was released from prison in 1770. He had by now become a cult hero, his followers marching under the banner "Wilkes and Liberty!" He was elected alderman and then lord mayor of LONDON (1774). Again chosen by the voters of Middlesex, this time he was seated in Parliament (1774–90). Wilkes had been exonerated in the case of general warrants and had won damages in a suit against the SECRETARY OF STATE. His group, the Society for the Supporters of the Bill of Rights, was an early model for the increasingly organized radical political community of the late 18th century.

Wilkinson, John (1728–1808)
ironmaster

Born to an ironmaster in Cumberland, Wilkinson created his own successful business, building the first blast furnace in Staffordshire and then a plant for boring cylinders. His work was of such precision that it was chosen for the machines of Matthew BOULTON and James WATT. His greatest success was in manufacturing cannons, for which he earned large orders from the government.

William III (1650–1702)
king of England and Scotland, 1689–1702, and Ireland, 1691–1702

William of Orange was the son of William, the Prince of Orange, and Mary, the daughter of CHARLES I. William became the stadtholder, or chief executive, of Holland and Zeeland during the struggle against an Anglo-French alliance. In 1677 he married his cousin Mary, daughter of

James, the duke of York (later JAMES VII AND II). He was thus in a key position when dissident Protestant Englishmen sought relief from the Catholic restoration imminent under James II. William was invited by a cross-section of English leaders to lead an expedition to ENGLAND. As he did so, James fled to the continent, and the way was open for William and Mary to take the English throne as well as that of SCOTLAND. Meanwhile, a Catholic revival in IRELAND supported the exiled king, and William had to lead an army there to seize power (1690–91). Part of the new king's design was to secure the resources of England in his fight against the French, which warfare resumed in 1689 and went on until 1697. At the end of it, France recognized his title in England, and it remained for William to secure the succession. His wife had died in 1694; her sister Anne had one surviving son who died in 1701. Thus an Act of SETTLEMENT was passed in the latter year, vesting the title in the House of HANOVER. William's reign had settled a Protestant line to the throne, and his own background and conduct of affairs had eased the transition to a constitutional monarchy.

William IV (1765–1837)
king of the United Kingdom of Great Britain and Ireland, 1830–1837

The third son of GEORGE III, William entered naval service at 13. He lived with an actress, Mrs. Jordan, for 20 years and had 10 children with her. Meanwhile he was made duke of Clarence (1789) and admiral (1799). He married a German princess in 1818 and had two daughters, both of whom died in infancy. His eldest brother, GEORGE IV, assumed the throne in 1820 after being regent for 10 years. The next brother, the duke of York, died in 1827, and thus William became the heir apparent. He became king at the age of 65 and was faced at once with the political crisis which resulted in the REFORM ACT of 1832. He opposed the measure, but after a resounding electoral victory for the WHIGS, he gave in. In 1834 he dismissed his Whig ministers and called Lord MELBORNE to be PRIME MINISTER.

But he was unable to win a majority at the next election, and the king had to accept the previous ministers. This was the last time a monarch tried to replace ministers who had the support of the HOUSE OF COMMONS. William died without (legitimate) heirs, and he was succeeded by his niece VICTORIA.

Wilson, Sir Harold (1916–1995)
prime minister, 1964–1970, 1974–1976

An economist, Wilson served in the CABINET of WORLD WAR II. Elected to PARLIAMENT in 1945, he became president of the BOARD OF TRADE under Clement ATTLEE. In 1963 he won the leadership of the LABOUR PARTY and then won the general election of 1964, but only with a margin of four seats. He was able to expand that lead to 97 seats in the 1966 election. His promise of a modern and technological approach to government was not fulfilled. Instead there were continuing economic problems which led to devaluation in 1967. Economic difficulty also barred policy agreement with the TRADE UNIONS, one of his main constituencies. Defeated by Edward HEATH in 1970, Wilson returned to power in 1974, but the economic problems persisted, and he resigned in 1976.

Wimbledon

The All England Club hosts its Lawn Tennis Championship in suburban Wimbledon in Southwest LONDON every year. The event began in 1877, with women's matches from 1884. In 1968 the open era began, with professional players being allowed to compete with the amateurs.

window tax

All dwellings except cottages were taxed in 1695, in an effort to support the military expenses of the country. This tax replaced the older hearth tax, and it was scaled for less than 10, 10 to 20, or more than 20 windows. The tax was revised, and rates were increased during the

1790s. It was impossible to evade, except by closing up or not building windows. But it was widely unpopular, sharply cut in 1823, and abolished in 1851, replaced by a house duty on all inhabited dwellings.

Windsor

The House of Windsor: the renamed royal family, originally German (Hanover, Brunswick, Saxe-Coburg). However, in WORLD WAR I, German names caused embarrassment; thus prince Louis of Battenburg had to resign his naval commission, and King GEORGE V was obliged to remove the honors bestowed on his cousin, the German Kaiser. The name Windsor was taken in 1917.

Windsor Castle: the largest castle in ENGLAND and a principal royal residence. Its construction was begun by William the Conqueror, and through many additions it grew into an imposing fortress and later a palatial residence. A serious fire in 1992 led to a series of concessions by Queen ELIZABETH II, from paying taxes to opening BUCKINGHAM PALACE to tourists, to help to defray the cost of repairs.

Windsor, duke of See EDWARD VII.

Wingate, Orde (1903–1944)
soldier

Born in INDIA, Wingate organized special forces in PALESTINE (1936–39), fought in The SUDAN, and captured Addis Ababa in 1941. Assigned to the Far East, he led a force ("Chindits") operating behind Japanese lines in BURMA, using gliders and air supply drops. He died in an plane crash in the jungle.

Winstanley, Gerrard (1609–1660)
reformer

An apprentice and farmworker, Winstanley was caught up in the turmoil of the 1640s, wrote tracts on millennial themes, and then founded the communal movement known as the "Diggers" (1649). They created communities on common lands in southern ENGLAND, and Winstanley wrote their manifestos about the evil of property and the dawn of common ownership and equality. The Diggers were attacked and dispersed by local farmers, and sometimes by COMMONWEALTH OF ENGLAND soldiers. Winstanley's last work, *The Law of Freedom in a Platform* (1652), was dedicated to Oliver CROMWELL.

Winthrop, John (1588–1649)
governor of Massachusetts

Born into a Suffolk family, Winthrop studied at Trinity College, CAMBRIDGE UNIVERSITY; and the Inner Temple (see INNS OF COURT). In 1630 he and other PURITANS left for America. Winthrop was subsequently chosen governor of the Massachusetts colony, a post he held intermittently for 15 of the next 20 years.

Wishart, George (1513–1546)
Scottish reformer

Born in SCOTLAND, Wishart was accused of heresy and migrated to ENGLAND, then to Germany and Switzerland, where he adopted Calvinist principles. He returned to Scotland and preached; one of his followers was John KNOX. Arrested in 1546, he was taken to St. Andrews, tried for heresy, and burned. Months later, Cardinal BEATON was murdered in an apparent reaction to Wishart's death.

Wodehouse, P(elham) G(renville) (1881–1975)
author

Son of a colonial civil servant, Wodehouse went to school at Dulwich College. The family had no money for university, so he was sent to work in a bank. He wrote industriously and became a freelance writer in 1902. He visited the United States in 1904 and began what became a transatlantic career that included writing lyrics for musicals by Jerome Kern and George Gershwin. From 1920 he devoted more time to his novels, many of which featured Bertie Wooster and his manservant Jeeves in addition to other characters (*Indiscretions of Archie*, 1921; *The Clicking of Cuthbert*, 1922; *The Inimitable Jeeves*, 1932; *Uncle Fred in the Springtime*, 1939). With his 98 books, including 16 volumes of short stories, plus his work on 31 musicals and 17 plays, he was one of the most prolific and popular 20th-century English writers.

Wolfe, James (1727–1759)
soldier

The son of an Irish general, Wolfe joined the ARMY at 14 and served in European wars and in the Battle of CULLODEN. He fought at Louisburg in 1758 and was made the commander of the British force sent to Quebec in CANADA in 1759. He led his troops in a dramatic victory there and died in battle.

Wollstonecraft, Mary (1759–1797)
author, feminist

Wollstonecraft began a school in LONDON and wrote *Thoughts on the Education of Daughters* (1787). A governess in IRELAND, she wrote a novel (*Mary*, 1788), and with the coming of the French revolution, she wrote a reply to Edmund BURKE, *A Vindication of the Rights of Man* (1790) followed by *A Vindication of the Rights of Woman* (1792). She traveled to France, wrote a commentary on the revolution, but had a personal crisis and attempted suicide. She was briefly married to William GODWIN and died after the birth of their daughter Mary, who would marry Percy Bysshe SHELLEY.

Wolseley, Garnet Joseph Wolseley, first viscount (1833–1913)
soldier

A noted Victorian soldier and ARMY reformer, Wolseley served in the CRIMEAN WAR, and fought in BURMA, INDIA, and China. He became famous for battles in the ASHANTI War (1874) and in EGYPT (1882). His effort to save General GORDON at KHARTOUM (1885) was too late, but Wolseley went on to become commander in chief of the army and was able to implement important reforms he had long advocated (1895–99).

Wolsey, Thomas (1472–1530)
cardinal, statesman

The son of a butcher in Ipswich, Wolsey was made a royal chaplain in 1507. He remained in royal service under HENRY VIII, and became a councillor in 1511. His diplomatic and administrative skills brought a rapid rise, and they helped him to accumulate offices and titles. He became LORD CHANCELLOR and cardinal of the church in 1515. In 1518 he was made legate *a latere* (special papal emissary, ranking above the ARCHBISHOP of CANTERBURY), and he negotiated the Treaty of London, a peace agreement among France, Spain, and ENGLAND. This gave way to alliances and wars in the next few years. But Wolsey's greatest challenge was the commission to gain an annulment of Henry's marriage to CATHERINE OF ARAGON. In 1527 he began this futile process, but his legal and administrative skill was offset by the pope's virtual captivity at the hands of Catherine's nephew, the Holy Roman Emperor Charles V. Thus stymied, and the king anxious to marry Anne BOLEYN, Wolsey fell from power. In 1530 he was arrested on a TREASON charge, and he died on the way to his trial in LONDON.

women's movement

The status of women in British society was fundamentally altered in the 19th and 20th centuries, a process that in one view was sweeping in its range, but in another view agonizingly slow and erratic in its pace. The status issues were essentially matters of LAW; the idea of equality between men and women went to the deepest senses of social and physical identity. At the beginning of the 19th century, a woman was the legal and social inferior of a man, a status affirmed in religion, political life, and employment. Except for a few aristocratic heroines (and an army of women laboring in mills, mines, and farms) there was no legitimate place for a woman outside of family and domestic work.

The first manifesto for women's rights was Mary WOLLSTONECRAFT's *Vindication of the Rights of Woman* (1792), which extended the arguments of Thomas PAINE to British women. A woman was still the legal property of her husband, with no rights of her own, and the unmarried woman had few opportunites for superior education and employment. The key areas of legal change came in divorce, property, and electoral laws. A civil divorce court was established in 1857, and though women were allowed to sue, they had heavier burdens of proof. In 1878 women were able to obtain legal separation and child support, but those rights were greatly strengthened after WORLD WAR I, and the grounds for divorce were successively widened between 1923 and 1969. In matters of property, married women first gained recognition in 1870, when they were allowed to hold £200 of their own earnings. Their rights were greatly expanded in 1882, as the married woman could now exercise the same rights over property as her unmarried sister. However, her opportunities in work and business were still limited. With the 20th century, they too expanded. Women worked at many new jobs during and after the wars. But they were not paid at the same rate as men, and only in 1970 was there an Equal Pay Act, which came into force in 1975.

The question of women's right to vote was perhaps the most dramatic dimension of the movement, if not the most significant. The suffragists and their volatile SUFFRAGETTE cousins forced the male politicians to recognize their rights, first in local government, then in school boards, and finally in national elections (1860–1918). In other areas, the barriers fell, slowly but surely: university admission, election to PARLIAMENT, admission to professions (law, medicine, clergy) were achieved in the half-century of 1870–1920.

See also ANDERSON, ELIZABETH GARRETT; BUTLER, JOSEPHINE; PANKHURST FAMILY.

Wood, Edward   See HALIFAX, EDWARD WOOD, EARL.

wool

The first major export and manufacturing industry in ENGLAND was wool. Sheep farming and wool production were important economic sectors from the 12th century. At first England exported raw wool to cloth manufacturers in the low countries (today's Belgium and the Netherlands). The subsidy or duty charged on this trade and collected in the STAPLE towns was the core of royal finance in the 13th and 14th centuries. By the 15th century the production of woolen cloth in England became dominant. Manufacturing was conducted by merchant clothiers who collected the material at different stages from home-based spinners and weavers, often spread across rural areas to avoid the TAXATION and regulation of urban centers. As the cotton industry grew in the 18th and 19th centuries, wool manufacture was concentrated in Yorkshire. Mechanized processes were slow to develop, but as they did, regional centers of production in the West and in SCOTLAND declined. The industry suffered serious decline in the 1920s, revived in the 1930s, but was unable to compete with manmade fibres from the 1960s on.

Woolf, Virginia (1882–1941)
novelist

The daughter of a literary family, Virginia Stephen and her siblings settled in LONDON, where they were among those who made up the BLOOMSBURY GROUP. In 1912 she married Leonard Woolf, and they founded the Hogarth Press. Her first novel, *The Voyage Out,* appeared in 1915. Her other works included *Mrs. Dalloway* (1925), *To the Lighthouse* (1927), and collections of essays. Her feminist classic *A Room of One's*

Own was published in 1929. Suffering from severe depression, she drowned herself in 1941.

Wordsworth, William (1770–1850)
poet

Born in Cumberland, Wordsworth attended St. John's College, CAMBRIDGE UNIVERSITY, and on a visit to France in 1791 he was moved by the experience of the revolution there. He had a child with a Frenchwoman but returned to ENGLAND and was stranded by the outbreak of war. Setting up housekeeping with his sister, his poems developed themes from the turmoil and hardship of the times. His *Lyrical Ballads* appeared in 1798. A few years later he married Mary Hutchinson and settled in his native Lake District in northern England. His long autobiographical poem *The Prelude* was composed over many years and not published until 1851. Meanwhile his innumerable individual and collected works made him a leading figure of the romantic movement (see ROMANTICISM).

Workers' Educational Association

Founded in 1903, this body aimed at providing workers with advanced education. Its founder, Albert Mansbridge, felt that university extension courses (begun in 1878) had become the province of the middle class. He found tutors from the UNIVERSITIES and worker students who initially wanted to study politics and economic and social issues. The movement went on to a wider curriculum, and it can be seen as one of the forerunners of the OPEN UNIVERSITY.

World War I
CAUSES

Decades of tension in Europe were reflected in rival military alliances—on one side imperial Germany, Austria-Hungary, and Italy in the Triple Alliance; countered by a Dual Alliance of France and Russia, joined by GREAT BRITAIN through diplomatic ENTENTES. The main concerns of Britain were the threat of German naval power and, behind that, her perceived ambition to dominate the continent and reach eastward into Asia. In short, Germany posed a very real threat to the BRITISH EMPIRE. In 1914 a crisis in the Balkans arose when the Austrian archduke was assassinated by a Serbian nationalist. There had been a number of crises in the area, and this time Austria insisted on punishing the guilty party. Germany supported her, and Russia vowed to protect the Serbs. Thus armies were mobilized in the East, but German military plans called for a first strike against France before launching the much larger and longer operation against Russia. Thus, in August 1914 Germany attacked through neutral Belgium. That invasion provided a pretext for British entry into the war, for while she had no open military agreement with France, she was a guarantor of Belgian neutrality. But if this was the pretext, the much deeper cause of imperial power rivalry clearly lay beneath the surface.

CAMPAIGNS

The collision of German and French armies, plus a small BRITISH EXPEDITIONARY FORCE, set the stage for a "western front"—a line of battle from the Swiss border to the North Sea—which dominated the military effort of both sides for the next four years. After early engagements, both armies dug in, fortified trenches, and employed heavy artillery, machine guns, and barbed wire against the other's assaults. Fearsome casualties mounted on both sides. At Verdun between February and June 1916, a million men died. The British launched an offensive soon after on the SOMME, where close to 60,000 were killed in the first day and a total of 400,000 by November. These battles did little to move the front line, and they seemed to mire the combatants in more and more deadly entanglement.

The second major front of the war was in Eastern Europe, where large armies moved over great distances, with Germany conquering Poland, allying with Turkey and Bulgaria, and eventually defeating the demoralized armies of

Russia (1917). In secondary campaigns, the British and French tried to outflank their enemies and form a link with Russia by invading the Dardanelles and taking Constantinople (1915). The GALLIPOLI campaign failed, as the NAVY could not force the straits, and an amphibious assault on poorly chosen beaches of the Gallipoli peninsula resulted in only more casualties and a withdrawal of the invaders. Armies in the Middle East and Mesopotamia were more successful in defeating Turkish opposition, Britain and France taking Syria and Palestine.

The other critical theater of operations was naval warfare. Unexpectedly, the high-seas fleets of Britain and Germany met only once, in the indecisive Battle of JUTLAND in 1916. However, submarine warfare by Germany against British shipping was a serious threat, nearly cutting off supplies to the islands. Submarine warfare was a point of friction with the United States and other neutrals, but in 1917 Germany chose to drop all restrictions on U-boat operations, calculating that British defeat would come long before American aid could reach the battlefront. They were very nearly right; however, the United States did declare war, and its troops reached the western front in 1918. Meanwhile, Britain survived the crisis, using convoys to reduce her shipping losses. On the western front, the last German offensive in 1918 was defeated, and the allied armies advanced in the late summer, bringing an armistice in November 1918.

POLITICS

The war was profoundly important in British domestic and foreign politics. Twice there were crises that resulted in coalitions. In May 1915 there was a "shell scandal," based on reports that not enough ammunition was being produced and shipped to the troops on the western front. This generated enough pressure to cause Herbert ASQUITH to form a coalition with the CONSERVATIVE PARTY. In 1916, after the unsatisfactory campaigns of that year, another coup resulted in the Liberal David LLOYD GEORGE replacing Asquith at the head of a national coalition dominated by Conservatives. These moves irreparably split the LIBERAL PARTY and provided a prolonged period without normal political activity (1914–1922).

In foreign affairs, the war brought the United States into closer contact through borrowing and military aid, but not into full diplomatic alliance, as the American Senate chose to boycott the LEAGUE OF NATIONS. Elsewhere, Russia was transformed by the 1917 revolutions there, new successor states rose in central Europe, and France alone remained as a major if untrusting ally.

CONSEQUENCES

PARLIAMENT was bypassed during long periods, as a small but powerful War CABINET made most decisions. There was consolidation of control in the name of the war effort through the DEFENCE OF THE REALM ACT (1914) and the formation of ministries to control munitions, food, shipping, and even information (i.e., propaganda). The resort to CONSCRIPTION, the vast employment of women in replacement positions, and the surge in TRADE UNION membership transformed the socioeconomic landscape. Postwar reconstruction programs promised education, housing, and unemployment insurance, but these were not all forthcoming. Thus the deaths and wounds and losses of property were not seen as worthwhile. Although the peace settlement and the treaties signed in Paris were supposed to close this chapter and open a new era of international cooperation, they became instead engulfed in economic, political, and ideological struggles, all too soon resulting in another global conflict.

World War II

CAUSES

From a European viewpoint, the Second World War flowed directly from the first, as German anger over the "diktat" of the Treaty of VERSAILLES (1919) fed the flames of nationalist resentment. This was cleverly manipulated by Adolf Hitler, leading to the invasion of Poland in 1939. But the war's origins were more diverse, as Japan forged an empire in Asia, invading China in 1937 and then pursuing a policy of expansion into Southeast Asia and finally into the islands of the Pacific. The British public was much more aware of and interested in Germany's aggressive steps. Hitler's reoccupation of the Rhineland, his rearmament of Germany, his demands for German national goals, and his annexation of Austria, also reclaiming parts of Czechoslovakia and of Poland, were all met at first by a policy of APPEASEMENT—accepting his demands and gaining time for rearmament. By 1939 this policy ceased and an alliance was made with Poland, but it was immediately sabotaged by the Nazi-Soviet nonaggression pact in 1939, Joseph Stalin's more brutal and effective brand of appeasement. He and Hitler agreed to divide Poland between them, and thus Germany invaded in September 1939, with little fear of resistance. GREAT BRITAIN was bound, as was France, to declare war in fulfillment of the guarantees they had given to Poland.

CAMPAIGNS

In the European theater, the war had several distinct phases: a period of British resistance and defensive campaigns (1939–41), a period of allied defensive actions (1941–43), and a period of offensive campaigns recapturing German gains and ultimately destroying the enemy's war machine. In the first phase, Britain did not engage German forces until April 1940, by way of an abortive invasion of North Norway. Ironically, the failure of this campaign, designed by Winston CHURCHILL, had to be defended by Neville CHAMBERLAIN in the HOUSE OF COMMONS. When Chamberlain's support dwindled, Churchill became the new PRIME MINISTER in May 1940. As he did, France was invaded and fell to Germany in six weeks. Britain thus was fighting alone and would have no ally for over a year. In this period she had to defend against the BLITZ and a possible German invasion as well as survive the submarine warfare that nearly cut her lifelines. At the same time, British forces in North AFRICA were threatened, as were the imperial outposts in other parts of the world.

In 1941 three events transformed Britain's strategic position. First, in March U.S. president Franklin Roosevelt inaugurated the LEND-LEASE program, making vital supplies available to Britain. Second, Hitler invaded the Soviet Union in June 1941, a move that created an alliance between Churchill and Stalin. This was an awkward and testy relationship, but the two were forced to join against their mutual enemy, and within a few years this would prove to be an unbeatable alliance. Finally, in December 1941 the Japanese attack on Pearl Harbor brought the United States into the war. Since Hitler had also declared war on the Americans in December, President Roosevelt agreed with Churchill to focus first on defeating Germany. The allied effort first aimed at clearing German and Italian forces from North Africa, and then an invasion of Sicily (1943) signaled the new offensive phase. In 1944 the invasion of Normandy began the long and bloody reconquest of France. Meanwhile Stalin's armies had been able to stop Hitler and go on the offensive after lifting the siege of Stalingrad in December 1942.

As the campaigns of 1944 and 1945 proceeded to victory in May 1945 in Europe, the United States, Britain, Australia, and New Zealand joined in attacking Japan's island conquests, winning back Southeast Asia while the nationalist Chinese under Chiang Kai-shek mobilized mainland China to evict their conquerors. To forestall an invasion of the Japanese home islands, the Americans dropped two ATOM BOMBS, on Hiroshima and Nagasaki, forcing a surrender in September 1945.

POLITICS

British politics were profoundly affected by the war. Another domestic coalition (first formed in 1931) was abruptly ended by a smashing LABOUR PARTY victory in 1945, evicting the war hero Churchill. Abroad, Britain seemed to be part of a victorious triumvirate and was engaged in leading the formation of a postwar United Nations, but at the same time her empire was critically weakened and would never recover. Churchill was an effective war leader, but not as a party politician. He had changed sides in his career and was distrusted by many, but he found a way to strike the right chord as a popular leader in war. He irritated and antagonized many subordinates and often tried to impose his strategic ideas on unwilling soldiers and sailors. Nevertheless he inspired tremendous loyalty. But when the war's end was near, an election was necessary. There had been none since 1935, and the memories of that decade were compounded by the sacrifices of the war years. Churchill's campaign tried to portray Labour as being dangerously authoritarian. However, Clement ATTLEE had been his deputy PRIME MINISTER and it was impossible to paint him as a man to be feared. Labour won 397 seats in PARLIAMENT and began to honor the commitments to postwar reconstruction, whatever their cost.

In foreign affairs, the war had greatly altered the picture. The United States was a partner, indeed the senior partner by 1945, whereas other European states were devastated by the war and unable to provide significant support. The Soviet Union, once an ally, soon appeared to have ambitions to expand its power in Western Europe, and its longtime dedication to communist revolution made relations tense. The one major improvement over 1919 was that in 1945 a new international body, the United Nations, was established. Given the experience of the LEAGUE OF NATIONS, improvements were made, and there was fuller participation than previously. This was both a plus and a minus. For Britain it was now important to play a part in a large effective international body; at the same time, her imperial role was reduced, even though it took 20 years for that to be generally accepted by political leaders and the public.

CONSEQUENCES

The war's 350,000 military and civilian deaths were about a third of the toll of WORLD WAR I, but the damage was felt in different and possibly more severe terms. Physically, the civilian population suffered far more, with increased air warfare and bombing of cities. The drain on British resources was proportionally greater, even though there was a vastly greater amount of American aid. There was, however, much less uncertainty about war aims, given the demonstrable brutality of the German concentration camps and Japanese mistreatment of war prisoners.

Wren, Sir Christopher (1632–1723)
architect

The son of a rector in Wiltshire, Wren was educated at Westminster School and Wadham College, OXFORD UNIVERSITY. In his early career he was an astronomer and mathematician, and he had a part in the founding of the ROYAL SOCIETY. He turned to architecture in 1663, and his first major project was the design of the Sheldonian Theatre in Oxford. He was the principal architect for the rebuilding of London after the Great FIRE OF LONDON (1666). Other projects included the Royal Observatory, Greenwich (1675); HAMPTON COURT PALACE (1689–1702); and ST. PAUL'S CATHEDRAL (1705–11).

writ

A royal command, later an order to hear a case before the royal courts. Writs were issued from the king's chancery and drawn up according to a formulary—the register of writs. They were subject to change, to be verified in court proceedings. Hence the writ, and its alterations ("forms of action" in the COMMON LAW courts) tell the story of the evolution of the LAW. There were only about 60 forms in the 13th century, but three centuries later the number was over 2,500. By the 19th century the form was standardized and eventually eliminated.

Wyatt, Sir Thomas (1521–1554)
rebel

Wyatt led a rebellion of about 3,000 men from Kent, against the announced plan of MARY I to marry Philip of Spain. He attempting to reach LONDON but was repulsed. Arrested and tried for TREASON, he was executed on Tower Hill. The revolt led to the execution of Lady Jane GREY.

Wycliffe, John (1330–1384)
theologian, reformer

Born in Yorkshire, Wycliffe studied at Merton College, OXFORD UNIVERSITY, and later became master of Balliol College at the university. As the protégé of John of Gaunt, he served on a number of diplomatic missions. He wrote works expressing radical opinions, such as *De dominio divino* and *De dominio civil* (ca. 1376). These works brought a denunciation from Rome. Wycliffe worked on a translation of the BIBLE and wrote *On the Eucharist* (1379), which stamped him as a heretic. His followers were known as LOLLARDS, and while Wycliffe was able to live out his life peacefully, the Lollards were later hunted down and persecuted.

Wyvill, Christopher (1740–1822)
reformer

Wyvill was a Yorkshire landowner and clergyman who initiated the Association Movement, an effort to form county associations to petition for limits on government spending and patronage. These objectives were thought to require an increase in the number of county members of PARLIAMENT—those elected on the broadest FRANCHISE, the 40-shilling freeholders. The movement spread quickly during the 1780s, but it was swept away in the turmoil generated by the revolution in France.

Y

Yalta Conference

In February 1945 Winston CHURCHILL, Franklin Roosevelt, and Joseph Stalin met in the Crimea to consider postwar plans. They discussed disarming Germany and reparations and agreed on a border between Poland and the Soviet Union. Stalin committed to joining the United Nations and entering the war against Japan three months after victory in Europe. Critics saw the conference as yielding too much authority to Stalin in central and eastern Europe, but Soviet armies had already taken care of that.

year books

Records of arguments in the COMMON LAW courts, kept from the 13th to the 16th centuries. These were a basis for procedural points as well as an invaluable historical source. Year books were succeeded by law reports, which noted the issues, arguments of counsel, and opinions of judges.

Yeats, William Butler (1865–1939)
poet

Yeats was an Irish nationalist who founded literary groups and a national theatre in the 1890s. His early work was part of the CELTIC revival of the 19th century (*Celtic Twilight,* 1893; *The Secret Rose,* 1897), though his mature work found a more distinctive voice (*Poems Written in Discouragement,* 1913; *The Wild Swans at Coole,* 1917). His nationalism was tempered with an appreciation of the Anglo-Irish contribution. He was a member of the SEANAD ÉIRANN (1922–28), and he received the Nobel Prize in literature in 1923.

yeoman

Not a precise term, "yeoman" applied mainly to freeholders below the rank of gentlemen but above the level of a tenant. A yeoman was usually someone who held some land in his own right, although the terminology varied by region and over time. In the "New Domesday" (1877), John Bateman classified "greater yeomen" as owners of 300–1,000 acres, "lesser yeomen" as those with 100–300 acres. The term "yeomanry" refers to volunteer cavalry formed as a MILITIA on a COUNTY basis. Used for the period of the 19th century, the yeomanry was absorbed in the Territorial Army after 1907.

York, house of

Edmund, first duke (1342–1402), the fifth son of EDWARD III, fought in the campaigns of the HUNDRED YEARS' WAR and was a supporter of HENRY IV when that king overthrew RICHARD II.

Edward, second duke (1373–1415), son of Edmund, was a supporter of Richard II and involved in various plots, but he served Henry IV and died in the Battle of AGINCOURT.

Richard Plantagenet, third duke (1411–60), nephew of Edward and son of the earl of Cambridge, was heir presumptive to the throne, 1447–53. Lord protector during the illness of HENRY VI, he was the leader of the Yorkists at the outset of the Wars of the ROSES, killed at Wakefield, and succeeded by his son, who became EDWARD IV.

Yorktown, Battle of (1781)

In the American Revolution, General CORNWALLIS had won victories in the southern colonies, returned to the Virginia coast, and fortified an encampment at Yorktown. There he was surrounded by an American army on land and a French fleet at sea. After heavy bombardment, lacking the relief he had expected from New York, Cornwallis surrendered to General George Washington, thus ending the American revolutionary war.

Young, Arthur (1741–1820)

writer

Young was the premier publicist for improved 18th-century farming. He inherited a farm in 1763 and made a *Six Weeks Tour through the Southern Counties of England and Wales* (1768) in which he surveyed the practice of farmers and inaugurated a long career of agricultural reporting. His *Annals of Agriculture* began in 1784 and ran to 46 volumes. In 1793 he became the secretary to the newly formed Board of Agriculture. He also traveled in IRELAND and France and published journals of those tours.

Young England

A group of TORY aristocrats opposed to the leadership of Robert PEEL and critical of the new industrial and commercial classes. Their solution to social problems was to extol the paternal role of the aristocracy. Benjamin DISRAELI was the most prominent figure associated with them, and his novels reflect some of their ideas.

Young Ireland

Irish middle-class intellectuals who were supporters of Daniel O'CONNELL's repeal movement but inclined to more militant action. Charles Gavan Duffy (1816–1903) founded and edited the *Nation* (1842). He and other leaders broke away from the Repeal Association and staged a futile rebellion in 1848.

Young Men's Christian Association (YMCA)

A small group of tradesmen founded this association in 1844. Prayer meetings and BIBLE study were the early energizing force. Soon, with patronage from Lord SHAFTESBURY and others, the movement spread and established facilities across GREAT BRITAIN and around the world. The first YMCA world conference met in Paris in 1855. That same year the Young Women's Christian Association (YWCA) was founded, at first around a hostel for Florence NIGHTINGALE's nurses, bound for the Crimea. The two groups were linked in 1877, and a world YWCA was organized in 1894.

Young Wales

A Welsh nationalist organization (*Cymru Fydd* = future Wales) was founded in 1886. It may have been inspired by YOUNG IRELAND, but it was a group less militant than the contemporary IRISH HOME RULE party there. In any case, it found very little support in WALES and did not survive the 19th century.

Z

Zambia

A republic formerly called Northern RHODESIA. The British South Africa Company controlled the area until it became a PROTECTORATE in 1924. Zambia became part of the Central African Federation in 1953 (with Southern Rhodesia and Nyasaland), but it gained independence in 1964.

Zanzibar

An island off the east coast of AFRICA, Zanzibar was made a British PROTECTORATE in 1890. Indirect rule was established in the 1920s, independence was granted in 1963, and a union with TANGANYIKA formed TANZANIA in 1964.

zeppelins

These German airships were used to attack British targets beginning in 1915. They were erratic, but in 51 raids they killed over 500 people. British defenders managed to shoot down 23 zeppelins, or more than a fourth of the total fleet.

Zimbabwe See RHODESIA.

Zinoviev letter

A letter allegedly from Grigori Zinoviev, president of the Communist International, to the British Communist Party, urging them to conduct subversive activity. Released to the press in October 1924, on the eve of a general election, it may have been a forgery or a genuine letter leaked by the intelligence services. In any event,

it was presumably aimed at scaring voters into opposing the LABOUR PARTY, which had just completed its first few months in office as a minority government, during which time one of its acts had been to grant diplomatic recognition to the Soviet Union. There is disagreement among scholars as to whether the letter did in fact have a significant impact on the election. The CONSERVATIVE PARTY won a majority, but at the expense of the LIBERAL PARTY. Labour actually gained a million votes over its tally in the previous election.

Zionism

Nationalist movement among Jews, aimed at restoring a Jewish state in PALESTINE. An idea present in some form in the Jewish communities of the diaspora for centuries, Zionism was expressed vividly in a world Zionist Conference at Basel in 1897. Theodor Herzl organized the group, and its activity helped to bring about the BALFOUR DECLARATION in 1917. After WORLD WAR II there was an irresistible sentiment to grant this wish, and when the British government withdrew from Palestine, the state of Israel was established in 1948.

Zulu

The natives of the colony of NATAL, they were known as fierce warriors. The Zulu were provoked into a war in 1879, in which they won the first battles but were eventually overwhelmed. Their territory was divided into districts and absorbed into the colonies of the British and the Boers.

CHRONOLOGY

1348

The "Black Death" (bubonic plague) first strikes England; mortality as high as 50 percent in some areas. Plague returns four times before 1400.

1351

Statute of Laborers attempts to freeze wages.

1352

Statute of Treason defines the offense as direct attack on the king.

1360

Treaty of Brétigny ends first phase of the Hundred Years' War.

1369

French renew warfare with raids on the channel coast of England.

1371

David II of Scotland dies; succeeded by Robert II.

1376

The "Good Parliament" meets; first impeachment in English history.

1377

Parliament passes the first poll tax.
Edward III dies, Richard II becomes king.

1381

Further poll taxes (1379 and 1380) produce poor returns, and resentment explodes in the Peasants' Revolt (June).

1382

John Wycliffe's works are condemned; the statute *de heretico comburendo* provides for burning of Lollard heretics.

1388

The "Merciless Parliament" impeaches Richard II's favorites for high treason.

1390

Robert II of Scotland dies, succeeded by Robert III.

1397

Richard II assumes absolute power; he annuls all acts of the Merciless Parliament.

1399

Richard banishes Henry Bolingbroke and seizes his estates (February). Henry returns to England (July), captures the king (August), and takes the throne himself (October) as Henry IV.

1400

Rebellion of Owen Glendower.

1403

Rebellion of the Percies; they ally with Glendower, and he is aided by some Scots and the French.

1405

Rebel forces are defeated by Prince Henry, who becomes a dominant figure in English government.

1406

James of Scotland is taken prisoner by the English, remains in captivity when he succeeds to the throne after the death of Robert III.

1408

Northumberland's third rebellion against Henry IV.

1410

End of Glendower's rebellion.

1413

Henry IV dies; Henry V succeeds to the throne.

1414

Revolt of Lollards fails; 40 are executed.

1415

Henry V renews the Hundred Years' War; invades France (August), captures the port of Harfleur (September), and wins the Battle of Agincourt (October).

1420

Treaty of Troyes: King Charles recognizes Henry V's claim to the French throne (April); Henry marries Catherine of Valois, daughter of the French king (June).

1422

Henry V dies during the siege of Vincennes (August); his infant son Henry VI becomes king.

1424

James I of Scotland is freed from English captivity.

1429

French recovery begins, led by Joan of Arc (April).
The Dauphin is crowned Charles VII (July).

1430

Joan of Arc captured.
Henry VI goes to France for his coronation there.

1431

Joan of Arc burnt as a witch by the English (May).
Henry is crowned in Paris.

1436

French army takes Paris.

1437

James I of Scotland is murdered, succeeded by James II (February).
Henry VI is declared of age (November).

1442

The French continue to recover power in Normandy.

1445

Henry VI marries Margaret of Anjou, and there is a two-year truce.

1449

The French recapture Normandy.

1450

Cade's Rebellion, triggered by losses in France and suspicion of treacherous royal advisers; rebels take London, disperse after the grant of pardons; further French victories in Normandy and Guienne.

1453

French take Gascony, English withdraw from all but the port of Calais, ending the Hundred Years' War.
The king's son Edward is born (October).

1454

Henry VI has mental collapse; duke of York named protector (March); Henry recovers (December).

1455

York dismissed as protector (February).
First Battle of St. Albans (May) sees capture of the king, and the Wars of the Roses begin.

1459

Queen Margaret raises troops; acts of attainder passed against Yorkists; after defeats, the Yorkists flee to Wales, Ireland, and Calais.

1460

Battle of Northampton; Henry VI captured by the Yorkists (July); duke of York returns to England, claims the throne, to succeed Henry VI.
James II of Scotland dies, succeeded by James III.

1461

Queen Margaret leads Lancastrian forces to victory at second Battle of St. Albans, releases Henry VI from captivity (February), but he is deposed and replaced by Edward, earl of March, as Edward IV. This is confirmed by the Yorkist victory at Towton (March).

1465

Henry VI is captured by Edward IV, kept prisoner until 1470.

1468

Norway surrenders Orkneys to Scotland.

1469

Rebellion against Edward IV; earl of Warwick captures the king, but they are reconciled.

1470

Edward challenges Warwick and the duke of Clarence; they flee to France and unite with Queen Margaret (May). The Lancastrians return to England and overthrow Edward (September) and restore Henry VI (October).

1471

Edward returns to England (March), deposes Henry VI (April), and defeats the rebels at the Battle of Barnet, where Warwick is killed. At the Battle of Tewkesbury (May), the Lancastrians are crushed, the son of Henry VI is killed, and later the old king is murdered in the Tower.

1475

Edward allies with Burgundy and invades France. A treaty is signed giving Edward a yearly pension (August).

1477

William Caxton publishes the first book printed in England (*The Sayings of the Philosophers*).

1478

The duke of Clarence is attainted for treason, later murdered secretly in the Tower of London.

1483

Edward IV dies, succeeded by his young son, Edward V. Richard, duke of Gloucester, takes custody of the new king, and is recognized as protector (May). The king and his younger brother are imprisoned in the Tower (June), and after the king is deposed, Gloucester takes the throne as Richard III. The two brothers are presumably murdered in the Tower (August).

1485

Henry Tudor lands in Wales.
At the Battle of Bosworth (August), Richard III is killed and his army defeated.
Coronation of Henry VII (October).

1486

Henry VII marries Elizabeth, daughter of Edward IV, uniting the Yorkist and Lancastrian lines.

1487

The pretender, Lambert Simnel, and his supporters are beaten at the Battle of Stoke.

1488

James III is defeated at the Battle of Sauchieburn, then murdered by his son and successor, James IV.

1489

Treaty of Medina del Campo between Henry VII and Ferdinand of Aragon.

1494

Poynings' Law enacted in Ireland, named after the king's deputy, Sir Edward Poynings. The Irish Parliament shall not meet or adopt legislation without English consent.

1497

Cornish rebellion; march on London in reaction to taxes levied for war with Scotland; rebels beaten and leaders executed.
The pretender Perkin Warbeck lands in Cornwall, is captured later but escapes in 1498.

1499

Warbeck recaptured and executed.

1501

Arthur, Prince of Wales, is married to Catherine of Aragon (November).

1502

James IV of Scotland marries Margaret, daughter of Henry VII.

Arthur, Prince of Wales, dies (April).

1505

Merchant Adventurers Company receives charter from Henry VII giving it a monopoly of cloth export to northern Europe.

1509

Henry VII dies and is succeeded by Henry VIII (April); the new king marries Catherine of Aragon (June).

1510

Richard Empson and Edmund Dudley, hated tax collectors for Henry VII, are charged with treason and executed.

1513

Henry VIII invades France; Scotland allies with France and invades England.

King James IV is killed at the Battle of Flodden and is succeeded by his infant son James V.

1514

Louis XII of France marries Mary Tudor, the king's sister.

1515

Thomas Wolsey made lord chancellor and cardinal.

1518

Wolsey negotiates the Treaty of London, involving England and the major powers of Europe.

1520

The "Field of the Cloth of Gold" meeting between Henry VIII and Francis I of France, where for two weeks the rivals hold jousts in ornate settings while affirming their alliance.

1521

Lutheran books are burned in London.

Henry VIII writes *The Defence of the Seven Sacraments* and is awarded the title "Defender of the Faith" by Pope Leo X.

1522

England goes to war with Scotland and France.

1525

William Tyndale publishes the New Testament in English at Worms. It is publicly burnt in St. Paul's Cathedral in 1526.

1527

Henry VIII appeals to the pope for annulment of his marriage to Catherine.

1529

The "Reformation" Parliament is summoned; complaints against clergy are aired in the House of Commons.

Wolsey loses property and positions, having failed to obtain the royal divorce.

1530

Wolsey is arrested and dies before his trial.

1531

Thomas Cromwell becomes a member of the privy council.

The clergy submit to the king, acknowledging his supreme authority.

1532

Act of Annates seizes revenues normally paid to Rome.

Anne Boleyn involved with the king.

Sir Thomas More resigns as chancellor.

1533

Act in Restraint of Appeals forbids legal appeal to Rome, formulates the king's constitutional position.

Henry VIII secretly marries Anne Boleyn (January), announces the annulment of his marriage to Catherine, declares his marriage to

Anne valid, she is crowned (May), and Princess Elizabeth is born (September).

1534

Act of Succession states that heirs of Henry and Anne Boleyn will succeed to the throne, and any who oppose the law are traitors.

Act of Supremacy formally recognizes the king's full power over the Church of England.

1535

Thomas Cromwell initiates the *valor ecclesiasticus,* a visitation of all monastic houses to assess their property and their performance.

Execution of Sir Thomas More and Bishop John Fisher for refusing to take the oath of succession (June).

1536

Dissolution of monasteries with incomes below £200. There is widespread public resistance, especially the Pilgrimage of Grace in northern England. The government subdues the revolt, executes its leaders, and creates a Council of the North to increase the king's authority there.

Anne Boleyn accused of treason and executed; her marriage is declared invalid. Henry VIII marries Jane Seymour 11 days after the execution.

Act of Union with Wales states in principle that the laws and government of Wales shall be the same as England. English law is to be followed, and five new shires are added to those of the principality, each to be represented in Parliament.

1537

The bible translation of Miles Coverdale is licensed by the Crown.

Jane Seymour dies, having given birth to a son, Edward.

1538

Thomas Cromwell issues injunctions to clergy to keep registers of baptisms, weddings, and burials for each parish.

1539

Dissolution of remaining monasteries.

Six articles: points of Catholic doctrine considered essential are established in an effort to retard the spread of Protestantism.

1540

Henry VIII marries Anne of Cleves (January) but the marriage is soon annulled (July) and Thomas Cromwell is attainted and executed.

Henry marries Catherine Howard (August).

1541

Henry VIII claims title of king of Ireland.

1542

Battle of Solway Moss. English raid is countered by a Scottish invasion, but a much smaller English force routs the invaders.

King James V dies after the birth of his daughter, Mary, Queen of Scots.

1543

Treaty of Greenwich signed, providing for marriage of Mary, Queen of Scots, and Prince Edward. The Scottish parliament repudiates the treaty and affirms the French alliance.

Henry VIII marries Catherine Parr.

1544

England invades France, and war resumes with Scotland.

Edinburgh is attacked and burned.

1546

Peace of Ardres ends fighting between England and France.

Murder of Cardinal Beaton at St. Andrews.

1547

Henry VIII dies and is succeeded by Edward VI. A regency council is meant to rule on his behalf, but Edward Seymour, the king's uncle, assumes the title Lord Protector and duke of Somerset.

Fighting in Scotland; the English win the Battle of Pinkie and capture Edinburgh.

1549

The first Book of Common Prayer is adopted, part of a growing Protestant reform campaign.

Kett's rebellion, a protest over economic grievances like enclosure of land, is beaten by royal forces and leaders are executed.

Somerset is removed as protector and imprisoned; John Dudley, earl of Warwick (later duke of Northumberland) becomes the new protector.

1552

The second Book of Common Prayer further advances the Protestant reform.

1553

The 42 Articles of religion drafted by Thomas Cranmer are published. Edward VI dies. Lady Jane Grey is proclaimed queen by the late king's will, but Mary Tudor eludes capture and raises forces to march on London. Lady Jane is deposed and Mary becomes queen. Mary repeals acts of Protestant reform and restores much of the traditional church.

1554

Wyatt's rebellion, triggered by Mary's plan to marry Philip of Spain. Thomas Wyatt captured and executed. Princess Elizabeth, suspected of involvement, is imprisoned in the Tower of London.

The pope is recognized as head of the English church.

1555

Trials of protestants for heresy. Leading protestants burned at the stake include Hugh Latimer and Nicholas Ridley.

1556

Thomas Cranmer is burnt at the stake.

1558

Mary dies and is succeeded by Elizabeth I.

1559

Elizabeth's church settlement includes restoration of the prayer book, the vernacular Bible, and closing of the monastic houses restored by Mary. Elizabeth becomes "supreme governor" of the church under a new Act of Supremacy.

Treaty of Cateau-Cambrésis brings peace between England and France.

1560

Lords of the Congregation in Scotland lead a popular reformation movement.

Treaty of Berwick is agreed between Elizabeth and Scottish reformers.

Treaty of Edinburgh between England, France, and Scotland arranges withdrawal of French troops and promises English noninterference.

1561

Mary, Queen of Scots, returns to Scotland after the death of her husband, Francis II of France.

The *Book of Discipline,* composed by John Knox, sets up a new church constitution in Scotland.

1562

Shane O'Neill comes to London, submits to Elizabeth.

Tyrone's rebellion in Ireland.

John Hawkins enters the slave trade.

1563

Thirty-nine Articles of religion adopted.

Statute of Apprentices gives justices of the peace power to set wages.

John Foxe's *Acts and Monuments* (alias *Book of Martyrs*) published.

1564

Peace of Troyes ends fighting between England and France.

1565

Tobacco introduced.

Royal College of Physicians allowed to conduct dissections of humans.

1566

Archbishop Matthew Parker's *Advertisements* enjoins the use of the cope and surplice, vestments denounced by some Puritans.

Thomas Gresham, the royal agent in Antwerp, begins construction of the Royal Exchange.

1567

Lord Darnley, husband of Mary, Queen of Scots, is murdered. She is abducted by the earl of Bothwell, and they are later married. Mary surrenders to opposing forces and abdicates in July. The earl of Moray is made regent to her infant son James VI.

William Salesbury translates the New Testament into Welsh.

1568

Mary, Queen of Scots, escapes confinement, but her forces are routed and she flees to England, where she is imprisoned in Carlisle Castle.

Archbishop Parker's new translation, the "Bishops' Bible," introduced.

William Allen founds college at Douai for English Catholics.

1569

Desmond rebellion in Ireland.

Northern rebellion led by earls of Northumberland and Westmorland tries to restore the Catholic faith and to arrange a dynastic marriage between the duke of Norfolk and Mary, Queen of Scots. Rebels are beaten and retreat into Scotland.

1570

Civil war in Scotland; the earl of Lennox replaces Moray as regent.

Elizabeth is excommunicated and declared deposed by Pope Pius V.

1571

Ridolfi plot aims at deposition of Elizabeth, replacing her with Mary. The plot is exposed, leading to executions of duke of Norfolk and earl of Westmorland.

1573

Desmond rebellion is crushed.

Pacification of Perth sees the end of fighting in Scotland and the end of threats to Elizabeth from that country.

Sir Francis Drake captures a shipment of Spanish silver in Panama.

1576

Peter Wentworth, staunch Puritan spokesman, claims that free speech in the Commons is denied, and he is sent to the Tower.

Edmund Grindal is made archbishop of Canterbury, but he refuses to abolish "prophesyings"—informal discussions of doctrine and scripture by Puritan congregations.

Martin Frobisher explores Canada in the course of his search for a northwest passage.

1577

Archbishop Grindal is suspended for continuing to refuse to ban prophesyings.

1578

Sir Humphrey Gilbert, with a patent to settle North America, conducts an unsuccessful expedition with Sir Walter Raleigh.

James VI assumes personal rule in Scotland.

1579

The Eastland Company chartered to trade with Scandinavia.

Duke of Anjou proposes marriage to Queen Elizabeth.

Munster rebellion in Ireland.

1580

Jesuit missionaries arrive in England.

Sir Francis Drake returns from his around-the-world voyage in the *Golden Hind*.

1581

Edmund Campion, Jesuit missionary, is executed.

1582

Sir Humphrey Gilbert reaches Newfoundland.

James VI captured by Protestant nobles who fear his Catholic favorites (the "Ruthven Raid").

1583

Sir Walter Raleigh lands in North America in what will later be Virginia.

Munster plantation begins.

Francis Throckmorton's plot to replace Elizabeth with Mary, Queen of Scots, is exposed; he is executed in 1584.

James VI escapes from his captors.

1584

Raleigh founds a colony on Roanoke Island.

Parliament forms "the Association" to root out conspiracies against the queen.

1585

War with Spain.

1586

Babington plot exposed; Mary, Queen of Scots, implicated, but her sentence is delayed.

Treaty between Elizabeth and James VI recognizes his right to succeed to the English throne and grants him a pension.

1587

Sir Francis Drake raids Spanish shipping.

Mary, Queen of Scots, is executed for her involvement in the Babington plot.

1588

The Spanish Armada sails (May) and attempts to rendezvous with the army of the duke of Parma in the Netherlands. English sailors disrupt the plan and defeat the Spanish fleet (August), forcing it to make a return voyage around the north coast of the British Isles.

William Morgan's Welsh translation of the New Testament is published.

1594

Hugh O'Neill leads a rebellion in Ulster, appeals for help from Spain.

1595

In a search for El Dorado, Raleigh explores the Orinoco.

Hawkins and Drake sail for the West Indies, but both die on the voyage.

1596

The English sack Cadiz; Spanish forces take Calais.

1597

The first poor law is enacted as the country is in the midst of prolonged agricultural distress.

1598

An act to establish workhouses and punish beggars passes.

English forces are defeated at the Battle of the Yellow Ford in Ulster.

1599

Tyrone's rebellion in Ulster. Robert Devereaux, earl of Essex, is made lord lieutenant of Ireland. Essex is defeated by Tyrone at Arklow, signs a truce, and returns to England. This action leads to arrest and banishment for Essex.

1600

Essex is tried for his conduct in Ireland, and he is deprived of offices.

William Gilbert discovers earth's magnetic field.

Charles Blount, Lord Mountjoy, is new lord lieutenant in Ireland.

Conspiracy to murder James VI is thwarted.

Charter is granted to the East India Company.

1601

Monopolies are abolished.

Poor law codifies legislation on poor relief.

Spanish fleet arrives to aid the rebels in Ireland, but it lands at Kinsale. A siege by Lord Mountjoy defeats the invaders, despite a relief force from Ulster led by Hugh O'Neill.

Earl of Essex rebels in London, is defeated and executed.

1603

Queen Elizabeth dies. James VI of Scotland succeeds as James I of England. His coronation is in July. There are plots against him: Sir Walter Raleigh is implicated in the Main Plot; Cobham's plot is to replace James with Arabella Stuart. Both Raleigh and Cobham are imprisoned.

1604

Treaty of London ends the war between England and Spain.

The Hampton Court Conference convenes to resolve church issues raised by puritans, but James I takes a conservative position on most matters.

A new translation of the Bible is authorized.

Parliament begins debate of the king's proposals for the union of England and Scotland.

1605

The Gunpowder Plot is exposed; Guy Fawkes and fellow conspirators planned to blow up the Houses of Parliament while the king met with the lords and commons in an opening session (November). The plotters are apprehended, tortured, and executed.

1606

The Virginia Company is chartered.

The Union Jack (combining the crosses of St. Andrew and St. George) is adopted as the flag of the kingdom of Great Britain, so named by James I.

1607

The English and Scottish parliaments reject the proposed union.

Calvin's Case affirms common citizenship for English and Scots born after James's accession to the English throne.

Flight of the Earls: earls of Tyrone and Tyrconnel go into exile with a small group of family and followers, rather than submit to English rule in Ulster (September).

First American colonial settlement established at Jamestown.

1610

Disputes over royal finances lead to the Great Contract, drafted by Robert Cecil, the lord treasurer. In exchange for a regular income, the king would surrender old feudal rights such as wardship. After bitter debates, the project fails.

1611

The King James Bible is printed.

The order of baronet (hereditary knighthood) created and sold by the crown.

1612

Prince Henry, the king's eldest son, dies.

1613

Sir Thomas Overbury is murdered; Robert Carr the king's favorite, is later accused of the murder.

1614

The "Addled" Parliament, King James's second parliament, meets and is bogged down by disputes over impositions.

1616

The king's continuing heavy expenditure and limited revenues produce extreme measures like the sale of peerages.

1620

The king begins negotiations with Spain for the marriage of his son Charles and the princess the Infanta Maria.

Pilgrims land at Plymouth, Massachusetts.

1621

Parliament is summoned, and it debates the policy of marital alliance with Spain as well as the tender issues of religious belief and royal finance.

1622

Prince Charles and Lord Buckingham travel to Spain to seek the hand of the princess.

1623

The prince's mission fails; the princess rejects him, and her father insists on Charles's conversion to Catholicism. Charles and Buckingham return and now seek war against Spain.

1624

A new Parliament resists delaring war on Spain, votes a ban on monopolies, impeaches the lord treasurer, Lionel Cranfield.

Treaty with France arranges the marriage of Charles and the Princess Henrietta Maria.

1625

James I dies and is succeeded by Charles I (March). The new king is married to his French princess (May). Due to the plague, the king's first Parliament adjourns to Oxford.

1626

The second Parliament of Charles impeaches Lord Buckingham, and Charles retaliates by arresting the leaders of the impeachment. Parliament insists on their release, which Charles grants.

The king begins to sell knighthoods as a source of revenue.

A forced loan is imposed on all taxpayers, provoking hostility.

1627

War with France; a failed expedition to La Rochelle to help French Huguenots is led by Buckingham.

Five knights are imprisoned for refusing to pay the forced loan, claiming that only Parliament should levy taxes. When they seek bail, arguing that no cause of detention had been given, the court rules against them.

Colonists settle on Barbados.

1628

Parliament debates the Petition of Right, insisting that there should be no taxation unless endorsed by Parliament, nor any arbitrary arrest or forced billeting or martial law. Charles accepts the petition, claiming that it only contained existing "rights and liberties."

1629

The king's opponents in the House of Commons insist on continuing discussion of finance and other issues. The king dissolves Parliament, but several members hold the Speaker in his chair, preventing him from announcing the dissolution, while they read out a set of resolutions containing their grievances. The king orders the arrest of these members and decides not to summon another parliament.

1630

Charles I uses distraint of knighthood, a feudal levy, to raise funds from the gentry.

1631

Colonists settle on St. Kitts.

1632

Colony of Maryland is founded, and Antigua is colonized.

1633

William Prynne is convicted by the Star Chamber; his book *Historio-mastix* is burnt by the hangman; his ears are cropped.

Thomas Wentworth, earl of Strafford, becomes lord deputy of Ireland.

William Laud becomes archbishop of Canterbury.

Charles visits Scotland, has coronation in Edinburgh.

1634

The medieval levy of ship money is revived as a means to raise revenue.

1635

Foundation of Rhode Island.

1636

Foundation of Connecticut.

1637

John Hampden refuses to pay ship money. The legality of the tax is upheld in court, but the returns begin to decline.

Scottish Prayer Book is introduced, arousing opposition.

1638

Scottish National Covenant is composed; it recites the founding documents of the reformed kirk, which signers vow to support.

A General Assembly meets in Glasgow and abolishes the office of bishop.

Scots form an army.

1639

Charles sends an army to Scotland; it meets the Scots at Berwick, where an agreement is signed. The first "Bishops' War" ends without fighting.

1640

Charles recalls Lord Strafford from Ireland and makes him chief adviser.

Parliament is summoned for the first time since 1629; for several weeks there is little but acrimonious debate, and Charles dissolves the session.

The second Bishops' War begins when Scots cross into England, defeat the English at Newburn, and occupy northern England.

Treaty of Ripon (October) provides payment to the Scottish army until a settlement can be made.

Charles is forced to summon another parliament in November.

Impeachment of Lord Strafford and Archbishop Laud.

1641

The Triennial Act provides that a parliament must be called every three years, and it must remain in session for 50 days.

Trial of Lord Strafford begins (March); leaders of the Commons change the procedure to a bill of attainder, which Charles signs, and Strafford is executed in May.

The prerogative courts—Star Chamber, High Commission, and the Court of Requests—are abolished. The Privy Council is deprived of judicial authority, thus limiting royal power and enhancing that of Parliament and the common law courts.

Rebellion in Ulster causes death of many Protestants and panic in London.

1642

Charles orders the arrest of five leaders of the House of Commons; the Commons refuses to give them up, and the king enters the House to arrest them. The leaders have hidden and later are protected by the London authorities.

Charles withdraws from London. Parliament enacts legislation to take control of the army, but Charles refuses to sign. Both sides prepare for war.

Charles raises the royal standard at Nottingham (August), signaling a state of war.

Battle of Edgehill (October), the first of the Civil War, is indecisive.

Royal army moves toward London, is repulsed at Turnham Green (November).

1643

The king makes his headquarters at Oxford. A three-pronged assault is planned, to the west country, toward London, and to the southeast. Prince Rupert takes Bristol, but other battles are inconclusive.

Parliament agrees to the Solemn League and Covenant with the Scots (September), promising to adopt a Presbyterian settlement in exchange for the support of a Scottish army.

Westminster Assembly convened to reform the church; it produces the Directory of Worship and the Westminster Confession.

1644

The Committee of Both Kingdoms is formed to direct the war (February).

The Battle of Marston Moor (July) is won by the allied armies.

The earl of Essex loses his army in Battle of Lost-
withiel (Cornwall).

Lord Montrose leads royalist highland forces on
victorious campaign in Scotland.

1645

Archbishop Laud is convicted by an act of attainder and executed (January).

Parliament passes the self-denying ordinance,
removing peers and members of Parliament
from military command (April).

The army is constituted on a "new model." Fairfax becomes commander.

The Battle of Naseby (June) brings defeat to main
royalist army.

Lord Montrose is defeated at Philiphaugh (September).

1646

Charles I surrenders to the Scots at Newark (May).

1647

The Scots hand Charles over to Parliament for
£400,000 (January).

Parliament disbands the army without settling
arrears of pay.

Army units seize the king (June).

Army enters London (August).

Putney Debates (October); army council debates
the Leveller constitution, "The Agreement of
the People."

Charles, in captivity on the Isle of Wight, signs a
treaty with Scottish supporters who commit
to restoring him by force (December).

1648

Scottish force enters England, beginning the
"second civil war" (July).

Battle of Preston (August): Oliver Cromwell defeats the Scots under the duke of Hamilton.

Charles is again taken captive by the army (December).

Pride's Purge: the Presbyterian majority of Parliament is excluded, the remaining "Rump" parliament has about 60 members, loyal to the army.
Parliament forms a special court to try the king.

1649

Trial of Charles I. Accused of treason, the king is
allowed no witnesses but makes a sturdy defense of his innocence and a powerful denunciation of the court conducting his trial.
The king is executed on January 30th.

Charles II is proclaimed in Edinburgh.

The monarchy and the House of Lords are formally abolished by the Rump. A Council of
State consisting of army officers and leaders of
the Rump forms a new government.

Cromwell leads an invasion of Ireland; the anni-
hilation of the garrison at Drogheda (September) marks a low point in English military
annals.

1650

Lord Montrose returns to Scotland, is defeated,
captured, and executed (April).

Charles II comes to Scotland, accepts the covenant, and is proclaimed king (June).

Cromwell invades Scotland, wins the Battle of
Dunbar (September).

1651

Coronation of Charles II at Scone (January).

Charles marches into northwestern England
(January).

After his defeat at the Battle of Worcester (September), Charles escapes to France.

Navigation Act, aimed at Dutch shipping, pre-
cipitates Anglo-Dutch war (October).

1653

Cromwell dissolves the Rump (April), replacing
it with a nominated parliament. This "Bare-
bones" Parliament takes its nickname from
"Praise-God" Barbon, a London preacher. A
collection of Independent ministers, its sessions are just as hard to control as those of its
predecessors.

Cromwell dissolves the Parliament and takes the
title of Lord Protector, governing with a
Council of State and occasional parliaments,
which now have members from each of the
three kingdoms (December).

1654

Treaty of Westminster ends the Anglo-Dutch war.

1655

Cromwell dissolves Parliament, and England is divided into 11 districts, each governed by a major-general (January).

Penruddock's rebellion in the west country fails (March).

1656

English expedition to Jamaica provokes war with Spain (February).

Second Protectorate Parliament meets (September).

1657

The Humble Petition and Advice offers the crown to Cromwell. He rejects the title, but names members to a new "upper house" of Parliament (March-June).

1658

Third Protectorate Parliament meets, but Cromwell dismisses it after two weeks (February).

Oliver Cromwell dies of pneumonia (September) and is succeeded by his son Richard.

1659

Richard Cromwell meets his first Parliament; disputes between that body and the army disrupt the session. It is dissolved in April.

Rump parliament restored (May).

Richard resigns title of protector.

Rump Parliament is expelled by the army (October), and a series of military coups lead to restoration of the Rump in December.

1660

General George Monck, the commander of the army in Scotland, leads his troops into London. He reconvenes the Long Parliament (February), which dissolves itself (March).

Charles issues the Declaration of Breda (April), promising a lawful settlement and some religious toleration.

Election held for a Convention Parliament to consider the king's restoration (April).

The Convention Parliament invites Charles to return; he is restored (May) to popular rejoicing. The army is disbanded, its arrears having been paid.

Parliament passes acts of indemnity and oblivion, restoring much of the land lost during the war.

1661

Charles summons a new parliament, to be known as the "Cavalier" Parliament.

The Church of England is restored, and parliament enacts strict controls, later dubbed the "Clarendon Code," after the king's first minister, the earl of Clarendon. The first of these is the Corporation Act, which requires a religious test for any elected member of a borough corporation.

1662

Act of Uniformity requires clergy to accept the prayer book. About 2,000 refuse and are ejected from the church.

Settlement Act says paupers may be returned to their parish of settlement.

Licensing Act requires books on theology to be approved by church.

Quaker Act penalizes Quaker meetings.

Charter granted to the Royal Society, the first body devoted to scientific investigation.

1664

The colony of New Jersey is established.

1665

Second Dutch War (March).

Plague in London; Parliament adjourns to Oxford (June).

Five Mile Act excludes dissenting ministers from towns.

1666

War with France (January).

Great Fire of London destroys large parts of central city (September).

Covenanters' revolt is crushed at the Battle of Pentland Hills (November).

1667

Dutch fleet sails into anchorage in the Medway and tows off the British flagship (June)

Dutch war ends with Treaty of Breda (July).

Clarendon falls, is impeached, and goes into exile (August–November).

New ministry is formed, known as the CABAL, for initials of its leaders: Clifford, Arlington, Buckingham, Ashley, and Lauderdale.

1668

Triple Alliance (Sweden, Holland, and England) is formed against Louis XIV (February).

1670

Founding of North and South Carolina.

Treaty of Dover with France. The public treaty pledged English support against Holland; the secret clause of the treaty said that Charles would announce his conversion to Catholicism, and Louis would provide a subsidy and an army to put down resistance (June).

1672

Stop of the Exchequer; Charles II defaults on loans (January).

Declaration of Indulgence (March).

War with the Dutch (May).

1673

The Dutch defeat English and French invasion attempts; Parliament passes the Test Act, driving Catholics and dissenters from public office by requiring religious oaths (April). James, the duke of York, resigns his post as lord high admiral rather than take the oath (June). He thus discloses his Catholic conversion. The duke then marries Mary of Modena, a Catholic princess (October).

1674

Treaty of Westminster ends the third Dutch war. The Dutch agree to pay an indemnity, and the English take control of New Amsterdam, thereafter New York (February).

1675

Founding of the Royal Observatory at Greenwich.

1678

Alliance between England and Holland (July).

The "Popish Plot" is revealed: Titus Oates and Israel Tonge report a conspiracy to assassinate the king and replace him with James, the duke of York, and a Catholic government (August). Amid general panic, Parliament bars Catholic members and conducts investigations which lead to the trial and conviction of many alleged conspirators.

The king's chief minister, Thomas Osborne, Lord Danby, resigns, is attainted, and imprisoned.

A movement begins to exclude James from the royal succession.

1679

Charles II dissolves the Cavalier Parliament and summons a new one (January).

Murder of Archbishop Sharpe near St. Andrews (May).

The Habeas Corpus Act promises the writ to all eligible prisoners (May).

Exclusion bill introduced into Parliament, leading to dissolution (May).

Rebellion of Scottish covenanters defeated at Bothwell Bridge (June).

1680

Petitions to exclude James are collected by Lord Shaftesbury. Those who sign or support them are called "Whigs." Their opponents are called "Tories."

Charles dissolves his third Parliament and summons another.

New Hampshire is founded.

The Scottish Cameronians denounce the king; their leaders are killed.

1681

Founding of Pennsylvania.

Charles summons his last Parliament, dissolves it when another exclusion bill is introduced (March).

Oliver Plunket, archbishop of Armagh, is accused in the Popish Plot and executed (July).

Lord Shaftesbury is prosecuted for treason; a London grand jury fails to indict, and he goes into exile (July–November).

1682

Edmund Halley observes and identifies the comet that comes to bear his name.

1683

The Rye House Plot—a plan to seize Charles II—is discovered (June).

The Whigs engaged in this plot are apprehended; Lord William Russell and Algernon Sidney are executed.

1685

Titus Oates (of the Popish Plot) is convicted of perjury and sentenced to life in prison.

King Charles II dies (February) and is succeeded by his brother James VII and II. The first parliament of James II makes generous and longterm grants of revenues.

Rebellion by the duke of Monmouth (England) and the earl of Argyll (Scotland) fails; both are executed (June–July).

The "Bloody Assizes" are held in western England, where George Jeffreys sentences several hundred of Monmouth's supporters to death. Many hundreds more are transported.

1686

James II begins a campaign of revising laws and charters in favor of Roman Catholics

Case of *Godden v. Hales* allows a Catholic to hold an army commission.

The Court of King's Bench rules that the king has the power to dispense with the Test Act.

Ecclesiastical commissions are established by James to administer discipline in the church, even though such a body had been declared illegal.

1687

James expels the Fellows of Magdalen College, Oxford, when they refuse to appoint a Catholic as president.

James appoints a Catholic as admiral of the fleet.

The king issues a declaration of indulgence, dispensing with the penal laws against Catholics.

1688

James issues another declaration of indulgence, stating his wish that "all the people of our dominions were members of the Catholic church." He orders this declaration read from all the pulpits, and when seven bishops petition him, pointing out that this will force them to violate the Test Act, he charges them with sedition.

A son is born to James (June 10), guaranteeing a Catholic successor.

The Seven Bishops are acquitted by a London jury (June 30).

A group of Whig and Tory leaders ask William of Orange to come to England to protect "their religion, liberties and properties" (July). William accepts the invitation (September), and James begins to retract some of his measures, but it is too late.

William lands in the southwest, at Torbay (November 5).

James flees into exile, having been unable to mount an effective resistance to William, who enters London in December.

1689

A Convention Parliament meets (January) to debate the terms of the new settlement. There is much discussion of whether James "abdicated" or was deposed. The crown is offered to Mary, with William as regent, but he rejects this, and they are offered the crown jointly (February).

With the crown comes a declaration of rights, listing James's errors: suspending and dispensing with laws, punishing petitioners, maintaining an army without the consent of Parliament. In addition, several principles are stated: elections shall be free, Parliaments shall meet frequently, there shall be freedom of speech in Parliament, and Parliament must consent to any taxation or to the formation of an army.

Scottish estates meet in convention (March) and recognize William and Mary, presenting a "Claim of Right" stating that James has been deposed, and that the office of bishop is a grievance.

In Ireland, a Catholic "Patriot Parliament" is chosen, and it welcomes the arrival of James from exile (March). Protestants loyal to William gather in the north.

Coronation of William and Mary (April).

Toleration Act removes religious disabilities of dissenters (May).

War with France (May).

Mutiny Act provides basis for exercise of military discipline, but its term is limited to six months (June).

Siege of Londonderry is lifted (July 28); James retreats to Dublin.

William sends army to Ireland under General Schomberg (August).

1690

William lands in Ireland (June), faces James at the Battle of the Boyne on July 1. The armies number about 25,000, and the Williamite forces seize victory with an assault across the river. The casualties are not heavy, but the result is decisive. James quickly leaves and returns to exile, but warfare continues until October 1691.

1691

William's army continues the campaign in southern Ireland, wins Battle of Aughrim (July 12), and besieges Limerick.

Treaty of Limerick marks the end of the war (October), allows the French troops to leave, and promises lenient treatment for Catholics—promises the Irish Parliament will later ignore.

1692

Massacre of Glencoe. Clan MacDonald had not submitted to King William before a deadline, and the Campbells kill many of their traditional enemies in a treacherous manner (February).

French plan invasion, but their fleet is destroyed at Cap de la Hogue (May).

1694

The Bank of England is incorporated by act of Parliament. It provides finance for the wars with France, initially raising £1.2 million, which is loaned to the government at 8 percent interest. Parliament has to approve any loans to the Crown, and it is responsible for raising the revenue to pay interest on the debt. This financial revolution establishes the basis for growing economic power.

Triennial Act requires a new Parliament to be elected every three years.

1695

The Bank of Scotland is founded.

1696

A plot to assassinate the king is discovered; Sir John Fenwick and others are arrested (June).

Treason Act requires two witnesses, allows prisoner counsel and a copy of the indictment.

Committee of Trade and Plantations (Board of Trade) founded.

Act for Settling Schools requires every Scottish parish to establish a school and landowners to pay for a schoolmaster.

1697

Sir John Fenwick is condemned by act of attainder (January).

Treaty of Ryswick between England and France ends the Nine Years' War. Louis XIV recognizes William as king and makes minor territorial concessions (September).

Rebuilt St. Paul's Cathedral is opened.

1698

London Stock Exchange founded, the number of licensed brokers is limited to 100.

1699

Company of Scotland's settlement at Darien (Panama) fails due to English intervention, Spanish opposition, and local problems in the colony. The large investment loss is a serious blow to the Scottish economy.

1701

Act of Settlement prescribes the royal succession after Princess Anne to be the Protestant descendants of the Electress Sophia of Hanover, the granddaughter of James I.

Louis XIV declares his grandson Philip the king of Spain, beginning the War of Spanish Succession.

William forms a Grand Alliance with the United Provinces and Austria to fight the French.

Former King James II dies; his son James Edward (the Old Pretender) is recognized as king of England, Scotland, and Ireland by Louis XIV.

1702

William III dies after a riding accident. Queen Anne succeeds him.

The first daily newspaper, the *Daily Courant,* is published in London.

John Churchill is made captain-general of English forces; a series of victories in the wars against Louis XIV gains him the title duke of Marlborough.

1703

Scottish parliament passes Act Anent Peace and War, claiming power to make separate decisions on peace and war under the next sovereign.

Methuen Treaty with Portugal; English wool and Portuguese wine are given preferential status.

1704

British forces capture Gibraltar (July).

Battle of Blenheim: Marlborough leads coalition forces to victory over France (August).

Scottish Parliament passes the Act of Security, which claims that the Scottish succession should not follow that of England but be determined in the Scottish Parliament.

Act for Preventing the Growth of Popery limits inheritance by Catholics.

1705

Alien Act by the English Parliament sets a deadline of December for Scots to begin negotiation for union, or be declared aliens in English law, thus losing rights to property and trade.

1706

Battle of Ramillies in Belgium, where Marlborough defeats the Franco-Spanish forces, ending the threat to the Netherlands and seizing the offensive against France (May).

Queen Anne appoints English and Scottish commissioners to negotiate terms of union. Treaty signed (July), and acts of ratification are passed in Scotland and England. The countries retain separate legal systems and established churches.

1707

Parliament of Great Britain meets for the first time, with 45 Scottish MPs and 16 elected peers added to the English Parliament.

1708

Jacobite invasion attempt, with French assistance, is defeated.

Battle of Oudenarde (July), another victory for Marlborough.

1709

Tatler begins publication (April).

1710

Dr. Henry Sacheverell is impeached for a sermon attacking Whig ministers for their support of dissenters. During his trial rioting breaks out in London, and half a dozen dissenting chapels are burned down (March).

1711

Formation of the South Sea Company.

Occasional Conformity Act tries to prohibit dissenters from qualifying for public office by taking Anglican communion.

Spectator begins publication (March).

1712
Newcomen's steam engine is invented.

1713
Treaty of Utrecht ends the War of Spanish Succession: France and Spain recognize the Hanoverian succession; Britain obtains Gibraltar and Minorca, Hudson's Bay, Nova Scotia, and Newfoundland; Spain surrenders lands in the Netherlands and Italy, and grants Britain the right to supply negro slaves to the Spanish empire (the *asiento*) (April–July).

1714
Schism Act requires licensed schoolmasters who are Anglican, but after the Tories leave office, it is not enforced.

Queen Anne dies, succeeded by George I (August), who arrives in England from Hanover in September. He installs a Whig ministry under Lord Stanhope.

Parliament enacts a prize of £20,000 for the measurement of longitude.

1715
Impeachment of the earl of Harley and Viscount Bolingbroke (March).

Riot Act passes (July) allowing justices of the peace to order dispersal of public meetings, which if disobeyed makes the participants guilty of felony and subject to the death penalty. The Act is triggered by the prospect of Jacobite rebellion.

The earl of Mar collects an army of 10,000 Highlanders, but they are stopped at Stirling by the duke of Argyll, and a small uprising in Lancashire is beaten (November). The belated landing of the pretender, James Francis Edward Stuart (December), is followed quickly by his return to exile.

1716
Leaders of the rebellion executed at Preston (February); forfeiture of estates enacted.

Septennial Act extends the life of a Parliament from three to seven years (May).

Mutual defense treaties with Austria and France.

1717
Triple Alliance with Britain, France, and Holland to uphold the Treaty of Utrecht is formed.

Meetings of the convocations of the Church of England are suspended.

A sinking fund is adopted; surplus government revenue is to be used to retire old debts and interest.

1718
Repeal of the Occasional Conformity and Schism Acts.

Quadruple Alliance of Britain, France, the Holy Roman Empire, and Holland against Spain is formed. Fleet is dispatched to Sicily, where it destroys the Spanish fleet.

1719
Spanish troops invade Scotland in support of the pretender, but they are beaten at Glenshiel (June).

Peerage Bill proposes to limit new creations and increase in Scottish representation; defeated in the House of Commons (December).

1720
Peace with Spain (January).

House of Commons accepts South Sea Company proposal to take over three-fifths of the national debt in exchange for exclusive trading rights (February).

South Sea shares reach highest level (June) but then collapse (August), causing heavy losses to investors. Robert Walpole engineers a plan to restore public credit, a committee investigates the company, and directors are expelled from the House of Commons.

Declaratory Act asserts British Parliament's power over that of Ireland and orders all legal appeals from Ireland to be heard in the British House of Lords.

1721
Walpole forms ministry. (Lord Townshend and John Carteret are secretaries of state).

1722

Francis Atterbury plot is discovered; Jacobites arrested (May). Parliament suspends habeas corpus and levies penal taxes on Catholics and nonjurors (October). Bishop Atterbury is banished.

1725

Treaty of Hanover between Britain, France, and Prussia.

1727

George I dies, succeeded by George II, who recalls Robert Walpole to lead the ministry.

Walpole introduces the first annual indemnity bill, to allow dissenters to avoid penalties in the Test and Corporation Acts.

1729

Treaty of Seville; Spain confirms *asiento* and cedes Gibraltar to England.

John Wesley and friends begin meeting in a strict religious society at Oxford, called "methodists."

1731

Treaty of Vienna. The Ostend East India Company is disbanded.

Captain Robert Jenkins loses an ear in a skirmish with Spanish authorities.

1732

Founding of the colony of Georgia.

Covent Garden Opera House opens.

1733

John Kay invents the flying shuttle.

Uproar over Walpole's excise bill (March). He offers to resign, later drops his scheme.

Molasses Act bans trade between the West Indies and the mainland colonies.

1734

Anglo-Russian trade treaty.

General election; Walpole wins a majority.

John Harrison produces his first marine chronometer.

1736

Riots in Edinburgh after the hanging of a smuggler, and Captain John Porteus allegedly orders the Town Guard to fire on the mob. He is charged with murder, sentenced to die, given a reprieve, and then lynched by another mob.

1737

Licensing Act submits all plays to censorship by the Lord Chamberlain.

Frederick, Prince of Wales, argues with his father and openly supports the opposition in Parliament.

1738

John Wesley returns from America, comes under the influence of the Moravian church.

George Whitefield begins missionary work in America.

1739

Agitation for war with Spain finally forces Walpole to adopt that policy; complaints of Spanish harassment lead to the "War of Jenkins' Ear."

Capture of Porto Bello by Admiral Edward Vernon (November).

John Wesley begins open-air preaching, attracting very large numbers. He employs lay preachers and begins building chapels.

1741

A motion to dismiss Walpole loses by 184 votes (February).

In a general election, Walpole's majority falls to 20 seats (April).

When Parliament reconvenes, Walpole loses in a series of votes (December).

1742

Walpole resigns and is replaced by John Carteret (February).

Britain allies with Prussia, supports Austria in the War of Austrian Succession, which had begun in 1740.

1743

Battle of Dettingen: when a British force is trapped by the French near the Main River, it is able to fight its way out. King George II is in the battle, the last time a British monarch personally fights in war (June).

Henry Pelham becomes first lord of the treasury.

1744

France declares war on Britain (March).

George Anson returns from his circumnavigation of the globe.

Carteret resigns from office and is replaced by Henry Pelham (November).

First Methodist conference in London.

1745

Battle of Fontenoy: the duke of Cumberland is defeated by Marshall Saxe (May).

Charles Edward Stuart ("Bonnie Prince Charlie") lands in Scotland and proclaims his father as king ("James VIII") (July). Highlanders support the prince, and he enters Edinburgh in September. Ten days later his army defeats an English force at Prestonpans. The Jacobites invade England. Prince Charles reaches Derby, but finding little support in England, he decides to retreat (December).

1746

Charles wins the Battle of Falkirk (January), retreats to Inverness (February), and faces the enemy at the Battle of Culloden (April). The duke of Cumberland takes command, and he defeats the smaller and lightly armed highlanders. Charles, who is commanding for the first time, flees the field and goes into exile. His troops are pursued and brutally dispatched. Later there are acts to ban the tartan, prohibit arms to highlanders, and end their hereditary jurisdictions. These were in addition to the usual executions and forfeitures.

1748

Treaty of Aix-la-Chapelle ends the War of Austrian Succession.

1750

Robert Clive captures Arcot.

The Bank of England assumes responsibility for the national debt.

1751

Clive defends Arcot against the French and secures control of southern India.

Frederick, Prince of Wales, is hit by a cricket ball and dies (March).

Gregorian calendar adopted: years begins on January 1 instead of March 25; 11 days will be omitted from the calendar between September 3 and 14, 1752, in order to conform to the new calendar.

1753

Jewish Naturalization Act passes, but there is strong popular resistance, and the act is repealed in 1754.

Lord Hardwicke's Marriage Act requires a license to marry and requires the banns of marriage to be published on three successive Sundays, in an effort to prevent clandestine marriages.

Government purchases the collection of antiquities of Sir Hans Sloane, thus beginning the formation of the British Museum.

1754

Henry Pelham dies, is replaced by Thomas Pelham, duke of Newcastle, as head of the ministry.

First iron rolling mill opened at Fareham.

Joseph Black discovers carbonic gas.

1756

War declared against France in May, beginning the Seven Years' War.

Admiral Byng sent to relieve Minorca, but fails (June).

In Calcutta the native ruler attacks the British; imprisonment in the "Black Hole of Calcutta" draws reprisals (June).

Henry Fox and the duke of Newcastle resign, are replaced by the duke of Devonshire and William Pitt.

1757

The duke of Cumberland loses two battles on the continent.

Admiral Byng is shot after being court-martialed for failing to relieve Minorca (March).

Clive wins the Battle of Plassey, secures control of Bengal.

Kings demands Pitt's resignation due to defeats; Newcastle joins Pitt in a reformed ministry.

Frederick the Great of Prussia has important victories at Rossbach and Leuthen (November and December).

1758

John Wilkinson's blast furnace at Bilston opens.

Second Treaty of Westminster gives Frederick the Great an annual subsidy, and parties promise not to make separate peace (April).

Louisberg captured (July).

Fort Duquesne is retaken by British and American forces (November).

1759

The capture of Guadaloupe (May).

Fort Niagara captured (July).

French fleet defeated at Lagos (August).

British forces capture Quebec; General James Wolfe dies (September).

British fleet defeats the French at Quiberon Bay (November).

1760

Montreal surrenders, leaving Canada open to British conquest (September).

George II dies, succeeded by George III (October).

Josiah Wedgwood opens pottery works in Staffordshire.

1761

Pondicherry (India) falls to the British (January).

William Pitt wants to declare war on Spain, close ally of France; opposed by colleagues, he resigns (October). The new ministry is headed by the duke of Newcastle and Lord Bute.

1762

War with Spain: British forces capture Havana, Martinque, St. Lucia, St. Vincent, Grenada, and Manila.

Bute succeeds Newcastle as first lord of the treasury (May).

John Wilkes begin publishing the *North Briton* (June).

1763

Treaty of Paris between Britain, France, and Spain: Britain gains Canada, Nova Scotia, Minorca, Tobago, St. Vincent, Grenada, Dominica, Senegal, and Florida (February).

Bute resigns under pressure of attacks in the press and in Parliament; he is succeeded by George Grenville (April).

Wilkes is arrested on a general warrant for attacks on the king in issue no. 45 of the *North Briton* (April). His arrest is declared illegal by Chief Justice Pratt (December).

1765

Stamp Act places a tax on legal documents in the American colonies, designed to provide revenue for defense of the colonies (March).

Grenville is dismissed by the king; Lord Rockingham forms a new ministry (July).

Six colonies petition against the Stamp Act.

Clive becomes governor of Bengal; East India Company assumes powers of taxation.

1766

Stamp Act repealed after the government passes the Declaratory Act, asserting full power to legislate for the colonies (March).

William Pitt becomes earl of Chatham, forms a new government, but is taken ill and unable to manage daily affairs.

1767

Charles Townshend's revenue act imposes duties on colonial imports.

1768

John Wilkes is elected MP for Middlesex (March). After he is sentenced to two years in prison for the acts of 1763, rioting breaks out in London, and a mob tries to free him. Eleven people are killed in the "massacre" of St. George's Fields (May).

Pitt resigns, and the duke of Grafton forms a ministry (October).

Royal Academy is founded; Sir Joshua Reynolds is the first president (December).

Richard Arkwright invents the water frame.

1769

Wilkes is expelled from the House of Commons after vote declaring him guilty of seditious libel on the massacre of St. George's Fields (February). The Supporters of the Bill of Rights is organized to support Wilkes and to promote parliamentary reform.

The anonymous "Letters of Junius" attack leading members of the government.

James Watt receives patent for steam engine.

1770

Grafton resigns, and Frederick, Lord North, becomes first lord of the treasury and chancellor of the exchequer (January).

Import duties are repealed, except that on tea (March).

Boston Massacre (March).

Edmund Burke's *Thoughts on the Causes of the Present Discontents* is published, condemning the influence of the Crown on politics.

1771

House of Commons debates are printed, and London officials are imprisoned for breach of parliamentary privilege (March). But debates continue to be printed from this time.

Captain James Cook returns from his first Pacific voyage.

1772

Warren Hastings becomes governor of Bengal.

1773

Robert Clive defends his actions in India before the House of Commons.

Regulating Act places the East India Company under government control.

Tea Act allows direct importation of tea to America (October). Colonists resist imports; in the Boston Tea Party 340 chests of tea are dumped into Boston harbor (December).

1774

Parliament closes the port of Boston; this and other "intolerable acts" fuel American resistance.

Quebec Act allows toleration of Roman Catholics in Canada.

Continental Congress meets in Philadelphia.

Robert Clive commits suicide.

Warren Hastings is made governor-general of India.

John Wilkinson patents cylinder-boring process.

John Wilkes is elected lord mayor of London.

1775

Proposals for conciliation of the American colonies are defeated in the House of Commons.

Clashes between colonists and British troops at Lexington and Concord (April).

Second Continental Congress meets (May), creates army under George Washington.

Battle of Bunker Hill (June).

Proclamation of state of rebellion in the colonies (August).

1776

British troops withdraw from Boston (March).

Declaration of Independence is drafted (July).

1777

Washington wins Battle of Princeton (January).

British win Battle of Brandywine Creek (September).

General Gates defeats General Burgoyne at Saratoga (October), which victory helps the colonists forge an alliance with France and Holland.

1778

War with France, renewed fighting in the West Indies and India.

Lord North's Reconciliation Bill (with the Americans) defeated.

Catholic Relief Act permits Catholic worship, and it inspires the formation of the Protestant Association.

1779

War with Spain.

Irish Volunteer Movement raises a force of 40,000 to defend Ireland.

Irish agitation against trade restrictions.

Christopher Wyvill conducts Yorkshire meeting for parliamentary reform.

1780

Petition from Yorkshire for parliamentary (and "economical") reform. The Yorkshire Association is replicated in many other counties.

Reformers' convention in London (March).

Famous resolution by John Dunning, "that the influence of the crown has increased, is increasing, and ought to be diminished," passes the House of Commons in April.

Gordon Riots: Lord George Gordon's Protestant Association presents a petition to repeal the Catholic Relief Act, an effort that leads to riots and general mayhem in which London is under mob rule for six days (June).

Robert Raikes founds Sunday schools in Gloucester; they become a national movement and an early step toward general elementary education.

War with Holland (December).

1781

Lord Cornwallis surrenders to Washington at Yorktown (October).

1782

Lord North resigns; Lord Rockingham forms a ministry (March).

Reform act disqualifies government contractors from sitting in the House of Commons (May).

Another act disenfranchises government revenue officers (June).

Civil List Act controls royal expenditure, pensions, and offices (July).

Rockingham dies, is replaced by Earl Shelburne (July).

Irish Parliament repeals Poynings' Laws and Declaratory Act.

Gilbert's Act allows parishes to combine for poor law purposes; the infirm to be sent to workhouses, the able-bodied to be given work.

1783

Shelburne replaced by the duke of Portland and the unnatural allies Lord North and Charles James Fox (April).

Treaty of Versailles between the United States, Britain, and France: the independence of the former colonies is recognized, and Britain and France exchange colonial territories elsewhere (September).

Fox introduces an India Bill, to place the authority of the East India Company under commissioners appointed by Parliament. The king opposes this and puts pressure on the House of Lords to reject the bill. Ministers are dismissed, and William Pitt (the younger) is asked to form a government (December).

1784

General election yields a majority of 100 for Pitt (March).

Pitt reorganizes government finance, reintroduces window tax and other indirect taxes, and sets up a Board of Taxes to supervise collection.

Pitt's India Act establishes a Board of Control to supervise the East India Company.

1785

Power loom invented by Edmund Cartwright.

Pitt presents moderate parliamentary reform proposals, and they are defeated by the Commons (April).

Warren Hastings resigns as governor-general of India, returns to England.

1786
Pitt reestablishes a Sinking Fund (May).
Commercial treaty with France (September).

1787
Anti-Slavery Society organized.
Impeachment of Warren Hastings begins.

1788
Penal colony at Botany Bay begins settlement of Australia.
Sierra Leone is used as a refuge settlement for Africans and ex-slaves.
George III has mental collapse, debate begins on a possible regency (November).

1789
King recovers (February).
Mutiny on the *Bounty* (April).
Storming of the Bastille and the beginning of the French Revolution (July).
The Revolution Society meets to commemorate the Glorious Revolution of 1688 and praises the events in France (November).

1790
Edmund Burke publishes his *Reflections on the Revolution in France,* attacking the upheaval and destruction of the French radicals.

1791
Thomas Paine publishes *The Rights of Man* (Part I) (March).
The Society of United Irishmen is founded.
Riots in Birmingham destroy dissenting chapels and the home of Joseph Priestley (July).
Canada Act divides that government into two provinces.

1792
Founding of the London Corresponding Society, a group of artisans in favor of reform (January).
William Wilberforce carries a motion to abolish slavery (April).
Proclamation against seditious publications issued.
Paine tried in absentia for seditious libel.

Loyalist associations formed.
The French Republic is established (September).

1793
Execution of Louis XVI (January).
French invasion of the Low Countries, declaration of war on Britain (February). Britain signs alliances with Russia, Spain, Sardinia, Sicily, and Prussia.
British Convention meets in Edinburgh (October).
Friendly Societies Act recognizes legal status of these mutual-aid groups and protects their funds.
Catholic Relief Act grants Roman Catholics in Ireland the franchise and the right to hold office, except as members of Parliament.

1794
Trials of leaders of British Convention (January–September).
Arrest and trial of English reformers; secret committees investigate radicals.
Britain agrees to subsidy for the Netherlands and Prussia.
Some provisions of the habeas corpus act suspended (May)
Treason trials of Thomas Hardy, John Horne Tooke, and John Thelwall end in acquittals (December).

1795
Food riots occur in many parts (July); antiwar demonstrations in London.
London Corresponding Society organizes a mass meeting.
Speenhamland system of outdoor poor relief inaugurated.
During the procession to open Parliament, stones are thrown at the king's coach by protesters (October).
Parliament passes a Treason Act and a Seditious Meetings Act, designed to stiffen the definitions and the punishments for those actions.
Methodists formally separate from the Church of England.
Orange Order founded by Irish Protestants to combat Catholics.

1796

Insurrection Act gives government powers to suppress insurgents in Ireland. United Irishmen take up arms and are suppresssed by the military.

French attempt to land in Bantry Bay fails (December).

1797

Bank crisis, cash payments suspended (February).

Spanish fleet beaten at Cape St. Vincent (February).

French landing in Pembrokeshire fails (February).

Naval mutinies at Spithead (April) and the Nore (June).

Dutch fleet defeated at Camperdown (October).

Pitt introduces plan for income tax (November).

1798

Rebellion in Ireland has early success in Wexford (May).

Defeat of rebels at Vinegar Hill (June).

Treaty with Russia and the Second Coalition against France (June).

French landing in Mayo (August).

Nelson wins Battle of the Nile (August).

French expedition to Lough Swilly; capture of Wolfe Tone (October).

1799

Income tax of 10 percent imposed on incomes over £200 (April).

Combination Act (July).

Military expedition to Holland (August–October).

Political societies (Corresponding Society, United Irishmen) banned.

1800

Peace proposals from Napoleon are rejected by Pitt (January).

Act of Union with Ireland (August); the Irish Parliament is dissolved, Ireland to send 100 MPs to the British House of Commons, 32 peers to the House of Lords when the Parliament of the United Kingdom convenes on January 1, 1801. Pitt wants to include a measure for Catholic emancipation, but that is blocked by George III.

1801

Pitt resigns over the failure to include Catholic emancipation; he is replaced by Henry Addington (February).

Nelson destroys the Danish fleet at Copenhagen (April).

Peace terms discussed with France (October).

The first census is taken.

1802

Peace of Amiens: English conquests (except Ceylon and Trinidad) are surrendered, and France evacuates conquests around the Mediterranean (March).

1803

War with France resumes (May).

British fleet captures Tobago and St. Lucia.

Emmet's Rebellion in Ireland is suppressed (July).

1804

Addington (Lord Sidmouth) resigns; Pitt returns to office (May).

Napoleon assembles a large fleet and an army of 150,000 at Dunkirk for an invasion of England (July).

British and Foreign Bible Society formed.

1805

Third Coalition formed by Britain, Austria, and Prussia (August).

Napoleon moves his army from the channel toward central Europe.

Nelson defeats the Franco-Spanish fleet at Trafalgar (October).

Napoleon wins Battle of Austerlitz (December).

1806

Pitt dies; George Grenville forms a new government (January–February).

Berlin Decrees: Napoleon orders all European ports closed to British shipping (November). Britain counters with Orders in Council, which require neutral vessels to clear British ports and pay duties.

1807

Administration of duke of Portland is formed (March).

Slave trade abolished (May).

Bombardment of Copenhagen (September).

Milan Decrees: Napoleon orders confiscation of neutral vessels which have used British ports (November).

Cotton weavers petition for minimum wage.

1808

Convention of Cintra: French withdraw from Portugal (August). Unrest in Spain, ruled by Napoleon's brother Joseph. Spanish guerilla forces request British intervention.

Cotton workers' strike in Manchester idles 60,000 looms.

1809

Battle of Corunna; Sir John Moore killed (January).

Committee investigates charges surrounding duke of York's sale of army commissions.

British win Battle of Talavera; Wellesley created duke of Wellington.

Walcheren expedition fails to take Antwerp (October).

Portland resigns; Spencer Perceval administration formed.

1810

George III loses his sanity; regency inaugurated.

Anglo-Portuguese alliance resists French assault at Torres Vedras.

London printers prosecuted for conspiracy.

Lancashire and Cheshire cotton spinners strike for four months.

1811

Luddite disturbances in the Midlands (March). Framework breaking spreads through Nottinghamshire, Derbyshire, and Leicestershire.

1812

Luddite riots spread to Yorkshire, Lancashire, and Cheshire.

Spencer Perceval is assassinated; Lord Liverpool becomes chief minister (May).

British victory at Salamanca (July).

Napoleon invades Russia, takes Moscow (September). The city is set afire, and Napoleon retreats, leaving disorganized army behind (October).

1813

The duke of Wellington wins Battle of Vittoria (June).

Fourth Coalition is formed. Napoleon is defeated at Leipzig (October).

Wellington enters southern France (November).

1814

Treaties of Chaumont maintain the alliance (March).

Napoleon abdicates (April).

First Peace of Paris (May) gives France her frontiers of 1792.

Congress of Vienna convenes (September).

1815

Napoleon returns from Elba (March); during his "Hundred Days" he raises the French army and faces the revived coalition forces of Britain and Prussia.

Napoleon defeated at Waterloo (June), exiled to St. Helena.

Congress of Vienna reconvenes (June).

Second Peace of Paris: France is held to 1790 frontiers, has to pay an indemnity and have an army of occupation (November).

Corn law passed, brings wave of petitions, London riots.

1816

Abolition of income tax (April).

Poverty and distress lead to riots, and depression follows the war as the ranks of unemployed are swollen by demobilized veterans.

Spa Fields Riot occurs when a crowd assembled to hear speeches on parliamentary reform, but agitators use the occasion for violent protest (December).

1817

Attack on the Prince Regent's coach after the opening of Parliament (January).

March of unemployed "blanketeers" is broken up by soldiers (March).

Coercion acts passed, banning seditious meetings; habeas corpus act suspended (March).

Derbyshire workers stage the Pentrich Rising (June).

1819

Outpost at Singapore is established by East India Company.

Factory Act prohibits children under nine from working in cotton mills, those over nine may only work a 12-hour day.

Meeting on parliamentary reform at St. Peter's Fields near Manchester is broken up by soldiers, and a dozen people are killed, hundreds injured in the "Peterloo massacre," as it is called (August).

In a panicked reaction to the massacre, Parliament passses the "Six Acts," which allow magistrates to seize arms, prevent drilling, control the press, and limit public meetings (December).

1820

George III dies, and he is succeeded by George IV (January). The new king's estranged wife Caroline returns from the continent to claim her place as queen (June).

The Cato Street Conspiracy is exposed. A radical plot to kill the cabinet and establish a provisional government, it leads to the trials and execution of the ringleaders, and it makes the achievement of moderate reform more difficult (February).

A bill is introduced to deprive Caroline of her title (July), but it is dropped when opposition mounts in the Commons (November).

1821

Coronation of George IV in Westminster Abbey; Caroline attempts but is not allowed to enter (July).

Rioting in London at Queen Caroline's funeral (August).

1822

Lord Castlereagh commits suicide, is replaced by George Canning as foreign secretary (August).

Congress of Verona. The old alliance breaks down when the absolutist states (Russia, Prussia, and Austria) use the "Holy Alliance" to stifle any and all radical or reform movements (October).

1823

Robert Peel, the home secretary, proposes abolition of the death penalty for a long list of crimes, as well as a major prison reform act.

William Huskisson, president of the Board of Trade, initiates Reciprocity of Duties Act, enabling bilateral tariff reductions between Britain and European states.

Catholic Association founded in Ireland by Daniel O'Connell.

1824

War in Burma; Britain moves toward annexation.

Singapore ceded to Britain.

Repeal of the Combination Acts (February).

Royal Naval Lifeboat Institution founded (March).

1825

Factory Act prevents children under 16 from working more than 12 hours a day.

Steam locomotive runs on the Stockton to Darlington railway.

Financial crisis with many failures of banks and businesses (November).

1827

Lord Liverpool has a stroke (February); George Canning becomes new prime minister (April).

Treaty of London with France and Russia to protect Greece (July).

Combined Anglo-Franco-Russian fleet destroys the Turkish-Egyptian fleet more than twice its size at Navarino (October).

Canning dies; Lord Goderich becomes prime minister (August).

1828

Goderich resigns after internal dispute in cabinet; the duke of Wellington forms government.

Repeal of Test and Corporation acts admits nonconformists to Parliament (May).

Foundation of King's College and University College, London.

Catholic emancipation passes in Commons, is defeated in the Lords.

Corn laws reformed by adoption of sliding scale of duties.

1829

Daniel O'Connell wins election in County Clare; as a Roman Catholic he is unable to take his seat in Parliament.

Wellington and Peel declare in favor of Catholic emancipation, splitting the Tory Party (February).

Emancipation passes, allowing Catholics to hold most public offices; the Irish franchise is raised from 40 shillings to £10 (April).

Metropolitan Police Act creates a force of 3,300 paid constables for London (September).

Formation of the Birmingham Political Union.

1830

George IV dies, is succeeded by his brother William IV (June).

At the opening of the Liverpool and Manchester Railway, William Huskisson is hit and killed by the locomotive "Rocket" (September).

Unrest in rural areas due to distress, protesters invoking a "Captain Swing" as leader; the incidents include arson, machine breaking, and rioting, and they continue sporadically until 1833.

Wellington opposes parliamentary reform, and his government resigns. Whigs take office, and Earl Grey becomes prime minister (November).

1831

Reform bill is introduced, but the government is defeated on an amendment, resigns, and calls a new election (April). Whigs win election and introduce second reform bill (June) which passes the Commons (September) and is rejected by the House of Lords (October), prompting riots in Nottingham, Derby, and Bristol. A third bill in December passes the Commons.

Cholera epidemic begins in Sunderland, spreads to major cities, causing 31,000 deaths in England and Scotland (October).

1832

House of Lords passes the third reform bill after the king threatens to create enough new peers for its approval (March). New franchise is uniform £10 for boroughs, 40 shillings for counties; 143 seats are taken from small "rotten" boroughs; 42 towns get new seats, 65 to counties, eight to Scotland, five to Ireland (June). Scotland (July) and Ireland (August) have separate reform acts.

1833

Tithe War in Ireland; coercion bill gives lord lieutenant powers to suppress public meetings (April).

Slavery is abolished in the British Empire; slaveowners promised £20 million in compensation for their "property" (August).

Irish Church Temporalities Act suppresses 10 Irish bishoprics and reduces church revenues (August).

Factory Act limits hours of work by children in textile mills; compulsory education (two hours a day) for the younger employees; state inspectors to be appointed.

Government makes first grant for education: £20,000 to be shared by the National Society and the British and Foreign School Society.

1834

Grand National Consolidated Trades Union organized by Robert Owen (February).

Six farm workers from Dorset (the Tolpuddle Martyrs) sentenced to transportation for administering illegal oaths to join union (March).

Grey resigns as prime minister; replaced by Lord Melbourne.

Poor Law Amendment Act removes direction of the law from parish authorities and vests it in new Boards of Guardians and Poor Law Commissioners; requires poor to enter workhouses to receive relief (August).

Fire destroys houses of Parliament (October).

Melbourne resigns and is succeeded by Robert Peel (November).

1835

During election campaign, Peel states the Conservative acceptance of the reformed government in his Tamworth Manifesto (January).

Peel resigns after defeat on the issue of Irish church revenues.

Melbourne wins 112-seat margin, returns as prime minister (April).

Municipal Corporations Act requires elected councils and published local accounts as well as a force of constables in 178 boroughs (September).

1836

London Working Men's Association founded (June).

Tithe Commutation Act requires payment in money, not in kind (August).

Marriage Act allows licenses to be issued in register offices and nonconformist chapels.

1837

William IV dies, is succeeded by Queen Victoria (June).

General election required after the death of the sovereign; Liberals win a reduced majority of 33 seats.

Vital registration begins (births, marriages, and deaths) under civil direction and on a compulsory basis, taking over the traditional role of the parish priest.

Electric telegraph invented.

1838

People's Charter published, calling for universal manhood suffrage, secret ballot, no property qualification for MPs, pay for MPs, equal districts, and annual parliaments (May).

1839

Chartist convention meets in London (February).

Convention moves to Birmingham (May), and divisions appear between factions.

Chartist petition presented to Parliament and rejected (July), followed by rioting in some cities, and by a small uprising in Newport, Wales, in November.

Anti–Corn Law League is established in Manchester (August).

Opium War with China.

1840

The penny post is introduced (January).

Victoria and Prince Albert are married (February).

Repeal Association is founded by Daniel O'Connell to repeal the Act of Union.

Committee on the Health of Towns publicizes slum conditions.

1841

Straits convention (Britain, France, Austria, and Russia) closes the Dardanelles to foreign shipping (July).

Government defeat followed by the administration of Robert Peel; Gladstone enters the cabinet (August).

1842

Second national convention of Chartists (April).

Assassination attempt on the queen by John Francis (May).

Peel brings in new sliding scale of duties; tariffs on over 700 imports are removed; income tax brought back (June).

Railway telegraph introduced.

Treaty of Nanking ends the Opium War: Hong Kong ceded to Britain, and five treaty ports are opened to British trade (August).

Mines Act bans employment of women and children underground.

"Plug Plot" in northern industrial areas: workers strike and pull plugs on boilers, forcing stoppage of production.

Edwin Chadwick writes *Enquiry into the Sanitary Condition of the Labouring Population of Great Britain.*

1843

Royal College of Surgeons founded (June).

Chartist convention in Birmingham (September).

O'Connell's Repeal Association plans a "monster meeting" at Clontarf, which is banned by the government (October). He and others are tried and convicted of conspiracy. Judgment is later reversed in the House of Lords.

Maori wars begin.

Annexation of Natal.

1844

Bank Charter Act redefines functions of Bank of England, including monopoly on printing money (May).

Railway mania sees massive extension of railway building.

First cooperative shop opened in Rochdale (December).

1845

Half of the Irish potato crop destroyed by fungus; debate intensifies over repeal of the corn laws.

1846

Total failure of the potato crop in Ireland; Peel's government sets up food depots; Whig government tries public works programs.

Peel proposes repeal of corn laws, which passes in June, but a reduced duty is retained until 1849, and thereafter becomes a nominal one shilling.

Government defeated on an Irish coercion Bill; Peel resigns, and Lord John Russell forms a government.

1847

Irish famine causes increasing mortality and emigration. Public works plan is dropped; soup kitchens are used but abandoned as the potato crop appears to improve.

Factory Act limits hours of women and older children in textile factories to 10 a day.

1848

Revolution in France; publication of the *Communist Manifesto* (February).

Chartist meeting on Kennington Common supports third petition to Parliament, but the meeting is dispersed, and the petition is rejected (April).

Young Ireland uprising in Tipperary is suppressed (July).

Public Health Act provide local boards of health and power to appoint medical officers.

Women admitted to London University (extramural classes for women at King's College).

1849

William Hamilton attempts to assassinate Queen Victoria (May).

Repeal of the Navigation Acts (June).

1850

Roman Catholic hierarchy is reestablished; Southwark Cathedral is the first Catholic cathedral of the modern era.

Don Pacifico Affair: a resident of Gibraltar claims compensation from Greece when his house in Athens is destroyed; Lord Palmerston, the foreign secretary, sends fleet to blockade Piraeus (April–June) and defends his policy on grounds that a British subject can claim imperial protection anywhere.

1851

Great Exhibition opens in Hyde Park (May).

Palmerston expresses approval of the coup of Louis Napoleon, without first referring to the queen; she dismisses him from office (December).

Reuters News Agency formed in London.

Amalgamated Society of Engineers founded, initially with 12,000 members.

Gold rush in Australia.

1852

Lord John Russell resigns; new government formed by the earl of Derby. Benjamin Disraeli is chancellor of the exchequer.

Conquest of Burma.

Transvaal independence recognized.

General election; conservatives win narrow victory.

Derby resigns in December.

1853

Lord Aberdeen forms a coalition government.

Cholera epidemic.

1854

Britain and France ally with Turkey, declare war on Russia (March).

Northcote-Trevelyan report proposes reforms of the civil service.

Troops land in the Crimea (September); siege of Sevastopol and the Battle of Balaklava (October); allied victory in the Battle of Inkerman (November).

Cheltenham Ladies' College founded.

1855

Aberdeen resigns, under attack for the conduct of the war (January).

Lord Palmerston forms a new government (February).

Russians abandon Sevastopol (September).

Stamp duty on newspapers is repealed.

1856

Treaty of Paris ends the Crimean War.

Britain and France at war with China.

County and Borough Police Act requires all counties and boroughs to maintain a police force; parliamentary inspectors to examine them, and if they qualify they receive a grant from the exchequer.

1857

Commercial crisis due to surplus of American wheat crop; failure of banks and commercial brokers.

Matrimonial Causes Act establishes divorce court and gives limited access to women.

Indian Mutiny begins in Meerut, spreads across northern India (May).

Liberals win general election by a margin of 126.

1858

Palmerston resigns, is replaced by Lord Derby.

Property qualification for MPs is abolished; Jews are admitted to Parliament.

Mutiny is suppressed with great violence in India. Government of India Act ends political role of East India Company, creates secretary of state for India.

Treaty of Tientsin ends war with China (June).

National Miners' Association formed.

Fenian Brotherhood established.

1859

After defeat on a reform bill, Derby resigns, is replaced by Palmerston.

Liberals win general election by a reduced majority of 60.

1860

Cobden-Chevalier Treaty reduces tariffs between Britain and France (January).

War in China ends when British and French troops enter Peking (October).

1861

British colony in Nigeria founded.

Establishment of Post Office Savings Bank.

"Trent Affair": two Confederate commissioners are seized aboard the British steamer *Trent* by a U.S. warship (November).

Prince Albert dies of typhoid (December).

1862
Companies Act creates limited liability.
"Cotton famine" strikes Lancashire textile industry.

1863
London Underground opens Metropolitan Line.

1864
Octavia Hill launches campaign to remove slum housing in London.
National conference of trade union delegates.

1865
Antiseptic surgery pioneered by Joseph Lister.
Great Eastern lays transatlantic cable.
William Booth founds the Salvation Army.
Palmerston dies; Lord Russell becomes prime minister (October).
Liberals win 82-seat majority in the general election.

1866
William Gladstone introduces parliamentary reform bill (February).
Thomas Barnardo opens home for deserted children.
Financial crisis (May). Failure of the finance company Overend and Gurney met by emergency measured by the Bank of England.
Cholera epidemic.
Sanitary Act give powers to limit air pollution.
Russell is replaced by Derby as prime minister after defeat of the reform bill (June).

1867
Disraeli introduces reform bill (February).
Fenian raid on arsenal at Chester; uprising in Ireland put down (February).
British North America Act establishes Dominion of Canada (July).
Parliamentary reform act introduces household suffrage in boroughs and a wider franchise in counties, adding nearly a million new voters (August).

Master and Servant Act limits prosecution of strikers; a royal commission recommends legalization of trade unions.

1868
Derby resigns; Benjamin Disraeli becomes prime minister (February).
General election in November gives the Liberals a majority of 116; William Gladstone forms his first administration.
Artisans and Labourers Dwellings Act empowers local authorities to compel owners to repair or demolish unsanitary housing.
Trades Union Congress (TUC) meets in Manchester with 34 delegates.

1869
Act for disestablishment of the Anglican Church of Ireland (July), to take effect in 1871.
Suez Canal opens (October).
TUC meets in Birmingham, with 40 delegates representing 250,000 members.

1870
Bankruptcy Act and the end of imprisonment for debt (January).
Peace Preservation Act increases power to deal with agrarian violence.
Married Women's Property Act allows women to retain £200 of their earnings.
Education Act creates system for elementary education in England and Wales.
Irish Land Act begins to recognize the grievances of tenants.
Home Government Association formed by Isaac Butt, a Dublin Protestant.

1871
In the first Rugby international, Scotland defeats England (March).
Religious tests abolished at Oxford and Cambridge (June).
Trade Union Act recognizes unions, grants protection to funds, but allows them to be prosecuted under old laws (June).
Purchase of army commissions abolished (August).

Newnham College, Cambridge, founded for female students.

1872
Ballot Act establishes the secret ballot in parliamentary elections.
Licensing Act restricts sale of intoxicating liquor.
Scottish Education Act.
Joseph Arch establishes National Agricultural Labourers Union.

1873
Irish Universities Bill plans to unite all colleges, Protestant and Catholic.
Gladstone is defeated, resigns, but returns to office when Disraeli declines to replace him (February).
Judicature Act creates the High Court of Justice (a merger of old royal courts) and a new Court of Appeal (February).
Agricultural depression.
Ashanti War begins.

1874
Gladstone loses general election (by 91 votes) and resigns. Disraeli forms a government (February). Irish nationalists win 59 seats.
Ashanti War ends; Gold Coast becomes British colony.
Strike by agricultural workers.

1875
Agricultural depression and strikes continue.
Artisans Dwellings Act gives local authorities power to make compulsory purchase of housing "unfit for human habitation" (June).
Conspiracy Act ends the use of that law against trade unions and allows peaceful picketing (August).
Government buys £4 million in Suez Canal shares from the Khedive of Egypt (December).

1876
Alexander Graham Bell, a Scot, invents the telephone.

Massacre of Christians in Bulgaria arouses a storm of protest in Britain.
Merchant Shipping Act regulates the seaworthiness of vessels.
Royal Titles bill creates the title Empress of India for Queen Victoria (April).
Medical schools opened to women.

1877
Transvaal annexed by the Cape Colony.
The first cricket Test Match won by Australia in Melbourne (March).
The first Wimbledon Men's tennis final played (July).
Socialist demonstration in Trafalgar Square and clashes with the police (November).

1878
Treaty of Berlin (July) embodies the Balkan settlements of the Congress of Berlin, plus the Anglo-Turkish agreement on Cyprus.
Anglo-French control established in Egypt.
Second Afghan war.

1879
Zulu war begins (January).
Treaty of Gandamak settles boundary between Afghanistan and India.
Agricultural depression continues.
Tay Bridge collapses, killing 74 aboard the Edinburgh-Dundee train (December).
Charles Parnell and Michael Davitt form the Irish Land League.

1880
In the general election, Gladstone wins 115 more seats than the Tories, and the Irish nationalists take 61. Gladstone forms his second administration (April).
Charles Bradlaugh, an atheist, declines to take the oath as a member of Parliament.
Education Act makes schooling between ages five and 10 compulsory.
Irish Land League organizes "boycotts," and Home Rule MPs use obstruction tactics in Parliament.

1881

Coercion Act for Ireland to deal with agrarian violence (April).

Irish Land Act (August) is unpopular with landlords and tenants.

Arrest of Parnell; he is confined in Kilmainham prison (October). His arrest triggers "No Rent" movement.

Flogging abolished in the army and navy.

1882

Parnell is released after the "Kilmainham Treaty," in which he promises to try to reduce violence. Only days later the new Irish chief secretary is a victim in the Phoenix Park murders (May).

Prevention of Crimes Act suspends jury trial and grants full powers to police in Ireland (July) to combat Irish terrorism.

British bombard Alexandria (July) and occupy Cairo (September).

Married Women's Property Act allows women to own and administer property.

1883

Corrupt and Illegal Practices Act limits spending in parliamentary campaigns (August).

British forces occupy Egypt, begin evacuating The Sudan.

1884

Parliamentary reform bill introduced.

Uprising in The Sudan; General Gordon sent to rescue the garrison at Khartoum, but he is trapped there.

Reform Act grants vote to almost a third of the adult population (December).

1885

Gordon is killed at Khartoum; the city falls (January).

Redistribution of Seats Act creates single-member districts (March).

Anglo-Burmese war: Burma is annexed.

Bechuanaland becomes a colony.

Secretary of state for Scotland is (re)created.

Gladstone resigns (June); Lord Salisbury becomes prime minister.

Ashbourne Act creates £5 million fund to subsidize Irish tenant land purchases (August).

General election gives Gladstone an 86-vote majority over the Conservatives, but the Irish nationalists have that exact number of seats (December). Gladstone appears to have decided to support Irish Home Rule.

1886

Gladstone forms new Liberal government (February); introduces Home Rule bill (April); bill defeated in the House of Commons, with large-scale defection of Liberal Unionists (June).

General election brings a Conservative victory; Lord Salisbury forms a government (July).

Discovery of gold in the Transvaal.

Kenya becomes a British colony.

1887

Queen Victoria's Golden Jubilee (June).

First Imperial Conference, discusses imperial defense.

A new coercion act for Ireland.

Social Democratic Federation calls meeting in Trafalgar Square, which is broken up by police, and dubbed "Bloody Sunday" (November 13).

1888

Miners' Federation founded.

County Councils Act.

Affirmation Act passed due to efforts of Charles Bradlaugh.

Commission investigates Parnell's involvement in Irish violence.

Murders by "Jack the Ripper" (August–November).

1889

Formation of the London County Council.

Board of Agriculture established.

London Dock Strike (August–September).

1890

Opening of the mile-long Forth Railroad Bridge in Scotland (March).

Parnell cited in O'Shea divorce; Home Rule party splits, majority rejecting Parnell's leadership (December).

1891
Gladstone presents the "Newcastle Programme," in which Liberals call for Irish Home Rule, Scottish and Welsh disestablishment, reform of the House of Lords, and three-year periods between elections, plus a number of other progressive proposals (October).

Joseph Chamberlain assumes leadership of Liberal Unionists, affirming the split in the Liberal party.

1892
General election returns a small advantage for the Liberals, but they have an overall minority.

Keir Hardie is elected, the first Labour MP.

Liberal government is formed by Gladstone (August).

1893
The Independent Labour Party is formed, with Keir Hardie as chairman (January).

The Second Home Rule Bill introduced, passes the Commons, but is rejected by the Lords, 419–41 (September).

Gaelic League founded.

1894
Local Government Act creates parish councils, urban district councils, and rural district councils. Women eligible to vote for parochial councils (March).

Gladstone resigns, and he is replaced as prime minister by Lord Rosebery (March).

Sir William Harcourt's budget includes death duties (August).

Second Imperial Conference meets in Ottawa and discusses the laying of a cable across the Pacific.

1895
Trial of Oscar Wilde. He is convicted of sodomy, sentenced to two years' imprisonment at hard labor (May).

Rosebery resigns, is succeeded by Salisbury (June).

General election returns an overall Conservative majority (July).

Britain and the United States dispute the boundary between Venezuela and British Guiana (the matter is settled in the Treaty of Washington, 1897).

The Jameson Raid into the Transvaal is repelled (December).

1896
The so-called "Kruger telegram" brings congratulations to the president of Transvaal from the German emperor (January).

Lord Northcliffe founds the *Daily Mail,* the first mass circulation newspaper, priced at 1/2 d. (May).

Sir William Harcourt takes the leadership of the Liberal Party after Rosebery resigns (October).

1897
Queen Victoria's Diamond Jubilee (June).

Third Imperial Conference agrees to hold regular meetings.

Committee reports on the Jameson Raid clear Chamberlain but censure Cecil Rhodes.

Workmen's Compensation Act creates fund to pay for industrial injuries after arbitration (August).

1898
Britain leases the New Territories in Hong Kong from China for 99 years (June).

Battle of Omdurman is won by Herbert Kitchener, winning control of The Sudan (September).

Kitchener proceeds to Fashoda, where he meets with French major Marchand.

1899
Efforts to resolve disputes in South Africa include a set of meetings between President Kruger and Lord Milner (May).

Hague Conference on peace and disarmament (May).

Boer War begins (October).

British troops suffer early defeats (December 10–15), and Redvers Buller is replaced by Lord Roberts (Lord Kitchener is chief of staff).

1900

As Boer War continues, Ladysmith is relieved (February).

Labour Representation Committee formed by varied socialist and union elements, dedicated to electing MPs sympathetic to workers.

Relief of Mafeking (May) brings widespread celebration in Britain.

General Frederick Roberts annexes the Transvaal (September).

General election is called "khaki election" as it is held in the middle of war; Conservatives want to exploit deep divisions within the Liberal Party over the war, but they actually lose a few seats (October).

1901

Queen Victoria dies; she is succeeded by her eldest son Edward VII (January).

The Commonwealth of Australia is formed.

British concentration camps are publicized: in fighting guerilla war, the British army had rounded up women and children and burned Boer farms; some 20,000 died of disease and malnutrition in the camps, a number far greater than the total losses on the battlefield.

1902

Anglo-Japanese Alliance is signed (January).

London School of Economics opens.

Boers sue for peace (March) and treaty signed at Vereeniging (May); British sovereignty is recognized by the Orange Free State and Transvaal, and a British payment of £3 million is promised to repair war damage.

Lord Salisbury resigns, A. J. Balfour becomes prime minister (July).

Education Act (Balfour Act) passes; school boards abolished, replaced by local education authorities, empowered to provide secondary education (December).

The Taff Vale Railway is to receive £23,000 in a judgment for damages against the Amalgamated Society of Railway Servants (December).

1903

Irish Land Purchase Act (Wyndham's Act).

Wireless news service between New York and London begins (March).

Joseph Chamberlain announces his plan for "imperial preference," challenging the orthodoxy of free trade (May). He resigns from the cabinet to promote the idea nationally (September).

The Women's Social and Political Union is founded by Emmeline Pankhurst (October).

1904

First electric train runs between Liverpool and Southport (March).

Entente between Britain and France resolves old colonial conflicts, especially over claims in Africa (April).

First ocean-going turbine steamship launched in Belfast (August).

Russian fleet sinks two English trawlers off the Dogger Bank, claiming that they appeared to be Japanese torpedo boats (October).

1905

Unemployed Workmen Act; registers established by local government boards (August).

Sinn Féin ("ourselves alone") founded in Dublin (November).

Balfour resigns; Liberal government is formed under Henry Campbell-Bannerman.

Anglo-French military and naval conversations (December).

1906

General election produces a Liberal landslide of 400 seats and an overall majority of 84. There are 29 Labour MPs elected as well (January).

HMS *Dreadnought* is launched (January).

Boer War Commission estimates the cost of incompetence and corruption at over £1 million (August).

Suffragetes imprisoned for disturbances in Parliament (October).

Trade Disputes Act passes, reversing the Taff Vale decision (December).

1907

Imperial Conference in London (March).

Anglo-Russian agreement on Asia; Russia joins the entente (August).

Founding of the Territorial Army, one of Haldane's army reforms (October).

1908

Campbell-Bannerman resigns, and Herbert Asquith becomes prime minister (April).

Old Age Pensions Act creates noncontributory pensions for those over 70 (July).

Large demonstrations for votes for women (June, October).

First airplane flight in Britain (October).

First woman elected mayor (Elizabeth Garrett Anderson, in Aldeburgh) (November).

1909

As naval arms race escalates, government proposes to build four more Dreadnoughts and another four if necessary (January).

The "People's Budget" is introduced by David Lloyd George (April).

House of Lords rejects the budget (November), triggering a constitutional crisis and serious discussion of reform of the upper house (November).

In the Osborne judgment, the House of Lords upholds a court ruling that trade unions cannot use funds to support a political party, thus threatening the future of the Labour Party (November).

Labour Exchanges provide register of vacant jobs for unemployed workers.

1910

General election fought on the issue of the budget and the powers of the House of Lords. Liberals win a smaller majority, and they are dependent upon support from the Irish nationalists (January).

The budget is passed; a parliament bill is introduced to trim the powers of the Lords (April).

Edward VII dies; George V takes the throne (May).

A conference of conservatives and liberals is held to resolve the question of reform of the Lords, but it fails (June–November).

Herbert Asquith obtains a pledge from the king to create enough peers to pass the parliament bill. Another election is held, and the major parties end in a tie (December).

Hulton Colliery disaster; 350 miners are killed (December).

1911

Suffragette demonstration in London produces a column four miles long (June).

Parliament Act forbids House of Lords to vote on money bills, deprives Lords of veto power over legislation, and shortens the life of a Parliament from seven to five years (August).

MPs get salary of £400 per year.

Suffragette demonstration is broken up by police; marchers break windows and destroy other property (November).

National Insurance Act provides sickness and unemployment benefits for selected trades and lowest incomes (December).

1912

Miners strike for national minimum wage (February–April).

Suffragettes raid the House of Commons; 96 arrests (March).

Coal Mines Act establishes principle of minimum wage (March).

Third Irish Home Rule Bill introduced (April).

Titanic hits iceberg and sinks; 1,500 lives lost (April).

Dockers strike in London (May).

Ulster Covenant is signed by 200,000 enemies of Home Rule (September).

Anglo-French naval agreement shares Atlantic and Mediterranean naval defense responsibilities (September).

1913

The Ulster Volunteer Force, composed of units which had been forming since 1911, is organized to resist the imposition of Home Rule (January).

Home Rule bill rejected by the House of Lords (January, July).

Suffragette bomb destroys house being built for Lloyd George (February).

Emmeline Pankhurst receives three-year sentence for the Lloyd George bombing (April). She and other prisoners go on hunger strikes; police respond with force feeding.

Government introduces "Cat and Mouse Bill," which permits temporary discharge (and re-arrest) of persons weakened by hunger strikes (April).

First oil-powered battleship, the *Queen Elizabeth,* is launched (October).

1914

British army officers stationed in Ireland resign their commissions to avoid enforcing Home Rule (March).

Welsh Church Disestablishment bill passes (May).

Home Rule bill passes the Commons (May), and the Lords propose an amendment to delay implementation in Ulster (June).

Railway workers and miners join building workers in strike, bringing the total of striking workers to 2 million (June).

Archduke Franz Ferdinand, crown prince of Austria, is assassinated in Sarajevo (June).

Buckingham Palace Conference fails to find compromise on Home Rule, and the European crisis leads to delay in enforcing it (July).

Germany declares war on Russia (August 2); German troops invade Belgium, and Britain declares war on Germany (August 4); British Expeditionary Force lands in France (August 17).

British forces defeated in Battle of Mons (August 23).

British and French forces advance after Battle of the Marne (September 5–12). Trench warfare begins.

A German U-boat sinks three British cruisers (September 22).

Battle of Ypres (October–November).

Britain declares war on Turkey (November).

Lloyd George warns of the need to double income tax due to cost of the war.

German ships shell Scarborough and Whitby (December).

1915

German blockade of Britain (February).

British blockade German ports (March).

Attempt to force the Dardanelles by a naval force fails (March).

Second Battle of Ypres (April–May).

Landing of British, Australian, and New Zealand troops on Gallipoli Peninsula meets heavy Turkish resistance (April).

Germans sink the liner *Lusitania,* killing 1,198 (May 7).

Rumors that troops are running out of shells causes an uproar; the government is forced to form a coalition with Conservatives (May 26).

Munitions Act places arms production under a Ministry of Munitions, headed by David Lloyd George. Strikes are banned, and tight regulations made (May).

U.S. protests lead to restricted submarine warfare by Germany (September).

Execution of nurse Edith Cavell (October 12).

Sir John French turns over his command to General Douglas Haig (December 15).

Troops withdraw from Gallipoli after losing 20,000 lives (December 20).

1916

Conscription is introduced (January).

Battle of Verdun begins; Germans launch heavy offensive, and fighting lasts from February to December with extremely heavy losses on both sides.

Easter Rebellion in Ireland: Irish nationalists seize several buildings in Dublin; expected German arms are intercepted, and the rebels are beaten in five days. Their swift executions arouse public sympathy (April).

The Battle of Jutland marks the sole occasion when the two high-seas fleets engage. British losses are somewhat heavier, but German ships return to port and do not venture out in force for the rest of the war (May–June).

Battle of the Somme sees Britain's heaviest losses of the war: 420,000 British lives lost in order to move the front line 10 miles (July–November).

Sir Roger Casement is hanged in London, a leader of the Easter Rebellion and the rebels' agent in Germany (August).

Asquith resigns, and Lloyd George becomes prime minister at the head of a coalition. He forms a War Cabinet with Andrew Bonar Law, Alfred Milner, George Curzon, and Arthur Henderson, the latter representing the Labour Party (December 7).

1917

Germany resumes unrestricted submarine warfare (February 1).

Revolution in Russia (February).

Offensive in Flanders (June).

Royal family drops its German titles (June), takes the name of Windsor.

Third Battle of Ypres (July).

Passchendaele captured by the British (November).

Balfour Declaration supports Jewish homeland in Palestine (November).

Bolshevik revolution in Russia (November).

Lord Allenby enters Jerusalem (December).

1918

Lloyd George makes statement of war aims (January).

Representation of the People Act gives vote to all adult males and to females over 30 (February).

Tetanus vaccine used widely on the battlefield.

Global influenza epidemic kills millions; at peak it kills 3,000 per week in London alone.

Formation of the Royal Air Force from the Royal Flying Corps and the Royal Naval Air Service (April).

Conscription extended to Ireland (April).

New German offensive on the Somme (April).

Allied counterattack (August).

German retreat (September) is followed by armistice (November).

German fleet interned at Scapa Flow (December).

General election: Lloyd George runs as the head of the coalition, wins 478 seats. Women vote for the first time for members of parliament (December).

1919

Peace Conference convenes in Paris (January).

Irish MPs remain in Dublin and declare themselves the Dáil Éireann, or Irish Parliament, and the Irish Republican Army (IRA) is formed under Michael Collins. Sporadic fighting between the republicans and British forces.

Eamon de Valera elected president (April).

Germany accepts terms of the Treaty of Versailles under protest (June).

German fleet is scuttled in Scapa Flow (June).

Government commission recommends nationalizing the coal industry.

Railway strike (September–October).

Nancy, Lady Astor, elected MP for Portsmouth, becomes first woman to sit in the House of Commons (December).

Sex Disqualification Removal Act allows women to enter the professions (December).

1920

League of Nations established in Geneva (January).

Conscription abolished (April).

Strikes and hunger strikes against British treatment of Sinn Féin prisoners in Ireland.

British volunteers ("Black and Tans") recruited to fight in Ireland (June).

Miners' strike (October–November).

British forces burn the city of Cork (December).

Government of Ireland Act divides the country into Ulster (six northern counties) and the south; both are provided with separate institutions.

Unemployment Insurance Act provides 15 weeks of assistance to those who contribute to the scheme.

1921

Coal Mines Act returns mines to their owners, ending government control (March).

Railways Act amalgamates over 100 railways into four regional companies.

Miners' strike (April–June) brings declaration of a state of emergency (April).

Truce called on the fighting in Ireland (July).

Conference on the status of Ireland (October) between high-level delegations; an Anglo-Irish Treaty is drafted, recognizing an Irish Free State as a dominion within the British Empire and giving separate status to Northern Ireland (December).

1922

Postwar slump; unemployment rises.

British protectorate over Egypt ends (February).

Washington Naval Conference agrees on 10-year holiday on ship construction and ratio of battleships between major fleets (February).

Michael Collins is assassinated by republican extremists (August).

Socialists and workers in Glasgow organize a hunger march on London (October).

Conservatives withdraw support from David Lloyd George and he resigns; Andrew Bonar Law becomes prime minister (October).

British Broadcasting Company organized (October).

General election gives Conservatives a majority of 73 seats (November).

1923

Bonar Law resigns because of ill health; Stanley Baldwin becomes prime minister (May).

Matrimonial Causes Act allows women to divorce adulterous husbands (July).

Housing Act gives subsidies for home building (July).

Southern Rhodesia gains autonomy (October).

General election is inconclusive: Conservatives 258, Labour 191, Liberals 159 (December).

1924

Conservative government loses a vote in the House and resigns. The first Labour government is formed, with Ramsay MacDonald as prime minister (January).

Diplomatic recognition is given to the Soviet Union (February).

Conference on Reparations convenes (July) and adopts Dawes Plan to moderate the settlement (August).

Agricultural Wages Act allows county boards to set wages.

Labour government loses a vote of censure; MacDonald resigns. Conservatives win large majority in the general election (October).

Stanley Baldwin becomes prime minister again (November).

1925

Britain rejects the Geneva Protocol, which is meant to strengthen the League's ability to moderate international disputes (March).

Britain returns to the gold standard (April).

"Red Friday" threat of strike by miners, railwaymen, and transport workers. Government sets up Samuel Commission to study the disposition of the coal mines (July).

Summer Time is made a permanent system (August).

Widows, Orphans and Old Age Pensions Act sets up contributory scheme for pensions from age 65 (December).

Treaty of Locarno (December).

Irish Boundary Agreement (December).

1926

British troops withdraw from the Rhineland (January).

Samuel Commission reports on ending subsidy to coal mines (March).

Miners refuse cut in wages, go on strike; they are supported by the Trade Union Congress, and the General Strike lasts for nine days (May 3–12). The government organizes emergency transport and other services, and the strike fails. Miners remain out until November, when they return to work at lower pay.

Imperial Conference in London agrees to a statement that dominions are of equal political status, and the name "British Commonwealth" is adopted (October–November).

1927

British Broadcasting Corporation reorganized (January).

Trade Disputes Act outlaws general strikes and forbids levy on unions for political purposes (May).

Naval disarmament conference (Britain, United States, Japan) fails (August).

1928

Voting age for women reduced to 21; universal suffrage arrives (April).

Revised Prayer Book is rejected by Parliament (May).

1929

Local Government Act takes farms and their buildings off the poor-rate system. Guardians of the poor are abolished, and functions transferred to local councils (March).

General election gives the victory to Labour but without a majority: Labour 288, Conservatives 260, Liberals 59. Ramsay MacDonald becomes prime minister (June). Margaret Bondfield, minister of labor, is first female cabinet member.

Wall Street crash is felt on London exchange, shares fall sharply (October).

Diplomatic relations resumed with the Soviet Union (October).

Viceroy of India makes a public promise of dominion status (October).

1930

Naval Disarmament Conference in London (April).

Britain recognizes the independent state of Iraq (June).

Roundtable Conference on the government of India convenes in London (November).

Depression worsens as unemployment reaches 2.5 million (December).

1931

Oswald Mosley forms the New Party (February).

Government appoints Committee on National Expenditure under George May (February).

The May Committee recommends severe economies in social services, including unemployment benefits (July).

Labour government resigns in dispute over financial economies; MacDonald forms a national coalition with the Conservatives (August).

Britain goes off the gold standard (September).

Second India Conference in London (September).

General election gives a large majority to the National Government (Conservatives 473, National Labour 13, National Liberals 35; Liberals 33, and Labour 52). MacDonald continues as prime minister (October).

1932

World Disarmament Conference convenes in Geneva (February).

Import Duties Act creates a general tariff of 10 percent, with some concessions for imperial trade (February).

Duties on manufactured goods raised to 20–33 percent (April).

Imperial Economic Conference convenes in Ottawa (July–August).

Oswald Mosley forms the British Union of Fascists (October).

Third India Conference in London (November).

1933

The Oxford Union resolves "That this house would in no circumstances fight for king and country." This marks the extent of pacifism and internationalism in some quarters (February).

World Monetary Conference in London fails to resolve problems; Britain continues to pursue nationalist economic policy (July).

1934

Unemployment Assistance Board established; benefit is distributed after means test.

British Union of Fascists rallies in Birmingham (January). A rally later in London brings clashes (September).

Anglo-Russian trade agreement (April).

Naval Disarmament Conference in London fails (October).

1935

Stresa Conference (Britain, France, and Italy) (April).

MacDonald resigns for health reasons (June); he is replaced by Stanley Baldwin.

The "Peace Ballot"—an unscientific poll conducted by the League of Nations Union—shows a large majority of the British public in favor of negotiated settlement of disputes (June).

Anglo-German Naval Agreement sets Germany's fleet at less than 35 percent of that of Britain (June).

Government of India Act lays down a program leading to independence (August).

Italy invades Abyssinia (October).

General election gives majority to the National Government (432 seats) over Labour (154) and Liberals (21).

Hoare-Laval Pact proposes to give Abyssinia to Mussolini; Samuel Hoare is forced to resign as foreign minister (December).

1936

George V dies; Edward VIII becomes king (January).

Germany reoccupies the Rhineland (July).

Civil war begins in Spain (July).

British military occupation of Egypt ends (August).

Jarrow Hunger March (October).

Public Order Act bars wearing of uniforms, grants powers to control public demonstrations by fascists and others (November).

Edward VIII abdicates in order to marry Wallis Simpson. His brother takes the throne as George VI (December).

1937

Anglo-Italian Agreement on Mediterranean interests (January).

Stanley Baldwin resigns; he is replaced as prime minister by Neville Chamberlain (May).

Imperial conference in London (June).

Lord Halifax meets with Adolf Hitler (November).

Irish Free State adopts new republican constitution as "Eire." (December).

1938

Opening of British base at Singapore (February).

Anthony Eden resigns as foreign secretary, is replaced by Lord Halifax (February).

German troops enter Austria and the "Anschluss," or annexation, to Germany is proclaimed (March).

Treaty with Italy recognizes authority over Abyssinia (April).

Nazi demands over the Czech "Sudetenland" raise fear of annexation (May).

Lord Runciman leads a mission to mediate the Sudeten crisis (July).

Chamberlain visits Hitler at Berchtesgaden and Godesburg (September 15 and 27), and finally at Munich the British and French endorse the cession of border lands to Germany (September 29). Hitler promises that he has no further territorial ambitions.

1939

Britain recognizes Franco's government in Spain (February).

Irish Republican Army begins bombing campaign in Britain.

British guarantee protection to Poland (March).

German troops invade Czechoslovakia (March).

Russia offers to make a treaty with Britain and France (April).

Britain extends guarantees to Greece and Romania (April).

Compulsory military service set up (June).

Nazi-Soviet Non-aggression Pact signed (August).

Germany invades Poland (September 1); Britain and France declare war on Germany (September 3); war measures implemented, including conscription, air raid precautions, government controls, and emergency powers.

Both sides exchange air raids. The first British ship (HMS *Courageous*) is sunk in the Atlantic, and British troops embark for France. While bombs fall in the Shetlands, a naval engagement takes place in the River Plate (where the Graf Spee is scuttled), and major fighting is in eastern Europe. There is no sign of battle in the west until 1940.

1940

Food rationing begins in Britain (February).

German invasion of Denmark and Norway (April 8).

British troops land briefly in Norway (April 15–May 2).

Germany invades Belgium, the Netherlands, Luxembourg, and France; Neville Chamberlain resigns and is replaced as prime minister by Winston Churchill (May 10).

British and French forces are cut off and evacuated from Dunkirk (May 17–June 4); 335,000 men are saved by a fleet of over 700 boats.

Italy declares war on Britain (June 10).

France surrenders (June 22).

Germany occupies the Channel Islands (July 1).

British forces attack the French fleet at Oran (July).

Battle of Britain: the Luftwaffe launch air raids against RAF installations, then switch to population centers (August).

The "Blitz" of London causes heavy damage, but Germans lose nearly twice the number of aircraft as the RAF (August–September). Bombing of major cities continues through the winter.

German U-boats blockade Britain, heavy losses of merchant ships.

British troops land in Greece (October).

1941

British forces in North Africa raid Tobruk, capture Benghazi (January–February).

Royal navy destroys Italian fleet off the coast of Greece (March).

United States enacts Lend-Lease (March).

Standard rate of income tax raised to 50 percent (April).

British troops evacuate Greece, retreat from General Rommel's advance in North Africa (May).

German bombs destroy the House of Commons (May).

Germany invades the Soviet Union (June). Anglo-Russian alliance (July).

Churchill meets President Roosevelt in Placentia Bay; they sign the Atlantic Charter, a statement of joint principles for international peace (August).

British invade Libya (November).

Japan attacks Pearl Harbor; Britain declares war on Japan, Germany and Italy declare war on the United States (December).

1942

Battle of the Atlantic sees mounting losses of merchant ships.

Japanese capture Singapore (February) and Rangoon (March).

India rejects terms for independence, remains neutral (April).

British launch 1,000-bomber raid on Cologne (May).

Raid on Dieppe (August).

Generals Alexander and Montgomery take commands in Middle East (August).

British victory at El Alamein; British and United States forces land in North Africa (November).

Beveridge Report on *Social Insurance and Allied Services* published (December).

1943

Churchill and Roosevelt meet at Casablanca, adopt policy of unconditional surrender (January).

British troops take Tripoli (April), German and Italian forces surrender in North Africa (May).

Allied invasion of Sicily (July) and Italy (September). Italy surrenders.

Foreign ministers of Britain, Russia, and the United States agree to form a postwar international organization (October).

Churchill, Rooosevelt, and Stalin meet at Teheran (November–December).

1944

Allies enter Rome (June).

Landing in Normandy (June).

Germans launch V-1 bombs on Britain (June); large-scale evacuation necessary.

Bretton Woods agreement on postwar economic order (July).

Butler Education Act passed, promising secondary education for all (August).

Allied armies enter Paris (August).

Allies capture Brussels and Antwerp (September).

Churchill and Roosevelt meet at Quebec, and Churchill travels to Moscow to meet with Stalin (October).

1945

Churchill, Roosevelt, and Stalin meet at Yalta to plan postwar European settlement (February).

Bombing of Dresden kills an estimated 100,000 civilians (February).

British troops cross the Rhine (March).

British troops liberate the Belsen concentration camp (April).

British capture Rangoon (May).

Germany surrenders (May).

Labour leaves the coalition; Churchill forms "caretaker" government.

United Nations Charter published (June).

General election produces Labour landslide: 393 seats to the Conservatives' 213 and 12 for the Liberals (July). Clement Attlee becomes prime minister.

Potsdam Conference (July–August).

Atom bombs dropped on Hiroshima and Nagasaki; Japan surrenders (August).

Lend-Lease terminated (October).

1946

Labour introduces programs of expanded social services and nationalization: Bank of England nationalized (March); cable and wireless; coal industry (July); National Health Service (November).

Churchill's "Iron curtain" speech (Fulton, Missouri; March).

Jewish terrorists attack British headquarters in Jerusalem (July).

Bread rationing; loans from the United States (July).

Trade Disputes Act repealed.

New Towns Act.

Arts Council founded.

1947

National Coal Board takes over (January); fuel crisis and strikes threaten the economy (February).

U.S. secretary of state Marshall suggests U.S. aid to Europe (June).

Sterling made convertible (July).

India Independence Act provides for partition into India and Pakistan; power is rapidly transferred by August.

Rail and road transport and electricity nationalized (August).

1948

British Railways organized (January).

Burma becomes independent (January).

Ceylon becomes a self-governing dominion (February).

Organization for European Economic Cooperation formed (April).

Marshall Plan aid is approved (April).

British mandate in Palestine terminated; state of Israel proclaimed (May).

Berlin airlift provides supplies to the city when it is blockaded by Russian occupation troops (July).

Bread rationing ends (July).

National Health Service begins operation (November).

Republic of Ireland Act (Dublin) (December).

1949

End of clothing rationing (March).

North Atlantic Treaty Organization established (April).

Republic of Ireland formally leaves the Commonwealth; Commonwealth prime ministers accept the membership of republics, India being the first (April).

Gas industry is nationalized (May).

Council of Europe inaugural meeting (May).

Sterling devalued (£1 = $2.80) (September).

Parliament act reduces the veto power of the House of Lords, legislation may only be suspended for one year instead of two (November).

Iron and steel nationalization passed (November).

1950

General election gives Labour a reduced majority with 315 seats to 298 for the Conservatives and 9 for the Liberals (February).

Petrol rationing ends (May).

Schumann Plan (May).

North Korean troops invade South Korea; the United Nations authorizes intervention (June). British troops enter action (September).

Soap rationing ends (September).

Stone of Scone taken from Westminster Abbey by Scottish nationalists (December).

1951

Government begins rearmament program (January).

Iron and Steel nationalization takes effect (January).

Festival of Britain (July–September).

Stone of Scone returned to Westminster (August).

British atom bomb testing begins (October).

British troops seize the Suez Canal (October).

General election won by the Conservatives (321) over Labour (298) and Liberals (9). Winston Churchill becomes prime minister (October).

General Certificate of Education introduced (England and Wales).

1952

George VI dies; Queen Elizabeth II succeeds to the throne (February).

First British atom bomb detonated in the Pacific (October).

State of Emergency in Kenya (October). Mau Mau rebels challenge British rule.

1953

Rationing of sweets ends (February).

Amnesty for wartime deserters (February).

Iron and Steel industry denationalized (March).

Road transport denationalized (April).

Sir Edmund Hillary climbs Mt. Everest (May).

Coronation of Elizabeth II is the first to be televised (June).

Korean armistice (July).

Sugar rationing ends (September).

Florence Horsbrugh (minister of education) becomes first Conservative female cabinet minister.

1954

Nuclear breeder reactor begins operation at Harwell (February).

Geneva Conference on Indo-China (April).

All food rationing ends (July).

Agreement to withdraw all British troops from the Suez Canal zone (July).

Formation of the Independent Television Authority (August).

South-East Asia Treaty Organization (SEATO) formed (September).

Western European Union formed (September).

The United Kingdom associates with the European Coal and Steel Community (formed in 1951) (December).

1955

Government announces plan to produce hydrogen bombs (February).

HMS *Ark Royal* is launched; it is Britain's largest aircraft carrier (February).

The United Kingdom joins Baghdad Pact (April).

Sir Winston Churchill resigns; he is replaced as prime minister by Sir Anthony Eden (April).

General election brings a majority for the Conservatives (344–277) (May).

Summit Conference at Geneva (Britain, United States, France, and the Soviet Union) (July).

The city of London is declared a "smokeless zone" in order to reduce air pollution (October).

State of Emergency in Cyprus (November).

Hugh Gaitskell succeeds Clement Attlee as leader of the Labour Party (December).

1956

The House of Commons rejects a motion to abolish the death penalty (February).

White Paper on full employment (March).

British troops withdraw from Suez (June).

Nasser nationalizes the Suez Canal (July).

Declaration against nationalization (Britain, France, United States) (August).

Anglo-French invasion of the Suez (October), opposed by the United States, United Nations; fighting ends (November).

British plan for European Free Trade Area (October).

1957

Eden retires, is replaced as prime minister by Harold Macmillan (January).

Macmillan meets Eisenhower in Bermuda (March).

Treaty of Rome establishes the Common Market (European Economic Community) [EEC] (March).

Gold Coast becomes independent Ghana (March).

National Service to end in 1960 (April).

British H-Bomb tested in the Pacific (May).

Independence for the Federation of Malaya (July).

Council on Prices, Productivity and Incomes (August).

Wolfenden Report recommends legalization of homosexual acts between adults in private (September).

Nuclear power plant at Windscale has serious fire and leak of radioactivity (October).

1958

Britain and the United States agree to build nuclear bases in Britain; Campaign for Nuclear Disarmament formed (February); antinuclear protest march is staged from London to Aldermaston (April).

State of emergency declared in Aden (May).

Clean Air Act (June).

Life Peerages Act allows creation of nonhereditary peers. (July).

Race riots in Nottingham and in Notting Hill, London (August–September).

British trawlers ignore Iceland's 12-mile territorial waters limit (September).

Jodrell Bank radiotelescope begins operation (October).

First female peers sit in the House of Lords (October).

Thalidomide found to be the source of birth deformities (December).

First Motorway section opened (December).

1959

Britain recognizes the regime of Fidel Castro in Cuba (January).

Agreement between Britain, Greece, and Turkey on independence for Cyprus (February).

Macmillan visits Moscow (February).

Hovercraft goes into service (May).

Radcliffe Report on the monetary system (August).

General election produces a majority of 100 for the Conservatives (October).

European Free Trade Association is organized (November).

1960

Macmillan visits South Africa, makes his "Winds of Change" speech in Parliament in Capetown (February).

Beeching Commission prepares reorganization of British Rail.

Somaliland becomes independent (June).

British rule in Cyprus ends (August).

Nigeria becomes independent (October).

Penguin Books tried and acquitted for publishing *Lady Chatterley's Lover* under the obscenity law (October–November).

HMS *Dreadnought,* Britain's first nuclear-powered submarine, launched (October). Plans announced for U.S. Polaris submarines to be based in the Firth of Clyde (November).

1961

Prescription charges in the National Health Service (February).

Geneva talks on ending nuclear weapons testing between Britain, the United States, and the Soviet Union (March).

South Africa decides to leave the Commonwealth (March).

Under the Betting and Gaming Act, authorized betting shops open (May).

British troops sent to Kuwait at the request of that government (July).

Britain to apply for EEC membership (July).

National Economic Development Council established (July).

Geneva conference fails; Russia resumes testing (August).

Independence for Tanganyika is granted (December).

Macmillan meets with President Kennedy in Bermuda (December).

1962

Consecration of the new Coventry Cathedral (May).

National Incomes Commission established (July).

Commonwealth Immigration Act (July).

Jamaica, Trinidad, and Tobago become independent (August).

Britain and France agree to develop the Concorde supersonic airliner (November).

Macmillan and Kennedy meet at Nassau; the United States offers Polaris missiles for use on British submarines (December).

1963

Britain is denied entry into the EEC (January).

Nyasaland becomes independent (February).

Harold Wilson is elected leader of Labour Party after the death of Hugh Gaitskell (February).

Terence O'Neill becomes prime minister of Northern Ireland (March).

Beeching report on British railways published (March).

Peerage Act allows peers to renounce titles (July).

Partial nuclear test ban treaty (Britain, the United States, and the Soviet Union) (August).

Macmillan retires; Sir Alec Douglas-Home becomes prime minister (October).

Robbins Report on Higher Education recommends rapid expansion of facilities and enrollment (October).

Kenya and Zanzibar become independent (December).

1964

Malta becomes independent (September).

Northern Rhodesia becomes independent and is renamed Zambia (September).

Forth Road Bridge opened in Scotland. At 3,300 feet, it is the longest suspension bridge in Europe (September).

Licenses granted for North Sea oil drilling (September).

General election results in a five-seat majority for Labour. Harold Wilson becomes prime minister (October).

Government imposes 15 percent import surcharge (October).

Ban is implemented on the sale of arms to South Africa because of its policy of apartheid (November).

International Monetary Fund loan of £500 million. The Trade Union Congress and employers sign a statement of intent on productivity, prices, and incomes (December).

1965

National health prescription charges abolished (January).

British rail announces plans to cut the network in half (February).

The Gambia is granted independence (February).

Prices and Incomes Board is set up (March).

Britain gets another £700 million from the IMF (May).

Sir Alec Douglas-Home resigns as Conservative Party leader. Edward Heath is chosen as his successor (August).

Oil is discovered in the North Sea (September).

Provisional abolition of the death penalty (November).

Race Relations Act (November).

Rhodesia makes unilateral declaration of independence (November).

Rent control act (December).

Miniskirt invented by Mary Quant.

1966

Trade ban against Rhodesia (January).

Nelson monument in Dublin is blown up (March).

General election gives Labour a majority of 97 (March).

Seamen's strike (May–June).

British Guiana becomes independent as Guyana (May).

Prices and Incomes bill introduced; government imposes wage freeze and deflationary measures (July).

Plaid Cymru wins Carmarthen by-election (July).

England wins the World Cup (July).

The first parliamentary commissioner, or ombudsman, is named (August).

Severn Bridge opens (September).

Bechuanaland becomes independent, as Botswana (September).

Basutoland becomes independent, as Lesotho (October).

Aberfan disaster as a slag heap slides into a junior school, killing 144 people (October).

Natural gas discovered in the North Sea (October).

Barbados becomes independent (October).

Import surcharge ends (November).

U.N. sanctions are imposed on Rhodesia (December).

1967

Abortion Act allows termination of pregnancy under specified conditions.

The tanker *Torrey Canyon* sinks off Land's End, producing a 300-square-mile oil slick (March).

Britain applies for entry into the EEC (May).

Government decides to make defense budget cuts and to withdraw from all stations east of Suez (July).

Decimal Currency Act plans for introduction of new currency in 1971 (July).

Steel industry nationalized (July).

Citizens of Gibraltar vote in favor of remaining British (September).

British troops withdraw from Aden (November).

Scottish National Party wins Hamilton by-election (November).

Devaluation of the pound (£1 = $2.40) (November).

France vetoes Britain's entry into EEC (December).

1968

Financial crisis: public expenditure cuts (January); rush for gold causes banks, exchanges to close (March); central bankers agree on two-tier system for price of gold (March).

Enoch Powell makes inflammatory speech on immigration, is sacked from the shadow cabinet (April).

Fulton Report on the civil service (June).

Prescription charges again in National Health Service (June).

Nuclear nonproliferation treaty is signed by 137 members of the United Nations (July).

Swaziland becomes independent (September).

Theatres Act abolishes censorship (September).

Antiwar demonstrations in London against the United States in Vietnam (October).

Fighting in Londonderry begins the troubles in Northern Ireland (October).

Squeeze on credit (November).

1969

London School of Economics forced to close by student protests (February).

British army units to be sent to Northern Ireland (April).

Voting age is reduced to 18 (May).

Divorce Act recognizes "irretrievable breakdown" of marriage (June).

Investiture of Prince Charles as Prince of Wales (July).

Street fighting in Londonderry; British army takes over security in Northern Ireland (August).

Abolition of death penalty for murder becomes permanent (December).

Open University is founded.

1970

Rhodesia proclaims itself a republic (March).

Equal Pay Act aims to prevent discrimination against women in terms of employment, effective 1975 (May).

General election gives the Conservatives a majority of 30; Edward Heath becomes prime minister (June).

1971

Postal workers strike (January).

Commonwealth meeting in Singapore (January).

Decimal currency comes into operation (February).

Prices and Incomes Board ended (March).

Upper Clyde Shipbuilders liquidated (July).

Industrial Relations Act (August).

Under a special powers act, Northern Ireland government interns a large number of suspected persons (August–September).

Immigration Act (October).

Heath meets with President Richard Nixon in Bermuda (December).

1972

Miners' strike begins (January).

Britain joins the EEC (January); effective January 1973.

"Bloody Sunday" in Londonderry, when 13 members of an unarmed Catholic protest are killed by British troops (January).

Miners' strike ends (February).

IRA bomb attack at Aldershot (February).

Heath imposes direct rule on Northern Ireland; William Whitelaw appointed secretary of state for Northern Ireland (March).

Major violence in Ulster when direct rule is imposed (April).

Bangladesh admitted to the Commonwealth (April).

British Rail is shut down by union "go-slow" (May).

Ceylon becomes independent as Sri Lanka (May).

Idi Amin expels 40,000 Asians from Uganda (August).

"Cod war" begins when Iceland extends fishing limit from 12 to 150 miles (September).

Congregational church and Presbyterian church combine to form the United Reform church (October).

90-day freeze on prices, pay, rent, and dividends (November).

Race Relations Act in force; discrimination on grounds of color is not allowed (November).

1973

Britain becomes member of the EEC (January).

Foreign exchange crisis (February).

Referendum in Ulster favors ties with Britain; new Northern Ireland assembly proposed, to be chosen by proportional representation (March).

Value-added tax is introduced (April).

New assembly elected in Ulster (June), but its first meeting is disrupted (July).

IRA bombings in London (August–September).

Arab-Israeli war (October).

Steep increase in price of oil is ordered by OPEC (October).

Kilbrandon Commission reports on devolution (October).

Cod war with Iceland ends (November).

A new power-sharing executive proposed for Northern Ireland (November).

Miners and power workers go on strike (November).

Emergency conservation measures enacted to meet fuel crisis (December).

Conference of leaders from the United Kingdom, Ireland, and Northern Ireland agree to form a Council of Ireland, the "Sunningdale Agreement" (December).

1974

Three-day week introduced to meet power shortage (January).

Northern Ireland executive takes office, ending direct rule; some members of the new assembly are expelled for disruption (January).

Miners go on strike, and Heath calls a general election. Labour has a narrow edge over the Conservatives 301 to 297 (February). Efforts to form a coalition with the 14 Liberals and the other smaller groups (12 from Northern Ireland, 7 Scottish nationalists, and 2 Welsh nationalists) are unsuccessful. Harold Wilson becomes prime minister, and miners return to work (March).

Britain demands renegotiation of terms of entry into EEC (April).

Protestant general strike against the new regime in Northern Ireland. The new assembly suspended and direct rule resumes (May).

Repeal of the Industrial Relations Act of 1971. Pay board and incomes policy abolished (July).

IRA bombings in Guildford (October).

General election gives Labour a slim overall majority (October).

IRA bombings in Birmingham (November).

Prevention of Terrorism Act proscribes the IRA and gives wide powers to police (November).

1975

Plan for the Channel tunnel abandoned (January).

Margaret Thatcher becomes leader of the Conservative Party (February).

Agreement on renegotiated terms of entry into EEC (March).

Referendum on membership in the EEC sees more than 2 to 1 in favor (June).

Oil is pumped ashore from the North Sea (June).

Iceland again extends its fishing grounds, from 50 to 200 miles (October).

Further IRA violence in London (October–December).

National Enterprise Board established (November).

Employment Protection Act creates advisory, conciliation, and arbitration service (November).

Comprehensive schools made compulsory by an Education Act (December).

End of internment without trial in Northern Ireland (December).

1976

Concorde enters passenger service (January).

Wilson resigns as prime minister (March).

James Callaghan wins election as new Labour Party leader and becomes prime minister (April).

Agreement ends the Cod War (June).

Britain receives £3 billion in standby credit from European and American banks (June).

European Commission on Human Rights reports on torture of Irish internees by British guards (September).

Roy Jenkins becomes president of the European Commission (September).

Government applies for £2.3 billion loan from the IMF (September).

Spending cuts, increased taxation, and sale of British Petroleum shares are needed to meet financial crisis (December).

Referenda on devolution for Scotland and Wales are announced (December).

1977

Talks on Rhodesian government fail (January).

IRA bombing in London continues (January).

Government loses motion on devolution bills (February) and forms a pact with Liberal Party to defeat a vote of no confidence by Conservatives (March).

Loyalist general strike in Ulster fails due to lack of support (May).

Government incomes policy moves into new stage, limits wage increases to 10 percent (July).

National Front march in London leads to violence (August). A march planned for Manchester is banned (September).

Firemen go on strike, demand 30 percent wage increase (November).

1978

Firemen's strike ends (January).

Scottish devolution bill amended: requires 40 percent of total electorate to approve the measure (January).

Internal agreement on majority rule in Rhodesia (March).

Devolution Acts for Scotland and Wales (July).

Series of strikes of public employees and others begins (September).

Labour Party conference opposes proposed 5 percent limit on wage increases (October).

Trades Union Congress objects to government's limit of 5 percent on wage increases; *The Times* is silenced by industrial dispute (November).

IRA bombings in Bristol, Manchester, Coventry, Southampton, and London (December).

1979

Strikes continue; road haulage strike and secondary picketing lead to production delays and layoffs of 150,000. Serious delays in health services, garbage collection, and other services (January).

Rhodesia votes for limited majority rule (January).

European Monetary System established (January).

Welsh referendum on devolution is a large "no" vote; in Scotland, the "yes" vote is only about 32 percent of total electorate, thus it fails (March).

Government loses a vote of confidence, and a general election is called (March).

Conservative MP is killed by an IRA car bomb at Westminster (March).

Conservatives win a 41-seat majority, and Margaret Thatcher becomes the first woman to be prime minister (May).

In the first direct elections for the European Parliament, the Conservatives win 60 of the 78 seats (June).

Commonwealth Conference in Lusaka and Lancaster House Conference set up free elections in Rhodesia (August).

Lord Mountbatten is assassinated by the IRA by a bomb that explodes on his boat (August).

The Times resumes publication (November).

Thatcher proposes cuts in Britain's EEC contributions (November).

Government introduces trade union bill to regulate picketing, balloting, and the closed shop (December).

1980

Steel workers go on strike (January–April).

A North Sea oil platform collapses, killing 100 (March).

Robert Mugabe forms the first black government in Rhodesia (Zimbabwe) (March).

Rioting in Bristol (April).

Inflation reaches 21.8 percent (April).

Argentina prepares to invade the Falkland Islands (*Las Malvinas*) (April).

Hostages taken in the Iranian Embassy in London (April); SAS troops storm the embassy and free them (May).

Agreement to reduce Britain's payments to the EEC (May).

Callaghan retires and is replaced by Michael Foot as Labour leader (October).

Unemployment reaches 2 million for the first time since 1935 (October).

1981

Special conference of Labour Party creates an electoral college to choose party leader (January). Four leading members resign and create Council for Social Democracy, and later the Social Democratic Party (March).

National Coal Board announces pit closures, which would mean the loss of 30,000 jobs, but it rescinds the plan after a strike threat (February).

Brixton race riots (April).

Bobby Sands, IRA prisoner in Northern Ireland, dies after a 66-day hunger strike in the Maze prison (May).

Rioting in London, Liverpool, and Manchester (July).

Wedding of Prince Charles and Lady Diana Spencer (July).

Liberal Party and Social Democratic Party form alliance (September).

Hunger strike ends at the Maze, after 10 men died (October).

Scarman Report on the race riots (November).

1982

Number of unemployed passes 2 million (January).

Falklands War begins with Argentine invasion; a British fleet sails, and a blockade on the islands is proclaimed (April).

Port Stanley is bombed by the British, and they sink the Argentine cruiser *General Belgrano.* An Exocet missile destroys HMS *Sheffield.* The British take several posts in the islands, while losing a number of other vessels to enemy fire (May).

Argentine troops surrender and a cease-fire is declared. General Galtieri, the Argentine leader, is deposed (June).

IRA bombs explode in Hyde Park and Regent's Park, London (July).

The Thames barrier, an engineering work designed to prevent flooding in London, is activated (October).

Nuclear weapons protest by 30,000 women at Greenham Common air base (December).

1983

General election produces landslide for the Conservatives (397), with Labour getting 209 and the Liberal/SDP Alliance only 23. Michael Foot resigns as Labour leader (June).

Escape of 38 IRA prisoners from the Maze prison (September).

Neil Kinnock is elected leader of the Labour Party (October).

Prime minister of Grenada is shot by troops; American forces invade and restore the governor-general (October).

American cruise missiles arrive at Greenham Common (November).

Large IRA bombs explode in London (December).

Inflation falls to 3.7 percent; unemployment down.

1984

Trade unions are banned at Government Communications Headquarters (GCHQ) in Cheltenham (January).

National Coal Board announces closing of 21 pits; Miners' Union calls strike (March).

Constable Yvonne Fletcher shot and killed outside the Libyan embassy in St. James's Square; police surround the building, relations with Libya are broken off, and 30 Libyans are deported (April).

Violence during picketing at Sheffield (May).

Talks between Britain and Argentina break down (July).

High Court declares the government ban on unions at GCHQ is illegal (July).

Trades Union Congress supports miners' strike (August).

Sino-British declaration on Hong Kong is signed, promising continued capitalist regime there for 50 years after Britain leaves in 1997 (August).

IRA bombs Grand Hotel in Brighton where Mrs. Thatcher and Conservative leaders are staying during the party conference. Five are killed, two party leaders are injured (October).

British Telecom privatized (November).

Law Lords uphold government's ban on unions at GCHQ (November).

National Coal Board begins back-to-work drive (November).

National Union of Miners funds are sequestered (December).

1985

Oxford University refuses to award an honorary degree to Mrs Thatcher because of opposition to her policies regarding universities (January).

IRA bomb attack on police station in Newry kills nine policemen (February).

Frontier between Spain and Gibraltar is reopened (February).

Miners vote to end strike (March).

Epidemic of "Legionnaires' Disease" in Stafford (May).

Football disasters: fire at Bradford kills 55, riot of Liverpool fans at Heysel causes 41 deaths. British teams are banned from European competition due to bad behavior of fans (May).

The Fédération Internationale de Football Association (FIFA) imposes a worldwide ban on British teams (June).

General Synod of the Church of England approves the ordination of women (July).

Greater London Council abolished (July).

Riots in Birmingham and Brixton result from friction between black communities and the police (September).

A policeman killed in riots in Tottenham after the shooting of a black woman by a policeman (October).

Dissident miners set up Union of Democratic Mineworkers (October).

Anglo-Irish Agreement at Hillsborough recognizes Dublin's interest in the affairs of Northern Ireland (November).

Ulster MPs resign in protest over the Hillsborough agreement, forcing 15 by-elections (December).

1986

Rupert Murdoch moves printing of his newspapers to a new site at Wapping; this is designed to resist the strikes of print unions (January).

Britain and France agree to build Channel tunnel (February).

European Court rules that retirement age should be the same for men and women; the government takes no action (February).

Royal proclamation recognizes legal independence of Australia (March).

Thatcher allows American planes to use British bases to bomb targets in Libya in retaliation for terrorist attacks (April).

Chernobyl nuclear reactor explodes; high levels of radiation in northern and western areas (April).

Northern Ireland Assembly dissolved (June).

Court bans publication of works by former MI 5 officer, Peter Wright.

Privatization of British Gas (December).

1987

Violent clashes outside the Wapping print works result in 300 injuries (January).

The printers' dispute ends (February).

British Airways privatized (February), as are British airports (July).

A channel ferry sinks, killing 200 (March).

After the government fails to halt the publication of *Spycatcher,* Peter Wright's memoirs, in Australia (March), the book is published in the U.S. and Canada (May).

General election gives the Conservatives a majority of 101 (June).

Thatcher is denied an honorary degree from Oxford a second time (July).

Hurricane strikes Britain and destroys an estimated 15 million trees; 17 people killed (October 16).

"Black Monday" sees fall in share values of £50 million (October 19).

Government announces plan to introduce "community charge"—a poll tax—to replace local rates in 1990 (November).

Unemployment falls to 2.65 million, lowest in five years (November).

1988

Mrs. Thatcher is the longest-serving prime minister in the 20th century (January).

MPs vote in favor of televising proceedings in the House of Commons on an experimental basis for six months (February).

Liberals and Social Democrats merge, forming the Social and Liberal Democrats (March).

Three IRA gunmen are shot by Special Air Service forces in Gibraltar; government fails to suppress a TV documentary on the shootings (March–April).

Education Act introduces national curriculum (July).

North Sea oil rig Piper Alpha explodes, killing 150 (July).

Law Lords reject government claim for permanent ban on publication of *Spycatcher* (October).

Pan Am jetliner blown up by a terrorist bomb, falls on Lockerbie, Scotland, killing all 270 people on board and 11 people on the ground (December).

1989

A Boeing 737 crashes on the M1 highway in Leicestershire, killing 47 (January).

Salman Rushdie's *Satanic Verses,* which had won the Whitbread Prize in 1988, is condemned by Iran's Ayatollah Khomeini, who orders Rushdie's execution for blasphemy (February).

Disaster at Hillsborough football stadium, where 95 Liverpool fans are killed in a stampede (April).

Britain rejects European Community social charter (May).

Violent protest in Parliament Square over Rushdie's book (May).

Water companies privatized (September).

"Guildford Four" released after police conduct in their arrest and trial for alleged role in IRA bombings is exposed (October).

Britain and Argentina sign peace treaty (October).

Sanctions proposed against South Africa by the Commonwealth are rejected by Britain (October).

Mrs. Thatcher defeats a challenge to her leadership of the Conservative Party (December).

1990

South Africa lifts bans on political parties; Nelson Mandela released from prison after 27 years (February).

Demonstration against poll tax in Trafalgar Square; rioting follows (March).

Strangeways Prison seized by inmates and held for 25 days (April).

Declaration by NATO leaders formally signals the end of the cold war (July).

Iraq invades Kuwait; the EEC, United States, and Japan place an embargo on Iraqi oil (August).

Britain joins the exchange rate mechanism (ERM); summit meeting in Rome sets timetable for monetary union, with Thatcher in outspoken opposition (October).

Edward Heath negotiates with Saddam Hussein for release of British hostages (October).

Mary Robinson is elected the first woman president of Ireland (November).

Mrs. Thatcher faces a revolt within her party; in a leadership election she falls short of a majority by four votes and withdraws. In the second ballot for the new leader, John Major wins and becomes the new prime minister (November).

Privatization of electricity (December).

British troops assemble in Saudi Arabia (December).

1991

U.N. coalition launches invasion of Kuwait and Iraq with an air assault on Iraqi positions. Operation "Desert Storm" begins (January).

IRA mortar attack on 10 Downing Street (February).

Kuwait is liberated, and the Iraqi army destroyed, followed by a cease-fire in the Gulf War (February).

Court of Appeal quashes convictions of the "Birmingham Six" (February).

The poll tax is scrapped, replaced by a tax primarily on property (April).

Mikhail Gorbachev resigns as head of Communist Party (April).

Helen Sharman, Britain's first female astronaut, joins two Russian astronauts on an eight-day mission to the MIR space station (May).

Government proposals to give polytechnics the same status as universities (May).

Conservatives lose 890 seats in local elections (May).

Convictions in Guildford and Woolwich bombings overturned (June).

Defense review called "Options for Change" (July).

Gorbachev dismisses Soviet government (August).

The EEC signs Maastricht Treaty for political and economic union (December).

1992

Meeting of a self-appointed Muslim Parliament of Great Britain (January).

All-party talks resume in Belfast (March).

Despite weak showing in the opinion polls, the general election gives the Conservatives a 21-seat majority (April). Neil Kinnock resigns as head of the Labour Party. Betty Boothroyd becomes the first female Speaker of the House.

Secret Intelligence Service (MI 6) is acknowledged to exist for the first time (May).

Tactical nuclear missiles are to be scrapped (June).

Denmark rejects the Maastricht Treaty in a referendum (June).

John Smith is elected leader of the Labour Party (July).

Lloyd's of London announces losses of over £2 billion (July).

Sterling crisis (August–September). Speculation puts pressure on the pound; U.K. membership in the ERM (exchange rate mechanism) is suspended.

Conservative Party conference divided over relations with Europe and over the announcement of closure of 31 coal mines, with a loss of 30,000 jobs (October).

General election in Ireland, plus referendum on abortion. Voters approve making information on abortion available and allowing travel to other EEC countries to obtain an abortion; abortion itself is not approved (November).

High court rules that the government's pit closure announcement was illegal, as it failed to consult unions and workers (December).

Prince Charles and Diana separate (December).

1993

Single European market begins (January). The EC is renamed the European Union (EU).

John Smith lays out new lines of Labour policy: less power for unions, less centralized government, abolition of the House of Lords (January).

The queen agrees to pay income tax and capital gains tax (February).

An IRA bomb in Warrington kills two boys and triggers a peace march in Dublin (March).

Government loses vote on Maastricht bill; budget includes doubling of VAT (value-added tax) on domestic fuel (March).

Large IRA bomb explodes in Bishopsgate, City of London (April).

Opinion polls show John Major has lowest support of any prime minister since polling began (June).

Government loses several votes but manages to win a vote of confidence (July).

Britain ratifies Maastricht Treaty (August).

Public sector pay freeze (September).

Defense cuts require privatizing dockyards (October).

Downing Street Declaration by Major and Irish prime minister Albert Reynolds plans all-party talks on Northern Ireland (December).

1994

Prime Minister Major testifies before the Scott Inquiry into arms sales to Iraq, the first such testimony by a sitting head of government (January).

IRA mortar attack on Heathrow Airport (March).

First women ordained in the Church of England (March).

IRA announces temporary ceasefire (April).

Conservatives lose heavily to Labour and Liberals in local elections (May).

John Smith dies of heart attack (May).

Channel tunnel opens (May).

Labour gains in European elections, Liberals win their first two seats in the European parliament (June).

Tony Blair is elected leader of the Labour Party (July).

IRA announces cessation of military operations (August).

Blair proposes reform of Labour Party constitution (October).

Coal industry privatized (December).

Government loses vote to extend VAT to fuel and power (December).

The United Kingdom holds talks with Sinn Féin in Belfast (December).

1995

Army ends daylight patrols in Belfast (January).

Collapse of Barings, the United Kingdom's oldest merchant bank (February).

Anglo-Irish Agreement on the future of Northern Ireland (February).

At a special Labour Party conference, Blair wins revision of Clause IV in the party constitution (April).

Conservatives lose more than 2,000 seats in local elections (May).

John Major resigns as Conservative Party leader, wins election over John Redwood (July), but a large number of MPs do not support Major.

David Trimble elected leader of the Ulster Unionist Party (September).

European Commission on Human Rights condemns the 1988 SAS shootings of IRA members in Gibraltar (September).

Metrication Day: Britain converts to metric units (October).

Nigeria suspended from the Commonwealth for the executions of human-rights activists, among them Ken Soro-Wiwa (November).

Referendum in Ireland narrowly approves divorce (November).

1996

Mitchell Commission reports on disarming of rival groups in Northern Ireland (January).

Scott Report on arms sales to Iraq finds that the government deliberately failed to inform Parliament of the sales (February).

Privatized passenger trains begin operation (February).

The Princess of Wales agrees to Prince Charles's request for divorce (February).

IRA cease-fire ends with a bomb blast in London's docklands, killing two (February).

Reports of links between Creutzfeld-Jacob disease and B.S.E. ("mad cow" disease) cause drop in beef sales and an EU ban on British beef exports (March).

Elections for constitutional forum in Northern Ireland (May).

Labour publishes plans for devolution for Scotland and Wales (June).

British and Irish leaders have talks with representatives of Ulster political parties; it is the first meeting of an elected assembly in 10 years (June).

IRA bomb in central Manchester injures hundreds of shoppers and workers (June).

1997

Geneticists in Scotland report first cloning of an adult sheep (February).

Major calls for general election after his government fails to keep its majority and comes under great public pressure due to scandals and policy problems (March).

IRA bomb and hoax campaign disrupts U.K. travel (April).

Labour wins election with 179-seat majority; Conservatives leave office after 18 years; Tony Blair becomes new prime minister; 120 women elected, nearly doubling the previous number; Liberal Democrats win 46 seats; Sinn Féin wins two seats, but the winners refuse to take oath and do not enter the House of Commons (May).

John Major announces his resignation as party leader (May).

Gordon Brown, chancellor of the exchequer, announces that Bank of England will determine interest rates in future (May).

William Hague elected Conservative Party leader (June).

House of Commons votes for ban on handguns (June).

McDonald's wins libel case against two environmental activists (June).

IRA resumes cease-fire of 1994 (July).

A former agent alleges that MI 5 had phone taps and secret files on prominent figures (August).

Princess Diana dies in an auto crash in Paris (August).

Devolution referenda pass in Scotland (74 percent) and Wales (50.3 percent). The Scottish Parliament also is granted powers to adjust tax levels (September).

The United Kingdom delays entry into European Monetary Union (EMU) (October).

Tony Blair meets with Gerry Adams, head of Sinn Féin (October).

1998

Sinn Féin suspended from peace talks (February).

Welfare reform featured in Gordon Brown's budget (March).

"Good Friday" peace agreement signed by the United Kingdom, Ireland, and eight Northern Ireland political parties (April).

Peace agreement endorsed in referendum (May).

Northern Ireland Assembly elected (June).

Tony Blair delivers "Annual Report" on his government's activities (July).

Strategic defense review sees cuts of over £915 million in the next three years (July).

Jenkins Commission on electoral reform recommends replacing the "first past the post" system with a form of proportional representation plus 150 seats from larger city and county areas (October).

1999

The "euro" is introduced as the common currency for 11 EU countries; note circulation is to begin in 2002 (January).

Northern Ireland Assembly creates a power-sharing executive (February).

Hillsborough Declaration by Prime Minister Blair and Irish prime minister Bertie Ahern (April).

Bombings in London aimed at ethnic minorities and homosexuals (April).

Elections for new assemblies in Scotland and Wales. Labour gains the most seats, but no majority (May).

Government loses votes in the House of Lords on the reform of that body (June).

Former Soviet KGB agent Vasili Mitrokhin reveals the identities of a number of British spies (September).

The House of Lords votes on its abolition; creates an interim chamber of 92 hereditary peers (October).

2000

London mayoral election is won by Ken Livingstone, maverick Labour politican and former London council chairman. Though he ran against the official Labour candidate and was expelled from the party for doing so, Livingstone polled 58 percent of the vote (May).

Fuel protest as farmers and truckers blockade oil refineries for a week. Tanker drivers and police do not force confrontation; petrol supplies dry up in days. Blair prepares emergency measures, but the protest is terminated. For a brief period, the Conservatives overtake Labour in opinion polls (September).

Human Rights Act comes into force. Passed in 1998, the act brings Britain into line with the European Convention on Human Rights. Similar legislation went into effect in Scotland in 1999 (October).

B.S.E. report reviews the history of the disease, suggests that the effects, and links to humans, were aggravated by bureaucratic and political lethargy and secrecy (October).

Millenium Dome exhibition criticized by National Audit Office report (November).

U.S. president Bill Clinton visits Northern Ireland, calls for implementation of the Good Friday accord and asks IRA to ensure arms decommissioning (December).

APPENDIXES

APPENDIX I
Maps

APPENDIX II
Genealogies

APPENDIX III
English Sovereigns from 899

APPENDIX IV
United Kingdom Prime Ministers from 1721

APPENDIX I

GREAT BRITAIN ADMINISTRATIVE BOUNDARIES, 2001

1 West Dunbartonshire
2 East Dunbartonshire
3 Falkirk
4 Inverclyde
5 Renfrewshire
6 Glasgow City
7 North Lanarkshire
8 West Lothian
9 East Renfrewshire
10 Blackburn with Darwen
11 Knowsley
12 St. Helens
13 Wigan
14 Bolton
15 Bury
16 Rochdale
17 Salford
18 Oldham
19 Warrington
20 Trafford
21 Tameside
22 Stockport
23 Manchester
24 Halton
25 Kirklees
26 Wakefield
27 Barnsley
28 Doncaster
29 Sheffield
30 Rotherham
31 City of Stoke-on-Trent
32 City of Derby
33 City of Nottingham
34 Telford and Wrekin
35 City of Wolverhampton
36 Walsall
37 Dudley
38 Sandwell
39 Birmingham
40 Solihull
41 Coventry
42 City of Leicester
43 City of Peterborough
44 Milton Keynes
45 Luton
46 Merthyr Tydfil
47 Blaenau Gwent
48 Caerphilly
49 Torfaen
50 Newport
51 Monmouthshire
52 South Gloucestershire
53 City of Bristol
54 North Somerset
55 Bath and North East
   Somerset
56 Reading
57 Wokingham
58 Windsor and Maidenhead
59 Bracknell Forest
60 Slough
61 Camden
62 Islington
63 Hackney
64 Hammersmith and Fulham
65 Royal Borough of
   Kensington and Chelsea
66 City of Westminster
67 County of the City
   of London
68 Tower Hamlets
69 Wandsworth
70 Lambeth
71 Southwark

ENGLISH TRADING COMPANIES, CA. 1550–1770

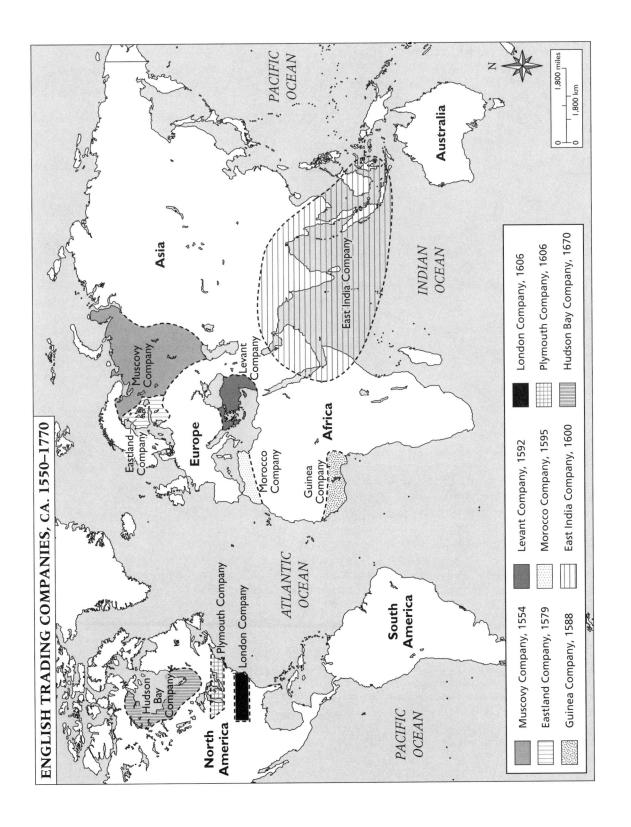

North America

Hudson Bay Company

Plymouth Company

London Company

South America

Europe

Eastland Company

Muscovy Company

Levant Company

Morocco Company

Guinea Company

Africa

Asia

East India Company

Australia

PACIFIC OCEAN

ATLANTIC OCEAN

PACIFIC OCEAN

INDIAN OCEAN

N

1,800 miles

1,800 km

Muscovy Company, 1554		Levant Company, 1592	
Eastland Company, 1579		Morocco Company, 1595	
Guinea Company, 1588		East India Company, 1600	
London Company, 1606			
Plymouth Company, 1606			
Hudson Bay Company, 1670			

CIVIL WAR IN ENGLAND, 1642–1643

District controlled by Crown, 1643

Districts conquered by Crown, 1643

District controlled by Parliament, 1643

Districts conquered by Parliament, 1643

★ Major battles

N

SCOTLAND

Isle of Man

Irish Sea

North Sea

Newcastle

Carlisle

Bolton Castle

Scarborough

York

Hull 1643

Preston 1643

Manchester

Liverpool

Sheffield

ENGLAND

Chester

Winceby 1643

Caernarfon

Belvoir Castle

Norwich

Litchfield 1643

Leicester

PRINCIPALITY

Edge Hill 1642

Northampton

Hereford

Cambridge

OF

Colchester

WALES

Oxford

Brentford 1643

Raglan Castle

Landsdown Hill 1643

Pembroke

Bristol

London

Dover

Bristol Channel

Roundway Down 1643

Newbury 1643

Maidstone

Bideford 1643

Wardour Castle

Southampton

Arundel

Stratton 1643

Exeter

Portsmouth

Brudock Down 1643

Corfe Castle 1643

Dartmouth 1643

English Channel

0 50 miles

0 50 km

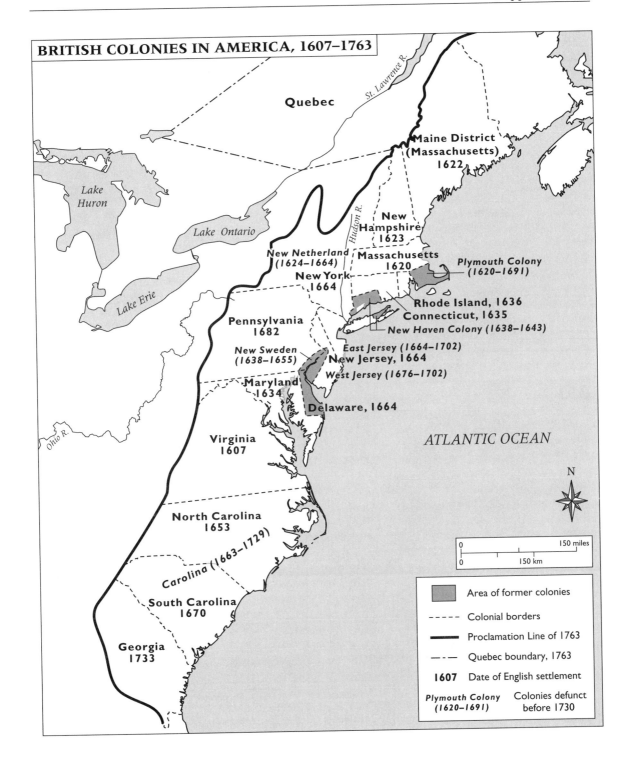

BRITISH COLONIES IN AMERICA, 1607–1763

Quebec

St. Lawrence R.

Maine District (Massachusetts) 1622

Lake Huron

Lake Ontario

Hudson R.

New Hampshire 1623

New Netherland (1624–1664)

Massachusetts 1620

Plymouth Colony (1620–1691)

New York 1664

Lake Erie

Rhode Island, 1636
Connecticut, 1635
New Haven Colony (1638–1643)

Pennsylvania 1682

East Jersey (1664–1702)
New Sweden (1638–1655)
New Jersey, 1664
West Jersey (1676–1702)

Maryland 1634

Delaware, 1664

Ohio R.

Virginia 1607

ATLANTIC OCEAN

N

North Carolina 1653

Carolina (1663–1729)

| 0 | | 150 miles |
| 0 | | 150 km |

South Carolina 1670

Georgia 1733

Area of former colonies

- - - - - Colonial borders

Proclamation Line of 1763

- · - · - Quebec boundary, 1763

1607 Date of English settlement

Plymouth Colony (1620–1691) Colonies defunct before 1730

BRITISH POSSESSIONS IN AFRICA, 1885–1924

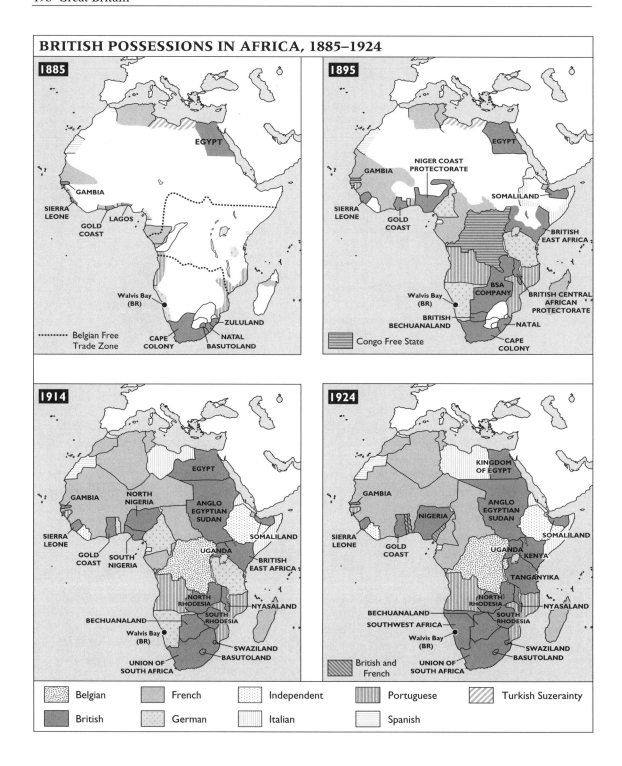

1885

EGYPT

GAMBIA

SIERRA
LEONE

GOLD
COAST · LAGOS

Walvis Bay
(BR)

ZULULAND

CAPE · NATAL
COLONY · BASUTOLAND

-------- Belgian Free
Trade Zone

1895

EGYPT

NIGER COAST
PROTECTORATE

GAMBIA

SOMALILAND

SIERRA
LEONE

GOLD
COAST

BRITISH
EAST AFRICA

BSA
COMPANY

Walvis Bay
(BR)

BRITISH CENTRAL
AFRICAN
PROTECTORATE

BRITISH
BECHUANALAND · NATAL

Congo Free State

CAPE
COLONY

1914

EGYPT

GAMBIA

NORTH
NIGERIA

ANGLO
EGYPTIAN
SUDAN

SIERRA
LEONE

SOMALILAND

GOLD
COAST · SOUTH
NIGERIA

UGANDA

BRITISH
EAST AFRICA

NORTH
RHODESIA

NYASALAND

BECHUANALAND

SOUTH
RHODESIA

Walvis Bay
(BR)

SWAZILAND
BASUTOLAND

UNION OF
SOUTH AFRICA

1924

KINGDOM
OF EGYPT

GAMBIA

NIGERIA

ANGLO
EGYPTIAN
SUDAN

SIERRA
LEONE

SOMALILAND

GOLD
COAST

UGANDA · KENYA

TANGANYIKA

NORTH
RHODESIA · NYASALAND

BECHUANALAND

SOUTH
RHODESIA

SOUTHWEST AFRICA

Walvis Bay
(BR)

SWAZILAND
BASUTOLAND

British and
French

UNION OF
SOUTH AFRICA

Belgian   French   Independent   Portuguese   Turkish Suzerainty

British   German   Italian   Spanish

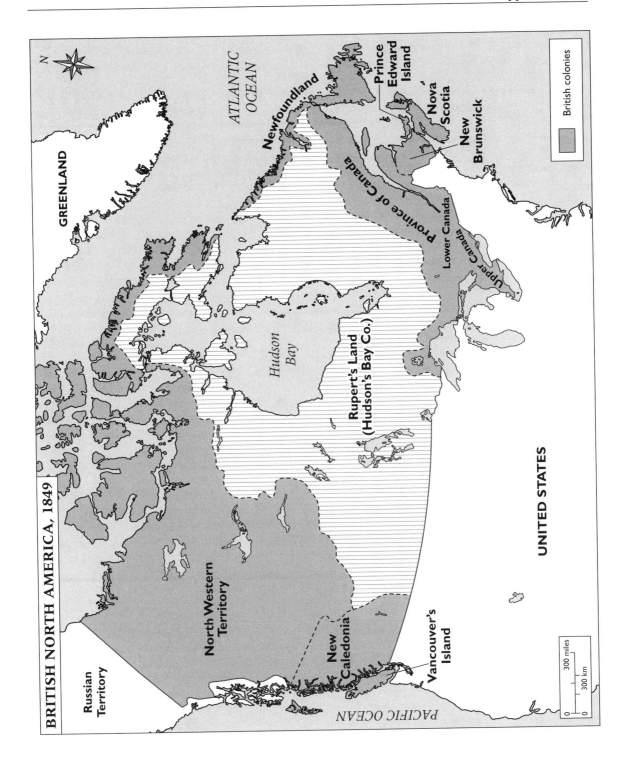

BRITISH NORTH AMERICA, 1849

British colonies

N

GREENLAND

ATLANTIC OCEAN

Newfoundland

Prince Edward Island

Nova Scotia

New Brunswick

Province of Canada

Lower Canada

Upper Canada

Hudson Bay

Rupert's Land (Hudson's Bay Co.)

Russian Territory

North Western Territory

New Caledonia

Vancouver's Island

UNITED STATES

PACIFIC OCEAN

300 miles

300 km

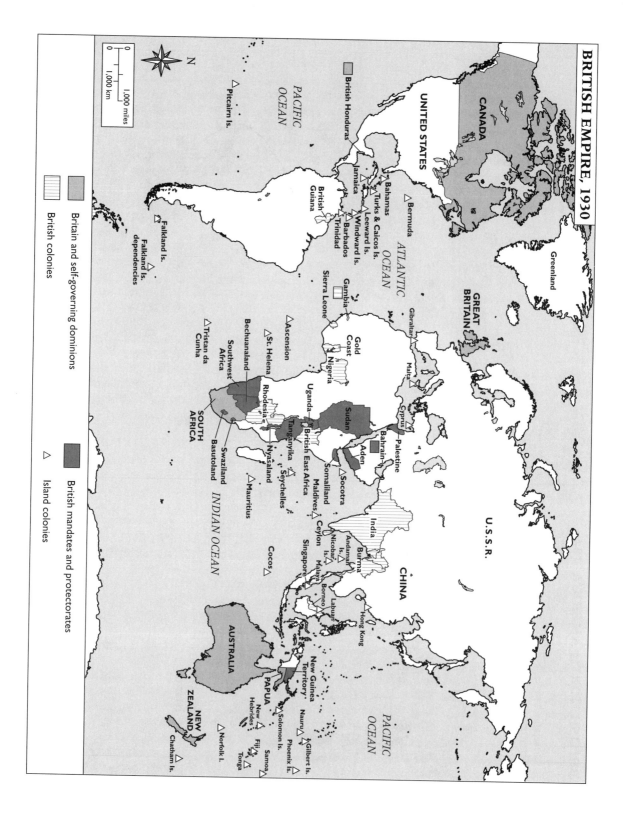

BRITISH EMPIRE, 1930

Britain and self-governing dominions

British colonies

British mandates and protectorates

Island colonies

PACIFIC OCEAN

ATLANTIC OCEAN

INDIAN OCEAN

PACIFIC OCEAN

UNITED STATES

CANADA

Greenland

GREAT BRITAIN

U.S.S.R.

CHINA

AUSTRALIA

NEW ZEALAND

SOUTH AFRICA

British Honduras

British Guiana

Falkland Is.
dependencies

Falkland Is.

Pitcairn Is.

Bahamas

Bermuda

Turks & Caicos Is.

Jamaica

Leeward Is.

Windward Is.

Barbados

Trinidad

Sierra Leone

Gambia

Gold Coast

Nigeria

Ascension

St. Helena

Tristan da Cunha

Bechuanaland

Southwest Africa

Rhodesia

Swaziland

Basutoland

Nyasaland

Mauritius

Uganda

British East Africa

Tanganyika

Seychelles

Sudan

Somaliland

Aden

Socotra

Maldives

Ceylon

Palestine

Bahrain

Gibraltar

Malta

Cyprus

India

Burma

Andaman Is.

Nicobar Is.

Malay

Singapore

Borneo

Labuan

Hong Kong

Cocos

New Guinea Territory

PAPUA

New Hebrides

Solomon Is.

Norfolk I.

Chatham Is.

Fiji

Tonga

Samoa

Phoenix Is.

Gilbert Is.

Nauru

N

0 1,000 miles
0 1,000 km

APPENDIX II

SAXONS, DANES, AND NORMANS (showing union of the Saxon and Norman lines)

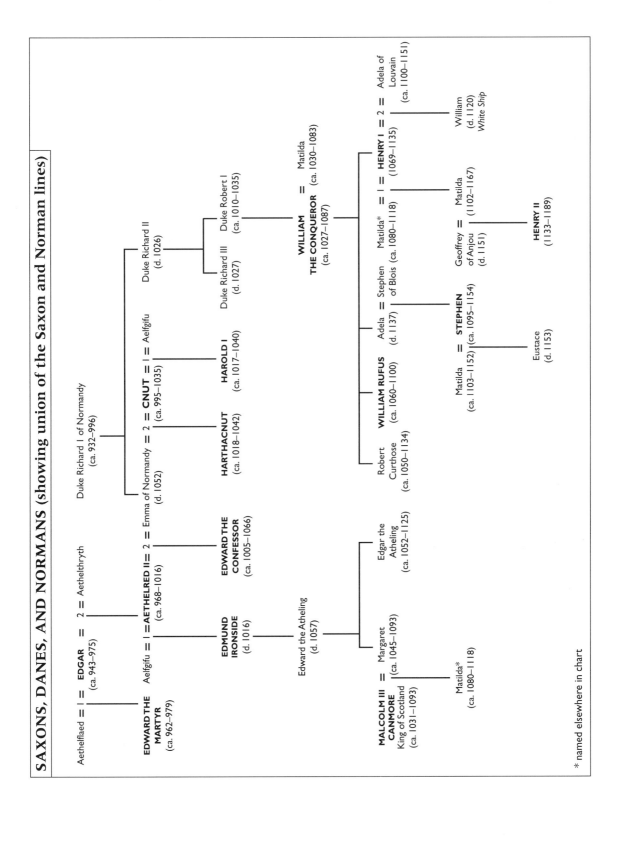

* named elsewhere in chart

THE PLANTAGENETS

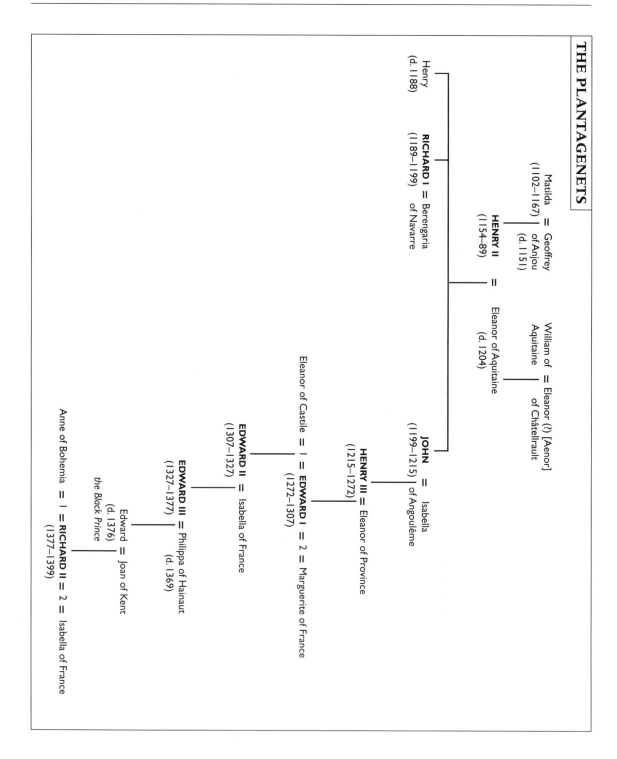

Matilda = Geoffrey
(1102–1167)   of Anjou
              (d. 1151)

William of = Eleanor (?) [Aenor]
Aquitaine   of Châtellrault

HENRY II
(1154–89)

=

Eleanor of Aquitaine
(d. 1204)

Henry
(d. 1188)

RICHARD I = Berengaria
(1189–1199)   of Navarre

JOHN = Isabella
(1199–1215)   of Angoulême

Eleanor of Castile = 1   = **EDWARD I** = 2 = Marguerite of France
                              (1272–1307)

HENRY III = Eleanor of Province
(1215–1272)

EDWARD II = Isabella of France
(1307–1327)

EDWARD III = Philippa of Hainaut
(1327–1377)   (d. 1369)

Edward = Joan of Kent
(d. 1376)
the Black Prince

Anne of Bohemia = 1 = **RICHARD II** = 2 = Isabella of France
                          (1377–1399)

HOUSE OF YORK, 1327–1485

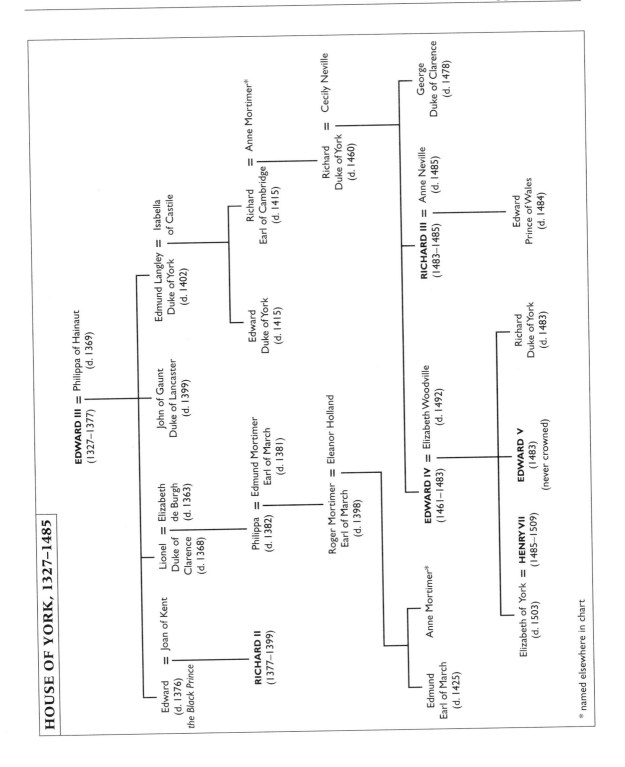

EDWARD III = Philippa of Hainaut
(1327–1377)   (d. 1369)

Edward = Joan of Kent
(d. 1376)
the Black Prince

RICHARD II
(1377–1399)

Lionel = Elizabeth
Duke of   de Burgh
Clarence   (d. 1363)
(d. 1368)

Philippa = Edmund Mortimer
(d. 1382)   Earl of March
(d. 1381)

Roger Mortimer = Eleanor Holland
Earl of March
(d. 1398)

Anne Mortimer*

Edmund
Earl of March
(d. 1425)

John of Gaunt
Duke of Lancaster
(d. 1399)

Edmund Langley = Isabella
Duke of York   of Castile
(d. 1402)

Edward
Duke of York
(d. 1415)

Richard = Anne Mortimer*
Earl of Cambridge
(d. 1415)

Richard = Cecily Neville
Duke of York
(d. 1460)

EDWARD IV = Elizabeth Woodville
(1461–1483)   (d. 1492)

RICHARD III = Anne Neville
(1483–1485)   (d. 1485)

George
Duke of Clarence
(d. 1478)

EDWARD V
(1483)
(never crowned)

Richard
Duke of York
(d. 1483)

Edward
Prince of Wales
(d. 1484)

Elizabeth of York = **HENRY VII**
(d. 1503)   (1485–1509)

* named elsewhere in chart

HOUSE OF LANCASTER, 1399–1471

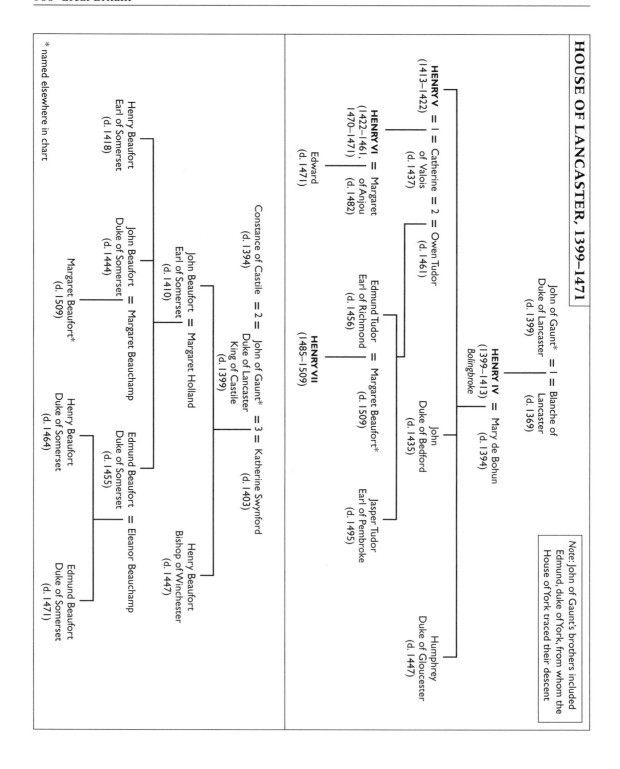

Note: John of Gaunt's brothers included Edmund, duke of York, from whom the House of York traced their descent

* named elsewhere in chart

John of Gaunt* = 1 = Blanche of
Duke of Lancaster   Lancaster
(d. 1399)   (d. 1369)

HENRY IV = Mary de Bohun
(1399–1413)   (d. 1394)
Bolingbroke

John
Duke of Bedford
(d. 1435)

Humphrey
Duke of Gloucester
(d. 1447)

HENRY V = 1 = Catherine = 2 = Owen Tudor
(1413–1422)   of Valois   (d. 1461)
                 (d. 1437)

Edward
(d. 1471)

HENRY VI = Margaret
(1422–1461,   of Anjou
1470–1471)   (d. 1482)

Edmund Tudor = Margaret Beaufort*
Earl of Richmond   (d. 1509)
(d. 1456)

Jasper Tudor
Earl of Pembroke
(d. 1495)

HENRY VII
(1485–1509)

John of Gaunt* = 3 = Katherine Swynford
Duke of Lancaster   (d. 1403)
King of Castile
(d. 1399)

Constance of Castile = 2 =

Henry Beaufort
Earl of Somerset
(d. 1418)

John Beaufort
Duke of Somerset
(d. 1444)

John Beaufort = Margaret Holland
Earl of Somerset
(d. 1410)

Margaret Beaufort = Margaret Beauchamp
(d. 1509)

Edmund Beaufort = Eleanor Beauchamp
Duke of Somerset
(d. 1455)

Henry Beaufort
Bishop of Winchester
(d. 1447)

Henry Beaufort
Duke of Somerset
(d. 1464)

Edmund Beaufort
Duke of Somerset
(d. 1471)

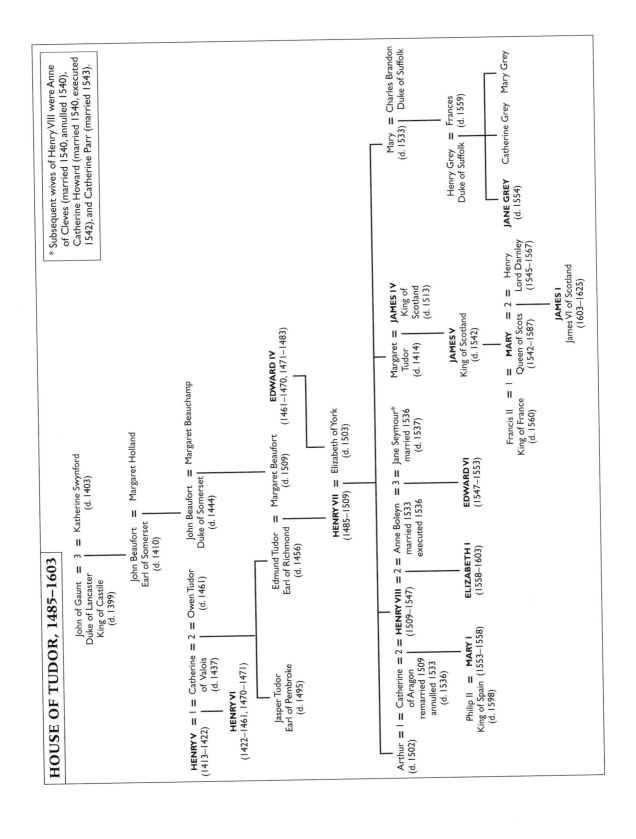

HOUSE OF TUDOR, 1485–1603

* Subsequent wives of Henry VIII were Anne of Cleves (married 1540, annulled 1540), Catherine Howard (married 1540, executed 1542), and Catherine Parr (married 1543).

HOUSE OF STUART AND HOUSE OF HANOVER, 1603–1837

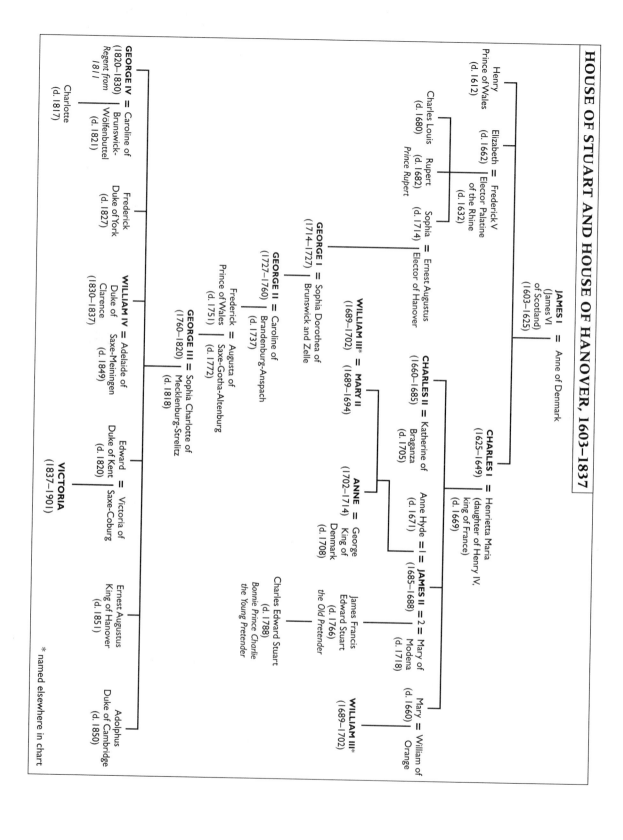

* named elsewhere in chart

HOUSE OF SAXE-COBURG-GOTHA AND WINDSOR, FROM 1837

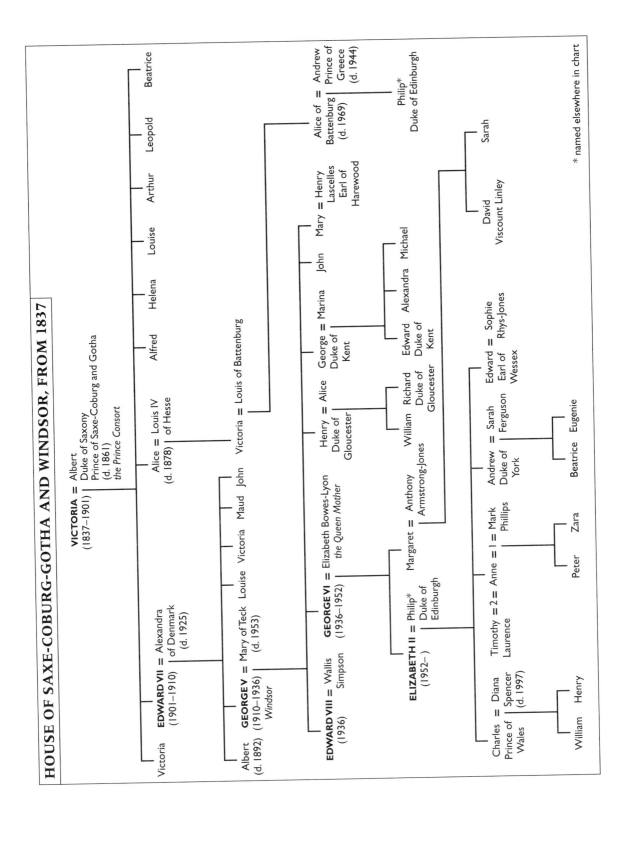

* named elsewhere in chart

APPENDIX III

Reign	Name	Relationship
West Saxon Kings		
899–924	Edward the Elder	son of Alfred the Great
924–39	Athelstan	son of Edward the Elder
939–46	Edmund	half-brother of Athelstan
946–55	Edred	brother of Edmund
955–59	Edwy	son of Edmund
959–75	Edgar	brother of Edwy
975–78	Edward the Martyr	son of Edgar
978–1016	Ethelred (II) the Unready	son of Edgar
1016	Edmund Ironside	son of Ethelred (II) the Unready
Danish Kings		
1016–35	Canute	son of Sweyn I of Denmark who conquered England in 1013
1035–40	Harold I	son of Canute
1040–42	Hardicanute	son of Canute
West Saxon Kings (restored)		
1042–66	Edward the Confessor	son of Ethelred (II) the Unready
1066	Harold II	son of Godwin
Norman Kings		
1066–87	William I	illegitimate son of Duke Robert the Devil
1087–1100	William II	son of William I
1100–35	Henry I	son of William I
1135–54	Stephen	grandson of William II
House of Plantagenet		
1154–89	Henry II	son of Matilda (daughter of Henry I)
1189–99	Richard I	son of Henry II
1199–1216	John	son of Henry II
1216–72	Henry III	son of John
1272–1307	Edward I	son of Henry III

ENGLISH SOVEREIGNS FROM 899 (*continued*)

Reign	Name	Relationship
House of Plantagenet (continued)		
1307–27	Edward II	son of Edward I
1327–77	Edward III	son of Edward II
1377–99	Richard II	son of the Black Prince
House of Lancaster		
1399–1413	Henry IV	son of John of Gaunt
1413–22	Henry V	son of Henry IV
1422–61, 1470–71	Henry VI	son of Henry V
House of York		
1461–70, 1471–83	Edward IV	son of Richard, Duke of York
1483	Edward V	son of Edward IV
1483–85	Richard III	brother of Edward IV
House of Tudor		
1485–1509	Henry VII	son of Edmund Tudor, Earl of Richmond
1509–47	Henry VIII	son of Henry VII
1547–53	Edward VI	son of Henry VIII
1553–58	Mary I	daughter of Henry VIII
1558–1603	Elizabeth I	daughter of Henry VIII
House of Stuart		
1603–25	James I (James VI in Scotland)	great-grandson of Margaret (daughter of Henry VII)
1625–49	Charles I	son of James I
1649–60	Commonwealth of England	
House of Stuart (restored)		
1660–85	Charles II	son of Charles I
1685–88	James II (James VII in Scotland)	son of Charles I
1689–1702	William III and Mary	son of Mary (daughter of Charles I); daughter of James II
1702–14	Anne	daughter of James II
House of Hanover		
1714–27	George I	son of Sophia (granddaughter of James I)
1727–60	George II	son of George I
1760–1820	George III	son of Frederick (son of George II)
1820–30	George IV (regent 1811–20)	son of George III

ENGLISH SOVEREIGNS FROM 899 (*continued*)

Reign	Name	Relationship
1830–37	William IV	son of George III
1837–1901	Victoria	daughter of Edward (son of George III)

House of Saxe-Coburg		
1901–10	Edward VII	son of Victoria

House of Windsor		
1910–36	George V	son of Edward VII
1936	Edward VIII	son of George V
1936–52	George VI	son of George V
1952–	Elizabeth II	daughter of George VI

THE KINGS OF SCOTLAND

Term	Name
The House of Alpin	
843–859	Kenneth Macalpin
860–863	Donald I
863–877	Constantine I
877–878	Aed
878–889	Eochaid
889–900	Donald II
900–942	Constantine II

The House of Dunkeld	
942–954	Malcolm I
954–962	Indulf
962–967	Dubh
967–971	Cuilean
971–995	Kenneth II
995–997	Constantine III
997–1005	Kenneth III
1005–1034	Malcolm II
1034–1040	Duncan I
1040–1057	Macbeth
1057–1058	Lulach (The Fool)

The House of Canmore	
1058–1093	Malcolm III (Canmore)
1093–1094	Donald Ban
May–November 1094	Duncan II

THE KINGS OF SCOTLAND (*continued*)

Term	Name
The House of Canmore	
1094–1097	Donald Ban and Edmund
1097–1107	Edgar (The Peaceable)
1107–1124	Alexander (The Fierce)
1124–1153	David I
1153–1165	Malcolm IV (The Maiden)
1165–1214	William (The Lion)
1214–1249	Alexander II
1249–1286	Alexander III
1286–1290	Margaret (Maid of Norway)
	The Competitors (Balliol and Bruce)
The House of Balliol	
1292–1296	John Balliol
The House of Bruce	
1306–1329	Robert I (The Bruce)
1329–1371	David II
The House of Stewart	
1371–1390	Robert II
1390–1406	Robert III
1406–1437	James I
1437–1460	James II
1460–1488	James III
1488–1513	James IV
1513–1542	James V
1542–1587	Mary, Queen of Scots
1567–1603	James VI

APPENDIX IV

Term	Name	Party
1721–42	Sir Robert Walpole	Whig
1742–43	Earl of Wilmington	Whig
1743–54	Henry Pelham	Whig
1754–56	Duke of Newcastle	Whig
1756–57	Duke of Devonshire	Whig
1757–62	Duke of Newcastle	Whig
1762–63	Earl of Bute	Tory
1763–65	George Grenville	Whig
1765–66	Marquis of Rockingham	Whig
1766–68	Earl of Chatham	Whig
1768–70	Duke of Grafton	Whig
1770–82	Lord North	Tory
1782	Marquis of Rockingham	Whig
1782–83	Earl of Shelburne	Whig
1783	Duke of Portland	coalition
1783–1801	William Pitt the Younger	Tory
1801–04	Henry Addington	Tory
1804–06	William Pitt the Younger	Tory
1806–07	Lord Grenville	coalition
1807–09	Duke of Portland	Tory
1809–12	Spencer Perceval	Tory
1812–27	Earl of Liverpool	Tory
1827	George Canning	coalition
1827–28	Viscount Goderich	Tory
1828–30	Duke of Wellington	Tory
1830–34	Earl Grey	Whig
1834	Viscount Melbourne	Whig
1834–35	Sir Robert Peel	Tory
1835–41	Viscount Melbourne	Whig
1841–46	Sir Robert Peel	Conservative
1846–52	Lord Russell	Liberal
1852	Earl of Derby	Conservative
1852–55	Lord of Aberdeen	Peelite

UNITED KINGDOM PRIME MINISTERS FROM 1721 (*continued*)

Term	Name	Party
1855–58	Viscount Palmerston	Liberal
1858–59	Earl of Derby	Conservative
1859–65	Viscount Palmerston	Liberal
1865–66	Lord Russell	Liberal
1866–68	Earl of Derby	Conservative
1868	Benjamin Disraeli	Conservative
1868–74	W E Gladstone	Liberal
1874–80	Benjamin Disraeli	Conservative
1880–85	W E Gladstone	Liberal
1885–86	Marquis of Salisbury	Conservative
1886	W E Gladstone	Liberal
1886–92	Marquis of Salisbury	Conservative
1892–94	W E Gladstone	Liberal
1894–95	Earl of Rosebery	Liberal
1895–1902	Marquis of Salisbury	Conservative
1902–05	Arthur James Balfour	Conservative
1905–08	Sir H Campbell-Bannerman	Liberal
1908–15	H H Asquith	Liberal
1915–16	H H Asquith	coalition
1916–22	David Lloyd George	coalition
1922–23	Andrew Bonar Law	Conservative
1923–24	Stanley Baldwin	Conservative
1924	Ramsay MacDonald	Labour
1924–29	Stanley Baldwin	Conservative
1929–31	Ramsay MacDonald	Labour
1931–35	Ramsay MacDonald	national coalition
1935–37	Stanley Baldwin	national coalition
1937–40	Neville Chamberlain	national coalition
1940–45	Sir Winston Churchill	coalition
1945–51	Clement Attlee	Labour
1951–55	Sir Winston Churchill	Conservative
1955–57	Sir Anthony Eden	Conservative
1957–63	Harold Macmillan	Conservative
1963–64	Sir Alec Douglas-Home	Conservative
1964–70	Harold Wilson	Labour
1970–74	Edward Heath	Conservative
1974–76	Harold Wilson	Labour
1976–79	James Callaghan	Labour
1979–90	Margaret Thatcher	Conservative
1990–97	John Major	Conservative
1997–	Tony Blair	Labour

BIBLIOGRAPHY

The titles listed in this bibliography include works which have been recently published and are available in most general-reference libraries. In the sections below, works are arranged by type, by national areas (Britain, England, Scotland, or Wales), and by the chronological periods they cover.

GENERAL REFERENCE

The titles in this section are guides to general information for Great Britain. They may be used to direct students to other sources and to provide similar information to that which is contained in this book. Since the field of British history is so large and so well supplied with printed information, no single work will adequately cover the field, and therefore the student usually needs to refer to several works of the same type for full coverage.

Bibliographies

World Bibliographical Series. Oxford: Clio Press.
  Day, Alan. *England.* 1993.
  Grant, Eric G. *Scotland.* 1982.
  Huws, Gwilym. *Wales.* 1991.
  Shannon, Michael O. *Irish Republic.* 1986.
  ———. *Northern Ireland.* 1991.
Bibliography of British History published by the Royal Historical Society and the American Historical Association.
Brown, Lucy, and Ian R. Christie, eds. *Bibliography of British History, 1789–1851.* Oxford, U.K.: Clarendon Press, 1977.
Graves, Edgar B., ed. *A Bibliography of English History to 1485.* Oxford, U.K.: Clarendon Press, 1975.
Hanham, H. J., ed. *Bibliography of British History, 1851–1914.* Oxford, U.K.: Clarendon Press, 1976.
Keeler, Mary Frear, ed. *Bibliography of British History: Stuart Period, 1603–1714.* 2d ed. Oxford, U.K.: Clarendon Press, 1970.
Pargellis, Stanley, and D. J. Medley, eds. *Bibliography of British History: The Eighteenth Century, 1714–1789.* Hassocks, U.K.: Harvester Press, 1977.
Read, Conyers, ed. *Bibliography of British History: Tudor Period, 1485–1603.* 2d ed. Hassocks, Eng.: Harvester Press, 1978.
Robbins, Keith, ed. *Bibliography of British History, 1914–1989.* Oxford, U.K.: Clarendon Press, 1996.

Dictionaries and Encyclopedias

Bennett, Martyn. *Historical Dictionary of the British and Irish Civil Wars, 1637–1660.* Lanham, U.K.: Scarecrow, 2000.
Cannon, John, ed. *The Oxford Companion to British History.* Oxford, U.K.: University Press, 1997.
Childs, Peter, and Mike Storry. *Encyclopedia of Contemporary British Culture.* London: Routledge, 1999.
Daiches, David, comp. *A Companion to Scottish Culture.* London: Arnold, 1981.
Donnachie, Ian, and George Hewitt. *A Companion to Scottish History.* New York: Facts On File, 1989.
Fritze, Ronald, and William B. Robison. *Historical Dictionary of Stuart England.* Westport, Conn.: Greenwood, 1996.
Gardiner, Juliet, and Neil Wenborn, eds. *The Columbia Companion to British History.* New York: Columbia University Press, 1997.
Gascoigne, Bamber. *The Encyclopedia of Britain.* London: Macmillan, 1993.
Gilbert, Martin. *Routledge Atlas of British History.* 2d ed. London: Routledge, 1996.
Haigh, Christopher. *The Cambridge Historical Encyclopedia of Great Britain and Ireland.* 2d ed. Cambridge, U.K.: University Press, 1990.

Hall, Simon, ed. *Hutchinson Illustrated Encyclopedia of British History*. Chicago: Fitzroy Dearborn, 1999.

Kurian, George. *Facts On File National Profiles: The British Isles*. New York: Facts On File, 1990.

Keay, John, and Julia Keay. *Collins Encyclopedia of Scotland*. London: HarperCollins, 2000.

Lenman, Bruce, ed. *The La Rousse Dictionary of British History*. New York: La Rousse, 1994.

Leventhal, F. M. *Twentieth-Century Britain: An Encyclopedia*. Westport, Conn.: Garland, 1995.

Newman, Gerald. *Britain in the Hanoverian Age, 1714–1837: An Encyclopedia*. Westport, Conn.: Garland, 1997.

Palmer, Alan. *Dictionary of the British Empire and Commonwealth*. London: Murray, 1996.

Panton, Kenneth. *Historical Dictionary of the United Kingdom*. 2 vols. Lanham, Md.: Scarecrow, 1998.

Wagner, John. *Historical Dictionary of the Elizabethan World: Britain, Ireland, Europe, and America*. Phoenix, Ariz.: Oryx, 1998.

Who's Who in British History (to 1901). 2 vols. Chicago: Fitzroy Dearborn, 1998.

Wood, Eric S. *Historical Britain: A Comprehensive Account of the Development of Rural and Urban Life and Landscape from Prehistory to the Present Day*. London: Harvill Press, 1995.

Chronicles

Chronicle of Britain, incorporating a Chronicle of Ireland. Farnborough, U.K.: JL International Publishing, 1992.

Cook, Chris, and John Stevenson. *Longman Handbook of Modern British History, 1714–1995*. London: Longman, 1996.

———, *Longman Handbook of Modern European History, 1763–1997*. London: Longman, 1998.

———, *Longman Handbook of the Modern World, since 1945*. London: Longman, 1998.

Thorpe, Andrew. *Longman Companion to Britain in the Era of the Two World Wars*. London: Longman, 1993.

SURVEYS

These broad accounts of British history are divided into three categories: first, the multivolume series which cover all or most of British history; second, the single-volume surveys of long periods of British history; and third, the treatments of national (i.e., English, Scottish, or Welsh) history, either in single volumes or series.

Series Surveys

Arnold History of Britain. London: Arnold.

O'Gorman, Frank. *The Long Eighteenth Century, 1688–1832*. 1997.

Rubenstein, W. D. *Britain's Century, 1815–1905*. 1998.

Pugh, Martin. *State and Society, 1870–1997*. 1999.

Foundations of Modern Britain. General editor Geoffrey Holmes. London: Longman.

Evans, Eric J. *The Forging of the Modern State: Early Industrial Britain, 1783–1870*. 2d ed. 1996.

Holmes, Geoffrey. *The Making of a Great Power: Late Stuart and Early Georgian Britain, 1660–1722*. 1993.

Holmes, Geoffrey, and Daniel Szechi. *The Age of Oligarchy: Pre-Industrial Britain, 1722–1783*. 1993.

Robbins, Keith. *The Eclipse of a Great Power: Modern Britain, 1870–1992*. 2d ed. 1994.

Smith, Alan, G. R. *The Emergence of a Nation State: The Commonwealth of England, 1529–1660*. 1997.

Thomson, John A. F. *The Transformation of Medieval England, 1370–1529*. 1983.

New History of England. London: Arnold.

Beloff, Max. *Wars and Welfare: Britain, 1914–1945*. London: Arnold, 1984.

Christie, Ian. *Wars and Revolutions: Britain, 1760–1815*. London: Arnold, 1982.

Hirst, Derek. *Authority and Conflict: England, 1603–1658*. Cambridge, Mass.: Harvard University Press, 1986.

Feuchtwanger, E. J. *Democracy and Empire: Britain, 1865–1914*. London: Arnold, 1985.

Gash, Norman. *Aristocracy and People: Britain, 1815–1865*. London: Arnold, 1979.

Jones, J. R. *Country and Court: England, 1658–1714*. London: Arnold, 1978.

New Oxford History of England. Oxford: Clarendon Press.

Hoppen, K. Theodore. *The Mid-Victorian Generation, 1846–1886*. 1998.

Hoppit, Julian. *A Land of Liberty: England, 1689–1727*. 2000.

Langford, Paul. *A Polite and Commercial People: England, 1727–1783.* 1989.

Williams, Penry. *The Later Tudors: England, 1547–1603.* 1995.

Penguin History of Britain. London: Penguin Books.

Brigdon, Susan. *New Worlds, Lost Worlds: Britain, 1485–1603.* 2001.

Clarke, Peter. *Hope and Glory: Britain, 1909–1990.* 1996.

Kishlansky, Mark. *A Monarchy Transformed: Britain, 1603–1714.* 1996.

Single-Volume Surveys

Childs, David. *Britain Since 1939: Progress and Decline.* New York: St. Martin's, 1995.

Frame, Robin. *The Political Development of the British Isles, 1100–1400.* Oxford, U.K.: University Press, 1990.

Lee, Stephen J. *Aspects of British Political History, 1815–1914.* London: Routledge, 1994.

McCord, Norman. *British History, 1815–1906.* Oxford, U.K.: University Press, 1991.

Morgan, Kenneth O. *Oxford History of Britain.* Oxford, U.K.: University Press, 1988.

———. *The People's Peace: British History, 1945–1989.* Oxford: University Press, 1990.

Morrill, John, ed. *The Oxford Illustrated History of Tudor and Stuart Britain.* Oxford, U.K.: University Press, 1996.

Pugh, Martin. *Britain Since 1789: A Concise History.* New York: St. Martin's Press, 1999.

Robbins, Keith. *Nineteenth-Century Britain. England, Scotland and Wales: The Making of a Nation.* Oxford University Press, 1988.

Williams, Glyn, and John Ramsden. *Ruling Britannia: Political History of Britain, 1688–1988.* London: Longman, 1989.

National Surveys

Black, Jeremy. *A New History of England.* Stroud, Eng.: Sutton, 2000.

Carr, A. D. *Medieval Wales.* New York: St. Martin's, 1994.

Davies, John. *A History of Wales.* London: Allen Lane, 1993.

Elton, Geoffrey R. *England under the Tudors.* 3d ed. Cambridge, U.K.: University Press, 1991.

Evans, D. Gareth. *A History of Wales, 1906–2000.* Cardiff: University of Wales Press, 2000.

Haigh, Christopher. *English Reformations.* Oxford, U.K.: University Press, 1993.

Jenkins, Philip. *A History of Modern Wales, 1536–1990.* London: Longman, 1992.

Jones, G. E. *Modern Wales: A Concise History.* 2d ed. Cambridge, U.K.: University Press, 1994.

Lynch, Michael. *Scotland: A New History.* London: Pimlico, 1992.

Mackie, J. D. *A History of Scotland.* 2d ed., rev. New York: Dorset, 1985.

Mitchison, Rosalind. *A History of Scotland.* 2d ed. London: Methuen, 1982.

Morgan, Kenneth O. *Rebirth of a Nation: Wales, 1880–1980.* 1981.

Morrill, John S. *The Nature of the English Revolution.* London: Longman, 1993.

Scott, Paul, ed. *Scotland: A Concise Cultural History.* Edinburgh: Mainstream, 1993.

Smout, T. C. *A Century of the Scottish People, 1830–1950.* London: Collins, 1986.

———. *A History of the Scottish People, 1560–1830.* New York: Scribner, 1969.

The Edinburgh History of Scotland. General editor Gordon Donaldson. Edinburgh: Oliver and Boyd.

Donaldson, Gordon. *Scotland: James V–James VII, 1965.*

Duncan, A. A. M. *Scotland: The Making of the Kingdom, 1975.*

Ferguson, William. *Scotland: 1689 to the Present, 1968.*

Nicholson, Ranald. *Scotland: The Later Middle Ages, 1974.*

New History of Scotland. London: Arnold.

Checkland, S. G. *Industry and Ethos: Scotland, 1832–1914.* 1984.

Grant, Alexander. *Independence and Nationhood, 1306–1469.* 1984.

Harvie, Chris. *No Gods and Precious Few Heroes: Scotland Since 1914.* New ed. 1993.

Lenman, Bruce. *Integration, Enlightenment and Industrialization: Scotland 1746–1832.* 1981.

Mitchison, Rosalind. *Lordship to Patronage: Scotland, 1603–1745.* 1983.

Wormald, Jenny. *Court, Kirk and Community: Scotland, 1470–1625.* 1981.

The History of Wales. Oxford: Clarendon Press, and Cardiff: University of Wales Press.

    Davies, R. R. *Conquest, Coexistence and Change: Wales, 1063–1415.* 1987.

    Jones, Gwynfor J. *Early Modern Wales, 1526–1640.* New York: St. Martin's, 1994.

    Williams, Glanmor. *Renewal and Reformation, 1415–1642.* 1993.

TOPICS

In this section, works have been chosen which amplify broader topics in British history (e.g., art, music, literature). They are general treatments, and more specific works (biographies, accounts of specific events, etc.) are not included.

Politics and the Constitution

Bennett, Martyn. *The Civil Wars in Britain and Ireland, 1638–1651.* Oxford, U.K.: Blackwell, 1997.

Branson, Noreen. *History of the Communist Party of Great Britain, 1927–1941.* London: Lawrence and Wishart, 1985.

Burgess, Glenn. *The New British History: Founding a Modern State, 1603–1715.* New York: St. Martin's, 1999.

Butler, David, and Gareth Butler. *Twentieth-Century British Political Facts, 1900–2000.* 8th ed. New York: St. Martin's, 2000.

Colley, Linda. *Britons: Forging the Nation, 1707–1837.* New Haven, Conn.: Yale University Press, 1994.

Cook, Chris. *A Short History of the Liberal Party, 1900–1992.* 4th ed. Basingstoke, U.K.: Macmillan, 1993.

Davies, Hywel D. *The Welsh Nationalist Party, 1925–1945: A Call to Nationhood.* Cardiff: University of Wales Press, 1983.

Dickinson, H. T. *The Politics of the People in Eighteenth-Century Britain.* New York: St. Martin's, 1995.

Ellis, Steven G. *Conquest and Union: Fashioning a British State, 1485–1725.* London: Longman, 1995.

———. *Tudor Frontiers and Noble Power: The Making of the British State.* Oxford, U.K.: Clarendon Press, 1995.

Finlay, Richard J. *Independent and Free: Scottish Politics and the Origins of the Scottish National Party, 1918–1945.* Edinburgh: John Donald, 1994.

Francis, Mark. *A History of English Political Thought in the 19th Century.* New York: St. Martin's, 1994.

Harrison, Brian. *The Transformation of British Politics, 1860–1995.* Oxford, U.K.: University Press, 1996.

Hutton, Ronald. *The British Republic, 1649–1660.* New York: St. Martin's, 1990.

Jeffreys, Kevin. *The Labour Party Since 1945.* New York: St. Martin's, 1993.

Lenman, Bruce. *The Eclipse of Parliament: Appearance and Reality in British Politics Since 1914.* New York: Arnold, 1992.

Levack, Brian. *The Formation of the British State: England, Scotland and the Union, 1603–1707.* Oxford, U.K.: Clarendon Press, 1987.

Morgan, Kenneth O. *Wales in British Politics, 1868–1922.* 3d ed. Cardiff: University of Wales Press, 1980.

Nairn, Tom. *The Enchanted Glass: Britain and Its Monarchy.* London: Radius, 1988.

Pakenham, Frank, earl of Longford. *A History of the House of Lords.* London: Sutton, 1999.

Porter, Bernard. *Britannia's Burden: The Political Evolution of Modern Britain, 1851–1990.* London: Arnold, 1994.

Pugh, Martin. *The Making of Modern British Politics, 1867–1939.* 2d ed. Oxford, U.K.: Blackwell, 1993.

Ramsden, John. *An Appetite for Power: A History of the Conservative Party Since 1830.* London: HarperCollins, 1998.

Smith, E. A. *The House of Lords in British Politics and Society, 1815–1911.* London: Longman, 1992.

Tilley, Charles. *Popular Contention in Great Britain, 1758–1834.* Cambridge, Mass.: Harvard University Press, 1995.

Waller, Robert, and Byron Criddle. *The Almanac of British Politics.* 6th ed. London: Routledge, 1999.

Wilson, A. N. *The Rise and Fall of the House of Windsor.* New York: Norton, 1993.

Wright, D. G. *Popular Radicalism: The Working Class Experience, 1780–1880.* London: Longman, 1988.

Empire

Louis, William Roger, ed. *Oxford History of the British Empire.* Oxford, U.K.: University Press.

    Brown, Judith, and W. R. Louis, eds. *The Twentieth Century.* Vol. 4. 1998.

    Canny, Nicholas, ed. *The Origins of Empire.* Vol. 1. 1998.

Marshall, P. J., ed. *The Eighteenth Century.* Vol. 2. 1998.

Porter, Andrew, ed. *The Nineteenth Century.* Vol. 3. 1998.

Winks, Robin, ed. *Historiography.* Vol. 5. 1999.

Bowen, H. V. *Elites, Enterprise and the Making of the British Overseas Empire, 1688–1775.* London: Macmillan, 1996.

Cain, P. J., and A. G. Hopkins. *British Imperialism: Innovation and Expansion, 1688–1914.* London: Longman, 1993.

———. *British Imperialism: Crisis and Deconstruction, 1914–1990.* London: Longman, 1993.

James, Lawrence. *The Rise and Fall of the British Empire.* New York: St. Martin's, 1996.

Marshall, P. J. *The Cambridge Illustrated History of the British Empire.* Cambridge, U.K.: University Press, 1996.

Porter, Bernard. *The Lion's Share: A Short History of British Imperialism, 1850–1995.* 3d ed. London: Longman, 1996.

Semmel, Bernard. *The Liberal Ideal and the Demons of Empire: Theories of Imperialism from Adam Smith to Lenin.* Baltimore: Johns Hopkins University Press, 1993.

Wilson, Kathleen. *The Sense of the People: Politics, Culture and Imperialism in England, 1715–1785.* Cambridge, Eng.: University Press, 1995.

Foreign Relations

George, Stephen. *An Awkward Partner: Britain in the European Community.* Oxford, U.K.: University Press, 1990.

Greenwood, Sean. *Britain and European Cooperation Since 1945.* Oxford, U.K.: Blackwell, 1992.

Jones, J. R. *Britain and the World, 1649–1815.* Brighton, Eng.: Harvester Press, 1980.

Pincus, Steven. *Protestantism and Patriotism: Ideologies and the Making of English Foreign Policy, 1650–1688.* Cambridge, Eng.: University Press, 1996.

Smith, Michael, et al. *British Foreign Policy: Tradition, Change, and Transformation.* London: Allen & Unwin, 1988.

Walker, William O. *Opium and Foreign Policy: The Anglo-American Search for Order in Asia, 1912–1954.* Chapel Hill: University of North Carolina Press, 1991.

Weigall, David. *Britain & the World, 1815–1986: A Dictionary of International Relations.* New York: Oxford University Press, 1987.

Young, John W. *Britain and the World in the Twentieth Century.* London: Arnold, 1997.

Economy

Berg, Maxine. *The Age of Manufactures, 1700–1820: Industry, Innovation and Work in Britain.* London: Routledge, 1994.

Daunton, M. J. *Progress and Poverty: An Economic and Social History of Britain, 1700–1850.* Oxford, U.K.: University Press, 1995.

Devine, T. M., and David Dickson. *Ireland and Scotland, 1600–1850: Parallels and Contrasts in Economic and Social Development.* Edinburgh: John Donald, 1981.

English, Richard, and Michael Kenny, eds. *Rethinking British Decline.* New York: St. Martin's, 2000.

Gamble, Andrew. *Britain in Decline: Economic Policy, Political Strategy and the British State.* 4th ed. New York: St. Martin's, 1994.

Healey, Nigel M., ed. *Britain's Economic Miracle: Myth or Reality.* London: Routledge, 1993.

Houston, R. A. *The Population History of Britain and Ireland, 1500–1750.* Cambridge, U.K.: University Press, 1995.

———, and I. D. Whyte, eds. *Scottish Society, 1500–1800.* Cambridge, U.K.: University Press, 1989.

Koehn, Nancy. *The Power of Commerce: Economy and Governance in the First British Empire.* Ithaca, N.Y.: Cornell University Press, 1994.

Pollard, Sidney. *Britain's Prime and Britain's Decline: The British Economy, 1870–1914.* London: Arnold, 1989.

Pope, Rex, ed. *Atlas of British Social and Economic History Since 1700.* New York: Macmillan, 1989.

Rubenstein, W. D. *Capitalism, Culture, and Decline in Britain, 1750–1990.* London: Routledge, 1993.

Saville, Richard, ed. *Economic Development of Modern Scotland, 1950–1980.* Edinburgh: John Donald, 1985.

Whatley, Christopher. *The Industrial Revolution in Scotland.* Cambridge, U.K.: University Press, 1997.

Whyte, Ian, and Kathleen Whyte. *The Changing Scottish Landscape, 1500–1800.* London: Routledge, 1991.

Wilson, Charles. *England's Apprenticeship, 1603–1763*. 2d ed. London: Longman, 1984.

Woods, Robert. *The Population History of Britain in the Nineteenth Century*. Cambridge, U.K.: University Press, 1995.

Wrigley, E. A. *Continuity, Chance and Change: The Character of the Industrial Revolution in England*. Cambridge, U.K.: University Press, 1990.

Society

Anderson, R. D. *Education and the Scottish People, 1750–1918*. Oxford, U.K.: University Press, 1995.

Bean, J. M. W. *From Lord to Patron: Lordship in Late Medieval England*. Philadelphia: University of Pennsylvania Press, 1989.

Becker, Marvin B. *The Emergence of Civil Society in the Eighteenth Century*. Bloomington: Indiana University Press, 1994.

Beckett, J. V. *The Aristocracy in England, 1660–1914*. Oxford, U.K.: Blackwell, 1986.

Cannadine, David. *The Rise and Fall of the British Aristocracy*. New Haven, Conn.: Yale University Press, 1990.

Clark, J. C. D. *English Society, 1688–1832*. Cambridge, U.K.: University Press, 1985.

Devine, T. M. *Clanship to Crofters War: The Social Transformation of the Scottish Highlands*. Manchester, U.K.: University Press, 1994.

Himmelfarb, Gertrude. *Poverty and Compassion: The Moral Imagination of the Late Victorians*. New York: Knopf, 1991.

Holmes, Colin. *John Bull's Island: Immigration and British Society, 1871–1971*. Basingstoke: Macmillan, 1988.

Humphreys, Robert. *Sin, Organized Charity and the Poor Law in Victorian Britain*. New York: St. Martin's, 1995.

Joyce, Patrick. *Visions of the People: Industrial England and the Question of Class, 1840–1914*. Cambridge, U.K.: University Press, 1992.

Langford, Paul. *Public Life and the Propertied Englishman, 1689–1798*. Oxford: Clarendon Press, 1991.

Lowe, Rodney. *The Welfare State in Britain Since 1945*. New York: St. Martin's, 1993.

Mitchison, Rosalind. *People and Society in Scotland, 1760 to the Present*. 3 vols. Edinburgh: John Donald, 1988.

Ormrod, W. M., and P. G. Lindley, eds. *The Black Death in England*. Stamford, Conn.: Watkins, 1996.

Sampson, Anthony. *The Essential Anatomy of Britain: Democracy in Crisis*. San Diego: Harcourt Brace, 1993.

Sullivan, Michael. *The Development of the British Welfare State*. New York: Prentice Hall, 1996.

Thompson, F. M. L., ed. *The Cambridge Social History of Britain, 1750–1950*. 3 vols. Cambridge, U.K.: University Press, 1990.

Wahrman, Dror. *Imagining the Middle Class: The Political Representation of Class in Britain, 1780–1840*. Cambridge, U.K.: University Press, 1995.

Women

Aaron, Jane, ed. *Our Sisters' Land: The Changing Identities of Women in Wales*. Cardiff: University of Wales Press, 1994.

Erickson, Amy Louise. *Women and Property in Early Modern England*. London: Routledge, 1993.

Holt, Constance. *Welsh Women: An Annotated Bibliography of Women in Wales*. Metuchen: Scarecrow, 1993.

Jewell, Helen. *Women in Medieval England*. Manchester, U.K.: University Press, 1996.

Johnson, Dale A. *Women and Religion in Britain and Ireland: An Annotated Bibliography from the Reformation to 1993*. Lanham, Md.: Scarecrow, 1995.

Kent, Susan. *Sex and Suffrage in Britain, 1860–1914*. Princeton, N.J.: University Press, 1987.

Leyser, Henrietta. *Medieval Women: A Social History of Women in England, 450–1500*. New York: St. Martin's, 1995.

Marshall, Rosalind Kay. *Virgins and Viragos: A History of Women in Scotland from 1080 to 1980*. London: Collins, 1983.

Perkin, Joan. *Victorian Women*. London: Murray, 1993.

Rogers, Katherine M. *Feminism in Eighteenth Century England*. Urbana: University of Illinois Press, 1982.

Shoemaker, Robert B. *Gender in English Society, 1650–1850: The Emergence of Separate Spheres?* London: Longman, 1998.

Religion

Burnett, Charles. *Magic and Divination in the Middle Ages*. Aldershot, U.K.: Variorum, 1996.

Cowan, Ian B. *The Scottish Reformation: Church and Society in Sixteenth Century Scotland*. London: Weidenfeld and Nicolson, 1982.

Davis, R. W., and R. J. Helmstadter, eds. *Religion and Irreligion in Victorian Society.* London: Routledge, 1992.

Dilworth, Mark. *Scottish Monasteries in the Late Middle Ages.* Edinburgh: University Press, 1995.

Donaldson, Gordon. *Scottish Church History.* Edinburgh: Scottish Academic Press, 1985.

Dowell, Susan. *Bread, Wine and Women: The Ordination Debate in the Church of England.* London: Virago Press, 1994.

Durston, Christopher, and Jacqueline Eales, eds. *The Culture of English Puritanism, 1560–1700.* New York: St. Martin's, 1996.

Gilley, Sheridan. *A History of Religion in Britain: Practice and Belief from the Pre-Roman Times to the Present.* Oxford, U.K.: Blackwell, 1994.

Haydon, Colin. *Anti-Catholicism in Eighteenth-Century England: A Political and Social Study.* Manchester: University Press, 1993.

Hempton, David. *Religion and Political Culture in Britain and Ireland from the Glorious Revolution to the Decline of Empire.* Cambridge, U.K.: University Press, 1996.

———. *The Religion of the People: Methodism and Popular Religion, 1750–1900.* London: Routledge, 1996.

Heeney, Brian. *The Women's Movement in the Church of England, 1850–1930.* Oxford, U.K.: Clarendon Press, 1988.

Hill, Christopher. *The English Bible and the Seventeenth-Century Revolution.* London: Allen Lane, 1993.

Hinde, Wendy. *Catholic Emancipation: A Shake to Men's Minds.* Oxford: Blackwell, 1992.

Jansen, Sharon. *Dangerous Talk and Strange Behavior: Women and Popular Resistance to the Reforms of Henry VIII.* New York: St. Martin's, 1996.

Jenkins, Geraint H. *Literature, Religion, and Society in Wales, 1660–1730.* Cardiff: University of Wales Press, 1978.

MacDougall, Norman, ed. *Church, Politics and Society: Scotland, 1408–1929.* Edinburgh: John Donald, 1983.

Marshall, Peter. *The Impact of the English Reformation, 1500–1640.* London: Arnold, 1997.

Medhurst, Kenneth, and George Moyser. *Church and Politics in a Secular Age.* Oxford, U.K.: Clarendon Press, 1988.

Neal, Frank. *Sectarian Violence: The Liverpool Experience, 1819–1914. An Aspect of Anglo-Irish History.* New York: St. Martin's, 1995.

Paz, Dennis G. *Popular Anti-Catholicism in Mid-Victorian England.* Stanford, Calif.: University Press, 1992.

Questier, Michael. *Conversion, Politics, and Religion in England, 1580–1625.* Cambridge, U.K.: University Press, 1996.

Rodes, Robert. *Law and Modernization in the Church of England: Charles II to the Welfare State.* Notre Dame, Ind.: University Press, 1991.

Scribner, Bob, et al. *The Reformation in National Context.* Cambridge: University Press, 1994.

Sommerville, C. John. *Secularization of Early Modern England: From Religious Culture to Religious Faith.* New York: Oxford University Press, 1992.

Stanley, Brian. *The Bible and the Flag: Protestant Missions and British Imperialism in the Nineteenth and Twentieth Centuries.* Leicester, U.K.: Apollos, 1990.

Swanson, R. N. *Church and Society in Late Medieval England.* Oxford, U.K.: Blackwell, 1989.

Williams, Glanmor. *The Welsh and Their Religion: Historical Essays.* Cardiff: University of Wales Press, 1991.

———. *The Welsh Church from Conquest to Reformation.* Cardiff: University of Wales Press, 1962.

Wolffe, John. *God and Greater Britain: Religion and National Life in Britain and Ireland, 1843–1945.* London: Routledge, 1994.

National Identity

Bradshaw, Brendan, and Peter Roberts eds. *British Consciousness and Identity: The Making of Britain, 1533–1707.* Cambridge, U.K.: University Press, 1998.

Davies, Charlotte Aull. *Welsh Nationalism in the Twentieth Century: The Ethnic Option and the Modern State.* New York: Praeger, 1989.

Harvie, Christopher T. *Scotland and Nationalism, 1707 to the Present.* London: Routledge, 1998.

Kidd, Colin. *British Identities Before Nationalism: Ethnicity and Nationhood in the Atlantic World, 1600–1800.* Cambridge, U.K.: University Press, 1999.

Langford, Paul. *Englishness Identified: Manners and Character, 1650–1850.* New York: Oxford University Press, 2000.

MacDougall, Hugh. *Racial Myth in English History: Trojans, Teutons, and Anglo-Saxons.* Hanover, N.H.: University Press of New England, 1982.

Murdoch, Alexander. *British History 1660–1832: National Identity and Local Culture.* New York: St. Martin's, 1998.

Pittock, Murray. *Inventing and Resisting Britain: Cultural Identities in Britain and Ireland, 1685–1789.* New York: St. Martin's, 1997.

Robbins, Keith. *Great Britain: Identities, Institutions, and the Idea of Britishness.* London: Longman, 1998.

Military

Chandler, David, ed. *The Oxford Illustrated History of the British Army.* Oxford, U.K.: University Press, 1994.

French, David. *The British Way in Warfare, 1688–2000.* London: Unwin Hyman, 1990.

Harding, Richard. *The Evolution of the Sailing Navy.* New York: St. Martin's, 1995.

Hill, J. R., ed. *The Oxford Illustrated History of the Royal Navy.* Oxford, U.K.: University Press, 1995.

Massie, Robert. *Dreadnought: Britain, Germany and the Coming of the Great War.* New York: Random House, 1991.

Strachan, Hew. *The Politics of the British Army.* Oxford, U.K.: Clarendon Press, 1997.

Strawson, John. *Beggars in Red: The British Army, 1789–1889.* London: Hutchinson, 1991.

Watts, Anthony. *The Royal Navy: An Illustrated History.* Annapolis, Md.: Naval Institute Press, 1994.

Art and Architecture

Archer, Lucy. *Architecture in Britain and Ireland, 600–1500.* London: Harvill Press, 1999.

Brewer, John. *The Pleasures of the Imagination: English Culture in the Eighteenth Century.* London: HarperCollins, 1997.

Durant, David N. *The Handbook of British Architectural Styles.* London: Barrie & Jenkins, 1992.

Ford, Boris, ed. *The Cambridge Guide to the Arts in Britain.* 9 vols. Cambridge, U.K.: University Press, 1988.

Girouard, Mark. *The English Town.* New Haven, Conn.: Yale University Press, 1990.

Graham-Dixon, Andrew. *A History of British Art.* Berkeley: University of California Press, 1999.

Johnson, E. D. H. *Paintings of the British Social Scene from Hogarth to Sickert.* New York: Rizzoli, 1986.

Lubbock, Jules. *The Tyranny of Taste: The Politics of Architecture and Design in Britain, 1550–1960.* New Haven, Conn.: Yale University Press, 1995.

Platt, Colin. *The Architecture of Medieval Britain: A Social History.* New Haven, Conn.: Yale University Press, 1990.

Pragnell, Hubert. *Britain: A Guide to Architectural Styles from 1066 to the Present Day.* London: Ellipsis, 1995.

Prest, John. *Illustrated History of Oxford University.* Oxford, U.K.: University Press, 1993.

Shanes, Eric. *Turner's England: A Survey in Watercolors.* North Pomfret, Vt.: Trafalgar Square Publications, 1990.

Strong, Roy. *Lost Treasures of Britain.* London: Viking, 1990.

———. *The Spirit of Britain: A Narrative History of the Arts.* New York: Fromm International, 2000.

Summerson, John. *Architecture in Britain, 1530–1830.* Harmondsworth, U.K.: Penguin, 1991.

Thompson, M. W. *The Rise of the Castle.* Cambridge, U.K.: University Press, 1991.

Thurley, Simon. *The Royal Palaces of Tudor England.* New Haven, Conn.: Yale University Press, 1993.

Waterhouse, Ellis. *Painting in Britain, 1530–1790.* 5th ed. New Haven, Conn.: Yale University Press, 1990.

Worsley, Giles. *Classical Architecture in Britain: The Heroic Age.* New Haven, Conn.: Yale University Press, 1995.

Literature

Brown, John Russell, ed. *Oxford Illustrated History of the Theatre.* Oxford: University Press, 1995.

Bryson, Bill. *The Mother Tongue: English and How It Got that Way.* New York: Morrow, 1990.

Cambridge Companion to British Romanticism. Cambridge, U.K.: University Press, 1993.

Cranston, Maurice. *The Romantic Movement.* Oxford, U.K.: Blackwell, 1994.

Davies, Ceri. *Welsh Literature and the Classical Tradition.* Cardiff: University of Wales Press, 1995.

Drabble, Margaret, ed. *The Oxford Companion to English Literature.* 5th ed. Oxford, U.K.: University Press, 1998.

Gillie, Christopher ed. *The Longman Companion to English Literature.* 2d ed. London: Longman, 1978.

Hartnoll, Phyllis, and Peter Found, eds. *The Concise Oxford Companion to the Theatre.* 2d ed. Oxford, U.K.: University Press, 1992.

McCordick, David, ed. *Scottish Literature: An Anthology.* New York: Peter Lang, 1996.

Ousby, Ian, ed. *Cambridge Paperback Guide to Literature in English.* New York: Cambridge University Press, 1996.

Rogers, Pat, ed. *Oxford Illustrated History of English Literature.* Oxford, U.K.: University Press, 1987.

Royle, Trevor, ed. *The Mainstream Companion to Scottish Literature.* Edinburgh: Mainstream, 1993.

Sanders, Andrew. *The Short Oxford History of English Literature.* Oxford, U.K.: University Press, 1994.

Sommerville, John, C. *The News Revolution in England: Cultural Dynamics of Daily Information.* Oxford, U.K.: University Press, 1996.

Stephens, Meic. *The Oxford Companion to the Literature of Wales.* Oxford, U.K.: University Press, 1986.

Trussler, Simon. *Cambridge Illustrated History: British Theatre.* Cambridge, U.K.: University Press, 1994.

Weinbrot, Howard D. *Britannia's Issue: The Rise of British Literature from Dryden to Ossian.* Cambridge, U.K.: University Press, 1993.

Music

New Oxford History of Music. Oxford, U.K.: University Press.

    Abraham, Gerald. *The Age of Humanism, 1540–1630.* Vol. 4. 1968.

    ———. *The Age of Beethoven, 1790–1830.* Vol. 8. 1982.

    ———. *Concert Music, 1630–1750.* Vol. 6. 1986.

    ———. *Romanticism, 1830–1890.* Vol. 9. 1990.

    Cooper, Martin. *The Modern Age, 1890–1960.* Vol. 10. 1974.

    Hughes, Anselm. *Ars Nova and the Renaissance, 1300–1540.* Vol. 3. 1960.

    Lewis, Anthony, and Nigel Fortune. *Opera and Church Music, 1630–1750.* Vol. 5. 1986.

    Wellesz, Egon. *The Age of Enlightenment, 1745–1790.* Vol. 7. 1973.

Fraser, David, ed. *Fairest Isle: BBC Radio 3 Book of British Music.* London: BBC Books, 1995.

Gammond, Peter. *Oxford Companion to Popular Music.* New York: Oxford University Press, 1991.

Historiography

Darwin, John. *The End of the British Empire: The Historical Debate.* Oxford, U.K.: Blackwell, 1991.

Jones, Gareth Stedman. *Languages of Class: Studies in Working-Class History, 1832–1982.* Cambridge, U.K.: University Press, 1983.

Kenyon, J. P. *The History Men: The Historical Profession in England Since the Renaissance.* 2nd ed. London: Weidenfeld & Nicolson, 1993.

Looser, Devoney. *British Women Writers and the Writing of History, 1670–1820.* Baltimore, Md.: Johns Hopkins University Press, 2000.

Mitchell, Rosemary. *Picturing the Past: English History in Text and Image, 1830–1870.* Oxford, U.K.: Clarendon Press, 2000.

Pittock, Murray. *The Invention of Scotland: The Stuart Myth and the Scottish Identity: 1638 to the Present.* London: Routledge, 1991.

Woolf, D. R. *Reading History in Early Modern England.* Cambridge, U.K.: University Press, 2000.

INDEX

Italic page numbers indicate
illustrations.

A

Abbot, Charles 153
Abbot, George 99
abdication crisis (Edward VIII) 99,
204, 225
Aberdeen, George Hamilton-
Gordon, fourth earl of (prime
minister) 99, 179
Aboukir Bay, Battle of (1798) 99,
317
Acadia 325
Act of. *See specific acts*
act of Parliament 99–100, 171, 263,
308, 342, 385, 387
Acton, John, first baron Acton 100
Adam, Robert 100
Addington, Henry, viscount Sidmouth (prime minister) 100
Addison, Joseph 100, 386
admiralty 101, 169, 244, 273, 404
Admiralty Board 101, 317
adult education, early 19th century
303
advocates. *See* barristers
Afghanistan 67, 101
Africa 101. *See also specific African
countries and territories*
  British possessions in
    (1885–1924), map 498
  British relations, history 101
  Dr. Livingstone 288, 385
  exertion of imperial power 64–65
  "indirect rule" of Baron Lugard
    292
  rebellion against British power
    66–67
  slave trade. *See* slave trade and
    slavery

Afrikaners. *See* Boer War
Age of Enlightenment 46–48, 208
Agincourt, Battle of (1415) 12,
101–102, 242, 252
agitators 37
"agnostic" 254
agricultural revolution 48–49, 102
  Coke, Thomas 166–167
AIDS 401
aircraft, first use in World War I 71
air raids 79, 102–103, 127, 428
Aix-la-Chapelle, Treaty of (1748)
115
Alamein, Battle of El (1942) 103,
310
Alanbrooke, Alan 103
Albany, duke of 103
Albert, Prince 58, 103–104, 181,
201, 231–232, 405
Alexander, Harold Rupert Leofric
George, first earl Alexander of
Tunis 104
Alfred the Great 4, 207
Allen, William 104
Allenby, Edmund Henry Hynman,
first viscount 104
almshouses 104
Alternate Service Book 129
Amboyna massacre (1623) 104, 195
American colonies 104–105, 167.
  See also Revolutionary War in
  American colonies; Stamp Act
  (1765); United States
  Battle of Bunker Hill (1775) 137,
    165, 251
  Board of Trade 128
  Continental Congress 185
  crises 104–105
  Declaration of Independence
    (1776) 185
  expansion 104–105
  map (1607–1763) 497

  Massachusetts Bay Company 302
  Quebec Act, effect of 349
  rebellion of 45, 53, 105, 130, 186
  settlement 104–105
  trade ties with new United States
    following rebellion 56
  transportation to 397
Amiens, Peace of 173
Amritsar massacre (1919) 105, 222,
258
Ancient Britons 220
Anderson, Elizabeth Garrett 106,
212
Angevin invasions 4–5
Anglican Church 106, 162, 237,
283. *See also* Church of England
Anglo-Dutch Wars. *See* Dutch Wars
Anglo-Irish Treaty (1921) 106, 167,
188, 230, 233, 263, 264, 266, 323,
328
Anglo-Normans 5
"Anglo-Saxondom" 189
Anglo-Saxon kingdoms 4, 307, 321.
See also Saxons
Anne, Princess 204
Anne (queen) 44, 45, 52, 106–107,
277
Anne of Cleves (queen) 20, 107,
181, 243
Anson, George 107, 251
anticolonialism 56
Anti-Corn Law League 55, 107, 166,
173, 304
antislavery movement 54, 107, 135,
164, 165, 373, 377, 378
antiterrorist legislation 195
apartheid 381, 390
Appeal, Court of 107–108, 143, 175,
179, 244, 273, 302
appeasement policy, pre–World
War II 77, 78, 108, 112, 154,
160, 197, 295, 393, 423

H